THE ROUGH GUIDE TO

Jamaica

There are more than one hundred and fifty Rough Guide titles
covering destinations from Amsterdam to Zimbabwe

Forthcoming titles include

Alaska • Copenhagen • Ibiza & Formentera • Iceland

Rough Guide Reference Series

Classical Music • Country Music • Drum 'n' bass • English Football
European Football • House • The Internet • Jazz • Music USA • Opera
Reggae • Rock Music • Techno • Unexplained Phenomena • World Music

Rough Guide Phrasebooks

Czech • Dutch • Egyptian Arabic • European Languages • French
German • Greek • Hindi & Urdu • Hungarian • Indonesian • Italian
Japanese • Mandarin Chinese • Mexican Spanish • Polish • Portuguese
Russian • Spanish • Swahili • Thai • Turkish • Vietnamese

Rough Guides on the Internet

www.roughguides.com

Rough Guide Credits

Text Editor:	Lisa Nellis
Series Editor:	Mark Ellingham
Editorial:	Martin Dunford, Jonathan Buckley, Jo Mead, Kate Berens, Amanda Tomlin, Ann-Marie Shaw, Paul Gray, Helena Smith, Judith Bamber, Orla Duane, Olivia Eccleshall, Ruth Blackmore, Geoff Howard, Claire Saunders, Gavin Thomas, Alexander Mark Rogers, Polly Thomas, Joe Staines, Andrew Tomičić, Richard Lim, Duncan Clark, Peter Buckley, Sam Thorne, Lucy Ratcliffe, Clifton Wilkinson (UK); Andrew Rosenberg, Mary Beth Maioli, Don Bapst, Stephen Timblin (US)
Online:	Kelly Cross, Anja Mutić-Blessing, Jennifer Gold, Audra Epstein (US)
Production:	Susanne Hillen, Andy Hilliard, Link Hall, Helen Ostick, Julia Bovis, Michelle Draycott, Katie Pringle, Robert Evers, Mike Hancock, Robert McKinlay, Zoë Nobes
Cartography:	Melissa Baker, Maxine Repath, Ed Wright
Picture Research:	Louise Boulton, Sharon Martins
Finance:	John Fisher, Gary Singh, Edward Downey, Mark Hall, Tim Bill
Marketing & Publicity:	Richard Trillo, Niki Smith, David Wearn, Jemima Broadbridge, Chloë Roberts, Birgit Hartmann (UK); Simon Carloss, David Wechsler (US)
Administration:	Tania Hummel, Demelza Dallow, Julie Sanderson

Acknowledgements

Polly, Polly and Adam would like to thank the staff of the Jamaica Tourist Board for their help and support, particularly Paula Dyke, Iva Walters, Dawn Smith, Judith Thompson, Dan Hammond and Marlon Stuart-Granger, and to all at Barclay Stratton. Thanks also to Paul Gray and Kate Berens for guidance, Lisa Nellis for cool editing, Sharon Martins for luscious photos, Robert McKinlay for smooth typesetting, Sam Kirby for excellent cartography, Sarah Tyson for painless proofreading, Narrell Leffman and Gerrard Kennedy for Australian and US Basics research, John Fortnum for the lowdown on movies, and Steve Barrow and Greg Salter for their original contributions to the music piece.

The editor would particularly like to thank the authors for their enthusiasm towards Jamaica which made working with them on the book so enjoyable.

Polly Thomas: Huge and heartfelt thanks go to all those in Jamaica who offered their help and expertise so freely, and who make the island so special. Extra respect and love goes to my girls: Andrea Lewis, Marjorie Morris, Victoria Bate and Simone Eschmeier. Thanks also to Petroline Lewis and family, the Morris family, Ricardo Hutchinson, Colin MacDonald, Jan Pauel, Andre McGann, Robert Kerr, Roger Williams, Martin Orr, the Dixon family in MoBay, Donahue Jarrett, Adam Miller, Jennifer Lyn, Linette Wilks, Albert "Jesse" Junior, Roydell Johnson, Daniel "Bozra" Barrett, Gibbs Ford, Herbert "Super" Kennedy, Shark, Trevor Porter, Ainsley Henriques, Dermott Hussey and Jean Causewell; also to Polly RB for being such a cool and lovely customer. Lastly, big kisses to the west London crew who supported me all the way: Imogen and Isabella Spencer, Emma Sturgess-Leif, Amanda Rolandini-Jensen, to mum and dad, Celia and Matt, and to all the family.

Polly Rodger Brown: special thanks to Polly Thomas for her support, encouragement and enthusiasm which went way beyond the call of duty... Many thanks also to the following for their generous advice, hospitality and friendship which helped to make my stay in Jamaica so much fun: Nancy Becker, Antonio Czmarko, English, Terry Facey, Gibbs, Jason Henzell, Besrick Hamilton, Paul Henningham, Jordan, Captain Brian Langford, Wynnsome Lewin at Prospective Car Rental, Frank Lohmann, Andre McGann, all at the Montego Bay Marine Park, Sam Petros, Phil Rock and Chuck Birkestrand at the Negril Yacht Club, Valerie, Hugh Veitch, Anna Wendt, Gary Winter.

This second edition published November 2000 by Rough Guides Ltd, 62–70 Shorts Gardens, London WC2H 9AH.
Distributed by the Penguin Group:
Penguin Books Ltd, 27 Wrights Lane, London W8 5TZ.
Penguin Putnam, Inc., 375 Hudson Street, New York, NY 10014, USA.
Penguin Books Australia Ltd, 487 Maroondah Highway, PO Box 257, Ringwood, Victoria 3134, Australia.
Penguin Books Canada Ltd, 10 Alcorn Avenue, Toronto, Ontario M4V 1E4, Canada.
Penguin Books (NZ) Ltd, 182–190 Wairau Road, Auckland 10, New Zealand.
Printed in England by Clays Ltd, St Ives Plc
Typography and original design by Jonathan Dear and The Crowd Roars.
Illustrations throughout by Edward Briant.

THE ROUGH GUIDE TO

Jamaica

Written and researched by
Polly Thomas and Adam Vaitilingam

With additional contributions by
Polly Rodger Brown
John Fortnum, Steve Barrow and Greg Salter

ROUGH
GUIDES

Help us update

We've gone to a lot of trouble to ensure that this second edition of *The Rough Guide to Jamaica* is accurate and up-to-date. However, things inevitably change, and if you feel we've got it wrong or left something out, we'd like to know: any suggestions, comments or corrections would be much appreciated. We'll credit all contributions and send a copy of the next edition – or any other *Rough Guide* if you prefer – for the best correspondence.

Please mark letters "Rough Guide to Jamaica Update" and send to: Rough Guides, 62–70 Shorts Gardens, London WC2H 9AH or Rough Guides, 4th Floor, 345 Hudson St, New York, NY 10014.

Email should be sent to:
mail@roughguides.co.uk

Online updates about Rough Guide titles can be found on our Web site at *www.roughguides.com*

The Authors

Polly Thomas is a freelance writer, full-time editor and newly converted cricket fan who first visited Jamaica in 1990 and who plans to retire to St Elizabeth one day. She has also co-written *The Rough Guide to Trinidad and Tobago*.

Adam Vaitilingam is a barrister, freelance writer and occasional sax player who lived in the West Indies from 1989 to 1993. He is author of the mini Rough Guides to Antigua and Barbuda, and also Barbados.

Readers' letters

Valeria D'Atanasio, Lee Azus, Channa Cajero, Ronald Catlow, Gabrielle Melchionda Chappell, Christopher A. Galaty, Mr and Mrs D. Hancock, Markus A.K. Holford, Marian Nicholson, Kirsty Rae, Yvonne Salmon and Steven Stothers.

Rough Guides

Travel Guides • Phrasebooks • Music and Reference Guides

We set out to do something different when the first *Rough Guide* was published in 1982. Mark Ellingham, just out of University, was travelling in Greece. He brought along the popular guides of the day, but found they were all lacking in some way. They were either strong on ruins and museums but went on for pages without mentioning a beach or taverna. Or they were so conscious of the need to save money that they lost sight of Greece's cultural and historical significance. Also, none of the books told him anything about Greece's contemporary life – its politics, its culture, its people, and how they lived.

So with no job in prospect, Mark decided to write his own guidebook, one which aimed to provide practical information that was second to none, detailing the best beaches and the hottest clubs and restaurants, while also giving hard-hitting accounts of every sight, both famous and obscure, and providing up-to-the-minute information on contemporary culture. It was a guide that encouraged independent travellers to find the best of Greece, and was a great success, getting shortlisted for the Thomas Cook travel guide award, and encouraging Mark, along with three friends, to expand the series.

The Rough Guide list grew rapidly and the letters flooded in, indicating a much broader readership than had been anticipated, but one which uniformly appreciated the Rough Guides' mix of practical detail and humour, irreverence and enthusiasm. Things haven't changed. The same four friends who began the series are still the caretakers of the Rough Guide mission today: to provide the most reliable, up-to-date and entertaining information to independent-minded travellers of all ages, on all budgets.

We now publish 150 titles and have offices in London and New York. The travel guides are written and researched by a dedicated team of more than 100 authors, based in Britain, Europe, the USA and Australia. We have also created a unique series of phrasebooks to accompany the travel series, along with the acclaimed series of music guides, and a best-selling pocket guide to the Internet and World Wide Web. We also publish comprehensive travel information on our Web site: *www.roughguides.com*

Contents

Chapter 3: Ocho Rios and the north coast 184

Chapter 4: Montego Bay and Cockpit Country 241

Chapter 5: Negril and the west 289

Chapter 6: The south 335

Part Three: Contexts 367

List of maps

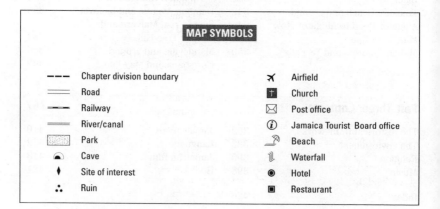

MAP SYMBOLS

- --- Chapter division boundary
- ═══ Road
- ━━━ Railway
- ═══ River/canal
- Park
- Cave
- Site of interest
- Ruin
- ✈ Airfield
- ✝ Church
- ✉ Post office
- (i) Jamaica Tourist Board office
- Beach
- Waterfall
- Hotel
- Restaurant

Introduction

R ightly famous for its beaches and music, beautiful, brash
Jamaica is much more besides. There's certainly plenty of
white sand, turquoise sea and swaying palm trees, but there's
also a huge amount to see away from the coast: spectacular mountains and rivers, tumbling waterfalls, and cactus-strewn savannah
plains. The towns and cities, meanwhile, affirm that the island is far
more than just a tourist attraction, particularly Kingston – the
dynamic, sprawling metropolis which helped to inspire the music of
Bob Marley and countless other home-grown **reggae** superstars.

Despite Jamaica's immense natural allure, it's not just the physical
aspect that makes the country so absorbing and, to many visitors, so
utterly addictive. Notwithstanding the invasion of tourists and
American satellite TV, Jamaica retains an attitude – a personality –
that's more resonant and distinctive than you'll find in any other
Caribbean nation. It's a country with a swagger in its step – proud of
its history, sporting success and musical genius – but also with a
weight upon its shoulders. For Jamaica has not avoided the familiar
problems of a developing country such as dramatic inequality of
wealth, and social tensions that occasionally spill over into localized
violence, or worldwide headlines. The mixture is potent, and has produced a people as renowned for being sharp, sassy and straight-talk-
ing as they are laid-back and hip. People don't tend to beat around
the bush here; Jamaicans get on with life, and this can sometimes
make them appear rude or uncompromising. Particularly around the
big resorts, this direct approach is taken to extremes at times, with
harassment reaching infuriating levels.

But there's absolutely no reason to be put off. As a foreign visitor,
the chances of encountering any trouble are minuscule, and the
Jamaican authorities have spent millions making sure the island
treats its tourists right. As the birthplace of the "**all-inclusive**" hotel,
Jamaica has become well-suited for those who (like many people)
want to head straight from plane to beach, never leaving their hotel
compound. But to get any sense of the country at all, you'll need to
do some exploring. It's undoubtedly worth it, as this is a country

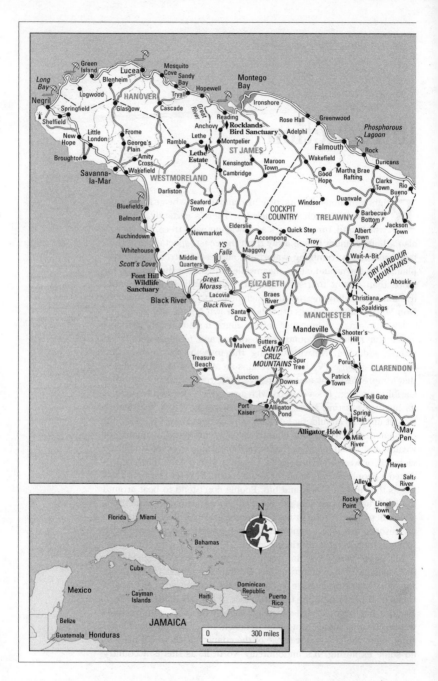

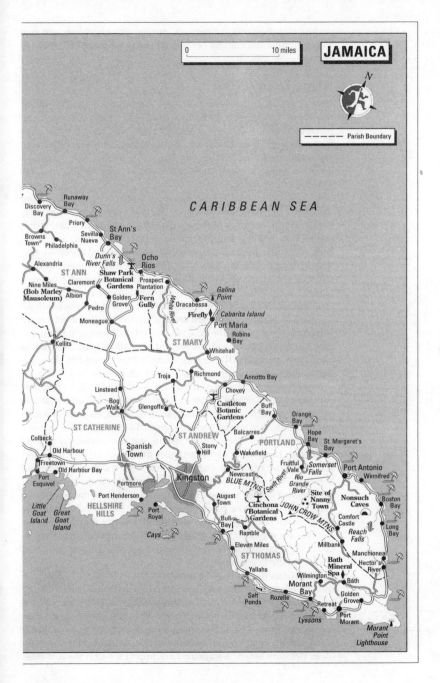

JAMAICA

0   10 miles

N

- - - - Parish Boundary

CARIBBEAN SEA

Discovery Bay
Runaway Bay
Priory
Browns Town
Philadelphia
Sevilla Nueva
St Ann's Bay
Alexandria
Dunn's River Falls
Ocho Rios
Nine Miles (Bob Marley Mausoleum)
Claremont
Shaw Park Botanical Gardens
Prospect Plantation
ST ANN
Albion
Golden Grove
Fern Gully
Pedro
White River
Galina Point
Oracabessa
Firefly
Moneague
Cabarita Island
Port Maria
Kellits
ST MARY
Robins Bay
Whitehall
Troja
Richmond
Annotto Bay
Linstead
Chovey
Castleton Botanic Gardens
Bog Walk
Glengoffe
Buff Bay
ST CATHERINE
Orange Bay
Balcarres
ST ANDREW
Hope Bay
St Margaret's Bay
Colbeck
Old Harbour
Spanish Town
Stony Hill
PORTLAND
Port Antonio
Freetown
Old Harbour Bay
Wakefield
Fruitful Vale
Somerset Falls
Winnifred
Port Esquivel
Portmore
Newcastle
Swift River
Port Royal
BLUE MTNS
Rio Grande River
Site of Nanny Town
Boston Bay
Little Goat Island
Great Goat Island
HELLSHIRE HILLS
Port Henderson
Kingston
August Town
Cinchona (Botanical Gardens)
JOHN CROW MTNS
Nonsuch Caves
Comfort Castle
Long Bay
Cays
Bull Bay
Ramble
Reach Falls
Manchioneal
Eleven Miles
Millbank
Hector's River
ST THOMAS
Bath Mineral Spa
Yallahs
Wilmington
Bath
Salt Ponds
Rozelle
Morant Bay
Golden Grove
Lyssons
Retreat
Port Morant
Morant Point Lighthouse

packed with first-class attractions, oozing with character, and rich with a musical and cultural heritage; if you're a reggae fan, you're in heaven.

Where to go

Most of Jamaica's tourist business is concentrated in the "big three" **resorts** of Montego Bay, Ocho Rios and Negril which, between them, pull hundreds of thousands of visitors every year. Probably the most evocative name in the Caribbean, **Montego Bay** is a busy, commercial city with hotels lined up along its main strip, a stone's throw from a couple of Jamaica's most famous beaches. Though "MoBay" has lost some of its old lustre, the place retains an appealing vitality, with a busy street life and a great entertainment scene, most obvious during the annual **Reggae Sumfest** festival. West of here, its low-rise hotels slung along seven miles of fantastic white sand and two miles of dramatic cliffs, **Negril** is a different type of resort – younger, more laidback, and with a longstanding reputation for unbridled hedonism that still carries a hint of the truth. East of MoBay, and the least individualistic of the big three, **Ocho Rios** embodies high-impact tourism – purpose-built in the 1960s to provide the ultimate package of sun, sand and sea. It's not an overly attractive place, and the beaches don't compare favourably with Negril and MoBay, but tourist infrastructure is undeniably strong – the place is packed with shops, restaurants, bars and watersports – and you're right by some of Jamaica's leading attractions, including the famous **Dunn's River** waterfall, dramatic **Fern Gully** and the lovely **botanical gardens** at Shaw Park.

Away from these resorts, you'll have to look a bit harder to find your entertainment – Jamaica's quieter east and south coasts offer a far less packaged product – but there are plenty of real gems worth hunting out, particularly if you're keen to escape the crowds. In the island's **east**, lush, rain-fed, sleepy **Port Antonio**, and it's increasingly popular neighbour, **Long Bay**, provide gateways to some of Jamaica's greatest natural attractions, like the cascading **waterfalls** at Reach and Somerset, and outdoor activities such as **rafting** on the majestic Rio Grande, and **hiking** through the dense rainforest of the John Crow Mountains. The **south coast** offers different pleasures, from gentle beach action at the terminally easy-going **Treasure Beach** – the perfect base for exploring local delights like the YS waterfalls and the gorgeous lagoon and beach at Gut River – to boat safaris in search of local wildlife on the **Black River**.

Last, but in no way least, **Kingston** is the true heart of Jamaica, a thrilling place, pulsating with energy and spirit, that is home to more than a third of the island's 2.5 million population. This is not just the nation's political capital but the focus of its art, theatre and music scenes, with top-class hotels, restaurants and shopping, a clubbing scene that is second to none and legendary fried fish on offer at the fabulous Hellshire beach. A stunning backdrop to the city, the cool **Blue**

Mountains are a captivating, gentle antidote, with plenty of marvellous hiking possibilities, while the nearby fishing village of **Port Royal**, once a great pirate city, and the former capital of **Spanish Town**, with its grand Georgian buildings, provide more historic diversions.

When to go

For many visitors, Jamaica's tropical **climate** is its leading attraction – hot and sunny all year. The weather is at its most appealing during the peak tourist season, which runs from mid-December to mid-April, when rainfall is lowest and the heat is tempered by cooling trade winds, known locally as the "Doctor Breeze". Things can get noticeably hotter during the summer and, particularly in September and October, the humidity can become oppressive. September is also the most threatening month of the annual hurricane season, which runs officially from June 1 to October 31, though it's worth bearing in mind that, on average, the big blows only hit about once a decade.

As you'd expect, prices and crowds are at their highest during peak season, when the main attractions and beaches can get pretty busy. Outside this period – from Easter to early December – everywhere is quieter and, though the main resorts throb with life pretty much year-round, quieter tourist areas like Port Antonio and Treasure Beach can feel a little lifeless. The good news is that hotel prices everywhere fall by up to 25 percent, there are more bargains to be had in every field of activity, and a number of **festivals** – including the massive annual Reggae Sumfest in Montego Bay – inject some summertime zip.

Climate

These figures are for Kingston, but are virtually identical island-wide with the exception of Port Antonio and the Blue Mountains, where rainfall is considerably higher.

	Climate chart	
	Average daily temperature (°F max/min)	**Average monthly rainfall**
Jan	86/67	0.9
Feb	86/67	0.6
March	86/68	0.9
April	87/70	1.2
May	87/72	4.0
June	89/74	3.4
July	90/73	3.4
Aug	90/73	3.5
Sept	89/73	3.8
Oct	88/73	7.0
Nov	87/71	3.0
Dec	87/69	1.4

Part 1

Basics

Getting there from North America

There's no doubt that the Caribbean, in general, is an extremely popular destination from North America, and Jamaica is no exception. However, the relatively low profile it has on cruise itineraries, the scarcity of cheap flights, and the negative image Jamaica still has in America, have had an adverse effect on its popularity with North American travellers, and many people stick to the confines of the all-inclusive enclaves. However, just one hour and twenty minutes from Miami, and easily accessible by sea, Jamaica is nothing if not convenient.

By air

There are few **cheap flights** to Jamaica. The airlines don't offer special student rates or air passes and the Caribbean doesn't fit too well into a round-the-world (RTW) itinerary. Apart from special promotions advertised from time to time (when the major carriers are engaged in a price war, for instance), the cheapest of the airlines' published fares is usually an **APEX** ticket, although this will carry certain restrictions: you have to book – and pay – seven, fourteen or 21 days before departure, spend at least seven days abroad (maximum stay three months), and you tend to get penalized if you change your schedule.

You can normally cut costs further by going through a **specialist flight agent** – either a **consolidator**, who buys up blocks of tickets from the airlines and sells them at a discount, or a **discount agent**, who in addition to dealing with cut-price flights may also offer complementary services such as travel insurance, car rental, tours and the like. Some agents specialize in **charter flights**, which may be cheaper than anything available on a scheduled flight, but again departure dates are fixed. With all reduced-rate operations, withdrawal penalties are high (check the refund policy). Myriad options are available on the Internet; check out deals on *www.cheaptickets.com, www.travelocity.com* or *www.lastminute.com*.

Regardless of where you buy your ticket, fares will depend on the **season**. Seasonal definitions vary from airline to airline – and some consider the island a domestic destination not subject to such distinctions – but the period from around mid-December to mid-April is generally classified as **high season**, with the rest of the year considered **low season** (although various one-off events, like Spring Break and the reggae festivals, see fares unseasonably high and seats at a premium). US flights from major airlines run daily year round. Flights from Canada depend on the time of year: in low season there are about five flights a week, during high season daily flights are available.

The following are typical high/low season **APEX fares** from US/Canadian cities to Montego Bay's Sangster Airport: Atlanta (US$598/450); Chicago (US$583/459); Charlotte, NC (US$485/382); Detroit (US$542/439); Orlando (US$469/447); LA (US$752/657); Miami (US$432/385); New York (US$489/386); St Louis (US$586/449); Toronto (CAN$899/726); Vancouver (flights from Vancouver include a stop in Toronto CAN$1259/1086). A few flights continue on, or fly direct, to Norman Manley Airport in Kingston – the extra leg will cost you anything between US$10 and US$65 on top of these prices.

AIRLINES

Air Canada ☎ 1-888/247-2262, *www. aircanada.ca.*

Air Jamaica ☎ 1-800/523-5585, *www. airjamaica.com.*

American Airlines ☎ 1-800/433-7300, *www.aa. com.*

Northwest Airlines ☎ 1-800/447-4747, *www. nwa.com.*

TWA ☎ 1-800/892-4141, *www.twa.com.*

US Air ☎ 1-800/622-1015, *www.usairways. com.*

DISCOUNT TRAVEL AGENTS AND CONSOLIDATORS

Adventure Travel, 785 Market Street, San Francisco (☎ 1-800/467-4595, *www.atntravel.com*). Specializing in discounted airfares and adventure holidays.

Airtech, 588 Broadway, Suite 204, New York, NY 10012 (☎ 1-800/575-TECH or 212/219-7000, *www.airtech.com*). Offers standby, last-minute, wholesale and courier tickets.

Council Travel, 205 E 42 St, New York, NY 10017 (☎ 1-800/226-8624, *www.counciltravel.com*). Branches in many other US cities. Specialists in student/youth budget travel.

Educational Travel Center, 438 N Frances St, Madison, WI 53703 (☎ 1-800/747-5551, *www.edtrav.com*). Student/youth and consolidator fares.

LTC Travel, 101 2 St W, Chaska, MI 55318 (☎ 1-800/216-9776, *www.ltctravel.com*). Discount ticket agent.

STA Travel, Head Office at 5900 Wiltshire Blvd. Suite 2110, Los Angeles, CA 90036 (☎ 1-800/777-0112 or 212/627-3111, *www.sta.com*). Branches in many other US cities. Worldwide discount travel firm specializing in student/youth fares; also student IDs, travel insurance and car rental.

TFI Tours International, 34 W 32nd St, New York, NY 10001 (☎ 1-800/745 8000 or 212/736-1140). Consolidator; also has other offices in Las Vegas and Miami.

Travel CUTS, 187 College St, Toronto, ON M5T 1P7 (☎ 416/979-2406 or 1-800/667-2887 in Canada, *www.travelcuts.com*). Other branches all over Canada. Organization specializing in student fares, IDs and other travel services.

Travelocity, *www.travelocity.com*. Online travel agent with discounted tickets on airfares and cruises to Jamaica.

Not surprisingly, **Air Jamaica** leads the field in flights to the island, with once-daily services to Montego Bay and Kingston from Atlanta, Baltimore, Chicago, Fort Lauderdale, Los Angeles, Miami, New York (Newark and JFK), Philadelphia and Orlando. The other chief contender is **American Airlines**, with one daily direct flight from New York (JFK) and Miami to Montego Bay or Kingston, with connections to New York from every major US city available. Plenty of other carriers are in the market, though, and it's worth calling around to see which are the most convenient for you – US Air, for example, offers the only direct flights to Jamaica from Charlotte, NC, and TWA flies from St Louis, while Nothwest Airlines operate a flight from Tampa to Jamica.

Finally, the Trinidadian airline BWIA International offers a thirty-day **air pass**, valid for travel around the Caribbean, which is available in the US. See p.26 for details.

By sea

The archetypal luxury vacation – a **Caribbean cruise** – is a relatively accessible reality in North America. A handful of corporate shipping companies peddle all-inclusive cruises of the Caribbean, and although prices on a luxury liner can scale the heights of silliness, a seven-day spin on a not-so-swanky ship should only set you back about US$500. The downside of choosing a cruise is that as you only get to see the tourist ports – and only for a few hours at that – the glimpse you get of each island is both hurried and unrepresentative. Mind you, the chance to live out your Jackie O fantasies might be ample compensation considering that the major cruise companies' ships can range from a whopping

CRUISE OPERATORS

The fares quoted below are for seven-day cruises, in single person/double occupancy "inside" (no ocean views) cabins, and are exclusive of port charges, which add an extra US$110 to US$140, depending on where you stop. All cruises operate year-round and leave from Florida (unless stated otherwise in the listing). In each case, there is only one stop in Jamaica. All prices are in US dollars.

DOCKING IN MONTEGO BAY

Commodore Cruise Line ☎ 1-800/832-1122 or 954/967-2100, *www.commodorecruiseline. com*. Operate a weekly cruise on the Enchanted Isle to Jamaica departing from New Orleans, with one stop in Grand Cayman, starting at US$580 and going up to US$880 depending on the season of travel.

DOCKING IN OCHO RIOS

Carnival Cruise Line ☎ 1-800/327-9501 or 305/599-2600, *www.carnival.com*. Probably the most well-known, if not well-publicized, cruises in North America operating a fleet of ships throughout the Caribbean with many departure points including Galveston, Houston, and Tampa. Five- or seven-night cruises are on offer; prices range from US$600 to US$770 for five nights and US$630 to US$1000 for seven-nights.

Celebrity Cruises ☎ 1-800/437-3111 or 305/262-8322, *www.celebrity-cruise.com*. As the name suggests, this cruise company likes to be flashy. Big boats cruise through the whole of the Western Caribbean. The 815ft Century cruises through Jamaica with prices begining at US$649 and climbing up to US$1400 – depending on whether or not you want the presidential suite.

Costa Cruise Lines ☎ 1-800/462-6782 or 305/358-7325, *www.costacruises.com*. "Cruising Italian style" is their motto, which basically carries over into everything they do. Cuisine, nightlife, general style and even the ship's crew are all Italian. This cruise company has lots of personality and boasts lots of activi-ties for children and special New Year's Eve cruises. Ships depart every two weeks from November to April. Prices start at US$569.

Holland America Line – Westours ☎ 1-800/426-0327 or 206/281-3535, *www .hollandamerica.com*. The most upmarket of the list, specializing in five-star cruises and attracting an older set in search of peace and quiet as opposed to activities galore. From October through December cruises set sail through the West Caribbean. Prices begin at US$750.

Norwegian Cruise Line ☎ 1-800/327-7030 or 305/445-0866, *www.norwegiancruise.com*. Well-established and very large cruise operator, offering a number of variations to the Caribbean throughout the year. Prices start at US$760.

Royal Caribbean Cruises ☎ 1-800/327-6700 or 305/539-6000, *www.rccl.com*. This company spe-cializes in trips to the Caribbean and promises that their boats have more glass on them than any other afloat. Offers numerous seven to eleven-day cruises. Prices start starts at US$649, rising to US$1099 depending on your level of luxury.

1000ft to a more intimate 600ft. They all seem to vary on the theme of "over-the-top", however, as all ships promise live entertainment and endless exotic drinks and many cruise liners also boast tennis courts, pools, gyms and some have Internet cafés for those who need to stay wired.

It may seem like there are an overwhelming range of options at first, but you'll find there real-ly are only a few large companies which seem to dominate the scene. The Internet is a good place to start your research. Web sites such as *www.cruise.com* and *www.cruisereviews.com* are helpful resources for deciding which cruise is best for you (price range, size of boat, length of trip). Travelocity.com (*www.travelocity.com*) also provide useful reviews of the major cruise com-panies. And if you're still unsure, you can always rent a yacht for US$50,000 a week as offered by *www.sailing-vacations.net/poweryachts/*.

Yachting

Yachting between the USA and the Caribbean is big business, and a very pleasurable way of getting to the island. In February, there's a race from Miami

TOUR OPERATORS

Air Jamaica Vacations ☎ 1-800/622-3009. All-inclusive trips to the island's premier tourist spots. Offer occasional good specials.

American Airlines Flyaway Vacations ☎ 1-800/321-2121, *www.aavacations.com*. Organize customized packages from budget to luxury with a large range of hotels in Jamaica to choose from.

Dragonfly Expeditions ☎ 1-888-9-WANDER, *www.dragonflyexpeditions.com/jamaica*. A well-run and energetic company offering eco-tours through Jamaica via snorkelling trips, bike rides, mountain trails, and other adventurous activities. Nine-day tours from Montego Bay include mountain biking, snorkelling, hiking and spelunking for US$1145 per person including lodging, food, transportation but not flights. Check out the helpful Website that explains its tour group philosophy.

Elderhostel ☎ 617/426-7788 or 426-8056, *www.elderhostel.org*. Educational program for seniors, such as a twelve-day course in marine biology and natural history for US$1330 per person, or an eight-day Coral Reef program for US$940 per person. Meals and lodging are included, but you have make your own way to the island.

Friendly Holidays ☎ 1-800/221-9748, *www.globetrottersvacations.com*. Independent, customized tours of Jamaica with a range of prices and options to suit your budget. Seven days during high season at a mid-range hotel costs US$1340 per person and includes air fare from New York to Montego Bay.

ITS Tours Limited *www.infohub.com*. Infohub is an online tour organizer sponsoring companies such as ITS Tours. ITS Tours specialize in Reggae Sumfest packages which include seven nights accommodation, concert tickets for five nights, access to Sumfest parties, and transportation for US$699 per person (based on double occupancy).

Spring Break Travel ☎ 1-800/678-6386, *www.springbreaktravel.com*. Large tour company specializing in what else but Spring Break holidays. Packages include airfare, hotel accommodation, transportation and drink coupons and begin at US$776 per person. Accommodation options range from small hotels for students to crash in, to larger, private beachfront bungalows.

STA Travel ☎ 1-800/777-0112 or 212/627-3111, *www.sta.com*. Seven-night hotel/air packages from New York to Jamaica.

StudentCity.com *www.studentcity.com*. Online Spring Break wholesaler – used by both travel agents and individuals. Lots of budget options and a range of package tours.

Sunburst Holidays ☎ 1-800/MONTEGO or 212/567-2900. All-inclusive customized packages to Jamaica. Seven days during low season in a superior hotel costs US$914 flying from Los Angeles to Montego Bay.

Sun Splash Tours ☎ 1-800/426-7710, *www.sunsplashtours.com*. Specializes in budget/self-catering tours for college students and is one of the largest Spring Break Tour organizers in the US (over 15,000 tours arranged per year). A week in Negril starts at US$420 per person, and can be up to as high as US$850.

Tour Host International ☎ 1-800/THE HOST or 212/953-7910, *www.tourhost.com*. Specialist tour operator with very helpful staff and an astonishing range of travel options, including adventure, natural history and eco tours, coffee-tasting day-trips, and trips to the big reggae festivals. Specializes in tours in Kingston.

TourScan Inc ☎ 1-800/962-2080 or 203/655-8091, *www.tourscan.com*. This Caribbean specialist scans some 18,000 tours from 200 brochures for the best-value deals (including hotels, flights & tours) on a variety of general and specialist packages, and publishes its findings in a catalogue. This is available for US$4, which is refundable if you use TourScan Inc to make your booking. They claim unique expertise as every member of their staff have toured the Caribbean extensively and are also one of the only tour operators offering sports tours in Jamaica – especially cricket.

Travel Jam ☎ 1-800/554-7352. Company which creates tailor-made packages only. For events such as Sumfest, they offer seven days, flying from New York and staying in Negril, for US$1077. Also offer various sight-seeing tours throughout the island.

to Montego Bay, The Pineapple Cup, and a lot of yachters go over for the Montego Bay Easter Regatta. Marinas pepper the coast, and on arrival you have to go through customs and immigration, and pay a hefty tax. The US Coast Guard in Miami will steer you in the right direction (☎305/535-4470), or you can call US Sailing (☎1-800/-US SAIL 1 or 401/683-0800) or, in Jamaica, the Montego Bay Yacht Club (☎979 8038).

Packages and tours

Although the island is so small it's easy to explore independently, you might well be tempted by the comfort and convenience of a vacation **package**. If you're considering specific events such as Spring Break, Sumfest and cricket matches, it may be worth having someone do the work for you. Regardless, remember to book early if you are heading down during high season. Beware of Spring Break deals, if it looks too good to be true it probably is, with so much money up for grabs there are a lot of less than desirable packages offered by less than desirable outfitters – although all those we have listed are among the best around.

If you decide on a package tour, there are no end of **all-inclusive** deals available, most geared around lying on a north-coast beach for a week or two, and comprising flights, transfers, accommodation and airport taxes. Prices start from around US$650 for seven nights in low season, but generally hover around US$900 for a fortnight, occasionally going as high as US$2800. A few specialist operators offer more thematically designed **tours**, with itineraries geared around special interests or occasions – including relaxing honeymoons and wild outdoor adventures.

If you arrive in Jamaica independently but then decide you want to join an organized tour of the island you can easily sign up at your hotel front desk.

Entry requirements

US and Canadian citizens don't need a passport to enter Jamaica but do need **proof of citizenship**. This can take the form of a valid passport, a birth certificate supported by a driver's licence with photo ID, or a voter registration card supported by a driver's licence with photo ID. You'll also need a ticket valid for return or ongoing travel, sufficient funds to support yourself, and details of the place you'll be staying for the first couple of nights.

JAMAICAN EMBASSIES, CONSULATES AND HIGH COMMISSIONS

The Embassy of Jamaica, 1520 New Hampshire Ave NW, Washington, DC 20036 (☎202/452-0660, *www.caribbean-online.com/jamaica/embassy/washdc*).

The Jamaican Consulate General, 767 Third Ave, 2nd & 3rd Floors, New York, NY 10017 (☎212/935-9000); 842 Ingraham Building, 25 SE Second Ave, Miami, FL 33131 (☎305/374-8431); 214 King St West, Suite 402, Toronto, Ontario, M5H 1K4 (☎416/598-3008).

The Jamaican High Commission, Standard Life Building, 275 Slater St, Suite 800, Ottawa, Ontario KIP 5H9 (☎613/233-9311).

Getting there from Britain and Ireland

The vast majority of British and Irish visitors to Jamaica are on some form of package tour, which includes a charter flight direct to the island and accommodation. This is certainly the simplest way of going about things, and even if you plan to travel independently and organize your own accommodation, a seat on a charter is normally the cheapest way to get out there. But charters do have their drawbacks, especially if your plans don't fit exactly into their usual two-week strait-jacket. As an alternative, a couple of airlines offer direct scheduled flights from London to both Kingston and Montego Bay, and you can find similar fares with other carriers that require a stopover in the USA. There are no direct flights from Ireland to Jamaica, but there are good connections via London and Manchester or, on Aer Lingus or Delta, via New York and Miami.

Fares and flights

Start by calling the **discount** and **specialist** travel agents listed below; most of these can quote fares on scheduled and charter flights, although

---

AIRLINES IN BRITAIN AND IRELAND

Aer Lingus, 64 Conduit St, London W1R 0AJ (☎ 0645/737 747); 40–41 O'Connell St, Dublin 1 (☎ 0645/737 747, *www.aerlingus.ie*).

Airtours, Wavell House, Holcombe Rd, Helmshore, Rossendale, Lancashire BB4 5NB (☎ 01254 358 3000, *www.airtours.com*).

Air Jamaica, Central House, 3 Lampton Rd, London TW3 1HY (☎ 020/8570 7999, *www.air-jamaica.com*).

American Airlines, 15 Berkeley St, London W1X 5AE (☎ 0345/789 789, *www.aa.com*).

British Airways, 156 Regent St, London W1R 5TA; Fountain Centre, College St, Belfast BT1 6ET (both ☎ 0345/222 111); in Eire (☎ 0141/222 2345, *www.british-airways.com*).

Continental, 1st Floor, Beulah Court, Albert Road, Horley Surrey RH6 7HP (☎ 0800/776 464, *www.continental.com*).

Delta Airlines, Oakfield Court, Consort Way, Horley RH6 7AF (☎ 0800/414 767); 989 Upper Newtonards Rd, Dundonald, Belfast 4 (☎ 028/9048 0526 or 1800/414467 in Northern Ireland). *www.delta-air.com*.

Virgin Atlantic, Ashdown House, High St, Crawley, West Sussex RH10 1DQ (☎ 01293/747747); Club Travel Offices, 30 Lower Abbey St, Dublin 1 (☎ 01/873 3388). *www.flyvirgin.com/atlantic/*.

DISCOUNT AGENTS IN BRITAIN AND IRELAND

American Holidays, Lombard House, Lombard St, Belfast 1 (☎ 028/9023 8762); 38/39 Pearse St, Dublin 2 (☎ 01/679 8800 or 679 6611).

Flightbookers, 177–178 Tottenham Court Rd, London W1P 0LX (☎ 020/7757 2000).

---

some, including STA and USIT (which both specialize in youth and student fares), can only quote for scheduled flights. Other good sources of information are the ads in London's *Time Out* magazine, and the travel pages in the *Observer* and other Sunday **newspapers**. For **last-minute** charter flights it's well worth looking at the Airtours, Caribbean and Worldwide pages on ITV's **Teletext**, checking out the deals at your local travel agent and those we recommend in the box below, and having a browse of cheap flight sites on the **Internet** (try *www.cheapflights.com*, *www.lastminute.com* or *www.deckchair.com*) – all of these options commonly turn up last-minute charter seats to Montego Bay for less than £200 return.

Regardless of where you buy your ticket, though, fares depend on the **season**. Seasonal definitions vary from airline to airline, but the period from around mid-December to mid-April is generally classified as **high season**, with the rest of the year considered **low season**. During Easter and in July and August, however, when many British-based Jamaican families take advantage of school holidays to visit relatives, mid-priced "shoulder season" fares come into play.

Air Jamaica offers **scheduled flights** from London Heathrow five times a week, on Wednesday, Thursday, Friday, Saturday and Sunday. The Thursday flight is direct to Kingston; the others stop at Montego Bay before continuing on to the capital. British Airways flies from London Gatwick four times a week, on Tuesday, Thursday, Friday and Sunday, stopping at Montego Bay and continuing on to Kingston. Return **fares** with both airlines start at about £320 in low season, reaching £550–650 in high season.

A less convenient but sometimes cheaper option is to change planes in the United States, normally in Miami. Delta, Virgin, American Airlines, Continental and British Airways all fly from London to Miami, with return fares as low as £200 to £250 during the low season. From Miami, American Airlines and Air Jamaica both offer direct flights into Montego Bay and Kingston, with return fares from around £140 to £170, according to season.

A number of **charter operators**, with the main player being Airtours, fly from London Gatwick and Manchester into Montego Bay. They are normally significantly cheaper than the scheduled flights but tend to arrive and depart at anti-social hours, and there is little or no flexibility once the ticket is booked. Fares start at as little as £200 in low season, rising to £550–600 in high season. Most charter flights are for two weeks, although you can also find one-week and three-week

---

Joe Walsh Tours, 69 Upper O'Connell St, Dublin 2 (☎01/872 2555); 117 St Patrick St, Cork (☎021/277959).

King Travel, 4 St John's Terrace, London W10 4RB (☎020/8964 3335).

The London Flight Centre, 131 Earls Court Rd, London SW5 9RH (☎020/7244 6411) and other branches across London.

New Look Travel, 111 High St, London NW10 4TR (☎020/8965 8212).

Newmont Travel, 55–57 Chase Side, Southgate, London N14 5DB (☎020/8920 1122).

North South Travel, Moulsham Mill Centre, Parkway, Chelmsford, Essex CM2 7PX (☎01245/608 291).

Ryan Travel, Suite 607, Langham House, Regent St, London W1 5AL (☎020/7580 8141).

Sackville Travel, 207 Stockwell Rd, London SW9 7BP (☎020/7738 7077).

STA Travel, 86 Old Brompton Rd, London SW7 3LH (☎020/7361 6262, *www.statravel.co.uk*) and offices nationwide.

Stratford Travel, 41 Broadway, London E15 4BQ (☎020/8519 4921, *www.stratfordtravel.co.uk*).

Thomas Cook Flights Direct In UK (☎0870/5101520); 11 Donegall Place, Belfast (☎028/9055 0232); 118 Grafton St, Dublin 2 (☎01/677 0469).

Trailfinders, 42–50 Earl's Court Rd, London W8 6FT (☎020/7938 3366); 4–5 Dawson St, Dublin 2 (☎01/677 7888), and offices nationwide. *www.trailfinders.co.uk*.

The Travel Bug, 125A Gloucester Rd, London, SW7 4SF (☎020/7835 2000); 597 Cheetham Hill Rd, Manchester M8 5EJ (☎0161/721 4000). *www.flynow.com*.

Usit Campus, in UK (☎0870/240 1010, *www.usitcampus.co.uk*).

options available. Your best bet for booking a charter is often ITV's Teletext (see p.9), though big-name high street travel agents can also turn up surprisingly low fares.

Finally, if you fancy flying around more than one Caribbean island, BWIA International offers 30-day **air passes**, available in Britain, which let you do just that; see p.26 for details.

Packages and tours

If you plan to do little more than stay in one place and soak up the sun, a **package holiday** can offer excellent value, often considerably cheaper (and more convenient) than arranging separate flights, transfers and accommodation yourself. There are all kinds of deals available, depending on whether you opt for an all-inclusive (hotel room plus all meals and drinks) room only, or self-catering option (usually a hotel room or villa with simple cooking facilities). Most packages are for two weeks, with one- and three-week deals slightly less common.

All-inclusive packages at a three-star hotel tend to start at around £775 per person for a week, £950 for a fortnight, while room-only deals start at about £400 per person for a week, £500 for a fortnight – prices are based on double occupancy. Self-catering rooms start at around £500 per person for a week, £650 for a fortnight, again based on two people sharing. All deals include the flight and transfers from airport to hotel.

A handful of tour operators offer **specialized tours**, centred, for example, around getting married or catching the West Indian cricket season (see box below). And if you just want to see Jamaica for a day, you could do worse than a **Caribbean cruise** (covered in more detail in "Getting There from North America"; see p.4); these start at around £1000 per person for a seven-day cruise, including a return flight to the embarkation point at Miami.

Entry requirements

Citizens of Britain and Ireland can enter Jamaica without a visa and stay for up to six months. You will, however, need a **passport** and a return ticket or proof of onward travel. You might also be

---

SPECIALIST PACKAGE AND TOUR OPERATORS

Airtours, Wavell House, Holcombe Rd, Helmshore, Rossendale, Lancashire BB4 5NB (☎01706/260000, *www.airtours.com*). One of the largest package operators into Jamaica, with a range of holidays in all the tourist hotspots.

Caribtours, 161 Fulham Rd, London SW3 6SN (☎020/7581 3517). Solid, upmarket group with expensive all-inclusive packages and luxury yacht charters.

Hammock, 19a Clapham High St, London SW4 7TS (☎020/7627 2323, *reservations@hammockleisure.demon.co.uk*). Small-scale, reliable company offering specialized packages to coincide with all the biggies in Jamaican's calendar, as well as weddings and all types of accommodation throughout the island.

Hayes & Jarvis, Hayes House, 152 Kings St, London W6 0QU (☎0870/8989890). Exotic packages to a range of hotels.

Kuoni Worldwide, Kuoni House, Dorking, Surrey RH5 4AZ (☎01306/742222). Flexible package holidays and good family deals.

Thomas Cook, 45 Berkeley St, London W1X 5AE and high streets across the UK (nationwide ☎0870/5666222); 11 Donegall Place, Belfast (☎028/9024 2341); 118 Grafton St, Dublin 2 (☎01/677 1721). *www.tch.thomascook.com*. Package holidays, charter and scheduled flights.

Time Out Travel, 207 Stockwell Rd, London SW9 7BP (☎020/7738 7077, *timeout@ sackville.demon.co.uk*). One of the best in the UK for destination management: airport pickups, accommodation and tours plus flights via sister-company Sackville Travel. Particularly good for first-time visitors to Jamaica.

Tropical Places, Freshfield House, Lewes Rd, Forest Row, East Sussex RH18 5ES (☎01342/825123). All-inclusive hotel packages only but a wide choice of places to stay.

Virgin Holidays, Ashdown House, High St, Crawley, West Sussex RH10 1DQ (☎01293/ 617181). General room-only and all-inclusive package deals.

---

asked to show that you have sufficient funds to cover your stay, and to confirm that you have accommodation arranged for the first couple of nights – if you're not sure where you're staying, giving the name of any hotel near the airport will usually suffice. If you can't satisfy the immigration authorities on all counts, they have the right to deny you entry.

The **Jamaican High Commission** in Britain is at 1–2 Prince Consort Rd, London SW7 2BZ (☎020/7823 9911, fax 408 2545). There is no embassy or consulate in Ireland.

Getting there from Australia and New Zealand

Jamaica is no bargain destination from Australasia. There are no direct flights from Australia or New Zealand, so you'll have to take a flight to one of the main **US gateway airports (Los Angeles, San Francisco, Miami or New York)**, and pick up onward **connections** from there.

The least expensive and most straightforward **route** is via Los Angeles, or Miami, from where there are frequent flights to Kingston and Montego Bay. If you're planning to see Jamaica as part of a longer trip, **round-the-world** (RTW) tickets are worth considering, and are generally better value than a simple return flight. Whatever kind of ticket you're after, your first call should be one of the **specialist travel agents** listed in the box on p.13. If you're a **student** or **under 26**, you may be able to undercut some of the prices given here; STA is a good place to start.

Fares and air passes

All the **fares** quoted below are for return travel during **low season**, and exclude airport taxes; flying at peak times (primarily Dec to mid-Jan) can add substantially to these prices.

Los Angeles and San Francisco are the main US gateway airports for flights **from Australia**; when they have surplus capacity, airlines frequently offer special fares to these gateways which can be as low as A$1599; from LA, Air Jamaica and American Airlines fly on to Kingston and Montego Bay for around A$650 return giving a total fare of A$2249. Otherwise, the best you're likely to find are the Air New Zealand and Qantas regulars to Los Angeles, with connecting flights to Miami, flying American Airlines, Delta or United: through return fares to Miami cost around A$2499 from eastern gateways in Australia, rising to A$2899 from Perth and Darwin. From Miami to Kingston or Montego Bay, return flights with American Airlines cost A$330. **From New Zealand**, Air New Zealand, Qantas and United Airlines return fares to Los Angeles start around NZ$1999, with connections on to Miami; through return fares to Miami start at NZ$2699 from Auckland; and the return to Kingston will add another NZ$380.

It may be worth looking into the various **US coupon deals** if you plan to visit more than one destination in the Caribbean. Coupon deals must be purchased with your main ticket, are valid in

AIRLINES

Air New Zealand, Sydney (☎13 2476); Auckland (☎0800 737 000 or 09/357 3000). *www.airnz.com*. Daily from Sydney, Brisbane, Melbourne and Adelaide to LA, either non-stop or via Auckland and one of Honolulu/Tonga/Fiji/Papeete, with onward connections to Miami and Jamaica.

Air Jamaica *www.airjamaica.com*.

American Airlines, Sydney (☎1300/650 747); Auckland (☎09/308 9159 or 0800/887 997); *www.aa.com*. Code-share with Qantas. Daily to LA from Brisbane, Sydney and Melbourne either non-stop or via Honolulu, and daily from Auckland via Sydney; onward connections to Kingston and Montego Bay.

Delta Air Lines, Sydney (☎02/9251 3211); Auckland (☎09/379 3370). *www.delta-air.com*. Daily flights from LA and San Francisco to Miami: code-share with Air Jamaica to provide daily services from Miami to Kingston and Montego Bay. Coupons are available for extended travel in the US and Carribean.

JAL Japan Airlines, Sydney (☎02/9272 1111); Auckland (☎09/379 9906). *www.japanair.com*. Several flights a week to LA and San Francisco from Sydney, Brisbane, Cairns and Auckland: flight often includes a free overnight stopover in Tokyo.

Qantas, Sydney (☎13 1211); Auckland (☎09/357 8900 or 0800/808 767), *www.qantas.com.au*. Daily to Los Angeles from Brisbane, Sydney or Melbourne either non-stop or via Honolulu and daily from Auckland via Sydney; onward connections to Miami and Kingston.

United Airlines, Sydney (☎13 1777); Auckland (☎09/379 3800). *www.ual.com*. Daily to LA and San Francisco from Sydney, Melbourne and Auckland either non-stop or via Honolulu; connections to Miami, Montego Bay and Kingston.

DISCOUNT AGENTS IN AUSTRALIA AND NEW ZEALAND

Anywhere Travel, 345 Anzac Parade, Kingsford, Sydney (☎02/9663 0411 or 018 401 014, *anywhere@ozemail.com.au*).

Budget Travel, 16 Fort St, Auckland, plus branches around the city (☎09/366 0061 or 0800/808 040).

Destinations Unlimited, 87 Albert St, Auckland (☎09/373 4033).

Flight Centres, 82 Elizabeth St, Sydney, plus branches nationwide (☎02/9235 3522 or 13 1600); 350 Queen St, Auckland plus branches nationwide (☎09/358 4310). *www.flightcentre.com.au*.

Northern Gateway, 22 Cavenagh St, Darwin (☎08/8941 1394, *oztravel@norgate.com.au*)

STA Travel, 855 George St, Sydney; 256 Flinders St, Melbourne and other offices in state capitals and at major universities (☎13 1776 or 1300/360 960); 10 High St, Auckland ☎09/309 0458 or 09/366 6673), and other offices in state capitals and at major universities. (*www.statravel.com.au*).

Student Uni Travel, 92 Pitt St, Sydney (☎02/9232 8444), plus branches in Brisbane, Cairns, Darwin, Melbourne and Perth.

Thomas Cook, 175 Pitt St, Sydney (☎02/9231 2877); 257 Collins St, Melbourne, plus branches in other state capitals (☎13 1771 or 1800/801 002); 191 Queen St, Auckland (☎09/379 3920). *www.thomascook.com.au*.

Trailfinders, 8 Spring St, Sydney (☎02/9247 7666); 91 Elizabeth St, Brisbane (☎07/3229 0887); Hides Corner, Shield St, Cairns (☎07/4041 1199).

Travel.com.au, 76–80 Clarence St, Sydney (☎02/9262 3555). *www.travel.com.au*.

Usit Beyond, cnr Shortland St and Jean Batten Place, Auckland (☎09/379 4224 or 0800/788 336) plus branches in Christchurch, Dunedin, Palmerston North, Hamilton and Wellington. *www.usitbeyond.co.nz*.

continental US, and offer add-on Caribbean extensions for US$330 for two additional flights/destinations. They are all fairly similar in price and a minimum purchase of three usually applies. American Airlines' Coupon Pass costs $US379 for the first three, and between US$60 and US$100 for subsequent tickets up to a maximum of ten. The best deal, however, is with

Delta, which actually includes Jamaica and other Caribbean destinations in their fare of US$409 for the first three. Alternatively, if you plan to indulge in some island-hopping around the Caribbean, BWIA **air passes** can be worthwhile; available for purchase in conjunction with any international carrier, these allow unlimited stopovers within the Caribbean within a thirty-day period. See p.26 for more details.

RTW tickets

Given these fares and routings, **round-the-world tickets** that take in **Los Angeles**, **San Francisco**, **New York** or **Miami** are worth considering, especially if you have the time to make the most of a few stopovers; see "Getting there from North America", p.3, for more on reaching Jamaica from Los Angeles, New York and Miami.

Ultimately, your choice of route will depend on where else you want to go besides Jamaica, but here are a few sample itineraries to whet your appetite: starting from either **Melbourne**, **Sydney** or **Brisbane**, flying via Auckland/Papeete/Los Angeles/London (surface) to Paris/Buenos Aires/ Melbourne, Sydney or Brisbane (from A$2499); or, starting from **Perth**, flying via Johannesburg/ Amsterdam/New York/Los Angeles/Honolulu/ Auckland to Perth (from A$2599). **From New Zealand**, you could fly from Auckland via Los Angeles/Rome/London/ Bangkok/Melbourne and back to Auckland; fares for this route start at NZ$2899.

Packages and tours

Package holidays from Australia and New Zealand to Jamaica are few and far between, and many specialists simply act as **agents** for US-based operators, tagging a return flight from Australasia onto the total cost. **Cruises** account for the largest sector of the market: most depart from Miami, and because prices are based on US dollar amounts, they fluctuate with the exchange rate. To give some idea of price all-inclusive three-day cruises start from A$599/NZ$699, while seven-day cruises cost upwards of A$1000/NZ$1200, both rates per person based on twin-share. The luxury end of the market is also catered for by Caribbean Destinations and Contours, both of which offer **resort- and villa-based holidays** as well as cruises, with a choice of accommodation. Prices for all of these are suitably rarefied, starting around A$3500/NZ$5000 for two-centre two-week resort holidays (based on twin-share three-star accommodation and low-season airfares from Australia), and rising inexorably.

None of the adventure-tour operators ventures to Jamaica; for independent travellers, the cheapest way to visit Jamaica is as part of a round-the-world or American holiday, making creative use of airpasses.

Entry requirements

Australian and New Zealand citizens do not need a visa to enter Jamaica for stays of less than sixty days, but do need a **passport** and an ongoing or return ticket, and you may be asked to prove that you have sufficient funds, and somewhere to stay for the first couple of nights. There are **no Jamaican embassies or consulates** in Australia or New Zealand.

Insurance

A typical travel insurance policy usually provides cover for the loss of baggage, tickets and – up to a certain limit – cash or cheques, as well as cancellation or curtailment of your journey. Most of them exclude so-called dangerous sports unless an extra premium is paid: in Jamaica this can mean scuba-diving and some motorized watersports. Read the small print and benefits tables of prospective policies carefully; coverage can vary wildly for roughly similar premiums. Many policies can be chopped and changed to exclude coverage you don't need – for example, sickness and accident benefits can often be excluded or included at

will. If you do take medical coverage, ascertain whether benefits will be paid as treatment proceeds or only after return home, and whether there is a 24hr medical emergency number. When securing baggage cover, make sure that the per-article limit – typically under £500 equivalent – will cover your most valuable possession. If you need to make a claim, you should keep receipts for medicines and medical treatment, and in the event you have anything stolen, you must obtain an official statement from the police. Bank and credit cards often have certain levels of medical or other insurance included and you may automatically get travel insurance if you use a major credit card to pay for your trip.

The **British** and **Irish** would do well to take out an insurance policy before travelling to Jamaica to cover against theft, loss and illness or injury. Travel agents and tour operators are likely to require some sort of insurance when you book a package holiday, though according to UK law they can't make you buy their own (other than a £1 premium for "schedule airline failure"). If you have a good all-risks home insurance policy it *may* cover your possessions against loss or theft even when overseas. Many private medical schemes such as BUPA or PPP also offer coverage plans for abroad, including baggage loss,

---

ROUGH GUIDES TRAVEL INSURANCE

Rough Guides now offer their own **travel insurance**, customized for our readers by a leading UK broker and backed by a Lloyds underwriter. It's available for anyone, of any nationality, travelling anywhere in the world, and we are convinced that this is the best-value scheme you'll find.

There are two main Rough Guide insurance plans: **Essential**, for effective, no-frills cover, starting at £12 for two weeks; and **Premier** – more expensive but with more generous and extensive benefits. Each offer European or Worldwide cover, and can be supplemented with a "Hazardous Activities Premium" if you plan to indulge in sports considered dangerous, such as scuba-diving. Unlike many policies, the Rough Guides schemes are calculated by the day, so if you're travelling for 27 days rather than a month, that's all you pay for. You can alternatively take out annual **multi-trip insurance**, which covers you for all your travel throughout the year (with a maximum of sixty days for any one trip).

For a **policy quote**, call the Rough Guides Insurance Line on UK freefone ☎0800 015 0906, or, if you're calling from outside Britain on ☎(+44) 1243 621 046. Alternatively, get an online quote at *www.roughguides.com/insurance.*

cancellation or curtailment and cash replacement as well as sickness or accident.

Americans and **Canadians** should also check that they're not already covered. Canadian provincial health plans usually provide partial cover for medical mishaps overseas. Holders of official student/teacher/youth cards are entitled to meagre accident coverage and hospital in-patient benefits. Students will often find that their student health coverage extends during the vacations and for one term beyond the date of last enrolment. Homeowners' or renters' insurance often covers theft or loss of documents, money and valuables while overseas, though conditions and maximum amounts vary from company to company.

Information and maps

Before you leave home, it's worth contacting the nearest branch of the Jamaica Tourist Board (JTB), which will send out plenty of glossy information on the country, including brochures on the main tourist attractions and forthcoming events, lists of recommended accommodation island-wide and a good road map. Once in Jamaica, you can get the same information from JTB desks at the Kingston and Montego Bay airports, and JTB offices in the main towns. The office in Kingston also has a small informative library, with clued-up staff who can usually help with local queries. None of the JTB offices provides an accommodation-booking service.

Jamaica has no entertainments **listing magazine**, so to find out what's going on, you have to rely on the radio (particularly Irie FM), on news-papers (the *Daily Gleaner* for arts and music events and *X-News* for dancehall parties and stageshows), and – the usual way of announcing forthcoming events – flyers and banners posted up around the towns. We've given more specific advice on finding out what's on in the individual chapters.

Lastly, there's a wealth of Jamaica-related sites on the **Internet**; we've listed some of the best and most useful sites below.

Jamaica on the Internet

There's a vast amount of information about Jamaica available on the Internet, and having a browse before you leave is an excellent way to get a taster of the place. You can, of course, book flights and accommodation online, and it's possible to make a considerable saving this way. For **Music**-related sites see Contexts p.406; many Web sites appear throughout the Guide wherever relevant.

General and travel-related sites

www.jamaicatravel.com

Official site of the Jamaica Tourist Board, with a regularly updated, searchable calendar of events, accommodation, resort and attraction listings, and hoards of local information. A good first stop.

www.villa-jamaica.com/links/db.asp? catalog=jamaica

Handy and extremely comprehensive list of links to all things Jamaican, with topics categorized for easy access and short reviews of each site.

JTB OFFICES ABROAD

Note: There are no JTB offices in Australia, New Zealand or Ireland.
Jamaican Tourist Board Web site *www.jamaicatravel.com.*

UNITED STATES

US Hotline ☎ 1-800/233-4JTB
Chicago, 500 N Michigan Ave, Suite 1030,
Chicago IL 60611 (☎ 312/527-1296, fax 527-1472).
Los Angeles, 3440 Wilshire Blvd, Suite 1207,
Los Angeles, CA 90010 (☎ 213/384-1123, fax 384-1780).

Miami, 1320 S Dixie Hwy, Suite 1101, Coral Gables, FL 33146 (☎ 305/665-0557, fax 666-7239).
New York, 801 Second Ave, New York, NY 10017 (☎ 212/856-9727, fax 856-9730).

CANADA

Canada Hotline ☎ 1-800/465-2624
Toronto, 1 Eglinton Ave East, Suite 616,

Toronto, Ontario M4P 3A1 (☎ 1-800/233-4582 or 416/482-7850, fax 482-1730).

UNITED KINGDOM

London, 1–2 Prince Consort Rd, London

SW7 2BZ (☎ 020/7224 0505, fax 224 0551).

JTB OFFICES IN JAMAICA

Black River, Hendriks Building, 2 High St, Black River (☎ 965 2074, fax 965 2076).
Kingston, 2 St Lucia Ave, PO Box 360, Kingston 5 (☎ 929 9200, fax 929 9375).
Montego Bay, Cornwall Beach, PO Box 67, Montego Bay (☎ 952 4425, fax 952 3587).

Negril, Coral Seas Plaza, Negril PO (☎ 957 4243, fax 957 4489).
Ocho Rios, Ocean Village Shopping Centre, PO Box 240, Ocho Rios (☎ 974 2582, fax 974 2559).
Port Antonio, City Centre Plaza, PO Box 151, Port Antonio (☎ 993 3051, fax 993 2117).

www.roughguides.com
The Travel Talk message board, on the Rough Guides' Web site, is a useful forum for swapping first-hand tips with other travellers.

www.afflictedyard.com/menu.htm
The antidote to the slicker Jamaican sites, including a suitably volatile "Informer Corner" message board, beautifully cynical features, incisive discussion of current events, clips filmed in Jamaica and sound system tapes from Kingston's best cassette vendors. Essential.

www.jamaica-netlink.com/jamaica-netlink/
Links, travel features, accommodation reservations, Jamaican products and a lot more.

www.top5jamaica.com
Links to the most popular Jamaican sites on the Web, divided by category.

www.lastminutejamaica.com
Last minute all-inclusive deals bookable from the US.

www.jamaicans.com
Entertaining, if rather pedestrian, with items on

language, culture, music and cookery, and popular themed message boards.

www.jamaica-irie.com
Good range of links and tourist information.

www.realjamaica.com
Interesting links to all things Yardie.

www.jam-web.com/tourism
Links to hotel and villa homepages, and hordes of other sites related to tourism in Jamaica.

Jamaican media

www.jamaicagleaner.com
Huge site from Jamaica's best-selling newspaper, with weather forecasts, a business directory, chatrooms, personals and a Webcam from the *Gleaner* building in Kingston as well as an electronic version of the newspaper itself, with brilliant searchable archives.

www.jamaicaobserver.com
Internet edition of the dependable Jamaican daily.

MAP AND TRAVEL BOOK SUPPLIERS

UNITED STATES

Adventurous Traveler Bookstore, 245 S Champlain St, PO Box 64769, Burlington, VT 05406 (☎ 1-800/282 3963, *www.adventurous-traveler.com*).

The Complete Traveler Bookstore, 199 Madison Ave, NY 10016 (☎ 212/685 9007).

Map Link, 30 S La Petera Lane, Unit #5, Santa Barbara, CA 93117 (☎ 805/692 6777, *www.maplink.com*).

The Map Store, 1636 1st St, Washington. DC 20006 (☎ 202/628 2608).

Rand McNally, 444 N Michigan Ave, Chicago, IL 60611 (☎ 312/321 1751); 150 E 52nd St, NY 10022 (☎ 212/758 7488). For the location of other branches and mail order call ☎ 1-800/333 0136 (ext 2111) or consult *www.randmcnally.com*.

Sierra Club Bookstore, 6014 College Ave, Oakland, CA 94618 (☎ 510/658 7470).

CANADA

International Travel Books and Maps, 552 Seymour St, Vancouver, BC V6B 3J5 (☎ 604/687 3320, *www.itmb.com*).

Open Air Books and Maps, 25 Toronto St, Toronto, ON M5R 2C1(☎ 416/363 0719).

Ulysses Travel Bookshop, 4176 St-Denis, Montreal, PQ H2W 2M5 (☎ 514/843 9447, *www.ulyssesguides.com*).

BRITAIN

Blackwell's Map and Travel Shop, 53 Broad St, Oxford OX1 3BQ (☎ 01865/792792, *bookshop@blackwell.co.uk*).

Daunt Books, 83 Marylebone High St, London W1M 3DE (☎ 020/7224 2295, fax 020/7224 6893); 193 Haverstock Hill, London NW3 4QL (☎ 020/7794 4006).

James Thin Melven's Bookshop, 29 Union St, Inverness, IV1 1QA (☎ 01463/233500, *www.jthin.co.uk*).

National Map Centre, 22–24 Caxton St, SW1H 0QU (☎ 020/7222 2466, *www.mapsworld.com*).

Stanfords, 12–14 Long Acre, London WC2E 9LP (☎ 020/7836 1321); other branches are located within Campus Travel at 52 Grosvenor Gardens, London SW1W 0AG (☎ 020/7730 1314), and within the British Airways offices at 156 Regent St, London W1R 5TA (☎ 020/7434 4744).

Waterstone's, 91 Deansgate, Manchester, M3 2BW (☎ 0161/837 3000, fax 0161/835 1534, *www.waterstones.com*) and branches country-wide.

Note: maps by mail or phone order are available from Stanfords (☎ 020/7836 1321, *sales@stanfords.co.uk*) and from James Thin Melven's Bookshop (☎ 01463/233500, *www.jthin.co.uk*).

IRELAND

Easons Bookshop, 40 O'Connell St, Dublin 1 (☎ 01/873 3811, *www.eason.ie*).

Hodges Figgis Bookshop, 56–58 Dawson St, Dublin 2 (☎ 01/677 4754, *www.hodgesfiggis.com*).

Waterstone's, Queens Bldg, 8 Royal Ave, Belfast BT1 1DA (☎ 028/9024 7355); 7 Dawson St, Dublin 2 (☎ 01/679 1415); 69 Patrick St, Cork (☎ 021/276 522). *www.waterstones.com*.

AUSTRALIA AND NEW ZEALAND

Mapland, 372 Little Bourke St, Melbourne (☎ 03/9670 4383).

The Map Shop, 16a Peel St, Adelaide (☎ 08/8231 2033).

Mapworld, 173 Gloucester St, Christchurch (☎ 03/374 5399, fax 374 5633, *www.mapworld.co.nz*).

Perth Map Centre, 1/884 Hay St, Perth (☎ 08/9322 5733).

Specialty Maps, 58 Albert St, Auckland (☎ 09/307 2217).

Worldwide Maps and Guides, 187 George St, Brisbane (☎ 07/3221 4330).

www.xnewsjamaica.com
Jamaica's most salacious tabloid, with lots of entertainment and music information alongside the personal adds and nubile ladies.

www.radiojamaica.com
News and sports stories, plus links to local radio stations in the RJR stable.

www.cvmtv.com
Fairly useful site of the Jamaican TV company, with news, archives and a few links.

Cricket and football

www-aus.cricket.org/link_to_database/ NATIONAL/WI/
Homepage of the West Indies cricket team, with reports on regional and international matches, and lots of features.

members.tripod.com/~kathylynn/
Windies supporters' cricket homepage, and well worth a visit.

www.footballjamaica.com
Bills itself as the number one resource on Jamaican football, and not far wrong, with loads of features, news and message forums.

www.jamfootballfed.com/index.html
Official site of the Jamaica Football Federation, with all the juice on the Reggae Boyz and the lesser-known local leagues and teams.

Education and reference

www.infochan.com/natlib
Homepage of Jamaica's National Library, with a huge list of links.

www.uwimona.edu.jm
Web site of the University of the West Indies, with all the college news and activities, and dedicated sections on natural history and island tours.

www.jis.gov.jm
Web site of the ever-helpful Jamaica Information Service, unsurprisingly heavy on facts, figures and links to government agencies. Also has clips from JIS TV programmes, and you can email staff at the JIS with specific questions.

Environment and conservation

www.nrca.org
Web site of the Natural Resources Conservation Authority; seldom updated, but worth a browse nonetheless.

www.greenjamaica.org
The Jamaica Conservation and Development Trust site, with lots of conservation information; you can also book cabins within the Hollywell National park in the Blue Mountains.

www.jnht.com
The Jamaica National Heritage Trust site has pages on places of historical significance throughout the island, plus regularly updated conservation news.

Maps

For touring or driving around the island, the best map to get hold of is the **JTB road map**, *Discover Jamaica*, which includes a 1:350,000 of the entire island, a 1:34,000 of Kingston, and small ones of the other main towns. The map is available from JTB offices abroad and, in Jamaica, from the offices in Kingston and Montego Bay – you may have to pay a small fee.

Of the other island maps, the two best are *Hildebrandt* (1:300,000) and *ITNB* (1:250,000). If you're after something more detailed, 1:50,000 Ordnance Survey maps are published by the Survey Department, 23 1/2 Charles St, Kingston 10 (Mon–Thurs 9am–1pm & 2–3.30pm; ☎922 6630). Twenty of them cover the island – with nos. 13, 14, 18 and 19 dealing with the Blue Mountains – and cost US$10 each. If you can, get them before you arrive in Jamaica, as obtaining them from the Survey Department can be a laborious process.

Costs, money and banks

In keeping with the rest of the Caribbean, traditionally thought of as a "luxury" destination, Jamaica is not a cheap country to visit. Some things, like car rental and international telephone calls, cost more than in Europe and a lot more than in the US; for the staples, like accommodation and food, there's usually something to suit every budget, though the pickings are slim at the bottom end of the lodging market. Don't be scared to negotiate on prices – particularly in taxis and at markets and roadside stalls, the first price quoted is often an opening gambit, and even hotels and guesthouses are generally fair game for a bit of bargaining, especially during low season.

Currency

Jamaica's unit of currency is the **Jamaican dollar** (J$), divided into 100 cents. It comes in bills of J$500, J$100, J$50, J$20 and J$10 and coins of J$5, J$1 J$0.50 and J$0.25.

At the time of writing the **rate of exchange** is roughly J$45 to US$1 and J$60 to £1, although it is prone to fluctuation, with the local currency inexorably falling in recent years. As a result, the **US dollar** has emerged as an unofficial parallel currency, particularly at the north-coast resorts, and prices for tourist services – hotels, restaurants, car rental and sightseeing tours – are usually quoted in US$. When paying a bill, though, check in advance that your change will be given in the same currency or, if in Jamaican dollars, at a decent exchange rate.

Costs

Accommodation is likely to be the major expense of your trip, although if you're prepared to put up with extremely basic options, you can find rooms in most of the main resort areas for around US$30. For something more salubrious expect to pay US$45–50, and closer to US$60–80 for a room with air-conditioning and cable TV. Accommodation apart, if you travel around by bus or shared taxi and get your food from markets and the cheaper cafés and roadside stalls, you can just about survive on a daily budget of around US$25–30 per day. Upgrading to one decent meal out, the occasional taxi and a bit of evening entertainment, expect to spend a more realistic US$35–50; after that, the sky's the limit.

Travellers' cheques and plastic

Travellers' cheques, in US dollars or English pounds, are the safest and most convenient method of carrying money in Jamaica. These are available for a small commission from most banks, and from branches of American Express and Thomas Cook; make sure you keep the purchase agreement and a record of cheque serial numbers safe and separate from the cheques themselves. Once in Jamaica, they can be cashed at banks and cambios (you'll need your passport or other photo ID to validate them) for a small charge.

Major **credit cards** – American Express, Visa, Mastercard – are widely accepted in the larger tourist hotels, but don't necessarily expect the smaller hotels and restaurants to take them. You can also use your credit card to get **cash advances** at most banks, though you'll pay both commission to the bank and hefty interest to your credit card company. **ATM cards** can be used to withdraw local cash at some banks, but don't rely on it – ask your issuing bank for a list of reciprocating Jamaican banks before you leave.

Banks and exchange

Banking hours in Jamaica are generally Monday to Thursday 9am to 2pm and Friday 9am to 3pm or 4pm. Other places to exchange money include **cambios**, which are found at some supermarkets across the country and usually offer a better exchange rate, particularly when the currency is fluctuating wildly – a firm favourite, with consistently good rates, are the islandwide branches of FX Trader, run by the Grace company and often conveniently situated within supermarkets and

shopping malls; you can find out the location of the nearest office by calling toll-free on ☎1-888 398 7233. **Exchange bureaux** at the main airports offer rates slightly lower than the banks, and at **hotels**, the rate is invariably significantly lower – it's only worth changing money at hotels if you have no other choice.

Keep the official receipts when you change money, as you'll need them to convert any Jamaican dollars back to dollars/sterling when you leave as you are not allowed to take Jamaican dollars out of the country. Whenever you exchange money, ask the cashier to give you some small bills – many shops, taxi/bus drivers and small restaurants won't be able to change a J$500 note.

The illegal **black market** is active in Jamaica, particularly when the currency is volatile, and you may well be approached to change money on the streets. The exchange rate offered may be a little better than the banks and even cambios, but bear in mind that counterfeit notes are common and scams rife on the black market, and that peeling off wads of cash in a public place makes you an obvious target for muggers. If you choose to risk it, never hand over your cash until you've counted the Jamaican dollars you're given.

Emergency cash

If you run out of money, you can arrange a **wire transfer** to Jamaica from your home bank account (or that of someone willing to lend you cash). Bear in mind, though, that this carries a steep handling fee, and should be considered a last resort. Western Union (☎0800/833 833 in the UK; ☎1-800/543-4080 in the US or Canada; ☎1800/649 565 in Australia; ☎09/270 0050 in New Zealand) has branches in banks as well as separate offices across the island; in Jamaica, call toll-free on ☎1-888-991 2056 for locations of outlets islandwide. You can also wire cash from post offices and branches of Thomas Cook in the UK via American Express Moneygram, which is slightly cheaper than Western Union (☎0800 8971 8971 in the UK; ☎1-800/543-4080 in the US; ☎1800/230 100 in Australia; ☎09/379 8243 or 0800/262 263 in New Zealand).

Getting around

A lot of people come to Jamaica, make straight for their hotel and spend the next fortnight lying on the beach. For those who want to see some of the island, and you'll have a far more rewarding stay if you do, there are a variety of ways to get around. Buses and minibuses run around the coasts, and to all towns and most rural communities in the interior. Renting a car offers maximum independence but will eat heavily into your budget, if you just want to make the odd excursion or short trip, it can work out cheaper to take a taxi, or even hire a private driver. For longer trips, internal flights are reasonably priced, and a good idea if you're short of time or considering a two-centre holiday – say, Negril and Port Antonio.

Buses, minibuses and coasters

According to the *Daily Gleaner* newspaper, Jamaica's public transport system is "a dreadful source of punishment and wasted time for those who are forced to use it". And there's no doubt that Jamaica's **buses** and **minibuses** – aside from the smarter **"coasters"** that ply the busier routes – can be a little disquieting if you're used to a more regulated system. Timetables, if they exist, are rarely adhered to, drivers can show little interest in the rules of the road, and passengers are often squeezed in with scant regard for their comfort.

On the other hand, public transport is a great way to meet people and get a window into a

different side of the island, is absurdly cheap – about J$50 per 50 miles for a bus and J$100–140 per 50 miles for minibuses and coasters – and, if like most Jamaicans, you can't afford to fly, take taxis or rent a car, you'll be doing a lot of it. Throughout the book we've explained where to catch buses and, at the end of each chapter, detailed the main routes and journey times.

Each town has a bus terminal of sorts, often near the market. The destination is usually written somewhere on the front of buses, minibuses and coasters, squeezed between the vehicle's name: "Ease Dem Off Cherry", "Nuff Vibes", "God's Property", "Rude Boy Strength" and the like. The conductor will shout out the destination repeatedly before departure, scouting the area for potential passengers and cramming in as many as the vehicle will take, before it screeches off, jam-packed with humanity and often pounding with music. Buses and minibuses will stop anywhere en route to pick up or drop off passengers (except in major towns, where they are restricted to bus stops and terminals). If you want to get off somewhere before the terminus, tell the conductor and fellow passengers where you're going when you get on; yelling "one stop", or something similar, at the driver is the usual method of getting the bus to stop when you get there. To get on a bus, just stand by the side of the road and flag it down.

Always keep as close as possible to your luggage – it's probably unwise to stow your shiny new pack on the roof. Fares are paid after boarding to a conductor, and having the right change, or at least small bills, will make your life easier. Try also to travel during daylight as arriving in an unfamiliar place at night will make things more difficult, especially if you have to find accommodation. In fact, the earlier in the day you travel the better – being stuck in a bursting Jamaican bus on a boiling afternoon is no picnic.

Cars

If you can afford it, **renting a car** is the best way of getting around and seeing Jamaica. Though some of the roads beggar belief – and knacker your suspension – it's a relatively easy country to

CAR RENTAL AGENCIES OVERSEAS

NORTH AMERICA

Avis ☎1-800/331-1084, *www.avis.com*.
Budget ☎1-800/527-0700, *www.budget.com*.
Dollar ☎1-800/800-4000, *www.dollar.com*.

Hertz ☎1-800/654-3001, *www.hertz.com*.
Thrifty ☎1-800/367-2277, *www.thrifty.com*.

Note: Web sites listed in the North America section are useable worldwide.

BRITAIN

Avis ☎0870/590 0500
Budget ☎0800/181 181

Hertz ☎0870/599 6699
Thrifty ☎0870/516 8238

IRELAND

Avis Northern Ireland ☎0870/5900 500; Eire ☎01/874 5844
Budget Rent-A-Car Northern Ireland ☎0800/181 181; Eire ☎0800/973 159; Dublin airport ☎01/837 9611

Europcar Northern Ireland ☎0345/222 525; Eire ☎01/874 5844
Hertz Northern Ireland ☎0870/5996 699; Eire ☎01/676 7476
Holiday Autos Northern Ireland ☎0870/5300 400; Eire ☎01/872 9366; freefax 1800/729 366, *info@holidayautos.ie*

AUSTRALIA

Avis ☎13 6333
Budget ☎1300/362 848

Hertz ☎1800/550 067
Thrifty ☎1300/367 227

NEW ZEALAND

Avis ☎09/526 2800 or 0800 655 111
Budget ☎0800/ 652 227 or 09/375 2270

Hertz ☎09/309 0989 or 0800 655 955
Thrifty ☎09/256 1405

drive in; distances are small, and a car can take you on some delightful back routes that you won't see if you're flying or travelling by bus. However, rental **prices** are high, starting at around US$70 per day in high season, including government tax (rates can go as low as US$40 at slow times). Third party insurance is normally included in the price; if you don't have a credit card that offers free collision damage waiver, you'll have to pay another US$12–15 per day to cover potential damage to the car. If you choose not to take out this cover, you're liable for every scratch on the car, whether caused by your own error or not.

There are rental companies all over the island, with the best selection in Kingston, Montego Bay and Ocho Rios, and we've listed them in the individual chapters. Renters range from reputable international chains to small but efficient local operators or dodgy one-man-and-his-dog outfits; though the latter may appear less expensive, you're often better off going with the known names, which will normally offer guaranteed

roadside assistance and are less likely to palm you off with a shoddy vehicle. Most larger companies will also allow you to pick up and drop off in different major towns for no extra fee. To rent a car you'll need a current licence from your home country or an international driver's licence and, in theory, you'll need to have held the licence for at least a year. Most rental companies stipulate that drivers must be at least 21-years-old (though some will rent only to drivers over 25). Before you set off, check the car fully to ensure that every dent, scratch or missing part is inventoried, and that the gas tank is full (bear in mind that you'll have to return the vehicle with the same amount of petrol). When returning the car undamaged, ensure that you collect and destroy any credit card deposit slip.

Rules of the road

Driving in Jamaica is on the **left**, and (unless otherwise specified) speed limits are set at 30mph in towns and minor roads and 50mph on highways. Wearing front seatbelts is now mandatory in Jamaica. The main A roads across the country are normally in pretty good condition, though once you come off them, you'll find the minor roads are often badly potholed. In parts of the country, including the Blue Mountains and Cockpit Country, roads are often little more than bare rock, and if you're planning to explore much in these areas, you should consider getting a **four-wheel-drive** (4WD) vehicle, though you'll pay a premium of around US$20 a day.

Jamaicans can be pretty cavalier behind the wheel, with many drivers (particularly those in charge of air-braked, diesel-spitting juggernauts) often dangerously macho and impatient. Always drive **defensively**; watch out for overtaking traffic coming towards you as overtaking a line of ten or more cars, even if it's impossible to see what's coming, is common practice. Be prepared to spend a lot of time stuck behind large lorries on smaller, winding roads, particularly the route between Ocho Rios and Kingston. At night, you'll also need to get used to being dazzled by other drivers' undipped headlights; to minimise the effects of the glare, keep your eyes on the left verge of the road and slow down. You should use your horn as freely as most Jamaicans do; a toot is just as likely to mean thank-you as it is an indication of some kind of hazard such as "I'm planning to overtake as soon as we get to this blind corner". If someone does hoot to indicate that they're about to overtake don't try to teach them a lesson by speeding up to prevent them from doing so, no matter how potentially dangerous you think they're being. Anywhere on the island, but particularly in Kingston, be extremely careful when driving in the rain; unsurprisingly, Jamaicans don't take kindly to being splashed, even if the water comes from a pothole that you didn't see. Daredevil stunts notwithstanding, you'll notice that on the whole Jamaican drivers are pretty courteous toward visitors, often offering loud vocal suggestions as to how best to handle situations and giving way to rental plates.

If you do have an **accident**, wait for the police before moving your car, and avoid making any admission of responsibility, or, for that matter, accusations of blame – you don't want to get embroiled in a heated roadside argument.

Finally, the Jamaican police often set up **speed traps** and **roadblocks**; seen by the more cynical as a way for officers to augment their wage packets as the weekend approaches. Jamaican drivers have an informal system of flashing their lights to other drivers to indicate police presence ahead. If you're stopped, be friendly and polite and you'll normally be sent on your way fairly quickly, but drug searches are not uncommon – for more on this, see p.54.

Local drivers

If you don't drive – or don't want to – but still want to travel independently around the island, it might be worth hiring a **local driver** to ferry you about; generally for between US$60 and US$100 a day. They often make excellent tour guides, but, especially if you're a woman alone, you might find the prospect of setting off in a car with a stranger a bit daunting. Obviously, we only recommend reliable drivers, whose names and numbers appear at relevant points throughout the Guide.

Hitching

Although many Jamaicans **hitch** rides – and will expect you to offer if you're driving through a rural area in a half-empty car – very few tourists do, and it's not something we recommend. There's a common assumption that tourists have plenty of money so, at the least, you'll be looked at as a curiosity; at the worst, you're exposing yourself to danger. If you're short of cash, you're better off sticking to buses or shared taxis.

Taxis

Although a rental car is useful for touring, if you're staying in one place for any length of time, you'll find that it often works out cheaper to get around by **taxi**.

What passes for a taxi in Jamaica varies from the gleaming white vans and imported cars of the **Jamaican Union of Travellers Association** (JUTA; ☎927 4534, 926 1537 or 952 0623), the official – and expensive – carriers, to beaten-up old **Ladas** that crawl along the island's roads. Officially licensed taxis carry red number plates with "PP" or "PPV" on them, but there are a number of rogue taxis, most of whom claim that their application for taxi status is being processed. The authorities advise against using the rogues but, obviously, it's up to you whether you trust them or not. Most towns have a reliable local taxi service that you can call (numbers are given throughout the Guide); during the day, it's usually just as easy to head to the local taxi rank or flag them down in the street.

On the whole, taxi **fares** are pretty reasonable in Kingston and the less touristed areas, even for long journeys; on the north coast, prices are rather more hefty – around US$20 for ten miles, and you'll always pay a little more if you take a taxi licensed to a hotel. Bear in mind, though, that few of the cars have meters, so always establish a price before you get in (or over the phone if you're calling for one). The first quoted price may well be just an opener, particularly if you hail a vehicle on the street; don't be afraid of negotiating. Once you've agreed on a price, a tip is unnecessary.

Shared taxis or "route taxis" are private Lada cars or, more commonly these days, imported Japanese estate cars known as "deportees" (so-called because like the wayward Jamaicans in other countries, they've been sent here in huge numbers as no-one else wants them). Crammed with as many passengers as the driver/owner can fit in, route taxis operate on short, busy set routes around the main towns, picking up and dropping off anywhere along the way in the same manner as the buses and minibuses. Some shared taxis are marked by the PPV number plate, though many more are not, making them difficult to identify, except by the squash of passengers. Though they're normally perfectly safe, they are used more by Jamaicans than visitors, and it's not uncommon for a driver to assume that you wish to charter the whole taxi if you flag it down, in which case he will throw the other passengers out – make it clear that this is not what you want. Prices are much closer to bus fares than to taxi rates.

Motorbikes and cycling

Jamaica should be much better for **cycling** than it is. Places like the Blue Mountains, perfect for biking, are not well geared towards independent cyclists, though several tours offer an easy, and expensive, way of seeing them on a bike (see p.132). Throughout the island, rental outlets are thin on the ground – we've listed them where they're available. If you're interested in a bit of off-road **mountain biking**, contact Rusty's X-Cellent Adventures in Negril (☎957 0155, rxad-ventures@cwjamaica.com); excursions are detailed in that chapter, p.304.

Renting a **scooter** or **motorbike** is easier, and can be an exhilarating way of touring the island. Outlets abound in the main resorts, and at US$30–40 per day, prices are very reasonable, and though in theory you'll need to show a driving licence, these are rarely asked for. Under Jamaican law, all motorcycle riders must wear helmets – you'd be a fool not to in any case.

Zooming about on two wheels, though hugely enjoyable, is fraught with **danger** in Jamaica, one of the most common forms of injury to visitors is "road rash" courtesy of a motorbike incident, and you'll need to be a confident rider to tackle the major roads and Kingston streets. Cyclists should stick to minor roads, and everyone should be on the lookout for potholes, madcap drivers and daft goats and dogs.

Planes

If you're heading across country – say from Kingston to Montego Bay or Port Antonio – it's well worth considering one of the **internal flights** provided by Air Jamaica Express (☎923 6664), which are quick, efficient and sensibly priced; numbers for Air Jamaica Express regional offices are given in

---

AIR JAMAICA EXPRESS FLIGHTS

Prices quoted are for a one-way trip; return fares are double the single rate. Note that as Air Jamaica Express flight schedules are somewhat labyrinthine and subject to frequent changes, we've listed the minimum number of direct flights per day; call the airport you want to travel from to check availability before you book.

Tinson Pen, Kingston to: Montego Bay (4 daily; 35 min; US$66); Negril (2 daily; 35min; US$72); Boscobel, Ocho Rios (2 daily; 15min; U$50); Port Antonio (2 daily; 15 min; US$50).

Montego Bay to: Negril (3 daily; 15 min; US$58); Boscobel, Ocho Rios (1 daily; 25min;

US$55); Port Antonio (1 daily; 35 min; US$66).
Negril to: Boscobel, Ocho Rios (1 daily; 35min; U$61); Port Antonio (1 daily; 45min; US$72).
Boscobel, Ocho Rios to: Port Antonio (2 daily; 15min; U$50).

---

the relevant chapters. There are domestic airports at Tinson Pen in Kingston (☎924 8850), Montego Bay (☎952 4300), Port Antonio (☎923 6664), Negril (☎957 4251), and Ocho Rios (☎975 3254). Private **charters** are available from Wings Jamaica at Tinson Pen (☎923 5416 or 6573) and from Timair at Montego Bay (☎952 2516, *www.timair.net/*) and Negril (☎957 5374). For **sightseeing tours** you're better off with Helitours, based in Ocho Rios (☎974 2265 or 1108, fax 974 2183); a 20min helicopter ride around Ochi costs

US$60 per person, while longer charters vary in price – see p.189.

Organized tours

There's plenty on offer if you're after an **organized tour**; hundreds of operators crowd the resorts, most schlepping off to well-known attractions like Rose Hall or Dunn's River Falls, or offering "highlight" tours of a specific area. At best, they're a hassle-free and comfortable means of getting around; at worst, they barely skim the surface of

---

TOUR OPERATORS IN JAMAICA

CONVENTIONAL TOUR OPERATORS

Caribic Vacations ☎953 2584 or 3658.
Holiday Services ☎974 2817, *holiday@cwjamaica.com*.
JUTA ☎952 0623 or 927 4532.
PRO Tours ☎978 6113 or 8129.

Tourwise ☎974 2323 or 952 6098, or toll-free on 1-888 991 1009.
Tropical Tours ☎952 0400 or 7575, *www.marzouca.com*.

ALTERNATIVE TOUR OPERATORS

Cockpit Country Adventure Tours, Albert Town PO, Trelawny (☎610 0818, fax 610 0819, *stea@cwjamaica.com*). Excellent, small-scale walks around Albert Town in the scenic fringes of Cockpit Country from US$15–50 per person. The Quashie River Sinkhole trek is particularly rewarding.

Destinations (formerly Sense Adventures), PO Box 216, Kingston 7; ☎702 0314. The original alternative operator – tales of its naked canoe trips are legendary – but, since the 1996 departure of its founder, no longer the best. Now concentrates solely on mountain hiking trips.

Heritage Tours, Kingston (☎928 2394, fax 927 4369, *ainsley@cwjamaica.com*). Run by the head of the Jamaica National Heritage Trust, and offering one- or two-week, custom-designed tours on every aspect of Jamaican culture and heritage from the sixteenth to the twentieth century. Established themes include art and culture, churches or Jewish-Jamaican history. All inclusive rates (excluding air fare) start at US$875 per person for a week.

Our Story Tours, Spanish Town (☎984 4165 or 943 8520, *crompton@cybervale.com*). Thoughtful, offbeat and fascinating historical-based islandwide tours, with an emphasis on Kingston, Spanish Town and Port Royal as well

as farther afield in St Thomas, St Andrew and St Catherine. Rates start at US$100 per person for 2–4 people for a full-day tour, plus cost of transport; shorter hops around Kingston, Spanish Town or Port Royal start at US$20 per person plus transport.

Safari Tours, Arawak PO, Mammee Bay, St Ann (☎ & fax 972 2639, *www.jamaica-irie.com/safari*). Ocho Rios-based company doing great business along the north coast. It's distinctively-painted jeeps plough through the Blue Mountains, then down to Kingston with a stop at the Marley Museum (US$75 per person), or trundle along the north coast and into the interior to Marley's mausoleum and a rum factory (US$70 per person). Bus-based tours (US$46–89) around the Ochi area include river tubing, horseback riding and Dunn's River Falls.

Sun Venture, 30 Balmoral Ave, Kingston 10 (☎960 6685, fax 920 8348, *www.sunventuretours.com*). Reliable, innovative and eco-friendly scheduled and custom-designed tours – the best on the island for off-beat tours. Mainstays include Blue Mountain hikes (from US$80 per person), Cockpit Country hikes (US$120 per person), south coast safaris (US$100 per person), caving (US$120 per person) and city tours (US$50 per person).

the country and its culture from the shelter of an air-conditioned bus. There also tends to be little variation in content from one company to another. Prices are generally comparable, too, starting from around US$35 for a simple half-day excursion to US$100 for full day-trips, including meals. Tours of specific sights are listed in the relevant chapters throughout the Guide. Listed in the box below are the largest operators, running trips throughout Jamaica, and several more **alternative-style** companies, which tend to be more rewarding and, consequently, more expensive – booking in a group spreads the cost and always ensures cheaper rates. Almost every hotel in Jamaica will be able to book you with one of the companies listed below.

Community tourism

Community tourism is a relatively new concept in organized tours in Jamaica, the idea being to encourage closer connections between the tourist and the community, through visits to private houses, farms, schools and craft centres. Countrystyle Ltd, based in Mandeville (☎962 3725, fax 962 1461, *countrystyle@cwjamaica. com*) is one of the main organizers, arranging accommodation and customized itineraries island-wide; for more details, see p.355. Other similar organizations include: the Bluefields People's Community Association (☎955 8792, fax 955 8791) in the southwest; the Oracabessa Foundation (☎975 3393), in St Mary on the north coast; Portland Environmental Protection Association (P.E.P.A.), 6 Allen St, Port Antonio (☎993 9632, fax 993 3407); and the Southern Trelawny Environmental Association (S.T.E.A.) in Albert Town Cockpit Country (☎610 0818, *stea @cwjamaica. com*).

CARIBBEAN ISLAND-HOPPING

People often like to do a bit of **island-hopping** while they're in the Caribbean. Many, certainly, can't resist the lure of **Cuba**, just seventy miles north. Cubana (☎978 3410) flies to Havana from Kingston twice a week, with return trips costing US$187; Caribic (☎979 0322) flies from Montego Bay to Havana (5 weekly; US$226) and Santiago de Cuba (2 weekly; US$214) for a similar fare. Both companies can arrange accommodation. North Americans should note that Washington presently allows US citizens to visit Cuba but not to spend dollars.

Air Jamaica (see p.24) uses Montego Bay as a hub airport, with connections to Cuba, Antigua, the Bahamas, Dominican Republic, Haiti, St Lucia, Barbados, Trinidad, Grenada, Bonaire, Dominica, the Cayman Islands and the Turks and Caicos Islands. At present, round-trip flights to these islands start at around US$150 for a round-trip to Cuba, US$284 to St Lucia – though the airline already offers discounts for travellers visiting Jamaica on certain package holidays. It's also well worth bearing in mind that if you book a flight with Air Jamaica to another Caribbean destination, you can stop over in Jamaica for free.

More economical if you want to see a few islands is to buy a Caribbean **air pass** before you leave home. The Trinidadian **BWIA International Airways** (☎1-800/538-2942 in the US; ☎020/8577 1100 in the UK; ☎01/2859 222 in Ireland; ☎02/9285 6811 in Australia) *www.bwee.com*, sells thirty-day air passes, valid for ten Caribbean destinations including Jamaica (St Maarten, St Vincent, St Lucia, Barbados, Grenada, Trinidad, Tobago, Guyana and Caracas). The pass allows unlimited stops, though you can't visit one island more than once. You must specify your routing, but not the dates, in advance, and each change incurs a fee of US$20 or the equivalent. Passes are available for purchase in conjunction with any international carrier if you're coming from Australia or North America, but only in conjunction with a flight into Jamaica with BWIA if you're coming from the UK. Passes cost US$449/£245/A$460/NZ$500.

Accommodation

Accommodation is likely to be your biggest single expense while travelling in Jamaica. Although the country has far more choice than you'll find on other Caribbean islands, it's rare to find anywhere to stay for less than US$20 per night in the large resorts, and you usually need to pay at least twice that for a place with reasonable security and comfort. At the other end of the scale, Jamaica has some of the world's finest luxury hotels, and there are also plenty of options in the middle. As you'd expect, you get what you pay for, although throughout the book we have emphasized places that we consider particularly good value.

The majority of visitors to Jamaica have their accommodation pre-arranged as part of a package deal, and though this can work out cheaper, you run the risk of being stuck in an unsuitable location. If you're not pre-booked, it's normally worth calling ahead to reserve a room for your first night or two to save hassle on arrival, and to satisfy immigration requirements (see pp.7,10 and 13). After that, it's easy enough to call the next place you're heading to arrange a room, although if you've got your heart set on staying in a specific hotel or guesthouse, you should try to sort it out earlier. There exist a couple of new initiatives to help get visitors out of the all-inclusives and into Jamaica's many small hotels. The Ring of Confidence, c/o 5a Port Royal St, Kingston (☎967 2641, www.in-site.com/ring) represents a network of small-scale properties all over the island; you book into one for your first night, and staff there advise and book accommodation to suit you for the rest of your stay. A similar scheme, run by the Port Antonio Guesthouse Association, operates in Portland, representing some of the nicest accommodation options in the Port Antonio area (see p.158).

A couple of times a year, the Jamaica Tourist Board publishes a list of approved accommodation island-wide, with details of their latest rates. It's a reasonable guide to what's available, but there are plenty of perfectly acceptable hotels and guesthouses which aren't included because they don't meet the JTB's sometimes rather pedantic requirements.

If you're in the mood, it is always worth **haggling** over the price of a room. Even in high season, a lot of hotels have surplus capacity and are sometimes desperate for custom – the boom in all-inclusives has hurt the independent sector badly. In low season, you have even more bargaining power, and it's not unknown for US$100 rooms to go for US$50. If you are going to negotiate, doing so over the phone will save you having to traipse around; if you do strike a deal, get the name of the person you're talking to in case the agreement has been forgotten by the time you arrive at the hotel.

Hotels and guesthouses

Jamaica has no youth hostels and the **cheapest** places to stay are usually small, family-run **guesthouses** with pretty basic facilities. At rock-bottom prices (US$20–35), rooms make little concession to comfort; the ones that we recommend are normally clean and have some measure of security, though you can expect them to be cramped and box-like, with spartan furniture, shared bathrooms and a fan. Moving up in price, and into **hotel** territory, US$40–60 will normally secure a more tolerable place with a comfortable bed, hot water and, usually, a bar and maybe a place to eat; for a little more money you'll get a television and a phone and possibly air-conditioning. Once you're paying US$75, you can expect your hotel to have a swimming pool, a restaurant and air-conditioning; over US$100 you'll get a considerable degree of luxury. The top-price hotels are beyond most budgets but are often worth a visit – expect top-quality architectural design, lavish artwork in the rooms and lobby, impeccably dressed staff, and swimming pools carved in exotic shapes or with their own tumbling waterfalls.

All-inclusives

Jamaica was the birthplace of the **all-inclusive** hotel, where a single price covers your room and all meals, and often all drinks and watersports too. *Sandals* and *Superclubs* are the best known of the all-inclusive chains, with around twenty hotels between them, but many other hotels are jumping on the bandwagon, offering all-inclusive deals side-by-side with room-only packages. Prices vary enormously, and it's possible to get bargain deals during low season.

The product offered by the all-inclusives is often excellent – sometimes verging on the madly luxurious – and, despite a blanket no-tips policy, staff are invariably as pleasant and accommodating as in other hotels. Also there is something undeniably seductive about the idea of unlimited access to a hotel's facilities without having to reach for your wallet every time. There is a downside, though. Jamaicans call these places tourist prisons, and indeed many guests do feel rather trapped after a couple of days – the fact that everything is already prepaid discourages them from getting outside the hotel compound to sample the island's many great restaurants and bars – and the giddy thrill of trying twenty different types of cocktail in an evening quickly evaporates. Most all-inclusives offer **day or evening passes** for lunch, dinner or drinks and entertainment, so you might find it

better to stay elsewhere and only visit once for a blow-out.

It's also worth bearing in mind that while all-inclusives remain the bedrock of Jamaican tourism, with high occupancy rates even when the independent resorts are struggling, many establishments do very little for the local economy aside from the filter-down effect of employees wages. Many foods are imported, and as the chains are often foreign owned, it's easy to see that Jamaica gets little direct benefit from their presence. For more on the ramifications of the all-inclusive trend, get hold of a copy of Polly Pattulo's *Last Resorts* (see Contexts, p.424).

Villas

Throughout Jamaica, there are hundreds of **villas** available for visitors to rent, normally by the week. Ranging from small beachside chalets to grand mansions, these are typically self-catering places, often with maid-service (occasionally with a cook and a security guard), and can make a reasonably priced alternative to hotels if you are travelling as a family or in a group. *JAVA*, the Jamaica Association of Villas and Apartments, PO Box 298, Ocho Rios (☎974 2508, fax 974 2967) has comprehensive details of three hundred or so places to suit most budgets.

Camping

There are surprisingly few **camping** options around Jamaica, although you'll normally find one or two in each of the main tourist areas, and some of the cheaper hotels will let you set up a tent on their grounds for a small charge. Treasure Beach is fast becoming popular for camping, with several small properties offering sites. Expect to pay US$5–10 per person per night. **Camping**

ACCOMMODATION PRICE CODES

All accommodation listed in this guide has been graded according to the following **price categories**:

① under US$20	② US$21–35	③ US$36–50	④ US$51–70
⑤ US$71–100	⑥ US$101–150	⑦ US$151–200	⑧ US$200 and above

Rates are for the cheapest available **double or twin room** during the off-season – normally mid-April to mid-December. During the high season, rates are liable to rise by up to 25 percent (though this is rare at the cheaper hotels), and proprietors may be less amenable to bargaining. Many of the all-inclusive hotels have a minimum-stay requirement – where this is the case, we have mentioned it in the text – and rates are quoted per person per night based on double occupancy. Although the law requires prices to be quoted in Jamaican dollars, most hotels give their rates in US dollars; payment can be made in either currency.

rough on the beaches is not recommended, as the risk of serious hassle and robbery is high. When camping at an official site, it's always wise to check on the security arrangements; fencing and an all-night guard are advisable unless you're in a quiet rural area or up in the Blue Mountains.

Health

Health-wise, travelling in Jamaica is generally very safe. Food tends to be well and hygienically prepared – though you should be wary of dirtier-looking roadside stalls – and the filtered and heavily chlorinated tap water is safe to drink, so bugs and upsets are normally limited to the usual traveller's tummy. In rural homes not connected to mains pipes you may be offered rainwater – while this is generally safe it is up to you to decide whether to risk it.

Vaccinations and other precautions

Unless you have travelled to Asia, Africa, Central or South America, the Dominican Republic, Haiti or Trinidad and Tobago within six weeks of landing in Jamaica, **no vaccinations** are required to enter the island (contact a travel clinic or doctor for up-to-the-minute advice on specific shots), though you might want to have hepatitis A, typhoid and polio shots if you're planning to hike or swim in rivers.

Jamaica is not malarial, but there are occasional outbreaks of **dengue fever**, carried by the *Aedes aegypti* mosquito, found throughout the island but particularly prevalent in Kingston. It's rarely fatal (only the infirm, very young or old are at serious risk), but at the first sign of symptoms – extreme aches and pains in the bones and joints, rashes around the torso, dizziness, headaches, fever and vomiting – you should take to your bed for a few days, and call a doctor if symptoms persist. There's no effective vaccination, so your best prevention is to avoid mosquitoes (see "Creepy Crawlies" on p.31).

Have a **dental check-up** before you travel and bring **prescription medicines** with you. A pre-prepared **medical kit** (see box) is also useful. The Yahoo! health Web site, *health.yahoo.com*, gives information about specific diseases and conditions, drugs and herbal remedies, as well as getting advice from health experts. In the UK, you might also want to pick up the Department of Health's free publication *Health Advice for Travellers*, a comprehensive booklet available from post offices (or by calling the Health Literature Line on ☎0800/555 777). It includes immunisation advice and is constantly updated on pages 460–464 of the BBC's CEEFAX, or, you can consult it on the Internet at *www.open. gov.uk/*. Another useful Web site *www.24dr.com* outlines health risks in most countries.

A TRAVELLER'S FIRST-AID KIT

Among items you might want to carry with you – especially if you're planning to go hiking (see "Sports and Outdoor Activities", p.47) are:

Antiseptic spray or powder
Insect repellent
Plasters/band aids
Lint and sealed bandages
Emergency diarrhoea treatment
Painkillers
Multi-vitamin and mineral tablets

Rehydration sachets
Calamine lotion or aloe gel
Hypodermic needles and sterilized skin wipes (more for the security of knowing you have them, than any fear that a local hospital would fail to observe basic sanitary precautions).

Staying healthy in the heat

If you're unused to it, Jamaica's **humid climate** can bring on a host of minor medical complaints. Open wounds take longer to heal and easily become septic: clean wounds scrupulously as soon as they occur, and dress with iodine, dry antiseptic spray or powder – creams just keep a cut wet and slow down healing; for the same reasons, avoid dressing minor wounds. If you've no antiseptic to hand, white rum is an effective substitute. Other bothersome ailments include **conjunctivitis** (pink eye) which thrives in heat and bright sunlight so wear sunglasses, and bring your usual treatment if prone, or try the local remedy, aloe vera (see box below). **Pityriasis** is a common, easily transmitted fungal infection that appears as circular crispy patches on white skin and as lighter patches of discoloration on black skin; it's easily treated with antifungal creams, sulphur-based lotions or anti-dandruff shampoos containing selenium. The same treatments apply for **athlete's foot** – to avoid it, wear open sandals as much as possible and flip-flops around pools and communal showers.

You'll need to be extra-scrupulous about personal hygiene, too, as blocked sweat ducts can cause uncomfortable and unsightly **prickly heat** rashes. To treat or avoid prickly heat, wear loose cotton clothes, take frequent cold showers without soap, dust with medicated talcum powder and don't use sunscreen or moisturiser on affected areas.

Given Jamaica's steamy heat, **dehydration** is easily achieved; it pays to dramatically increase your intake of water or coconut water (not fizzy drinks, alcohol, tea or coffee), and remember that if you feel thirsty, you're probably already dehydrated; it's wise to carry an insulated bottle of water wherever you go. **Heat exhaustion** is another potential (and more serious) problem; at the first sign of light-headedness, headache, or nausea, lie down in a cool place and drink as much as possible – packed with goodness, fresh coconut water is especially effective. If you become seriously dehydrated, a salt/sugar rehydration solution helps replenish lost minerals (see "Stomach problems", below). In case of serious **sunstroke** – signalled by vomiting and blurred vision – get to a doctor.

Stomach problems

While serious stomach disorders are rare among travellers in Jamaica, the climate and unfamiliar food might well result in a bout of **diarrhoea** – or "running belly", as the locals call it. Washing and peeling fruit and vegetables, being choosy about where you eat and always washing your hands before you do so lessen the risk, but if you do come a cropper, rest and drink plenty of water, herb tea, fruit juice or clear soup; coconut water has excellent calmative properties and is packed with vitamins. Make up for lost minerals by drinking a glass of water mixed with a teaspoon of sugar and half a teaspoon of salt after every motion and once an hour. Eat plain foods like rice or bread and avoid fruit, fatty foods and dairy products. Conventional diarrhoea remedies

---

ALOE VERA

Jamaicans are so convinced of the curative power of fast-growing **aloe vera** or "sinkle bible" (a corruption of the botanical name *Sempervivum*) that many dispense with titles altogether and simply call it the "healing plant". Noticeable for its thick, spiny-edged clusters of leaves growing close to the ground, aloe is the workhorse of Jamaican medicine – used to treat sunburn (for which it's particularly effective), heat rashes, cuts, bruises, burns and all insect bites; mixed with water to make an eye wash that soothes conjunctivitis; used to condition sun-damaged afro hair; prepared as a treatment for skin conditions like eczema and psoriasis; and drunk with garlic to cleanse the blood – a daring feat, as it's very bitter.

Rastafarians use aloe in place of the Biblical hyssop, but you're most likely to encounter it in the hands of hustlers who peddle bottles of "aloe massage" (aloe gel mixed with water) on north-coast beaches. As aloe plants flourish throughout the island, you can usually find it for free, but anyone will collect a stem for a few Jamaican dollars, and it's much more effective (and hygienic) to use aloe straight from the plant rather than in a preparation. To extract the gel, slice the stem in two, cut off the serrated edges, lightly scrape the mauve jelly and wipe it on. Be careful not to get it on clothing – it leaves a stubborn purple stain. You'll also find pure aloe gel in a tube on the shelves of health food stores at home.

alleviate symptoms but reduce the body's natural response to flush out the infection and should only be used if you cannot get to a toilet, such as before a long journey.

Creepy crawlies: bites and stings

Prevention really is better than cure when it comes to encounters with insects. Avoid being bitten by **mosquitoes** by wearing long sleeves and trousers, and by applying lots of DEET-rich repellent – especially in the early evening or after rain. Mosquito coils are sold everywhere and can be effective, if a bit smelly, and the widely available Skin So Soft has miraculous anti-mosquito properties, particularly if you're unwilling to spray on the chemicals. Another natural repellent, citronella, is also catching on in Jamaica, but even though sprays, oils – look for "Oil of No Mosquito" in the Starfish aromatherapy range – and scented candles are available from resort gift shops, you'll pay less if you bring it from home. Once you've been bitten (and you will be), anoint the bites with aloe or calamine – and **leave them alone;** though hellishly tempting, scratching (or even a light investigative rub) will always lead to more irritation, and possibly infected sores and scarring.

Tiny and innocuous-looking, **sand flies** amass on beaches at dusk, inflicting a small, shiny bite with a lingering itch; Jamaicans use rubbing alcohol to soothe. Present wherever there is livestock, **ticks** and **grass lice** wait on grass stems to feast on passing feet; defy them by wearing trousers tucked into socks, as repellent is ineffective. Though present year-round, tick populations peak between October and January, but even then they're only a problem in rural areas. They can be safely plucked from the skin, though you should apply antiseptic and ensure that you have removed the head as well as the body – leave infested clothes out to air. A lighted cigarette efficiently despatches the larger grass lice; locals dab with kerosene.

There are no **poisonous snakes** in Jamaica, and **black widow spiders** are shy enough to make an encounter unlikely, though you should see a doctor if you think you've been bitten. Watch out for the red and black **"forty legs" centipede,** which measures up to five inches and imparts a nasty scarring bite if touched, even when dead.

Hazards of the sea

Though they look vicious, **moray eels** and **barracudas** only attack if threatened, so keep away from them when snorkelling or diving. Other than the **nurse shark** occasionally seen around the reefs, and again only dangerous if cornered or harassed, sharks are rare along the heavily populated coast. **Spiny black urchins** are easily missed in a bed of sea grass – if you tread on one, remove the spines immediately, soak the skin in vinegar (or urine) and see a doctor; water heated as hot as you can stand is also useful for getting out the spines. Colourless **jellyfish** are quite common, particularly in harbours; the sting is painful but not serious and is easily treated by a doctor. Supreme care should be taken to avoid the trailing purple **Portuguese man o' war,** which is rare but toxic. Never touch **coral;** apart from the fact that contact usually kills the organism, it can cut and you'll come away with a painful, slow-to-heal rash. Fire coral is particularly nasty. If you do have a brush with the reefs, don't touch the affected area directly, but wash it with a diluted vinegar or ammonia solution; again, urine can be used if nothing else is available.

Sexual health

Government figures put the number of people with **AIDS** in Jamaica at 3109, with roughly ten per cent more **HIV positive**. However, US Peace Corps workers estimate that some 60,000 Jamaicans are HIV positive. Given the high level of holiday liaisons and the local propensity for casual sex, figures seem set to rise and, even officially, have so far doubled every two years since the late 1980s. HIV is primarily a heterosexual problem in Jamaica, with tourist areas the worst affected; one in ten citizens in the Montego Bay area are HIV positive and one in five female prostitutes carries the virus. With an estimated 80,000 cases of other **STDs** (including syphilis) each year, Jamaica has a long way to go in sexual health education; as recently as the late 1990s, a radio advertising campaign saw fit to dispel the (widely believed) myth that STDs can be cured by having sex with a virgin.

Advice and information on AIDS, HIV and STDs is available on ☎ 0888 991 4444 (toll free) or 929 9408 or 9409.

Always use **condoms**. Bring them with you even if you don't plan on having sex. The main Jamaican brand, Rough Riders, and some US imports, including Durex, are available from pharmacies and street vendors – check the expiration date. If you notice unusual symptoms get treatment right away. In an attempt to sell safe sex to the ghetto massive, dancehall queen Carlene has lent her name to a new range of condoms, Slam (the brand-name employs a local epithet for sex), complete with a suitably alluring picture of the lady herself on the packet.

Women's health

It's an irritating inevitability that time in the tropics creates the perfect conditions for a bout of **thrush** – bring bifidum acidophilus capsules with you, and take them daily to balance yeasts. Canesten cream or pessaries are effective treatments, as is the more messy natural yoghurt, which is difficult to find in Jamaica. To avoid thrush, avoid using heavily perfumed products in this area and always wear cotton underwear. Dehydration and the stress of travel can encourage **cystitis**; to avoid it, drink copious amounts of water and be rigorous about personal hygiene. If you suffer regularly, bring sachets of acidifying remedies that contain potassium citrate.

You should bring more than enough **sanitary protection**, as your usual brand will be more expensive, and bear in mind that flushing towels and tampons down the toilet is usually a straight route to the sea.

Hospitals, doctors and pharmacies

There are tiny regional **hospitals** throughout Jamaica, but most are overcrowded, underfunded and poorly equipped; the general rule is the larger

---

BUSH MEDICINE

Many Jamaicans, particularly in rural areas, still make frequent use of "**bush medicine**" or "**balm**", a system of African herbal medicine introduced to Jamaica by slaves, fundamental to Maroon civilization for 300-odd years and still an important part of Myalist practice (see "Religion" in Contexts, p.393). Most Jamaicans have a rudimentary knowledge of plant medicine, using natural remedies for minor complaints as a matter of course, but balmists or herbalists have a lifetime's experience, if no formal qualifications. One or two of these respected elders still prescribe from the traditional setting of a **balmyard**, distinguishable from other rural dwellings by coloured flags and hanging talismans. Consultations can be enlightening, but balmists tend to be secretive souls and you'll find a good one only through word of mouth.

Herbs can be taken as an infusion or decoction (usually as a tea), as a poultice, or in a hot "bush bath". Many households have a pot of cure-all **bush tea** permanently on the hob, made up of diverse ingredients like lemon, fevergrass, soursop, breadfruit leaves and pepper elder. Perhaps the most widely used single herb is **cerassee**, a climbing vine made into a very bitter tea – you can buy ready-made teabags if you develop a taste. It's said to cure practically everything, but is particularly good as a blood purifier and allegedly discourages mosquitoes. Inevitably, there are loads of plants geared around **male virility** – chainy root, jack-in-the-bush, medina, janta (or cow-hoof leaf), quassia – the list of "front end lifters" goes on and on, and many concoctions are now commercially bottled (see "Food and drink, opposite). **Ganja** is boiled into a tea for asthma and eye problems; **leaf of life** conquers colds, hypertension and bronchial problems; **tuna cactus** treats dandruff, nerves and chronic pain such as arthritis. Many of the medicinal herbs have rather fanciful names; among the best are **search mi heart** and **shame o' lady**, both used for colds and stomach problems, but the prize goes to **ram goat dash along**, good for arthritis and debility. Simple **fruits and vegetables** are also attributed with specific healing properties – soursop is said to calm the nerves, and it's leaves are used to help testy babies go off to sleep. Papaya (paw-paw) is reputed to relieve indigestion, guava leaves are good for diarrhoea, tamarind soothes itchy skin and chicken pox, and coconut water cleanses the bladder.

Though most balmists stick to medicine, some are associated with **obeah**, or witchcraft, prescribing what's said to be grave dirt mixed with substances such as "**Oil of Keep the Dead**" or "**Oil of Deliver Me**" to banish duppies, "**Oil of Come Back**" to win back a straying lover, or even "**Oil of Fall Back**" which dooms the imbiber to fail in everything they attempt. These days, though, most Jamaicans regard such potions with a healthy degree of cynicism.

---

the town, the better the hospital. There are two good, sizeable public hospitals in Kingston, while Cornwall Regional in Montego Bay (see p.272) is the best equipped on the north coast. The easiest way to find a **doctor** in a hurry is to ask at your hotel; some have a resident nurse, and all will be able to recommend someone locally as every town has a doctor or medical clinic. Most of these are reliable, but you'll have to fork out for

the treatment and claim on your insurance once back home, so make sure you get receipts.

Every town has at least one **pharmacy**, with those in resort towns well stocked with expensive brand-name products; they will only issue antibiotics with a doctor's prescription.

Hospitals, private doctors, clinics and pharmacies are found throughout the island and listed in each chapter.

Food and drink

Jamaica's food reflects its motto – "Out of many, one people" – with distinctive contributions from each of the groups to have peopled the island, and though it's never made great strides outside West Indian communities overseas, Jamaican cuisine is undeniably excellent. From fiery jerk meat, probably the island's best-known culinary creation, to its inventive seafood and ubiquitous rice and peas, the national diet is surprisingly varied – though vegetarians may tire quickly of endless versions of sautéed cabbage and carrots with rice and peas. Snacking is good, too, with patties the staple fare, and there is a vast selection of fresh fruit and vegetables. Outside Kingston and the north-coast resorts, international eating options are limited, although you will find pizza and Chinese restaurants in most towns alongside an ever larger smattering of interna-

tional fast-food chains such as *McDonald's, Burger King, KFC* and *Pizza Hut.*

Eating out

Cosmopolitan Kingston has the variety of eating options you'd expect in a capital city but elsewhere on the island, Jamaica's **restaurants** tend to be of two types: either the no-frills filling-stations patronized mostly by locals and with a standard menu of West Indian staples, or tourist restaurants with more in the way of decor and a menu geared towards American and European palates. We've listed a cross-section of options throughout the Guide, but for quality of cooking (as well as cheaper prices), it's almost always best to go for Jamaican food; bear in mind, though, that such places often close early in the evenings – usually before 9pm.

In the cheapest of Jamaican places, expect to pay the equivalent of J$100–200 for a substantial plateful for breakfast, lunch or dinner. Going up a notch, moderately priced restaurants, which tend to price in US$, will charge more like US$10–15 for a main course, while at the upper end of the scale you'll be looking at US$20 plus for a similar dish.

Breakfast

The classic – and totally addictive – Jamaican breakfast is **ackee and saltfish**. The soft yellow flesh of the otherwise bland ackee fruit is fried with onions, sweet and hot peppers, fresh tomatoes and boiled, flaked salted cod, producing a

Despite forming one half of Jamaica's national dish, **ackee** is a rather hazardous foodstuff. The fruits of the ackee tree must be picked only when their red pods have burst open to reveal the pale yellow arils inside; if forced open when unripe, ackees emit a toxic gas (hypoglycin), so poisonous that it's not unknown for people to die from what's known as **"Jamaica poisoning"**.

dish similar to scrambled eggs in looks and consistency but wildly superior in taste. You'll usually find it served with the leafy, spinach-like **callaloo**, boiled green bananas, a hunk of hard-dough bread (a dense, slightly sweet white loaf) fried or boiled dumplings, or **Johnny cake** – a sweet bread that varies widely in appearance from region to region. Other popular morning options include delicious and filling cornmeal, plantain or peanut porridge, steamed fish or smoked mackerel **"rundown"** – flaked fish boiled with coconut milk, onions and seasoning. Inevitably, tourist demands have resulted in a wider availability of the continental breakfast (rolls, jam, juice and coffee), or American breakfast (bacon, pancakes and scrambled eggs), and most moderate and expensive hotels and restaurants will also have a good selection of local fruits.

Lunch and dinner

Most of Jamaica's cheaper restaurants and hotels offer **chicken** and **fish** as the mainstays of lunch and dinner. Chicken is typically fried in a seasoned batter, jerked or curried, while fish can be grilled, steamed with okra and pimento pods, brown-stewed in a tasty sauce or **"escovitched"** – served in a spicy sauce of onions, hot peppers and vinegar (tastier than it sounds). Red snapper and parrot are probably the most common varieties of fish, but you'll also be offered juicy steaks of kingfish, jackfish, tuna and dolphin (not the mammal). Other staples include stewed beef, curried goat, oxtail with butterbeans and **pepperpot soup**, made from callaloo, okra and beef or pork. More adventurous palates might fancy **"mannish water"** – goat soup that includes the testicles, traditionally an aphrodisiac served to a groom on his wedding night – and **cowfoot** (a gelatinous and arguably delicious stew of bovine hooves) or **cow cod soup** (made from a bull's genitals and, unsurprisingly, touted as an aid to virility).

The tradition of **"jerking"** meat dates back to the seventeenth century, an invention of Maroon warriors keen to preserve the meat of wild pigs, and it has since become the island's most idiosyncratic – and flavoursome – cooking style. Seasoned in a mixture of island-grown spices, including pimento, hot peppers, cinnamon and nutmeg, the meat – usually chicken or pork, but occasionally sausage – is grilled slowly, often for hours, over a fire of pimento wood and under a cover of wooden slats or corrugated zinc sheets.

You'll find jerk on the menu at most tourist restaurants, though not so often in local places, and on the street in every town, where it's sold from smoking barbecues fashioned from oil drums. With hard-dough bread and some roast breadfruit, yam or sweet potato (usually sold by the same vendors), it's the perfect picnic – head for the vendor with the longest line. If you're after the real McCoy, head for Boston Bay in Portland (see p.168), where you can get great meat from one of the original jerk centres, and a bottle of fiery marinade to take home.

Seafood is another Jamaican joy, with fresh **lobster** – occasionally curried but usually simply grilled with lemon or butter sauce – and **shrimp** on every upmarket restaurant menu. Freshwater **crayfish** (known locally as janga) are pulled from rivers across Jamaica, and you'll occasionally see groups of vendors offering bags of them, hotly peppered and ready to eat; however, a better alternative is janga soup, a fortifying combination of whole janga and vegetables that's a popular aid to sexual potency. Though it's not the most visually appealing fruit of the sea, **conch** (the inhabitant of the huge pink shells sold in the resorts) is dense and delicious, cooked up into soup (yet another so-called source of virility) or curried in silver-foil parcels at roadside stalls and served with bammy; the more adventurous prefer to eat it raw in a lime and garlic marinade, Cuban-style. **Seapuss**, also occasionally on menus, is octopus.

Once known as the Jamaican coat of arms, **rice and peas** (rice cooked with coconut, spices and red kidney beans) is the accompaniment to most meals, though you'll sometimes get **bammy** (a substantial bread made from cassava flour which is soaked in milk or water and then fried or steamed), **festival** (a deliciously light sweet fried dumpling), sweet or regular **potatoes** (the latter known as Irish potatoes), yam, dasheen, Johnny cakes or fried or boiled **dumplings**.

Though the island produces a fabulous array of fresh produce, **vegetarians** are only really catered for at Rastafarian **Ital** restaurants, where meals are exclusively meat-free, and in theory, cooked without salt. Mainstays include ackee and vegetable stews served with rice and peas; tofu, gluten and soya are cooked up in various forms as an alternative source of protein. You should usually be able to get patties filled with pulses, soya chunks and ackee. The best places to eat Ital are in Kingston, though there are a couple of good eateries in Ocho Rios; many double up as health food stores, stocking soya- or rice-based alternatives to dairy products.

In a bid to boost decimated fish stocks, the Jamaican government has enforced **closed seasons** on lobster and conch during their reproductive cycles – April 1 to June 30 and July 1 to October 31 respectively. It is **illegal** for restaurants to serve lobster or conch caught during these times, and while many will tell you that the stock is frozen and predates the deadline, this is obviously not always true, and you should avoid restaurants that don't comply with the law.

Snacks

Along with jerked meat (see opposite), **patties** are Jamaica's best-known snack, a flaky pastry case usually filled with highly spiced minced beef, though occasionally with chicken, shrimp, ackee and saltfish or vegetables, and widely available in bakeries, cafés and snack bars. Many Jamaicans prefer **"bun and cheese"** – a sweet bun sold with a hunk of processed cheese that often passes for lunch – or **meatloaf** and **callaloo loaf**, both made with bread rather than pastry. Bakeries also offer buttery folds of **coco bread** (eaten wrapped around a patty for the classic working man's lunch), **bullas** (flat, heavy ginger cakes, improved upon in the Portland area by the creation of lighter "holey bullas"), rock cakes, fruit cakes and **gizzadas** (small tarts filled with shredded coconut and spiced with nutmeg and ginger). If you're lucky, you'll find **duckanoo** (also known as "blue drawers"), an African dessert made from cornflour, sugar and nutmeg, wrapped in a banana leaf and steamed.

Jamaican's are enthusiastic **roadside** eaters, and you shouldn't miss out on breaking long journeys with a cup of fish tea (a tasty broth that's nicer than it sounds), conch or pepperpot soups, or a chunk of buttered roast yam with saltfish, which are all sold from steaming mobile cauldrons. Peanuts and cashews are also hawked at major road junctions, sold salted or "Ital"; if he's not holding a pile of them aloft, you'll recognize a "nuts man" by the high-pitched, steam-driven whine that emanates from the push-cart roasting equipment.

Fruits and vegetables

One of the delights of touring around Jamaica is stopping off at markets and roadside stalls to try the dozens of different **fruits** on sale. Bananas, oranges, pineapples and paw-paws (papaya) are the most common but, in season, there are plenty of others to choose from. **Mangos** come in all shapes and sizes (though the juicy, non-stringy Julie variety is a universal favourite), the suitably named **ugli fruit** looks like a disfigured grapefruit but is more tasty, while the origins and flavour of the Jamaican-bred **ortanique** are described by its hybrid name – orange, tangerine, unique. Something like a green-skinned lychee, with delicate flesh around a large pip, **guineps** (only available from July to October) are sold on the roadside all across the island; the brown, orange-sized **naseberries** (sapodilla) are sweeter and slightly gritty; **sweetsops** or custard apples look like pine cones and, as they ripen, the sections separate for eating. Other options include: **guavas**; **soursops** (a bigger, sharper and indescribably better version of the sweetsop); deep-purple, milky-fleshed **star apples**, and the perfumed, rose-tinted flesh of **otaheite** (or "Ethiopian") **apples**, crimson-red and pear-shaped.

Ubiquitous **vegetables** include pumpkin and **dasheen**, like a yam but chewier. Of a variety of squashes, the watery **cho-cho** (also known as christophine) is the most common, and you'll also find **callaloo**, **pak-choy**, **okra**, **yams**, **cassava**, **breadfruit** and **plantains**, the latter ripened and served as a fried accompaniment to main meals.

Drinking

Jamaica's water is perfectly safe to drink (see p.29), and locally-bottled **spring water** is widely available, though not as cheap as you might expect – look out for the attractive red-gold-and-green labelling of the Cool Runnings brand. For a tastier non-alcoholic **drink** during the day, look no further than the roadside piles of coconuts in every town and village, often advertised with a sign saying "ice-cold jelly". The vendor will expertly open one up with a few strokes from a machete, and you drink straight from the nut (with a straw if you're lucky), after which the vendor will split the shell so you can eat the soft flesh, using a piece of the shell as your scoop. **Sky juice** – cones of shaved ice flavoured with sticky fruit syrup or fresh cane juice – is also popular, usually served in a plastic bag with a straw, though the hygiene element is sometimes questionable.

Elsewhere, you'll find the usual imported **sodas**, plus Jamaica's own Ting (a refreshing sparkling grapefruit drink), Malta (not surprisingly a malt drink), throat-tingling ginger beer and fresh limeade. Most places also sell "box drinks" – additive-filled, over-sweetened peanut punch (curiously popular), egg-nog or orange juice. **Fresh fruit juices** – tamarind, June plum, guava, soursop, strawberry and cucumber – are always delicious if a bit over-sweet, while blended fruit juices are a meal in themselves; if you haven't got a sweet tooth, ask for yours to be made without syrup.

Jamaican **coffee** (see p.139) is usually excellent. The Blue Mountain brand, grown only on Jamaica's far eastern mountain slopes, is among the best and most expensive in the world, though the other local brews, such as High Mountain, Low Mountain or Mountain Blend, are also good. Made from balls of locally-grown cocoa spiced up with cinnamon and nutmeg boiled up with water and condensed milk, **hot chocolate** is a traditional but rather labour-intensive breakfast drink. **Tea**, in Jamaica, means any hot drink and includes regular tea, fish tea, herbal tea or even ganja tea; make sure you specify which one you want.

Alcohol and bars

Jamaica's national **beer** is the excellent Red Stripe, available in distinctive squat bottles (and occasionally in the inferior draught variety) island-wide. If you need an alternative, Heineken is widely available, as is locally-brewed Guinness (stronger than British varieties), which competes with the sweeter Dragon as the island's stout of choice. Major hotels and restaurants as well as supermarkets sometimes stock a couple of other brands; if you find it, try Carib, a light lager from Trinidad and Tobago. Decent **wine** is a little more difficult to come by, and if you order a glass in a restaurant, you pay a premium. A rum shop staple, the local Red Label plonk is pretty grim

---

STAMINA POTIONS

Ever careful to safeguard their powerful libidos, the average Jamaican man couldn't live without gallons of age-old potions concocted to ensure sexual stamina. With self-explanatory names such as **tanpon-it-long**, these drinks are taken to thicken and enrich semen and supplement the diet, and deemed necessary to see the Jamaican male through extended sessions of sexual olympics.

The most popular ingredient is **Irish moss**, a seaweed boiled and strained into a glutinous milky-white potion. Now available ready-processed in tins (as well as by the bag in its pure form from supermarkets and roadside vendors), Irish moss is the main component in many stamina drinks including **magnum** (Irish moss and linseed), **strong back** (Irish moss, oats, peanuts, paw-paw, Dragon stout and a decoction of the strong back herb) and **pep-up** (Irish moss, Dragon stout, Red Label Wine and liquified green corn). Most people have their own favourite blend and a suitably libidinous name to match.

Another popular tonic is **roots wine**, usually made by Rastafarian herbalists, who mix various quantities of roots and herbs such as arrowroot, chainy root, bridal wisp, strong back and occasionally ganja, boiling them with molasses or honey to make an evil-smelling brew. Most people have their own recipes, but as preparation is time-consuming, many prefer to visit their favourite "juice man" who sells old rum bottles full of the stuff in most markets. If you're female, don't be surprised if a potential purchase is refused on the grounds that such drinks are a "man's ting". These days, you can also buy commercially bottled roots wine from health food stores: look out for the wonderfully-named "Put It In Wine" brand.

---

fortified tipple, while the sweetish Rosemont is marginally better. However, you can buy imported wines in most large supermarkets, and while the variety is never huge, prices are reasonable.

Rum is the liquor of choice, with a huge variety at a range of prices. Wray and Nephew make the classic white overproof rum: the poor man's friend – cheap, potent, available everywhere and best knocked back with a mixer of Ting, though most hardened drinkers prefer water. Even more lethal is John Crow Batty, it's often over 80 percent proof and said to be as strong as the stomach acids that "John Crow" vultures need to digest their diet of rotting meat. There are plenty of better, less caustic, brands of white rum, the smoothest being C.J. Wray Dry, made principally for export but sold in larger supermarkets. If you're after taste rather than effect, you might prefer simple gold rums

and the older, aged varieties, left to mature in (and taking their colour from) charred oak barrels; Appleton produce delicious twelve- and twenty-one-year old blends. Rum-based **liqueurs** are the other local speciality; Sangster's make award-winning rum creams and liqueurs flavoured with orange, coffee, pimento and more. Finally, the coffee-flavoured Tia Maria is made on the island and widely available.

Jamaica's **bars** – or rum shops – are generally rather macho enclaves, with groups of men sitting around drinking rum, playing dominoes and gazing at the scantily-clad ladies on the Red Stripe posters. They can present a good opportunity to meet local people, though single women won't always feel at home. Within the resorts, there are hordes of drinking holes, from sports bars to English-style pubs.

Communications

Though fairly efficient, Jamaica's telephone system is expensive for overseas calls; local calls are far cheaper, but you'll need to watch out for the shocking surcharges imposed by most hotels. The mail service is less dependable and, particularly within the island, can be extremely slow. Jamaica is fast catching onto travellers' online needs, and Internet access is available in

all of the major resorts for anything from J$$150 to US$6 for half an hour. It's a good idea to set up an Internet-based email account, via Hotmail, Yahoo, Excite and the like, before you leave.

Phones

Finding a **phone** is never a problem in Jamaican towns (though rural areas are less well-served), most hotel rooms have one and phone booths litter the island. **Rates** for local and long-distance calls within Jamaica are low, but if you're calling from your hotel, check the service charge first – most hotels impose a hefty mark-up on calls, sometimes over 1000 percent.

For calls within Jamaica, it's always much cheaper to use the public booths operated by Cable and Wireless. These accept **phonecards** only, available – in denominations of J$50, J$100, J$200 and J$500 – from hotels, post offices and gift shops.

All Jamaican telephone numbers (except some freephone ones) have **seven digits**. To dial locally (within the same parish), simply key in the number. To get a number in another parish, prefix the number with "1"; you also use the "1" prefix when dialling mobile (cellular) numbers. Finding numbers is easy – if there is no telephone directory in your hotel room or phone booth, call **directory enquiries** on ☎114.

International calls are more problematic, though the widespread availability of international calling cards such as "Worldtalk" has made the situation simpler. Sold at supermarkets, pharmacies and giftshops in denominations of JS$50, $100, $200 and $500, you can use them to call home from a hotel room or a phone booth. First of all scratch off the silver strip on the back to reveal the security code, dial the access number (☎958 2273), key in your code and you'll be told how much time you have before you place your call. However, keep your security number very private – a common fraud is for someone to read it over your shoulder as you key it in, then transfer your credit to their card. Another good option for overseas calls and faxes are privately operated **call-direct centres**, where a call is placed on your behalf and you're directed to a phone. Most are open daily from mid-morning until around 11pm, in order to take account of time differences. Details of all of these places are given throughout the Guide. If you do find a phone booth that permits direct-dial international calls, dial ☎113, wait for the tone, press the # sign, and wait for the tone again before dialling your number.

Mail

Considering how small Jamaica is, it's amazing how long it can take for inland mail to get

across the country. Don't expect a letter from Kingston to the north coast (or vice versa) to arrive in less than a week. International mail is also slow – reckon on around ten days to a fortnight for airmail to reach Europe or North America. Always use airmail, as surface mail takes forever. If you're really in a hurry to send something overseas, DHL (☎922 7333) or FedEx (☎926 1456) have offices in larger towns; call for your nearest location. Within Jamaica, Tara Couriers (☎926 7982) will get packages from one side of the island to another within a day, as will Airpak Express (☎923 0371 or 952 5299).

Most towns and villages have a **post office**, normally open Monday to Friday from 9am to 5pm; smaller postal agencies in rural areas keep shorter hours. Those in larger towns have **poste restante** facilities – mail is held for about a month, and you'll need your passport or other identification to collect it – and a few have **fax machines**.

Stamps are sold at post offices and in many hotels. Rates are reasonable at J0.90 for postcards to anywhere in the world, and the rate per half-ounce for airmail letters at J$12.50 to Canada and the USA, J$10 to the UK and Europe and J$16 to Australia, New Zealand, Asia and the Far East. Finally, think carefully before sending anything valuable through the post; postal theft is increasingly common, particularly around Christmas time, when Jamaicans traditionally send gifts to family back home.

INTERNATIONAL CALLS

To **call Jamaica from abroad,**	To call **abroad from Jamaica,**
dial your international access code (see below) + 876 + seven-digit number.	dial 00 + country code (see below) + area code minus first 0 + number
UK ☎001	UK ☎44
USA ☎011	USA ☎1
Canada ☎011	Canada ☎1
Australia ☎0011	Australia ☎61
New Zealand ☎00	New Zealand ☎64

The media

As in most countries, the best way to tap into the mood of Jamaica is to read its papers, tune in to its radio stations, or take a look at its television.

Newspapers

Of Jamaica's three daily **newspapers**, the broadsheet *Daily Gleaner*, founded in 1834, is the market leader, both in terms of circulation and quality journalism. Rarely afraid to voice an opinion, particularly during the 1970s when it regularly condemned the Manley administration, it eschews political partisanship these day, and regularly harangues all parties. The paper's coverage of local news and sport is excellent, it enjoys the pick of the feature writers and has the best listings; overseas news is perfunctory but adequate.

The *Observer* was founded by Gordon "Butch" Stewart (owner of Sandals and Air Jamaica) in the early 1990s. Tabloid in form but broadsheet in content, much of its news and feature journalism rivals the *Gleaner*, though it seems confused about its target readership. The *Star* is the island's tabloid, an afternoon publication from the *Gleaner* stable, full of salacious tittle-tattle. *X News* plumbs even lower depths, but is excellent for entertainment listings and music news; the truly enlightening "Dear Pastor" problem page is also worth a glance, and the personal columns give an interesting insight into Jamaican relationships. Regional titles include the *Western Mirror*, published in Montego Bay on Wednesdays and Saturdays and covering news and events on that side of the island, and the *North Coast Times*, based in Ocho Rios with good tourist-oriented features and listings.

Sunday brings weekend issues of the *Gleaner* and *Observer*, similar to the dailies with a few advertisers' supplements, and the rather dull but weighty *Sunday Herald*.

International newspapers – the main US dailies and the UK's Sunday broadsheets – are sold in major pharmacies and the gift shops of the bigger hotels, usually a couple of days out of date.

A couple of glossy, full-colour **magazines**, published every other month, will appeal if you're interested in Jamaican music: *Jammyng* and *Reggae Times* print interviews with artists, features on the music scene and entertainment news; both cost J$100 and are usually available from bookshops and some gift shops.

Radio

Jamaica's **radio stations** are predictably awash with island sounds – including stageshow broadcasts, talent showcases and festival coverage – though music faces tough competition from the daytime talk shows and sports coverage. Radio is much more popular than television in Jamaica, and an excellent way to appreciate the culture.

Irie FM is probably the most listened-to music station, easy skanking oldies in the morning giving way to harder core reggae and dancehall as the day wears on – for more on Irie, see p.197. Irie has edged ahead of the more long-standing **RJR** (Radio Jamaica Rediffusion, which bought out the government-owned JBC, now **Super Supreme**, in 1997), where talk and sport dilute the music. For many Jamaicans, talk shows are essential listening, as evidenced by the animated groups you'll see gathered round radios during their broadcasts. The anarchic Wilmott Perkins is the most entertaining presenter (Hot 102, daily 10.30am–2.30pm), his ferocious attacks on authority figures attracting regular death threats and healthy ratings for his show *Straight Talk*. Lawyer Ronnie Thwaites hosts *Independent Talk* (Hot 102, Mon–Fri 5.30–9am), a more measured breakfast-time analysis of topical issues, while Beverley Manley's *Breakfast Club* (Klas FM

Radio stations and frequencies

Hot 102 102FM
Irie 105.5/107.7FM
KLAS 89.7FM
Love 101.1FM
Power 106.5FM
Roots 96.1FM (in Kingston area only)
RJR 90.5/91.1/92.9/94.5/103.3FM
Super Supreme 91.1/103.3/105.7FM

Mon–Fri 6–9am) is another good morning news brief. For something altogether different, radical dub poet Mutabaruka's *Cutting Edge*, (Irie FM, Wed 10pm–2.30am) lays down a Rastafarian viewpoint. Obviously, schedules change; if you can't find what you're after, ask around.

Reception of the **BBC World Service** is patchy; early morning and late evening are the best times to find it. Consult the Web site *www.bbc.co.uk/worldservice* for further information.

Television

You'll find a **television** set in most hotel rooms, usually hooked up to the cable network with around thirty American-based channels as well as the two domestic channels, **TVJ** and **CVM**, competent if rarely thrilling; look out, though, for the excellent music-based programme *Entertainment Report* on TVJ. Output is dominated by news, local sport and US re-runs, though if you're a soap fan you'll want to catch the island's very own *Royal Palm Estates*. If you're desperate for international sports coverage then most towns have one or two bars with big-screen TV for major US sporting events – NFL and NBA games and occasionally baseball – though you won't find much from Europe. Try *Margaritaville* in Montego Bay and Negril, the *Jamrock Sports Bar* in Kingston, or the *Little Pub* in Ocho Rios.

Opening hours, festivals and entertainment

The main **national holidays**, when virtually all shops and offices close, are:

New Year's Day (January 1)
Ash Wednesday
Good Friday
Easter Monday
Labour Day (May 23)
Emancipation Day (August 1)
Independence Day (first Mon in August)
National Heroes Day (third Mon in October)
Christmas Day (December 25)
Boxing Day (December 26).

Jamaican offices are normally open for business between 8.30am and 4.30pm Monday to Friday, often closing for an hour at lunch, while shops are typically open from 8am to 5pm Monday to Saturday, although some close at noon on Saturdays. Sunday trading is rare, although you will find one or two pharmacies open in Kingston and at the major resorts, and we have listed these in the Guide. Museums normally close for one day a week, either Sunday or Monday, while most other places you'll want to visit – private beaches, waterfalls, gardens, churches and so on – are generally open daily.

Festivals and special events

Most of Jamaica's special events are timed to coincide with the winter tourist season the main exceptions are: **Reggae Sumfest** in August, and

CALENDAR OF EVENTS

JANUARY

Accompong Maroon Festival, Accompong, St Elizabeth (contact Kenneth Watson or Ava Simpson on ☎952 4546). All-day celebration of the 1739 Maroon peace treaty, held on January 6. Food and craft stalls, drumming, traditional dancing, speeches and a sound-system dance till dawn.

Annual National Exhibition, National Gallery, Kingston (☎922 1563). Annual showpiece exhibition of new artists and established names.

Heineken Startime, various locations (contact Michael Barnett on ☎960 2812). Veteran artists perform at this consistently excellent reggae stageshow showcasing the cream of Jamaica's veteran performers. There's usually a show in January, but events take place throughout the year all over Jamaica; check with the JTB or call ahead to confirm dates.

LTM National Pantomine; see "December" on p.43.

Rebel Salute, Brooks Park, Mandeville (contact Patrick Barrett on ☎969 1111). Annual concert with cultural artists and DJs from Tony Rebel's Flames stable that attracts a large roots crowd. Sometimes held in February.

Reggae Superjam, various locations (☎929 9200). A mix of top-rated singers and DJs in a friendly, laid-back atmosphere. Also takes place at other times of the year.

White River Reggae Bash, White River Reggae Park, Ocho Rios (☎974 2619 or 2489). Annual culmination of Irie FM's year-round series of open-air concerts which attract the best veteran and DJ artists.

FEBRUARY

Bob Marley Birthday Bash, Bob Marley Centre, Nine Miles, St Ann (☎0999 7003); contact Marjorie Scott at the Bob Marley Foundation on ☎978 2991, *marleyfoundation@cwjamaica.com*. Celebrations for the king of reggae are held on and around the anniversary of Marley's birthday on February 6. Ziggy Marley and the Melody Makers often perform alongside other cultural artists, and you're guaranteed a party through the night. Impromptu celebrations are also held throughout the island, particularly in Negril.

Hague Agricultural Show, Hague Showground, Trelawny (contact Beverly Harvey on ☎954 3373). Though not on the scale of the summer Denbigh extravaganza, this annual farming expo showcases local products and craft.

LTM National Pantomine; see "December" on p.43.

Negril Fat Tire and Music Festival, Good Hope, Negril Hills (contact Rusty's X-cellent Adventures on ☎957 0155, *rxadventures@cwjamaica.com*). Week long celebration of music and mountain biking, including scavenger hunts on bikes, cave parties and a street festival.

MARCH

Jamaica Music Industry Awards, Kingston (contact Pulse Investments on ☎968 1089 or 1090). The annual JAMI awards see the best of the island's performers collect awards in categories that include folk, gospel, jazz, classical and, of course, reggae.

Spring Break. In early March, American college students descend on the main resorts (particularly Negril) for a two-week JTB-sponsored orgy of beer drinking and slapstick antics. Student ID obtains discounts on hotels and events.

APRIL

Carnival, Kingston, Ocho Rios and Montego Bay (contact Tony Cohen on ☎923 9138, Courtney Sylvester on ☎922 1000, or JTB offices on the island and worldwide). The main festivities begin in Kingston in early April with J'Ouvert – costumed parades, reggae and soca live-music tents featuring Jamaican and Trinidadian soca artists and all-night fêtes. The show then moves around the island, with a big party at Chukka Cove in St Ann towards the end of the month.

Drax Hall Kite Festival, Drax Hall, Ocho Rios (contact Maria Protz on ☎927 9607). Affable family day attracting giant, flamboyant homemade kites as well as huge numbers of spectators. Stunt-flying, pony rides, clowns and lots of fun.

Continues over

CALENDAR OF EVENTS (continued)

Trelawny Yam Festival, Albert Town, Trelawny (contact Hugh Dixon on ☎610 0818). This tiny town, with a stunning setting on the outskirts of Cockpit Country, plays host to an incongruously large open-air party. As well as the prize tubers, competition categories include cooking, best goat and best dressed donkey, while sound systems and live entertainment take care of the music. A 10km race and a yam symposium complete the fun – unmissable.

JUNE

Ocho Rios Jazz Festival, Ocho Rios (contact Jazz Hotline on ☎927 3544, *www.ochorios-jazz.com*). Jamaica's original jazz festival, attracting top performers from all over the world. Concerts take place in hotels and open spaces in Ocho Rios, with a few events in Montego Bay and Kingston.

National Finals of the Performing Arts, Little Theatre, Kingston (contact Jamaica Cultural Development Commission on ☎926 5726). Annual presentation of Jamaica's traditional art forms, including dance, music and drama.

National Music Finals, Ward Theatre, Kingston (contact Jamaica Cultural Development Commission on ☎926 5726). Final round in the JCDC's annual songfest.

JULY

Columbus Annual Regatta, Portside Villas and Puerto Seco Beach, Discovery Bay, St Ann (contact Frederick Marsh on ☎974 1400). New event that hopes to breathe some life into the normally somnolent Discovery Bay, with watersports competitions, sailing and swimming races, fishing tournament, a triathlon, beachwear fashion shows and parties.

Mello Go Roun', Ranny Williams Entertainment Centre, Kingston (contact Jamaica Cultural Development Commission on ☎926 5726). Cultural extravaganza showcasing the winners of JCDC's Independence celebration competitions.

National Dance Theatre Company's Season of Dance, Little Theatre, Kingston (☎925 6129). Modern dance from this fabulous company throughout July and August.

National Festival Queen Competition, Kingston (contact Jamaica Cultural Development Commission on ☎926 5726). As part of the JCDC's annual heritage celebrations, the fourteen giggling Parish Queens from the all around the island descend on Kingston to battle it out; the winner is judged on political, cultural and historical awareness, talent and deportment as much as on looks.

National Song Competition Finals, Ranny Williams Entertainment Centre, Kingston (contact Jamaica Cultural Development Commission on ☎926 5726). National talent competition to find the nations best amateur musicians in the rather strange category of pop-reggae. The highlight of the 1999 show, though not the winner, was a catchy little anti-litter song: *Pick Up Your Papers from the Ground*. The entrants get plenty of local media coverage, and the finals are great fun.

Negril Carnival, Negril (contact Bernice Sinclair on ☎957 3528). A mixture of Trini-style carnival and traditional Jamaican festival, this features costume parades, mento bands, soca fêtes and concerts, traditional dance performances and sound-system jams in the streets.

Spring Break (see p.41) when young Americans take over the big resorts for a fortnight of raucous, beer-fuelled cavorting. April is **carnival** time – though not on the same scale as in Trinidad, Jamaica's Carnival is a growing event, with more and more parades each year. Other mini-carnivals to look out for are Mandeville's Mangerine effort and the smaller Negril Carnival. If you're in Jamaica in late July to early August, you're sure to come across **Emancipation Day** and **Independence Day** celebrations, which range from concerts to dance and theatre performances, family fun days, talks, parades; contact the JTB for details of each years' programme.

We haven't given specific **dates** for most events listed in the box above, as these change from year to year; all events (and each year's crop of new ones) appear in the JTB's annual

AUGUST

Denbigh Agricultural Show, Denbigh Showground, May Pen (☎922 0610). The best in everything from beasts to beets in a carnival atmosphere; sometimes held in July.

Independence Day Street Parade, Kingston (☎926 5726). Giant street parade through central Kingston to Liguanea Park to celebrate independence from the British. Colourful costumes and cultural performances, from traditional costumed Jonkonnu dancers to more contemporary gyrators.

Miss Jamaica World Coronation, Kingston (contact Mr Haughton-James on ☎927 7575). Beauty pageants are still big business in Jamaica, and this is the crowning glory; it's sometimes held in September.

Reggae Sumfest (see box, p.44).

OCTOBER

All That Heritage and Jazz Festival, Montego Bay (☎979 2567 or 2584, or Ute Clarke on ☎979 2498). A series of concerts and cultural seminars, performances and displays that gets the town going in the slow (and rainy) season.

National Mento Yard; contact Jamaica Cultural Development Commission on ☎926 5726. Usually held in Kingston, this growing celebration of Jamaican culture offers dance and performance groups from all around the island (and some from the wider Caribbean) the opportunity to show off their party pieces.

Oktoberfest, Jamaica German Society Headquarters, Kingston (☎927 6408, or Emile Finlay on ☎960 0617). Annual celebration of all things Teutonic, with stalls, German food, dancing, games, top Jamaican bands and the obligatory beer drinking contest.

Peter Tosh Birthday Celebration, *KD's Keg*, Belmont, Westmoreland (contact Worrel King on ☎957 4605). Annual roots and culture tribute concert in memory of the reggae great held on or around the anniversary of his October 19 birthday. Friendly and one of the highlights of the stageshow year.

NOVEMBER

Air Jamaica Jazz and Blues Festival, James Bond Beach, Oracabessa, St Mary (contact Marjorie Robinson on ☎922 3460 or JTB offices worldwide). Fabulous setting for this increasingly popular event, with a big enough purse to attract some excellent international performers.

Caribbean Heritage Festival, Jamworld, St Catherine (contact Mr Samuels at the Social Development Commission on ☎967 4414). Held just outside Kingston, this is a similar event to Mento Yard, featuring many of the same performers.

DECEMBER

LTM National Pantomime, Ward Theatre, Kingston (☎926 6603 or 968 0759). Unmissable annual theatrical institution, with ribald jokes, great costumes, political commentary and traditional Jamaican song and dance. The whole shebang moves to Kingston's Little Theatre in February, and occasionally tours around the island.

Reggae Kwanzaa, various venues island-wide. Kwanzaa, the African Christmas (Dec 26–Jan 1), is celebrated in a large annual concert, held at venues across the island and featuring the best in cultural reggae.

Sting, Jamworld Entertainment Centre, Portmore and other venues across the island. Annual New Year celebrations featuring current top DJs and singers. The atmosphere can get a bit hairy.

"**Calendar of events**" booklet, available from offices worldwide. Most of the bigger events are advertised nationally; local events are heralded on billboards

Entertainment

If you don't mind a musical policy of reggae, reggae and more reggae, then you'll find plenty on offer in the way of **live music**. Though touring American soul artists and the annual jazz festivals provide occasional alternatives, it's the home-grown scene that dominates. Jamaican **theatre** – particularly roots plays (see p.46) and the annual pantomime – is also hugely enjoyable, an idiosyncratic insight into the Jamaican way of life, and though the best productions are normally Kingston-based, many tour the island as well.

JAMAICA'S REGGAE FESTIVALS

Every year, Jamaica's best-loved art form overwhelms Montego Bay as the massive **Reggae Sumfest festival** takes to the stage. The original fiesta, Reggae Sunsplash, has paled into insignificance in recent years, but is still held in Ocho Rios – for an update, contact JTB offices worldwide, call ☎960 1904 in Jamaica, or check the Web site *www.reggaesunsplash.com*. The build-up to Sumfest, however, is still pretty frenetic: flights from the US and Europe become overbooked, beaches throng with fans from all over the globe and the line-up – which usually reads like a reggae hall of fame – is worried over in rum bars and on radio talk shows. By the time the sound equipment and lights arrive from Miami, Montego Bay's hotel rooms are pretty much booked-out, the cost of living increases overnight and every available scrap of cardboard is appropriated by small-time entrepreneurs to be sold in the show-grounds as a "reggae bed" – an essential piece of equipment for tired legs, though only the foolhardy actually sleep on them.

A heady combination of ganja, rum, sea breezes and simply brilliant music, Jamaica's festival tradition began in 1978 when a small crowd of revellers enjoyed five trouble-free nights of roots reggae at Montego Bay's Jarrett Park. Jamaica's first Reggae Sunsplash set a positive tone; international attention was captured and two years on a capacity crowd of Jamaicans and tourists alike rocked to a killer line-up featuring Bob Marley and a host of other headline acts. Promotion in the US and Europe drew huge crowds to the quintessential shows of the 1980s, which coincided with reggae's strongest phase and were characterized by the legendary, laid-back "good musical vibes" that still differentiate them from the cool reserve and farcical posturing of regular stageshows.

By the beginning of the 1990s, however, legal wrangles and a series of venue changes – including a couple of dismal years in Kingston that scared off tourists and journalists alike – left Sunsplash struggling to recapture its early success. Sunsplash's future seems even more uncertain; recent developments include another (unconfirmed) venue change and a shift from a summer to a winter festival – leaving the traditional August dates free for its mightier rival. In 1993, Reggae Sumfest muscled in, snapping up the coveted Montego Bay location (by then shifted to Catherine Hall Entertainment Centre) and outshining its rival in terms of line-up and fun factor.

Yet even with the success of this Johnny-come-lately, the festival scene is not what it used to be; where crowds once reached 30,000 nightly, even Sumfest is lucky to draw 20,000 today. As artist fees have risen, so ticket prices have become prohibitive for many Jamaicans, who increasingly prefer to attend sound-system jams rather than live shows. Some even argue that the changing focus of reggae – from the Bob Marley-style roots to today's immensely popular DJ-based dancehall – is just not appropriate to live performance any more. Despite all this, even today, with each festival boasting an average of around 100 acts spread over five themed nights, you'll get no better overview of the Jamaican music scene.

Sumfest usually takes place during the first week of August, kicking off with a beach party on the Sunday, a sound clash at the Pier One club on Tuesday nights, and the festival proper from Wednesday to Saturday. Wednesday is usually "Legends Night" when reggae stalwarts take to the stage, Thursday

Stageshows

Most concerts – or **stageshows** as they're locally known – are well worth attending, as you'll see artists who seldom perform off the island sharing the bill with more familiar reggae luminaries like Beenie Man, Buju Banton, Freddie McGregor and John Holt. Most take place in open-air venues and are generally peaceful, with a friendly atmosphere and plenty of stalls selling drinks and food; however, some of the DJ-based shows attract a younger, predominantly male crowd and can get a bit fractious, so unless

you're familiar with the scene, you might want to go with a Jamaican companion. Many are one-off affairs, but others – including **Sting** or **Heineken Startime** – are established events that hire a fixed roster of artists and tour the island's venues; see the "Calendar of events" for further details.

Clubs

The party spirit is deeply imbedded in most Jamaicans, who like to dress up (turn up in a floppy T-shirt and shorts and you're guaranteed and Friday centre on dancehall, and Saturday is "International Night", when big-name R&B acts from overseas perform alongside the hottest names from Jamaica. Specialist Caribbean travel agents in the US, UK and Australia (see pp.6, 10 & 13) sometimes offer packages that include accommodation and entrance fees; you are issued with a voucher to be redeemed for a ticket in Jamaica. Designated **ticket** outlets (including JTB offices) are found in all the resorts. Entry to the Sumfest beach party and sound clash cost around US$15, tickets for the shows on Wednesday, Thursday and Friday are US$28, and Saturday night US$38. Season tickets for all events cost US$90, VIP season tickets (which allow you backstage) cost US$140; you can also buy weekend passes which cover Friday and Saturday nights (non-VIP US$44/VIP US$60). Bear in mind that all prices are likely to increase annually, and that you'll pay less if you purchase tickets in Jamaican dollars; for specific rates for Sunsplash, consult the Web site. **Information** on both festivals is available from JTB offices worldwide (see p.16); for Sumfest information, call ☎ 952 0850 in Jamaica, or check the Web site: *www.reggaesumfest.com*.

HELPFUL HINTS FOR JAMAICAN STAGESHOWS

• Sumfest and Sunsplash adhere to published timetables and things are improving elsewhere, but none-the-less, Jamaican stageshows remain notorious for starting late; the gates may open at 10pm, but it's not uncommon for the first act to take to the stage at 1am. Ask local opinions (some promoters do have a good reputation for good timekeeping), but in general, it's not a great idea to leave your hotel too early; arriving at midnight will ensure an adequate view and enough stamina to last until the end.

• If it rains on the evening of an outdoor show, it's likely to be a washout – most Jamaicans won't leave home if it means getting wet.

• Wear clothing suitable for the night-time chill and the early morning sun – traditionally, stageshows continue well past daybreak. Despite having to stand in a field for ten hours, there are few pleasures more satisfying than watching the sun come up as the cream of the performers take to the stage.

• Jamaican entertainers can be uncompromisingly unreliable, and it's well worth checking that the artists you've come to see have actually turned up, and bear in mind that even if the doorman confirms their presence, big names are unlikely to perform for a tiny crowd. Similarly, it's common for shows with mixed billings of veteran singers and dancehall DJs to rapidly empty once the latter have left the stage, leaving the vocal acts with no audience and an excuse to slope off early.

• Don't worry about eating before a show. Vast quantities of curry goat, mannish water and fried fish are available at almost every stageshow – mobile vendors sell cigarettes and confectionery as well.

• Don't be alarmed by the practice of throwing firecrackers or employing home-made flame throwers (achieved by way of a can of bug spray and a lighter) to demonstrate appreciation of an act; it's not aimed at hapless tourists, so move away if you don't like it. However, it may be wise to think about a taxi home if people start substituting real gunshots for the traditional finger salute – only really likely to occur in the roughest of DJ-based dancehall events.

to feel underdressed) and let rip at the weekend. There's a lively **club scene** in Jamaica, at its most authentic in Kingston but also reasonably good along the north coast. Held indoors, most nights are sweaty and smoky in the extreme: the music is super-loud and dancers vie with each other as to who can wear the least and move the most. Away from some of the more sterile in-hotel establishments, many of which are all-inclusive, meaning your entry fee covers drinks all night, clubbing is lots of fun and generally inexpensive; you'll rarely encounter a cover charge of more than US$5, and the frequent "ladies nights" and weekday drinks promotions are well worth taking advantage of. Most towns also have a **go-go club** – generally full of men gawping at topless dancers, moving as rudely as only Jamaicans can.

Sound-system parties

Altogether less formal, **sound-system parties** (known as "dances" or "jump-ups") take place all over the island at weekends (see Contexts p.403). Loyal followers travel for miles to hear their favourite selectors (usually well-known figures) spinning exclusive tracks and, on a good night, see an established DJ take to the mike to improvise lyrics over the latest dancehall rhythms. Part-club and part-stageshow, most sessions are held in the open air at hurriedly fenced-in "**lawns**", and carry on until the early hours with the beer, rum and ganja consumption intensifying as the night rolls on. Most Jamaicans agree that the best dances are those held in remote country areas; noise restrictions are seldom enforced and the atmosphere is usually a lot more friendly than at city sessions or at "clashes" between two well-known sound systems, where aggressive undercurrents often mar the fun. Tourists are infrequent but welcome visitors at dances; it's rare to be harassed – most Jamaicans are pleasantly surprised to see visitors taking an interest in this side of their culture – but as you're well off the beaten track and possibly in the company of drunken undesirables, you may want to tag along with a Jamaican escort.

Theatre

Less energetic entertainment – though no less raucous – is available via a trip to the **theatre**, Jamaican-style. **Roots plays** are an institution, usually bestowed with titles – *Boops*, *Baby Faada* and so on – that reflect their bawdy vernacular content. With rich patois dialogue, plenty of easy-to-miss colloquial references and oceans of interaction from the audience, most performances are a riot and you're sure to get the overall gist of a play even if you don't catch on to the more complex themes. Roots plays are staged at impromptu venues all around the island (listed in the relevant chapters throughout the Guide), but particularly in larger towns, and details of performances are advertised in local papers – don't

miss the chance to get a uniquely unfettered view of the Jamaican psyche. Increasingly, local comedians such as Tony "Paleface" Hendricks are clubbing together with local performers to stage achingly funny comedy reviews such as *8 o'clock Jamaica Time*; grab the opportunity if you're in Jamaica when they're in production.

If you're after more conventional drama, you're restricted to Kingston's Ward or Little theatres and the Fairfield Theatre in Montego Bay. If you're on the island between December and February, it would be a crime to miss out on the annual Little Theatre Movement **pantomime** (see "Calendar of events", p.43), a blend of folklore, song, dance and jokes that gets better every year. The Little Theatre is also the venue for performances by Jamaica's superb national **dance** company, NDTC, who combine African steps with European themes to great success, and often perform with the venerated NDTC singers. Other companies to look out for include the innovative L'Cadco.

Cinema

If you tire of culture or partying, consider a trip to the **cinema**; most large towns have at least one, and away from the martial arts epics or cheesy b-movies that dominate matinee schedules, you'll usually find programming on a par with release times in America. Be prepared for a lot more audience participation than you're used to, particularly in the less salubrious establishments, and you might be required to stand up for the national anthem at the start of a performance. The Jamaican film scene has been enlivened in the last few years with the release of homegrown classics such as *Dancehall Queen* and *Third World Cop* – for more on Jamaican movies, see Contexts, p.418.

Sports and outdoor activities

As you'll quickly discover, sport is a Jamaican obsession – hardly surprising in a country that has produced so many world-class athletes. In bars, buses and taxis, if the music isn't blaring then the chances are that they're tuned into the cricket, football or horse-racing, while the newspapers are awash with sports reports and statistics from Jamaica and overseas. The island is also a great place to indulge your own sporting passion, with excellent watersports and top-class golfing in particular.

Spectator sports

Virtually every Jamaican has an opinion on **cricket**, the national game, and bringing it up in conversation is a sure-fire way to break the ice. If you get the chance to catch a match, you'll find the atmosphere very Jamaican – thumping reggae between overs and vendors hawking jerk chicken and Red Stripe. The Jamaican team is normally in action twice a year. In January, several matches of the Busta Cup – four-day games against the likes of Barbados, Guyana and Trinidad and Tobago – are held at Sabina Park in Kingston, Chedwin Park near Spanish Town and Alpart Sports Club in Nain, St Elizabeth. The more exciting one-day Red Stripe limited overs competition – against the same teams – is occasionally hosted in Jamaica in September/October, at Sabina Park, Jarrett Park in Montego Bay, Chedwin

Park and Kaiser sports ground in Discovery Bay, St Ann. On a grander scale, during March to May the West Indies team plays a series of international Test matches; one of the Tests is always held at Sabina Park and is definitely worth catching if you can.

Since Jamaica's national team, the **Reggae Boyz**, qualified for the World Cup, **football** (soccer) has become another national obsession that threatens to overtake even cricket in popularity. Although international matches, held at the National Stadium in Kingston (popularly known as "The Office"), are relatively rare, the team's success has inevitably boosted local interest with amateur leagues attracting large and passionate crowds at grounds across the island. Despite there being no professional league (many of the best players play in the UK and United States), the participation of the Reggae Boyz in the World Cup has proved them to be one of the best teams in the Caribbean.

Athletics is Jamaica's most internationally illustrious sporting field, winning Olympic sprint medals consistently from Arthur Wint in 1948 (when the island first entered the competition) through to the success of Deon Hemmings and Merlene Ottey in 1996. Most of the country's top athletes study and train abroad, and so major track meets on the island are unusual.

Finally, the influence of satellite television and the enormous salaries on offer have led to a growing interest in American sports, particularly **basketball**. You don't see that much of it being played around the country, but there is concern (as throughout the Caribbean) that this new enthusiasm is deterring youngsters from traditional sports, especially cricket, whose star players earn relatively little. Michael Jordan and rising star Vince Carter are idols for most young Jamaican males and, though few Jamaicans have yet made a big name for themselves in US sports, once they do, the rush to follow suit and abandon the cricket field is inevitable.

Participatory sports

Fabulous weather, excellent watersports, the widest variety of golf courses in the Caribbean

THE RULES OF CRICKET

The laws of cricket are so complex that the official rule book runs to some twenty pages. The basics, however, are by no means as Byzantine as the game's detractors make out.

There are two teams of eleven players. A team wins by scoring more runs than the other team and dismissing all the opposition – in other words, a team could score many runs more than the opposition, but still not win if the last enemy batsman doggedly stays "in" (hence ensuring a draw). The match is divided into innings, when one team bats and the other fields. The number of innings varies depending on the type of competition: one-day matches have one per team, Test matches have two.

The aim of the fielding side is to limit the runs scored and get the batsmen "out". Two players from the batting side are on the pitch at any one time. The bowling side has a bowler, a wicket keeper and nine fielders. Two umpires, one standing behind the stumps at the bowler's end and one square on to the play, are responsible for adjudicating if a batsman is out. Each innings is divided into overs, consisting of six deliveries, after which the wicket keeper changes ends, the bowler is changed and the fielders move positions.

The batsmen score runs either by running up and down from wicket to wicket (one length equals one run), or by hitting the ball over the boundary rope, scoring four runs if it crosses the boundary having touched the ground, and six runs if it flies over. The main ways a batsman can be dismissed are: by being "clean bowled", where the bowler dislodges the bails of the wicket (the horizontal pieces of wood resting on top of the stumps); by being "run out", which is when one of the fielding side dislodges the bails with the ball while the batsman is running between the wickets; by being caught, which is when any of the fielding side catches the ball after the batsman has hit it and before it touches the ground; or "LBW" (leg before wicket), where the batsman blocks with his leg a delivery that would otherwise have hit his stumps.

These are the bare rudiments of a game whose beauty lies in the subtlety of its skills and tactics. The captain, for example, chooses which bowler to play and where to position his fielders to counter the strengths of the batsman, the condition of the pitch and a dozen other variables. Cricket also has a beauty in its esoteric language, used to describe such things as fielding positions ("silly mid-off", "cover point", etc) and the various types of bowling delivery ("googly", "yorker", etc).

and a host of hiking opportunities make Jamaica a dream destination for **active sports** enthusiasts.

Watersports

A calm Caribbean sea bursting with sumptuous coral reefs make **watersports** Jamaica's most obvious attraction.

Scuba-diving and snorkelling is concentrated on the north coast, between Negril and Ocho Rios. The state of the reefs is variable – pollution and aggressive fishing techniques have affected many areas, and the whole stretch around Montego Bay is under enforced protection as a national marine park – but there are still some gorgeous sites very close to the shore. The fish are just as impressive, with multitudes of parrot fish, angel fish and trigger fish, as well as moray eels, turtles and the evil-looking barracuda. There are a handful of wreck dives – including several plane wrecks off the coast of Negril – and good trenches, overhangs and wall-dives. There are fewer decent sites on the south coast, and visibility is usually worse, but

Port Royal in Kingston is a divers' heaven, with hundreds of wrecks, excellent visibility and the possibility of turning up some real sunken treasure, tipped in – alongside most of Port Royal – during the earthquake of 1692.

See p.389 of Contexts for more on the ecological aspects of Jamaica's marine environment

The main resorts are packed with operators offering dive trips and snorkelling excursions; the most reputable are listed throughout the Guide. For beginners, the most popular options are the one-day introductory **resort courses**, for US$50–100, which offer basic instruction and a short supervised shallow dive close to shore. The longer **PADI** (Professional Association of Diving Instructors) **open-water certification course** costs US$300–350 and takes a few days, with practical and theoretical tests, safety training and

JAMAICA'S GOLF COURSES

KINGSTON

Caymanas Golf Club ☎922 3386. 18 holes, 6844 yards, par 72.
Constant Spring Golf Club ☎924 1610. 18 holes, 6196 yards, par 70.

MANDEVILLE

Manchester Club ☎962 2403. 9 holes (18 tees), 2863 yards, par 35.

MONTEGO BAY

Half Moon Golf Club ☎953 3105. 18 holes, 6196 yards, par 70.
Ironshore Golf and Country Club ☎953 2800. 18 holes, 7119 yards, par 72.
Tryall Golf and Beach Club ☎956 5681. 18 holes, 6920 yards, par 71.
Wyndham Rose Hall Country Club ☎953 2650. 18 holes, 6800 yards, par 72.

NEGRIL

Negril Hills Golf Resort ☎957 4638. 18 holes, 6333 yards, par 72.

OCHO RIOS

Sandals Golf and Country Club ☎975 0119. 18 holes, 6600 yards, par 71.

PORT ANTONIO

San San Golf and Country Club ☎993 7645. 9 holes, 6124 yards, par 40.

RUNAWAY BAY AND BRACO

Grand Lido Braco Golf Club ☎954 0010. 9 holes, 1357 yards, par 28.
Breezes Golf Resort ☎973 2561. 18 holes, 6870 yards, par 72.

---

several dives. Once you're certified, you can dive without an instructor, though you'll still need to go with a licensed operator – expect to pay around US$65 for a two-tank dive, and remember to take your certification with you.

Parasailing, jet-skiing, water-skiing, kayaking, glass-bottomed boats and **sailing** are also available at all of the major resorts and you can **surf** at Long Bay in Portland (p.171), though you're better off bring your own board. **Deep-sea fishing** is best around Portland, particularly during October's Blue Marlin tournament. Fully equipped boats are available for rent in all the major resorts; at about US$350 per half-day, the pursuit of big fish doesn't come cheap though.

Away from the coast, **river rafting** is the big aquatic attraction, first popularized in the 1950s by movie idol **Errol Flynn** who saw that the bamboo rafts used to transport bananas along Portland's Rio Grande could be used for pleasure punting. The Rio Grande remains the most spectacular spot for an idle glide, but operators have also set up in Ocho Rios, Falmouth and Montego Bay (see pp.197, 237 and 278). Costs start at around $45 for a two-person raft.

Swimming is idyllic in Jamaica, particularly the Rio Grande and White River in Ocho Rios. Dunn's River in Ocho Rios (p.194) offers the island's ultimate **waterfall climb**, but there are plenty more cascades, many untouristed. More relaxingly,

mineral springs and **natural spas** are Jamaica's hidden gems – locals flock to Bath in St Thomas (p.151), Rockfort in Kingston (p.105) and Milk River in Clarendon (p.348) for the restorative powers of the radioactive water, and **river rising pools**, such as Roaring River in Westmoreland (p.329) or Cranbrook in St Ann (see p.219), are a delight.

Golf

Jamaica boasts no fewer than twelve **golf courses**, from the magnificent championship Tryall course near Montego Bay – home to the annual Johnnie Walker international – to less testing nine-hole links in Mandeville and Port Antonio. All are open to the public, except during tournaments (Tryall sometimes closes to non-members in winter). **Green fees** vary from US$10 to US$100 in winter, less in summer, and there are additional charges for caddies, club and cart rental.

Hiking

Though the heat doesn't encourage strenuous exercise, **hiking** is by far the best way to get a flavour of the Jamaican countryside. The best opportunities are in the dense wildernesses of the **Blue and John Crow mountains** and **Cockpit Country**, where trails originally blazed by Maroon warriors lead deep into the Jamaican interior, though there are enjoyable minor walks elsewhere; all are fully covered in the text.

JAMAICA'S SPORTING CALENDAR

As cricket, golf and polo fixtures change each year, we haven't listed individual events. For an up-to-date rundown, get hold of a copy of the Jamaica Tourist Board's annual events calendar, available from offices worldwide. For more details on cricket in Jamaica, contact the Jamaica Cricket Association (☎967 0322). If you're interested in watching a polo match, contact Leslie Ann Masterton at the Jamaica Polo Association (☎922 8581); fixtures are held throughout the year. Golf events are also held regularly at several of Jamaica's courses; contact the JTB for details. Lastly, the Dover Raceway in St Ann hosts dozens of motor racing meets throughout the year; contact Hilary Jardine at Jamaica Motor Racing for more details (☎960 9100).

JANUARY

High Mountain 10km Road Race, Williamsfield, Manchester (contact Mr Minott Jnr on ☎963 4211). Strenuous annual mountain run undertaken by some of Jamaica's best athletes.

FEBRUARY

Jamaica International Marathon, Kingston (contact Teddy McCook on ☎927 5331 or JTB offices worldwide). A challenging run from the National Stadium to Kingston Harbour, up to Port Royal and finishing at the Rockfort Mineral Baths.

Pineapple Cup Yacht Race, Montego Bay Yacht Club (contact Felix Hunter on ☎979 8038 or 8262). Yacht race from Fort Lauderdale, USA, to Montego Bay, where the winner is crowned.

MARCH

Bowden Invitational Marlin Tournament, Bowden, St Thomas (contact Sir Henry Morgan Angling Association on ☎923 8724). A major local fishing event centred around this quiet ex-sugar cane wharf.

APRIL

Montego Bay Yacht Club Easter Regatta, Montego Bay Yacht Club (☎952 8262 or 979 8038). Annual boating fest that draws participants from the USA as well as Jamaica, with a feast of maritime events.

Motor Sports Championship Series, Dover Raceway, St Ann (☎978 2430). Championship motorcycle and car races in the hilly setting of Dover Raceway overlooking Runaway Bay. Local, amateur and international competitions. Other meets in the series take place in June, August, October and December

---

It is strongly recommended that you use a **guide** for all but the shortest of hikes, as it's perilously easy to get lost (see p.133 for major operators). Always stick to paths and trails; veering off into uncharted foliage not only encourages disorientation, but can destroy plants and lead to soil erosion. Never throw rubbish when hiking; even cigarette butts should be pocketed – a carelessly discarded cigarette can easily start a massive bush fire.

Other activities

A labyrinth of caves networks Jamaica's limestone interior, and as many have been opened up as attractions with lights and stairs, you don't have to be an experienced spelunker to enjoy them. Best of the bunch are Nonsuch Cave in Portland (p.174) and Roaring River and Runaway caves in St Ann (p.224). Serious cavers should head for Cockpit

Country, where the limestone is at its thickest and many of the caves are unexplored; Windsor (p.284) is the only easily accessible cavern. Contact Sun Venture Tours (see p.133) for caving trips. More on caving in Jamaica is available on the Internet at users.skynet.be/sky33676/index.html.

Horseback trail riding is a lovely way of exploring the island, though some stables and their mounts are rather run-down; stick to those listed in the chapters or check with the JTB. The best stables are Hooves or Chukka Cove in St Ann, and Rocky Point in Ironshore, just outside Montego Bay (see p.219, and 274); the latter two also offer **polo, dressage** and **show-jumping** lessons.

Cycling is surprisingly under-promoted in Jamaica (see "Getting Around" p.24). An alternative to demure processions aboard colour-co-ordinated resort cycles is a guided **mountain-bike tour**, available in the Blue Mountains (see

Negril Sprint Triathlon, Negril; contact JTB offices worldwide. Organized in conjunction with the Jamaica Triathlon Federation, this JTB-sponsored event takes place along Negril's luscious coastline.

Treasure Beach Off-Road Triathlon, Treasure Beach, St Elizabeth (contact Jason Henzell at *Jakes* hotel on ☎965 0552, *jakes@cwjamaica.com*). An arduous 400 metre swim, 18km mountain bike ride and a 4km run, with lots of parties alongside.

SEPTEMBER

Montego Bay Yacht Club Blue Marlin Tournament, Montego Bay (contact the Yacht Club on ☎979 8038 or 8262). Forty years old in 2000, this event is still attracting top fishermen from the Caribbean and US.

OCTOBER

Discovery Bay Marlin Tournament, Discovery Bay, St Ann (☎ 925 0893 or 2253). Big boats congregate on a little town in search of big fish.

James Bond Oracabessa Blue Marlin Tournament, Oracabessa, St Mary (☎9686792). Stylish setting for an ever-more popular competition.

Port Antonio Blue Marlin Tournament, Port Antonio Marina, Portland (contact Joe Kieffer on ☎923 8724 or 923 7683). One of the oldest and most prestigious fishing competitions in the Caribbean, this still attracts anglers from all over the world.

Treasure Beach Hook'n'Line Fishing Tournament, Treasure Beach, St Elizabeth (contact Jason Henzell at *Jakes* hotel on ☎965 0552, *jakes@cwjamaica.com*). If you want to go to a fishing tournament, pick this one as it's a million miles away from the big-boys-and-their-toys feel of the marlin fishing events. This one invites local fishermen to catch what they can with only the simplest of equipment, and with sound systems and other events, it's a huge amount of fun.

NOVEMBER

Holland Bamboo Run, St Elizabeth (contact JTB in Kingston on ☎929 9200). Part of the St Elizabeth homecoming celebrations, this is a 5km run through pretty Bamboo Avenue which finishes in Santa Cruz.

DECEMBER

Jammin International Regatta-Am Yacht race, Montego Bay Yacht Club (☎952 8262 or 979 8238). All kinds of watery events.

p.132); more serious mountain bikers should contact Rusty's X-cellent Adventures in Negril; ☎957 0155, *rxadventures@cwjamaica.com* (see p.304).

Finally, many upmarket hotels offer **tennis courts**, and for those who can't survive without their workout, the top-notch resorts normally provide **gyms** and **aerobics classes**.

THINGS TO BRING ON A HIKE

Clothes – warm, waterproof layers are best, especially in the wet and chilly Blue Mountains. Always wear long trousers or leggings to protect against scratchy ferns, brambles and grass ticks.

Shoes – unless you're planning to do a lot of walking hiking boots aren't essential, a pair of stout shoes with good grip should suffice. Sneakers (training shoes) aren't advisable; they have less hold and don't allow feet to breathe. Clipping your toenails short will help avoid blistered toes, a particularly painful hazard of the descent from Blue Mountain Peak (see p.142).

Food and drink – concentrated high-energy foods such as chocolate, dried fruit or nuts keep you going, while a bag of cut sugarcane will maintain energy levels and quench thirst. Always bring water; isotonic sports drinks are available from larger supermarkets.

First-aid kit – see p.29 for a list of recommended medicaments.

Sundries – insect repellent, high-factor sunscreen, good sunglasses, a good flashlight with spare batteries, toilet paper and a rubbish bag.

Shopping

The Jamaican souvenir industry is precisely that, with many of the carvings and knick-knacks mass-produced on a small scale with little variation from maker to maker. However, the most common products tend to be the best, and though your lignum vitae Lion of Judah may be a pitch pine copy of a thousand others, quality is generally good. Haggling is a natural part of the trade at crafts markets and stalls, but not in hotel boutiques and the more expensive air-conditioned shops.

Where to shop

Virtually every town in Jamaica has at least one **market**, most selling fruit, vegetables and other produce, and often a limited selection of crafts. The main tourist centres have dedicated crafts markets, and these, along with the **craft stalls** (same products, higher prices) you'll see by the roadside everywhere, are the most enjoyable places to browse and buy. The range of T-shirts, wooden carvings, jewellery, straw goods, hats and assorted knick-knacks varies little from place to place, but the main **Crafts Market** in Kingston (see p.79) is the cheapest.

Specialist **souvenir stores**, found island-wide, also have a good stock of crafts and indigenous art as well as rum and cigars, while local galleries often have paintings, sculptures and wood-carvings for sale. Both tend to be pricier than the markets and stalls, but the standard of merchandise is higher.

In-bond – or duty-free – shops are usually clustered together in glitzy plazas and malls, and their stock of perfume, spirits, designer clothes, brand-name watches, crystal, porcelain, diamonds and gold varies little. Savings range from twenty to forty percent; all goods must be paid for in foreign – basically that means US – currency, and major credit cards are usually accepted. You'll need your passport and proof of onward travel.

What to buy

There are many alternatives to "Rasta" tams with attached fake locks or Bart Marley (yes, Bart Simpson with dreadlocks and a spliff) T-shirts and bamboo shakers: a custom-designed pair of leather sandals, the ubiquitous string vests, bandanas and red-gold-and-green tassels for car mirrors are all available in market areas of most towns.

Not surprisingly, **reggae music** is big business in Jamaica, and fans will have a field day rooting through the record racks. The best music stores are in downtown Kingston (see p.101), and there are adequate outlets in most towns, though the latter are usually a little thin on older releases – don't expect to find a Studio One classic in downtown Ocho Rios, for example. As well as buying CDs, tapes and vinyl, compilation tapes are available from roadside vendors throughout Jamaica; they also sell recordings of the most recent sound-system dances, like gold-dust to dancehall fans back home.

Other good Jamaican gifts include the prettily packaged range of essential oils, soaps, candles and bodycare accessories from Blue Mountain Aromatics, made from natural local ingredients, and Starfish Aromatherapy oils also make classy gifts; both ranges are available from more upmarket gift shops. You can even take some Jamaican **flowers** home with you: Exotic Flowers To Go (toll-free ☎888 991 4234) offers a choice of thirty tropical blooms and foliage packed in a checkable travel-ready box for about US$40.

> Especially on the north coast, you'll see **coral** (particularly black coral) and **"tortoiseshell"**, products made from the endangered hawksbill turtle, on sale, but the trade in these protected species is **illegal** – don't buy; you're liable to serious fines if you're caught with them. Though not illegal, conch shells, too, should be avoided, as demand has eclipsed supply and conch are slowly disappearing from Jamaican waters.

Food and drink

For a taste of Jamaica back home, you can pick up fiery **jerk sauce** or viscous **guava jelly** at any supermarket – the main locally made brands, such as Walkers Wood or Busha Brown, are substantially cheaper when purchased in non-tourist shops. Jamaican **vanilla essence**, used in blended drinks, cakes and puddings, **cocoa tea** balls used to make the local version of hot chocolate, fresh **nutmeg** or the delectable **logwood honey**, sold in old rum bottles at any market, will all bring your memories flooding back.

Rum is an obligatory memento (see p.37) – gift shops sell cardboard "Jamaica Farewell" packages holding two or three bottles for easy transit, though these are usually cheaper in the airport departure lounge; savings can also be made if you buy from a wholesale liquor shop or supermarket. The Sangster's company produces excellent **liqueurs**, on sale everywhere, and the ubiquitous Tia Maria coffee liqueur is another must-have. Finally, a packet of **Blue Mountain coffee**, sold all over the island but most reasonably in situ, is essential; by far the best brand is Alex Twyman's Old Tavern, available in more upmarket outlets.

Groceries and provisions

Most sizeable towns have fairly large **supermarkets** selling most items you'll find in shops at home, but **food**, particularly imported goods, is not cheap. Fresh **fruit and vegetables** are best bought at the markets, though expect to bargain over price, and ask for your "brawta" (a little extra) when finalizing a purchase. Women market traders will give tips on preparation and will not usually rip you off, though prices may be a little higher for foreigners, black or white. Sadly, you'll find yourself paying more for produce grown in Jamaica, which is often better quality than the imported factory-farmed stuff grown on a huge scale in the US or Canada.

Smokers will find that the cheapest way to buy Jamaican brands (Craven A, Matterhorn, Rothmans and Benson and Hedges) is by the carton at any wholesaler – you pay more at street stalls and small shops. Foreign brands are available at larger supermarkets, hotels and tourist gift shops.

Drugs, trouble and harassment

Jamaica has a terrible reputation for violent crime; foreign documentaries flash images of poverty and gangsterism around the world,

and the image that lingers is of drug-crazed, uzi-toting political rivals battling it out in the bloodbath of Kingston. Such adverse publicity encourages international perceptions of a "dark" land in political and social turmoil. However, while the island's murder rate is undeniably high – the average is about 1000 per year – Jamaica's nightmare image is vastly exaggerated, a hangover from the late 1970s when the election violence that erupted during Michael Manley's turbulent administration (see Contexts, p.379) made headlines around the world.

The negative publicity has been difficult to shake off and, for a while, in the early 1980s, potential visitors stayed away in droves. In response, the government initiated a massive clean-up of the island's north-coast resorts.

Today, brigades of blue-uniformed tourist police patrol the boulevards, and the JTB are keen to stress that you are more likely to be mugged in New York than Montego Bay. You may even find that young men in the resorts are unwilling to be seen talking to, or walking with, tourists in case they're carted off by the tourist police for harassing visitors.

Most tourists still steer clear of the capital – even rural Jamaicans are wary of going into "Town", and you'll be warned against going at all of the resorts – but such trepidation is largely misplaced, and you'll be surprised at how safe and friendly Kingston feels. Drug-related organized crime is a frightening reality, but it's a reality that affects poor Jamaicans rather than tourists, and is restricted to isolated ghetto areas – pockets of west Kingston that you're never going to go to – and elsewhere, the vast majority of visitors experience no crime or violence during their stay. When the nation took to the streets in spring 1999 to protest against a forty-per cent hike in gas prices, the troubles spread as far as Montego Bay and Negril – but not a single visitor was harmed, and most frolicked on the beach completely unaware of the demonstrations.

At the same time, robberies, assaults and other crimes against tourists do occur, and it's wise to apply the **precautions** you'd take in any foreign city. Don't flaunt your wealth with fat rolls of bank notes, avoid walking alone late at night, don't go mad smoking ganja in the street – in short, use your common sense and you'll prevent potential problems before they happen.

Police

The **emergency number** for the Jamaican **police** is ☎ 119. Individual police stations are detailed throughout the text.

Hustling

Hustling – the hard-nosed, hard-sell pitches you'll be endlessly subjected to on the north coast – can be the chief irritation of time spent in Jamaica. Especially in Montego Bay, the tourist trade has long been adversely affected by the stream of young hopefuls aggressively (or humorously) accosting foreigners in the street with offers of transport, ganja, aloe massages,

hair-braiding and crafts. It's wearisome, to be sure, but much of what is perceived as harassment is really nothing more than an attempt to make a living in an economically deprived country, and while an inevitable few see tourists as easy prey for exploitation, most street touts are genuine. Hustling is a game played in the true entrepreneurial Jamaican spirit; the sales pitch is finely honed and modified to match the perceived nature of the potential client, and the national aptitude for "lyrics" (artful banter designed to break down even the most hardened sensibility) can make encounters with street vendors an entertaining and educative experience rather than a trial.

Tourists are not the only victims of the entrepreneurial urge; city traffic lights are haunted by regulars selling everything from a window wash to brooms, flowers, doughnuts or newspapers, and the travelling peanut or cigarette vendors that pop up in the most unlikely places are often very convenient.

For a humorous insider's view of the hustler's art consult *Hustling Jamaican Style – A Guide to Tourist Service* (see Contexts, p.425) which lists the most popular products and provides suggested responses; p.255 of this book also has some suggestions.

Homophobia

Anyone familiar with the theme of Buju Banton's infamous hit *Boom Bye Bye* will know that Jamaica is overwhelmingly **homophobic**. Homosexuality is illegal in Jamaica, condemned as a sin by the church and the moral majority, and fuel for much hysterical press coverage. Attempting to argue with freely expressed prejudices is almost always a lesson in futility. This doesn't mean that you should avoid Jamaica if lesbian or gay – many hotels are managed by gay men and a lot of the smarter ones won't turn a hair if you ask for a double room – but don't expect to be able to display affection in public without attracting catcalls, sniggers, downright aggression, and possibly physical violence.

Drugs

Though tourism officials are loathe to acknowledge it, many people do come to Jamaica in search of what aficionados agree is some of the finest marijuana in the world, and certainly, **ganja** is part-and-parcel of the culture here to a greater degree than in other Caribbean islands. Be warned that quite apart from being **illegal**, Jamaican ganja, or "herb", packs a mightier punch than anything you've probably experienced before, so don't plan on doing much if you decide to partake; yellow-eyed Jamaicans who've been smoking since their teens can cope with a spliff before breakfast – fresh-off-the-plane visitors probably can't.

Most Jamaicans smoke their ganja **pure** in carrot-sized spliffs or a water pipe (chillum or cutchie), though some make a "blend" with ordinary cigarettes or whole tobacco leaf; this last, known as "fronta", is also used alongside dried sweetcorn husks or even paper bags as an alternative to rolling papers.

Bear in mind, though, that despite the stereotypical view of an island populated by ganja fiends, those Jamaicans who smoke are in a minority; most islanders are highly religious and neither take drugs, nor approve of those who do. And despite its links with the Rastafari religion (see p.397) and frequent use as a medicinal draught, possession, use and export of any quantity of ganja is **against the law** and carries stiff penalties. Tourists are just as eligible for prosecution as Jamaicans; at any one time there are around a dozen foreigners awaiting trial in Jamaican jails.

If you choose to smoke ganja, trust your instincts. You will be approached with offers; buy only from someone you feel you can trust, and never accept a rolled-up spliff from someone you don't know – it may be what Jamaicans call a "seasoned spliff", laced with cocaine or crack. You should be equally wary of carrying ganja around the island; if you pass a car at the roadside flanked by a worried-looking white person and a swarm of cops, you can bet that the police are conducting one of their routine searches.

Finally, tempting as it may seem, do not attempt to smuggle ganja out of the country under any circumstances; however devious you think your method, customs officials have seen hollowed-out sculptures, training shoes or roasted breadfruits before. Even carrying rolling papers can prompt protracted questioning.

Other drugs

Though better known as a weed-smokers' paradise, **cocaine** and **crack** are also increasingly widespread in Jamaica, with addiction to both a major contributing factor in violent crime. Powder cocaine has long been the drug of choice for rich young Kingstonians, but the introduction of crack in the late 1980s ensnared a far wider following. Use is not restricted to the Kingston ghettos; Negril's reputation for drugs has attracted the inevitable quota of crack users, and cocaine has been a part of the scenery since wealthy tourists first brought it here in the 1970s. If you're fairly young, expect to be offered cocaine – and, less frequently, crack – in the tourist areas; if you're not interested, refuse calmly and firmly.

Women travellers

Violent sexual attacks against female tourists are very rare, and women travelling in Jamaica are likely to be more bothered by trivial catcalls than any serious threat – prepare yourself for a quite unusual degree of scrutiny. In the resorts particularly, unaccompanied women can expect to receive a barrage of attention from Jamaican men, from hopeful innuendo – "gal, me a cry for you"– to frankly pornographic propositions, and a walk down the street will have you sized up by a thousand eyes – all of which is somewhat wearing after the first couple of days, particularly if your idea of a good holiday doesn't include "climbing aboard the big bamboo".

As casual sex is part and parcel of Jamaican culture, and lots of women do come to the island in search of so-called "exotic" romance, it will inevitably be assumed that you are in Jamaica to find a man – or several. The news that you're not will often be greeted with incredulity, and the semi-professional gigolos (and full-blown male prostitutes) who work the resorts will do their best to get you to change your mind. Foreign black women are just as much of a target as white, though you might be treated to a "roots sister" approach. If you're not interested, saying "no" and meaning it, not wearing skimpy clothing off the beach and avoiding eye contact and idle chat with men you don't know are good lines of defence. As a last resort, you may want to assert that you already have a Jamaican boyfriend, though this can be seen to signify that you are playing the game and are a feasible challenge. Incidentally, the boyfriend-back-home excuse will only elicit, "but you're here for how long? Too long to go without".

In a social situation, Jamaican men are refreshingly direct, and while an open invitation to bed within the first five minutes of meeting can be disconcerting, you at least know where you stand; once the possibility of sex is out of the way you can move on to other agendas. Learn to listen to your instincts; the slightest hint of flirting means that you are probably about to be propositioned, so assume that even the most innocent reaction may be interpreted as a sign of acquiescence – agreeing to play a game of pool, for example, may well be read as a come-on.

If passion is on your agenda, don't have more than one partner in the same area; gossip spreads extremely quickly and Jamaican men do not take kindly to being "insulted" in this way (of course it's OK for them). Though most men will help if they see a sister being seriously bothered, don't expect men (even friends) to extricate you from sticky situations of your own making, as this would encroach on another's machismo. Cope with your new status as a sex goddess with humility and humour; most of it probably has more to do with your foreign allure – or economic clout – than your personal charms, and a lot of the come-ons can be extremely amusing.

Jamaican women

As tourist centres are generally the preserve of male hustlers, it can be difficult to meet **Jamaican women**, and while many women are friendly

---

Women's organizations

Most women's organizations are based in Kingston, and are presided over by the **Association of Women's Organizations in Jamaica**, 2 Waterloo Rd, Kingston 10 (☎968 8260, fax 968 0862), an umbrella group which aims to direct, unite and empower women as well as lobbying for change in the law and female opportunities. It can act as a conduit if you want to make contacts or want information on specific groups.

Woman Inc, 18 Ripon Rd, Kingston 5 (☎929 9038) runs a counselling service and crisis centre for victims of incest, rape and domestic abuse; the number above is a national helpline.

Sistren Theatre Collective, 20 Kensington Crescent, Kingston 5 (☎929 2457) is an internationally recognized feminist theatre company, with a sideline in publishing. It regularly tours the island with consciousness-raising plays and produces a monthly magazine.

---

and older ladies inclined to shower you with maternal protection, some display an understandable resentment towards the carefree, wealthy female visitors pursued by their men. Besides, most women are far too busy juggling childcare, cooking, cleaning and breadwinning to have time for idle chat.

From the dancehall queen to the market higgler, it's pretty obvious that strong women rule Jamaica. They make up 46 percent of the labour force, the highest per capita ratio in the world, many employed at garment assembly factories or as domestic helpers, and earn an average weekly wage of J$1000 (US$22). On top of this, they bear almost sole brunt of childcare responsibilities. Single parentage is an institution in Jamaica – eight out of ten children are born out of marriage, with women usually having several children by several partners, and the commonly used terms "**baby mother**" or "**baby father**" refer to parents who live apart. The impetus for women to have more than one baby father is more often economic than libidinous – if one man doesn't recognize his responsibilities, perhaps another will – and the family court in Kingston has dealt exclusively with paternity disputes for the past twenty years.

Despite the respect they earn as matriarchs and wage-earners, Jamaican women have it tough in this sexist, macho and economically challenged country. They face an increasing threat of violence; the 1000 or so rapes reported annually are estimated to be only a fraction of those that take place, and marital rape is not legally recognized. Incest and domestic violence are also on the increase, there are virtually no sexual harassment laws and legal abortions are so difficult to get that they might as well be barred; thousands of botched back-street attempts kill and maim every year.

Directory

Airport Departure Tax For international flights, the departure tax is presently J$750, payable, in local currency only, at the airport when you leave. There is no tax on domestic flights.

Children Pellucid seas, gently shelving beaches, no serious health risks and an indulgent attitude toward kids make Jamaica an ideal destination if you're travelling with babies, toddlers or children. Though many of the larger hotels (the Sandals chain in particular) operate a couples-only policy, most welcome families. The Montego Bay *Holiday Inn* (☎953 2485), *Franklin D Resort* in Runaway Bay (☎973 4591), *FDR Pebbles* in Trelawny (☎954 0000), *Boscobel Beach* in Oracabessa (☎975 7331) and *Beaches* in Negril (☎957 9270) are all self-styled family resorts with extensive facilities, daily events and personal nannies, but there are plenty of others with kids' clubs for an afternoon off.

Customs and immigration Entering Jamaica, customs allow a duty-free quota of 200 cigarettes, 25 cigars, a pound of tobacco, a quart (two pints) of any liquor except rum and a quart of wine. The import of weapons and farm products (including plants, fruit and meat) is heavily restricted and if you're crazy enough to try to smuggle drugs into the country you'll risk severe penalties. When leaving, craft made in Jamaica attracts no duty.

Note that visitors are given an immigration card on arrival, which must be returned to the Jamaican customs on departure.

Disabled travellers Only the largest hotel chains, such as *Holiday Inn*, *Superclubs* and *Sandals*, have ramps or lifts on their properties; the JTB can provide a full list of hotels with suitable facilities. The Combined Disabilities Association at 53 Lyndhurst Rd, Kingston 5 or PO Box 220, Liguanea, Kingston 6 (☎929 1177, fax 920 9389) acts as an umbrella for other groups on the island, lobbies on behalf of Jamaicans with disabilities, and is a useful source of further contacts and information. General holiday information for travellers with disabilities is available in the US from Access First, 239 Commercial St, Malden, MA 02148 (☎1/800-557-2047 or 781/322-1610); in the UK from RADAR (Royal Association for Disability and Rehabilitation), 12 City Forum, 250 City Rd, London EC1V 8AF (☎020/7250 3222, minicom ☎020/7250 4119, *www.radar.org.uk*); in Ireland from the Disability Action Group, 2 Annadale Ave, Belfast BT7 3JH (☎028/9049 1011); in Australia from ACROD, PO Box 60, Curtin ACT 2605, (☎ 02 6282 4333), and in New Zealand from the Disabled Persons Assembly, 4/173-175 Victoria St, Wellington (☎04/801 9100).

Electric current The island standard is 110 volts, with two-pin sockets, though a few of the older hotels still use 220 volts. Take adapters for essential items – some of the upmarket hotels and guesthouses have them, but you shouldn't rely on it.

GCT (General Consumption Tax) A government tax of fifteen per cent is levied on goods and services in most hotels, restaurants and stores, and is usually added to the bill (rather than included in the advertised price).

Getting married Jamaica is a hugely popular wedding destination. Only 24 hours' residence on the island is required before you can apply for a marriage licence. You'll need a valid passport or a certified copy of your birth certificate; if you're under 21 you'll also need written parental consent; if divorced, a certified copy of the decree absolute, and if widowed, a copy of your previous partner's death certificate. Most people leave the bureaucracy to someone else and arrange the wedding through their hotel or tour operator – expect to have to provide the documents at least one month in advance. Alternatively, you can apply in person at the Ministry of National Security and Justice, Kingston Mall, 12 Ocean Blvd, Kingston (☎922 0080; Mon–Thurs 8.30am–5pm, Fri 8.30am–4pm;) – the paperwork costs US$150.

Laundry Most hotels have a laundry service, but check prices before handing over a huge load as some charge as much as US$5 for a single shirt. Most large towns have at least one public laundry (listed in the relevant chapters) but in rural areas, your best option is to follow Jamaicans and have clothes washed by hand – ask around for a trustworthy lady and bear in mind that your best garments may receive over-enthusiastic bleaching and scrubbing. A bag of clothes should cost US$8–12.

Measurements The country is slowly converting from the Imperial to the metric system – road signs, for instance, now give distances in kilometres – but the former still dominates and is used throughout this book. The archaic measurement of a chain – 22 yards – is still used, though if you're asking directions, "a few chains" can mean anything from 100 yards to a mile or more. Treat the direction "it's not far" or "just over there" with the same scepticism.

Photography Jamaica is made for pretty pictures. Take plenty of film and all the equipment you'll need – local costs for both are high, and you'll have difficulty finding good filters and lenses, even at the in-bond stores. Humidity is the photographer's main enemy – carry packets of silica gel in your camera bag, keep film cool and develop it quickly. Over-exposure can also be a problem: watch out for the glare from sea and sand, and try to take pictures early or late in the day when the sun is less bright. When photographing people (or their homes and property), always ask permission – some like it, others don't – and anticipate a request for a donation.

Time Jamaica is on Eastern Standard Time and does not adjust for Daylight Saving Time. Accordingly, it is on the same time as New York (one hour behind from spring to autumn) and five hours behind London (six hours from spring to autumn).

Tipping No tip is necessary at any restaurant that imposes an automatic service charge; ten to fifteen percent is the norm anywhere else. Tip taxi drivers at your discretion; route taxi drivers do not expect a tip.

Visa extensions If you want to extend your stay, you can either leave and re-enter the island or apply to the Ministry of National Security and Justice, 12 Ocean Blvd, Kingston (☎922 0080; Mon–Thurs 8.30am–5pm, Fri 8.30am–4pm), or the Immigration Office, Overton Plaza, Union St, Montego Bay (☎952 5381; Mon–Fri 8am–1pm, 2–4pm).

The Guide

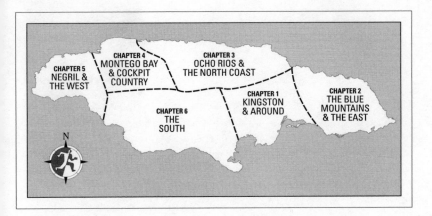

The Guide

Chapter 1

Kingston and around

O verwhelming and fascinating in equal measure, **Kingston** is quite unlike anywhere else in the Caribbean. Given its troubled reputation, it's hardly surprising that few tourists visit, and while the scare stories are absurdly exaggerated, Kingston is certainly not a place for the faint-hearted. In the 1950s, Ian Fleming called it a "tough city", and that still holds true today: Jamaica's capital is rough and ready, a little uncompromising, but always exciting.

With a population fast approaching the million mark, Kingston seethes with life, noise and activity, and if you venture downtown, you'll see the rough edges, some of them very much so indeed. Nonetheless, the capital offers a sharp insight into Jamaica that couldn't be more of a contrast to the resorts. As well as the seat of government and the island's administrative centre, Kingston is Jamaica's cultural heart, the city that spawned Bob Marley, Buju Banton, Beenie Man and countless other reggae stars, and the only place on the island to fully appreciate the best of Jamaican art, theatre and dance. If you do decide to visit – and it's well worth the effort for anyone with even a passing interest in Jamaican culture – you'll find that not only is it easy to steer clear of the troubled areas,

---

Accommodation price codes

All the hotels detailed in this guide have been graded according to the following price categories. Note that the prices have been calculated as those for the cheapest **double** or **twin room** during low season, normally mid-April to mid-December. During high season, rates are liable to rise by up to 25 percent (though this is rare at the cheap hotels), and proprietors may be less amenable to bargaining. Although the law requires prices to be quoted in Jamaican dollars, most hotels give rates in US dollars; payment can be made in either currency. For more details see p.27.

① under US$20	④ US$51–70	⑦ US$151–200
② US$21–35	⑤ US$71–100	⑧ US$200 and above
③ US$36–50	⑥ US$101–150	

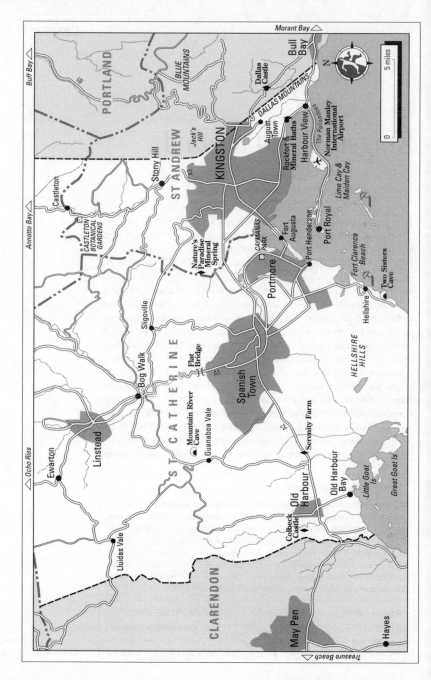

but that there's little of the persistent **harassment** which bedevils parts of the north coast. In comparison to Ochi or Negril, the capital feels refreshingly real, with most Kingstonians far more interested in going about their business than wasting time on a trifling tourist. That's not to say that city-dwellers are unfriendly; in fact, it's far easier to strike up a decent conversation here than in more conventional tourist honeypots, where every interaction can seem like a precursor for a sales pitch. The pulsating, live-for-today vitality of the place injects a shot of adrenaline that often proves addictive, and its exuberant atmosphere is tempered by a cool elegance and a strong sense of national history. If you follow the herd and avoid the capital, you'll have missed one of Jamaica's undoubted highlights.

For many, the sights and sounds of the capital's non-stop street life are entertainment in themselves, but the city is packed with more substantial draws besides. A handful of interesting museums, galleries and churches can easily fill a couple of days of sightseeing; the island's best clubs, theatres and some great restaurants will take care of the evenings. Nearby, quite apart from the lovely Blue Mountains which overlook Kingston (and are covered in Chapter Two), plenty of other attractions surround the city. The area is littered with historic sites – Georgian monuments in **Spanish Town**, the forts of the English buccaneers in atmospheric **Port Royal** and **Taino caves** from pre-Columbian times at **Mountain River** – and, for those who just can't cope without a beach, the white-sand **Hellshire beaches** and **Lime Cay** are the perfect places to get away from it all.

Kingston

Founded at the tail-end of the seventeenth century, **KINGSTON** fast became the greatest city in the West Indies. The main impetus to growth was its fabulous location, built on an expansive **natural harbour** – the seventh largest in the world – which was to prove the cornerstone of Kingston's future trading success. Since those early days, the city streets have gradually found their way north and now reach as far as the foothills of the **Blue Mountains**, a truly glorious backdrop.

Kingston's main sights are divided between the area known as "downtown", which stretches north from the waterfront to the busy traffic junction of Cross Roads, and "uptown", spreading up into the ritzy suburbs of Jack's Hill and Cherry Gardens at the base of the mountains. **Downtown** is the city's industrial centre, its factories and all-important port providing most of the city's blue-collar employment; the law firms, stock exchange and the Bank of Jamaica are also prominent features. The peaceful, grassy waterfront is a marked contrast to the busy streets of most of downtown, particularly the manic **Parade** square – a maelstrom of traffic and animals where vendors flog cassettes, yams, sky juice and bootleg designer gear, yelling over a backdrop of booming reggae and honking traffic.

Uptown is different, and you may be surprised at how attractive and easygoing it feels, as suited businessmen and office workers go about their daily routine. Most of Kingston's hotels, restaurants, clubs and shopping centres are here, and it's where you'll spend most of your time. Some of the residential districts – places like **Mona** and **Beverly Hills** – are simply beautiful, while the central high-rises suggest a modern city anywhere in North America – although the coconut vendors and the odd stray goat tend to give the game away.

In terms of **highlights**, many visitors make straight for the **Bob Marley Museum**, former home of the island's greatest reggae star and musical ambassador, but there are also some grand old **colonial houses**, recently restored as museums, and an excellent **national art gallery**. There are plenty of good hotels and restaurants, and the city is the heartbeat of the country's music industry, with top-quality clubs and a busy live music scene, including an extravagant annual **Carnival** – well worth catching if you're on the island in April.

Some history

Though the Spanish first settled in Jamaica in 1510, replaced by British colonists in 1655, there was little development in present-day Kingston until 1692. The area held just a small pig-rearing village, glamorously known as Colonel Beeston's Hog Crawle, and a handful of fishing shacks. All of the action was across the harbour on the island of Port Royal, then Jamaica's second city (after Spanish Town) and home to most of the country's leading lights. In 1692, however, a violent **earthquake** devastated Port Royal; several thousand people died instantly and the rest went scurrying for a more hospitable place to live. The Hog Crawle was the obvious choice – on the mainland but beside the harbour – and the former citizens of Port Royal promptly snapped up two hundred acres of land there. The population was further expanded in 1703, when more Port Royalists fled to the other side of the harbour after a devastating **fire**.

Within a few months, the plans for the new town had been drawn up. New-born Kingston took its name in honour of William of Orange, king of England since 1688, and the town was laid out beside the water to take advantage of the existing **sea trade**. The road plan mostly followed a grid system (which remains largely intact today) with the big central square of **Parade** left open in the heart of town.

By the early eighteenth century, Kingston had become a **major port** for the transhipment of English goods and African slaves to the Spanish colonies of South America. Merchants, traders and brokers made rapid fortunes and began to build themselves ostentatious homes, while fresh waves of **immigrants** piled in to the booming city – some from Europe, some from other Caribbean islands, some from other parts of Jamaica, all in search of opportunity.

With its swelling population and rising wealth, the city soon began to challenge for the role of the **nation's capital**, though the authorities in Spanish Town – comfortably ensconced in their grand Georgian buildings – proved stubborn in handing over the title to their upstart neighbour. By 1872, when Kingston finally became Jamaica's capital city, many wealthy families were already moving beyond the original town boundaries to the more genteel areas that today comprise **uptown** Kingston. Meanwhile, the less affluent huddled downtown and in the **shanty towns** that began to spring up on the outskirts of old Kingston, particularly west of the city, their ranks swollen by a tide of former slaves hoping to find prosperity beyond the sugar estates

Jamaica's turn-of-the-century boom, engineered by tourism and agriculture, largely bypassed Kingston's poor and helped to reinforce the divide between uptown and downtown. While the rich got richer and sequestered themselves in the new suburbs uptown, the **downtown** area continued to deteriorate, neglected by government and hit by a catastrophic earthquake in 1907 that destroyed almost all buildings south of Parade. Those who could afford to do so continued to move out, leaving behind an increasingly destitute population that proved fertile recruitment ground for the **Rastafari** movement during the 1920s and 1930s.

There were major **riots** during the 1930s, with the city feeling the knock-on effects of an island-wide economic crisis sparked by the plunging price of key crops like bananas and sugar on world markets. The riots led to the development of local trade unions and political parties during the 1940s to speak for the workers and the dispossessed, but improvements in working conditions and the physical infrastructure were slow in coming. Finally, in the 1960s, the city authorities began to show some interest in reversing the decay. Efforts were made to give the old downtown area a face-lift; redevelopment of the waterfront resulted in a much-needed expansion of the city's **port facility** (still a vital part of the city's commerce today) and a smartening up of the harbour area with the introduction of shops, offices and even the island's major art gallery.

A mini-**tourist boom** was sparked by the new-look Kingston (and by the growing popularity of Jamaican music abroad), with cruise-ships arriving to inject a fresh air of hope into the city. Sadly, the optimism proved short-lived. For the people of West Kingston, the redevelopment of downtown was only cosmetic. Crime – an inevitable feature in the crowded ghettos – was getting out of control, sponsored by irresponsible politicians who distributed weapons and patronage to their supporters. At election time (particularly in 1976 and 1980) hundreds of people were killed in bloody campaigns, many of them innocent bystanders. Tourists ran for cover, heading for the new beach resorts on the island's north coast, and the city sank into a quagmire of unemployment, poverty and crime.

Patrick Leigh Fermor's The Traveller's Tree *paints a vivid picture of the Rastafari movement in Kingston's wastelands; Orlando Patterson's* Children of Sisyphus *provides a more home-grown perspective. See "Contexts", p.421.*

For more on West Kingston's history, see p.82.

Kingston

Today, Kingston remains a divided city. The wealthy have moved further and further into the suburbs, coming in to work in the smart uptown area of New Kingston but rarely venturing near downtown, while the ghettos remain firmly under the control of area "dons". You have to look hard to find rays of hope, but there are hints that the city's fortunes may be turning. For the first time, senior politicians are starting to address the problem of the city's gangs and party factions and – a crucial development – admitting their own role in creating them. At the same time, there are proposals, from government and the private sector, to pour tourist development funds into the city, with the return of the cruise-ships the main priority. With tourism-generated money and a serious approach to tackling crime, Kingston has a good chance of regaining some of its former glory.

Arrival and information

All international and some domestic **flights** land at **Norman Manley International Airport** (☎924 8546 or 8452) on the Palisadoes – a strip of land that juts out into the Caribbean Sea southeast of the city. A number of **car-rental** firms have desks right alongside the arrivals area (see p.103); others will normally meet you there on request. A city **bus** runs from just outside the arrivals area to downtown roughly every half-hour (around J$30); however, you're far better off opting for a **cab** – the fare for the thirty-minute journey to New Kingston is around J$700.

The domestic airport of **Tinson Pen** (☎978 8068) is just to the west of downtown on the fringe of some of the city's less salubrious communities. A cab into central Kingston from here should cost around J$300. A few drivers usually hang around to meet the flights; otherwise, call one of the operators listed on p.103.

If you're arriving by **car**, there are four main **entry points** to the city. Most visitors come in from the north coast on the busy A3 road, which runs straight through the northern suburbs of Stony Hill and Constant Spring and into the heart of uptown Kingston. Also from the north coast, the more tortuous but scenic B3 from Buff Bay through the Blue Mountains will eventually bring you out at Papine, northeast of town; following the main Old Hope Road due west, then Hope Road from Matilda's Corner, and turning left at Trafalgar Road, brings you into New Kingston. Coming from the west, Spanish Town Road divides at Six Miles on Kingston's western edge, take the left fork for New Kingston, carrying straight along on Washington Boulevard and Dunrobin Avenue and turn right onto Constant Spring Road, which takes you to Half Way tree. Here, turn left along Hope Road for New Kingston. From the east, Windward Road swings in past the turn-off to Port Royal and the airport – to get uptown, turn right on Mountain View Avenue or South Camp Road.

Most of the **buses** into Kingston pull in at the swarming **terminal** at the junction of Beckford and Pechon streets, just west of the crowded Parade. Local services run from there into New Kingston, although as Kingston's bus system is in such a state of disrepair (see below), you're best off hopping straight into a **taxi** from the busy rank here. Many buses from the north and west also stop at **Half Way Tree** in the uptown area, closer to most of the hotels.

Information

The main office of the **Jamaica Tourist Board** (☎929 9200; Mon–Fri 9am–4.30pm) is at 2 St Lucia Ave in New Kingston. It has maps, booklets, lists of places to stay and a useful little library. There's a smaller branch at Norman Manley airport (☎924 8024; normally open to meet flights). The most useful **map** of the Kingston area is on the back of the JTB's island map in the *Discover Jamaica* booklet, with a handy separate plan of the city's downtown area. A little more unwieldy, though more detailed and covering a wider area, is the JTB road map.

There is no good **listings** section in any of the newspapers, but most of the theatres, cinemas and clubs advertise their activities on Irie FM or the national *Daily Gleaner*. Look out, also, for flyers slapped up around town heralding forthcoming stageshows and parties.

Getting around

Finding your way around Kingston is pretty straightforward. Downtown uses a grid system while uptown is defined by a handful of major roads. You'll quickly get used to the main landmarks and, as a reliable fallback, the mountains to the northeast serve as a good compass reference. The heat and the distances between places mean you're not going to want to do a lot of **walking**, though the downtown sights, in particular, are easily navigable on foot. It's not advisable to walk the streets at night in any part of the city; most Kingstonians don't.

Taxis are the best way of getting around the city and reasonably cheap; a ride from New Kingston to downtown costs around J$250. Bear in mind cabs rarely carry meters and you'll need to fix a price before you get in. Although it is standard practice to call for a taxi, particularly at night, they can almost always be flagged down on the main streets (look out for red "PP" or "PPV" plates), and there's a bustling rank downtown at Parade and an unofficial one in New Kingston along Knutsford Boulevard.

A list of Kingston's reliable taxi firms appears on p.103

Unfortunately, public transport in Kingston is simply not a viable option, as the city's **bus system** is a chaotic nightmare. The government handed control to private operators in the 1980s and the resulting free-for-all has seen any notions of timetables and passenger comfort fly out of the window. Since then, various attempts to re-regulate the system have had little discernible effect, though there are plans for a new terminal near the Parade, and the purchase in 1995

Safety and harassment

The **pestering** of visitors, irritatingly widespread on the north coast, is relatively and refreshingly uncommon in Kingston. Nevertheless, as with any big city, there are plenty of scare stories and some places that you should steer clear of. There is serious poverty and political tribalism in large parts of West Kingston (see p.82); it's not a place for some casual sightseeing and you shouldn't even think of straying in there without a good reason and the company of someone who knows the area well. Downtown, too, has its dodgy areas and, once the business crowd has gone, it can be a bit risky; unless you're seeing a show at the brightly lit Ward Theatre, there is little reason to head downtown after dark.

With an average 500 murders per year, the crime statistics for the city are ugly, although you should bear in mind that the majority of violent crime is domestic or the result of drug-related gang disputes in the ghettos. Of course, criminal elements do venture out of these areas, and the well-to-do are increasingly protected behind high fences, barbed wire, security guards and dogs. During the day, though, the uptown area (and most of downtown) feels fine, particularly once you're familiar with the main roads; at night, you're best off getting a taxi if you're travelling any distance.

of 150 smart new Mercedes Benz buses for use in the corporate area has at least ensured more vehicles on the road. Fares are absurdly cheap – no more than J$50 for any journey around the city – but the serious overcrowding and madcap driving deter all who can afford to do without, and you're likely to feel pretty conspicuous. If you're really determined (and foolhardy enough) to use them, Parade and Half Way Tree are the main terminals.

For details of tour companies and individuals that can take you on tours of Kingston and its surrounds, see p.104.

There are good reasons not to **drive** in Kingston. Car rental is expensive; it can work out cheaper to take taxis even if you're going as far afield as Spanish Town (around J$1000) or Port Royal (around J$1700). City traffic is increasingly hellish, particularly at peak hours, and navigation is hindered, especially at night, by a paucity of street lights and road signs and an excess of potholes and jaywalking animals. Only if you're staying outside the city or planning to tour extensively should you need a car; rental firms are listed on p.103.

Accommodation

Most of Kingston's **hotels** are scattered around the small uptown district of **New Kingston**, a convenient base for sightseeing and close to many of the restaurants, theatres, cinemas and clubs. Some of the cheaper places are in slightly insalubrious locales and, if you're staying there, you'll need to watch yourself at night. Few of the city's hotels cater specifically for the tourist trade, relying instead on a steady stream of Jamaican and international business visitors; as a result, prices are not as seasonal as in the resort areas and there are few discounts available during the summer. Although it is normally

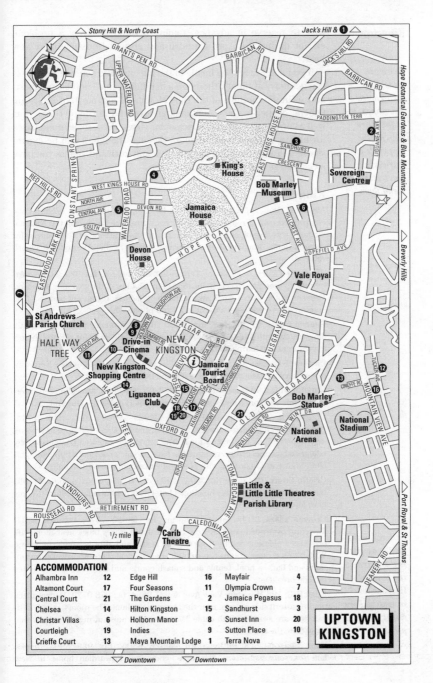

Hope Botanical Gardens & Blue Mountains ▷

GRANTS PEN RD

BARBICAN RD

JACK'S HILL RD

BARBICAN RD

UPPER WATERLOO RD

PADDINGTON TERR

LIGUANEA AVE

❷

RED HILLS RD

CONSTANT SPRING ROAD

WEST KINGS HOUSE RD

SANDHURST

❸

CRESCENT

EAST KINGS HOUSE RD

King's House

Sovereign Centre

NORTH AVE

CENTRAL AVE

❹

Bob Marley Museum

SOUTH AVE

WATERLOO ROAD

DEVON RD

❺

Jamaica House

HILLCREST AVE

CHRISTAR VILLAS ❻

▷ Beverly Hills

EASTWOOD PARK RD

Devon House

HOPE ROAD

HOPEFIELD AVE

❼ ▷

HAUGHTON AVE

Vale Royal

St Andrews Parish Church ✝

TRAFALGAR

LADY MUSGRAVE ROAD

❽
❾ **Drive-in Cinema**

NEW KINGSTON

HALF WAY TREE

❶❶

❿

New Kingston Shopping Centre

CECILIO AVE

OLD HOPE ROAD

❶❷

❶❸

CRIEFFE RD

TUCKER AVE

❶❻

MOUNTAIN VIEW AVE

i **Jamaica Tourist Board**

HALF WAY TREE ROAD

❶❹

Liguanea Club

❶❺

❶❼

Bob Marley Statue

❶❽
❶❾ ❷⓿

OXFORD RD

❷❶

National Stadium

RIPON RD

ARTHUR WINT DR

SWALLOWFIELD RD

National Arena

LYNDHURST RD

ROUSSEAU RD

RETIREMENT RD

TOM REDCAM AVE

Little & Little Little Theatres

Parish Library

CALEDONIA AVE

PORT ROYAL & ST THOMAS ▷

DEANERY RD

BEVERLY RD

0   ½ mile

Carib Theatre

UPTOWN KINGSTON

ACCOMMODATION

Alhambra Inn	12	Edge Hill	16	Mayfair	4
Altamont Court	17	Four Seasons	11	Olympia Crown	7
Central Court	21	The Gardens	2	Jamaica Pegasus	18
Chelsea	14	Hilton Kingston	15	Sandhurst	3
Christar Villas	6	Holborn Manor	8	Sunset Inn	20
Courtleigh	19	Indies	9	Sutton Place	10
Crieffe Court	13	Maya Mountain Lodge	1	Terra Nova	5

Kingston

There are some dirt-cheap hotels downtown, but as these are only for the desperate and fearless, we don't recommend them.

wise to reserve in advance, finding a room is rarely a problem, except during the April Carnival and around Christmas and New Year.

If you don't fancy the hustle of the big city (and some of the hotels can get noisy at night), there are a handful of small hotels and guesthouses in the foothills of the Blue Mountains just north of Kingston. Others, deeper in the mountains, are covered in Chapter Two – as well as offering peace and spectacular views, these make good bases for hiking. If you want to explore the city, though, it can be expensive and time-consuming getting back and forth and, unless you have a car, you're better off staying in town.

Kingston

Alhambra Inn, 1 Tucker Ave; ☎978 9072–3, fax 978 9074, *alhambra@ cwjamaica.com*. Pretty complex set back from the road near the National Stadium, with a pool, outdoor restaurant and lots of greenery. The rooms offer parquet floors, king-size beds, telephone, a/c and cable TV, and are superb value. ⑤.

Altamont Court, 1 Altamont Terrace; ☎929 4497-8, fax 929 2118, *altamont@n5.com.jm*. Excellent location in the shadow of the gleaming *Jamaica Pegasus* hotel, with a small swimming pool, jacuzzi, restaurant and bar. The comfortable rooms have a/c, cable TV and phone. ⑤.

Central Court, 47 Old Hope Rd; ☎920 1026. Reasonably priced but slightly dingy rooms with phone and cable TV; you pay a little more for a/c, and there's a restaurant and bar on site. ②.

Chelsea, 5 Chelsea Ave; ☎926 5803. Cheap and in the heart of New Kingston, rooms have a/c, fan, cable TV and hot and cold water. ②.

Christar Villas, 99 Hope Rd; ☎978 3933, fax 978 8068. Appealing self-catering studios and suites and a small pool near the Bob Marley Museum. ⑤.

Courtleigh, 85 Knutsford Blvd; ☎929 9000, fax 926 7744, *courtleigh@cwjamaica.com*. A New Kingston old-timer that's fast eclipsing its competition as the best in town. The brand new building contains a fully equipped business centre, restaurants, bars, a gym, a pool and a popular nightclub. Rooms are luxurious with plenty of extras; some have balconies. ⑥.

Crieffe Court, 10 Crieffe Rd; ☎927 7908, *crieff@cwjamaica.com*. No-frills but reasonable value at this functional hotel near the National Stadium. Rooms have kitchenettes. ②.

Another alternative, handy for the airport, is the charming Morgan's Harbour Hotel *in nearby Port Royal; see p.111.*

Crowne Plaza, 211a Constant Spring Rd; ☎925 7676, fax 925 5757. Towering over northern Kingston, this plush ten-storey block near Stony Hill provides a pleasant respite from the city centre and affords wonderful views. With all mod cons, rooms are suitably elegant, and there are several restaurants and bars, a pool, tennis and squash courts and a gym on site. ⑥ Rates include breakfast.

Edge Hill, 198 Mountain View Ave; ☎927 9854, fax 978 0779. Decent place on the eastern side of town near the National Stadium. The rooms, mostly self-catering, are sizeable, with cable TV, but can be noisy at night – ask for one away from the road. ④.

Four Seasons, 18 Ruthven Rd; ☎926 8805, fax 929 5964, *www. hotelfourseasonsja.com*. Attractive, converted Edwardian home in New

Kingston. Rooms in the original house are more atmospheric than those in the modern wing. ⑤.

The Gardens, 23 Liguanea Ave; ☎927 5957, fax 978 6942, *www .forrespark.com*. With centrality, seclusion and a homely, relaxing feel, this delightful complex of expansive two-bedroom townhouses, set in gorgeous flowered gardens and with a pool, is one of Kingston's best choices. Rooms and apartments with living room and kitchen (sleeping four) are available. ③.

Hilton Kingston (formerly the *Wyndham*), 77 Knutsford Blvd; ☎926 5430, fax 929 7439, *www.hilton.com*. Liveliest of the three high-rise New Kingston hotels with a fabulous swimming pool, small casino, nightclub and all the top-class facilities you could wish for. ⑧.

Holborn Manor, 3 Holborn Rd; ☎926 0296, fax 906 5281. Friendly, rather basic family property in New Kingston. Rooms have fan and cable TV costs a little extra. ③ The excellent rates include breakfast.

Indies, 5 Holborn Rd; ☎926 0989, fax 926 2879. Compact, clean, slightly overpriced little hotel next to *Holborn Manor*, set on two levels around a garden courtyard and small restaurant. ④.

Jamaica Pegasus, 81 Knutsford Blvd; ☎926 3690–9, fax 929 5855, *www .jmpegasus.com*. Plush high-rise, attracting mostly business travellers, with a gym, tennis courts and outdoor pool ⑥.

Maya Mountain Lodge, Jack's Hill; ☎702 0314. Budget place beautifully situated on the flanks of the Blue Mountains, a twenty-minute drive, geared as a base for hikers but feasible for seeing Kingston if you've got a car or patience to wait for the bus. Rustic cabin rooms, and a campsite (with questionable security). ④.

Mayfair, 4 W King's House Close; ☎926 6160 or 929 3703, fax 926 7741. A sound choice in a quiet area, with a pool, restaurant and bar. Rooms have phone, TV and a balcony, and suites have a dining/living room and kitchenette. ③–⑤.

Olympia Crown, 53 Molynes Rd; ☎923 5282, fax 901 6688. Roomy complex near Half Way Tree with restaurant, bar, gym and a large pool. Rooms are comfortable, with cable TV, phone and fan; you pay more for a/c. ③.

Sandhurst, 70 Sandhurst Crescent; ☎927 8244. Excellent value in a peaceful spot near King's House and the Bob Marley Museum, with a nice pool and a terrace restaurant overlooking the Blue Mountains. ③–④.

Sunset Inn, 1A Altamont Crescent; ☎926 2017. Rather cramped and functional but central. Rooms have a/c, phone, cable TV and fridge; some have small kitchens. ③.

Sutton Place, 11 Ruthven Rd; ☎926 4580, fax 926 8443, *www.sutton-place .com*. Large, comfortable if impersonal hotel with a pool and restaurant, popular with local business travellers. A reliable fallback at busy times. ④.

Terra Nova, 17 Waterloo Rd; ☎926 2211, fax 926 9334, *terranova @cwjamaica.com*. Very smart little hideaway set in landscaped gardens, with a small pool and elegant rooms. ⑦ Rates include breakfast.

The City

Most people divide Kingston into two sectors – **downtown** and **uptown** – and we've adopted the same distinction. It'll take you half a day or so to check out the sights downtown, a little more to catch

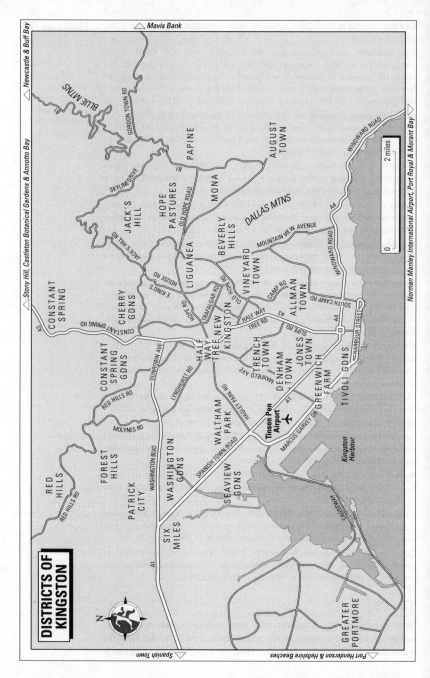

DISTRICTS OF KINGSTON

those uptown. Downtown, the **National Gallery**, by the waterfront, is the high-culture highlight, while the nearby **Crafts Market** and Orange Street **record stores** are throbbing with a more gritty atmosphere. The breezy waterfront is also the departure point for the **ferry** to Port Royal (see p.105). Ten minutes' walk north, the cacophonous **Parade** – one-time marching ground of the British army – is flanked by a couple of interesting **churches**, while a little further from here, **Headquarters House** is a grand old colonial home stuffed with historical relics.

Uptown has the more popular attractions, including the must-see **Bob Marley Museum** and the striking **Devon House** – home to the island's first black millionaire – with its clutch of gift shops, landscaped gardens and superb home-made ice cream. Also uptown, at Half Way Tree, the seventeenth-century **St Andrews Parish Church** remains one of the key churches in Jamaica, second in historical importance only to the cathedral in Spanish Town (see p.115), while the **Hope Botanical Gardens** offer a quiet refuge from the noise of the city.

Downtown

Flattened by an earthquake in 1907, **downtown Kingston** has lost most of its grand eighteenth-century architecture, though a handful of historic buildings can still be found along Rum Lane, Water Lane and King Street, and if you peer into the most unlikely yards you can occasionally find evidence of the intricate buildings that used to proliferate here.

Much of Kingston's economic strength still derives from its impressively huge natural harbour, one of the world's best but grimly polluted these days. Once buzzing with trading ships, the windwhipped **waterfront** is a good spot to start a tour of the downtown area, close to the **National Gallery** and the **Crafts Market** and a short walk from the main **Parade**, above which you'll find **Headquarters House**, and, just outside the old city boundaries to the north, **National Heroes Park**. Nearby, and very much off the beaten track, **West Kingston** is home to the country's most depressed ghetto areas – the stuff of many a reggae lyric – Trench Town, Jones Town, Tivoli Gardens and Greenwich Farm are explosive and creative; the birthplace of many of Jamaica's most successful musicians.

The Bench and Bar restaurant (see p.94) serves as an informal information centre for the downtown area; it's also a marvellous place to escape the dust and heat for a while.

The waterfront

Despite the fuel silos, loading cranes and container ships moored just offshore, the **waterfront** is a surprisingly pleasant place: people and pelicans fish off the concrete piers, couples and the odd vagrant sit on the harbour wall or walk the grassy boulevard, and planes swoop overhead en route to Norman Manley airport across the water. The chief beneficiary of the city council's 1960s' bid to beautify elements of downtown, the waterfront saw its historic buildings

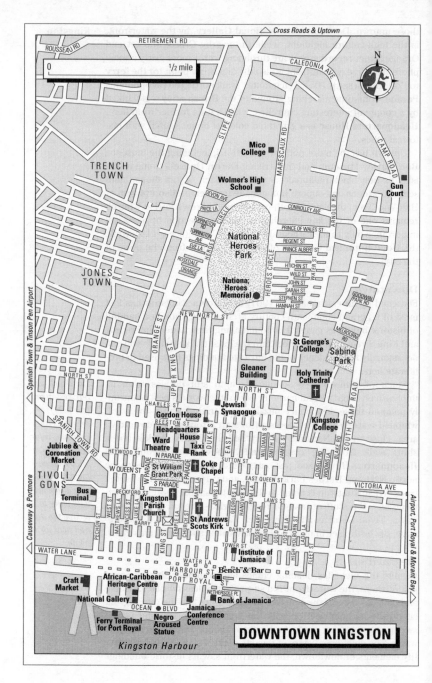

DOWNTOWN KINGSTON

swept away and replaced by spanking new high-rises – the icons of the era. Today, these modern monuments define the eastern end of the waterfront's main strip, Ocean Boulevard. They include the head-quarters of the Bank of Jamaica on Nethersole Place, whose **Coin and Note Museum** (Mon–Fri 9am–4pm; free) has a collection of the country's currency that should fascinate the numismatic. Nearby at 14 Duke St, you can get a free tour of the **Jamaica Conference Centre** (Mon–Fri 9am–4pm), built in 1981 to host meetings of the United Nations' International Seabed Authority. This in itself proba-bly won't have you queuing at dawn, but the building's lofty design and abundant use of glass and local crafts make it feel unlike any-where else in the city.

West of here, the large, pink, forlorn-looking building on Ocean Boulevard was, until the late 1980s, the **Oceana Hotel**, built as the government's flagship for Kingston in an attempt to entice business travellers – and their expense accounts – downtown. The target guests ignored it entirely and continued to enjoy the smarter hotels and better nightlife of New Kingston, and the hotel flopped; the long-standing official claim that private investors are on the verge of reopening it seems more than a little optimistic. Further along the boulevard, at the bottom of King Street, is a reproduction of the sculpture **Negro Aroused** by the late Edna Manley, one of Jamaica's leading artists and wife and mother, respectively, of former prime ministers Norman Manley and Michael Manley. One of the icons of twentieth-century Jamaican art, the bronze sculpture perfectly cap-tured the incipient labour movement and the spirit of unrest of the 1930s, and is dedicated to the workers of Jamaica.

The National Gallery and the African-Caribbean Heritage Centre

The icily air-conditioned **National Gallery**, at 12 Ocean Blvd on the corner of Orange Street (Mon–Thurs 11am–4.30pm, Fri 11am–4pm; J$40), is one of the unexpected highlights of a visit to Kingston. The permanent collection here is superb, ranging from delicate wood-carvings to flamboyant religious paintings, while of the several tem-porary exhibitions held each year, the Annual National Exhibition (normally Dec–Feb) showcases the best of contemporary Jamaican art.

Just inside the front door, Christopher Gonzales' statue of Bob Marley was commissioned for Kingston's proposed Celebrity Park (see p.87); the statue (which bears little resemblance to Marley) was too eccentric, and was consigned to relative obscurity here. Look out also for Rafiki Karikuli's *Donman*, a posturing rude boy with pierc-ing eyes, in the hall that leads into the gallery rooms.

At the core of the permanent collection are ten chronological gal-leries, housed on the first floor, representing the **Jamaican School**, 1922 to the present. Their era is generally deemed to begin with Edna Manley's 1922 *Bead Seller*, a dainty little statue which married

The lavishly illustrated Modern Jamaican Art *is the ultimate souvenir of the National Gallery's collection, and is available on site*

See p.410 of Contexts for more Jamaican art.

a contemporary artistic trend (cubism) to a typical local image (the Kingston "higgler", or female street vendor) to create something distinctly Jamaican. Manley's sculpture and the absorbing paintings of John Dunkley (1891–1947) dominate the first galleries. Dunkley was a Kingston barber, and the first and most important of Jamaica's self-taught artists; his dark, brooding local scenes are a far cry from the jaunty colours of modern landscape painters – *Lonely Road* is particularly powerful. He and Manley paved the way for others to paint what they saw around them and, in the work of artists like Albert Huie and David Pottinger – see his *Nine Night*, with its mourners turned trance-like during the ritual nine nights of grieving after a death – you can detect the early stages of a movement giving value and artistic identity to its own people and places.

The ferry to Port Royal departs from the pier at the bottom of Princess Street, near the National Gallery; see p.107 for details.

The paintings of the prolific Carl Abrahams in the later galleries show a move towards abstraction that is capped by the idiosyncratically Jamaican surrealism of Colin Garland and the unsettling ghostly images of David Boxer, long-time curator of the gallery and a key figure in Jamaican modern art. Realism returns with the spooky and powerful recreation of a Trench Town ghetto, complete with Kisco wrappers and political graffiti, in Dawn Scott's *A Cultural Object*, which has you walking in ever-decreasing circles through graffiti-splattered corrugated tin alleys to a disturbing climax. Look out, also, for the funky colours of Rastafarian Everald Brown whose vivid *Drum* sculpture recurs in his spiritual painting *Ethiopian Apple*. An entire room houses the **Larry Worth Collection** of African-style sculpture and paintings by revivalist Shepherd Mallica "Kapo" Reynolds that depict themes from the revivalist faith. As well as the hordes of beautiful wood sculptures, particularly striking are paintings *Watching Over Me* and *Peaceful Quietness*.

Downstairs, the **A.D. Scott Collection** displays a selection of Edna Manley's sculptures alongside some of the finest works of the island's biggest names, including Gloria Escoffery and Barrington Watson. Highlights include Watson's *Banana Loaders*, beautifully capturing the toiling banana workers in Post-Impressionist style, and Escofferey's *The Old Woman*, which suggests the esteem in which elders are held in Jamaica.

The rest of the permanent collection is rotated from time to time and includes a modern photographic display, a pre-twentieth-century exhibit, with its series of landscapes by itinerant European painters, and an international collection featuring such diverse sections as modern Cuban painters and the English Bloomsbury Group.

Orange Street holds some of the island's best record stores – see p.101.

Just north of the gallery on Orange Street, the tiny, uninspired **African-Caribbean Heritage Centre** (Mon–Fri 9am–3.30pm; free) is a library and small art gallery with a few African drums and musical instruments and a long-standing exhibition on Marcus Garvey.

The Craft Market

The **Craft Market** (closed Sun), housed in an unprepossessing iron building at the western end of Ocean Boulevard, is all that's left of the formidable market that for centuries was held at the bottom of nearby King Street. Originally a Sunday market drawing thousands of slaves on their day off, it got shunted a few hundred yards west during the 1960s' redevelopment of the waterfront. Shopping here is generally a hassle-free experience, and you'll find loads of little stores selling t-shirts, carvings, jewellery and other souvenirs – some of the stock appears marvellously antiquated. Unlike most places, though, don't expect to be able to bargain much as prices remain the lowest on the island.

The Parade and around

Opposite Edna Manley's *Negro Aroused* statue, King Street runs north to the **Parade**, a large square left open by the original city planners and used as a parade ground by British troops during the eighteenth century, as well as for public floggings and hangings – most famously the hanging of the slave hired to assassinate Cuban independence leader Simon Bolivar during his visit to the island in 1818 (he failed, but perished for trying). Today, it's one of the busiest spots in town, with traffic racing around the central park, music blaring from radios and shop-front speakers, crowds milling around the taxi rank and the bus terminus, and vendors hawking sky juice and cheap baubles. In the middle of the Parade is **St William Grant Park**, originally Victoria Park but renamed in 1977 for the 1930s' leader of the infant Jamaican trade union movement who was cynically upstaged by the more charismatic Alexander Bustamante; he ended his life as a security guard for the Ministry of Social Security. Rather fierce statues of political rivals Norman Manley and Alexander Bustamante guard its north and south entrances, while Queen Victoria – the onetime "Supreme Lady of Jamaica" – stands to the east, looking a little lost among all the mayhem. There's an elaborate fountain in the centre of the park, prettily illuminated at night. Though it looks like a shady spot to catch your breath, the park is probably best avoided as these days it serves as a makeshift home for vagrants.

Just north of the park on North Parade, looking like an elaborately iced birthday cake, the elegant **Ward Theatre** occupies a site with a long theatrical tradition. It is reckoned that public performances have been staged here since at least the mid-eighteenth century and probably earlier – although the present building dates only from 1911, bestowed to the city by one-time Custos and rum baron Colonel Charles Ward. It now hosts an annual **pantomime** every December and regular music and dance shows throughout the year. If you want to poke around, the building is normally open.

See p.100 for further details of perfomances at the Ward Theatre.

On South Parade, just below the park, the **Kingston Parish Church** was first built in 1699, although little of the present structure pre-dates the 1907 earthquake. Airy and spacious, the church is used for important state funerals and such, although the regular congregation has dwindled to almost nothing due to migration out of the downtown area. The south wall has a marvellously wordy elegy to midshipman Edward Baker, who died in 1796 in a sea battle off Santo Domingo, and there are plenty of marble monuments by John Bacon to such notables as British Admiral John Benbow, and John Wolmer, founder of Wolmer's School (see p.85). An eloquent testament to colonialism hangs on the west wall, where plaques honour soldiers of the West Indian regiment who died (mostly of fever) on unheard-of campaigns in West Africa in the 1890s.

Queen Street runs west and east of the park. To the west, the enormous **Jubilee Market** (Mon–Fri) spills over onto the Parade, a colourful place to wander and pick up fresh fruit and vegetables, though the crowds can make it rather daunting. Further west along Barry Street, Jubilee melts into **Coronation Market**, the islands biggest, busiest and loudest – and an experience even if you're not here to buy. Coronation has a distinctly chaotic feel; tattered tarpaulins flap over piles of everything from home-made graters fashioned from nail-punched tin cans to washing powder, underpants and, of course, artistically displayed produce amongst a backdrop of vegetable peelings and discarded corn husks. The dingy indoor section, its iron roof beams festooned with impressive cobwebs, is laced by alleys patrolled by customers prodding, poking and bargaining, and the sales banter of the vendors is always a joy; you'll need your wits about you to keep up with it. Backing onto the fringes of the volatile Tivoli Gardens area, Coronation is not a traditional tourist spot, and probably best experienced in the company of someone who knows where they're going and can keep you out of the way of the wildly-steered push-carts that weave though the shoppers.

Marley disciples could be interested by the Bob Marley Foundation Web site: www .bobmarley -foundation .com.

If you're a Bob Marley devotee, you might want to take a taxi west of the markets, via Temple Lane, south of St William Grant Park, turning right onto Port Royal Street, which becomes Marcus Garvey Drive, a battered but wide thoroughfare lined with warehouses and factories. At 220 Marcus Garvey Drive, you'll find the state-of-the-art **Tuff Gong Recording Studios** (☎923 9383), established by Bob Marley and now run by his daughter Cedella, with help from other assorted Marleys including Ziggy of Melody Makers fame. A pressing plant and re-mastering facility, it's a commercial venture rather than a tourist site, but nonetheless, it's sometimes possible to look around (though, obviously, you may not be allowed in if the studios are in use) to see the self-same mixing board used on Wailers' classics such as *Stir It Up, Concrete Jungle* and *No Woman, No Cry*. While not wildly exciting, it's a nice stop for Marley disciples, with a gift shop for that essential CD or souvenir.

Coke Chapel and around

East of the markets and St William Grant Park, the large red-brick **Coke Chapel** is a Methodist church that dates from 1840 and was erected over the remains of a smaller eighteenth-century chapel built by Thomas Coke, an early missionary. Methodism, along with other nonconformist religions, played an important role in Jamaica, its missionaries actively fighting for improvements in the conditions of slaves and, eventually, against slavery itself. Because of this, the Methodist church found itself in conflict with the Jamaican authorities and, like others, the Coke Chapel was ordered to close for several years in the early nineteenth century. There's little to see in the rather spartan interior, but it's a quiet retreat from the sun and the crowds; the caretaker can usually be found nearby with a key – ask at the little shop in the compound.

Just south of Coke Chapel on Mark Lane, the bizarre octagonal **St Andrews Scots Kirk**, was founded in the early nineteenth century by local merchants of Scottish ancestry; the St Andrews Cross can still be detected in the church's stained glass window. If you want to have a look around the resident caretaker has the key.

The Institute of Jamaica

Four blocks east of Coke Chapel, East Street runs south to the **Institute of Jamaica** (Mon–Thurs 9am–5pm, Fri 9am–4pm; free). Here you'll find the **National Library** (*www.infochan.com /natlib/*), home to the best collection of books and old newspapers in the country, and the eminently missable **National Museum** (entrance round the corner on Tower Street) of Jamaica's natural history. Alongside the ranks of musty cabinets filled with dust-gathering stuffed birds, one of the more interesting displays explains the origins of the country's most important "economic plants" – sugarcane, bananas, coconuts and pineapples – almost all imported from areas of Asia during the early years of Spanish and British colonialism, and now widely grown for export. The museum has plenty of other interesting odds and ends – Taino *zemis*, African jewellery, old musical instruments – but, infuriatingly, these are only occasionally on display, spending most of their lives mouldering away in the basement.

Headquarters House and Gordon House

Two blocks west of East Street and just north of Parade, **Headquarters House** on Duke Street (Mon–Fri 8.30am–4.30pm; free) affords a brief glimpse of Jamaican history. Built in 1755 by Thomas Hibbert, a wealthy local merchant, the house was part of a wager between four friends as to who could construct the most elegant building to impress a local woman (Hibbert lost the bet, but the winning house is no longer in existence). Jamaica's legislative assembly met here briefly in 1755 and moved in full-time between

Kingston

Perry Henzell's movie The Harder They Come *(see p.111) is the classic account of a country boy falling in with the gangsters of West Kingston; for a contemporary update on life in the city, take in* Dancehall Queen *or* Third World Cop.

West Kingston

West Kingston is the capital's urban nightmare. Bob Marley sang fondly of growing up in the "government yards in Trench Town", but the reality of it is of a huge underclass confined to crowded makeshift tenements enclosed by rusting, graffiti-daubed zinc. The area – basically west of Parade, both north (Trench Town, Jones Town) and south (Tivoli Gardens, Greenwich Farm) of the main Spanish Town Road – has seen some sporadic clean-up campaigns but it's an endless, and seemingly hopeless task.

In the city's early years, West Kingston was a popular residential zone – well laid out and central. Over the last century, though, an exodus of the wealthy to more chi-chi districts uptown led to West Kingston's decline, and a subsequent influx of the less well-off – men and women from rural Jamaica who headed for Kingston's bright lights but were unable to find either work or welfare. Crowded together, the very worst-off built their makeshift homes on the "Dungle" (dunghill) by Kingston harbour, where all the city's excrement was dumped before the introduction of a sewage system. There, they fought with each other, as well as with the dogs and John Crow vultures, for scraps of garbage from the dust-carts.

Criminal elements were quick to take advantage of the conditions, recruiting and arming gang members from the ranks of the poor, especially young men looking for the identity and protection offered by allegiance to a "posse". Robbery, muggings and drug sales brought in money and, with it, a measure of street credibility. The crime problem was exacerbated in the 1970s as feuding political factions provided guns and favours for their supporters, asking them to intimidate opponents or drive them out of their "garrisons" or constituencies. The fading "PNP zone" or "JLP enter at your own risk" graffiti plastered over West Kingston walls stands testament to the strong political loyalties of the area. The weapons helped the criminals to establish ever stronger and more extensive drug empires that soon became profitable enough for political allegiances to take a lower profile.

Today large areas of the West remain little more than **armed camps**, and the graffiti hails the power of area **dons** rather than Seaga or Manley. While political violence still flares up at election times, the people of the ghettos (like the rest of the population) have largely washed their hands of a system that seems to have done them no long-term favours despite the years of promises. Instead, many prefer to give their allegiance to high profile area leaders such as **Dudus**, son of the infamous original area don Jim Brown, or the equally powerful **Zekes**, who earn the favour of their communities as much as by staging free "fun days" for local people and doling out school books and cash to the needy as through sheer fire-power. Zekes is said to have initiated a kind of alternative justice system to police the notorious Matthew's Lane community, his downtown stronghold and a place where the official officers of the law rarely dare to tread.

Laurie Gunst's Born Fi Dead *(see "Contexts", p.424) is a gripping explanation of the development of Kingston gang culture.*

West Kingston continues to be seen by most politicians as being beyond hope, and despite the occasional highly publicized campaign to revitalize the area, there seems to be little physical improvement. In February 2000, Britain's Prince Charles visited Trench Town and Jones Town to see the yard formerly occupied by Bob Marley and hear of the somewhat ambitious plans to redevelop it as a tourist attraction, which should, in turn, bring some badly-needed foreign dollars to the area. Until that happens though – and it's a very long way off – West Kingston is clearly not a place to venture without an experienced guide and a very deep breath.

1872 and 1960. During the intervening years the house was commandeered by the armed forces to serve both as its military headquarters and as the residence of the local general in charge.

Today, Headquarters House is the home of the **Jamaica National Heritage Trust** (☎922 1287, *www.jnht.com*), whose offices are installed in the former bedrooms and on the now walled-in veranda, but you're free to look around the rest of the house. The debating chamber, where the legislative assembly used to meet, is on the ground floor, filled with original furniture and a fine mahogany public gallery for visitors, and the walls hold large portraits of Jamaica's first political leaders and some of its National Heroes, including Sam Sharpe, Nanny and Paul Bogle. In the basement, the cool storage rooms contain more offbeat relics, including a bronze statue of Marcus Garvey and a painting by Noel Coward of his adopted home at Port Maria on the north coast (see p.212). Upstairs, you can climb to the look-out tower for great views over downtown Kingston, Port Royal and the Blue Mountains. From here Hibbert would watch his ships coming into the harbour and, later, the generals could keep an eye on any enemy boat movements.

For more on Jamaica's National Heroes see p.85.

Next to Headquarters House is the rather less imposing **Gordon House**, home to the parliament since 1960 and named after National Hero George William Gordon. Gordon, a lay preacher who consistently advocated the rights of the poor, proved a constant thorn in the side of the establishment. In 1865, the authorities found a flimsy pretext to accuse him of involvement in the Morant Bay Rebellion and he was summarily executed, despite widespread protest from black Jamaicans. Today, the House of Representatives meets here most Tuesdays at 2pm (and at the same time on Wednesdays and Thursdays if there is sufficient business) while the Senate sits in the chamber on Fridays at 11am; at these times, surrounding streets are sometimes cordoned off. Entrance to the public gallery is free, and when the chamber is empty you can ask the marshall to show you around. The debates are normally pretty soporific for spectators, though you might want to catch political veterans like the Jamaican Labour Party's Edward Seaga in action.

See p.148 for more on the Morant Bay Rebellion.

The Jewish Synagogue

The striking white building on Duke Street above Gordon House is the **Jewish Synagogue**. It's kept locked, but you can normally find the caretaker on the premises during the week; you'll need to pay a small donation for him to open the place up. Jews were among the first Europeans to settle in Jamaica during the sixteenth century, fleeing the inquisition in Spain. Even here, though, they were still obliged to practise their religion in secret, a fact remembered today by the sand scattered on the floor of the modern building, which symbolically muffles your footsteps as you wander around.

In 1882, the synagogues of the two Jewish congregations, the Ashkenhazi and the Sephardic, were both destroyed by fire and an amalgamated synagogue was built on this site (although a handful of rebel members of each congregation refused to mix and went off to found their own synagogues). The present building dates from after the 1907 earthquake, with substantial repairs effected after Hurricane Gilbert in 1988. The exodus of Jamaica's Jews, both from downtown Kingston and from the island (part of the general flight of whites during the 1970s), means that the present congregation is tiny, but the building, with its mahogany staircase and gallery, is still worth a visit if you're passing.

East of Duke Street

A couple of blocks east of the synagogue, the **Gleaner Building** (closed to visitors) on the corner of North and East Streets holds the offices of the *Gleaner* and *Star* newspapers. The *Gleaner* has reported on events in Jamaica since it was founded as *de Cordova's Advertiser* in 1834; never afraid to voice its strident opinions, and particularly scathing during the first administration of Michael Manley, the paper remains the most influential and widely read of the country's three dailies. Five minutes' walk further east along North Street and you come to the Catholic Church's large-domed **Holy Trinity Cathedral**. A caretaker is supposed to guard the premises but don't hold out too much hope of finding him there, or the cathedral open, except during services. During termtime, hundreds of schoolchildren mill around the area, spilling out of nearby high schools **Kingston College** and **St George's College**, the latter founded by the Jesuits in 1850. Just around the corner from the cathedral is **Sabina Park**, home of the Kingston Cricket Club – the oldest sports club in the Commonwealth Caribbean – and venue for international test matches and many of the inter-island games.

See "Basics" p.48, for more on Jamaica's cricket fixation.

National Heroes Park and around

Ten minutes' walk north from the Gleaner Building, **National Heroes Park** (better known locally as the Racecourse) is a large stretch of scrubby grass enclosed by iron railings. If you're on foot it offers a chance to escape the traffic that hammers around it, but it's not really a popular spot for a promenade these days, favoured more by grazing goats than casual strollers. The park held the city's racecourse for more than a century before it got shifted to the more salubrious New Kingston, and from there to its present location west of the city at Caymanas Park. After independence, the government converted the southern portion of the park into a monument to Jamaica's **National Heroes** (see box); newly landscaped and guarded by two po-faced JDF sentries sweltering in full ceremonial uniform, it feels a lot less hairy than in previous years. Norman Manley, Alexander Bustamante and Marcus Garvey are buried beneath the futuristic Shrine of Monuments – a series of stone, marble and bronze memorial busts and figures dedicated to each of the Heroes –

at the south end of the park. Other local luminaries buried here include ex-prime ministers Michael Manley, Donald Sangster and entertainer Ranny Williams. When the reggae star **Dennis Brown** died on June 1 1999, controversy ensued when a Heroes Circle plot was made available. Detractors argued that Brown's long-term use of cocaine was hardly a motivation for official recognition, but in the end, the remarkable career of the honey-toned "Crown Prince of Reggae" was deemed reason enough for such honour. Adjacent to the main heroes' plots is a bust of Antonio Maceo and a statue of Simon Bolivar, independence leaders in Cuba and South America respectively and inspirational to Jamaica's early nationalists.

At the north end of the park, on Marescaux Road, are the colourful, wooden buildings of **Wolmers High School** and **Mico College**. Wolmers, founded in 1729, has proved a formidable centre of academic achievement, counting prime ministers and governor generals among its alumni. Nearby Mico, the largest teacher-training school in the West Indies, owes its foundation in 1834 to the eleventh-hour refusal of Englishman Samuel Mico to marry one of the six nieces of his aunt, Lady Mico, back in 1670. The intended dowry was invested for a number of charitable purposes, and eventually used to found teacher-training colleges in various parts of the Caribbean. Dedicated to "liberating minds from the bondage of

Kingston

Makeshift stalls selling boiled corn, land crab, roast yam and saltfish are set up on the outskirts of Heroes Circle at the corner of New North Street.

Jamaica's National Heroes

Since independence, the Jamaican parliament has elevated seven of the island's greatest people to the status of **National Hero**, all of whom carry the title "The Right Excellent". As yet, none of the Heroes hail from the worlds of sport or music, but it is widely anticipated that Bob Marley will be next to join the pantheon. Michael Manley, who died in 1997, is another popular candidate. The present National Heroes are:

Paul Bogle (unknown–1865). Baptist preacher who led the 1865 Morant Bay Rebellion, and was executed for his participation.

Alexander Bustamante (1884–1977). Labour leader, founder of the Jamaica Labour Party and first prime minister of the independent country from 1962 to 1967.

Marcus Garvey (1887–1940). Founder of the Universal Negro Improvement Association and widely viewed as the father of the black power movement.

George William Gordon (1820–65). "Free coloured" leader of Jamaica's nationalist movement after slavery, accused of involvement in the Morant Bay Rebellion and executed.

Norman Manley (1893–1969). Lawyer, founder of the People's National Party and leader of Jamaica's movement for independence.

Nanny (birth and death unknown). Legendary eighteenth-century female leader of the Windward Maroons in their battles with the English.

Sam Sharpe (1801–32). Baptist preacher executed after leading the 1831 slave rebellion in Jamaica's western parishes.

ignorance", Mico was founded to fund education for newly-emancipated Africans, and was one of the only colleges in Jamaica that operated on non-racial grounds. Inside the main building is a **museum** (☎929 5260; Mon–Thurs 9am–5pm, Fri 9am–3pm, Sat & Sun 10am–3pm; J$100), with a section on Mico's history as well as the excellent INAFCA (Indian, African and Caribbean Artefacts) collection of African (and a few Caribbean) artefacts donated by old Miconian Dr Aston Taylor, which includes spears, shields, sculptures and masks. If you want a guided tour of the museum and the college – at no additional charge – you'll need to book a day in advance.

East of here on Camp Road are the headquarters of the island's army, the Jamaica Defence Force (JDF), and the notorious **Gun Court**. Established in 1972 during the early years of Michael Manley's first administration to deal with the proliferating number of firearms offences, the place is still a harsh prison, protected by high-security fences and reams of barbed wire. The hugely busy **Cross Roads**, quarter of a mile above Mico and the dividing line between uptown and downtown, marks the intersection where Kingston's principal roads – Half Way Tree Road, Slipe Road, Caledonia Avenue/South Camp Road, and Old Hope Road – meet. There's little to it other than a busy market and the **Carib Theatre**, the city's oldest cinema, which has been lavishly rebuilt after a catastrophic fire destroyed it in 1996.

Uptown

Uptown Kingston is shown on the map on p.71.

The phrase "uptown Kingston" is used as a catch-all for areas of the city north of Cross Roads, including the business and commercial centres of **Half Way Tree** and **New Kingston** as well as residential areas like **Hope Pastures**, **Mona** and **Beverly Hills**. Up until the late eighteenth century, uptown was mostly rural, sprinkled with livestock farms (known as pens) and sugar estates. Gradually, as Kingston's wealthy merchants acquired this land in a bid to escape from the noise and crowds downtown, the city began to spill out of its original waterfront site. The process has accelerated during the past half-century and newer and more fashionable districts have been created further and further north of the old city, extending right across the old Liguanea Plain and into the foothills of the Blue Mountains.

Most visitors make a beeline for the **Bob Marley Museum** and the colonial-era **Devon House**, both just above New Kingston on the traffic-crazed Hope Road, uptown's central thoroughfare. Further east are the pleasant if ramshackle **Hope Botanical Gardens**, and Mona, home to the capacious **University of the West Indies** campus, while, to the north, the main arteries fan out into the Blue Mountains and the ritzy suburbs of Red Hills, Stony Hill and Jack's Hill.

New Kingston

The heart of uptown is the high-rise financial district of **New Kingston**, found in an eccentric triangle bounded by Trafalgar Road, Old Hope Road and Half Way Tree Road. In the early twentieth century this was an attractive grassy area, the location of the Liguanea Golf Club and later, briefly, the Knutsford Park racetrack. During the 1950s and 1960s, though, with the commercial areas of downtown getting increasingly choked and congested, the city planners decided to create a new self-contained business district. The horse-racing moved west to Caymanas Park, the Liguanea Club contracted, and bank, hotel and office buildings started to shoot up.

The chances are that you will stay and do much of your eating and drinking in or around this area; some of the interesting sights are within walking distance, the rest are a short bus- or taxi-ride away. There are few places of note in New Kingston itself, although the **Liguanea Club**, opposite the *Jamaica Pegasus* hotel on Knutsford Boulevard – in theory members only, but easily accessible if you're passing – still retains its old colonial buildings as well as lots of lovely tennis courts (available for hire).

The Liguanea Club served as the setting for the fictional Queens Club, the colonial hangout where James Bond took cocktails on the veranda with Professor Dent in Dr No.

The National Stadium and around

The 40,000 capacity **National Stadium**, known locally as "The Office", which hosts most of Jamaica's premier sporting fixtures, is just east of New Kingston on Arthur Wint Drive. The stadium was built to coincide with Jamaica's independence celebrations in 1962; the first event was the raising of the new nation's black, green and gold flag, followed soon after by the 1962 Commonwealth Games. Although the centrepiece soccer pitch looks a little the worse for wear, the facilities for athletics and cycling are first-rate. Just inside the railings by the car park is a statue of Jamaican athlete Herb McKinley coming off the starting blocks; at the 1952 Helsinki Olympics, McKinley became the first man in the world to run in the 200, 400 and 800 metres races (see box on p.88). A smaller adjacent stadium, to be used for minor events, is currently under construction.

The **National Arena** next door houses smaller-scale sporting events and other shows. There are plans to convert the grassy area opposite into a **Celebrity Park**, with statues of the island's leading names, but at present only a slightly mournful figure of Bob Marley, by local sculptor Alvin Marriot, stands by the road. The hills to the east house Jamaica's **Beverly Hills**, almost as affluent as the Los Angeles suburb it was named after. No longer the first-choice neighbourhood for wealthy Kingstonians since the exodus of the rich that followed Michael Manley's admonishments during his socialist 1970s administration – his famous comment that there were five planes a day to Miami and that anyone who didn't like his policies should get on one was taken up by those with the most to lose, and

For information on events at the National Stadium and National Arena, call ☎929 4970.

Jamaica at the Olympics

Although, like other West Indian islands, Jamaica is world-famous for its cricket, it also has a tremendous record of achievement in other sports, particularly athletics. The country first entered the Olympic Games in 1948 when it was still a British colony. Arthur Wint and Herb McKinley took gold and silver in the 400 metres, and Wint picked up silver in the 800 metres. That record of achievement, remarkable for such a small country, has been kept up over the years, with sprinters like Don Quarrie and Merlene Ottey winning medals and acquiring a devoted following in the process. The success of Jamaican-born athletes who have run under the flag of other countries – Britain's Linford Christie is just one example – has only enhanced the country's reputation.

Two explanations are usually given for Jamaica's athletic excellence. First, success (as in most sports) offers a quick way out of the ghetto – Merlene Ottey, born and raised in a poor rural village, was *the* role model for many young Jamaican women. Although her usually exemplary conduct took an international knocking after she tested positive for the banned steroid nandrolone in July 1999, Ottey's reputation at home remained relatively unscathed, with most Jamaicans insisting that she'd been treated erroneously, and that the presence of nandrolone in her sample was down to a natural excess caused by her menstrual cycle combined with traces of the substance contained in a supplement she was taking. The fans' suspicions were confirmed when Ottey was cleared by the Jamaican Athletics Federation in November 1999, and then had her IAAF ban lifted in June 2000, clearing the way for her to participate in the Sydney Olympics and restoring nationwide enthusiasm for the island's chances in the future. Second, the vision of political leaders like Norman Manley – who himself held a sprinting record in schoolboy athletics for over forty years – made sure that young athletes were given top-class facilities, particularly the National Stadium, and the opportunity to compete for track scholarships to colleges in North America – used by many Jamaican athletes as a springboard to international success.

The LTM's pantomime is premiered at the Ward Theatre; see p.79.

many of Beverly Hills' swankiest homes were swiftly deserted. Those brave enough to remain snapped up the properties, and it's often said that many of the newer homes were built by drug money. Nonetheless, the area still provides stunning views across the city and out to sea, which are best viewed by taking a trip along Beverly Terrace/Montclair Drive from Old Hope Road.

Further south from the National Arena, on Tom Redcam Avenue, the squat, wooden Little Theatre was built in 1961 to house the Little Theatre Movement, which from its inception in 1942 pioneered organized theatre in Kingston. The theatre hosts the LTM's annual pantomime and seasons by the globally recognized National Dance Theatre Company and the Jamaican Folk Singers. The wooden memorial outside is to Greta Fowler, energetic founder of the LTM, while the small building next door is the site of the innovative Little Little Theatre, where modern Jamaican playwrights are given an airing. The unimposing Parish Library (Mon–Fri 9am–6pm, Sat

See p.100 for further details of performances at the Little and Little Little theatres

9am–5pm; free), half a block further down Tom Redcam Drive, has an expansive if somewhat disorganized West Indian collection, and visitors can borrow books on payment of a small deposit.

Half Way Tree

On the other side of New Kingston, a mile or so away, is the congested area known as **Half Way Tree**. Before it got swallowed up by the expanding city, Half Way Tree was a tiny village and the capital of the parish of St Andrew. Its central plaza – today a busy shopping area and one of Kingston's key road intersections – once provided a resting-place for farmers travelling into the city's markets. The eponymous cotton tree under which they sheltered is long gone, and a clock tower now stands in its place, a 1913 memorial to British King Edward VII. With back-to-back traffic sweltering under the sun, vendors hawking anything from doughnuts to sound-system tapes and queues of hungry workers standing in line at the pretty-pink *Tastees Patties* outlet, Half Way Tree today is about as far away from a resting place as it's possible to imagine.

A handful of restored colonial buildings stand near the square, the most notable of which is the red-brick **St Andrews Parish Church** (always open; free). Though largely submerged by the modern buildings that have arisen around it, this is still a tranquil and gently alluring edifice. Built in 1666, it's one of the oldest religious sites on the island, though the present model is the fourth incarnation, renovated (with typical Victorian vigour) in 1879 after earlier ones were wrecked by hurricane and earthquake. Grand Latin memorials in the floor date back to 1692, the marble tablets on the walls commemorate English soldiers and Jamaican civil servants, and there are some delicate stained-glass windows. Outside, the massive **graveyard**, with its crumbling tombs, ancient and modern, is a fascinating spot to kill some time if you don't mind the company of large numbers of goats.

Devon House

Fifteen minutes' walk east from Half Way Tree, the immaculate **Devon House** at 26 Hope Rd (Tues–Sat 9.30am–5pm, tours run throughout the day and last half an hour; J$200 including guided tour) was built in 1881 by Jamaica's first black millionaire, and is still the grandest house in the city.

Born in Kingston in 1820, building contractor George Stiebel made his fortune gold mining in Venezuela, returning home in 1873 to snap up 99 properties throughout Jamaica (ownership of 100 was prohibited by law). Among these was Devon Pen, where he built the house that was his Kingston home until he died in 1896. Bought by the Jamaican government in 1967, the house has gradually been furnished with West Indian and European antiques as well as more modern Jamaican reproductions. It makes for a diverting hour's

Striking north from Half Way Tree, Constant Spring Road boasts Kingston's largest con-glomeration of shopping malls; it's also the route to the cool greens of the Constant Spring Golf Course (see p.103).

exploration, despite the enforced tour, which can be rushed and monosyllabic – don't be afraid to take your time. Some eccentric pieces – a folding bagatelle table, unique porcelain chandeliers and an 1821 Broadwood piano – offset the obligatory portraits and rather predictable furniture. There are a couple of obituaries of Stiebel on display in the games rooms; look out also for the print of French Admiral de Grasse surrendering to Admiral Rodney after the crucial naval battle of les Saintes in 1782, which confirmed British naval superiority in the Caribbean.

The landscaped grounds of Devon House make a fine place for a leisurely stroll, with plenty of breezy benches and shady spots to while away the midday heat, and you've a good chance of running into one of the numerous wedding parties who come here for their photos. The former stables now house a handful of gift shops, stocking a good range of rather expensive ephemera, but chief attractions are the shop selling heavenly home-made "I Scream" (soursop and Guinness flavours are sublime), and the *Brick Oven* bakery, which sells excellent gooey cakes and some of Kingston's best patties. You can also get a decent sit-down lunch at the *Grog Shoppe*, which is not as painfully quaint as its name would suggest, or even afternoon tea or a gourmet meal at the elegant *Norma's on the Terrace*; for details of both, see "Eating" p.93.

Rumour has it that nearby Lady Musgrave Road, which circuitously bypasses Devon House, was built at the request of the wife of Anthony Musgrave, Jamaica's governor from 1874 to 1883, so that she could get to King's House (see below) without having to pass such a fine house owned by a black Jamaican.

Jamaica House and King's House

The governor general, the Queen of England's representative in Jamaica, has the notional powers of a head of state although, like the Queen, he retains only vestigial political authority

Guardhouses further up Hope Road from Devon House, mark the entrances to **Jamaica House** (closed to visitors), used as the prime minister's office, and **King's House** (☎927 6424; Mon–Fri by appointment; free), official residence of the governor general. You can get a tour of a few of the latter's rooms, including the ballroom, with its portraits of Jamaica's governors through the centuries, and the banqueting room, which has full-length portraits of Britain's George III and Queen Charlotte. Bond fans might want to note that King's House served as Government house in the first 007 movie, *Dr No*. A little south of here on Montrose Road, **Vale Royal** is the official residence of the prime minister but is closed to visitors.

The Bob Marley Museum

For reggae fans, the **Bob Marley Museum** at 56 Hope Rd (☎927 9152, *www.bobmarley-foundation.com*; Mon–Sat 9.30am–5pm, tours every 20min last tour at 4pm; J$350) is the whole point of a visit to Kingston, and even if you're not a serious devotee, it's well worth an hour of your time. Marley's Kingston home from 1975 until his death from cancer in 1981, and still much as it looked when he lived here, the building is a gentle monument to Jamaica's greatest musical legend. The hour-long tour starts as soon as you pass through the gates (as no photography, filming or taping is allowed, you leave your equipment in safekeeping here), where the guide usually points out the mural *The Journey of Bob Marley Superstar* which decorates the outside wall, and Rasta artist Jah Bobby's colourful statue of Marley with his preferred guitar and football. Inside the house, you'll see in the room where Marley was almost assassinated during the 1976 election campaign – the bullet holes still much in evidence – after which he left Jamaica for a two-year exile in Britain. The stage dresses of the I-Threes, Marley's backing singers, and his own favoured denim stage shirt are on display below the stairs, alongside the famed rod of correction and the Order of Merit presented to him by the Ethiopian Orthodox Church and the Jamaican government respectively.

Upstairs, there is a recreation of Wail 'n' Soul – Marley's tiny, shack-like Trench Town record shop, where he once hung out with band members Peter Tosh and Bunny Wailer – and a room wallpapered with thousands of newspaper articles and a chart of all the cities he played worldwide, with prominence given to shows in Africa, particularly the independence celebrations in Zimbabwe in 1980. Gold and platinum discs rewarding sales of the albums *Exodus* (1977), *Uprising* (1980) and *Legend* (1984) hang above the stairs, and familiar tracks are played as you explore the building.

For more on Bob Marley, see the box on p.230.

The tour ends behind the house in the theatre that once housed Marley's Tuff Gong recording studio. There's moving footage of the "One Love" concert held during the bloody election year of 1980, at which Marley brought together rival party leaders Michael Manley and Edward Seaga, and a film of interviews with the great man cut together with appropriate music videos – the return to Africa and *Exodus*, celebration of "herb" and *Easy Skanking*. Afterwards, you can escape from the clutches of the guide to look at the excellent photo gallery, with pictures of Marley in New York during his final tour, with the police after the assassination attempt, and playing a lot of football. You'll also get a chance to buy CDs and items from the Tuff Gong clothing range at the gift shop, and the on-site *Queen of Sheba* restaurant offers a small menu of vegetarian Ethiopian food and fruit juices. Don't be surprised if you see Ziggy or other Marley family members hanging around the house or playing soccer on the tiny pitch out front.

Ziggy Marley's Tuff Gong studios are in downtown Kingston; see p.80.

Hope Botanical Gardens

Hope Road forks a quarter of a mile east of the Marley museum, just past the Sovereign shopping centre. Its eastern continuation, Old Hope Road, heads towards Papine and the Blue Mountains, passing the ample grounds of Jamaica College, one of the island's premier schools that includes both Norman and Michael Manley in its ex-pupils. In the early days of English settlement in Jamaica, Major Richard Hope, an officer with the invading forces of Penn and Venables (see p.370), set up a thriving sugar estate here, with a stone aqueduct (parts of which can still be seen today) bringing water down from the Hope River. In 1881 the government acquired 200 acres of land from the Hope Estate and laid out the **Hope Botanical Gardens** (daily 6am–7pm; free) in much the same form as you see them today.

Entered on your left as you head up Old Hope Road, the gardens have been neglected in recent years, particularly since Hurricane Gilbert struck in 1988, but despite the raggle-taggle feel, the expansive lawns are good for escaping the din of the city, and are popular with weekend strollers. Adjacent to the gardens is a small and equally underfunded **zoo** (daily 10am–7pm; J$20), with lions, crocodiles, monkeys, mongooses, tapirs, peccaries, snakes and tropical birds. A wooden tower overlooks the lot, and provides a handsome view of the city. If you're driving from downtown or New Kingston, turn off the Old Hope Road about 400 yards past the main entrance to the gardens (following the signs for Coconut Park); take the road under the aqueduct and around to the left to a small parking area.

University of the West Indies to Dallas Castle

A few hundred yards west of Hope Gardens along Old Hope Road, and just before the Sovereign Centre mall, Mona Road swings southeast towards the expansive campus of the **University of the West Indies** (*isis.uwimona.edu.jm*), usually just called UWI. Though it's not exactly scintillating stuff, the ordinarily quiet campus with grassy lawns and colonial relics – including sections of an aqueduct that once sluiced water from the Hope River in the Blue Mountain foothills to a sugar processing works that was part of the old Mona and Papine estates – provides the opportunity for a soothing stroll.

Southeast past UWI, Mona Road inches into **August Town**, a somewhat impoverished community with a volatile history. During the period of religious fervour that followed the 1860–61 Great Revival, one Alexander Bedward founded his Native Baptist Church here. Bedward's self-made faith struck a chord with the disenchanted masses, and the pro-Black religion attracted thousands of converts, but sadly, his tendency toward insanity was revealed when he failed to live up to his promised pledge to sprout wings and fly up to heaven on December 31, 1921. You're unlikely to see any Bedwardites in August Town these days; indeed, it's not a place accustomed to visitors at all, but reggae fans might want to check out the flag- and banner-adorned home of cultural reggae star Sizzla.

After the perimeter fences of the UWI campus, Mona Road becomes University Road. Take the first right, Golding Road, and the houses rapidly fade away as you climb into the Dallas Mountains, the

For further information on Alexander Bedward, see "Contexts" p.391; for more on Sizzla, see p.407.

foothills of the massive Blue Mountain range. Follow the signs (turn right at Lindo's Gap), and a forty-minute drive along some rather rough road takes you to *Dallas Castle* (☎927 5666 or 5198), a superbly situated restaurant in the lush Cane River valley. The house that stands today was built over the old Dallas Castle Estate, which was established by George Miflin Dallas of Texas oil fame, and the ruins of the sugar factory and coffee mill still stand in the car park. It's an amazing spot for **Sunday brunch** (J$750); once you've worked your way through the huge spead of Jamaican dishes, you can wander around the gardens, which are bursting with tropical flowers and nicely shaded by giant trees bedecked with rubber plants and bromeliads; you can even take a dip in the water. If you want to eat here at any other time, the remoteness of the location means you're best off arranging your visit in advance.

Skyline Drive and into the Blue Mountains

It is only a short drive from Kingston into the Blue Mountains. Even if you don't have time to make the trip, it's worth going up onto **Skyline Drive** for spectacular views across the city. To get there, follow either East King's House Road or Barbican Road to their northern end where they join Jack's Hill Road for the climb onto Skyline Drive itself. The drive presents you with a series of great panoramas of Kingston and across the harbour to Port Royal – imagine watching the catastrophic earthquakes of 1692 or 1907 from up here – before bringing you out on the Gordon Town Road. From there you can turn right, to return to Kingston through Papine, or left to travel up into the mountains (see Chapter Two). Opposite the junction, woven bamboo walls and Rasta flags mark the **Black Lion Foundation**, a Rastafarian hangout better known by the nickname of its owner, the genial Daddy D. Perched on the side of the hill and affording appealing views of Mona below, it's a good spot for a Guinness, an ital meal or even a discourse on the merits of Rasta; roots reggae blasts through the speakers each evening from Friday to Sunday.

Eating

After the sun goes down and the heat lifts, the Kingston area is hard to beat for open-air eating. Particularly uptown – which is where you'll want to be in the evenings – you'll find a wider choice of **restaurants** than anywhere else in Jamaica and an excellent standard of food. Most places offer variations on traditional Jamaican fare, from tiny jerk bars to exquisite local seafood establishments, but if you snoop around, you'll also find good Chinese, Indian, Italian and even Middle Eastern cuisine. Places downtown are less refined, usually doling out lunch to local workers or snacks to those on the move. **Fast-food** chains – *McDonald's, Burger King, KFC, Taco Bell* and the Jamaican-owned *Island Grill* and *Mother's* – have boomed around the city recently, concentrated downtown around the Parade, uptown in New Kingston in the shopping malls along Constant Spring Road and the Sovereign Centre grounds. *Island Grill* on Constant Spring Road is particularly good for JA-style jerk chicken sandwiches and fish on the hop. Knutsford Boulevard is also good for a fast-food blowout, with all the big names as well as the unimaginably tacky *Kenny Rogers Roasters*, a chicken chain owned by the country crooner himself. More substantial lunches of all kinds are available from the **food courts** at Sovereign Centre in Hope Road (where you can get a passable roti), Island Life Plaza on St Lucia Avenue, and the huge Marketplace complex in the Constant Spring Arcade or the two Manor Plazas on Constant Spring Road.

Lastly, if you're after truly authentic **jerk chicken**, try any of the smoking oil-drum barbecues that set up on street corners; an excellent choice is the vendor just outside Northside Plaza in the Liguanea section of Hope Road, who sells from Thursday to Saturday.

Downtown

In restaurant listings, we have given a phone number only for those places where you might need to reserve a table.

Bench and Bar Restaurant, 5A Port Royal St. Opposite the ScotiaBank tower, this is an essential downtown stop, even if you don't want to eat, as the genial owners make a point of going out of their way to assist visitors. Housed in a cool colonial building that once served as the tourist office, the food centres on inexpensive and tasty Jamaican staples, and it's a popular lunchtime choice amongst office workers as well as drawing an after-work crowd in the early evenings.

King Ital, 41 Half Way Tree Rd. Vegetarian café popular with Rastas, and adorned with signed photos of the reggae musicians who seem to be regular visitors. Great, inexpensive tofu and ackee stew, pastries, patties and natural juices.

Moby Dick, cnr Orange and Port Royal Streets. Simple, low-key joint for Jamaican staples – curry goat is particularly good.

Uptown

For a memorable meal with an equally wonderful view, head up to Strawberry Hill Hotel *in the Blue Mountains (see p.133), where the Sunday brunch is a local institution.*

Akbar, 11 Holborn Rd; ☎922 3247. The best Indian food in town, in a tastefully decorated but rather dark air-conditioned indoor dining room. All the regular dishes, roti and plenty of vegetarian choices. The Monday to Friday lunchtime buffet (J$500) is well worth it if you're hungry – you eat as much as you like.

Boon Hall Oasis, 4 River Rd, Stony Hill; ☎942 3064. Quite a drive from town (turn right at Stony Hill square and follow the small green signs), this outdoor restaurant on the banks of the Wag Water River is wreathed with flowers and greenery, and is best for the good but pricey Sunday brunch.

Carlos Café, 22 Belmont Rd. Friendly place off Oxford Road with appealing decor and excellent service. Decent and inexpensive, food ranges from salads and sandwiches to steaks, seafood and pasta. Monday is crab night, and "Fat Tuesday" offers two-for-one on drinks and meals.

Chasers Café, 29 Barbican Rd. Busy and popular with an older crown, this indoor/outdoor restaurant is a pleasant place for moderately-priced Jamaican lunches (weekday specials), dinners, Sunday brunch or just a drink. Theme nights include Caribbean on Wednesday and seafood splash on Thursday.

Chilito's, 166 Old Hope Rd; ☎977 9523. With funky decor and smiling service, this new Mexican place is a winner, serving excellent vegetarian or meat-based tostadas, enchiladas, fajitas, burritos and a host of more obscure fare including mole dishes. Puddings are equally sublime.

Ciao Bella, 19 Hillcrest Ave; ☎978 5002. Classy Italian restaurant with tables on the veranda as well as indoors. The cooking is pretty sophisticated, with daily pasta specials, imaginative sandwiches and salads (greens, roasted onions, bell pepper and goats cheese is great) and specialities such as pizza verde or homemade shrimp ravioli. Sunday brunch is a main draw.

Dakta Feelgood, 5 Southdale Plaza. Compact Ital diner serving up delicious breakfasts (ackee, callaloo, cabbage, steamed fish and okra or peanut, banana or bulgur porridge), and filling lunches (bean or gluten stew, veg rice), while natural juices are made up on the spot.

Devonshire Restaurant, Devon House; ☎929 7029. Classy, costly dishes – pasta, chicken Dijon, steak, roast suckling pig, flambéed shrimp – in a cool and elegant setting. Closed Sunday.

Dragon City, Northside Plaza, Liguanea. Almost opposite the Liguanea Shopping Centre on Hope Road, this inconspicuous place serves up some of the tastiest and cheapest Chinese food around, and reasonably priced to boot.

Eden, Central Plaza, Constant Spring Rd. Good Ital food (tofu, gluten, vegetable stew and patties) and natural juices served in this shopping-centre diner until 8pm.

The Emperial Kish-Inn, 2 Hillview Ave, off Eastwood Park Rd. Ital eatery for bargain-priced breakfast and lunch, such as stew with soya mince, fried fish and vegetables. Natural juices and home-made cakes are available, as are lengthy discussions on Rastafari.

Fish Place, 136 Constant Spring Rd. A bit of a ride from the centre of town but worth it for the spicy conch soup alone, quite apart from excellent fish, scallops, crab and lobster.

The Grog Shoppe, Devon House; ☎929 7029 (closed Sun). Shady setting in the oasis of the Devon House grounds, serving standard Jamaican meals at lunchtime and a more European flavour (and prices) in the evening. Theme nights include all-you-can-eat-crab combined with live jazz each Tuesday.

Guilt Trip, 20 Barbican Rd; ☎977 5130. Interesting variation on traditional Jamaican dishes with a regularly changing menu. Popular amongst a fairly fashionable crowd, many of whom pop in for a post-club (and very expensive) slice of cake – it's open until 2am. Closed Monday.

Heather's Garden Restaurant, 9 Haining Rd. Solid Jamaican food in a quiet location with an extensive, medium-priced menu and a daily seafood speciality.

Hilton Kingston, 77 Knutsford Blvd; ☎926 5430. The *Terrace Café* here serves up roast beef and Yorkshire pudding on Monday evenings, while the *Pool Bar* offers Tortilla night on Tuesday, Jamaican barbecue, with a steel band accompaniment on Wednesday and Kebab night on Thursday.

Hot Pot, 2 Altamont Terrace. Popular spot for typical Jamaican meals in the heart of New Kingston, with excellent breakfasts, including cornmeal and banana porridge and the unusual combination of baked beans and saltfish, and lunches of fish and bammy, curry goat, stewed beef and the usual Jamaican staples.

Indies Pub and Grill, 8 Holborn Rd, opposite *Indies Hotel*. Easy-going outdoor café with an eclectic, inexpensive menu featuring steaks, fish and chips,

With a gorgeous setting on the waterfront across Kingston harbour, the restaurant at Morgan's Harbour Hotel (see p.111) is ideal for a romantic seafood supper.

Scenes from the movie Dancehall Queen were filmed in the King Bebo Plaza, home of the Emperial Kish-Inn restaurant.

Kingston

pizza and Lebanese dishes. Specials are cooked each night, currently ribs on Monday, Hellshire-style fish on Tuesday, curry conch on Wednesday, while the rest of the week is given over to the drinking side of things (see "Bars" p.99). Closed Sunday.

Jade Garden, Sovereign Centre; ☎978 3476. Smart business-set restaurant with some of the best Chinese dishes in town, most of them J$500–800.

JamRock, 69 Knutsford Blvd. A perfect and always busy combination of bar, hangout, restaurant and patisserie; favourite among Jamaican dishes is the sumptuous "Jerk Nyamwich", and you can also get salads, burgers, tuna melts, pastrami sandwiches, excellent patties, pastries and espresso or cappuccino.

Mother Earth, 13 Oxford Terrace. Centrally located and businesslike vegetarian restaurant doing a cracking trade. The menu changes daily; expect good Jamaican staples for breakfast and imaginative lunches with lots of pulses, soya and tofu. Patties – chick pea, lentils, veg mince, ackee – are excellent, as are the natural juices and soya ice-cream.

Norma's on the Terrace, Devon House. Kingston's newest upscale eatery, situated on the terrace of the old Devon House stables and serving gourmet Jamaican food with an international twist. Menu highlights include peppered beef salad, smoked marlin or a chowder of crab, shrimp, conch and lobster, while afternoon teas feature delectable, light pastries. Besides full meals, it's also good for a late-night cappuccino, latté or espresso accompanied by one of the superb desserts.

Pegasus Café, *Jamaica Pegasus Hotel*, 81 Knutsford Blvd; ☎926 3690–9. Competing with *Norma's* as the best place in town for afternoon tea – sandwiches and fabulous cakes from J$150.

Peppers, 31 Upper Waterloo Rd. If you want a lively atmosphere while you eat, and perhaps a drink or a dance afterwards, *Peppers* is ideal, with inexpensive Jamaican food alongside "international" favourites, and Caribbean staples such as Trinidadian roti, and bake and shark.

Raquel's, 38c Trafalgar Rd. Reliable seafood-based restaurant, with good-value lunch specials and moderately-priced dinners. Cajun blackened shrimp and crab backs are highlights, and there's also steak, chicken and pasta.

Red Bones Blues Café, 21 Braemar Ave; ☎978 8262. Stylish, upmarket restaurant-cum-music venue with a distinguished but laid-back atmosphere, serving imaginative Jamaican-style food embellished with contemporary flavour.

Sugar Daddies, Gordon Town Rd, Papine. Simple, no-nonsense take-away serving tasty, inexpensive, no-frills Jamaican food – a good place to buy your lunch if you're heading into the mountains for a picnic.

Outside Kingston

Blue Mountain Inn, Gordon Town Rd; ☎927 1700. Gourmet food – seared breadfruit chips, exquisite steaks, lobster and fantasy desserts – in a fabulous setting, a 20min drive into the mountains. Expect to pay upwards of J$1250 for dinner.

Rock Pub, Gordon Town Rd. Small shack, peacefully situated on the far side of Hope River just opposite the turn-off to Skyline Drive; park by the sign, walk across the bridge and it's on your left. It's a great place to get away from it all and offers decent seafood and jerk chicken.

Drinking and nightlife

Kingston has legions of great places to head to for a **drink**, and many
of them also double up as restaurants; hotel bars uptown also make
decent venues for a swift beer or a more protracted soak. In many
parts of the city, the typical **rum shop** is a tiny room where a handful of men sit around drinking rum and playing dominoes. If you are
walking around downtown during the day you'll probably pop into
one or two of these places; remember that foreigners are rarely seen
here and, although it can be a good opportunity to meet local people
(and drink pretty cheaply), you may encounter some initial suspicion
or aloofness. When choosing a bar, bear in mind that you'll rarely
want to walk between places at night, and taxis are the best way of
getting around.

Kingston's active **club** scene ranges from smart laser shows with
big-name DJs, state-of-the-art equipment and the latest dancehall to
small dark oldies clubs for the more mature dancers. Anticipate a
cover of around J$100–200 – more if there's a band on; the *Gleaner*
advertises regular ladies' nights when women get in free. As you'll
find island-wide, nothing much happens before midnight except on
Friday, when after-work jams at places like *Peppers* and *Cactus* pull
an early-evening crowd of bright young things. **Security** at most of
the clubs is tight and you'll often be searched on your way in. You'll
occasionally find impromptu **street parties** happening around town,
with a sound system stacked up and beer and jerk vendors ready at
hand. Feel free to join in – everybody's welcome. If you're after some
real Kingston ambience, check out the Sunday night open-air dances
in downtown **Rae Town** – though you're probably best-off going with
someone who attends regularly.

*There are
street parties
in Port Royal's
main square
on Friday and
Saturday
nights; see
p.111.*

Live music in the capital is less predictable, but often more interesting, than the anaesthetised reggae dished up for tourists on the
north coast; some of the best shows to look out for are the annual
round of Heineken Startime concerts, featuring the best of Jamaica's
vintage artists. The big event is **Carnival**, a riotous street party in April,
adopted from the Trinidadian event, though on a smaller scale and
with a bigger ration of reggae to soca. Jamaica's top DJs, singers and
bands are usually in action around the city, playing anywhere from the
regular clubs to open-air gigs at the Hellshire beaches (see p.113) and
in the grounds of various hotels and the UWI campus. Unusually for
Jamaica, you'll find plenty of Trinidadian and Bajan calypsonians, soca
and rapso stars and steel bands playing too, reflecting the influence of
the Eastern Caribbean, and, undoubtedly, the island's own soca stars
Byron Lee and the Dragonaires; bandleader Byron Lee was heavily
instrumental in bringing carnival to Jamaica. The concluding weekend,
an intoxicating cacophony of sound and colour, sees marching bands,
brightly-painted floats and extravagant costume parades through the
city streets. For more on Carnival, contact Tony Cohen (☎923 9138),
Courtney Sylvester (☎922 1000), or the JTB (☎929 9200).

Kingston

For more on Jamaica's current music scene, see p.406 of Contexts.

Even if you can't make Carnival, the build-up can be almost as lively, with full dress rehearsals noisily spilling out onto the streets for several weeks before the main event and a party atmosphere taking hold of the city. Otherwise, the busiest times, musically speaking, are during the summer, when the annual round of **Jamaica Cultural Development Commission** arts competitions swing into action, when there are performances of traditional music and dance, by both amateur and professional artists, all around town as well; look out for amateur dramatics and music at the Ward Theatre, and the finals of the National Song Competition – the venue of which varies, often held in either the Ranny Williams Entertainment Centre or the Hilton. In Kingston, Christmas means **panto season**, and the annual LTM pantomime is unmissable.

Bars

For a drink with the Kingston lights twinkling in the distance, head over to Morgan's Harbour Hotel in Port Royal (see p.111). Closer to the centre, Daddy D's Rasta bar on the Gordon Town Road (see p.93)is a great place to get away from it all.

Bench and Bar Restaurant, 5A Port Royal St. Opposite the ScotiaBank, this genial restaurant is good for afternoon drinks, and there's a Friday evening happy hour (5–7pm).

The Bistro, *Crowne Plaza Hotel*, 211a Constant Spring Rd. Poolside bistro/bar that's a popular upmarket drinking spot, with karaoke each Wednesday, and 1970s and 1980s oldies on Thursday.

Carlos Café, 22 Belmont Rd. Small and very friendly place to sink a few drinks or shoot some pool, with various theme nights throughout the week, including Games night on Wednesday, Latin night on Thursday, with a show from Cuban dancers, and the genial Friday chill-out. See also "Eating", p.94.

Chasers Café, 29 Barbican Rd. Popular hangout with a decent beer selection; Monday offers karaoke, there's oldies on Tuesday, the Peter Phillips disco plays each Friday night, and sports events are shown on TV throughout the week. See "Eating", p.94.

Friends on the Deck, 51 Hope Rd. Easy-going and central outdoor bar under a mango tree, popular with a friendly, older set. Different snacks on offer each night, and low-key music from a DJ; women get half-price drinks each Thursday between 5 and 8pm.

Grasshoppers, 195 Constant Spring Rd. Occupying a sizeable portion of the Manor Centre shopping mall roof, with indoor and outdoor sections, this is a breezy spot for a drink and popular amongst young Kingstonians. Wednesday nights offer karaoke and a pool tournament, while for the rest of the week, it's more of a place to go and dance (see "Clubs and live music", p.100). Closed Monday.

The Grog Shoppe, Devon House. In the grounds of Devon House, this is a good place to finish your day's sightseeing with a drink outside under the giant cotton tree, especially on Friday when a band (usually Jazz) plays. See "Eating" p.95.

Half Time Sports Bar, 69 Knutsford Blvd. Laddish upstairs pool hall with plenty of fair-quality tables, a few arcade games and TVs showing sports events or karate movies. Good for a quiet drink or a game of pool; JS$100 admission for men after 7pm.

Harry's Bar, 80 Constant Spring Rd; ☎755 0514. Pretty, laid-back outdoor bar and restaurant set off from the road in gardens. The music policy of reggae, alternative and rock doesn't extend to dancehall, and there's a dancefloor and occasional live music.

Indies, 8 Holborn Rd, opposite the *Indies* hotel. Central location and a mellow atmosphere that's popular with mature late-night revellers from Thursday to Saturday, when it opens until 2am. Thursday is Country and Western night, Friday has an early-evening Happy Hour, and Saturday is Alternative night.

JamRock Sports Bar and Grill, 69 Knutsford Blvd. Shiny, neon-clad US-style sports bar with an authentically Jamaican twist, popular for lunchtime and after-work drinks or a late-night espresso and a pastry. Headline sports events are shown on the sprinkling of TV monitors.

Mingles, *Courtleigh Hotel*, 85 Knutsford Blvd; ☎929 9000. Indoor and outdoor sections of this in-hotel nightclub make a pleasant setting for a drink during the week, with backgammon and dominoes being the main distractions, while the dancefloor fills up on Friday and Saturday nights. See "Clubs and live music", p.100.

Peppers, 31 Upper Waterloo Rd. Late-opening and permanently popular outdoor bar that pulls in post-work drinkers and then younger clubbers, who come for a snack or to dance to sound-system DJs.

Pool Bar, *Hilton Kingston*, 77 Knutsford Blvd; ☎926 5430. Adjacent to the *Hilton's* lavish pool, this is a pleasant spot for a cocktail with a sense of being away from it all. A mento band play live on Monday, the Hummingbird Steel Orchestra accompany Tortilla night each Wednesday, there's karaoke on a Thursday, and Sunday evenings see a live jazz band.

Priscilla's, upstairs at 109 Constant Spring Rd. Pleasant and easy-going roof bar with views over the city; Sixties and Seventies Jamaican music on Friday and Saturday nights attracts the older media and professional set.

Raquel's, 38c Trafalgar Rd. Central and fairly smart with lots of fish tanks and excellent service; good for a quiet drink or a meal.

Red Bones Blues Café, 21 Braemar Ave; ☎978 8262. Good for a quiet drink amongst a fairly sophisticated crowd; look out for live music sessions.

Sandhurst Hotel, 70 Sandhurst Crescent. Spreading terrace with views up to the mountains and a very relaxed atmosphere. Not as popular as it used to be, but a reasonable option if you just want a quiet drink.

Kingston's parties

During the summer and Christmas periods (and, on a lesser scale, throughout the year), Kingston weekends see the more well-heeled of the capital's youth gather together for huge **outdoor parties** staged at venues on the outskirts of town, such as Caymanas Park or Temple Hall in Stony Hill. Most of them – RAS, Pip & Ting, Beer Vibes or a variety of names, many taken from costume bands that parade at carnival time – are **all-inclusive**. Your entrance fee of around J$2000 covers food and drink all night, as well as music from Jamaica's hottest **sound systems** – Renaissance, Adonai, Stone Love, Skyy Disco, Travellers – and live DJ performances. Each party draws a slightly different, though usually fairly peaceful, crowd of loyal revellers, but you'll need to enlist local help to decide which ones are likely to go with a bang. They're all advertised by way of flyers posted up around the capital.

Broadcasting only in Kingston, Roots FM (96.1) often publicises upcoming stageshows.

Kingston

As club nights are likely to change regularly, it's always worth calling your venue to check what's on before you set out.

Although Kingston has no listings magazine or newspaper, the Daily Gleaner *advertises most of what's going on in the city.*

In Jamaica, "Alternative" music on a club billing usually means house, techno, trance and the odd pop hit.

Clubs and live music

Asylum, 69 Knutsford Blvd; ☎929 4386. Fully refitted and packed with Kingstonians checking out the latest dances under the dry ice and UV glare. Currently, Monday is the house and techno "rave" night; Tuesday is ladies' night, with dancehall on the decks and free entry and drinks for women; Wednesday (probably the best time to make your first foray) is a little more sedate, with 1970s and 1980s reggae and R&B; Thursday is a hardcore, rude boy-filled dancehall night with Stone Love; Friday is a regular after-work jam, with dancehall and drinks promotions; Saturday sees a popular "dance party", with soul, hip hop and R&B in amongst the reggae, and Sunday is reserved for oldies.

Cactus, 13 Portmore Plaza, Portmore; ☎988 2319. Competes with *Asylum* for number one spot in the Kingston area, but its location – a 20min drive west of the city over the causeway in Portmore – is an impediment. Still, it's usually packed at weekends and on Wednesday (dancehall night), and worth the trip for the live shows. Open Wednesday to Sunday.

Countryside Club, 19–21 Eastwood Park Rd; ☎926 3010. Well-designed outdoor venue that hosts some of Kingston's main gigs, hidden behind security gates close to Half Way Tree, and usually opened up only for a big do.

Grasshoppers, 195 Constant Spring Rd; ☎941 3788. Capacious rooftop dancefloor attached to the small indoor bar that plays host to "Alternative" night each Thursday (currently the busiest time to go); Latin night on Friday, with live music and/or DJs; Saturday is your basic jam, with music from sound systems such as Renaissance or Stone Love, and Sunday is oldies night.

Jonkanoo Lounge, *Hilton Kingston*, 77 Knutsford Blvd; ☎926 5430. Relatively sedate, as you'd expect from a hotel-based venue, but a good and very upmarket (if rarely crowded) disco and occasional live bands. Currently, the Thursday Latin night (J$200 after 8pm) is popular.

Mingles, *Courtleigh Hotel*, 85 Knutsford Blvd; ☎929 9000. Though its former popularity is ebbing a bit since the hotel's move to its new location, *Mingles* remains an essential part of any night on the town. The best nights are Friday's After Work Jam, with free snacks and alternative music, but still the busiest is the Saturday Latin party, when a cover charge applies and the place is packed. A live band play most Tuesdays.

Peppers, 31 Upper Waterloo Rd; ☎925 2219 or 969 2421. One of Kingston's most consistently popular venues, with a heaving outdoor dancefloor, bigname stageshows every month and DJs most nights; usually packed and a lot of fun.

Playaz, 69 Knutsford Blvd (no phone). Spanking new place that occasionally serves as an upmarket go-go club; when girls get the night off, it's a good alternative to the sweatier *Asylum* next door.

Turntable Club, 118 Red Hills Rd; ☎969 2966. Oldies, ska and rocksteady club a couple of miles west of central Kingston; Thursday is the best night. Keep an eye out for one of the excellent one-off shows occasionally held here.

Theatre and cinema

Next to popular music, **theatre** is Kingston's strongest cultural suit. The performance scene is limited but buoyant, with a small core of first-rate writers, directors and actors – including Trevor Rhone,

Oliver Samuels, Aston Cooke and David Heron – producing work of a generally high standard. Most of the plays are sprinkled with Jamaican patois, but you'll still get the gist. Comedies (particularly sexual romps and political satire) are popular, and the normally excellent annual **pantomime** – a musical with a message, totally different from the English variety – is a major event, running from December to April at both the **Ward Theatre** (☎922 0453) and, later, the **Little Theatre** (☎925 6129).

Kingston's **cinemas** invariably screen recent mainstream offerings from the States. Tickets are around J$250, and there's usually a snack interval in the middle of the show. Most of the cinemas are uptown and include the **Palace Cineplex** (☎978 3522) at the Sovereign Centre, the **Island Cinemax** (☎920 7964) at the Island Life Centre on St Lucia Avenue and the **Odeon** (☎926 7671) at 11 Constant Spring Rd. Recently rebuilt and suitably plush, the **Carib Cinema** at Cross Roads (☎926 6106) is probably the most atmospheric choice. There's a **drive-in** cinema on the eastern outskirts of town at Harbour View; at present, the New Kingston Drive-In (☎929 5670) on Dominica Drive is not showing movies.

Kingston

Dance comes to the fore during the National Dance Theatre Company's annual summer residency at the Little Theatre.

For more on Jamaican film see "Contexts" p.418.

Shopping and galleries

A multitude of American-style malls means that **shopping** in Kingston is nothing if not convenient. The major players – the New Kingston Shopping Centre on Dominica Drive, the Sovereign Centre on Hope Road and the multitude of malls on Constant Spring Road – house everything you can imagine buying, although the heaving Jubilee Market downtown (see p.80) and the smaller markets at Cross Roads and, particularly, Papine (friendly and rich with super-fresh produce bused in from the Blue Mountains) are more exciting places to look for fresh **food**.

For **books**, the University Bookshop at the UWI in Mona is far and away the superior choice for both novels and books on Jamaica, though Sangster's (branches at Ward Plaza, 106 Old Hope Rd and 33 King St) and Bookland, 53 Knutsford Blvd, are reasonable and more central, while Reader's, at Liguanea Plaza, 134 Old Hope Rd, has a decent second-hand collection. Downtown, Headstart Books, 54–56 Church St concentrates on all things African and roots Jamaican, with an excellent collection of hard-to-find titles as well as Rasta-made crafts, greeting cards and posters, as does Books About Us and Blakk Muzic, 2 Hillview Ave, owned by broadcaster and dub poet Mutabaruka.

As you'd expect, reggae fans are in shopping heaven in Kingston, and downtown's Orange Street is the place to go – you'll find loads of **record stores**, many of them attached to studios and pressing plants. GG's Records, on the corner of Orange Street and Parade, is particularly well stocked, and as vibrant and loud as its location, while Prince Busta's further down Orange Street is known for its collection of rare oldies. Rockers International, 135 Orange St, carries an extensive stock of old rocksteady and reggae classics, and Techniques, at no. 99, has a good selection of old and new stock alongside (unaccountably) in-car accessories. Elsewhere, good places to check are Rock and Groove Mix, adjacent to *Pizza Hut* at 8 Northside Plaza in Liguanea; Nuff Tings Ltd at 17 Roosevelt Ave, great for vintage reggae; Aquarius, at 2–4 South Odeon Ave, and Derrick Harriot's One Stop in Twin Gates Plaza, Constant Spring Road both good for old and new reggae.

For **souvenirs**, try the Crafts Market downtown (see p.79); more expensively, check out the gift shops at Devon House or Patoo, in the Upper Manor Park Centre, which have prints, books, spices, coffee and a host of other items. It's also worth browsing the malls on Constant Spring Road, which hold hordes of excellent, reasonably-priced craft shops; Craft Cottage at 24c is particularly good. For the ultimate toothsome souvenir, look out for the coffee rum cakes and coffee fudge produced by the owners of the *Bench and Bar* restaurant in downtown Kingston using Blue Mountain coffee and Wray and Nephew white rum; it's a knockout. If you don't see it in gift-shops, head straight for the source.

Kingston also has a vibrant art scene and there are excellent **galleries** across the city. The Frame Centre Gallery at 10 Tangerine Place (Mon–Fri 9am–5pm) is a fine place to start, with a good variety of local work on display and for sale. The Grosvenor Galleries at 1 Grosvenor Terrace and the Chelsea Galleries at 12 Chelsea Ave (both galleries Mon–Fri 9am–5pm) both host exhibitions by contemporary Jamaican artists, while if you want to splash out, try the art shops at Devon House (Tues–Sat 9.30am–5pm) and the *Pegasus* and *Hilton* hotels (the latter has a great collection of paintings by Portland artist Ken Abendana Spencer in its lobby). Finally, the Art Centre (Mon–Fri 9am–5pm & Sat 10am–4pm), near Papine at 202 Old Hope Rd, sells local art, and there is a chaotic jumble of paintings and sculptures in the gallery opposite.

Listings

Airlines Air Canada, Norman Manley Airport (☎924 8211); Air Jamaica, 72 Harbour St (☎922 4661), Norman Manley Airport (☎924 8231); American Airlines, 26 Trafalgar Rd (☎920 8887), Norman Manley Airport (☎942 8308); British Airways, 25 Dominica Drive (☎929 9020), Norman Manley Airport (☎924 8187); BWIA, 19 Dominica Drive (☎929 3770), Norman Manley Airport (☎924 8364); Cayman Airways, 23 Dominica Drive (☎926 1762); Cubana, 22 Trafalgar Rd (☎978 3406).

Airport The information number for Norman Manley International Airport is ☎928 6077; the number for Tinson Pen domestic airport is ☎978 8068.

Ambulances Call ☎110 for a public ambulance, ☎926 8624 for a private one.

Banks The main banks have branches city-wide including: Bank of Nova Scotia at 2 Knutsford Blvd, 6 Oxford St and 125 Old Hope Rd; Citizen's Bank at the

Sovereign Centre, 17 Dominica Drive and 15A Old Hope Rd; Mutual Security Bank at 18 Trafalgar Rd, 134 Old Hope Rd and 37 Duke St. Most of those uptown have ATMs.

Car Rental Reliable firms include: Avis, Norman Manley Airport (☎924 8013); Bargain, Norman Manley Airport (☎924 8293); Caribbean, 31 Old Hope Rd (☎926 6339); Don's, 1 Worthington Ave (☎926 2181); Econocars, 11 Lady Musgrave Rd (☎927 6761); Island, 17 Antigua Ave (☎926 8012).

Doctors and dentists Ask your hotel to recommend a doctor or dentist, or contact the University Hospital (see below).

Embassies Almost all of the embassies and consulates are based in New Kingston. They include the British High Commission, 26 Trafalgar Rd (☎926 9050); the American Embassy, 2 Oxford Rd (☎929 4850); and the Canadian High Commission, 3 West Kings House Rd (☎926 1500).

Golf Kingston has two excellent golf courses open to the public, west of the city at Caymanas Park (☎922 3388) and north at Constant Spring (☎924 1610).

Hospitals Kingston's public hospitals are the University Hospital at Mona (☎927 1620) and the Kingston Public Hospital downtown on North Street (☎922 0227). There are a number of private hospitals in New Kingston, including Medical Associates, 18 Tangerine Place (☎926 1400) and Andrews Memorial, 27 Hope Rd (☎926 7401).

Internet One Stop Computers at shop 16, Island Life Mall on St Lucia Avenue in New Kingston (Mon–Fri 9am–6pm, Sat 10am–5pm) offers Internet access in pleasant, air-conditioned surroundings for JS$150 per hour.

Laundry All of the hotels will wash laundry and there is a drop-off/pick-up service at Supersuds, 13–15 National Heroes Circle (☎967 3791), and Speedy's, 108 Red Hills Rd (☎924 5846). Supercleaners at the Sovereign Centre (☎978 5116) offers a pricey dry-cleaning and laundry service.

Newspapers Sunday newspapers from England and many US publications can be found at Bookland, 53 Knutsford Blvd, in larger pharmacies and at the gift shops at the *Hilton* and *Pegasus* hotels in New Kingston.

Pharmacies There are pharmacies at most of the shopping malls. Monarch, at the Sovereign Centre (Mon–Fri 8am–10pm, Sat 9am–10pm, Sun 9am–8pm), and York Pharmacy at the Half Way Tree junction (daily 8am–11pm).

Police The main station is at 79 Duke St (☎922 9321). In an emergency, call ☎119.

Post Offices The GPO is at 13 King St downtown (☎922 2120) and there are a number of branches around town. Stamps can also be bought at most hotels.

Sports International and major domestic soccer and cricket matches are played at the National Stadium (☎929 4970) and Sabina Park (☎967 0322) respectively. Horse-racing and (occasionally) polo can be seen at Caymanas Park (☎922 3338). There's a fully equipped fitness centre at the *Crowne Plaza* hotel, 211a Constant Spring Rd (☎925 7676), where you can work out, take an aerobics class or sauna or play a game of squash; courts cost J$200 per hour.

Taxis Reputable operators include Blue Diamond (☎937 1604); Blue Ribbon (☎928 7739); Candy (☎925 0649); Checker (☎922 1777); Eagle Force (☎923 4236).

Telephone Telecommunications of Jamaica, downtown at 15 North St and uptown at 52 Grenada Crescent (both Mon–Fri 8am–4pm), has cardphone booths that allow international calls cheaper than anywhere else in town.

Otherwise, there's a cheap privately-owned international call centre on the Half Way Tree roundabout, and many more scattered around town.

Travel Agents Grace Kennedy Travel, 19 Knutsford Blvd (☎929 6290); ITS, 75 Old Hope Rd (☎978 7038).

Around Kingston

There are some excellent options around Kingston if you want to escape from the city for a day or two. The one-time pirate haunt of **Port Royal** in particular is worth a half-day visit, with nearby **Lime Cay** providing a good spot for a swim afterwards. **Spanish Town**, the nation's capital from 1534 to 1872, offers the third limb of Jamaica's "Historic Triangle" (with Kingston and Port Royal); again, half a day is more than ample to see the remains of the city's superb Georgian architecture and to tour the oldest Anglican cathedral in the "New World". Fragments of a more ancient culture remain in the old Taino haunts of **Mountain River Cave** and **Two Sisters Cave**, although both are tricky to reach without a car, while the **Blue Mountains** (see Chapter Two) and **Castleton Botanical Gardens** offer hiking and undisturbed nature. For something even more relaxing, **Rockfort Mineral Baths** have reasonably priced spas while **Hellshire's** lovely white-sand bays, just south of the city, are immensely popular at the weekend; you're best washing off the salt at the **Nature's Paradise mineral spring** behind Caymanas Polo Club.

Tours from Kingston

All of the places around Kingston can be explored on an **organized tour** from the city. Although you shouldn't need a tour to see Port Royal, easy to reach on the ferry and small, safe and relaxed enough to wander around alone, it's not a bad option for Spanish Town, which is a bit awkward to get to and – as a major industrial city – can feel rather unwelcoming. However, you'll get a fuller perspective on all the sights by engaging the services of a tour company, many of which offer individualized, small-scale jaunts. **Our Story Tours** (☎984 4165 or 943 8520, *crompton@cybervale.com*) is brilliant for historical perspectives, offering custom-designed tours of Kingston, Spanish Town and Port Royal as well as farther afield – Colbeck Castle, Mountain River Cave, Sligoville, St Thomas; costs start at US$100 for 2–4 people, plus cost of transport, shorter hops around Kingston or to Spanish Town or Port Royal start at US$20 per person plus transport. Another good option are Kingston-based **Sun Venture** (☎960 6685, fax 920 8348, *sunventure@hotmail.com*), who offer an interesting, professional half-day city tour of the more conventional sights – the Bob Marley Museum, Devon House etc – for US$35 per person for a group of four or more; Sun Venture are also your best choice if heading into the Blue Mountains. Funky, offbeat and extremely enjoyable **Nutourious Adventures'** tours of Kingston – Hellshire, Caymanas Mineral Spring, Blue Mountain picnics – provide an insiders' insight into the capital and start at US$20 per person (☎927 7619, fax 977 3719, *mmorris@bigplanet.com*).

East of Kingston

Windward Road, the main route east out of the city, follows the coastline out of Kingston, scything through an industrial zone of oil tanks and a cement works that towers over the ruined defensive bastion of Fort Rock, now the **Rockfort Mineral Baths**. If the scenery looks familiar, you may be recalling the classic scene in the **James Bond** movie, *Dr No*, in which Bond leaves Norman Manley airport in a nifty red Sunbeam Alpine. A mile or so further on, turning right at the roundabout takes you on to the **Palisadoes**, a narrow ten-mile spit of land that leads out past the international airport to the ancient city of **Port Royal**, from where it's a short hop to the tiny island of **Lime Cay**.

Rockfort Mineral Baths

Rockfort Mineral Baths (daily 8am–6pm; J$90 to use the pool, J$550 for a two-person spa) offer one of the few public swimming pools in the Kingston area as well as some rather luxurious private spas. This was the site of the British Fort Rock, first strengthened against a threatened French invasion in 1694 and remanned in 1865 amid fears that the Morant Bay Rebellion further east might spread to Kingston. Today, the baths sit in a neat modern facility – an oasis in the surrounding dusty terrain – and offer a laid-back chance to enjoy some pampering. The small mineral spas, which seat two people comfortably, are all fitted with jacuzzis and you're allowed to wallow in them for up to 45 minutes. Piped from a local spring, the mineral water is moderately radioactive; it's claimed that the radioactivity helps to infuse the therapeutic minerals into the body, though obviously it puts some people off.

The hills above Rockfort rise up to the **Dallas Mountains**, named after Robert Dallas, a local eighteenth-century plantation-owner whose grandson, George Miflin Dallas, became Vice President of the United States in 1845 and founded the eponymous city in Texas.

See p.93 for an account of the current incarnation of Robert Dallas's Blue Mountain plantation.

Port Royal

PORT ROYAL, a short drive or ferry ride from downtown Kingston, captures the spirit of early colonial adventure better than any other place in Jamaica. Originally a tiny island, this little fishing village is now joined to the mainland by the **Palisadoes**, a series of small cays that silted together over hundreds of years and, with a bit of human assistance, now form a roadway and a natural breakwater for Kingston's harbour. The cactus-strewn Palisadoes provided the setting for the opening scenes of the James Bond movie *Dr No* – it was here that the chauffeur of Bond's Sunbeam Alpine car tried unsuccessfully to poison him with a cyanide-laced cigarette.

For several decades in the late seventeenth century, Port Royal was a riotous town – the notorious haunt of cut-throats and buccaneers, condemned by the church as "the wickedest city on earth".

Around Kingston

Only a few traces of those days remain – much of the old town is now a sunken city, submerged under fifty feet of water – but the Jamaican government and the private sector are slowly beginning to appreciate the potential allure of its romantic past. A major archeological museum is in the pipeline and there is even talk of a cruise-ship port, though the "soon come" attitude combined with lack of funding have ensured that none have yet been realized. For now, Port Royal retains a deliciously eerie, antiquated feel, a perfect place to catch a whiff of pirates and pieces of eight, and of an egregiously proud city brought to its knees by natural disaster.

Some history

When Britain captured Jamaica from Spain in 1655, most of the country's population of two or three thousand lived in the capital city of Spanish Town, a few miles from what is now Kingston harbour. Two things were immediately obvious to British tacticians: to prevent any other power from repeating the simple strategy with which they had conquered the island, strong **defences** were required all around the harbour, and with their navy tied up with wars in Europe, they also needed to recruit local support to help defend the new colony.

Port Royal at this time was uninhabited but, surrounded by deep water, it had been a perfect place for the Spanish to moor up their

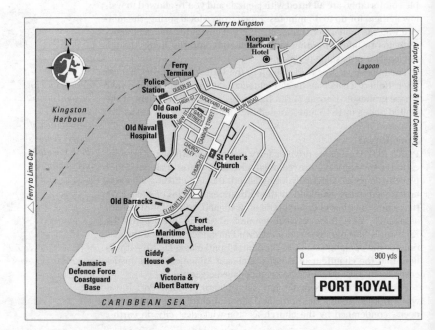

sailing ships for cleaning and caulking. Now the British turned it into a **battle station**, with five separate forts covering all of the angles from which enemy ships could approach, and a palisade at the north to defend against attackers coming over the cays. As added protection they encouraged the buccaneers who had for decades been pillaging the area to sign up as **"privateers"** in the service of the king.

See the box on p.110 for more on Port Royal's pirates.

Port Royal boomed. Merchants took advantage of the city's great location to buy and sell slaves, export sugar, logwood and import bricks and supplies for the growing population. The privateers wreaked havoc on the ships of Spain, and the fabulous profits of trade and plunder brought others to service the town's needs; brothels, taverns and gambling houses proliferated, and by 1692 the population had swollen to six thousand. Rents were as high as in the most fashionable parts of London and the world's finest wines and silks were readily available.

The huge **earthquake** that struck the city on June 7, 1692, dumped sixty percent of Port Royal into the sea, killing two thousand people in seconds; within a week, a thousand more had died. Of the remaining population, most fled for Kingston (see p.66), while almost all of the rest died or deserted when a massive fire swept the island in 1703.

Despite the destruction, Port Royal continued to serve as the country's **naval headquarters**. All the great British admirals of the eighteenth and early nineteenth centuries were stationed here at some point in their careers, plotting the downfall of the French, whose presence in the area grew increasingly threatening up until the time of the Napoleonic Wars. However, the advent of steam ships saw the British Navy close its dockyard in 1905, and following the rapid expansion of Kingston during the last century Port Royal has become increasingly marginalized – the settlement suffered further blows when Hurricanes Charlie and Gilbert wreaked havoc in 1951 and 1988 respectively. Though Port Royal still retains its naval traditions as home to the JDF Naval wing and the Jamaican coastguard, it's a far less exotic – though nonetheless beguiling – place today, a small and tidy fishing village, proud of its very low crime rate and happy to serve up some of the tastiest fresh **fish** you'll find anywhere in Jamaica.

Port Royal was a parish in its own right until the title was abolished in 1867, when Port Royal, along with Kingston and the southern slopes of the Blue Mountains, were incorporated into today's parish of St Andrew.

Getting there

Unless you are **driving** – in which case follow signs southeast from Kingston to the airport and keep going past the turn-off – the most pleasant and convenient way to get to Port Royal is on the little blue-and-white **ferry** (J$20 each way; 30min) that leaves regularly from the pier at the bottom of Princess Street in downtown Kingston, near the National Gallery.

An uncharacteristically smart (and usually empty) **bus** (J$20; 25min) runs several times a day between the Parade and Port Royal Square, via Harbour View, while a **taxi** will set you back around US$25 in each direction.

Around
Kingston

*The ferry leaves
Kingston
Monday to
Friday at 6am,
7am, 10am,
12.30pm, 3pm,
5pm & 7pm, on
Saturday at
6am, 8am,
10.30am,
12.30pm, 2pm
& 6.30pm, and
on Sunday at
11.30am,
2.30pm, 4.30pm
& 6.30pm,
returning from
Port Royal
30min later.
The one-way
fare is JS$20,
and journey
time is about
half an hour.*

The Town

Port Royal makes an impression before you even reach dry land; look back to sea as the ferry docks on the northwest shore and you'll get not only a great view of the harbour, but a clear idea of the area's strategic military importance and a glimpse of its former limits. The **old city** once extended way out across the harbour, but since the 1692 earthquake, sixty percent of it has been submerged under fifty feet of water, its key sites marked by several buoys.

Once on land, what remains of Port Royal is easily navigable on foot. Five minutes' walk from the ferry terminal, behind the old garrison wall, are the decaying red bricks of the **Old Naval Hospital**. Built by the Bowling Ironworks in Bradford, England, the two-storey iron prefab, that was shipped over and put up here in 1819, remains the oldest prefabricated structure in the "New World". Despite its ramshackle state (it has somehow managed to survive hurricanes Charlie and Gilbert), it now serves as offices for the National Heritage Trust, but was put into use in the aftermath of Hurricane Charlie as a refuge for displaced townspeople. Although numerous artefacts have been recovered from the sea and stored in the building (you may be able to get staff to show you the collection of pewter and china), plans to reopen to the public remain on hold at the time of writing. Take a wander around if there's no one to show you the place: a few rusting naval artefacts gather dust outside, but don't head upstairs without permission – only one of the staircases is strong enough to be climbed.

Ten minutes' walk away and on the main Church Street, **St Peter's Church** (irregular opening hours) was built in 1726 and, apart from the roof, has survived largely intact since. It's unremarkable apart from an intricately carved mahogany and cedar organ loft, which was made in 1743 by W.G. Dowles of Bristol, England; the organ was restored in the late 1990s by the same company, which still trades to this day. Marble tablets on the church walls emphasize the role of the navy in this area, and you should be able to get someone to show you a collection of silver plates, bowls and a jug said to have belonged to Henry Morgan. More interesting are the ancient tombs in the small and rambling graveyard, particularly that of the Frenchman **Lewis Galdy**. Swallowed by the earthquake in 1692, an eruption seconds later spat him out into the sea from where, amazingly, he scrambled to safety. No doubt a pillar of the church thereafter, Galdy lived until 1739. Next to Galdy's grave is a tomb for three small children who died in the earthquake and whose remains were found in the rubble of their collapsed house during underwater excavations in 1992.

*In the likely
event that St
Peter's is
locked up
when you
visit, ask
around for
local vendor
Patsy, who
usually has the
key; failing
that, try the
staff at Fort
Charles.*

A left turn out of the church leads down the main road to fascinating **Fort Charles** (daily 9am–5pm; J$130), approached through an expansive parade ground that was formerly Chocolata Hole – a part of the harbour and a sheltered spot for mooring ships before natural sea and land movements combined with artificial filling during the eighteenth and nineteenth centuries created the dry land of today. Originally known as Fort Cromwell (but renamed after King Charles II was restored to the British throne in 1660), Charles was the first of the five forts to be built here, though it never saw any action. The first structure was wooden but, following the Great Fire of London in 1666, British laws required that all such buildings in the colonies be made of brick. The present fort looks much as it did in 1692, except that then it was immediately bordered by the sea on three sides. The red-brick building to your left as you enter is the storage room, where the all-important gunpowder was kept dry. In the courtyard, the **Maritime Museum** gives a lucid history of Port Royal and displays items – bottles, coins, cannonballs, shipwrights tools and a set of ankle shackles used to restrain slaves – dredged up from the underwater city. Look out, in particular, for the National Geographic recreation of the city at the time of the 1692 earthquake.

The raised platform on the other side of the small parade ground is known as **Nelson's Quarterdeck**; the great commander (incredibly still under 21) used to pace up and down here spoiling for a fight with the French. From the quarterdeck you can see how the land has built up around the fort – over a foot per year – as the sea has continued to deposit silt against the former island. The two structures that now stand between the fort and the water both date from the 1880s. The squat, rectangular **Giddy House** was an ammunition store, while the circular bunker beside it was the **Victoria and Albert Battery** – an emplacement for a nineteenth-century supergun which was fired only once, at a British soldier who's attempt to desert was swiftly curtailed. The 1907 earthquake dropped the gun turret several yards into the earth, while the store room somehow remained intact but tilted at a seventeen-degree angle. Try walking across it without slipping over.

Nelson's Quarterdeck affords marvellous views of the Blue Mountains.

There are two other points of minor interest in Port Royal. Heading back towards the main square, turn left after St Peter's Church, then right and third left onto Gaol Street. The distinctive block building on your right is the **Old Gaol House** (closed to visitors), built before the 1692 earthquake and once used as a women's prison. Slightly out of town on the road back to Kingston the **Naval Cemetery** – its entrance marked by an anchor-shaped memorial to the crew of *HMS Goshawk*, who drowned when their vessel sank in Port Royal harbour – marks the final resting place of many of Port Royal's long-forgotten sailors. Buccaneer-turned-politician Henry Morgan (see box on p.110) was buried here too, but the earthquake tipped his body into the sea along with a large part of the old graveyard. What remains today of the cemetery was laid out by the British in 1762, following successive outbreaks of yellow fever; Port Royalists still avoid what they perceive as a contaminated area to this day.

Finally, there are a couple of **beaches** around Port Royal, but both sea and sand are pretty dirty; if you want to **swim**, you're better off

Pirates and buccaneers

The early history of Port Royal is inextricably linked with adventurers. The first **buccaneers** were a ragged crew of outlaws and fugitives, European outcasts who banded together on the island of Tortuga, north of present day Haiti. They lived by hunting wild pigs and cattle (first brought to the island by the early European explorers) which they smoked on a wooden frame known as a *boucan* (hence the name). As they grew more organized and more daring, they began to raid the treasure ships sailing between Spain and its "New World" colonies.

After Britain conquered Jamaica in 1655, the newly installed authorities embarked on an open-door policy, issuing a general invitation to these buccaneers to set themselves up in Port Royal and use it as their base for attacks on the Spanish enemy. In return for official status as **"privateers"**, they were obliged to deliver ten percent of their haul to the Crown. Privateering flourished and Port Royal turned into a city marked by extreme wealth and a constant threat of violence.

The privateers' reversal of fortune came in 1671 when a peace treaty was signed between Britain and Spain. Despite the treaty, **Henry Morgan** – the most famous of the buccaneers – sailed from Bluefields Bay in Jamaica to plunder the wealthy Spanish colony of Panama. Although there is some evidence that the British authorities connived at this attack, Morgan and the Jamaican governor, Thomas Modyford, were recalled to the mother country to face official sanction. Modyford was sacked to appease the Spanish while Morgan, having insinuated his way into royal favour, was made lieutenant-governor in his stead, returning to Jamaica with a new brief – to stamp out piracy by persuading his former colleagues to adopt a life of peace.

Many of the buccaneers, now officially termed **"pirates"** to mark their loss of favour, refused to give up their exciting and profitable lifestyles and continued to plague ships throughout the Caribbean. In turn, they were ruthlessly hunted down by Morgan and his successors, and hangings at a spot called Gallows Point on Port Royal were frequent until as late as 1831. The most famous success for the authorities came in 1720 when "Calico Jack" Rackham and his sidekicks, female pirates Anne Bonney and Mary Read, were captured during a party on Negril beach. Rackham was executed, his body squeezed into a tiny cage and left on Rackham's Cay, just east of Port Royal, as a warning to others; conveniently, the women both declared themselves pregnant and were spared the gallows; Bonney disappeared without trace, but Read contracted yellow fever, died in prison and is buried in St Catherine.

See p.302 for more on Calico Jack, Anne Bonney and Mary Read.

taking a boat out to Lime Cay (see opposite). Otherwise, the Buccaneer dive shop at *Morgan's Harbour Hotel* runs scuba certification courses (from US$300) as well as **diving** (US$65 per dive) and **snorkelling** (US$15 per hour) excursions to some of the best sites on the south coast, many of them centred around wrecked ships and frequented by the usual array of tropical fish and nurse sharks. You can also arrange deep-sea **fishing** (4hr US$400; 8hr US$650), and evening drop-line fishing (4hr; US$400) through the hotel. Alternatively, you could take a gentler **boat ride** into the mangrove swamps that parallel the Palisadoes road for a look at the local birdlife, particularly impressive during the pelican breeding season from February to April; at all times, though, you'll also see frigate birds and egrets rooting in the trees.

Lime Cay and other islands
Just fifteen minutes from Port Royal, **Lime Cay** is a tiny uninhabited island with white sand, blue water and easy snorkelling. It was here that Ivanhoe ("Rhygin") Martin – the cop-killing gangster and folk-hero immortalized in the classic Jamaican movie *The Harder They Come* – met his demise in 1948 (see "Contexts" p.418). Boats run regularly from *Morgan's Harbour Hotel* (see below) or you can ask the fishermen at the pier to take you – the going rate is J$250 per person round-trip. On Sundays, when a good-natured crowd of Kingstonians descend, food and drink stalls are set up on the beach; at other times, take your own picnic.

If you desperately want your own private island, ask to be dropped at **Maiden Cay**, a tiny, shadeless sandspit, or **Twin Cays**, shadier but with poorer swimming than at Lime Cay. En route to any of these, you'll pass the once heavily-armed **Gun Cay**, still bearing evidence of its eighteenth-century fortification by the British, and the fast-disappearing **Rackham's Cay**, a palpable victim of beach erosion.

Practicalities
The best place to **stay** in Port Royal (convenient also for the airport, five minutes' drive away) is the elegant and atmospheric *Morgan's Harbour Hotel* (☎967 8030 or 8040, fax 967 8073; ⑥), all dark wood and seafaring charm with a pool and a salt-licked open-air bar. Otherwise, ask in the town square about one of the private homes in the small housing development behind Church Street; a couple have been refurbished in readiness to rent to visitors.

Morgan's Harbour Hotel has a good and reasonably priced restaurant, *Sir Henry's*, which affords marvellous views of the city and cooks up excellent seafood and "International" dishes. Several cheaper **eating** options near the ferry pier serve Port Royal's best fish, the stuff that Jamaicans will drive miles to get. The most popular place is *Gloria's Rendezvous* at 5 Queen St, where you can enjoy a tasty plate of fish and bammy and watch the pelicans and frigate birds fishing just offshore. Otherwise, there's the similar *Buccaneer's Roost* around the corner, a patty store on the same block, and local women selling fried fish in the main square. The *Angler's Club/MacFarlane's Bar*, at the corner of the square on Dockyard Lane, opens up for some hard drinking, and at weekends, speakers are stacked up in the square for an outdoor **party**, playing dancehall on a Friday and oldies on Saturday. A big crowd piles down from Kingston, and it's a great opportunity to enjoy a very easy-going Jamaican street party. *Gloria's* is also the focus for a

Room 105 at Morgan's Harbour Hotel was the setting for the Dr No scene in which James Bond is woken by the attentions of a large spider. Bond also tumbles amongst crates of Red Stripe at the hotel bar, transformed for the movie into "Puss Fellers" nightclub.

marvellous Sunday oldies party, and there's a small indoor club, *Brave Star*, which stages late-night dances at the weekends, around the back of town.

West of Kingston

Southwest of Kingston, a **causeway** connects the city to the bland but booming dormitory town of **PORTMORE** in the neighbouring parish of St Catherine. Home to an estimated 120,000 people (and built to accommodate far fewer, as the recent strain on the sewage system illustrates), Portmore itself has nothing much of interest save a few shopping malls, one of which holds the *Cactus* nightclub (see p.100) – but **Port Henderson**, a brief detour away, has a handful of colonial-era relics and fine views across Kingston harbour. Below Portmore, the road cuts across the eastern fringe of the **Hellshire Hills** – a vast and scrubby limestone expanse – and down to Hellshire's white-sand **beaches** and the ancient Taino base of **Two Sisters Cave**. Further northwest, the former capital city of **Spanish Town**, a run-down shadow of its former self, still retains some graceful architecture, while the less accessible **Mountain River Cave**, **Colbeck Castle** and **Old Harbour** each offer a distinct glimpse into Jamaica's varied history.

Port Henderson

Established as a port in the 1770s, when it was the embarkation point for the ferry which provided a fast route to Spanish Town (then the capital city), **PORT HENDERSON** became a popular spa town and fashionable resort area during the Victorian era. It's now a small village with a few restored eighteenth- and nineteenth-century buildings, including the bar and restaurant at **Rodney's Arms**, named for the British admiral in charge of the local naval station during the late 1900s. Past here, towards the Jamaican Defence Force base, a trail leads up to **Rodney's Look-Out**, from where the admiral kept an eye peeled for French warships. The JDF keep-out signs aren't exactly welcoming, however, and you may prefer to take in the panorama by simply walking or driving up the hill past the restaurant.

To get to Port Henderson, take the left-hand exit as you cross the causeway from Kingston, then turn right onto Augusta Drive and left at the roundabout. En route, it's worth stopping off to look at the substantial old English fort at **Fort Augusta**, back at the far end of Augusta Drive, built by the British in 1740 as their main sea defence on Kingston's western side. It's now used as a women's prison and is closed to visitors, though you can drive up as far as the gates.

Practicalities

Buses and **minibuses** run to Port Henderson from Parade and to Portmore from Parade and Half Way Tree. There is nowhere to **stay** in Port Henderson itself, but Augusta Drive is lined with accommodation options, most of them short-time "love hotels" for couples escaping Kingston for a discreet rendezvous, though there's little reason to stay here. Of the more traditional places, *La Roose* (☎998 4654; ③) has very reasonable air-conditioned rooms, while *Jewels* (☎988 6785; ③), a little further on, has a nice pool beside its oceanfront restaurant. *Rodney's Arms*, justifiably the most popular local **eatery**, serves excellent seafood; the restaurant at *La Roose* is also good, dishing up fried chicken, fish and lobster, and there are plenty of fried fish shacks along the causeway. In terms of **entertainment**, *La Roose* serves as an occasional venue for dancehall events, and there's the odd **club** night at *Rodney's Arms*, which draws Kingston's good-timers. Otherwise, *Cactus* (see p.100) in nearby Portmore is livelier.

Hellshire and around

Covered in low, dense scrub and bushy cacti, the arid **Hellshire Hills** extend for around a hundred square miles west of Kingston. Around 500 to 1000 years ago, this forbidding landscape was home to Taino Indians and, later, to runaway slaves. For now, though, virtually the only inhabitants are the migrant birds, a few conies and a handful of Jamaican **iguanas**, thought extinct for half a century until their redis-covery here in 1990 by a local man who had the foresight to bring the specimen to the university for identification. Low rainfall and the unwelcoming limestone terrain have deterred people from settling out here, although the expansion of the suburb of Portmore threat-ens to encroach on the area's eastern half. It's not a bad place to **hike** if you're interested in seeing one of the island's genuine wilderness zones. Don't try it on your own – it's easy to get lost and there are some nasty sinkholes; Sun Venture Tours (see p.104) have excellent guides.

The best way to see Portmore, Hellshire and beyond is to arrange a trip with Our Story Tours (see box on p.104).

From Port Henderson, the signposted road to the Hellshire beach-es runs under the flanks of the Hellshire hills, passing a huge scar in the mountainside gouged out to provide marl for construction of Portmore's homes. Just before the quarry stands an abandoned, lonely-looking high-rise building, formerly the *Forum Hotel*, built by the government in an unsuccessful attempt to entice tourists to the area. Past here, the road hits the coast again beside the **Great Salt Pond**, an old Taino fishing spot and a site of ecological significance that continues to be polluted by excesses from Portmore's woefully inadequate sewerage system, and carries on to **Fort Clarence beach** (Mon–Fri 10am–5pm, Sat & Sun 8am–6pm; J$100), a pretty if ram-shackle stretch of white sand with scuzzy but soon-to-be-renovated showers and a passable café. The beach is often used as a venue for dancehall stageshows, and during the week, it's usually very quiet, though lifeguards are on duty during opening hours.

Buses from Parade and Half Way Tree in Kingston run roughly every hour to the Hellshire beaches.

If you're after beachlife, though, it's far better to press on to **Hellshire beach** (no set hours; free), separated from Fort Clarence by a barrier reef which makes the Hellshire water a lot calmer. As the closest beach to the capital, Hellshire is buzzing at the weekends, with booming sound systems (particularly on a Sunday) and a party atmosphere which keeps the powdery dunes peppered with family groups who haven't been able to nab one of the wooden loungers set up under the shady eaves of the area's multiple **fish restaurants**, which compete to sell the freshest fish, lobster and festival. Most Jamaicans come here for the food as much as the sea and sand, and Hellshire fried fish, best eaten with home-made pepper sauce, beats anything you'll find in town. Many local fishermen keep their pirogues here, and boats returning from their deep-sea sorties generate a flurry of excitement as would-be buyers attempt to secure the best of the catch. Also present at the weekends are **watersports operators** offering jet ski rental and snorkelling equipment, while horses (wearing fetching eye-gear to protect against flying sand grains) parade up and down giving children rides.

Beyond the beaches, the road leads south to the intriguing **Two Sisters Cave**, signposted on the left but currently closed for refurbishment. Ancient earthquakes in the area created subterranean chambers here, with streams trickling through them and a series of brackish pools – a perfect shelter (later a hideaway) for the island's first inhabitants, the Tainos (see "Contexts" p.369). Until the restoration is complete (and there's no sign that it'll happen any time soon), you can't go inside, but you might be able to make out a painted face, drawn beside the entrance to ward off evil spirits. It's a windswept, sun-parched place, with huge cacti poking through the "makka" thorn bushes all around, and an appropriately isolated lovers' spot.

The only place to **stay** in the area is the incongruous but friendly *Hellshire Beach Club* (☎989 8306; ④), a cavernous white building with a pool and restaurant. The clean, tiled rooms have a/c, fan and TV; the ceiling mirrors are a hint as to why most people rent by the hour.

To get to Nature's Paradise from Hellshire, follow the signs to Spanish Town; when you meet the A1 Nelson Mandela highway, go straight across and take the road signposted for the Caymanas/ Kingston Polo Club.

Nature's Paradise mineral spring

As there's no fresh water at Hellshire, a favourite way to sluice off the salt after a day on the beach is to head for the **Nature's Paradise mineral spring** (daily during daylight hours; J$20). Coming from central Kingston, follow Washington Boulevard west out of town; just past the Ferry police station, turn right at the sign for the Caymanas/Kingston Polo Club. A ten-minute drive through the lush surrounds of Caymanas estate brings you to the small community of Caymanas Bay. Here, to the right of the road, tall bamboo fences have been erected by the spring's Rasta caretakers, who open the gates so you can drive in and park within the compound. Seldom visited by tourists, and something of a Rasta hangout, the spring is actually the point where the Fresh River rises from underground. You can see the water bubbling up from pipes once used to irrigate the cane fields, and the river is clear, cool, refreshing and, at weekends, teeming with

Jamaican swimmers who come to lark about and chill out to the music pumped from the small bar, where you can get snacks and drinks.

As the facilities are pretty basic (there's no piped water in the toilets and no changing rooms), you're best off arriving in your swimming gear.

Spanish Town

Capital of Jamaica from 1534 to 1872, and still the island's second city, teeming, industrial **SPANISH TOWN**, twelve miles west of Kingston, today shows only vestigial traces of its former glory. Few tourists visit and, to be honest, it's not a place that you'll want to linger in for long, but the Georgian **square** – with possibly the finest collection of Georgian architecture in the Americas – and the great old **cathedral** – Jamaica's premier church and the oldest surviving Anglican cathedral outside England – repay the small effort involved in getting here from Kingston.

Some history

Spain's first attempt to create a city in Jamaica foundered when its chosen site at **New Seville** on the north coast proved well-suited only

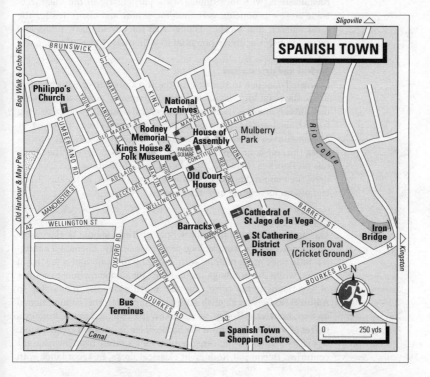

to the spread of disease (see p.218). Its second choice at St Jago de
la Vega (as Spanish Town was then known) proved more durable;
there was fertile ground, no mosquito-ridden swamps and it was only
a short march from two good south-coast harbours (present-day Old
Harbour and Kingston). The site also had great look-out points over
the surrounding plains, although this proved of little help during
English invasions in 1596 and 1643, when the city was comprehen-
sively sacked. Sadly, there are almost no relics of the Spanish-era
wooden and adobe buildings left today, although an extensive tunnel
system is believed still to run under the centre of town – a hiding
place for the Spaniards and their booty during English raids.

Soon after the English captured Jamaica, the country experienced
a boom in trade and, gradually, the newly created port city of
Kingston began to flourish as the centre of population and commerce. Although huge sums were spent on Spanish Town's major
public buildings in the late eighteenth century to boost the city's
prestige, the authorities cut their losses and eventually moved the
capital to Kingston in 1872, leaving Spanish Town to decay. Today,
parts of the city are desolate, rumoured to be entirely controlled by
political gangs. More optimistically, though, there is some economic
revitalization, with local industries – particularly in the busy free-
trade zone – producing garments for export and cigarettes for the
local market, and locals pushing hard for development funds and
recognition of the area's potential as a "heritage tourism" site.

Arrival and orientation

Spanish Town lies to the west of the Rio Cobre river with Bourkes
Road, the main highway from Kingston, running across its southern
end, fifteen minutes' walk from the central square. If you're driving
from Kingston, follow Washington Boulevard (from uptown) or
Marcus Garvey Drive (from downtown) out of the city. Regular buses
make the half-hour trip from Parade and Half Way Tree to the terminus on Bourkes Road (J$30), while a taxi costs about US$20. Once
here, the main sights can easily be explored on foot, as the city is still
laid out on its original neat grid system.

Parade Square

The starting point for any visit to Spanish Town should be the graceful **Parade Square**, centrepiece of the whole city. There is a charming little park at its middle, with a shabby fountain and a few royal
palms, while the buildings around are splendid showcase examples
of Georgian architecture. On the north side, the **memorial to
Admiral Rodney** by English sculptor John Bacon was commissioned
by the Jamaican House of Assembly to commemorate Rodney's
defeat of the French navy at the battle of les Saintes, off Guadeloupe,
in 1782 – a victory which ensured Jamaica's safety from invasion for
centuries. Bacon put Rodney in classical dress, in accordance with

the artistic convention of the time, and the seaman is flanked by a couple of rare and intricate Louis XIV cannons, taken from the French flagship and still bearing the herald of the Sun King. In the 1870s the memorial was briefly moved to Kingston, but the aggrieved citizens of Spanish Town banded together and intimidated the authorities into returning it. Check out the mural above Rodney, depicting his arms and motto and a picture of the French ship sinking. A number of Spanish buildings, including a sixteenth-century tavern, were demolished to make way for the memorial and the adjoining buildings, which today include the **National Archives** (Mon–Fri 9.30am–4pm), with records dating back to the early days of English settlement, and, opposite, the ruined **courthouse**, built early in the nineteenth century in symmetry with the memorial but badly damaged by fire in 1986.

On the west side of the square is the porticoed, red-brick facade of the **King's House**, built in 1762 and the official residence of the Governor of Jamaica until the capital was moved to Kingston. The facade is all that remains of the building, following a catastrophic fire

---

Jamaica's death row

The jail at Spanish Town, built right behind the cathedral, is home to Jamaica's notorious **death row**, the only place in the country that carries out capital punishment. In the recent past hundreds of men have awaited their execution here in appalling conditions, some of them for as long as fourteen years. In 1993 the cases of Earl Pratt and Ivan Morgan were brought before the Privy Council in London, which still sits as Jamaica's final court of appeal. Convicted of murder in 1979 and sentenced to hang, Pratt and Morgan had on three separate occasions heard the death warrant and been taken to the cells adjoining the gallows. Each time they received a last-minute reprieve. The Privy Council overturned the death sentence on the two men, finding that the length of time they had spent on death row was "cruel, inhumane and degrading". The verdict, which made future executions increasingly unlikely, didn't go down well with the vast majority of Jamaicans, who, in the face of soaring crime figures, express widespread support for the penalty. It has also increased pressure on the government to abandon the archaic reliance on the British House of Lords as the ultimate arbiter in Jamaica's legal matters, a hangover from colonial days.

In a bid to remove one less international body to which death row inmates could lodge an appeal and to speed up the process, Jamaica – to the horror of human rights organizations such as Amnesty International – withdrew from the Optional Protocol to the International Covenant on Civil and Political Rights in January 1998, and in February 1998, Stanford Dinnal and Nathan Foster promptly went to the gallows. The hanging of nine men in Trinidad and Tobago in June 1999 did much to fuel Jamaican debate on capital punishment, with popular opinion urging the government to follow Trinidad and Tobago's example, and the fate of the forty-plus men who remain on Spanish Town's death row seems increasingly imminent.

For more on Jamaica's death row and the issues surrounding capital punishment on the island, visit Amnesty International's Web site: www .amnesty.org.

in 1925, but there's a great little **People's Museum** in the former stables at the back (Mon–Fri 9am–5pm; J$40). Artefacts include an animal-operated press for extracting juice from sugar cane and copperpot boilers for separating the sugar crystals from the juice. The main body of the museum has displays on Jamaican architecture and crafts, with the emphasis firmly on upholding African traditions. To get into the museum, you must first pass through the *Wine Bar*, an elegant drinking hole decorated with first-rate Jamaican art (look out for pieces by David Pottinger, Ras Dizzy and Carl Abrahams) and a huge waterwheel shipped in from a nearby estate. If owner Derryk Roberts is around, you might be treated to an excellent rundown of Spanish Town past and present with your glass of wine.

The former **House of Assembly**, opposite the King's House, was built in the same year and to the same dimensions. The Assembly – representatives of the plantation owners and other bigwigs – met here until 1865 when, following the Morant Bay Rebellion (see p.148), Jamaica abandoned its constitution and became a Crown Colony with direct rule from Britain. Today, the building is the seat of local government, reflecting Spanish Town's fall in the rankings. It is not officially open to the public but you can normally sneak in to look at the grand mahogany staircase and the chamber upstairs.

The cathedral

From Parade Square, a five-minute walk south down White Church Street leads to the **Cathedral of St Jago de la Vega** (daily 9am–5pm; free), Jamaica's most important church and the oldest Anglican cathedral outside England. It stands on the foundations of the sixteenth-century Church of the Red Cross, and the black-and-white tiles in the aisle are thought to date from that Spanish building. Important monuments crowd the cathedral, many of them carved in England by leading sculptors of the time like John Bacon and John Wilton, reflecting the status and wealth of the colony during the eighteenth century.

The **Blessed Sacrament Chapel**, to the left of the altar, holds a memorial to Basil Keith, governor of Jamaica during the 1770s; the sculpture by Wilton was the first monument in the country to be built with public funds. The **Lady Chapel**, on the other side, has a cherubic monument to another governor, Thomas Effingham, sculpted by Bacon. Slightly differing versions of the Jamaican coat of arms, with its Taino figures, crocodile and pineapples (once a sign of great wealth), can be seen on the Effingham monument and on the stained-glass window behind the altar. Also in the Lady Chapel, the memorial to one Hugh Lewis on the south wall features the only **death mask** in the Caribbean.

Throughout the cathedral are eloquent memorials to former governors, bishops and other leading figures of Jamaican society. William Chadwick was the only principal of Jamaica's first university – the

Queen's College – which opened in 1873 for seven students but survived for just one year. Matthew Gregory established a benevolent fund for poor whites in 1765, aimed at getting a trade for the boys and a husband for the girls. John Colbeck, whose tomb is by the south door, was a soldier with the original English invading force in 1655 and is believed to have been the designer of Colbeck Castle, a few miles west from Spanish Town. Other tombs were mass burial sites for victims of cholera epidemics or those who died on ships en route to the colony.

Outside, you can spend an hour exploring and deciphering the ancient gravestones under the mango trees. Note the **gargoyles** with African features – considered to be unique anywhere – standing guard over a south window. Below them, a number of early governors found their final resting place, including Modyford and Lynch, as well as Martha Ducke, an early settler "most barbarously murdered by one of her own Negro slaves" in 1678.

Other sights

The old **iron bridge** spanning the Rio Cobre near where you drive into town was erected here in 1801 after being cast in England, and was the first of its kind in the Americas. In town, the attractive old English **barracks** building, west of the cathedral along Barracks Street, dates from the late eighteenth century. Before this the soldiers had been based in private houses dotted around town, which was seen as a threat to discipline. Cannons stand at the entrance to the barracks, as they once did at each of the public buildings, as a place to hitch up your horse.

A short walk from Parade Square down Constitution Street brings you to **Mulberry Park**, formerly the site of a monastery where mulberry trees were grown to produce silk and today an infirmary for the indigent. It has also been a Jewish cemetery and, though now overrun with banana trees, the old headstones – some in English, others in Hebrew – have been propped up around the park's perimeter.

North of the square, on the corner of French and William Streets, is an unremarkable Baptist church, first built in 1827 but badly damaged by the 1951 and 1988 hurricanes. It is popularly known as **Philippo's Church** for its associations with James Philippo, a missionary who campaigned for the abolition of slavery and the establishment of "free villages" for emancipated slaves and who set up the first such community at **Sligoville** (see p.121). These free villages were an important part of the development of Jamaican society after emancipation. The plantation owners were strongly opposed to allowing slaves to set up their own communities, hoping that they would be forced to return to semi-serfdom on the plantations. They didn't reckon on the missionaries, however, mostly Baptists like Philippo, who bought up old estates, sub-divided them and sold them off to the former slaves on generous terms. A church and a school were usually the first buildings erected in these new villages, with the houses going up around them, and this pattern of development can still be seen in parts of the country.

Practicalities

There are no good **hotels** or guesthouses in Spanish Town, and most people visit as a day-trip from Kingston. A smattering of **restaurants** around the town centre serve typical if unexciting chicken and fish meals; try *Cecil's* on Martin Street, five minutes from Parade Square, or there are a couple of snack-bars on Bourkes Road near the bus stop. The market, on Old Market Street, is good for a wander, and is busiest from Thursday to Sunday.

Around Spanish Town

A handful of places near Spanish Town merit a quick stop, particularly if you're driving. Eight miles to the northwest, **Mountain River Cave** – home to some rare Taino cave paintings – takes quite a lot of effort to reach, but rewards the trouble, while ten miles to the north, and a few thousand feet above, the historical settlement of **Sligoville**, one of the first "free villages" established after the abolition of slavery, provides a cool perspective on the area. If you're heading west, you'll pass through the bustling little town of **Old Harbour** – if you're in a car, the ruins of nearby **Colbeck Castle** invite a quick detour – while the route north from Spanish Town passes through the dramatically scenic **Bog Walk Gorge**.

Mountain River Cave and Guanaboa Vale

Mountain River Cave is best visited with Our Story Tours (see p.104).

Although Taino petroglyphs or stone-carvings have been found throughout the Caribbean, very few instances of their **paintings** survive. Accordingly, the fifty or so black drawings on the ceiling of **Mountain River Cave** – human figures, a turtle, lizards, fish, frogs – are a significant historic relic. The emphasis on food suggests that the cave might have been used for religious rites intended to ensure successful hunting. Don't expect anything spectacular; the figures are small, amateurish in the extreme and it's not always easy to make out what they are supposed to be. The real pleasure of this isolated spot is the tiny glimpse offered by the paintings – among the few visible markers left by the island's first inhabitants – into Jamaica's pre-Columbian history.

First uncovered in 1897, the small cave has been thoroughly documented by the Smithsonian Institute in Washington DC and is now a National Trust site. To reach it, drive northwest from Spanish Town towards Lluidas Vale, where a monument commemorates Juan Lubolo, a slave turned maroon turned guerrilla, who assisted British forces in the fight against the Spaniards, through the pretty and ancient village of **Guanaboa Vale**, childhood home of Jamaican National Hero and former political leader Norman Manley. A **church** has stood here since 1675 – very early in the period of English rule – although the present structure mostly dates from 1845, after repeated hurricane damage to the original. A couple of miles uphill beyond Guanaboa, *Cudjoe's Cavern* restaurant (good for drinks and basic Jamaican meals) and a small signpost on your right mark the entrance to the site; ask at the adjoining house for a guide to take you to the cave. It's a gruelling half-mile walk, involving a couple of steep slopes through cocoa, coffee and jackfruit trees. You'll also cross the narrow Thompson's river which, a hundred yards downstream, has a small **waterfall** and a refreshing swimming spot.

Bog Walk Gorge and the road to Ocho Rios

The smooth but busy main road from Spanish Town to Ocho Rios, a couple of hours' drive, runs north past Bog Walk and Ewarton. The first part of the drive is very scenic, the road cutting through the deep **Bog Walk Gorge**, a towering limestone canyon carved out of the rock by the deep green waters of the Rio Cobre over the centuries. Cars cross the river at **Flat Bridge**, an eighteenth-century stone bridge that has no sides and occasionally loses reckless drivers into the eddying river. Just past Flat Bridge, a Jamaican companion may be able to point out "Pum Rock" a very vagina-like cavity in the Rio Cobre's rocky banks. All along the route you'll see farmers selling their colourful crops – bananas, oranges, sweet potatoes and, in season, fabulous mangoes and luscious naseberries. If you're passing on a Saturday, **LINSTEAD**, eight miles north of Flat Bridge still has a traditional weekend market, immortalized in the folk song *Linstead Market*: "Carry me ackee go a Linstead Market/Not a quattie would sell".

SLIGOVILLE, six miles east of Bog Walk and several hundred feet above, was the first free village in Jamaica, named in honour of the pro-emancipation Marquis of Sligo, Howe Peter Browne, who arrived from Britain as Jamaica's governor in 1834 to supervise the six-year "apprenticeship" period (in effect, semi-slavery) that followed the initial abolition of the trade in the same year, and who bestowed land at Sligoville to the Reverend James Philippo in order to establish a settlement for ex-slaves. Unsurprisingly, Browne's stance on emancipation didn't go down too well with the white planters in Jamaica, who regarded their governor as an "annoying" man who "interpreted the law in favour of the Negro". Exasperated by his opponents, Browne resigned two years later and returned to Britain to press for full emancipation, testifying in the commission of enquiry that led Queen Victoria to grant full freedom.

Sligoville is a peaceful, serene place today, and there's not much to it; turn left just before the police station to the Marquis' former **summer house**, Highgate, built to take advantage of the cool mountain climate and now occupied by the US Peace Corps, who are developing the building into an environmental education centre. Highgate

For more on
the abolition of
slavery in
Jamaica, see
"Contexts",
p.373.

affords utterly fabulous views of shimmering Portmore below, and
makes a pleasantly different place to stay for a night or so, though
you need your own transport. Currently there's only hostel-type
bunks (US$20) and shared facilities, and meals are available. To
reserve a space, call ahead or email (☎749 1845, *sligoville1@
hotmail.com*).

On a ridge opposite Highgate is the boxy **Mount Zion church**,
originally established by black Baptist George Lyle (see p.392) but
rebuilt after hurricane damage. Inside is a plaque presented by
Jeremy Ulick Browne, the eleventh Marquis of Sligoville and a
descendent of Howe Peter Browne, when he visited Sligoville in
1996 to attend a service commemorating the end of slavery in
Jamaica.

West to Old Harbour

West of Spanish Town, the main A2 road to **OLD HARBOUR** is lined
by small businesses, shops, go-go clubs and bars decorated with
some gaudily gorgeous exterior paintwork – the *"No To The System"*
bar is particularly psychedelic. Four miles or so from Spanish Town,
a Texaco garage on the right marks the turnoff for the **Serenity
Fishing and Wildlife Sanctuary** (daily 9am–6pm; J$200); if you
pass the sign, you've gone too far. Owned and operated by the
Guardsman security company (the inane barking that echoes around
the place emanates from the guard dogs kept here), Serenity is a
neatly-landscaped complex of **fishing ponds** stocked with tilapia,
and a small **zoo**, inhabited by ostriches, ponies, llamas, monkeys and
a long row of reptile cages. Less exotic are the "frizzle" chickens, also
known as "peel neck" fowl for their scrawny, featherless necks and
rumpled plumage. The menagerie is generally the preserve of school
groups, who come for educational days out, while the ponds are popular with Jamaican anglers who come to fish for their supper or cool
off at the bar. Rods and lines are included in the entrance fee, and
you pay for your catch by the pound; you can either have it cooked
up here at the restaurant/bar area, or take it home. Boat rides and
horseback treks are also available, and it's a nice, breezy spot to
break your journey.

Past Serenity, and just before the A2 swings into Old Harbour
proper, look out for the sign on the left of the road for the Mighty
Gully Youth Project, behind which is the simple studio and shop of
accomplished woodcarver **Lancelot Bryan**, a former tractor driver
who won a scholarship to the Jamaica School of Art after coming second in a national art competition. Working only in lignum vitae roots,
which must be seasoned for ten years before being set upon with a
chisel, Bryan produces exquisite, delicate figures, deemed good
enough to have been presented to Desmond Tutu and Queen
Elizabeth by the Jamaican government. He also runs a training
school for young local artists.

From Bryan's studio, it's a short hop to the busy little town of Old Harbour, nine miles west of Spanish Town. Crowded, noisy food markets spill over onto the road near the town centre and traffic always seems to get clogged up around the central square, giving you time to admire the **clock** in the Victorian tower, which has kept pretty much perfect time since it was first installed here in the seventeenth century. Three miles south, the fishing village of **OLD HARBOUR BAY** was, four hundred years ago, an important harbour for the Spanish as they settled in and around Spanish Town. Columbus stopped here to meet with Taino leaders in 1494, and in 1845 the first wave of Jamaica's Indian indentured labourers docked here (see box). Columbus named the area Cow Bay, after the **manatees** or seacows that once proliferated offshore. Few of the gentle creatures have survived centuries of slaughter at the hands of local fishermen, and the only things you'll find here now are fishing boats, shacks and a few stalls selling fresh fish and lobster – as you'd expect, it's a good place to stop for a tasty fried-fish lunch. Just offshore, the virtually uninhabited **Great Goat Island** was used as a US Navy base during World War II, and is now home to a few fishermen who shelter in the crumbling barracks.

There are plenty of small shops and Jamaican restaurants in Old Harbour, ideal if you need sustenance whilst on the road.

Two and a half miles from Old Harbour lie what's left of **Colbeck Castle** (unrestricted access). These are among the oldest ruins in the country and, like Fort Charles at Port Royal, speak of the constant fear of invasion held by the early English settlers. The castle was

Indians in Jamaica

In 1845, just over a decade after slavery was ended in Jamaica, *The Blundell* landed at Old Harbour Bay. The event marked the start of a new bout of colonial social-engineering in Jamaica, for the ship carried the first load of indentured Indian labourers. The abolition of slavery and the subsequent refusal of many ex-slaves to work for their former masters provoked a drastic need for cheap labour on the sugar estates. The estate-owners, having failed to import the required workers from Europe, China and Africa, turned instead to the poverty-stricken states of northern India.

Thirty-five thousand Indians came to Jamaica before the Indian government put a stop to it in 1917. In theory, the labourers were to work on the estates to pay the cost of their passage from India and would have the chance to earn money to send home before returning themselves at the end of their contracts (generally 5–7 years). In fact, almost all were forced to work under appalling conditions of semi-slavery for miserly pay (if any) and the majority remained and died in Jamaica, establishing close communities and continuing to celebrate traditional Hindu festivals like Diwali, Holi and Hosay. They still constitute probably the largest ethnic minority in the country (although on nothing like the scale of Trinidad and Guyana), but in recent decades their separate identity has begun to disappear as they have been assimilated into the wider community. Today their most potent legacy is a taste for curry and for ganja, introduced to Jamaica by the first wave of labourers.

built on land granted to John Colbeck, an officer with the English invasion force that captured Jamaica from the Spanish in 1655, and strategically placed within ten miles of both the coast and the capital Spanish Town. It is probable (though the date of construction is uncertain) that it was Colbeck who had it fortified with the massive walls of imported brick and local cut stone. A perimeter wall had a smaller guardhouse – probably a combination of a living quarters and a defensive position – at each corner.

No records have been found detailing the identities of the workmen, but it seems likely that the work was done by slaves under the guidance of skilled artisans from England. The circular brick windows on the ground floor are unusual, and the brick arches that front the main building are equally striking, suggesting that decoration, as well as defence, was important to the architect. The rest of the castle is rather dilapidated, with collapsed staircases and exposed timbers hinting at a grand design.

It's a bit of a palaver to get to Colbeck. Turn inland at the clock-tower in Old Harbour and continue until the road splits in three; take the centre route and follow the winding road lined with fields of tobacco plants (the ruins loom up on your left after a while) until you cross a bridge. After about four hundred yards take the first left down a gravel road/dirt track. Follow this for just over a half a mile to the castle – if it has been raining you may want to walk rather than risk getting your vehicle stuck.

North of Kingston

The main A3 artery shoots north from Kingston, shearing first through the affluent Stony Hill suburbs, all electric gates, expansive driveways and barking guard dogs. First stop, fourteen miles along, is **Castleton Botanical Gardens** (daily 9am–5pm; free), which occupy fifteen acres adjacent to the Wag Water River. Established in 1862, with support from London's Kew Gardens, Castleton quickly became the best-stocked garden in the Caribbean, and many of the plants that now dominate the island – the ubiquitous **poinciana** for example – were first introduced here. Despite the damage caused by recent hurricanes (and by official neglect) the gardens are still an important research station and well worth a stop if you're passing. The guides, who are no longer paid and survive only on tips from visitors, are quite excellent; chief guide Roy Bennett has been here for over sixty years, and his tours are a delight.

The gardens are well set out and easy to explore. There is a bewildering variety of palm trees, as well as coffee, cocoa and ebony, all of the island's perfume and spice plants, and a diverse collection of foreign plants and trees, including the startling cannonball tree. You'll also be offered the opportunity to taste fruits in season, such as the unusual African Velvet Apple. The peace and quiet attracts a lot of birdlife, and you may well spot Jamaica's national bird – the streamer tail hummingbird also known as the "**doctor bird**", supposedly for its resemblance to a doctor in Victorian costume – and the tiny bee hummingbird, one of the smallest birds in the world. When you've finished your tour, there is a small **bar** on the other side of the road, where you can also buy Mr Bennet's accomplished bamboo carvings, and, further down, more open space with access to the river if you want to swim or take a picnic.

Beyond Castleton, the A3 winds a beautiful – but demanding if you're driving – route to Annotto Bay on the north coast (see Chapter Two, p.181). The road runs parallel to the Wag Water River and offers occasional marvellous views of the rocky riverbed below. About halfway to the coast, the tiny community of **Friendship Gully** – better known to all as Junction – offers a couple of places to break your journey with a snack at a fried chicken/Chinese food joint or a small Jamaican eatery.

Travel details

It is impossible to predict accurately the frequency of buses and minibuses in the Kingston region – service is often chaotic and delays and cancellations are frequent – so the figures below are only general guidelines. However, on the most popular routes you should be able to count on getting a ride within an hour if you travel in the morning; things normally quieten down later in the day. On less popular routes, you're best off asking for probable departure times the day before you travel.

Buses and minibuses

Kingston to: Black River (4 daily; 4hr); Mandeville (6 daily; 3hr); Montego Bay (3 daily; 5hr 30min); Negril (2 daily; 6hr); Ocho Rios (4 daily; 3hr 30min); Port Antonio (via Annotto Bay, 4 daily, 4hr; via Morant Bay, 3 daily, 4hr 30min); Port Royal (7 daily; 25min); Spanish Town (12 daily; 30min).

Spanish Town to: Black River (2 daily; 4hr); Mandeville (6 daily; 2hr 30min); Montego Bay (3 daily; 5 hr); Negril (2 daily; 5hr 30min); Ocho Rios (3 daily; 2hr 30min).

Ferries

Kingston to: Port Royal (Mon–Sat 7 daily, Sun 4 daily; 30min).

Flights

Kingston to: Montego Bay (Mon–Fri 8 daily, Sat & Sun 5 daily; 35min); Negril (1 daily; 1hr); Port Antonio (1 daily; 40min).

Chapter 2

The Blue Mountains and the east

Towering behind Kingston and enticingly visible from anywhere in the island's eastern third, the **Blue Mountains** conform with few people's mental image of Jamaica, land of sand, sea and reggae. At 28 miles, the mountains form one of the longest continuous ranges in the Caribbean, and their cool, fragrant woodlands, dotted with coffee plantations and often shrouded in mist, offer some of the best hiking on the island and a welcome break from the heat of the coast. The most popular hike is to **Blue Mountain Peak** – at 7402ft, the highest point in Jamaica – but there are dozens of other trekking possibilities, and more relaxed options for non-hikers, including a lovely undeveloped **waterfall** at Fishdone, down towards the north coast, the **botanical gardens** at Cinchona and a chance to visit the estates producing some of the most expensive **coffee** on earth.

Bisected by the mountains, the island's two easternmost parishes are relatively unknown outside Jamaica. Spreading back from the coast south of the range, **St Thomas** is historically one of the country's

---

Accommodation price codes

All the hotels detailed in this guide have been graded according to the following price categories. Note that the prices have been calculated as those for the cheapest **double** or **twin room** during low season, normally mid-April to mid-December. During high season, rates are liable to rise by up to 25 percent (though this is rare at the cheap hotels), and proprietors may be less amenable to bargaining. Although the law requires prices to be quoted in Jamaican dollars, most hotels give rates in US dollars; payment can be made in either currency. For more details see p.27.

① under US$20   ④ US$51–70   ⑦ US$151–200

② US$21–35   ⑤ US$71–100   ⑧ US$200 and above

③ US$36–50   ⑥ US$101–150

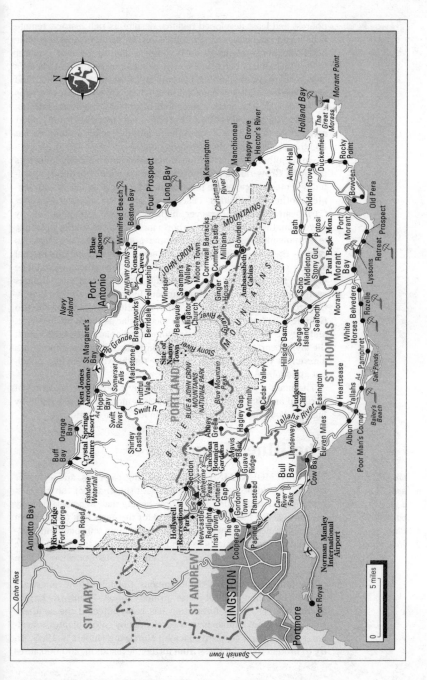

poorest and least developed regions, despite its rich history, remote beaches and stunning scenery; tourist development remains negligible here, but there's plenty to do if you're willing to get into explorer mode. A handful of hotels are slowly springing up on the south coast's best beaches, particularly at **Lyssons** and **Retreat**, where you'll find small swathes of deserted golden sand. These are good bases for trips to the delightful mineral springs and botanical gardens at **Bath**, an attraction for several centuries but neglected since Hurricane Gilbert ravaged the area in 1988, or to the deserted beaches around Morant Lighthouse, Jamaica's most easterly point.

On the other side of the Blue Mountains (here officially known as the **John Crow** range), the northeastern parish of **Portland** is justifiably touted as one of the most beautiful parts of Jamaica, with jungle-smothered hillsides cascading down to postcard-perfect Caribbean shoreline. However, high rainfall and a longish, bumpy drive from the island's main airports mean that the tourist presence is less conspicuous than in other main resorts. All the more reason to come – the wetter climate supports some truly stupendous natural scenery and, if you stay in the parish capital, **Port Antonio**, you'll be close to the lovely waterfalls of **Reach** and **Somerset** and fabulous swimming at the magical **Blue Lagoon**. Inland, you can hike in pristine tropical **rainforest** or take a more gentle rafting trip on the **Rio Grande**. The **beaches** are equally spectacular as those further west, and they're far less crowded with some lovely places to stay to boot: the idyllic, surf-pounded stretch at **Long Bay** is fast developing into a haven for younger visitors, who come for the waves and the chilled-out atmosphere.

The main **A4 highway** runs all the way around the coastline of Portland and St Thomas, and most points along it are reachable by bus, but you'll need a car to explore much of the interior.

The Blue Mountains

Rainfall averages 75 inches a year in some parts of the Blue Mountains.

The **BLUE MOUNTAINS** begin where Kingston ends, and a starker contrast would be hard to imagine, with the chaos of the city fast replaced by a tranquillity and a gentle beauty that, at its best, is truly staggering. The mountains are named for the mists that colour them from a distance, and their craggy slopes form an unbroken, undulating spine across Jamaica's easternmost parishes, a fabulously fertile tropical wilderness with a cool, wet climate found nowhere else in Jamaica.

The northern slopes of the mountains, the John Crow range, are covered by a huge quilt of dense, primary forest – easily the largest on the island – but deforestation has badly affected the southern side, where great chunks have been cleared by coffee planters, farmers, squatters and (catastrophically) Hurricane Gilbert in 1988. To try to protect the wilderness from further devastation, 200,000 acres

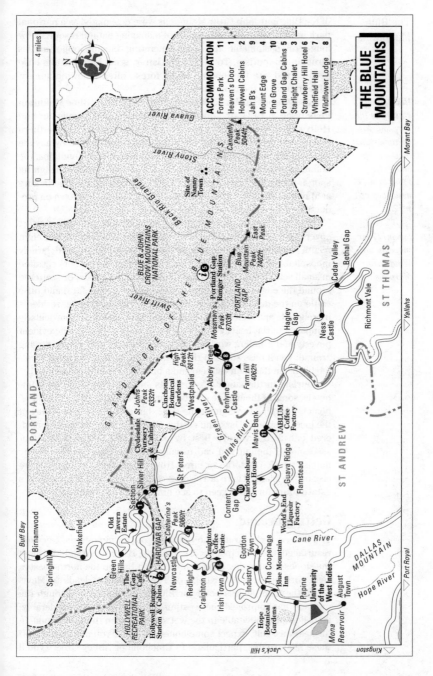

THE BLUE MOUNTAINS

ACCOMMODATION

Forres Park	11
Heaven's Door	1
Hollywell Cabins	2
Jah B's	9
Mount Edge	4
Pine Grove	10
Portland Gap Cabins	5
Starlight Chalet	3
Strawberry Hill Hotel	6
Whitfield Hall	7
Wildflower Lodge	8

Hiking and rafting in the gorgeous Rio Grande valley, on the north side of the mountains, is described on p.175.

See p.177 for more on the Windward Maroons.

of the Blue and John Crow Mountains were designated as a **national park** in 1993, with the stated aims of managing natural resources for long-term sustainable use and generating income opportunities through eco-tourism. To help in the latter, great **hiking trails** have been carved into the interior of the forest, often following ancient mule trails over the mountains.

Most visitors to the park come here to hike up **Blue Mountain Peak** (see p.142) or follow the well-maintained trails around **Hollywell** (see p.136); though exceptionally beautiful, the northern reaches are too remote and tough-going to be attempted by anyone except the most determined hikers. Elsewhere in the mountains, the botanical gardens at **Cinchona** (see p.138) are another delightful spot, a magical splash of colour 5000ft up, while the coffee factory at **Mavis Bank** (see p.138) is the place to go for the lowdown on production of the world's best coffee.

In population terms, though the dense forest provided perfect cover for the Windward Maroons during the seventeenth and eighteenth centuries, the mountains have historically proved largely inhospitable. Even today, the population remains low, concentrated in small settlements like **Gordon Town** and **Newcastle**, or scattered around the edges of the national park, where people farm and raise cattle on the denuded slopes. Many visitors find mountain residents more gentle and welcoming than Jamaicans elsewhere – particularly compared to the heavily touristed north coast – despite the evident poverty and grinding workload many of them face. If you're driving around, you'll pass some of the women who walk miles to pick coffee beans on the main estates, and a lift will be much appreciated.

Tourism in the mountains remains small-scale. There are a few hotels, some of them quite spectacular, and a couple of backpackers' hostels (detailed throughout the text), but **coffee** is the mainstay of the local economy. Dark and earthy, Blue Mountain coffee is considered one of the world's best by experts, and prices reflect that assessment, though you can usually find it cheaper here – at the hotels or coffee factories or direct from the farmers – than anywhere else on the island. There are also several moderately diverting **coffee estate tours** for those keen to see how the stuff is produced.

Getting around

You'll need a **car** to get the most out of the mountains. Recently resurfaced, the principal access road, the B1, cuts straight through the slopes, connecting Kingston with Buff Bay on the north coast; a right fork at the small village of **The Cooperage** leads to Mavis Bank, the main access point for Blue Mountain Peak. Though the upgrade has improved the weather-battered tarmac considerably, landslides are inevitable in the wet season, when the roads come in for heavy assault; expect some bone-rattling. If you plan to head off these main routes, particularly to Cinchona or Abbey Green, you'll need a four-wheel-drive, otherwise, a regular rental car should suffice. Whatever you drive, though, you'll need to be extra-attentive when behind the wheel here. Though the roads appear wide enough only for a single vehicle, snorting delivery trucks loaded with precariously balanced crates of Red Stripe frequently barrel up the slopes, sounding their presence with mighty blasts on the horn.

The mountain environment

The Blue Mountain range is Jamaica's oldest geographical feature, formed in the Cretaceous age (between 144 and 65 million years ago). Though the peaks are named for their cerulean tint when seen from afar, some of the rock actually is coloured blue by crossite minerals.

See p.382 of Contexts for more on Jamaica's environment.

Categorized as montane (the technical term for high-altitude woodland), the **forests** are mostly native cedar, soapwood, sweetwood and dogwood evergreens with a few blue mahoe, mahogany and teak, but the eucalyptus and Caribbean pines introduced in the 1950s are starting to dominate even in the primary forest above Hollywell. The primeval-looking cyathea (**tree fern**), with its diamond-patterned trunk and top heavy fronds is particularly distinctive; the tallest are over 150 years old. Below the dense canopy is a layer of **shrubs**, of which the red tubular flowers of the cigar bush are the most identifiable. Every tree trunk or exposed rock is festooned with brightly coloured epiphytic ferns, mosses and lichen; most common are the inexhaustible swathes of dirty lime-coloured old man's beard. Wild strawberries, raspberries, blackberries and rose apples provide a free feast at middle altitudes, and you'll doubtless encounter the prickly vines of climbing bamboo, the only variety native to Jamaica. The tiny white flowers appear only once every 33 years, when each and every one blossoms simultaneously – but as they last bloomed in 1984 your next chance to see them is 2017. The mountains support over five hundred species of **flowering plant**, including around 65 varieties of orchid. Begonias, blue iris, agapanthus, lobelias, busy lizzies and fuschias proliferate, while wild ginger lilies lend a delicate perfume to the fresh mountain air.

Other than mongooses, coneys and the wild pigs which roam the northern slopes, there are few **mammals** in the mountains. You may hear the scuffles of feral cats, mice and rats in the undergrowth, and Jamaican yellow boas inhabit the lower slopes in small numbers. The presence of bats is poorly documented; you're most likely to see them around the limestone slopes of the John Crow Mountains. By contrast, **birdlife** flourishes; the forests ring out with the evocative whistle of the rufous-throated solitaire, and mockingbirds, crested quail doves (known as mountain witches), white-eyed thrushes, blackbirds and Jamaican todys add to the cacophony, backed by the squeaking mating calls of tree frogs.

The mountains are the sole habitat of one of the rarest and largest **butterflies** in the world, the six-inch **Giant Swallowtail**, but its distinctively patterned dark brown and gold wings rarely flutter into view – again, the warmer John Crow range yields the most sightings. Insects, on the other hand, are multitudinous, particularly during the summer months when it's common to see thousands of **fireflies** (locally known as peenie-wallies) clustering on a single bush and lighting it up like a Christmas tree.

It's wise to turn off the radio here and listen out for oncoming traffic, and announce your presence with regular toots as well.

Public transport will only take you as far as the main settlements – from Papine in northeast Kingston, **buses** (roughly J$40) go to Newcastle via Irish Town (with the occasional minibus managing to get up as far as Hollywell), and to Mavis Bank via Gordon Town. Ask around in Papine square the day before you plan to travel, and avoid starting out on a Sunday. **Cycling** is an attractive option if you've got your own mountain bike (finding one to rent can be difficult). Several hotels run day-long biking expeditions, among them the *Mount Edge Guesthouse* (☎944 8151; US$60; see p.135), calling in at small coffee farms and private homes. Blue Mountain Tours (☎974 7075 or toll-free on 1-800 982 8238; US$85 including transfer, brunch, lunch and refreshments) picks you up from Port Antonio or Ocho Rios, drives you up into the mountains and lets you freewheel sixteen miles or so down to a waterfall near Buff Bay (see p.137).

Hiking

Extreme weather conditions, ecological protection projects and lack of funding mean that of the thirty recognized **trails** in the park, only twenty or so are open at any given time; any ranger station will provide a current update. If possible, avoid hiking in the rainy season (May–June & Sept–Oct), when you're almost guaranteed to get drenched.

All the usual common-sense guidelines apply to mountain hiking. Bring the standard equipment (see p.41), including **drinking water** – wild pine bromeliads hold over a pint of water between their leaves, but as they're home to insect nymphs and tree frogs, you'll only be tempted to sup in an emergency. Bins are rare, so carry a plastic bag to take every scrap of your rubbish home.

If you're heading into the mountains as a day-trip from Kingston, pick up simple picnic supplies and hot food in Bigga's Plaza, on Gordon Town Road just beyond Papine Square.

North to Newcastle

At Papine in northeast Kingston (see p.91), the city slams to an abrupt halt as it meets the southern edge of the Mona valley. From here Gordon Town Road (B1) winds slowly upward into the riverine hills; almost immediately, the contrast between the lush, seemingly impenetrable countryside that leaks onto the battered tarmac couldn't be more stark to the concrete maelstrom you've left behind. Passing the Hope River, its banks reinforced with high concrete walls that carry floodwater into the Mona Dam, the first place you reach is the tiny village of **THE COOPERAGE**, which is wrapped around a road junction and named for the Irish coopers who worked here in the early nineteenth century, making the wooden barrels in which Blue Mountain coffee was shipped abroad. The right fork leads toward Mavis Bank, and ultimately, Blue Mountain Peak (covered on pp.140–143), while the left fork leads up a winding road for three miles to **IRISH TOWN**, where the coopers lived. Just over 3000 feet

HIKING IN THE BLUE MOUNTAINS

PARK PRACTICALITIES

There's no charge to enter most parts of the Blue Mountains; however, since 1999, visitors pay US$5 to enter the managed Hollywell Recreation area, and an additional US$5 to walk its orderly, way-marked trails. Park information is available from each of the park's three **ranger stations**, located at **Hollywell**, **Portland Gap** and **Millbank**. Theoretically always open (though Hollywell is the liveliest and by far the most accessible), these can provide advice on weather conditions and trail access, and ordnance survey maps are on display for reference. None of the ranger stations has a phone, but you can make prior contact through the administrative **park office** at Guava Ridge (☎0997 8044 or 8069; Mon–Fri 10am–4pm):

GUIDES AND ORGANIZED GROUPS

No matter where you're walking in the Blue Mountains, it's almost always advisable to use a **guide**; given the changeable weather conditions and poor hiking maps (in a terrain with few obvious landmarks), it's very easy to get lost. Security can also be a problem for unaccompanied hikers, particularly on the Kingston side of the mountains. A guide will ensure your safety, clear overgrown paths and provide an informed commentary.

Climb Every Mountain, Mavis Bank (☎977 8541; ask for Ms Campbell). This rather disorganized but knowledgable local outfit offers a huge range of excursions with guides who've lived in the area all their lives; walks and scenic drives start at US$70, though rates are often negotiable.

Destinations, *Maya Mountain Lodge* (☎702 0314). Based at the lodge (see p.73), this outfit offers a variety of hikes, some starting right at its door, others on the Hollywell trails or to Cinchona or Blue Mountain Peak. Groups of five or more pay about US$60 per person per day for a guide, transport and lunch, or approximately US$30 for a guide alone; ask to walk with Willie.

Sun Venture, 30 Balmoral Ave, Kingston 10 (☎960 6685, fax 920 8348, *www.sunventuretours .com*). By far the best option for Blue Mountain hikes, including various day-long mountain walks (US$60–80), as well as the peak, with a night at *Wildflower Lodge* in Abbey Green (US$130). Other options include wilderness trails through the northern slopes and an ambitious three-day crossing of the entire Grand Ridge, a mighty range of peaks that forms a boundary between Portland and St Thomas. These prices are based on groups of two to four people and transport is included.

Just above Papine, Gordon Town Road passes the left-hand turnoff of Skyline Drive, the route to Jack's Hill and hiking base Maya Lodge (see p.73).

above sea level, today it's a small farming community, dominated by one magnificent **hotel**, *Strawberry Hill* (☎944 8400, fax 975 8408, *www.islandlife.com*; ⑧). The brainchild of Island Records magnate Chris Blackwell, this former plantation opened as a hotel in 1994 to a blaze of architectural awards, and is one of the most attractive places to stay in all Jamaica, with beautifully landscaped gardens

The Blue Mountains

(look out for the jade vine, with its unusual green flowers), a glorious decked pool affording panoramic views, and a state-of-the-art spa. *Strawberry Hill* has a strong rock and roll pedigree – the Rolling Stones and U2 are regular visitors, and Bob Marley was brought here to convalesce after being shot in 1976 – but the stunning setting is far more absorbing than the celebrity credentials. Perched on the hillsides and offering fabulous Kingston or mountain views, the twelve luxury cottages – from studios to two-bedroom villas with full kitchens – are all made from local materials and imaginatively designed with Jamaican heritage in mind. The cottages boast hand-carved fretwork, louvered windows, muslin-draped mahogany four-poster beds with heated mattresses (it gets cold at night) and antique furniture; some feature private jacuzzis.

The fabulous Strawberry Hill Sunday brunch, at US$45 per person, is an unmissable institution.

Even if you can't afford to stay here, eating at *Strawberry Hill* is a must. Set on the Great House terrace, the restaurant is the ultimate spot for a romantic dinner, and the eminently successful combination of fresh local ingredients and sophisticated international-style cooking, ranging from dasheen and sweet potato gnocchi, pasta with ackee or gorgeous salads to more conventional meals of jerk chicken roti or snapper in lemon sauce, is just sublime. If you're after a less formal meal in Irish Town, the *Roseberry Bar*, at the roadside just south of the village, cooks up a lovely janga or red peas soup and the usual Jamaican curry goat and brown stew chicken.

Victorian artist and traveller Marianne North painted a series of Blue Mountain scenes, now on display in London's Kew Gardens, when she stayed at Craighton Great House.

Beyond Irish Town, the B1 passes the near-vertical driveway for **Craighton Coffee Estate** (☎944 8224; Mon–Fri 8am–4pm; US$20; call ahead to ensure that a guide will be there to meet you), a Japanese-owned coffee plantation. Caffeine addicts will enjoy the enthusiastically presented (though heftily priced) hour-long tour, which reveals how the seedlings are nurtured into mature plants, and lets you taste the finished product in the small but charming eighteenth-century great house. The tour also includes a short uphill walk through coffee groves to a shady, thatched gazebo that provides a glorious panoramic view of Kingston and the mountains.

From Craighton, the road passes the ridiculously high boundary walls of a private house (known locally as the Great Wall of China) built by the owner to protect his property from landslides and subsidence, and continues through the tiny village of **REDLIGHT**, named for the former brothels that kept the Irish coopers entertained. There are a couple of basic bars here for a cold Red Stripe or warming white rum, and a couple of hole-in-the-wall stores where you can buy basic provisions. If you're staying in the mountains for a while, you may want to take advantage of the Hi-Way Laundry Centre here; call the owner, Birdman, on ☎944 8240. If you need a bed for the night, Birdman is also a good first point of call.

The **Gordon Town Trail** loops downhill from Redlight, passing through small coffee plantations and precipitous fields of broccoli and scallion, and offering lots of opportunities for river swimming, with plenty of mini-waterfalls and deepish pools; it's easy to follow once you get on to it – ask anyone in Redlight to direct you to the start, from where it'll take about two and a half hours to get to Gordon Town.

Four thousand feet up from Redlight is **NEWCASTLE**, an old British military base established by Major William Gomm in 1841 to escape the yellow fever raging on the hot, swampy plains below. The main road cuts across the **parade ground**, now a training ground for the Jamaica Defence Force, which still features old cannons and the insignia of the various regiments stationed here during the past century or so, while the nearby military graveyard remembers the dead of that period with its neat, white crosses. From the parade ground the views across the mountains and down to Kingston are dazzling and almost vertiginous, while behind you, immediately above Newcastle, **Catherine's Peak** (5060ft) – named after Lady Catherine Long, the first woman to climb it, in 1760 – marks the highest point in the parish of St Andrew. You can make the steep, misty hike to the pylon-topped summit of Catherine's Peak via a concrete road that branches off the B1 just north of Newcastle and winds its way up, affording excellent views of Kingston when the mist clears.

For **accommodation**, just below Newcastle and clinging to the side of the valley, *Mount Edge* (☎944 8151; ②–③) is a laid-back guesthouse-cum-restaurant run by wily local personality Michael Fox. The simple rooms inside the main house, and separate but small units just outside, are perfect for backpackers, while the bar is a great place to chill out. Meals (cooked to order; call ahead for dinner) are also available, ranging from crab in coconut milk to crayfish. Otherwise, you'll have to press on to the cabins at Hollywell (see p.136).

Hollywell Recreational Park

A couple of miles past Newcastle, the mountain pass 4000ft up at **Hardwar Gap** is named for a British army captain who supervised the construction of the road from here to Buff Bay. On the left is the atmospheric **Gap Café** (☎997 3032; Mon–Thurs 10am–5pm, Fri–Sun 10am–6pm), constructed in the 1930s and originally designed as a way-station for those traversing the mountains by horse and carriage. American or Continental breakfasts, and lunches or dinners of pizza, sandwiches, smoked marlin, escovitched fish, steaks or pasta are excellent here, costing J$300–500; the charming garden terrace or snug dining area are also perfect places to sink a cocktail or a beer. The owners also run regular "**Full Moon Frolics**", with music, drinks and food for about J$1500.

Just beyond the café is the entrance to the **Hollywell Recreational Park**, where you pay your US$5 entry fee (US$10 including guided walks of the trails within). Over 4000ft above sea level, the deliciously fresh, fragrant mountain air here is always cool, and

The Blue Mountains

If you're only planning to take one Blue Mountain coffee tour, the best ones are at JABLUM (see p.140) or Twyman's (see p.137).

Newcastle soldiers operate a small, sporadically opened tuckshop where you can buy beers and basic snacks.

The word "Gap", which features in placenames all over the mountains, refers to the valleys between the peaks.

Hollywell is often bathed in mist; when it clears, you get a spectacular unbroken view over the shimmering streets of Kingston, Port Royal and Portmore below. This 300-acre "park within a park" is the gateway to the mountains proper and had protected status before the rest of the area. Easily accessible from the city, it's the busiest part of the mountains, and is latticed with enjoyable, well-maintained hiking trails. Call at the ranger station – 100 yards beyond the *Gap Café* – if you plan to hike further afield than the basic trails in the immediate area, best of which is the gentle Oatley Mountain jaunt (see below). On the opposite ridge you'll find a picnic spot with tables, covered gazebos, water faucets and a toilet. Extensively replanted with Caribbean pines after Hurricane Gilbert, and a sanctuary for a wide variety of birds, the forest rising up sharply behind the ranger station is **Oatley Mountain** itself, while to the east is Mount Horeb and the ecologically sensitive (and so off-limits) Fairy Glades trail, where pines are outnumbered by the twisted trunks of soapwood and dogwood trees laden with clusters of orchids and wild pines.

The popularity of **trails** around Hollywell, detailed on boards dotted around the area, means that most are well maintained, but as rain can wreak havoc overnight, check in at the ranger station before you set off; you'll also need to be accompanied by a ranger for many of them. The best Hollywell hike is the **Oatley Mountain trail** (2 miles; 40min) an easy, varied circular hike through the tunnel-like jungle. There are a couple of lookout towers and viewing platforms from which to enjoy the views, and several information boards explaining the flora and fauna found in the area. You can continue on to the **Waterfall trail** (1.5 miles; 1hr 30min) – a mildly testing scramble along a river bed to the Cascade Waterfall; however, landslides have reduced the icy waters and swimming hole to a trickle.

If you want to **stay**, there are three cabins (③), which you'll need to book well in advance through the Jamaica Conservation and Development Trust, 95 Dumbarton Ave, Kingston 10 (☎960 2848 or 2849, fax 960 2850, *jcdt@kasnet.com*). These sleep four to six people, and the basic facilities – foam-mattressed beds without bedding, indoor cooking range, fridge and cold shower – take second place to the marvellous setting, a Kingston view from your balcony, complete seclusion and plenty of pure mountain air. You can also camp for US$5 per person. At weekends, you can buy fresh produce and a few basic food items from stalls set up as the "Hollywell Market Place". Otherwise, you'll need to bring all supplies with you.

Section and around

Three miles past the Hollywell ranger station, **SECTION**, a friendly little setttlement straggled around the road, is home to several small-scale coffee farmers, and is a great place to both enquire about a local hiking guide and buy some coffee (a pound of beans should cost about JS$250). The small shop can supply you with beers and snacks, and coffee farmer James Dennis offers cheap and very basic **accommodation** (②) in his anomalously large concrete house right on the road; ask anyone to direct you.

At Section, the road forks; turning left carries you toward the coast at Buff Bay (see below), while turning right and to the east takes you toward **Silver Hill**. There are a couple of **accommodation** options here, both offering complete seclusion. Perfect for those with an alternative bent, *Heaven's Door* (contact via Sun Venture Tours on ☎960 6685, fax 920 8348, *sunventure@hotmail.com*; ③) is an expansive open-sided wooden private home and a great, atmospheric base; rates include a lovely, healthy breakfast. Past here, the road negotiates switchback turns before passing the signposted entrance to the more organized *Starlight Chalets* (☎ & fax 969 3116 or 985 9380, fax 906 3075, *www.jamaicamarketplace.com/starlight*; ③), an isolated and extremely appealing hotel on a gorgeous flower-filled bluff overlooking Silver Hill Gap. The carpeted rooms are modern and comfortable, with balconies and private hot-water bathrooms. You also enjoy access to a shared TV lounge as well as a sauna and small gym. You can use the kitchen, but after a day of mountain air, you'll probably prefer to eat the good, inexpensive Jamaican meals served up in the **restaurant**. This, and the attached bar, are also open to non-guests; call ahead if you plan to eat. There are a couple of bicycles available for guests to use, and several short trails surround the property, one leading down the valley to a swimmable river; guides are available.

Past Starlight Chalets, *the road winds a torturous but wonderfully scenic route toward Clydesdale and Cinchona Botanical Gardens (see p.138).*

Back at Section, the B1 begins its attractive seventeen-mile descent to Buff Bay on the north coast (see p.181), with fantastic clear views over the mountain gaps planted with neat rows of coffee. Most of them are part of the 120-acre **Old Tavern Coffee Estate** (☎1-999 7070 or 924 2785), run by Alex and Dorothy Twyman from their cottage, just below the road a couple of miles past Section. Due to archaic laws that insist all coffee beans grown in the Blue Mountains be processed at the JABLUM factory in Mavis Bank (see p.140), the Twymans were forced to fight long and hard for the right to process their own crop. In 1997, they became the only growers in the country to be awarded a licence to self-process, and the result is unquestionably the best Blue Mountain coffee you'll find anywhere in Jamaica, roasted to perfection right here. If you call ahead, you should be able to arrange to tour the farm, and learn a little of the incredibly tricky progression from plant to bean to pot. The estate is also laced with hugely enjoyable trails, and there's an appealing waterfall for swimming; you're welcome to walk them by prior arrangement.

You can buy any of the Old Tavern blends directly from the source at a far lower price than in the resorts. You can also have it Fed-Exed right to you door; call the numbers above or visit www .exportjamaica .org/oldtavern.

Beyond Old Tavern, the B1 continues to snake through lushly vegetated hillsides and groves of coffee and starts its descent proper. Other than the odd rum shop or farmers' cottage tucked into the jungle, there's little of specific interest to see, but the one essential stop

is for a dip at **Fishdone waterfall**, about nine miles before Buff Bay
– turn left just before the white Silver Hill bridge at a sign for the
Avocat Primary School. The fat, gushing cascade offers opportunities for a natural power shower, and the wide, clear pool of cool
water is a fabulous place for a secluded swim.

Gordon Town and around

Back at the Kingston foothills of the Blue Mountains, the right fork
off the B1 at The Cooperage heads past the tiny riverside village of
Industry, where the Gordon Town river provides lots of swimming
spots, to undistinguished **GORDON TOWN** itself, the only sizeable
settlement in the Blue Mountains, built around a neat central square
with a couple of small snack bars and the usual giggling gaggles of
smartly turned-out schoolchildren. Crossing the bridge here and
heading three miles east brings you past the colourful mural-painted
walls of what was once the **Sangster's World's End liqueur factory**
(☎926 8888), the production centre for one of Jamaica's smallest
rum-makers until it went into receivership in 1999. Tours are on hold
until the company's future is decided, but you may still be able to
poke around.

Flamstead and Cinchona Botanical Gardens

Heading east from World's End, the road splits at the hilltop junction
of Guava Ridge, left takes you toward Section, while two consecutive
right turns will take you past **Nyumbani** – the late Michael Manley's
mountain home and coffee estate – to the **Flamstead plantation** (call
ahead to arrange a tour on ☎960 0204; US$50), once the site of a
magnificent great house that was home to Governor Edward Eyre
(see box on p.148), British Admiral Horatio Nelson and subsequent
naval captains, but has since been turned to rubble by a series of hurricanes. Today, the tourable plantation grows Blue Mountain coffee,
and in an area where every turn you make offers jaw-dropping vistas,
the panoramic view over Port Royal and the Caribbean Sea is unsur-
passable.

The northern fork of Guava Ridge takes you into the heart of coffee country. At the tiny hamlet of **CONTENT GAP**, you can stay in
the plain but clean rooms or studios with kitchenette at *Pine Grove*
(☎977 8001, fax 977 8477, *pinegrove@hotmail.com*; ④), set in
peaceful gardens that look down over the mountains and over to the
peak itself. You can take a good, inexpensive Jamaican meal (call
ahead) or sup a drink on the delightful garden terrace, listening to
the wind whistle through Caribbean pines.

Two miles further north of here, tucked into a remote pocket of
the mountains and accessible only by foot or four-wheel-drive, is
Clydesdale, an old coffee plantation converted into a nursery in
1937 by the Forestry Department. It's the only commercial tree

plantation remaining in the mountains, with row upon row of
Caribbean pines neatly arranged up the hillsides, networked by several paths that make for a pleasantly shady walk. It's usually completely deserted so you'll need to bring a guide. Just before the road
swings to the right toward Cinchona, you'll see a charming white-
painted house by the riverbank, originally built to process coffee
beans; it's an idyllic spot to stop and swim.

From here, you can drive within a mile of **Cinchona Botanical
Gardens** (no set hours; free), bearing left up the steep path that
snakes through the precipitous vegetable patches and coffee groves
that cover Top Mountain – the road is abysmal, however, and you'll
need a 4WD and a guide (see box on p.133). The gardens are at the
summit, and their orderliness is a surprise after the rugged and wild
hillsides below. Clinging to the ridge opposite Blue Mountain Peak
and overlooking the Yallahs River valley, the ten-acre maintained
gardens were initially a commercial venture, planted with Assam tea
and cinchona trees – which produce quinine, used as an anti-malari-
al before the advent of modern drugs – in 1886. However, the inac-
cessibility of the site and competition from Indian plantations led to

---

Blue Mountain coffee

The story of **Blue Mountain coffee**, rated as one of the world's finest, is a
long and turbulent one. Coffee trees were introduced to Jamaica from
Ethiopia in 1728 by Governor Sir Nicholas Lawes, and found to flourish on
the cool slopes of the Blue Mountains. Cultivation of the crop reached new
heights of excellence in 1801 when expert coffee growers flooded into
Jamaica from revolution-torn Haiti. At the same time, the craze for coffee
houses in Europe fuelled a massive demand for the beans and, during the
first half of the nineteenth century, Jamaica was among the world's main
exporters, producing up to fifteen thousand tons of beans per year.

The industry suffered its first crushing blow with emancipation in 1838,
as streams of former slaves left the plantations to set up their own small
farms. Soon afterwards, Britain abolished preferential trade terms for its
colonies; under free trade, direct competition from the excellent coffees of
South America crippled the small Jamaican farmers. The industry's decline
continued into this century, with periodic hurricanes wiping out entire
plantations.

After World War II, the government took belated steps to save the Blue
Mountains plantations. It established quality guidelines for both cultivation and processing, stipulating that only coffee grown at a certain altitude
could claim the Blue Mountain name (you'll see other Jamaican coffee
around the island called High Mountain or Low Land). This exclusivity
heightened the coffee's cachet, and helped to underpin its reputation
worldwide. The biggest boost for the industry came during the 1980s as
Japanese companies, with a big domestic market for Blue Mountain coffee, invested huge amounts in the best of the plantations. More than nine-
ty percent of the stuff is now sold to Japan, reducing the amount available
for export elsewhere and contributing to the extremely high price that
you'll pay for it in Europe and North America.

---

the project's decline and it became a government-run public garden in 1968; it's still an important centre for botanical research.

The cinchona trees have all died out now, battered by the hurricanes, but the gardens are magical nonetheless. Several varieties of eucalyptus whistle in the breeze, and Norfolk Island pine, Japanese cedar, weeping cypress, rubber and camphor trees flourish in the mist. The vivid walled flower beds are bursting with blooms, and wild coffee smothers the slopes. You can see it all on the **Panorama Walk**, preferably accompanied by one of the gardeners (leave a tip), which takes you through a tunnel-like thicket of Holland bamboo, past a broken-down old caretaker's house and back to the main house, an ancient oblong of stone that still contains most of its original fittings. There are several other trails to enjoy around Cinchona; the garden supervisor will rustle up a guide for a nominal fee. Of the most rewarding paths are the sticky six-mile hike down to Mavis Bank (see below), and the historic, ten-mile **Vinegar Hill** trail to Buff Bay, an old trading route that the British used to transport supplies from Kingston to the north coast.

If you want to **stay** in Cinchona, US$5 will buy you floor space in the house, but you'll need to bring food and bedding with you; you can also camp in the grounds.

Mavis Bank, Abbey Green and Blue Mountain Peak

Heading east from Guava Ridge, the next settlement along is **MAVIS BANK**, nestled in the Yallahs River valley. Accessible by bus from Papine, neatly arranged Mavis Bank is the last full-scale village on the route to Blue Mountain Peak. If you're driving, this is the place to park – in the lay-by opposite the police station – as only the sturdiest Land Rover can tackle the terrain beyond. There's little to the village itself: the town's single street consists of a police station, a shop selling basic foods, a church and a smattering of homes. The main organized attraction is the government-owned **JABLUM coffee factory** (tours by appointment on ☎977 8015; Mon–Fri 9.30–11.30am & 12.30–3.30pm; US$8) on the west side of the village. In business for around 100 years and handling some 70,000 bushels of coffee per year, the factory is Jamaica's main Blue Mountain coffee processing plant. Beginning with the obligatory infusion of steaming caffeine, the tour takes you through the entire process "from the berry to the cup". It's an engaging journey, particularly as the place is very much a working factory, and well worth an hour or so of your time. At the end, you can buy bags of beans far cheaper than in the shops.

Coffee aside, though, the main motivation for visiting Mavis Bank is undoubtedly hiking; with the peak temptingly close and legions of fabulous walks nearby, you'd be crazy not to test out some of the trails. A fairly new option for **guided hikes**, chaotic but enthusiastic Climb Every Mountain are a locally-run outfit operating from a tiny office on the main street (ask for Ms Campbell on ☎977 8541). They can arrange all manner of Blue Mountain walks with one of seven knowledgeable guides (all living in Mavis Bank) for around US$70 per person; offerings include the Peak and Governor's Bench near Flamstead. They also operate scenic driving tours; you should also be able to arrange 4WD transport to Abbey Green if you're intending to climb the peak. As Climb Every Mountain is operated by Seventh Day Adventists, bear in mind that there are no trips on Fridays and Saturdays.

If you want to linger in Mavis Bank, the best place to **stay** is *Forres Park* (☎927 8275 or 5957, fax 978 6942, *www.forrespark.com*; ③–④), a delightful collection of self-contained wood cabins set around a large house which holds simple, comfortable rooms with private bathroom. **Meals** are available on request (non-guests are also welcome), as are walks in the surrounding countryside and longer hikes such as Blue Mountain Peak and Cinchona Botanical Gardens. Though it was closed at the time of writing, the *Blue Mountain Taverna* is another comfortable accommodation option, set in a neat white house in the middle of the village; call ahead to see if it has reopened (☎967 2641).

Abbey Green

You can start the hike up to Blue Mountain Peak from Mavis Bank, along the steep and strenuous Farm Hill Trail from the church, but most people prefer to begin from **ABBEY GREEN**, just over five miles northeast. At some 4500 feet above sea level it's a completely different world, where wind whistles through eucalyptus trees and seemingly impenetrable mists billow over the mountainside only to evaporate after a few rays of sun. It's a magical, intensely beautiful place, and you're unlikely to meet anyone save the odd coffee-grower or scallion farmer. Two rustic **hostels** here (call ahead; see below) act as bases for peak hikers, and offer Land Rover pick-up from Mavis Bank for US$20–30 per carload. On the way up, you'll turn left through **HAGLEY GAP** – a steeply inclining one-street village where you can buy last-ditch provisions and get a hot meal from a couple of small-scale cookshops – after which you'll traverse one of the least road-like roads in Jamaica, with huge gullies carved through the clay by coursing water and a constant scree of small boulders in your path.

Both the Abbey Green hostels provide guides for the peak hike for around US$25.

Of Abbey Green's hostels, *Whitfield Hall* (☎926 6612 or 927 0986; ①–④) is the most atmospheric, set in an old stone planters' house, with a huge grand piano, a log fire, and geese in the yard. The low ceilings and pre-war kitchen add to the archaic feel, but it's all a bit run-down these days. You sleep in bunks or in a self-contained cottage, and you should be able to arrange to camp for a nominal fee. A few hundred yards down the road is the more comfortable *Wildflower Lodge* (☎929 5394; ①–④), a modern two-storey house set in gorgeous flowered gardens. Bedding choices are similar,

Whitfield Hall sells its own canned peaches for J$60

though there are private double rooms as well as bunkbeds and a self-contained cottage; there's also a gift shop, cavernous kitchen and dining room. Whichever lodge you choose, it's a good idea to arrange to have a **hot meal** prepared ready for your return; you'll need it. Another option, on the hillside just below *Wildflower*, is the simple, friendly guesthouse run by local Rasta Jah B (c/o ☎977 8161), where bunkbeds cost US$12 and meals are available.

Blue Mountain Peak

Undeniably the most rewarding hike in all of Jamaica, **Blue Mountain Peak** (7402ft), the highest point on the island, seems daunting but isn't the fearful climb you might imagine – though it's hardly a casual stroll, either. It is magnificent by day, when you can marvel at the opulence of the canopy, the thousands of orchids, mosses, bromeliads and lichens, the mighty shadows cast by the Peak, and the coils of smoke from invisible dwellings below; and thrilling by night, when after a magical moonlit ascent, Kingston's lights occasionally twinkling in the distance, you find yourself at Jamaica's zenith as a new day dawns – a completely heart-stopping experience.

From Abbey Green, the climb to the peak is around eight miles, and can take anything from three to six hours depending on your fitness level. If you're staying at one of the hostels, you can start at around 1am and catch sunrise at the Peak (at around 5.15 to 6.15am, depending on the time of year); if you synchronize your walk with a full moon, you'll get beautiful natural floodlighting, if not take a flashlight. Regular signposts make the route easy to follow without the aid of a guide, but in this remote area it's sensible to go with someone who knows their way. Don't stray onto any of the tempting "short cuts" – it's illegal, you'll damage the sensitive environment, and you'll almost certainly get hopelessly lost. Rescue patrols can take days to find you, by which time you'll be in serious trouble.

The first stretch of the trail, aptly named **Jacob's Ladder**, is said to be the most arduous (though you might disagree after a few hours more of tramping without a peak in sight) – a steep series of switch-back turns through thick forest. The halfway point – around 4.5 miles, or two hours' walking – is **Portland Gap Ranger Station**, where you can rest at the gazebo, fill up water bottles and let the rangers know that you're walking the trail (leave a note if you arrive in the early hours). A coffee shop is planned, but for now there's just a tuck shop, some pit toilets, a water pipe, a barbecue and two very basic cabins (①) where you can rent a bunk or some floor space – bring your own bedding and cooking utensils. Tent sites cost J$80. The cabins must be booked in advance via the Jamaica Conservation and Development Trust on ☎960 2848.

Once past Portland Gap, it's another three and a half miles to the peak through twisted montane and eventually low-lying elfin forest, in which the gnarled soapwood and dogwood evergreens are so stunted by low temperatures, exposure and lack of nutrients that they grow no higher than eight feet. You're still only about 6000ft up, but you might already be feeling dizzy or faint from the rising altitude; if so, take it slowly and eat a high energy snack. At around 7000ft, the plateau at **Lazy Man's Peak** is where many hikers call it a day, but it's worth struggling on for another twenty minutes, as a far more spectacular panorama awaits you at the peak.

If you've arrived before dawn, you'll be completely bowled over. The inky black slowly melts into ever-intensifying pinks, oranges and purples until finally a hint of wispy blue heralds the sun and reveals ranges unravelling like a sea of crumpled corrugated cardboard. It's quite possible you'll be here alone, the highest person in Jamaica and feeling –literally – on top of the world. As the sun burns off the mist, the panorama becomes recognizable; you can make out Cinchona and, on a good day, Buff Bay and Port Antonio's Navy Island to the north and Kingston, Portmore and coastal St Thomas to the south – and if visibility is especially good, you may even catch a glimpse of Cuba, seventy miles away to the north. You get a heady perspective of the ranges you've crossed to get here, although a rather depressing view unfolds of the deforestation towards Kingston.

This is the furthest you can go into the Blue Mountains, as thick forest and treacherous, unexplored terrain means that even the burly pig hunters seldom venture further east, preferring to enter the John Crows from Millbank in Portland (see p.178).

St Thomas

ST THOMAS, nestling below the Blue Mountains is probably the most neglected of Jamaica's parishes. Historically volatile, it has traditionally suffered from lack of government support; as a result, most of the villages you'll pass through are pretty impoverished, and tourist facilities remain meagre throughout. For some, however, this is the area's draw: a slice of the "real" Jamaica, untouched by the demands of tourism and boasting plenty of historical intrigue as well as some fabulous little-visited beauty spots. Largely because of the presence of the descendants of free Africans, brought to the island after the abolition of slavery, St Thomas is also the cradle of Jamaica's African-based religions (see Contexts, p.392). Traditions from the mother country are more a part of daily life here than anywhere else in the island; it's not uncommon to see a Kumina session taking place right by the roadside. The region is also a favourite retreat for Kingstonians, who head for the beaches at weekends and stage large-scale sound system parties and stageshows during holiday periods. Though the St Thomas coastline is served by buses barrelling between Kingston and Port Antonio, it's difficult to reach the more remote attractions without a car, but if you have your own transport or hire a driver for the day, it's well worth the effort.

The coastline between Kingston and **Morant Bay**, the parish capital, is mostly scrubby and less attractive than the north coast, despite the backdrop of the Blue Mountains, and there is little to Morant Bay itself. East of here, though, the scenery improves, becoming quite spectacular in places, while inland, sweeping vales and lush pastures are as pretty as any in Jamaica. **Lyssons** and **Retreat** are a couple of good beaches and the rambling old spa town of **Bath**, up in the foothills of the mountains and close to the historic village of **Stony Gut** – birthplace of National Hero Paul Bogle – merits a visit in its own right. The romantically inclined can make for the deserted **Morant Point**, where a candy-striped lighthouse overlooks a stunning beach that marks Jamaica's most easterly point.

East of Kingston

Heading east from Kingston, past the Palisadoes turnoff to Port Royal (see Chapter one), the A4 hugs the coastline, sweeping past the unappealing, litter-strewn Cable Hut beach, used more for sound system parties than for swimming. Beyond the beach, the road barrels past the tiny settlements of **Bull Bay** and **Cow Bay** – named for the manatees that were caught and slaughtered here in the seventeenth and eighteenth centuries, but these days more notable for the red-gold-and-green-painted buildings of the Bobo Shanti Rastafarian camp in the hills above Bull Bay, populated by orthodox followers of the late Prince Emmanuel Charles Edward. Unless you're serious about learning something of Bobo Shanti ways, and are willing to dress appropriately modestly, it's not really a place to visit, particularly without someone to introduce you. In the hills behind the commune the **Cane River Falls** offers fresh-water swimming, although it's little-visited by tourists, and you're best off going in local company. To reach the falls turn off the A4 just before Bull Bay (it's marked by a BITU sign and the *Nature's Law* restaurant) and follow the marl-covered road for a mile or so, just before a small Bailey Bridge, a path leads down to the thin-but-strong cascade said to have been Bob Marley's favourite place to wash his locks.

Back on the A4, the village of **ELEVEN MILES** holds a roadside marker that recalls **Jack Mansong**, a nineteenth-century Jamaican Robin Hood figure (see box opposite). North off the main highway here (turn inland at the Eleven Miles community noticeboard), a road leads up into the scrubby, forested hills – look out for good Blue Mountain views around the sixteen-mile marker – towards the tiny village of **Llandewey**; turn right here, at Bethlehem Church, and you can take in the thousand-foot wall of **Judgement Cliff**. It was created by a massive landslide in 1692, caused by the same earthquake that flattened Port Royal a few miles west (see p.105). Local legend claims that its fall buried a particularly cruel and rapacious local planter and his estate – hence the name. As the cliff is smothered in vegetation these days, it's not exactly a startling sight. Heading back down towards the coast the road runs parallel to the **Yallahs River**, one of Jamaica's longest waterways, now partially diverted to provide the capital with water, and passes the still-sturdy stone buttresses of Easington Bridge, which looks unfeasibly large in the dry season, when the river slows to a trickle. Just past the buttresses, you can either continue on to rejoin the coast at **Albion**, or cross the new bridge and head towards the sea via **Heartsease**. A string of rum bars and jerk vendors stand sentry at Heartsease, as if in wait for the regular spells of activity when the Yallahs River turns into a raging torrent during the rainy months, often flooding the A4 and forcing coastal traffic on an inland detour despite the new fording at Poor Man's Corner.

Back on the highway, the arid landscape is broken at **Poor Man's Corner**, the wide, boulder-strewn mouth of the Yallahs River, where a large new fording has been built in an attempt to keep the road passable when the river floods. Yet more rum bars herald your entrance into busy little **YALLAHS**, best known for its **twin giant salt ponds**, divided from the sea by a narrow spit of land and said to

As well as its jerk stands, Yallahs offers simple Jamaican meals at the A&I restaurant.

Three Finger Jack

Named Three Finger Jack for his battlescars, Jack Mansong was a runaway slave turned bandit, the scourge of British soldiers and travellers but, in the best tradition of the romantic nineteenth-century highwayman, unfailingly courteous to women and children. A formidable figure of nearly seven feet tall, Mansong's criminal activities began with the bungled attempted murder of one Captain Henry Harrop, the slave trader who'd transported Mansong's parents from Africa to Jamaica. Harming a white planter ensured a particularly grisly death sentence, but the night before his execution, Mansong escaped from his cell, capturing Harrop and carrying him to a cave deep in the St Thomas interior where, with delicious irony, he forced his former master to become his slave, eventually leaving him shackled to the cave wall where his remains were found years later. Using various hideouts – including caves near the Cane River Falls – Mansong then embarked on a reign of terror, gaining an almost mythical reputation in the process. By 1870, the House of Assembly had offered a reward of £100 and freedom to any slave who could capture him; a year later, with Jack still at large, the reward had been raised to £300 – a massive sum at the time. Fuelled by the promise of such riches, Quashie, the Maroon who had relieved Mansong of his fingers, managed to track him to his hideout. After a bloody battle, Mansong was shot in the stomach. Cutting off his head and hands and preserving them in a bucket of rum, Quashie proceeded to Spanish Town to claim his reward – reputedly, he was still receiving a generous pension from the state some sixty years later. Back in England, Three Finger Jack's legend was equally persistent – contemporaneous fascination with a man seen as a romantic hero inspired several plays and a West End musical.

have been created by the tears of an English estate owner, distraught when his brother married the woman he loved. Up to eight times saltier than the ocean, the larger of the two ponds (and the second one you pass if driving east) has the highest saline levels; however, though it's a source of rock salt, it's not suitable to be made into table salt, as demonstrated by the scummy foam that laps the banks. Bacteria occasionally go on the rampage, turning the ponds a reddish colour, and scientists reckon that some of the micro-organisms are actually archeo-bacteria, among the earliest of the earth's life forms. A UWI research team, based at the lagoon edge, are currently studying the ponds, concentrating on artemia, a shrimp-like creature that's one of the few animals able to survive in such harsh surroundings.

The Fish Castle *restaurant, on some appealing coastline at Botany Bay, east of Phamphret, is a worthy place for a seafood meal.*

Continuing east of Yallahs, the A4 slips into the village of **WHITE HORSES**, named for its white limestone cliffs (though some say the moniker stems from the white-tipped waves of the choppy waters hereabouts). It's a relaxed, easy-going place to break your journey, with fruit sellers constantly present, and an opportunity to swim at **Rozelle Beach**, a pebbly, brown-sand strip paralleled by the tarmac that gets busy at weekends, when Kingstonians pile in for a day on the beach, queuing up to shower under the mini-waterfall that gushes from the rocks on the inland side of the road. **Food** is available from a couple of beach shacks, and fried fish stands set up at weekends – if only for the name (though the food is fine), check out the *HotTaurant* restaurant in White Horses.

Just beyond the beach, you'll pass the fertile **Rozelle** and **Belvedere** districts. The family of Captain Dow Baker (see box on p.155) once owned much of this land; today, it's still made up of large sugar cane, coconut and papaya plantations.

Morant Bay

Paul Bogle Day is celebrated yearly in Morant Bay on October 11, with a road race starting from his home village of Stony Gut, six miles away, and a big party in the town square.

Some two miles east of Rozelle, the lengthy span of the Bustamante Bridge over the Morant River takes you into the dusty town of **MORANT BAY**. Parish capital of St Thomas, Morant Bay is best known for having witnessed some of the ugliest moments in Jamaica's post-emancipation history. Edna Manley's grim-faced, life-size (but not that life-like) statue of National Hero **Paul Bogle** stands in front of the courthouse in the town square, where he was hanged after leading the 1865 **Morant Bay Rebellion** (see box on p.148); a plaque honours the "patriots" who died alongside him. With a wide, double-spiral stone stairway leading up to a columned portico, the courthouse you see today was built as a replacement after the original building was razed in the rebellion. Bogle is buried behind it, alongside those who were tipped into a mass grave here after the uprising, and who were only afforded a proper burial when their remains were dug up by chance in 1965. Today, a memorial erected, "in gratitude from the generation who now realize that they did not die in vain," marks the spot, poignantly dedicated to those "who fell because they loved freedom." Nearby are three of the original nine 24-pound cannons that were installed here when the site housed a **British fort**.

There's not much else to the town, though walk west across the square from the courthouse, past the attractive red-brick **Anglican church**, built in 1865, and you're on Morant Bay's main street, home to the crowded **market** (Thursday to Saturday), bursting out of its long-standing home and a good place to pick up fresh fruit and vegetables.

The coastal road runs below Morant Bay's main street; to get to the square, turn uphill at the businesslike *Morant Villas Hotel* (☎982 2418 or 2637; ③–⑤) and the road leads up to South Street, where you can park by the courthouse. The **hotel** itself is fine, with a restaurant, bar and pool, and adequate, clean rooms and suites with fan, a/c and some with kitchenette, though there's not much reason to base yourself here when you can stay alongside the beaches further east. If you've business to do, though, you'll find a small **shopping mall** on the main street opposite the courthouse, with a branch of FX Trader for **currency exchange** and a supermarket. **Buses** and shared **taxis** en route to all parts of the island pull up on the main street or at the car park next to the petrol station on the coast road.

Hillside Dam and Stony Gut

From the roundabout at the western outskirts of Morant Bay, a pock-marked road winds inland through luxuriant cattle pastures to a couple of little-visited attractions. Just past the Paul Bogle Junior High School are the tattered fronds of what was the Morant Banana Farms plantation, closed during the restructuring of the Jamaican banana industry following the WTO ruling against preferential prices paid by EU countries for Caribbean bananas. Another minor road forks off to the right here, leading toward Bogle's birthplace, **Stony Gut**; carrying straight on takes you into residential **Seaforth**, where the roadside is sprinkled with small-scale shops, bars and restaurants. From here, bear left and cross a bridge over the Morant River toward the pastoral surrounds of **Serge Island**, a dairy farm based on the site of an old sugar plantation, where the Blue Mountain views are fabulous and the fields of fat Jamaica Hope and Jersey cattle munch idly. A rough track to the right of the factory gates (in rainy season, you'll need to walk it unless you have a 4WD) leads towards the Johnson River, where the shallow but fast-flowing waters meander along the centre of an improbably wide, boulder-strewn riverbed, with the foothills of the Blue Mountains shelving off behind. Proceed left along the riverbank and you'll reach **Hillside Dam** after a few minutes' walk. Once a hydroelectric plant (closed after floods swept away most of the machinery), the water cascades over the dam's concrete lip these days, creating a deep swimming pool at its base. You

St Thomas

Places to eat around Morant Bay are listed on p.150

The Morant Bay Rebellion

A generation after emancipation, living conditions for Jamaica's black population remained abysmal. High unemployment and heavy taxation hit the poor hard, and the transition to a free society was hindered by the bias of the authorities. Courts invariably supported white landholders in cases for trespass or squatting against the small farmers, who struggled to find decent land to cultivate, and there were frequent dissenting outbreaks across the island. Some of these were over rumours of re-enslavement, others were protests at taxes, food shortages or lack of access to property, and it was only a matter of time before black Jamaicans registered their grievances with a more organized, premeditated uprising.

In St Thomas, Baptist Deacon **Paul Bogle** – supported by **George William Gordon**, a wealthy mulatto member of the National Assembly whom Bogle had campaigned for (and who owed his seat to the support of Bogle's Native Baptists in St Thomas) – began to organize demonstrations against the inequity of the legal system. In August 1865, he led a group that marched 54 miles from St Thomas to Spanish Town to protest to the island's governor, Edward Eyre – Eyre refused to meet them. After being turned away, the group returned to St Thomas, and made plans to create a "state within a state" at **Stony Gut**, Bogle's home village and the site of his church, with Bogle himself as priest, judge and chief. Getting wind of what they saw as seditious plans, the police had two of Bogle's supporters, Alexander White and Lewis Miller, arrested on trumped-up charges of assault and trespass. On October 7, Bogle and his men marched military-style to the Morant Bay courthouse where White and Miller were being tried, in an attempt to disrupt the proceedings against them (though only by surrounding the building). Despite the peaceful nature of the protest, the authorities saw their chance to arrest a "troublemaker" and issued warrants for Bogle's arrest. The police who tried to capture him were thwarted by the sheer power of numbers, and forced to swear oaths that they would no longer serve public officials before they could escape.

On October 10, six policemen and two constables set out for Stony Gut in a bid to arrest Bogle and 28 of his followers; however, they underestimated

The Morant Bay library on the town's main street (Mon–Fri 9am–6pm, Sat 9am–1pm) holds lots of tattered but interesting material on Paul Bogle and his rebellion.

can climb the huge rocks at the side to get to the top of the dam. It's a fabulously secluded place to spend a day, and you're unlikely to meet another soul – for that reason, you're probably best-off going in a group.

Stony Gut and the Paul Bogle Monument

Back on the inland road from the Morant Bay roundabout, the first right fork, at the hamlet of Morant, heads up into the hills towards **STONY GUT**, a half-hour drive from the coast and the former home of **Paul Bogle**, National Hero and leader of the Morant Bay Rebellion (see box). Though Stony Gut looks no different to the other communities you've passed through on the way up, with neat houses and flower-filled gardens lining the roadside, chickens pecking around on tarmac and curious eyes following any vehicle that makes it up this far, the village is central to the history of St Thomas and of his support, and were quickly overpowered and forced to swear allegiance to Bogle. Once back in Morant Bay, the officers impressed the seriousness of the situation to the then-Custos Baron Von Ketelhadt, who promptly contacted his Kingston superiors for support; accordingly, one hundred soldiers set sail aboard the *HMS Wolverine*. On October 11, Bogle and his men again marched into Morant Bay from Stony Gut, raiding the police station for arms before attacking the courthouse where the local council was meeting. Eighteen soldiers and council members were killed as the crowd's frustration erupted; the courthouse was burned to the ground, and arms, gunpowder and foodstuffs were taken from the town's shops. The unrest quickly spread throughout St Thomas, but the government troops aboard the *Wolverine* were too late to quell the disturbance in Morant Bay when they put to shore on the morning of October 12. Fearing that the whole country would soon be engulfed, the authorities gave free rein to the army, and the protesters were crushed with brute ferocity. A staggering 437 people were executed; another six hundred men and women were flogged and over a thousand homes razed to the ground. Paul Bogle evaded capture and fled to the hills, where he remained undetected for several days. In Kingston, Governor Eyre declared Martial Law in the then-parish of St Thomas in the East and hand-wrote a warrant for the immediate arrest of his chief political opponent, George William Gordon, who was transported to Morant Bay for trial and was hanged outside the courthouse on October 20. With his chief advocate silenced, there was nowhere for Bogle to hide; he was captured at Stony Gut on October 23, and went to gallows two days later.

The rebellion marked a key political and social watershed for Jamaica. Governor Eyre, the man behind the repression, was immediately recalled to England and stripped of his position. Jamaica's constitution was suspended and replaced with direct rule from the home country, allowing British governors to impose reforms, for example in education and the legal system, that would never have got past the local elite under previous governments. Although progress for the poor was still painfully slow, Bogle's defiant legacy ensured that Jamaica remained relatively peaceful until well into the next century.

The Jamaican government eventually recognized Paul Bogle as a National Hero, and a monument to him stands in Heroes Circle in Kingston (see p.84).

Jamaica as a whole. From here, Deacon Bogle built the rockbed of support that enabled him to lead his rebellion, and it was also here that he was eventually captured by the authorities. Opposite the Methodist church, a battered, barely-legible sign for the **Stony Gut Monument** points downhill to Bogle's simple stone memorial, shaded by Otaheite apple trees and bearing a plaque that outlines his deeds. Bogle's late great-grandson was caretaker of the site for many years, and was interred behind the monument in 1995 at the request of the Jamaica National Heritage Trust.

Even if you've no interest in seeing Bogle's memorial, it's worth taking the trip for the scenery alone, with constant vistas of the Blue Mountains over verdant, fruited vales. From Stony Gut, you can drive further into the mountains via Middleton and Soho, looping back to the coast by way of Bath Mineral Spa (see p.151) or Serge Island.

Lyssons and around

Back on the coast, and a mile or so east of Morant Bay, the road swings into **LYSSONS**, a pretty residential community notable chiefly for its palm-fringed **beach**, easily the best in the area and presided over by the aptly named but unobtrusive *Golden Shore Beach Hotel* (☎982 9657 or 734 0923; ②), at the end of the track opposite the Forever supermarket. With cool tiled floors, a/c and cable TV, rooms are practically on the sand, and there's a restaurant and a small gazebo bar on site. Non-guests can use the hotel showers and changing rooms for J$100.

Lyssons slides imperceptibly into **RETREAT**, an unassuming sort of place which holds the majority of St Thomas's **accommodation** options, including the prominently signposted but chaotic *Goldfinger Guest House* on the main road (☎982 2644; ②), where the rooms are basic with fan, double bed and cable TV; some have a private bathroom and cooking facilities are available. *Goldfinger* is at the corner of Crystal Drive; at the bottom of the road, right at the sea's edge, is the more elegant *Whispering Bamboo Cove* (☎982 2912, fax 734 1049; ③–⑤ breakfast included), where there's a restaurant, a flowered garden with a gazebo overlooking the sea, and rooms ranging from rather cramped but spotless doubles with private bathroom, cable TV and fan, to spacious suites. Back on the main road and a few hundred yards east, the wide lawns of the supremely friendly *Brown's Guesthouse* (☎982 6205; ①–②) sweep down to the sea; rooms are immaculate and home-style Jamaican, and meals are available. Set back from the main road in the East Prospect housing development, the *Bluemah Palace* (☎ & fax 982 6250; ②–③) is a cavernous hotel, restaurant and bar. With huge beds, cable TV, a/c and the odd balcony, the rooms are great, and the atrium area serves as a venue for **Friday night jams**, with oldies reggae and plenty of food. All of Retreat's hotels are steps away from a pretty, unadorned strip of brown-sand beach. The only other facilities are slightly further on at **PROSPECT** itself, which merges with Retreat. The **Hymans Bathing beach** at Prospect boasts a bar-cum-restaurant and rudimentary changing rooms (J$20). The quiet charm hereabouts, is slowly starting to attract a loyal following of European backpackers, and dances are occasionally held at Prospect Beach House by the ocean.

For **food**, the restaurant at the *Morant Villas Hotel* (see p.147) in Morant Bay is adequate for a sit-down meal, and offers inexpensive local dishes of fried fish and chicken. The enormous *Chef's Sea View* on the Lyssons road just east of Morant Bay is also good, serving Jamaican breakfasts, lunches and dinners daily; both venues are occasionally used to stage parties and the odd reggae show. If you fancy a **drink**, head for the *Morant Villas Hotel* bar, or better still, the mural-covered *Jack Palance Palace*, a friendly rum shop just east of Morant Bay, where the white rum flows and the owner's record collection is a treasure.

Hurricane Gilbert

In September 1988 **Hurricane Gilbert** pulverized Jamaica. By the time the carnage had stopped, 45 people had died, 500,000 were left homeless – their tin shacks went down like ninepins – and agriculture was laid waste, with US$50 million worth of damage to banana, coffee, sugarcane and other crops. Sections of the Blue Mountains were denuded as the winds uprooted trees and hurled them down the slopes and, with electricity out for days, looting was widespread, particularly in Kingston. Aid poured into the island – US$125 million from the USA alone – and, in many parts of the island, particularly the main tourist areas, life returned to normal with remarkable speed. However, in the hardest-hit eastern parishes of Portland and St Thomas, it has taken a lot longer to repair the damage, and even today you can still find traces of Gilbert, as at the *Bath Fountain Hotel* (see below), still coping with the consequences more than a decade on.

Bath

Heading east from Morant Bay, a road cuts inland at Port Morant. Six miles from the coast, and right on the edge of the John Crow Mountains jungle, the little-visited village of **BATH** was born when a runaway Spanish slave stumbled across some hot mineral springs here in the late 1690s. He found that the springs cured wounds he had incurred during his escape and, slowly, the word spread; ironically, though, his "master" claimed the spring and some 1130 acres of land that surrounded it, and sold it to the British government in 1699 for £400. They swiftly carved a road through the hills from the coast to get here (still an exceptionally pretty drive today) and erected a spa building in 1747.

Colonists came from all over the island to treat their various ailments, the wealthy built their fashionable summer homes nearby, and for a while in the early 1700s Bath glittered in the spotlight. However, the atmosphere was soon soured by disputes between political factions (specifically, supporters of the Jacobite and Hanoverian dynasties competing for the throne back in England); hurricane damage also took its toll, and Bath fell from favour. By the late eighteenth century, it had become a ghost town, with only ten residents. Today, it's a quiet and rather backward country village, surrounded by jungle, with a straggle of visitors coming to take the waters. You may run into the odd tourist or someone up from Kingston taking treatment for rheumatism or arthritis, but it's just as likely that you'll have the place to yourself.

Reached along a signposted one-mile road from the town centre, opposite the church, the **spa** (daily 8am–9.30pm; J$100) now adjoins the rambling old *Bath Fountain Hotel* (see p.152), with a dozen small cubicles each housing a sunken, two-person tiled bath. The water is high in sulphur and lime and, like most mineral baths, slightly (though not, they insist, dangerously) radioactive. The charge covers use of a towel and a twenty-minute bath (any longer is not recommended in

A daily bus (2hr 30min) runs to Bath from the Parade in Kingston; buses from Port Antonio will only get you as far as Morant Bay, from where you can connect with the Kingston bus or take a taxi.

case you dehydrate). The private cubicles provide a secluded soak, but for a prettier bathe in the open air, surrounded by a thick forest of trees, vines and lianas, head up the path to the left of the hotel/spa building, which follows the "Sulphur River" to the point where the natural hot and cold springs gush out from the rocks (the two are diverted to the spa and mixed to provide you with water of a more even temperature). Just beyond the spot where the hot water is piped as it comes out of the rock, you can scramble down the bank to swim in the river and partake of the thermal springs. Waterfalls tumble prettily through the trees, and hiking trails lead from here for miles across the Blue Mountains and into Portland; the hotel may be able to help out with a guide – otherwise, contact Sun Venture Tours (see p.133). Before you start to head up to the spring mouth, though, you'll probably be accosted by a group of hangers-on offering a completely unnecessary, unofficial "guide" service to the spring; if you're female, they'll also proffer amateur massages and "spa" treatments (having your towel dunked in the water and wrapped around you). Rates for such services are inevitably exorbitant; if you take up any offers, make sure you agree on a reasonable price first.

If you want to **stay**, the *Bath Fountain Hotel* itself (☎703 4345, fax 703 4154; ②–③) is supremely quiet and old-fashioned, and rates include free access to the baths. The dining room of the hotel offers tasty Jamaican **meals** and some excellent fruit juices, and the town also holds a couple of tiny rum shops and snack bars.

At the bottom of the road to the hotel and spa, and adjacent to the cut-stone Bath Anglican Church, are the **Bath Botanical Gardens** (daily dawn to dusk; free). The gardens were established in 1779, a small patch of land where many plants – including cinnamon, jacaranda, bougainvillea and mango – were first introduced to the island. For a century or more, this was a thriving little spot, but the ravages of time and Hurricane Gilbert have ensured that little remains of the original, carefully ordered scheme. None of the trees are labelled anymore, but you'll see descendants of the **breadfruit trees** first brought from Tahiti by Captain Bligh of HMS *Bounty* in 1793. The gardens also house guava trees, royal palms, bamboo and crotons, and it's a pleasant and shady spot to stroll for fifteen minutes or so and test your botanical knowledge.

See p.161 for more on Captain Bligh and the bread-fruit.

If you're in no hurry to get back to the coast, and you have your own transport and an eye for scenery, it's worth taking an inland detour. Double back on the road to Port Morant from Bath, then turn off at tiny Potsoi, where two pretty rugged roads weave through the luscious interior, both passing the Paul Bogle Monument at Stony Gut (see p.148) and returning to the coast at Morant Bay.

The southeastern corner

About five miles east of Morant Bay, the tiny fishing village of **PORT MORANT** was a key harbour and banana shipping point during the eighteenth century, protected in its heyday by several bristling forts that dotted the coastline. These are now long gone, and, except when the fishing boats are unloading their catch, the place has a sleepy and somewhat melancholy feel. A mile or so on from Port Morant itself, a minor road swings off the A4 along the coast towards **Bowden Wharf**, though the water is masked by vegetation and the odd house. As you reach the water, a pair of large red gates mark the impromptu headquarters of an **oyster-farming** operation – the only commercial operation here since bananas ceased to be exported. Attached to pieces of tyre suspended in the water from wooden poles, the molluscs take around three months to grow to maturity. Oysters are as much a delicacy in Jamaica as anywhere else, and are most often enjoyed gulped down with a fiery sauce of Scotch bonnet peppers, scallion, thyme, pimento, sugar and vinegar. If any of the workers are around, they'll usually let you poke about.

East of Port Morant, the main highway skirts the far southeastern corner of the island, and it's a gorgeous six-mile drive, a seamless feast of banana, sugar and coconut plantations – look out for the neat but dilapidated rows of roadside homes, built on stilts to accommodate cane cutters working at the still-operational Duckenfield sugar plantation. The next sizeable village is the rather shabby **GOLDEN GROVE**. You won't want to stop here, but a quick detour south, past the dishevelled-looking Duckenfield factory, will bring you to **Rocky Point Bay**, one of the best and most secluded beaches in this part of the country. A sizeable fleet of small fishing boats is based here, normally out from dawn until the early afternoon when some of their catch starts frying at the bar.

A direct and extremely scenic road to Bath Spa (see p.151) swings inland from Golden Grove.

Also starting at Golden Grove, innumerable tracks weave through the Duckenfield canefields, and then the swampy mangroves of the Great Morass, out to the serenely isolated hundred-foot **Morant Point lighthouse**, cast in London in 1841 and put up here by Kru men from Sierra Leone, among the first free Africans to be brought to the island after the abolition of slavery. It's a deserted and windswept spot, with the sea crashing onto the rocks and sand; climb the lighthouse and look out over the bay and back to the Blue Mountains. As you approach the lighthouse (and on the other side of the lighthouse promontory to Rocky Point), you'll pass the utterly gorgeous **Holland Bay**, a deserted swath of fine white sand and pellucid water overlooked by a few ragged palms – the perfect place to live out your Robinson Crusoe fantasies.

You'll probably need to ask directions to get to both Rocky Point and the Morant Point lighthouse.

Back on the A4, and continuing north from Golden Grove, the road leads uphill, with a magnificent panorama behind you over Holland Bay and the mangrove swamps of the Great Morass. A little further on, **Hector's River**, halfway up Jamaica's eastern tip, marks the boundary between Portland and St Thomas.

Portland

PORTLAND, north of the Blue Mountains, is generally considered the most beautiful of Jamaica's parishes – a rain-drenched land of luscious foliage, sparkling rivers and pounding waterfalls. Eastern Jamaica's biggest resort, the small town of **Port Antonio** is your most likely destination, a good base for sightseeing with a couple of fabulous **beaches** a short ride away. The waterfalls at **Somerset Falls** and (a bit further afield) the gorgeous **Reach Falls** are within striking distance while, if you head into the interior, you can be poled down the **Rio Grande** on a bamboo raft or hike through the rainforest along the centuries-old trails of the Windward Maroons. An increasing number of visitors are venturing east of Port Antonio for the more laid-back pleasures of **Long Bay** – with a growing young travellers' scene and the best surf in Jamaica – while the roadside vendors in **Boston Bay** continue to offer some of the most authentic jerk pork in the country in a dazzling oceanside setting.

Some history

Even after the conquest of Jamaica by Britain in 1655, Portland was one of the last of Jamaica's parishes to be settled. Although its obvious capital-to-be, Port Antonio, blessed with two natural harbours, was superbly located for trade and defence, reports of the difficult terrain and the constant threat of Maroon warfare deterred would-be settlers. Eventually, the Crown was obliged to offer major incentives, including land grants, tax exemptions and free food supplies, before the parish was officially formed in 1723.

Like the rest of the country, Portland's early economy was dependent on sugar, with large estates scattered around the parish. However, as the industry declined in the nineteenth century, Portland's fertile soil proved ideally suited for the surprise replacement crop – **bananas** (see box). As the country's major banana port, Port Antonio boomed, ushering in a golden era of prosperity for the town and the region. Steamer lines and businessmen poured in from Europe and North America and, in 1905, the town's first **hotel** was built on the Titchfield peninsula. Cabin space on the banana boats was sold to curious tourists, who found themselves rubbing shoulders with the rich and famous – publishing magnate William Randolph Hearst, banker J.P. Morgan, actress Bette Davis et al – swanning in on their private yachts.

The reign of the banana was to prove relatively short-lived – blighted by hurricane damage and Panama disease from South America – but the high-end tourism it had helped to engender soon became a key revenue-earner. With the enthusiastic patronage of movie stars like Errol Flynn (see p.171), Port Antonio's place in the

Bananas

First brought to Jamaica from the Canary Islands as early as 1520, the banana was long considered an unpalatable vegetable, fit only for animals and slaves. The turning-point in its popularity came in 1871, when sea-captain **Lorenzo Dow Baker** took a shipload of bananas from Port Antonio to Boston to see whether he could drum up any interest for the fruit in the United States. His gamble paid off handsomely – he had barely unloaded the crates before the entire stock was sold for a healthy profit, setting off a mass demand for the "new" fruit that would bring him (and others like him) colossal fortunes over the next couple of decades.

With sugar already in decline by the second half of the nineteenth century, Jamaica's farmers rushed to plant the new crop of "green gold", and Portland's high rainfall and fertile soil secured its position as the island's leading production centre. Banana production went ballistic, with output hitting highs of around thirty million stems per year. With little employment available elsewhere, armies of workers arrived from all over the country to earn the pitiful sustenance wages available to planters and pickers, who lived in wretched conditions on the edge of the plantations.

The arrival of banana ships at the wharves was signalled by blasts on a conch shell throughout the interior, followed by frenetic activity as the labourers cut the stems and carried the fresh fruit off the estates and onto the waiting trucks. At the dock the bananas were unloaded from the trucks and taken to the checkers, who ensured that the stem had the nine hands of bananas required for it to count as a bunch – hence, in the banana boat song, *Day O* "six hands, seven hands, eight hands, bunch!". Once the stem was carried aboard the ship, the tallyman gave the carrier a tally to redeem for pay later, and the workers made their weary way back to the plantation or to the nearest bar.

Sadly for Portland, the boom didn't last for long. By the 1920s, a combination of disease and hurricane damage had decimated Jamaica's banana crops, and the decline was compounded by the disruption of shipping during World War II. Nevertheless, the precious banana remains the country's second most important official agricultural commodity (behind sugar) and still accounts for around four per cent of Jamaica's total exports.

---

glitterati's global playground was assured. The first luxury hotel in Jamaica, *Frenchman's Cove*, was built here, and remains a testament to faded glamour to this day.

Celebrities still sequester themselves in Portland, and there's a burgeoning backpacker scene at Long Bay, but the area can't yet compete for the mainstream vacationer, losing out to the more accessible and better-marketed resorts of Montego Bay, Negril and Ocho Rios. Agriculture is still important, though, and the region's lush vegetation provides vast amounts of fruit and vegetables for domestic and export markets. The movie business, too, periodically injects much-needed cash into the economy – films shot here include *Cocktail*, *The Mighty Quinn*, *Club Paradise* and *Lord of the Flies* – but the area is a long way from the prosperity of its heyday.

Port Antonio

A magnet for foreign visitors during the 1950s and 1960s, the quiet town of **PORT ANTONIO** feels more like an isolated backwater these days. There's not a huge amount to see, nightlife is limited and there is little in the way of watersports or shopping, but, to be frank, you're not here for the town. The highlight of this area is the great **outdoors** – waterfalls, river trips, hiking, splendid tropical scenery and some lovely beaches – and Port Antonio is the perfect base for exploring it all.

Arrival and information

Flights arrive at **Ken Jones Aerodrome**, six miles west of town in St Margaret's Bay, from where a taxi into town costs around US$10. **Buses** and **minibuses** from Kingston (3hr 30min) and Montego Bay (5hr) pull in at the main terminus by the seafront on Gideon Avenue, or by the town's central square on West Street (which also serves as the main **taxi rank**). If you're **driving**, the A4 highway runs straight into and through the town, whether you're coming from the east or the west. Both Huntress Marina and the Port Antonio Marina offer **boat mooring** and maintenance facilities.

The **Jamaica Tourist Board** office (☎993 3051; Mon–Fri 9am–4pm) is upstairs at the City Centre Plaza on Harbour Street, although it doesn't have much in the way of local information, just a few scant brochures on hotels and attractions. The **Portland Parish Library** is at 1 Harbour St (☎993 2793; Mon–Fri 9am–7pm, Sat 9am–1pm).

Getting around

When asking directions, bear in mind that local people often use different names to those printed on maps; Allan Avenue to the west of town, for example, is usually referred to as Folly Road.

Sandwiched between the mountains and the sea, Port Antonio is small and easily navigable. To get your bearings, head up to the *Bonnie View Hotel* (see p.158), overlooking the entire town and providing great views of the area. You can comfortably **walk** between the handful of sights in a couple of hours, while most places of interest outside town (and all of the beaches) can be reached by

---

Safety and harassment

Most people find Port Antonio something of a relief after the harassment of the north coast, and any hassle you do encounter tends to be fairly half-hearted. There is also a relatively low crime rate, despite the odd night-time robbery on the Titchfield peninsula. Even so, it is worth taking the normal precautions: don't flash wads of cash around or wander off the main streets after dark. The local police often set up roadblocks east of town, and it's not unusual for tourists to have their cars thoroughly searched for drugs. If this happens to you, be helpful and friendly and you shouldn't be detained long.

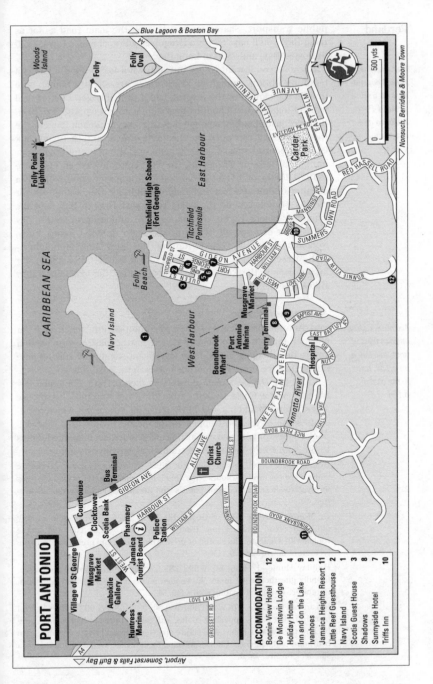

PORT ANTONIO

Blue Lagoon & Boston Bay

Nonsuch, Berridale & Moore Town

Airport, Somerset Falls & Buff Bay

Woods Island

Folly

Folly Oval

ALLAN AVENUE

AVENUE

EAST PALM

N

500 yds

0

EVELEIGH PK ROAD

Carder Park

Folly Point Lighthouse

CARIBBEAN SEA

Titchfield High School (Fort George)

East Harbour

RED HASSELL ROAD

MANINGS AVE

SUMMERS TOWN ROAD

Navy Island

Folly Beach

Titchfield Peninsula

TITCHFIELD ST

QUEEN ST

KING ST

FORT GEORGE ST

GIDEON AVENUE

HARBOUR ST

WILLIAM ST

WEST ST

BRIDGE ST

BONNIE VIEW ROAD

10

12

West Harbour

Musgrave Market

LOVE LANE

W BAPTIST AVE

Boundbrook Wharf

Port Antonio Marina

Ferry Terminal

8

9

EAST BAPTIST ST

Hospital

WEST PALM AVENUE

Annotto River

HALL'S AVE

NUTTALL RD

RICE PIECE ROAD

BOUNDBROOK ROAD

BOUNDBROOK ROAD

SPRINGBANK ROAD

11

Village of St George

Courthouse

Bus Terminal

ALLAN AVE

Christ Church

BRIDGE ST

Clocktower

Scotia Bank

GIDEON AVE

Musgrave Market

Jamaica Tourist Board ⓘ

Pharmacy

HARBOUR ST

Police Station

WILLIAM ST

BONNIE VIEW

Ambokile Gallery

WEST ST

LOVE LANE

GROSSETT RD

Huntress Marina

ACCOMMODATION

Bonnie View Hotel	12
De Montevin Lodge	6
Holiday Home	4
Inn and on the Lake	9
Ivanhoes	5
Jamaica Heights Resort	11
Little Reef Guesthouse	2
Navy Island	1
Scotia Guest House	3
Shadows	8
Sunnyside Hotel	7
Triffs Inn	10

Car and bike rental companies in and around Port Antonio are listed on p.164.

public transport. Shared taxis run along the main road as far as Long Bay; you'll pay JS$40 to Dragon Bay/Frenchman's Cove, J$50 to Boston Bay, and J$60 to Long Bay.

Because you'll want to get out of town a lot, renting a **car** is a tempting option, though as rental rates are slightly higher here than in the capital or the resorts, you'll probably get a better deal with a Kingston- or Ocho Rios-based company (see p.103 & p.204). If you're just planning a single day-trip – say to Reach Falls or the Rio Grande – it can work out cheaper to use a **taxi**; the main rank is in the central square, alternatively, call the cheerful Mr Palmer on ☎993 3468 or 772 9648, the Port Antonio taxi co-operative (☎993 2684), or JUTA (☎993 2684). A **moped** or **motorbike** is a cheaper option and just as handy, though, as ever, watch out for vicious potholes along the coast road past Dragon Bay, and the usual boy-racers. If you want an easy life, and are prepared to pay for it, you can see all of the area's main draws – Reach Falls, Nonsuch caves, Rio Grande Rafting, the John Crow Mountains – with Attractions Link, at 5 West Street (☎993 2102 or 4828); for hiking trips in the Rio Grande valley, contact the excellent Valley Hikes (see p.176).

Accommodation

Accommodation options west of town are listed on p.180, and to the east on p.168.

Port Antonio has plenty of good **accommodation**, much of it far cheaper than in more heavily-visited north coast resorts, and if you're on a budget, you'll make significant savings by staying here rather than the more glamourous hotels to the east of town.

From her *Drapers San* guesthouse (see p.168), the supremely friendly Maria Carla Gullotta runs the Port Antonio Guesthouse Association (☎ and fax 993 7118, *www.go-jam.com*), which represents some of the most appealing properties in the area. She will book rooms for you, and can also provide tours, accompanied forays to the *Roof Club*, and nights of traditional African drumming.

Bonnie View Hotel, Bonnie View Rd; ☎993 2752, fax 993 2862. Fantastic views over the twin harbours from this long-standing hotel, which also has lovely gardens and a nice pool, but it's a bit overpriced and in need of renovation. ⑤.

De Montevin Lodge, 21 Fort George St; ☎993 2604. Good value in a lovely old gingerbread house, a relic from colonial days. Clean, cool and simple rooms with a balcony and shared or private bathroom, and great food from the restaurant downstairs. ③.

Holiday Home, 12 King St; ☎993 2882, *www.go-jam.com*. Comfortable, friendly guesthouse set in an old wooden house on the Titchfield peninsula. Rooms are clean and inviting with a fan. ②.

Inn and on the Lake, 17a West Palm Ave; ☎993 3468, fax 993 3332. Cheerful place offering clean, appealing rooms with fan and private bathroom, at the back of the owner's home. A separate apartment has a private entrance, two bedrooms and a kitchen. Clothes-washing facilities are available, and there's a sun deck on site. ③–⑤.

Ivanhoes, 9 Queen St; ☎993 3043. Scrupulously clean and tidy no-frills guest-house opposite the ruins of the old *Titchfield Hotel*. The appealing, reasonably priced rooms have private bathrooms with hot and cold water and a fan; meals are available. ②.

Jamaica Heights Resort, Spring Bank Rd; ☎993 2156, fax 993 3563. Mellow guesthouse that offers excellent value and pleasant rooms in a great location, high up in the hills, with its own "private" river and waterfall, as well as a small pool. Taxis from town charge around J$300. ④.

Little Reef Guesthouse, 1 Queen St; ☎993 9743. Disorganized but extreme-ly friendly place where the plain rooms have double beds and a private bath-room. The genial owners usually throw in local tours as well. ①.

Scotia Guest House, 15 Queen St; ☎993 2681. Very basic option set in an atmospheric, mural-bedecked wood house near *Ivanhoes*; most rooms share bathrooms, or you pay a little more for the en-suite option. ①.

Shadows, 40 West St; ☎993 3823. Conveniently located in the centre of things and set back from the road, these small rooms have a/c, fan and cold water only in the bathrooms, but they're excellent if you're on a budget. ②.

Sunnyside Hotel, 5 Fort George St; ☎993 9788. Extremely basic (and equal-ly inexpensive) place opposite the *De Montevin Lodge*, just above the ocean. Rooms vary greatly – several look out to sea – but all are pretty bare with a fan and shared or private bathrooms; the most expensive has cable TV. ①–②.

Triffs Inn, 1 Bridge St; ☎715 4358, fax 993 2162, *triffs@in-site.com*. Good mid-range option in the centre of town, popular with Jamaican business trav-ellers. Rooms have a/c, cable TV and private bathroom with hot and cold water, and there's a decent restaurant attached. ③.

The Town

The obvious starting-point for a stroll around Port Antonio is its **cen-tral square**, with a landmark **clocktower** opposite the red-brick, two-storey Georgian **courthouse**, built in 1895 and fronted by an ele-gant fretworked veranda supported by cast-iron columns courtesy of the William MacFarlane company in Glasgow, Scotland. The area is always milling with people on court business or visiting the post office below. On the other side of the road, your eyes can't help but be drawn to the **Village of St George** shopping mall, a mish-mash of architectural styles from medieval to Tudor and Renaissance built over the old Delmar Theatre; some like it, many hate it, but some-how, its opulent exterior, richly embellished with murals and sculp-tures, manages to complement the surrounding buildings. The brain-child of the locally infamous Zigi Fami, owner of the equally exuber-ant *Jamaican Palace* hotel and the woman behind Trident Castle (see p.166), St George's boasts a handful of stores and snack bars and a gorgeous upstairs restaurant, closed at the time of writing but sure to reincarnate soon.

Due north from here, the **Titchfield peninsula** juts out into the Caribbean Sea, bisecting Port Antonio's **twin harbours**. The tip of the peninsula once held the British **Fort George**, whose ancient can-nons and crumbling walls today form part of Titchfield High School, alive with noisy open-air lessons and frenetic games of football and netball. The short wander up from town takes you past the **De Montevin Lodge** hotel – high-Victorian gingerbread architecture at its best – and the ruins of the **Titchfield Hotel**, Port Antonio's first and once owned by Errol Flynn. It's referred to by most as the "folly", but there's little to see there these days. Walking up Queen Street, and heading towards the ruins, which occupy a wasteland that parallels the street, a footpath leads down to the small but pretty **Folly beach**, a meagre scrap of sand which meets a grassy lawn, and a nice spot for a swim or a drink at the open-air bar whilst looking out to Navy Island and the lighthouse. You can also get simple Ital meals.

Back in the centre of town on West Street, which shoots off from the clocktower, compact **Musgrave Market** is the liveliest spot in town, friendly, easy-going and crammed with stalls. Fresh fruit and vegetables are the market's strong point, but there's also a busy trade in fish, meat and clothes, and a handful of crafts and souvenirs – try Honest Jon's stall at the back near the library. The rest of West Street reeks of faded glory; particularly nostalgic is the once beautiful wooden house at no. 22, now home to the small **Ambokile art gallery**, where resident artist and owner Philip Henry sells his own marvellous work alongside that of other local luminaries, including Burnett Anderson and Henry's wife, Marcia. The tasteful selection of craft and jewellery is the best you'll find in town. Opposite the gallery, the office of the local MP is equally easy on the eyes.

Further up West Street, past the grassy lawn where the **ferry** leaves for Navy Island (see opposite), **Boundbrook Wharf** is still the loading point for bananas being shipped to Europe and the United States. This is the place that inspired the banana boat song *Day O* – "Work all night for a drink of rum, daylight come and me wanna go home" – though the back-breaking work is now much simplified, with the bananas packaged centrally and mechanically loaded at the wharf.

Back in town, the red-brick Anglican **Christ Church** on Bridge Street, Romanesque in design, is the most prominent of Port Antonio's many houses of worship. Built on the site of an earlier church in 1840, its numerous memorials date as far back as the late seventeenth century. The eagle lectern was donated in 1900 by the Boston Fruit Company, a firm owned by Captain Dow Baker (see box on p.155) which owed its foundation and much of its profits to the trade in bananas between Port Antonio and North America. You'll probably be grabbed by one of the ancient assistants who guard the church and dish out nuggets of local history to visitors – you might want to leave a donation.

Across the road from the church, a stiff half-mile walk up Bonnie View Road takes you to the **Bonnie View Hotel**. A long-established, though rather run-down hotel (see p.158), this is a great place to head to on arrival as the views are magnificent. From the front you look over the town and the twin harbours while, from the lovely back garden, you can see into the heart of the Blue and John Crow Mountains. Hiking trails into the hills start from here and, with a bit of advance notice, the hotel can organize half-day horseback tours of the area (from US$30 per person).

Navy Island

The largest of the small islands that dot the Portland coast, **NAVY ISLAND** is a five-minute boat ride from the mainland. The British navy used it for storage and barracks in the early eighteenth century – hence the name – and Captain Bligh landed here in 1793, bringing breadfruit plants from Tahiti. A later adventurer, Errol Flynn, came to Port Antonio in 1947 and, taken with the beauty of the island, immediately bought it as a private retreat for entertaining Hollywood

Ferries (daily 9am–5pm) run to Navy Island on demand from the West Street pier; the J$100 charge includes the return journey and use of the facilities.

The breadfruit and the Bounty

Up until the late eighteenth century, Jamaica – like most of the West Indian islands – was not self-sufficient in food, relying on imports (particularly from North America) to feed the ever-increasing slave population. As a result, the American War of Independence (1775–81), which severely disrupted food supplies, brought tragedy to the islands, with thousands of slaves dying of malnutrition and related disease. To eliminate this catastrophic dependence, planters immediately lobbied the British government for a source of cheap food that could be grown in the islands, with the starchy, nourishing **breadfruit** – about which the great explorer Captain Cook had rhapsodized, "if a man plants ten of them... he will completely fulfil his duty to his own and future generations" – top of their wish list. In due course, the British designated *HMS Bounty* to bring breadfruit plants from their native Tahiti, and appointed one **Captain William Bligh** to command it.

Setting sail from England in 1787, the *Bounty* arrived in Tahiti the following year after a long and dangerous journey around Cape Horn, and captain and crew were treated as royalty by the islanders, garlanded with flowers and showered with gifts and hospitality. But Bligh had little time to waste, and insisted on loading up the breadfruit plants and moving on. Three weeks later, facing another arduous crossing under a captain who seemed to care more for his plants than for his men, the ship's crew, led by second-in-command Fletcher Christian, mutinied. Bligh was cast adrift in the middle of the Pacific Ocean with a handful of loyal followers, while Christian and his acolytes made for Ascension Island and their place in history.

Incredibly, Bligh survived. He eventually found his way back to England, where he was cleared of any blame for the loss of the *Bounty* and entrusted with command of another ship, *HMS Providence*, to complete his mission. The Jamaican House of Assembly voted him a substantial gift of 500 guineas to encourage his endeavours on their behalf, and the *Providence* left England in 1791, finally delivering the breadfruit to the island in February 1793. The plants were sent on to Bath Botanical Gardens (see p.152) for propagation, and eventually spread throughout the island, an important step towards Jamaican self-sufficiency.

---

starlets. Local legend – one of the myriad Flynn myths – says that he lost it in a poker game less than a decade later. It's rumoured that the island has recently been bought up by the actor Louis Gosset Jnr; however, at the time of writing, he's yet to make any changes.

The island's 64 acres are home to a rather run-down **hotel** (☎993 2041, fax 993 2667; ⊚), with its restaurant area covered in posters and stills from Flynn's movies; outside, the wreck of his fishing boat sits mournfully by the water's edge. Gentle nature trails carve through the island's lush vegetation, where you can spot ducks, cows and egrets among the coconut-palms, and look out over the derelict remains of Flynn's cottage, all bug-eaten bare boards and crumbling plaster. There are a couple of good **beaches** – the best one is to the east of the island – and although there's lots of sea grass near the shore, a rickety boardwalk leads out to deeper waters where, at low tide, you can swim out and bask on a sandbank. At the northern side, a totally private but narrow strip of tree-lined sand serves as a nudist beach; the volcanic rocks at one end provide a pretty view of the Port Antonio lighthouse.

Eating

As you leave town to the west, look out for jerk barbecues and stalls selling silverfoil parcels of spicy curried conch.

A number of inexpensive **restaurants** in town offer a standard Jamaican menu, and there are cheap Italian and Chinese options, too. If you're after something more international, you'll need to head east of town to the *Blue Lagoon* or one of the ritzier hotels (see p.168). Coronation bakery on the outskirts of town has been made famous for producing the "**holey bulla**", a smaller and far more toothsome version of the traditional pastry with, unsurprisingly, a hole in the middle; buy some freshly-baked from CC's Bakery at 25 West St. For bread, you might be better off following those who prefer the brick-oven baked stuff at the Three Star Lion Bakery, 27 West St.

Anna Bananas, Allan Ave. Fetching seaside restaurant on a raised wooden boardwalk overlooking the bay that's one of the best inexpensive places to eat in the area, with excellent, smiling service. Popular with tourists and locals alike, the food is reliable Jamaican; breakfast, lunch and dinner are served daily.

In restaurant listings, we have given a phone number only for those places where you might need to reserve a table.

Blue Marlin, Port Antonio Marina; ☎993 3209. With funky decor and a "contemporary Jamaican" menu, this is an atmospheric restaurant right on the water overlooking Navy Island. Lots of salads (including Greek with feta), and main meals such as fish and shrimp curry, grilled kebabs and lobster. Good also for Sunday brunch in the high season.

Cartoons, 15 West St. A good place to pick up snacks during the day, with patties, home-made cakes, Devon House I Scream and fruit juices.

Chenel's Pizza Pub, 26 West St. Reasonable if tiny place serving pizza, chicken and chips, roti and Jamaican staples.

Debonaire, 22 West St. Hole-in-the-wall eatery, serving up daily from 7am to midnight. Jamaican breakfasts, and lunches and dinners of JA-style roast pork and beef, curry goat and chicken, and brown stew, escovitched, steamed or sweet and sour fish.

De Montevin Lodge, 21 Fort George St; ☎993 2604. A great spot for a semi-formal feast of good-value traditional Jamaican food – like pepperpot soup and escovitched fish – served in a charming old dining room.

Dickie's Sweet Banana Stop, on the A4 just west of Port Antonio. Nestled on a knoll as you round the far bend of Port Antonio's west harbour, this simple wooden shack is easily missed, but is one of the best – and most unusual – choices around. Cooked by owner Dickie and served in his kooky lounge, the beautifully presented, moderately priced, four-course dinners are fabulous (order the morning before you want to eat) and include dishes such as ackee on toast, garlic lobster and steamed fish; you can also drop by for breakfast, lunch or afternoon tea.

Gallery Café, Village of St George. Cool upstairs diner that's good for breakfast (omelette, pancakes and toast), or lunches of quiche, pizza, sandwiches and Jamaican hot meals.

Golden Happiness, corner of Harbour and West streets. The best Chinese food in town, with a huge menu of chop suey, sweet and sour and masses more, and very cheap to boot.

The Hub, 2 West Palm Ave. Just west of the main drag and tucked off the main street near the old train station, this is a popular place for Jamaican food: rundown, liver or calalloo for breakfast, stew beef, stew peas, cow foot, chicken or baked chicken for lunch and dinner.

Huntress Marina, West St. Great place to hang out on the waterfront, with grilled lobster as good and as reasonably priced as you'll find anywhere.

K-S Kozy Knook, Allan Ave. Excellent seafood – the steamed fish with okra is seasoned to perfection and supremely fresh, and it's served up right by the sea. The bar is also a friendly place to stop for a drink.

Shadows, 40 West St. Excellent omelettes for breakfast and good Jamaican and Chinese meals served at a pleasant bar with gazebo or in the smarter, less atmospheric restaurant.

Troy's, Allan Ave. Simple hut on the beach just beyond the bridge serving good-quality veg patties, seafood and a huge array of great natural juices.

Drinking, nightlife and entertainment

Port Antonio isn't exactly bursting with good places to **drink**, and the few places that exist are often very quiet. The oceanfront *Huntress Marina* on West Street normally has the most people and atmosphere, though the *Blue Marlin* bar at Port Antonio Marina on West Palm Avenue (☎993 3209) is an equally breezy but slightly more upmarket choice, with occasional **live entertainment**. The terrace at the *Bonnie View Hotel* offers the town's best harbour views – simply spectacular. *Giggy's Pool Hall*, above Homelectrix on West Street, is a popular local hangout, with pool tables (J$40 per game) and lots of good spirited drinking, particularly on a Friday. *Shadows*, 40 West St, is a little more salubrious, with bars upstairs and down and a weekend disco, where the reggae, soca and hip hop draws a mixed but mellow older crowd; the outdoor bar is good for a drink at any time. If you fancy a drink with Port Antonio's officers of the law, *The Hub*, 2 West Palm Ave, is a good, if rather testosterone-charged choice, with late-night drinking on a Friday and Saturday. Just out of town and right by the sea on Allan Avenue, the friendly *K-S Kozy Knook* is the archetypal Jamaican drinking hole, with a fairylight-strewn circular bar and lots of white rum drinkers fuelling the chit-chat.

On the **club** scene, the fluorescent-streamer-bedecked UV palace of the *Roof Club* at 11 West St (daily; J$100) is the place for clubbing in Port Antonio, and busiest at the weekends (though rarely before midnight); DJs pump out the latest dancehall, reggae, soca, hip hop and R&B, with the occasional oldies night. Women get in free for the popular Thursday "Ladies' Night". Though it's a fair drive east of town, *Club Tiffany* at the *Jamaica Crest* resort near Dragon Bay is fairly popular on Fridays and Saturdays; music policy is dancehall, R&B, soul and soca.

Port Antonio's take on **cinema** consists of a couple of rooms set up with chairs with a video projected onto a whitewashed wall; try the Showtime at 16 West Street, or try the unnamed one upstairs at the back of Musgrave market near the library. Programmes usually centre on action or karate movies.

In October, the prestigious **Port Antonio Blue Marlin Tournament** attracts serious anglers from all over the world who carouse the streets in the evenings. For more information, contact the JTB on ☎933 3051.

If you want to go deep sea fishing, ask at Huntress Marina or call ☎993 7525.

Listings

Airlines Air Jamaica Express at Ken Jones Aerodrome; ☎913 3692.

Airport enquiries The information number for Ken Jones Aerodrome is ☎993 2405.

Banks and money There are plenty of banks, along Harbour and West streets. Better exchange rates are available at the town's cambios; FX Trader is in the City Centre Plaza on Harbour Street, but Kamal's supermarket, 12 West St, has longer opening hours (Mon–Thurs 8.30am–8.15pm, Fri & Sat 8.30am–9pm, Sun 9.30am–3pm).

Car and bike rental Eastern Car Rentals at 26 Harbour St (☎993 3624 or 2562) will deliver to your hotel, as will Derron's, east of town at Drapers (☎993 7111, fax 993 7253). High-season prices start at US$70 per day plus insurance. Sox, at 7 Harbour St (☎993 4805), is slightly cheaper than Eastern for cars, and has Honda scooters for US$35 per day. Bikes are also available from Olimett, 5 Market Square (☎993 4656) for a similar rate.

Doctors Dr Daniella Speed in Boundbrook (☎993 3564) is recommended; also in Boundbrook, Dr Speck is a German-speaking practitioner (☎993 3564).

Hospital The public hospital is on Nuttall Road; ☎993 2646.

Internet access Ela Systems, shop 7, Village of St George (☎715 3180; Mon–Sat 9am–5pm), offer Net access at J$150 per hour.

Laundry Tru Wash in Musgrave Market near the library (☎993 2563) will wash clothes for around J$250 per load; they also offer a pick-up and drop-off service.

Pharmacy City Centre Plaza Pharmacy (Mon–Sat 9am–7pm) is opposite ScotiaBank on Harbour Street.

Police The main station is on Harbour St (☎993 2546). Call ☎119 in an emergency.

Post Office The main branch is on Harbour St opposite the clocktower (Mon–Fri 9am–5pm).

Scuba diving Lady G'Diver (☎993 8988), based at *Dragon Bay Hotel* to the east of town (see p.168), is the only scuba operator in the area, offering dives, certification courses and equipment rental.

Shopping Crafts and souvenirs are sold at the new Port Antonio mall near the clocktower, in Musgrave Market and in the small arcade near ScotiaBank. The best supermarket is Kamal's at 12 West St (for opening hours, see cambios above), and three or more of the same item are sold at budget prices by G&L Wholesale, 5 Harbour St (Mon–Thurs 8.30am–5pm, Fri & Sat 8.30am–7pm).

Taxis The main rank is in the central square, or call the Port Antonio taxi co-operative (☎993 2684) or JUTA (☎993 2684).

Telephone Eastern Communication at 28 Harbour St (Mon–Sat 8am–10pm, Sun 10am–10pm) offer inexpensive international calls.

East of Port Antonio

Made all the more alluring for its delicious sense of faded glamour and relative lack of visitors, the rugged stretch of coast east of Port Antonio is one of the most attractive parts of Jamaica. A fairy-tale landscape of lush, jungle-smothered hills rolling down to a coastline studded with fantastic beaches such as **Frenchman's Cove**, **Dragon Bay** and **Winnifred**, and swimming inlets such as the **Blue Lagoon**, a fabulous aquamarine pool of salt and fresh water made famous by the eponymous 1980 movie. A series of smart hotels vie for business with a handful of less expensive guesthouses, and you can plump for dinner-jacketed feasts at their salubrious restaurants or for more authentic jerk cooking at **Boston Bay**.

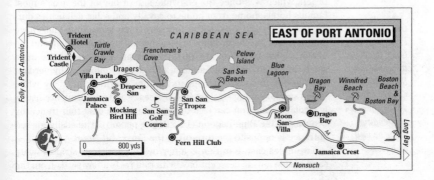

The Folly

Perched on Folly Point peninsula, on the eastern coastal outskirts of Port Antonio, the **Folly** is the sorry ruin of what was, briefly, one of the grandest houses in Jamaica. Built in 1902 for American banker Alfred Mitchell and widely applauded as a model of mock-Grecian architecture, the concrete house was a model of ostentation – until the roof collapsed in 1935, a victim of shoddy construction and the shortsighted use of saltwater in the cement mix, and the place was left to decay. Only the pillars and half a staircase remained standing, and today, graffiti-daubed and strewn with litter, they form a grim testament to lost glamour. Quirky and evocative, the shell's dramatic presence is not lost on film-makers, and it has featured in many movies as well as pop videos by the likes of Shabba Ranks and Lauryn Hill.

Just across the water, tiny **Woods Island** was once joined to the mainland by a stone causeway, and Mitchell had a small zoo built on it for his pet monkeys. Nothing remains from that time, but swimmers can cover the short distance to create their own private retreat. Take care if you're swimming – undercurrents can be strong.

Trident Castle, Frenchman's Cove and San San

Looming up suddenly as you make your way east, the fantasy **Trident Castle** is the most prominent landmark for miles around – a huge, white Disney-like edifice with each of its gleaming towers topped by a pointed roof. The castle began life in the 1970s as a relatively modest home for European baroness Zigi Fami, who has big land-holdings in the area, including the *Jamaica Palace* hotel. She was forced to sell after running into financial trouble, and the new owners got increasingly carried away with elaborate additions. Robust enough to have survived Hurricane Gilbert with barely a lost slate, the castle is occasionally rented out for private functions (contact *Trident Hotel*; see p.169) but is not otherwise open to the public. Continuing three miles east from Port Antonio, you arrive at **Frenchman's Cove**, with its lavish tropical gardens and stunning beach, which was once the erstwhile site of one of the area's most famous hotels, home from home to royalty and A-list celebrities during the 1950s and 1960s. The formerly sumptuous hotel villas have deteriorated, but the grounds are still beautifully maintained, and the **beach** (daily 9am–5pm; J$100), though small, is one of the most splendid in Jamaica, with a curve of fine sand enclosed by verdant hills, and a fresh-water river, its bottom alluringly lined by white beach sand, running straight into the sea. Food and drink are usually available, and you can rent loungers or take a boat tour to nearby beaches or the Blue Lagoon (US$10 per person). The easily missed entrance is opposite the turn-off to the *Fern Hill Hotel*.

Two miles east, **San San** is a narrow but gorgeous strip of white sand beside a wide crescent bay, with rich reefs a few yards from the

Just east of Trident Castle, the Gallery Carriacou at Mockingbird Hill Hotel (☎ 993 7134) stages excellent regular exhibitions, most focusing of the work of local artists; prints are available to buy.

To rent one of the extremely overpriced but beautifully situated villas at Frenchman's Cove call ☎ 993 7270 or 8211. ⑦.

Opposite Frenchman's Cove, the eighteen-hole San San Golf Course (☎ 993 7645) offers a challenging game as well as lessons.

shore that provide some of the best snorkelling around. These days, though, San San has fallen to the more unsavoury demands of the tourist industry; once a lively spot, popular with Jamaican bathers, it's now fenced-off, presumably to stop "undesirables" (in other words, regular Jamaicans) from getting anywhere near foreign guests. You'll be charged US$8 to go in. Just across from the beach is the tiny but beautiful **Pelew Island**, also known as Monkey Island despite a lack of primates, great for snorkelling or lazing if you're up to the swim out there.

The Blue Lagoon, Dragon Bay and Winnifred

The **Blue Lagoon** is where fourteen-year-old nymphet Brooke Shields (and the now obscure cherub Christopher Atkins) – child castaways on a desert island – frolicked naked in the movie of the same name. Enclosed by high cliffs that give a deep green tint to the noticeably turquoise depths, the lagoon is a result of several underwater streams running down from the mountains. Surrounded by rocks, trees and flowers, the whole effect is very picture postcard, the water a remarkable shade of blue and dropping to 198ft at its deepest spot. It's a peaceful place to swim, made more unusual by the thermal waves as warm sea water mixes with chilly gushes of fresh. You can swim for free from a pebbly "beach" straddled between the buildings, but if you're going to make a day of it, you're best off paying the J$100 entry fee to use the facilities at the purpose-built Blue Lagoon complex (☎993 8491; daily 10am–10pm). A wooden **restaurant** area hangs over the water (your entry fee is refunded if you eat), and snorkel gear is available to rent at US$9 for four hours.

There's more marvellous swimming a couple of miles east at **Dragon Bay**, where a protected sandy beach adjoins the *Dragon Bay Hotel*, half a mile from the main road and open to the public for a daily fee of J$150. It offers a lovely cove to swim and snorkel in – the hotel's Lady G'Diver (☎993 8988) also offers **scuba diving** – and access to the self-same beach bar where Tom Cruise juggled his bottles in *Cocktail*.

A mile or so on, **Winnifred's** (also known as Fairy Hill), is one of the biggest and most appealing public beaches on this side of the island. Used as the setting for the Robin Williams movie *Club Paradise*, the wide, golden crescent of sand is justly popular with Jamaicans. The small reef just offshore is perfect for snorkelling (you'll probably need to bring your own gear), and protects the bay from the waves ensuring clear, calm, bright-blue water that shelves gently from the sand. At the western end, a small mineral spring offers a fresh-water rinse (the changing facilities are best avoided). In keeping with its supremely laid-back, hassle-free atmosphere, Winnifred has good, unobtrusive food and drink facilities. Near the ramshackle changing rooms in the centre of the beach, *Roots Man*

Portland

Frenchman's Cove hosts an immensely popular all-inclusive all-day party each October, which pulls the Kingston crowds; look for posters slapped up around Port Antonio.

At weekends, local operator Scotty offers childrens' horseback rides along Winnifred's sands (J$100); fishermen will also provide boat trips to nearby Monkey Island (1hr; US$10).

Portland

Corner sells beer and soft drinks as well as Ital or fish meals, while tucked into the eastern corner, the larger *Painter and Cynthia's* offers delicious, delicately seasoned platefuls of ackee and saltfish or grilled chicken and fresh fish – food is cooked to order, so you're best off putting in lunch requests when you arrive.

The coast road swings away from the sea parallel to Winnifred; to get to the beach, take the road opposite the *Jamaica Crest Resort* and follow it for half a mile or so through a neat housing scheme. You can park and walk down to the sand where the tarmac ends; if it hasn't been raining recently, you should be able to drive right down onto the beach.

Boston Bay

Though blessed with a perfectly good public beach, twinkling with fishing boats and packed with Jamaicans at the weekends, **BOSTON BAY**, further east along the A4, is better known for its collections of **jerk stands**. Jerking of meat originated in this part of the country – the Maroons hunted wild pigs here and smoked the meat to preserve it – and the pork and chicken on sale here is still reckoned to be the best in Jamaica: tasty, succulent and truly authentic. You'll pay around J$200 for half a pound of chicken, and J$250 for a pound of pork; both are best eaten with roast yam, breadfruit or a hunk of fresh hardough bread – take your picnic down to the beach below. If you've room in your bags, buy a jar of the fiery home-made jerk sauce – you won't find better anywhere. **Buses**, minibuses and shared taxis run to Boston Bay from Port Antonio.

Accommodation

The coastline east of Port Antonio is packed with good **places to stay**, though none is as cheap as you'll find in town. Bear in mind, though, that transport links around here are poor, and if you don't have a car, you'll be reliant on taxis – expect to pay J$150–200 for a charter to Port Antonio from any of these places, and around J$50 for shared taxis. All the hotels listed here are marked on the map on p.165.

Dragon Bay; ☎993 8751–3, fax 993 8971, *www.dragonbay.com*. The classic Caribbean resort, with sweeping lawns, 55 lavish acres of grounds, gorgeous beach and a fantastic atmosphere. Extensive facilities include tennis courts, a pool, fitness centre, sauna, a dive shop and two restaurants, and you can stay in rooms, or one-, two- or three-bedroom villas. The best choice in the area by miles. ⑥–⑧.

Drapers San, Drapers; ☎ and fax 993 7118. Funky, friendly, Italian-run guesthouse with an eclectic collection of rooms, some with kitchen, some with shared bathroom. All have fans and mosquito nets. ③ Breakfast is included in the rates.

Fern Hill Club, Mile Gully Rd; ☎993 7374, fax 993 7373. Good-value, slightly ramshackle hillside hotel just under a mile uphill off the main road, with a

See "Basics" p.34 for more on jerk cooking.

Boston Bay's water can get choppy; unless you want to body-surf (no boards are available to rent), you're better off at the calmer waters of Winnifred (see p.167).

large airy terrace overlooking San San, spacious grounds, several pools and friendly staff. Rooms have a/c, fan, satellite TV and phone. ④.

Jamaica Crest, Fairy Hill; ☎993 8400 or 8401, fax 993 8432. Spanking new complex with a pool, restaurant and disco; the modern one- or two-bedroom villas have full kitchen, a/c, satellite TV and phone. ⑤.

Jamaica Palace; ☎993 7720, fax ☎993 7749, *pal.hotel@cwjamaica .com*. Bizarre fantasy hotel, with the pretensions of a European chateau, a huge black and white tiled patio and a swimming pool in the shape of Jamaica. ⑦.

Mocking Bird Hill; ☎993 7267 or 7134, fax 993 7133, *www .hotelmockingbirdhill.com*. Eco-friendly hotel, set in a peaceful location in the hills above San San and filled with sculptures and paintings by artist and co-owner Barbara Walker. The airy rooms feature bamboo furniture and balconies, and there's a pool and a good restaurant. ⑥.

Moon San Villa, Blue Lagoon; ☎993 7600, *www.moonsanvilla.com*. Gorgeous airy villa 300 feet from the Blue Lagoon with surprisingly reasonable rates. With lovely, clean decor, mosquito nets and fans, the four bedrooms can be rented separately, in which case you get access to the kitchen and living room. Passes to San San beach and the lagoon are included, and meals are available. ⑥.

San San Tropez, San San; ☎ and fax 993 7213. This genial Italian-run restaurant has extremely spacious rooms which sleep four (for the same price per room as for two people) and have king-size beds, a/c, cable TV and private bathrooms with hot and cold water. ⑤.

Trident Hotel; ☎993 2602, fax 993 2590. The epitome of tasteful luxury, with lawns (including one set up for croquet), topiary, peacocks and delightful cottages by the sea. Small private beach, two pools, tennis courts and a suitably elegant restaurant. ⑦ Rates include breakfast.

Villa Paola; ☎993 7525, fax 993 7524. In the shadow of the *Jamaica Palace* hotel, the airy, clean rooms in this Italian-oriented place vary in size and price; all are simple with double beds, ceiling fan and private bathroom. ② Rates include breakfast and children stay free.

Eating

On this side of Port Antonio there's a good selection of **places to eat** with a clutch of hotel restaurants at the pricier end, and several fine roadside joints too, which are good if you're watching the purse-strings or fancy some more authentic Jamaican fare. The renowned jerk stands at Boston Bay (see opposite) also offer excellent, inexpensive fare.

In restaurant listings, we have given a phone number only for those places where you might need to reserve a table.

Blue Lagoon; ☎993 8491. Right beside the lagoon and one of the prettiest locations in the country, serving jerk meat, fresh fish and lobster, though prices are a little steep. Daily 10am–10pm for lunch and dinner.

Fern Hill Club; ☎993 3222. Marvellous views and reasonable, moderately priced Jamaican food make this a good lunch spot.

Jamaica Palace; ☎993 2020. Elegant, expensive European-style restaurant, big on steaks.

Mille Fleurs, *Mocking Bird Hill Hotel*; ☎993 7267. A soothing terrace setting and imaginative – and often delicious – concoctions based on

Jamaican staples. There's a daily vegetarian option, and puddings are sublime. Great for an early evening cocktail while watching the sun set over the mountains.

Nazarite, between Folly Point and Trident Castle. Roadside shack, marked by a colourful fruit stall, with Ital food and superb fresh juices. Closed Thursday.

San San Tropez, San San; ☎993 7213. Flavoursome, authentic Italian cooking. Homemade spaghetti and fettucini with tomato, seafood or pesto sauces, fantastic thin-crust pizzas and Italian-style grilled fish with tomatoes. Made on site, the crème caramel is delightful.

Trident Hotel; ☎993 2602. Excellent haute cuisine Jamaica-style at the poshest and priciest option on this coast, with white-gloved waiters and a smart dress code to go with the genteel atmosphere.

Woody's. Inexpensive and friendly family-run café, a little way east of *Jamaica Palace*, with good Jamaican staples of fish with pumpkin rice, pepperpot soup, jerk and curries.

Drinking and nightlife

The area east of Port Antonio is perfect for a quiet sunset **drink** but if you're after serious nightlife, you'll need to head into Port Antonio. You can have a quiet beer or rum on the waterfront at the *Blue Lagoon* restaurant (an excellent spot for a sunset cocktail) or in the *Drunken Dragon Pub* or *Cruise Bar* at the *Dragon Bay* hotel (see p.168). Some of the major hotels lay on evening **entertainment**, although they often don't advertise outside the hotel itself; *Dragon Bay* is particularly good for floorshows, live music and karaoke, and as it's not all-inclusive, entry is free and you pay only for drinks and dinner – call ahead to see what's on (☎993 8751). *Trident Hotel* (see p.169) has a live calypso band most nights. The smart *Tiffany's* nightclub at the *Jamaica Crest* resort (see p.169) pulls a crowd from Port Antonio at the weekend.

Long Bay to Manchioneal

The rolling pasturelands below Boston Bay are **Errol Flynn country**. The erstwhile screen idol bought much of the land between Boston Bay and Fair Prospect in the 1950s, and his widow, Patrice Wymore, still manages the 2000-acre estates, growing coconuts and guavas and raising beef cattle. Past the ranch, **Long Bay**, with its gorgeous swath of surf-pounded honey sand and laid-back counter-culture atmosphere, is a marvellous place to get away from it all, and conveniently close to the fabulous **Reach Falls**, where Tom Cruise got amorous in the movie *Cocktail*. Past the falls, Jamaica's eastern tip is refreshingly pretty much indifferent to tourism, and a couple of simple accommodation options near the fishing village of **Manchioneal** are perfect if you're after some unaffected charm.

Errol Flynn

By the time he arrived in Jamaica in 1947, **Errol Flynn**'s movie career was already in decline. The era of the swashbuckler was drawing to a close, and the Australian actor – star of classic Hollywood action movies like *The Sea Hawk* and *Captain Blood* – had begun to fall from favour with the studios. Nonetheless, sailing ashore at Kingston in his yacht *Zaca* (now owned by the Superclubs hotel chain), Flynn quickly worked his way into local legend. Even today, you'll occasionally find people recounting (increasingly improbable) stories of his strength, powers of seduction, formidable drinking and addiction to gambling – he reputedly lost Navy Island, just off Port Antonio, in one particularly unfortunate poker bet.

Flynn loved Jamaica. Soon after his arrival, he bought the *Titchfield Hotel* in Port Antonio as well as Navy Island; later, with third wife Patrice Wymore, he set up a ranch near Boston Bay and planned a castle-like home up in the John Crow Mountains. For a while, he threw wild parties at his hotels – pulling a string of celebrities to the island – but unsuccessful efforts to resurrect his movie career and continuing bouts of heavy drinking and ill-health were already taking their toll.

During his final years Flynn spent much of his time in Jamaica, living at Titchfield with the teenage actress Beverley Aadland. After his death in 1959, Aadland asked that he should be buried in Jamaica, but Wymore insisted that his body go to Hollywood. Today, despite the tarnishing of Flynn's reputation over the years, the people of the area remember the one-time heart-throb with considerable affection.

Long Bay

East of Boston, the main road cleaves to the coastline, offering great views of the surf pounding in on this unprotected side of the island. After five miles of bumpy, potholed tarmac, the road swings into **LONG BAY**, where a mini-tourist industry – unusual on the barely developed east coast – is swiftly growing. A wide crescent of sand with a laid-back atmosphere and the best surf in Jamaica, the bay has been attracting a smattering of European backpackers for the last decade, some of whom have settled here and opened guesthouses. Simple, friendly beach bars cater to the demand for entertainment, and it's a far cry from the developed resorts on the north coast. Tourists are outnumbered on the beach by local people, and the whole place feels a bit like Negril must have in the 1960s – good-natured and vaguely alternative, with a lot of ganja-smoking and general hanging out.

Negril is covered in Chapter Five; see p.299.

There isn't much to the village, which has grown up piecemeal on either side of the main road. The north end of the beach is where you'll find Jamaica's premier **surf** scene, though you'd never know it from the paucity of board-rental outlets; try the *Fisherman's Park* beach bar, which also has showers for a fresh-water rinse and hammocks for lounging. The locals propping up the beach bars should be able to help find a board, and they'll also know of anyone who'll take you out **fishing**. **Swimming** is excellent here, too, particularly if you're feeling a little jaded toward the usual placid Jamaican shores, but watch out for a dangerous undertow and rip tides; it's best not to swim out further than you can stand. If you stay in Long Bay, try to get up early to catch the **sunrise** over the ocean – it's staggering.

Practicalities

Buses and **minibuses** run daily to Long Bay from Port Antonio and, less frequently, from Kingston. A shared taxi from Port Antonio will cost about JS$70.

There's an increasing wealth of budget **accommodation** in Long Bay, though as there are no phones in the area, you'll have to turn up and take a chance. Some of the best options, simple but reliable, are up the hill toward the east end of the bay. *Rose Garden* (②) is a pretty, flower-wreathed, child-friendly place owned by a Jamaican/German couple, with nicely-decorated but small rooms in the main house. All rooms have fans and mosquito nets, and there's a shared hot-water bathroom and a plunge pool. Also on the hill, the laid-back *Skanka Heights* (①) affords gorgeous views over the surrounding coastline, and is a perfect backpackers' hangout. Rooms are in the main house or private cottages; all have fans, mosquito nets and access to the kitchen; meals – from pizza to Jamaican staples – are also available. If you want the option of being totally self-contained, there's the pretty *Rose Hill Cottage* (③), which has a kitchen and a sea-facing verandah; rates usually include dinner. Down on the beach, *Likkle Paradise* (①) is probably the best choice, run by the ever-gracious Herlette Kennedy. The spotless rooms have fans and private bathrooms, and you can use the kitchen. For a greater degree of luxury, try the businesslike, American-owned *Seascape Villa* (*www.jamaica-beachvillas.com*; ③) right on the beach, where you can rent a room, or, for a little more, the whole three-bedroom villa. Otherwise, the concrete block of *Rolling Surf Guesthouse* at the eastern end of the bay (①) offers sparse, basic rooms with fan, private bathroom and balconies overlooking the sea, while at the opposite end of the beach, *Long Bay Chalets* (①) is a quirky little place that's usually busier, with small rooms with fan and private bathroom. If you're on a seriously tight budget, the staff at *Fishermen's Park* can to direct you to some basic, dirt-cheap units in an old house set just back from the sea, where rooms come with bed, fan and little more; some have private bathrooms. All these places will provide meals on request.

Chill Out *hosts sound-system parties and the occasional stageshow; ask at the bar to see what's on.*

Evenings in Long Bay are usually centred around the appropriately named *Chill Out* French-run beach bar and restaurant, an open-sided thatch-roofed joint where you can get good seafood, chicken or pizza **meals**, or have a **drink** at the lively bar, complete with a table-football game. For solid Jamaican food, head for *Fishermen's Park*, also a good spot for a drink. There's a sort of informal, Round Robin-type agreement between Long Bay bars, with everyone heading for a different place each night; considering the size of the place, you'll have no trouble finding the action.

Reach Falls and Manchioneal

South of Long Bay, the road passes by some marvellously rugged coastline, with waves crashing against the cliffs. Before crossing the Christmas River, you'll pass the tiny village of **Kensington**, four miles on from Long Bay, birthplace of Father Hugh Sherlock, who composed Jamaica's national anthem in 1962. Just over the river, the *Ranch Bar* (☎993 6138; ②) is a peaceful, rootsy place with basic **rooms** and shared bathrooms. A rugged slip of beach is steps away (though the water gets pretty rough), and if you've a tent, you can camp for US$6. Cooked up by Rasta owner Stanford Johnson, the Ital **meals** are flavoursome, and the *Ranch Bar* itself also makes a soothing place to stop for a drink.

Enclosed by a thick covering of trees and utterly pitch black at night, the tunnel-like, hairpin-bend punctuated stretch of road near Kensington is locally known as "see me no more".

Halfway along Jamaica's eastern edge, and a mile or so on from the *Ranch Bar*, a road swings left off the main to **Reach Falls** (daily dawn to dusk; J$40) is one of the loveliest spots on the island, with the Drivers River running through some sumptuous rainforest before cascading over the falls into a wide, green pool. The thirty-foot waterfall itself is pretty spectacular, and you can stand right underneath it for an invigorating water massage. From the base of the falls, tour guides charge J$100 to take you on a thirty-minute trek upriver through the rainforest – climbing up beside the waterfall, picking your way across slippery rocks, swimming through deep pools and wading along the riverbed. You can ask to be taken to the base of **Mandingo Cave**, though it's quite a tricky climb. You follow the same route returning downriver, ending (if you can muster the courage) with an exhilarating jump into the pool at the base.

You might recognize Reach Falls as the place where Tom Cruise cavorts with his lady love in the movie Cocktail.

The side road from the main coast road to the falls winds for a little over three miles through some dazzling countryside to a small car park, where there's a small bar and, on weekends, stalls selling excellent janga soup and roast corn; further back from the car park are changing rooms and toilets. Just off the main A4, the falls are only practically accessible by car. A round-trip taxi from Port Antonio costs around US$50, although at quiet times you may be able to persuade a driver to do the job for half that.

Half a mile beyond the turnoff for Reach, the coast road inches into the pretty fishing village of **MANCHIONEAL**, where brightly-painted stalls selling roast fish and conch soup border the road and canoes line up on the sand; there's also a petrol station, and you can sup a Red Stripe at the diminutive *Titus Bar*. Protected by the headlands, Manchioneal bay is frequented by a family of **manatees** (locally known as sea cows); the four-strong brood can often be seen gambolling in the water. Across the bay, and offering gorgeous views of the harbour, there's a wonderful **accommodation** option in the shape of *Zion Country Cottages* (☎993 0435, fax 993 0551, *www.go-jam.com*; ②), well-signposted and 100 yards down a dirt track off the main road. Run by an enthusiastic Dutch couple who've built Rasta sensibilities into their eco-friendly outlook, the complex spreads down the cliffs to a small shingle beach complete with hammocks for catching the evening breezes, while lovingly-tended flowers and plants wreathe the pathways. The four simple, bright cabins share showers, and meals are available. If you want to **camp**, you can rent a tent for J$100 per night; otherwise, a pitch and breakfast costs U$12. The owners run excellent informal **tours** of the surrounding area, including hikes along the volcanic rocks of the local coastline to impressive blowholes and natural swimming pools, and also offer islandwide excursions.

The Rio Grande valley

Portland's interior – the **Rio Grande valley** – is a fantastically lush and partially impenetrable hinterland of tropical rainforest, rivers and waterfalls. The **Rio Grande** – one of Jamaica's major rivers – pours down from the John Crow Mountains through the deep and beautiful valley of real virgin forest, with none of the soil erosion and deforestation found on the south side of the Blue Mountains.

Despite its beauty, the area is little explored and many people only get as far as the **Nonsuch Caves** on its outskirts. Those tourists who do venture in are here to **raft** the river, though a few are discovering the superb **hiking** options, which range from gentle riverside walks to strenuous overnight pilgrimages up into the mountains. This is Maroon country, and many of the rivers and springs are named after local leaders – Nanny, Quao, Quashie and Quako. The major remaining Maroon settlement is **Moore Town**, though its past is more of a draw than its present, and while some of the other **villages** have a lovely setting and fascinating names – Alligator Church, Comfort Castle – you'll only want to visit if you're craving rustic isolation.

For more on the Maroons, see p.370.

Nonsuch Caves and Athenry Gardens

Four miles south of Port Antonio, on the outer fringes of the Rio Grande valley, the **Nonsuch Caves and Athenry Gardens** (daily 9am–5pm; US$5) are an obvious and mildly entertaining first stop in the interior. The fourteen ancient subterranean chambers were used by Taino Indians in pre-Columbian times (although their relics were removed to the University of the West Indies long ago), and now house some impressive stalactites and plenty of bats. The guides who shepherd you through the well-lit passages deliver a well-oiled patter, and they'll point out fossils of fish, coral and sea sponges from the days – around one and a half million years ago – when the whole of Jamaica was still underwater. Once you've emerged back into the sunshine, take a stroll around the expansive **gardens** adjacent to the caves; they command a magnificent view over the coastline and are packed with ginger lilies, bougainvillea, royal poinciana trees and the like.

For more on the Tainos, see "Contexts", p.369

The road up to the caves is in a dreadful condition, although your slow progress will allow you to appreciate some spectacular views of the John Crow Mountains.

Rafting the Rio Grande

Once just an easy way to transport bananas to the loading wharf in Port Antonio, **rafting** down the majestic Rio Grande has been Portland's most popular attraction ever since Errol Flynn began organizing rafting races for his friends in the 1950s. Today, it's a delightfully lazy way to spend half a day, although the sun can get fierce, so take a hat or umbrella.

From the put-in point at **Berridale**, six miles southwest of Port Antonio, thirty-foot rafts – made of lengths of bamboo lashed together, with a raised seat at the back that can hold two people and a small child – meander down the river on a three-hour journey through some outstanding scenery before terminating at the *Rafters' Rest* restaurant at St Margaret's Bay (see p.179). The raft captain stands at the front and poles the craft downstream, stopping periodically to let you swim or buy snacks from vendors positioned along the route.

Tickets are sold at the put-in spot by Rio Grande Attractions Ltd (☎993 5778; US$45 per raft), or occasionally by hotels and tour groups in Port Antonio. Because it's a one-way trip, **transport** can be a problem. If you're driving, you can leave your car at Berridale and have an insured driver take it down to *Rafters' Rest* for around US$5. A taxi to Berridale and back to Port Antonio from *Rafters' Rest* costs around US$10 each way. If you're desperate to save cash, the Berridale bus from Port Antonio runs close by the put-in point, and buses to Port Antonio from Kingston and Buff Bay pass the entrance to *Rafters' Rest* approximately once an hour.

You'll occasionally find people touting **unofficial rafting trips** for a lower price; don't hand over the cash until you've finished the journey at *Rafters' Rest*, and don't go with anyone unless you feel completely comfortable with them.

Hiking in the Rio Grande

Although some of the villages they once connected are long gone, the old parish council "roads" provide the basis for a number of **hiking trails** into the Rio Grande valley; others follow traditional pig hunters' routes. Many of them feature occasional reminders of Maroon occupation, from half-buried sugar pans to the remains of a deserted village above the Quako River.

Valley Hikes can also be contacted via the Mocking Bird Hill *hotel (☎993 7267 or 7134, fax 993 7133, www. hotelmocking birdhill.com).*

Hiking in the valley is an entirely different experience to the Blue Mountains. The lower limestone John Crow Mountains are hotter and wetter – a waterproof is essential – and the humidity can make walking uncomfortable, though the proliferation of mineral springs and Rio Grande tributaries means that you're never far from somewhere to cool off.

Portland

Rio Grande Valley hikes

The hikes listed are merely the most popular, pleasant or spectacular, but there are many more to explore; contact Valley Hikes for details.

Guava River Trail, (7 miles; 7 hours) A difficult trail, run by Valley Hikes, that's well worth the effort; from Bellevue head straight into the jungle and follow the Guava River for most of the way. Opportunities abound for swimming and waterfall-spotting, and there are even some hot springs if you fancy a dip.

Nanny Town (10–15 miles; 2 days). This extremely difficult two-day excursion from Coopers Hill through untouched forest of unparalleled beauty to the site of the eighteenth-century Maroon hideaway demands determination, a love of nature and a tent to do it; enlist a Valley Hikes guide.

Scatter Water Falls (0.75 miles; 20min). The shortest, easiest and most popular hike in the area, usually done from Berridale (see p.175). From there, a raft takes you across the Rio Grande, and it's then a twenty-minute walk to the falls, where there are swimming pools and a bar. A further fifteen-minute hike up the falls leads to the Foxes Caves, which you'll need a flashlight to explore properly.

White River Falls (4 miles; 7hr). Starting from Millbank, this tough climb traces the beautiful White River through virgin rainforest to a series of fabulous high waterfalls. The trail is strenuous and slippery with lots of uphill scrambling, but at the first cascade you get your reward – a swim in the freezing froth. There are seven falls in all, but most people go only as far as the first two or three.

Once a sizeable village, Nanny Town is today a scattering of crumbling and overgrown ruins, but remains an important symbol of Maroon history, allegedly haunted with the ghosts of vanquished British soldiers.

One or two of the peripheral hikes, such as Road End, can be done on your own, but a **guide** is essential if you're heading deep into the valley. You can easily find someone to guide you once you're up in Millbank (ask at *Ambassabeth Cabins* at Bowden – see p.179), but far and away the best official organization is Port Antonio-based Valley Hikes (☎993 3881, fax 993 4962, *valleyhikes@cwjamaica.com*), an excellent, eco-friendly, non-profit group employing well-trained certified guides from the area who really know their stuff. The per person rates are extremely reasonable, ranging from US$20–35 for two to four hour Lower Rio Grande treks, to US$150 for an overnight trip up to Nanny Town high up in the hills. Valley Hikes, in addition to offering most of the hikes covered in the box above, also offer combination **hiking and Rio Grande rafting trips** from US$20 plus US$45 to cover the cost of the raft, and **horseback riding** in the valley at US$40 for four hours. You can even rent a pair of rubber boots for US$3 if muddy going is anticipated.

The only other reputable organization is Kingston-based Sun Venture Tours (☎960 6685, fax 920 8348, *sunventuretours @hotmail.com*), which can arrange hikes on request along pig hunters' trails in the area; contact them in advance for rates.

Moore Town

Eleven miles inland from Port Antonio, **MOORE TOWN** is Jamaica's principal Maroon settlement, founded, so the legend goes, by **Nanny** (chieftainess of the Windward Maroons and now a National Hero) in the mid-eighteenth century. Today, it's a small, quiet place at the end of a winding rocky road, with few signs and little apparent sense of its historical importance. The road goes straight into the heart of the village, with houses and small shacks scattered beside it and across the adjacent fields. You should, as a matter of protocol, check in by saying hello to the Maroons' **Colonel** or chief. There are presently two of them: Colonel Harris, a knowledgeable elder whose house is the first on the right after the post office, and Colonel Stirling, to whom leadership was officially passed in 1995, who lives a little further up. There's no charge for looking around, but you may be asked for a donation to a planned (though probably far-off) Maroon museum.

The Windward Maroons

When the Spanish left Jamaica in 1660, they armed and freed most of their African slaves and encouraged them to fight a guerrilla war against the new British colonists. Over the years, the ranks of these guerrillas – known to the Spanish as *cimarrones* (meaning wild or untamed), and corrupted to **Maroons** by the British – were boosted by runaway slaves from the sugar plantations. They set up small communities in inaccessible parts of the island, with the **Windward Maroons** establishing themselves in the Blue and John Crow Mountains and the Trelawny Maroons making a base in Cockpit Country (see p.282). As they grew in confidence, the Maroons raided British settlements for weapons and supplies and, by the 1720s, they had become such a serious threat that the British decided to send the troops in.

The Windward Maroons had their headquarters 2000ft up in the mountains at **Nanny Town**, virtually inaccessible to the British soldiers who were unfamiliar with the area. They only discovered it after a black slave led them there in 1728, and were periodically slaughtered on their forays into the rainforest to destroy the settlement. Eventually, in 1734, British army captain Stoddard dragged swivel guns up the south side of the John Crow Mountains and bombarded Nanny Town, destroying most of the 140 homes and scattering the Maroons, forcing many of them to move south. Still the British couldn't flush them out completely, though, and five years later a peace treaty was signed, giving the undefeated Maroons a semi-independent status that they retain today, as well as five hundred acres of land in the Rio Grande valley, on which they established their new base at Moore Town (see above).

Today, the Windward Maroons have been virtually assimilated into the wider Jamaican population. Though some of the elders remain fiercely proud of their heritage – and a handful still speak the traditional Coromantee language – most young Maroons see little opportunity in their mountain villages, and move to the cities for work, inter-marrying with other Jamaicans. Within a generation there are likely to be few pure-blood Maroons left.

The former village of Nanny Town is visitable on an arduous but deeply satisfying two-day trek from Millbank; see opposite.

Bump Grave, a monument to Nanny and supposedly the place where she's buried, is in the town's small central square, and is pretty much the only thing to see. It's a stone tomb, with a plaque to the "indomitable and skilled chieftainess", and the Maroon and Jamaican flags fly side by side overhead. Otherwise, apart from the usual profusion of schoolchildren, Moore Town feels deserted. Many villagers live scattered around the nearby hills, and you'll see houses perched in the most unlikely places.

If you're lucky you'll catch a **cricket game** in the grassy square across from the monument – given the precarious position of the pitch at the edge of the Wildcane River, several fielders normally stand up to their ankles in water to catch any well-struck balls before they disappear downstream. Alternatively, you can hike up to **Nanny Falls**, following the track north through town for around forty minutes. A guide will help you to find the best places to swim and can take you on a longer hike through the jungle if you wish; ask around for a suitable person and arrange a fee. **Valley Hikes** (see p.176) will also provide a guide to Nanny Falls, who'll pick fruits for you to sample and point out medicinal plants along the way (US$25 per person); longer walks along trails around the town are also available (US$30 per person).

Moore Town is served by two daily **buses** from Port Antonio, one in the early morning, the other early afternoon (J$20 each way). Each bus takes about ninety minutes and comes straight back down, so your best plan is to go up on the first bus and come back on the second. Take a **picnic** as there are no restaurants, and don't miss the bus back as there's nowhere to **stay**; if you get stuck, the colonels might know someone with a room for the night.

Millbank

Little-visited **MILLBANK** – the last sizeable town in the Rio Grande valley – nestles deep in the John Crow Mountains five miles south of Moore Town. Sizeable here means a couple of basic shops, a playing field and a community centre, but the town also contains one of the three Blue and John Crow Mountains National Park **ranger stations** (see box on p.133), which, if there's anyone there (rangers are often out on patrols) acts as an unofficial information centre. You're in prime Maroon country here, and many of the town's older inhabitants (a healthy diet and clean mountain air mean that many residents are pushing 100) will happily tell you tales of Maroon history, while the younger locals can escort you to derelict settlements that don't appear on the maps.

Millbank's setting is spectacular; rainforest rises up all around and the perfume of wild ginger lilies hangs heavy in the air. It's also the starting point for several good **hikes**, the most popular (detailed on p.176) heading to **White River Falls**, seven high cascades on the other side of the Rio Grande river; ask around for a guide or pre-arrange with Valley Hikes (see p.176).

Kingston lights from Jack's Hill

Exterior decoration

Carnival queen

Devon House, Kingston

IAN CUMMING

Kingston - downtown looking up

IAN CUMMING

IAN CUMMING

Papa San at Sabina Park, Kingston

Blue Mountain peaks

Long Bay, Portland

Carnival, Chukka Cove

Frenchman's Cove, Portland

Bamboo rafts on the Martha Brae

Bob Marley's Mausoleum, St Ann

Good Hope Estate, Trelawny

As the road stops just beyond Moore Town, getting to Millbank involves taking the right fork at Seaman's Valley via **Alligator Church**. You'll pass the diminutive communities of **Ginger House** and **COMFORT CASTLE**, where the *Gingerbread House* bar is the area's only source of entertainment, with loud rocksteady and reggae played well into the night. The only **place to stay** in the area is the wonderful *Ambassabeth Cabins and Campsite* (☎938 5036, fax 977 8565; ①) at **BOWDEN**, a half-hour walk southeast of Millbank – a regular car should be able to handle the road if there's been no rain; otherwise, you might be able to scrounge a lift in Millbank square or from the ranger station. The down-to-earth wooden cabins have no electricity or running water (though fresh water is readily available from mineral springs), but bags of atmosphere and ingenuity, and traditional Maroon meals are prepared on an open fire. Baths are taken in the Rio Grande or at a small spring nearby. If you're on a budget, you can rent floor space in one of the larger cabins for US$5, camping is also possible for a nominal fee, and guides are available for walks in the area. As *Ambassabeth* is so remote, it's best to arrange your stay in advance; the owners can also arrange transportation from Kingston or Port Antonio.

Between Millbank and Bowden, a rope and board **suspension bridge** provides the only dry means of crossing the Rio Grande for miles around and is an important link for locals. Once past *Ambassabeth*, the road widens into an improbably large thoroughfare, built in the late 1970s by British ex-servicemen granted large tracts of crown land. Harsh conditions and lack of modern conveniences prompted a swift exodus and the now grassy track melts abruptly into the bush at Road End, less than a third of the way to its intended destination at Bath.

West of Port Antonio

The A4 winds west from Port Antonio, criss-crossing the old railway track torn up by Hurricane Allen in 1980 and threading through a series of tiny fishing villages, peppered with stalls selling local fruit and vegetables. You can stop for a fresh-water splash at **Somerset Falls**, or head inland to Swift River or River's Edge, or explore the towns of **Buff Bay** and **Annotto Bay**, both bursting with small-town character.

Buses run between Port Antonio and Annotto Bay every hour or so in both directions and will stop wherever you ask.

St Margaret's Bay and Somerset Falls

About five miles west of Port Antonio, the first settlement of note is tiny **ST MARGARET'S BAY**, where the Rio Grande empties into the sea underneath an iron bridge dating back to 1891. Just by the bridge, a side road leads towards **Rafters' Rest**, a pretty colonial-style building that serves as journeys end for Rio Grande rafting

Fabulous fun days at Bryan's Bay, just east of Port Antonio, are advertised by way of fly-ers slapped up around town.

excursions (see p.175). You can also book a trip here, and a posse of raft operators usually hang out by the bridge touting for business. Past *Rafters' Rest*, you enter St Margaret's Bay proper, an appealingly neat settlement spreading back from the roadside. St Margaret's Bay was the last stop-but-one of the Jamaica Railway until Hurricane Allen dispensed with most of the track here in 1980, ten years before the railway was shut down islandwide. The railway buildings now serve as homes, and the old station itself operates as a simple restaurant/bar. If you want to **stay** in the area, *Rio Vista* (☎993 5444, fax 993 5445, *riovistavillaja@jamweb.net*; ④–⑤) is beautifully situated on a bluff that affords fantastic views of the Rio Grande river and the Blue and John Crow Mountain foothills. You can stay either in a room in the main house (rates for these include breakfast), or a self-contained one-bedroom villa with a kitchen. A little further west, the friendly *Paradise Inn* (☎993 5169, fax 993 5569; ③–⑤) has simple rooms and a grander selection of studio apartments with a/c, fan, phone and a kitchen; there's also a pool and restaurant on site. Otherwise, the hills above town hold the quiet *Pleasant View Guesthouse* (☎913 3058; ②), where the spacious rooms have private hot-water bathrooms, two double beds, fans and TVs, and the pool faces verdant mountain slopes. St Margaret's Bay has a couple of roadside shacks selling cheap **meals**. Slightly classier, the *Rafters' Rest* restaurant has typical Jamaican dishes as well as hamburgers and sandwiches.

Just outside St Margaret's Bay, lush landscaping and sizeable signs mark the entrance to the concrete complex built around **Somerset Falls** (daily 9am–5pm; J\$120), part of the cascading Daniels River. Guides lead you through to the main falls, passing a stairway that provides access to the "cool pool" – a refreshing place to have a dip and slide over the rocks. Past here, your entrance fee gets you a boat ride through a chink in the gorge-like rocks to the spectacular "hidden falls" beyond, cascading into a 20-foot deep pool and perfect for a natural power shower. There's a simple **café** serving drinks and light snacks.

Hope Bay and Swift River

West of St Margaret's Bay, past the turnoff to Ken Jones Aerodrome, the road swings into the busy little village-cum-fishing-community of **HOPE BAY**, home of a string of shops and rum bars. At the police station, you can turn inland for some marvellous **river swimming** in the upper reaches of the Swift River, a half-hour drive through cocoa groves and mountain valleys. Follow the roadsigns and keep bearing left to the tiny and supremely friendly settlement of **Swift River** itself, where you turn left off the main road at a small suspension bridge and follow the path of the river. The further you go upstream, the quieter it gets, and there are innumerble deep pools for a dip.

In the hills above Hope Bay, Content *(☎913 0690 or 953 2387; ②) is the perfect place to stay if you've an interest in Ital living and the willingness to eschew modern comforts; book via the numbers above, or call in at the Sundial health food shop in town.*

Burkies is the best spot for **food** in Hope Bay, and you can get passable meat from the *Buss Di Place* jerk centre, while the slightly more ambient *Railway Drive-In Bar*, in the old clapboard train station, makes a pleasant spot for a drink.

Crystal Springs, Buff Bay and Annotto Bay

Heading west from Hope Bay, the **Crystal Springs nature resort** (daily dawn to dusk; J$100) is a quasi-botanical gardens signposted off the main road just before Buff Bay, on the site of a seventeenth-century sugar plantation. A river runs through the rambling gardens, where there's a fine collection of orchids and an old waterwheel. The **mongoose** was introduced to Jamaica here in 1872, in an attempt to wipe out the cane rats that were wrecking the local sugar harvest. The plan backfired badly as the mongooses, showing more catholic taste than had been anticipated, turned their attention to the island's harmless coneys and iguanas and devastated their respective populations. Mongooses are still all over the place and, if you're driving around the country, you'll often see them legging it across the road with gay abandon.

Beyond Crystal Springs, the road affords some awesome views of the Blue and John Crow Mountains, the peaks poking above the endless fields of coconut palms and banana groves that were planted as part of the United Fruit Company's Kildaire Estate, itself occupying land that was previously a colonial-era sugar plantation. Kildaire's former great house, on the A4, serves as an efficient rest stop these days, with a good restaurant, a well-stocked gift store and sparkling bathrooms, which are quite a rarity in these parts.

It's another half-mile along bumpy, potholed tarmac before you get to the easy-going market town of **BUFF BAY**, where Blue Mountain farmers come to sell their wares in the dingy covered market. Aside from the piles of produce and a rickety metal arch over the main street – a relic from the 1962 independence celebrations – there's not a lot to see, but you might want to poke around **St George's** Anglican church, the oldest building in town. There's been a church on this site since 1681, although most of the present structure dates from 1814.

Aside from Kildaire, the best place to **eat** in Buff Bay is the excellent *Pacesetter*, almost opposite the church, with great curry goat and rice and peas, and a lovely selection of cakes and pastries.

Ten miles west of Buff Bay, the road enters **ANNOTTO BAY**, a busy, tatty little one-street town named after the red annatto dye once produced here from the pulp of indigenous trees (though locals argue that the name comes from the colour of the bay after rain). A commercial centre for surrounding communities which, since the scaling-down of local banana and sugar industries, when produce was loaded from the wharves, has become a lot quieter.

Portland

At the time of writing, the wooden cabins at Crystal Springs were closed for refurbishment; you can call ☎996 1400 to see if they're open again.

Just outside Buff Bay on the knoll of a hill, the A4 passes the Blueberry Hill jerk centre, which offers meat that some say is better than Boston Bay's.

Buff Bay is the start of a spectacular drive through the Blue Mountains to Kingston.

The town boasts a police station, courthouse and a market behind the main square (main days Friday and Saturday). Pause to admire the red and yellow **Baptist church**, built in 1892, its entrance guarded by old cannons, the meagre remains of British Fort George.

The grey-sand beach to the west of Annotto Bay isn't a particularly appealing place for a swim, but you might want to take advantage of the JTB-run *Travel Halt*, where there's a restaurant and bathrooms. Almost opposite, *Siloah Bar* is a more representative example of a Jamaican rest stop, with lots of character and friendly staff. For **food**, head to the *Human Service Station*, just east of town, for adequate Jamaican fare; just past here, the bamboo *Seaview Jerk Centre and Pub* is good for chicken and a Red Stripe. A tight corner in the road just beyond the outskirts of town causes drivers to slow down and offers vendors a prime opportunity to flog Irish Moss seaweed and peppered shrimp, the latter freshly caught in the rivers of the Blue Mountains above.

The fertile pastures inland of Annotto Bay are the home of the small but coveted long mango, an elongated, sweet and non-stringy fruit. In season, you should be able to pick some up at the town's market.

The countryside **inland of Annotto Bay**, sheltering under the eaves of the Blue Mountains, makes a welcome change from the endless coastal vistas of the A4; turn in at the Annotto Bay All Age School and follow the signs to **River Edge** (☎944 2673, fax 944 9455), twenty minutes' drive from the coast. On the way, you'll pass grove upon grove of bananas, and a commercial palm and flower farm nestled at the bottom of a pretty valley. Built around the cool, clear waters of the Pencar River, *River Edge* is a friendly, family-run combination of restaurant, swimming spot and guesthouse. Shallow swimming pools offer a refreshing dip (or a natural jacuzzi), and you can have a drink, a tasty Jamaican meal or even a massage in the shady waterside gazebo. If you want to **stay** here, there's the option of pleasant, airy dorm beds (U$20), or private studio apartments with bathrooms and cooking facilities (④). If you fancy camping, pitches hooked up to electricity, with showers and bathrooms nearby, cost U$6 per person if you have your own tent, U$10 per person if you need to rent one.

If you're not staying on site, the best time to visit River Edge is for the excellent Sunday brunch (J$500).

Travel details

Buses and minibuses
It is impossible to predict accurately the frequency of buses and minibuses in the Blue Mountains and the East – service is often chaotic and delays and cancellations are frequent – so the figures opposite are only general guidelines. However, on the most popular routes you should be able to count on getting a ride within an hour if you travel in the morning; things normally quieten down later in the day. On less popular routes, you're best off asking around for probable departure times the day before you travel.

Bath to: Kingston (1 daily; 2hr 30min).

Morant Bay to: Kingston (3 daily; 2hr); Port Antonio (2 daily; 2hr 30min).

Papine to: Mavis Bank (2 daily; 1hr 20min); Newcastle (2 daily; 1hr 10min).

Port Antonio to: Boston Bay (4 daily; 20min); Buff Bay (4 daily; 1hr); Kingston (via Buff Bay, 4 daily, 3hr 30min; via Morant Bay, 2 daily, 4hr 30min); Long Bay (4 daily; 50min); Montego Bay (1 daily; 5hr); Moore Town (2 daily; 1hr 30min); Morant Bay (2 daily; 2hr 30min); Ocho Rios (1 daily; 3hr).

Flights

Port Antonio to: Kingston (2 daily; 15 min); Montego Bay (3 daily; 35min); Negril (2 daily; 45min), Ocho Rios (2 daily; 20min).

Chapter 3

Ocho Rios and the north coast

Potholed as it is, the north coast road is the busiest tourist route on the island. Traffic belts between the most commercial of Jamaica's resorts, and hundreds of hotels, bars, jerk stands and craft shacks line up to catch the possible trade which passes by but rarely stops. The attraction of the north coast is obvious – barrelling through the diverse parishes of St Mary, St Ann and Trelawny, the road passes sparse mangrove coastline, luscious farmland and sweeping cane or coconut plantations, and runs parallel to miles of white-sand beaches with reefs less than a hundred feet out to sea. Yet the "tourist" coast can seem like Jamaica at its most forlorn – many of the sights appear contrived, much of the accommodation is in fenced-in all-inclusives, and the ingrained practice of tourist hustling in the resorts can make every interaction feel like a sales pitch. Nonetheless, the area does offer Jamaica's highest concentration of things to do, and boasts an energetic atmosphere that's noticeably absent in more tempered parts.

Much of the tourism development is centred on the "garden parish" of **St Ann**, so called because of the area's immensely fertile

---

Accommodation price codes

All the hotels detailed in this guide have been graded according to the following price categories. Note that the prices have been calculated as those for the cheapest **double** or **twin room** during low season, normally mid-April to mid-December. During high season, rates are liable to rise by up to 25 percent (though this is rare at the cheap hotels), and proprietors may be less amenable to bargaining. Although the law requires prices to be quoted in Jamaican dollars, most hotels give rates in US dollars; payment can be made in either currency. For more details see p.27.

① under US$20	④ US$51–70	⑦ US$151–200
② US$21–35	⑤ US$71–100	⑧ US$200 and above
③ US$36–50	⑥ US$101–150	

---

soil. St Ann has also spawned luminaries such as **Marcus Garvey**, **Bob Marley** and **Winston "Burning Spear" Rodney**, and is considered the spiritual centre of the island. The nucleus of the parish and the home of the famous **Dunn's River Falls**, **Ocho Rios** is fast becoming Jamaica's most popular holiday destination, with all the high-rise blocks, buzzing jet-skis and thumping nightlife you could ask for, while just a few miles to the east, the quiet coastal villages of **Oracabessa** and **Port Maria** are disturbed by little other than birdsong, with miles of deserted coastline nearby and lots of possibilities for hiking and waterfall-hunting. West of Ocho Rios, **St Ann's Bay**, parish capital and site of ruined Spanish settlement **Sevilla Nueva**, makes a refreshing change to the glitz of its neighbour, while the developing resort towns of **Runaway Bay** and **Discovery Bay**, where tourism is largely restricted to all-inclusives, maintain communities relatively unaffected by the influx of foreigners. Small villages and brashly advertised rest-stops punctuate the scenery as far as the windswept market town of **Falmouth**.

Inland, smack in the middle of St Ann, is **Nine Mile**, Bob Marley's birthplace and mausoleum, where an obligatory cache of Rasta guides welcome hordes of reggae disciples. Away from this star attraction, though, you can drive for hours through the mostly undeveloped **interior** with only cattle for company and some marvellous scenery to distract you from the wheel.

Ocho Rios and around

Light years away from the "sleepy fishing village" of a few decades ago, **OCHO RIOS** (usually just called "Ochi") is unabashedly dedicated to the tourist industry these days. The first town in Jamaica to be developed specifically as a resort, Ochi's growth has been rapid, and in some places, the planners have overlooked aesthetics in the chase for foreign dollars. The town thrives on the spending power of regular tourists and the thousands of cruise-ship passengers who disembark each week, and is fully geared up to cater to easy-access tourism. The streets abound with neon-fronted in-bond stores, fast-food chains, bars, clubs and visitor-oriented restaurants, while several slickly packaged attractions are within a few minutes' drive. Local culture takes a bit of a back seat to the tourist trappings, though, and Ochi is not a place to get an authentic flavour of Jamaica; nor is it the best choice amongst the island's "big three" resorts for the classic Caribbean beach holiday – the meagre strip of hotel-lined sand just can't compete with the beaches of Negril and Montego Bay, and the club and bar scenes are less vibrant. Nonetheless, the nightlife is improving, and Ochi compensates for its scenic deficiencies with a certain infectious energy. Though still in evidence away from the main streets, harassment has declined since resort police became a permanent

presence, and as Ochi's town and tourist area are one and the
same, there's less of the "sitting duck" atmosphere of the Montego
Bay strip.

Some history

"Ocho Rios" – literally "Eight Rivers" – is a corruption of the Spanish
name *chorreros* or *chireiras*, referring to the "gushing water" of the
many local waterfalls. Less poetically, the town's surrounds were the
site of several bloody battles, which took place when local Spanish
governor **Don Christobel Arnaldo de Yssasi** – whose family had
been in Jamaica for over 100 years – refused to give in to the British
after their capture of the island in 1655. Major skirmishes took place
at Dunn's River in 1657, Rio Nuevo in 1658 (see p.198) and Shaw
Park in 1659, when Yssasi's men were attacked by a group led by his
erstwhile ally, **Juan De Bolas**, a former slave who had defected to the
British. In April 1660, Yssasi fled the island in a dug-out canoe from
Don Christopher's Point in St Mary, and the local Spanish legacy
remains only in a smattering of place names and the ubiquitous presence of the fragrant **pimento** tree, first discovered by the Spanish in
St Ann, and commercially planted in the parish ever since.

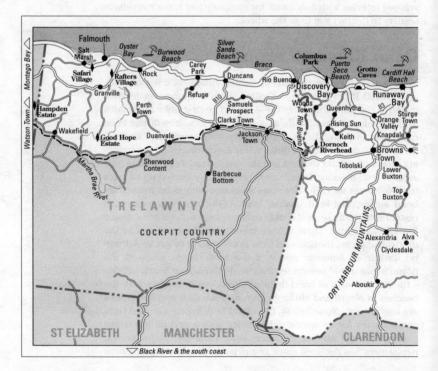

The **British** left a more pervasive mark, with their huge sugarcane, pimento, lumber and cattle farms, but most of the planters were absentees and Ocho Rios remained little more than a fishing harbour until the twentieth century, when the dual concerns of **tourism** and **bauxite** began to physically sculpt the land and secure local prosperity. In 1923, the great house of a struggling citrus plantation at Shaw Park became Jamaica's first exclusive **hotel**. By 1948, it had been joined by four others – *Sans Souci Lido*, *Silver Seas*, *Dunn's River* (now *Sandals Dunn's River*) and *Eden Bower* (now *The Enchanted Garden*) – and Ocho Rios looked set for a glowing future. However, though there were a few glorious beaches nearby, most were overhung by steep cliffs or cut off from the mainland by mangrove swamps, a significant problem in a destination sold on the premise of sand and sea. Meanwhile, perpetual crop failures led local planter **Alfred DaCosta** to chemically analyze the St Ann earth; he found that the soil contained high levels of **bauxite**, the chief raw material used to produce aluminium. Foreign-owned companies Reynolds and Kaiser bought up huge tracts of land, and in 1968, the newly formed St Ann Development Company clubbed together with Reynolds Jamaica Mines and the Urban Development Corporation to

Ocho Rios and around

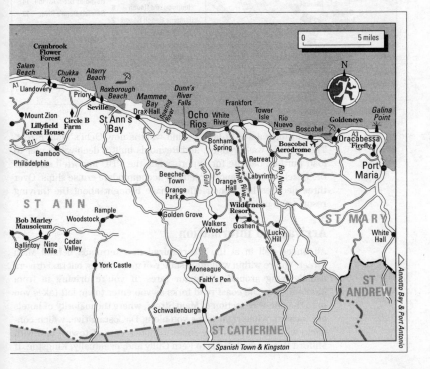

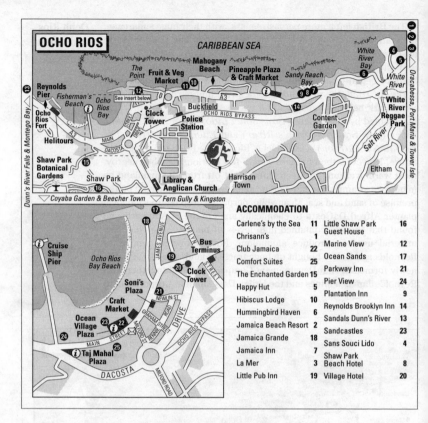

OCHO RIOS

CARIBBEAN SEA

White River Bay

Reynolds Pier

The Point
Fruit & Veg Market
Mahogany Beach
Pineapple Plaza & Craft Market
Sandy Reach Bay

White River

Fisherman's Beach
Ocho Rios Bay
See insert below
Clock Tower
Buckfield
OCHO RIOS BYPASS

White River Reggae Park

Ocho Rios Fort

Police Station
Content Garden

Helitours

Salt River

Shaw Park Botanical Gardens

Shaw Park
Library & Anglican Church
Harrison Town

Eltham

Coyaba Garden & Beecher Town   Fern Gully & Kingston

Dunn's River Falls & Montego Bay

Oracabessa, Port Maria & Tower Isle

Cruise Ship Pier
Ocho Rios Bay Beach
Bus Terminus
JAMES AVENUE
EVELYN STREET
Clock Tower

Soni's Plaza
Craft Market
Ocean Village Plaza
Taj Mahal Plaza
NEWLIN ST
GRAHAM STREET
FENNY ROAD
MILFORD DRIVE
OCHO RIOS BYPASS
MAIN STREET
DACOSTA
MILFORD ROAD

ACCOMMODATION

Carlene's by the Sea	11	Little Shaw Park Guest House	16
Chrisann's	1	Marine View	12
Club Jamaica	22	Ocean Sands	17
Comfort Suites	25	Parkway Inn	21
The Enchanted Garden	15	Pier View	24
Happy Hut	5	Plantation Inn	9
Hibiscus Lodge	10	Reynolds Brooklyn Inn	14
Hummingbird Haven	6	Sandals Dunn's River	13
Jamaica Beach Resort	2	Sandcastles	23
Jamaica Grande	18	Sans Souci Lido	4
Jamaica Inn	7	Shaw Park Beach Hotel	8
La Mer	3	Village Hotel	20
Little Pub Inn	19		

reclaim forty acres of land behind what is now Ochi's Main Street. The harbour was dredged, and Reynolds built a deep-water pier to load purified bauxite for export, while the UDC imported sand for the beach and built another jetty to accommodate cruise ships. Over three decades later, their efforts have brought about the thriving resort town of today.

Arrival and information

All buses pull in at the disorganized new terminus behind Main Street. You're within walking distance of most hotels, but taxi drivers usually hang around plying for fares. If you're **driving** in from Montego Bay, the coast road forks as you enter town; left takes you onto the one-way section of Main Street, where the majority of hotels are located, while right takes you along DaCosta Drive, which connects with the bypass (the route to hotels east of town), and with Milford Road, which leads to Fern Gully and, eventually, Kingston. If you drive in from the east, you enter town via the bypass and there are numerous signposted exits onto Main Street. Domestic **flights** touch down at Boscobel Aerodrome, a thirty-minute drive from town; a cab should cost about US$25.

The main **JTB office** (☎974 2582 or 2570; Mon–Fri 9am–5pm, Sat 9am–1pm) in Ocean Village Plaza on Main Street (go up the staircase at the side of the building, and it's the first door on the left) has flyers on activities and hotels and dispenses useful local maps as well as general information. There are smaller **information booths** at Pineapple Place Craft Market, Taj Mahal Plaza on Main Street and at the cruise-ship pier. Look out also for *Focus on Jamaica – Ocho Rios*, an annual free guide to local attractions,

---

Organized tours from Ocho Rios

In terms of quality and choice, the Ocho Rios roster of **organized tours** (see Basics, p.25) is second only to Montego Bay. Scores of comparably priced operators (most with in-hotel desks) will whisk you off to Dunn's River Falls or Nine Mile, though it's often more interesting to go without the company of twenty other camera-toting tourists. Of the more conventional operators, the best bet is **Safari Tours** (☎972 2639 or 1-800 919 7900); excursions (usually aboard zebra-painted jeeps) include a downhill mountain bike tour from Murphy Hill to Dunn's River Falls (5hr; US$49), tubing along the White River from Spanish Bridge (3.5hr; $49) and various full- or half-day round-the-island trips, from north coast jaunts to a tour of the Blue Mountains and Kingston (all around US$70, including return transportation to your hotel).

An alternative to taking an organized tour is to hire a local driver and do some independent sightseeing; try Alton Smith (☎1-997 7573 or 933 7978).

Among the more adventurous possibilities, try the exhilarating ATV (or quad bike) tours offered by Wilderness Resorts in the St Mary interior (☎974 5189 or 4613; see p.198). Their valley tour (1hr; US$60) goes through the lush landscape that surrounds the Wilderness farm, while the country tour (2hr; US$103) takes you to the Spanish Bridge Blue Hole with stops for swimming and photos. All trips include transport to and from your hotel, and can be combined with other Wilderness activities such as fishing, hiking and horse riding. G & B at 6 James Ave (☎974 8247) offer day-long guided **motorbike tours** to places such as Port Antonio, the Blue Mountains and the Bob Marley mausoleum; you pay for the cost of your bike plus US$30 for the guide, and usually buy his lunch as well. Hooves (☎972 0905) offer **horseback trail rides** around the Seville Great House at St Ann's Bay (see p.219); they also offer inland hacks, and can do private rides on request. Finally, Helitours, 120 Main St, (☎974 2265 or 1108, fax 974 2183), offers expensive but unforgettable **helicopter** jaunts – call a day ahead to book. Its "Jamaican Showcase" takes in Linstead, Bog Walk Gorge, Spanish Town, Port Royal, Kingston, the Blue Mountains and Port Maria (1hr; US$225 per person). A half-hour tour over Ocho Rios and down the coast to Port Maria costs US$110 per person, and the cheapest option is twenty minutes above Ochi for US$65 per person. In conjunction with Wilderness Resorts, Helitours also offer a combination tour of road transportation to Wilderness, a 1hr ATV tour and a helicopter ride back to Ochi, which costs US$520 for a group of four.

The "no pedalling" downhill bike trip from Blue Mountain Tours (US$85; see p.132) is one of Ochi's most popular tours.

---

and *The North Coast Times*, a valuable weekly source for one-off entertainment events.

Orientation and getting around

*Watson's
Shopping
Shuttle (☎974
5169 or 995
3277) offers
cheap rides –
between
US$1.50 to
U$3.50 –
between Ochi's
shopping cen-
tres and main
attractions,
and will pick
up from most
local hotels.*

Both the clocktower and the car park next to Ocean Village Plaza are unofficial **taxi ranks**; see p.205 for reliable firms if you want to call a taxi. The abundance of tourist dollars can mean unreasonably inflated fares – haggle, as there is always another waiting; as a rule of thumb, expect to pay about J$250 to charter a taxi from downtown to the Tower Isle area. **Shared taxis** running along Main Street can be flagged down anywhere at the roadside; for most drives around town, you'll pay around J$20, rising to J$40 to Boscobel or Oracabessa. **Car rental** agencies abound, and rates are as you'd expect for a major tourist destination. If you can find one, a **bicycle** is a good option for nipping around town (US$10 per day), as is a **motorbike** (from US$35 for a Suzuki 200). For reputable car and bike rental companies, see Listings, p.204. If you're spending most of your time in town you'll probably find it's easier to walk.

Accommodation

While the fashion for **all-inclusives** is embraced even by some of the small central hotels, there are alternatives. The sheer volume of accommodation here means good deals, particularly during the low season, and a decent spread of budget options, but prices overall are higher than in less developed areas. There are hordes of self-contained **villas** in and around Ocho Rios; the more luxurious units can rent for up to US$10,000 per week, others go for as little as US$1000 – not bad considering some sleep up to eight. Most villas are bookable via JAVA, the Jamaica Association of Villas and Apartments, PO Box 298, Ocho Rios (☎974 2508, fax 974 2967); good choices include villas at Mammee Bay Villa Complex, 74 Main St (☎974 5762) and Prospect Plantation (☎974 2058, fax 974 2468), or condos at the Columbus Heights complex overlooking the bay (☎974 2940).

Carlene's by the Sea, 85 Main St; ☎974 5431. Great location and fantastic value, this friendly place has pleasant rooms with cable TV, fan and hot and cold water. ③.

Chrisann's, PO Box 11, Tower Isle, St Mary; ☎975 4467. Clean, well-maintained studios and one- to three-bedroom apartments with a/c, cable TV, fully equipped kitchen and access to the pool and mini private beach. ④–⑧.

Comfort Suites, 17 DaCosta Drive; ☎974 8050, fax 974 8070, *comfortsuites @cwjamaica.com*. Overlooking the town, these agreeable self-contained units have a/c, satellite TV, phone, balcony and kitchenette. There's a large pool, a restaurant and tennis courts on site. ⑥.

Happy Hut (formerly *Marastilda*), White River; ☎974 1223. Situated on the far reaches of Main Street just past *Sans Souci Lido*, these very sparse but spacious and clean rooms have a fridge and ceiling fan; one has a kitchenette, and the others have access to the main kitchen. ②.

Hibiscus Lodge, 83–87 Main St; ☎974 2676, fax 974 1874. Set back from the road in beautiful gardens, this is Ochi's most attractive hotel. The clean, pleasant cliffside rooms each have balconies, and there's a pool, jacuzzi, tennis court, sun deck, sea access, excellent restaurant and a bar with swinging seats. ⑤ Rates include breakfast.

Hummingbird Haven, PO Box 95, White River; ☎974 5188. Youthful budget-style complex of hexagonal wooden cabins that can take four at a push; though there's no security, the grassy campsite (US$10) is surrounded by a high razor-wire fence. ①–②.

Jamaica Beach Resort, Tower Isle; ☎975 4582, fax 975 5599. Located a fifteen-minute drive east of town means reasonable rates. The clean, comfortable rooms have fan and cable TV; studios upstairs have a kitchenette and there's a restaurant, bar and pool on site. ④.

La Mer, PO Box 335; ☎ 974 5187, fax 974 2359. Spacious one- to three-bedroom apartments with a/c, cable TV and kitchen, facilities include a pool and tennis court. A good bargain but a fifteen-minute drive east of town. ④–⑤.

Little Pub Inn, PO Box 256, 59 Main St; ☎974 2324, fax 974 5825. The restaurant and entertainment-cum-shopping-mall make this one of the busier spots in town. Rooms are quirky, some are split-level with platform beds, most have attic-style sloping roofs, and all are spotless and inviting with a/c and satellite TV. ④ Rates include breakfast.

Little Shaw Park Guest House, 21 Shaw Park Rd; ☎974 2177, fax 974 8997. Easy-going, family owned place set in gardens overlooking town with space for camping (US$25). Homely rooms with cable TV, fan and hot and cold water; some share bathrooms, others have kitchen facilities and meals are available. ③.

Marine View, 9 James Ave; ☎974 5753, fax 974 6953. Comfortable, clean rooms and a pool, restaurant and bar, but you might not want to walk home late at night as it's at the far end of James Ave. ③.

Parkway Inn, 60 Main St; ☎974 2667. Centrally located, these clean, affable rooms have phone and cable TV, and there's a good restaurant. ④.

Pier View, PO Box 134, 19 Main St; ☎974 2607, fax 974 1384. Busy, friendly and laid-back apartment development, next to the beach and popular with younger travellers. Rooms or self-catering units with kitchenette have fridge, cable TV, fan or a/c, and access to the pool and sun roof. ③–④.

Plantation Inn, PO Box 2, Ocho Rios; ☎974 5601, fax 974 5912, *winglobal @aol.com*. Graceful colonial-style resort just east of town offering rooms, suites and villas, all amenities such as watersports, a great private beach and tennis courts with professional tuition. Breakfast and afternoon tea are included, but most guests book all-inclusive plans. ⑥–⑨.

Reynolds Brooklyn Inn, 188 Main St; ☎974 2480. Small budget guesthouse above a bar/restaurant, with simple but clean rooms with shared bathroom and a predominantly Jamaican clientele. ②.

Sandcastles, 120 Main St; ☎974 5626, fax 974 2247, *sandcastles @cwjamaica.com*. In front of the beach (guests get a pass), these airy studios and one- or two-bedroom apartments have cable TV and kitchenette. Good for families – the pool has a slide and a children's area. ⑤–⑥.

Village Hotel, 54 Main St; ☎974 9193, fax 974 5440, *villagehtl@toj.com*. Friendly, family-run property slap in the centre of town and five minutes' walk from the beach. Rooms have queen bed, cable TV, a/c and phone, and there's a pool, restaurant and bar. ⑤.

All-inclusives

Club Jamaica, Box 342, Ocho Rios; ☎974 6632, fax 974 6644. Very central, busy all-inclusive overlooking the beach, with functional but uninspiring rooms, a nightclub, pool, watersports and PADI dive operator (additional charge). ⑥.

The Enchanted Garden, PO Box 284, Ocho Rios; ☎974 1400–9, fax 974 5823 (US & Canada call ☎1-800/847-2535). This capacious all-inclusive boasts fourteen natural waterfalls, five restaurants, two pools, private beach club, tennis courts, spa centre, fitness programmes, the largest aviary in the Caribbean and every other imaginable frippery. ⑧.

Jamaica Grande, PO Box 100, Ocho Rios; ☎974 2201, fax 974 2162 (in US ☎1-800/228-9898, fax 602/443-6543). Jamaica's largest hotel with 720 amenity-packed rooms, a man-made waterfall in the lobby, five restaurants, nine bars, private beach, fitness centre, three pools, gym, tennis courts, disco, mini-casino, children's activity programme and the atmosphere of a ritzy shopping mall. ⑧.

Jamaica Inn, PO Box 1, Ocho Rios; ☎974 2514, fax 974 2449, *jaminn@infochan.com*. Quietly elegant place surrounded by a gorgeous private beach, pool and manicured croquet lawns, the tasteful rooms have a/c, beautiful decor and ocean-facing balconies. No children under 14; jacket and tie required for dinner. ⑧ Rates include breakfast and dinner.

Sandals Dunn's River, PO Box 51, Ocho Rios; ☎972 0653, fax 972 1611. A ten-minute drive west of town, this is luxury for couples only, with smart but gaudy rooms, three restaurants, seven bars, private beach and the largest freshwater pool in Jamaica. Nightly entertainment and gazebos that see plenty of weddings. Three night minimum stay. ⑧.

Sans Souci Lido, PO Box 103, White River; ☎974 1206, fax 974 2544. Ten minutes' drive east of town, this adults-only all-inclusive is the best in the area. Full spa facilities, three excellent restaurants, two pools, a magnificent white-sand beach, fitness centre, tennis courts, golf and all watersports. The strolling saxophonist, gazebos and low-key landscaping ensure an emphasis on romance. Three night minimum stay. ⑧.

Shaw Park Beach Hotel, PO Box 17, Ocho Rios; ☎974 2552, fax 974 5042, *shawparkbchhtl@cwjamaica.com*. Ochi's oldest hotel, on the eastern outskirts of town. The wooden fittings and plantation-style decor are pretty; some of the concrete accommodation blocks are not. But the atmosphere is friendly and there's a pool, superb beach, all watersports, tennis courts, gym and nightly entertainment. Three night minimum stay. ⑦.

The Town

Apart from trawling the shopping malls or hanging out in a bar, activities in Ocho Rios are limited. Compact enough to explore on foot, the permanently busy streets hold little interest for sightseeing, though, and unless you're heading out to one of the nearby attractions, days in Ochi are best spent lazing on the beach. Running parallel to the sea (but hidden from it by all the concrete), **Main Street** houses the majority of hotels, bars, banks, shopping plazas and restaurants, as well as the craft markets and the post office, while **DaCosta Drive** is Ochi's quieter back entrance and a slip road for

Watersports

Although there isn't that much to see underwater at the main beach – you'll find much richer pickings east of the harbour or at the reef at the bottom of Dunn's River (see p.194) – the sand is lined with **watersports concessions**. Prices are fairly high – even snorkel equipment can cost as much as US$20 per day, though bargaining usually brings this down a bit and you might get better deals toward the quieter, western edge of the beach. Touts roam the sand offering jet ski rides (30min; US$35–45); banana boat rides (30min; US$25); water-skiing (about US$45 for three laps of the bay), and parasailing (10–15min; US$45). You can also take a glass-bottom boat ride; many, such as *Lady G*, go along the coast to Dunn's River Falls, at a cost of around US$20 per person plus US$6 entry to the falls. For **scuba diving**, try Resort Divers at 2 Island Plaza (☎974 5338), which also offers deep-sea fishing from US$300 per half day. Alternatively, try Oras Divers on the beach, which operates from the *Silver Seas* hotel, 66 James Ave (☎974 5005, fax 974 5739).

The coast reverberates to the sound systems of the many private boats offering **pleasure cruises**. Day-trips go to Dunn's River for snorkelling and climbing the falls, with an open bar and lunch or snacks; sunset cruises include drinks only, but most operators offer dinner cruises too. Most people book via the agents who stake out the beaches, and some of the cruises are racier than others. Among the better organized operators are Red Stripe (☎974 2446), who do a day cruise (3hr; US$45), a sunset soca cruise (2hr; US$25) and a dinner cruise (2hr 30min; US$50). All prices are per person.

fast traffic. Opposite the clocktower and forking off toward the sea from Main Street, **James Avenue** has a somewhat seedy feel, despite it's official reincarnation as the "Reggae Strip", and is home to plenty of low-key, Jamaican style eateries, the odd ganja hustler and the Thursday night "Reggae Strip" shenanigans.

During the day, most of the town's tourist activity centres around the lone **beach** – variously known as Mallards, Turtle and Ocho Rios Bay (daily 9am–5pm; J$50, children J$20). Tucked under the tower blocks and accessible from the western end of Main Street near the *Pier View* and *Sandcastles* hotels, the white-sand beach is wide, fairly attractive and well maintained, with showers, changing rooms, bars and plenty of general hanging-out and activity. However, the water is prone to patches of sea grass, and occasional reports of unacceptable pollution levels mean that this isn't one of the north coast's most appealing beaches, particularly when it's overshadowed by the bulk of docked cruise ships across the bay. It's also a lot smaller than it used to be, as a prime section at the eastern end has long been appropriated by the island's largest hotel, *Jamaica Grande*.

Ocho Rios Fort and Dunn's River Falls
Heading west of town along Main Street, a boardwalk allows easy pedestrian access to Ochi's biggest attraction, Dunn's River Falls. It

passes the town's only historical feature, **Ocho Rios Fort**, sandwiched between the cruise terminal and a former slaughterhouse. The fort was built by the British in the seventeenth century and restored in 1780 to defend against a feared French attack, but there's little to see other than two cannons, taken from the now derelict Mammee Bay Fort and placed here by the Reynolds bauxite company in the 1960s. Just past the fort and the Helitours landing pad, Clarke's Art Studio, a flower-wreathed, green-painted wooden house on the cliffside, makes a nice stop even if you don't want to buy any crafts, with gorgeous views of a small waterfall cascading down to the beach below, itself accessed via a dirt track from the roadside.

Ten more minutes' along the boardwalk is **Dunn's River Falls** (daily 9am–5pm, beach closes 6pm; US$6, plus a tip for the guide). Jamaica's best-loved waterfall and a staple of tour brochures, the falls are a little overdeveloped but still breathtaking, and remain the area's major tourist honeypot. Masked from the road by restaurants, craft shops and car parks, the wide and magnificent 600ft waterfall cascades over rocks down to a pretty tree-fringed white-sand beach that's far cleaner than the one in town. There's a lively reef within swimming distance, and snorkel gear is available to rent from several touts.

Impressively proportioned, with water running so fast you can hear it from the road below, the falls are surrounded by dripping foliage and more than live up to their reputation, despite the concrete and commerciality. The main activity is climbing up the cascade, a wet but easily navigable hour-long clamber. The step-like rocks are regularly scraped to remove slippery algae, and the done thing to prevent a stumble is for visitors to form a hand-holding chain led by one of the very experienced guides. It's thoroughly exhilarating, as you're showered with cool, clear water all the way up – wear a bathing suit. There's a restaurant and bar, craft and hair-braiding shacks and full changing facilities at the beach and at the top of the falls.

An alternative to the crowds and the admission price are the unmaintained waterfalls above the enclosure; to get to them, take the main route to Dunns River but carry on up past the car park to where the tarmac ends. Follow the first dirt path into the bush to your right for five minutes. There are several more waterfalls further up the road which you can drive or walk to, but you may need a local companion to find them.

Shaw Park and around

From the main roundabout at Ochi's western outskirts, a twenty-minute walk starting along Milford Road takes you to two of Ochi's better known pastoral attractions, both on the ill-maintained Shaw Park Road (turn right from Milford Road 100ft from the junction at the Shaw Park signpost). About 100 yards from the main round-about, Shaw Park Road forks; a left turn and a steep twenty-minute drive brings you to the 1922ft peak of **Murphy Hill** (sometimes called Governor's Hill), which provides handsome views over Ocho Rios bay. A right turn from the fork brings you past some swanky private homes to the **Shaw Park Botanical Gardens** (daily 8am–4pm; US$3.50), a mere 550ft above sea level but boasting stunning aerial views of town nonetheless. The former grounds of a long-gone hotel, Shaw Park does a cracking trade with cruise-ship passengers these days. The creatively planted 25-acre gardens are resplendent with unusual flowers, plants and trees – including a huge banyan – set amidst grassy lawns, as well as a near-perpendicular (but non-swimmable) waterfall. You can walk unaccompanied, but the knowledgeable gardeners-cum-guides will initiate you into the wonders of tropical horticulture. There's an on-site bar, and crafts and jewellery on sale at the gift shop.

About five minutes further up Shaw Park Road, the more intimate **Coyaba River Garden and Museum** (daily 8am–6pm; US$4.50) is another favourite stop-off for tour buses, and while not the most exciting of Ocho Rios's packaged attractions, this meditative and restful miniature hothouse of lush, well-watered flower beds is worth an hour of your time. Wooden walkways allow easy viewing of the heliconias, anthuriums, hot-pink ginger lilies and rampant vines, and the flower beds are bisected by streams teeming with mullet, koi carp, crayfish and turtles, with occasional glass panels embedded into the banks to provide a view of the underwater goings-on. Housed in an elegant cut-stone building, the museum has a limited but thoughtful collection of exhibits spanning Jamaican history, from Taino *zemis* (talismans used to ward off evil spirits) to a nineteenth-century man trap and photographs depicting post-emancipation Jamaican life; special weight is given to St Ann's own Marcus Garvey and Bob Marley. There's a good café and gift shop on site.

Fern Gully and beyond

Carrying on along Milford Road past the Shaw Park Road turnoff brings you into **Fern Gully**, a densely vegetated and steeply inclining three-mile stretch of the A3/A1 road to Kingston, made famous by the arboreal splendour of the 500 or so varieties of fern that smother the roadside banks. First planted in the 1880s, the ferns are overhung by tall trumpet and mahoe trees that meet overhead, filtering the sunlight to create a cool, green-tinged tunnel. Moist and sheltered, the gully environment is ideal for ferns, but exhaust fumes from the heavy traffic have damaged and even wiped out some of the species, and there are regular calls for Fern Gully to be closed to traffic and redeveloped as a beauty spot. This proposition makes even more sense in bad weather – after heavy rains the gully is reduced to an impassable series of potholes, causing traffic jams that stretch

To the right just as you turn onto the road for Murphy Hill, Millford Falls are a pretty spot for a fresh-water splash.

If the Shaw Park and Coyaba gardens whet your appetite for things botanical, a pricey US$10 buys you a half-hour tour of the Enchanted Garden hotel's waterfalls, fish tanks, aviary and flower beds. Trips leave daily at 10am, 11am, noon, 2pm & 3pm.

right back into town. You can walk up from Ochi in about twenty minutes, but the whizzing traffic, lack of pavements and persistent roadside vendors make pedestrians vulnerable.

While you're in the area, the **Wassi Art pottery works** (Mon–Sat 9am–5pm; free) at Great Pond make an interesting distraction; turn off Milford Road at the colourful signposts just before Fern Gully. A small, family-owned commercial factory producing some of the island's better ceramic craft, Wassi's tours take you through each stage of production, from clay processing to pot-throwing, painting and firing, and you can buy the works at cheaper prices than at local gift shops.

Once at the top of the Fern Gully hill and out of the undergrowth, the landscape opens up with eye-popping views across the pastures and hillocks of the eastern interior, with the misted Blue Mountain peaks just visible in the distance. Continuing along the A3, through emerald fields dotted with dilapidated gingerbread houses and restored plantation homes, you eventually reach **MONEAGUE**, a quiet roadside town that's worth a stop for its sole **restaurant**, the elegant *Café Aubergine* (☎973 0527; Tues–Sun noon–9pm). Set in a beautiful colonial-era building, the linen tablecloths and tastefully rustic decor here come as a bit of a surprise after all the roadside cook-shops you've passed. The menu is as sophisticated as anything you'll find in Ochi, and is well worth the forty-minute drive from town. With starters from mussels in a herbed tomato and wine broth to mains of salad nicoise, lamb chops in a honey and mustard sauce, or grilled chicken breast with linguine and callaloo, the cooking is complemented by a supremely soothing atmosphere. Easily missed, the restaurant is marked by a nondescript sign on the left of the road just as you enter town; be careful when driving out after your meal, as the entrance/exit is a bit of a blind spot and traffic on this section of road is invariably fast.

If *Café Aubergine* is beyond your budget or time constraints, a ten-minutes drive along the A3 north of Moneague brings you to one of Jamaica's best-loved street-food institutions, **Faith's Pen**, a string of smoking food stalls housed in a purpose-built layby. Blackened by years of barbecue cooking, the stalls do a cracking trade with the steady stream of traffic passing between Kingston and Ochi. Though some are more popular than others (go for the cook with the longest queue), each stall sells a variation on the same theme: roast yam and saltfish, jerk chicken or pork, ackee and saltfish, roast corn, curry goat, mannish water or fish/conch soup, alongside the usual array of cold beers and natural juices. You eat at a bench by the stall to a background music of whizzing cars and the strains of Irie FM blaring from the vendors' ghetto blasters, and though not the most picturesque place for a meal, Faith's Pen is the consummate on-the-road eating experience.

*See "Contexts"
p.398 for a
wider discus-
sion of
Jamaican
music.*

East of town

The clamour of Ocho Rios's Main Street recedes as you head east of town, but one place you shouldn't pass by is **Mahogany Beach**, a bar with a beach just off Main Street past the *Hibiscus Lodge* hotel. Occupying a pretty strip of beach with good snorkelling, swimming and watersports (though some of these are heftily priced), and boasting a beach bar and grill, swimming pool, volleyball and basketball courts, all set in beautiful landscaped gardens, Mahogany is Ochi's newest chill-out spot, worth a visit by day or night. On Sundays, there's a buffet brunch and live jazz in the afternoon, and different activities take place every evening (see p.201).

Beyond *Mahogany*, in amongst the glamorous frontages of the all-inclusive hotels, the studios of **Irie FM** are marked by a colourful billboard and set back from the road opposite the Coconut Grove shopping centre. Jamaica's most popular radio station, Irie was the island's first reggae-only station – the airwaves were previously dominated by American soul, gospel and country and western. Since its first transmission in June 1990, Irie has championed the artistic and cultural legitimacy of a musical genre branded subversive until the early 1970s. Today, the station provides the soundtrack for the nation – wherever you go you'll hear the music, the massively popular talk shows, and the patois jingles: "Irie FM – a fi wi station" or "My radio dial stuck pon Irie FM, and guess what – me nah bother fix it". Steel Pulse, Burning Spear, Aswad and Third World among others have recorded at Irie's Grove Studios, and the station has brought a bit of Kingston-style culture to the town.

Past Irie FM, Main Street merges into the A3 coast road and crosses the bridge over the wide but sluggish **White River**, which marks the parish boundary of St Ann and St Mary. Just before the bridge, Bonham Spring Road winds inland, taking you through Ochi's satellite communities and past the sumptuous Sandals eighteen-hole golf course at Upton (see p.49 for details). This is also the route to the fabulous **Irie Beach**, a landscaped portion of White River banks with a deep swimming pool. It's currently closed, but if you're a river-swimming enthusiast, it's well worth calling the owners to check if you can go in (☎974 5044).

Back on the main road and half a mile into St Mary, the former haunt of British planter Harold Mitchell has been reincarnated as a tourist attraction, **Prospect Plantation** (☎974 2058; 1hr 25min guided tours Mon–Sat 10.30am, 2pm & 3pm, Sun 11am, 1.30pm & 3pm; US$12). Designed to introduce the more sedentary visitor into the delights of tropical farming, the tour consists of sitting with 38 others on an open trailer and listening to an inaudible commentary while trundling through sugar cane patches and groves of coconut palm, pimento, lime, ackee, breadfruit, mahoe and soursop trees, stopping only to sample fruits, admire the bay views from Sir Harold's lookout, and potter around a stone church. You'll feel less

Ocho Rios and around

See p.206 for the East of Ocho Rios map.

For more on Jamaican radio, and a complete list of frequencies, see "Basics" p.39.

You can raft White River with Calypso Rafting (☎974 2527; 45min; US$40 per raft).

*Check out
Harmony Hall
art gallery in
Tower Isle (see
p.203) for the
north coast's
best collection
of Jamaican
artwork; they
also hold craft
fairs in April
and November.*

*Campbell's
Lawn in Rio
Nuevo stages
extremely pop-
ular open-air
parties most
Saturday
nights, with
oldies reggae
from Irie FM
maestro Bob
Clarke.*

like a member of a cattle herd if you do the tour aboard a **mountain bike** (1hr; US$12), or on **horseback** (1hr; US$20). Other **trail rides** cover the property and go down into White River gorge (1hr 30min; US$35), the site of Jamaica's first hydro-electric plant, while the "View Jamaica" trek goes down to the river and up into the hills (2hr 15min; US$50). You'll need to book all rides one day in advance, and the horses rest on Sundays.

A few minutes' drive east of Prospect along the A3 is **Reggae Beach** (Mon–Fri 9am–5pm, Sat & Sun 9am–6pm; J$100). A pretty curve of somewhat coarse yellow sand, it's cleaner than the strip in town, though there's also some sea grass. The brightly painted show-ers and changing rooms add a touch of panache, though, and there are rope swings from the trees, plenty of shade and a good snack shop. As it's a fair drive from town, you'll usually have the place to yourself during the week.

Beyond the beach, the coast road is intermittently lined with clumps of hotels and condos that have sprung up in the hope of cap-italizing on Ochi's resort status. One of these new developments has almost obscured **Rio Nuevo Park**, a rather nondescript monument at the ocean side of the road commemorating the final skirmish which made Jamaica a British rather than a Spanish territory. The area was donated to the Jamaica National Heritage Trust by its owner the Beckfords, and their efforts have ensured that the rather decrepit memorial plaque and gazebo remain despite the new building.

Inland to Wilderness

Just past Prospect Plantation, the coast road whips past a narrow inland turn at Frankfort, where you'll see the signposts for **Wilderness Resort** (☎974 5189 or 4613; Tues–Sun 10am–5pm; US$3), a 447-acre commercial cattle and fish farm that's been opened up to the public. From the coast, the narrow road winds a snakelike parallel of the White River Gorge – you can hear the gushing water far below – before the overhanging trees recede and the stunning views of the rolling St Mary countryside open up: cat-tle pastures, banana plantations, citrus orchards and banks of yam plants are broken only by the tiny settlements of Cascade, Labyrinth and Goshen; signs directing you to Wilderness are pre-sent at all the junctions. In the late nineteenth century, the entire area was part of a 40,000 acre estate owned by one Judge Roper, who converted what had formerly been a vast sugar plantation into a successful cattle and horse rearing farm. At Gayle, the site of today's Wilderness Resort, he built a racetrack, a polo field and a showground which became a favourite haunt of the St Ann planter elite, who came to lay their bets and parade their prize cattle and horses. Judge Roper bestowed portions of his property to each of his nine children, but as bauxite began to eclipse agriculture as the area's main industry, only two of the farms remained in the family, run by his sons, Leicester and Harold. The Roper connections persist today, though: these days Wilderness is owned and run by the judge's grandson, Alex Lanigan, and it's easily the most appealing of the managed attractions that surround Ocho Rios. Ensconced in a wonderfully lush, riverine valley 1000 feet above sea level (it's usually about ten degrees cooler here than on the coast), Wilderness boasts 37 **fishing ponds** stocked to bursting with fresh water snapper, as well as hiking trails, kayaking, paddle-boating, a stable full of **horses** for country hacks, a **petting zoo** of Jamaican animals and birds, and a garage filled with well-maintained ATV **quad bikes**. Unless you can drive up independently (and pay for all the activities separately), you'll get the best out of Wilderness by booking one of their combination packages, which include return transportation from local hotels. If you simply want to see the property and hang out at the clubhouse/restaurant, you'll pay US$21 per person (US$14 for children under 12); otherwise, prices start at US$40 for catch and release fishing and lunch; US$40 for a 1hr horse ride; US$27 for a 1hr 30min hike, and US$60 for a 1hr guided ATV tour in the Wilderness valley. Perhaps the best of the bunch is a 2hr ATV tour to Spanish Bridge, a fabulous, deep swimming pool on the White River at US$103. Combinations of all the activities work out much cheaper: fishing, lunch and a 1hr ATV tour, for example, costs US$81.

Eating

As many of Ochi's **restaurants** aim to please the foreign palate, Italian, Indian, Chinese and American cuisine vie for your custom alongside the Jamaican staples, and there are a couple of excellent vegetarian options – a rarity along the north coast. Most places here stay open late, so you'll rarely be stuck for a midnight feast. For a truly tasty – and inexpensive – Jamaican meal, try the outdoor cookshop at the fishermen's beach west of town, where you'll be served hearty fish tea and well-prepared lunches of fish, rice and peas and vegetables.

Snacks

The recent influx of international **fast-food chains** divides office workers between those who opt for *Burger King* or *Kentucky Fried Chicken* (both on Main Street) and those who stick with the traditional callaloo loaf, patties and coco bread – the best place for the latter is *Taste Pleasures* in Island Plaza; for vegetarian patties, try *Afiya* or *The Healthy Way* (see p.200). The ubiquitous *Mother's* has a 24hr branch at 17 Main St, serving patties, burgers, chicken and ice cream, and there's a branch of *Island Grill* at 12 Main St, good for jerked chicken, pork and fish. If you've a sweet tooth, the *Baskin' Robins* chain has a branch in Ocean Village Plaza, but the far-superior Devon House I-Scream is sold at various outlets along Main Street.

Ocho Rios and around

In restaurant listings, we have given a phone number only for those places where you might need to reserve a table.

Inexpensive

Afiya, shop 11, Island Plaza, Main St. Delicious vegetarian soups and patties, salads, veggie burgers and full hot meals to take away or eat in.

Coco's, 17–19 Ocean Village Plaza. Squeaky-clean, busy indoor café serving up appetizing Jamaican cuisine as well as seafood, pasta salads, bagels, cakes and pastries. Natural juices, iced coffee and frozen drinks are good, too.

Fish World, 3 James Ave. Popular place for a late supper; fish is served any which way, with bammy, festival or rice and peas, and the outdoor seats are perfectly placed for soaking up the shenanigans of the "Reggae Strip". Open Monday to Saturday until 2am.

The Healthy Way, Ocean Village Plaza. Energetic and efficient vegetarian takeaway, with a couple of tables, offering veggie/tofu burgers and patties, soups, Ital juices, fruit salad, cakes and a different main dish each day.

Mr Humphrey's Pizza Café, 10 Evelyn St, off Main St; ☎974 8319. Fast and tasty pizzas, sub sandwiches, jerk chicken and pitta pockets. Free delivery if you call ahead.

Jack Ruby's, 1 James Ave. A little glossier since the transformation of James Ave into the "Reggae Strip", but the menu remains reliable – ackee and saltfish or callaloo with all the trimmings, fish and lobster any style, Ital stew, cow foot, oxtail and chicken.

Jeff's, 10 Main St. Solid, reasonably priced Jamaican food, from ackee and saltfish, mackerel run-down, fruits or omelettes for breakfast to seafood, oxtail, pepper steak, cow foot and curry chicken or goat for lunch and dinner.

Mayflower, Island Plaza, Main St. Good Cantonese food served up in an air-conditioned indoor dining room – seafood specialities, pleasant service and reasonable prices.

Mo' Time, 1 James Ave. Colourful Rasta-oriented indoor diner offering good, Ital-style breakfasts (including cornmeal, plantain and oats porridge), and various vegetarian delights for lunch and dinner as well as the full array of natural juices.

Ocho Rios Village Jerk Centre, just before the roundabout on DaCosta Drive. Renowned for the consistently good jerk pork, chicken, fish and barbecued spare ribs as well as the piped dancehall which draws in an evening crowd of drinkers. Daily 10am to midnight.

One Stop, Cnr Main St and James Ave. Conveniently located diner-cum-grocery shop serving tasty Ital takeaways and lovely unsweetened fruit juices. Open daily from noon until around 2am.

Parkway Inn, 60 Main St, entrance on DaCosta Drive. Cavernous air-conditioned restaurant serving up large portions of tasty Jamaican food to predominantly local clientele – breakfast is particularly good.

Three Girls and a Coffee Shop, shop 5, Island Plaza, Main St. Brilliant for daytime refreshment, with good cappuccino, espresso, latte and various flavoured coffees as well as an admirable variety of teas. Sandwich fillings include smoked chicken, beef and tuna, and there are bagels, muffins and excellent cheesecakes.

White River Ranch, White River. Busy, late-opening jerk joint with tables outside, cooking up sizzling chicken, pork and fish for an enthusiastic crowd – the conch soup and roast or steamed fish are pretty good, too

Moderate

Bibibips, 93 Main St. Set back from the road, with tables overlooking the sea, this is one of the better choices in town. The menu includes devilled jerk chicken, coconut curry chicken, seafood crepes, vegetable stir-fry, Rasta pasta, Red Stripe shrimp and all the usual Jamaican favourites – fish is a definite winner, and service is excellent.

Café Mango, Main St, opposite the entrance to *Jamaica Grande*. Semi open-air diner in a shady, central location serving Jamaican and American breakfasts, interesting lunches of calamari, nachos, chicken wings, salads, some Mexican dishes, pasta and pizza. A nice spot for a long lunch or an outdoor dinner.

Little Pub, 59 Main St; ☎974 2324. American and Jamaican breakfast and lunch in a roadside café with a juice bar on site. Dinner – from filet mignon or surf 'n' turf to lobster thermidore – is dished up in the "entertainment area".

Passage to India, Soni's Plaza, 50 Main St; ☎795 3182. Fairly new, attractively decorated rooftop restaurant serving excellent Indian cuisine. From tandoori meats to chicken jalfrezi or masala, rogan josh, lots of seafood and a vast array of vegetarian dishes, the menu is pretty comprehensive. Breads are particularly good, as are the lassi yogurt drinks and desserts.

Toscanini, Harmony Hall; ☎975 4785. Under the eaves of pretty Harmony Hall a ten-minute drive east of the centre, and easily one of Ochi's best. Service is great and the menu features all the Italian classics, from carpaccio to home-made pasta, and meat dishes such as veal escalope with prosciutto and parmesan. Vegetarians are well catered for, daily specials are displayed on the blackboard and the puddings are sublime. Closed Monday.

Expensive

The Almond Tree, *Hibiscus Lodge Hotel*; ☎974 2813. Romantic clifftop setting, friendly service and a great gourmet menu, featuring superb seafood.

Evita's, Eden Bower Rd; ☎974 2333. The best-advertized pasta on the north coast, served on a gingerbread verandah overlooking the bay. Huge choice of starters, salads and soups; main courses including fettucine bolognaise, linguine with pesto, seafood, and "Lasagne Rastafari" with ackee, callaloo and tomatoes, plus calorie-packed desserts.

For a sophisticated alternative to Ochi restaurants, try Café Aubergine *in Moneague, a forty-minute drive from town towards Kingston (see p.196).*

Nightlife and entertainment

Though it's not Kingston or Negril, Ocho Rios does have **bars** and **clubs** open every night of the week, and in a somewhat misguided attempt to inject a little "homegrown flavour" into Ochi's nightlife, local tourism bigwigs have transformed James Avenue, the town's seediest street, into **"Reggae Strip"**, repainting everything in bright shades for that "carnival" touch, and closing it to traffic from around 9pm each Thursday to accommodate steel bands, sound systems and the occasional reggae show. In essence, a free outdoor reggae party is a great idea, but the fun can be marred by persistent hustle. Also on James Avenue, Jack Ruby's lawn, behind the restaurant, is a regular venue for sound system dances and concerts.

Otherwise, **Mahogany Beach**, at the far end of Main Street (see p.197), may well develop into the town's best place for evening

Billboards advertising one-off stageshows and sound-system dances – a truly Jamaican experience – spring up overnight around town.

entertainment, with themed activities in the evenings and dancing on the sand à la Negril; music policy is more eclectic than elsewhere in town, with soul, R&B and jazz alongside the reggae. *Evita's* restaurant (see p.201), holds occasional theme nights (Latin and the like) with dancing, and if you fancy taking in a standard Caribbean-themed **floorshow**, try the *Little Pub*. Another possibility is an evening pass to one of the all-inclusive hotels. These cost from US$55, and cover a meal and unlimited drinks as well as entertainment – call individual properties for details.

Finally, the stellar **Ocho Rios Jazz Festival** brings Ochi to life every June, with concerts at venues around town – for more information call the tourist board or the Jazz Hotline (☎927 3544). Jazz Festival lineups and information are posted on the Web site prior to the event: *www.ochoriosjazz.com*.

Bars

Bibibips, 93 Main St. Laid-back clifftop bar popular with upscale Jamaicans, and one of the best places in town for a drinking session.

Cocktail Lounge, 47 Main St, behind *Gem Palace* in-bond shop. Popular, lively and very central bar-cum-disco, with satellite TV, occasional karaoke, dancing every night and excellent cocktails – they often do two-for-one drinks promotions, too.

Jamaican Hard Rock Café, Coconut Grove Shopping Centre. Not part of the international chain, but a Jamaican version of an American bar. Popular with guests from the all-inclusives at Ochi's eastern outskirts, and with occasional live music at weekends.

Little Pub, 59 Main St. Right in the centre of Ochi and one of the town's most enduring nightspots, with football games and boxing via satellite TV in the busy bar area (also great for people-watching), and different entertainment put on each night of the week in the stage/dancefloor area. From karaoke to comedy, discos and the spangly-costumed "Jamaica Farewell" cabaret – details are posted on a board outside and entrance fees vary.

Mangy Dog Beach Bar, *Mahogany Beach*, off Main St just past the *Hibiscus Lodge* hotel (☎974 3026). Appealing and friendly drinking spot at the sea's edge, with movies shown on a big screen (J$100) and theme nights, most of which are focused around happy hours and drinks promotions. Currently, highlights are the all-you-can-eat beach barbecue and party held on Wednesday (call a day ahead to reserve), and the Friday beach bonfire bash.

Ocho Rios Village Jerk Centre, just before the roundabout on DaCosta Drive. Well-patronized jerk centre with good food and lots of rum bar-style banter.

White River Ranch, White River. Busy, open-air circular bar, five minutes east of the centre, of this popular restaurant, good for white rum drinking alongside the predominantly local clientele.

Clubs

Amnesia Disco, above the Mutual Security building, 70 Main St (Wed–Sun). The new incarnation of the former *Acropolis* nightclub, still with an indoor, air-conditioned dancefloor and an outdoor bar area. Wednesday is the quiet "warm up night"; women get in free on Thursday for the ever-popular "Ladies Night"; Friday is "After Work Jam" with drinks promotions; on Saturday, everyone dresses up for the "Marathon Dance Party", and Sunday is quieter "oldies night". Music policy is dancehall, R&B, hip-hop and dance, and entrance is J$200.

Jamaika-Me-Krazy, *Jamaica Grande* (Closed Tues). Popular in-hotel disco with good sound and lights and a happy holiday crowd taking advantage of the all-inclusive bar. Cover US$30.

The Marine Disco, 6 James Ave (nightly, but best at weekends). Next door to *The Roof* and competing with it to see who can make the most racket; music policy is dancehall and more dancehall, with some R&B thrown in. Women get in free most nights, but it's a place to avoid if you're feeling fragile or want to be left alone. Cover J$100.

Silks Disco, *Shaw Park Hotel* (Closed Tues). Touristy in-hotel disco which can be entertaining at the weekend; music policy is Jamaican and "international" – expect some cheesy dance standards. Cover around US$8.

Ocho Rios and around

If you need reviving after a night on the tiles, the Natural Health Care Centre on DaCosta Drive (☎ 973 2834) offer massages and reflexology.

Shopping

Shopping is big business in Ocho Rios. The town's three **craft markets** (daily 7am–7pm) have enticed many a hapless soul to leave Jamaica laden with "Yeh mon it irie" and "Same shit, different island" T-shirts or Rasta hats complete with "comedy" fake dreadlocks. A frantic free-for-all on cruise-ship days, these are otherwise great places to shop – among the dross you'll find really nice T-shirts and sculptures, and vendors have a wicked line in sales banter. The main market is to the right of Ocean Village Plaza, while the smaller Pineapple Place and Coconut Grove markets are further east towards *Hibiscus Lodge* and the all-inclusive hotels.

As well as the craft markets, Main Street houses no less than eleven **shopping malls**, open-air courtyards set back from the road and lined with near-identical **in-bond shops** selling imported jewellery, watches and china, as well as upmarket craft shops that are the scourge of market vendors who claim that deals struck with cruise ship companies ensure that prospective souvenir-buyers are ferried straight into the air-conditioned calm rather than making their purchases on the street. Prices in the stores are higher than in the markets, but the quality of merchandise is reliable; alternatively, go directly to the source at Clarke's Art Studio, a tiny, green-painted wooden shack just west of town – the sculptures, carvings and acrylic paintings are beautiful. **Ceramics** and various other creative souvenirs are sold at the Wassi Art Factory Outlet at Great Pond in the hills above town (see p.196), though you can buy the products in most local craft stores and the markets. Living Wood in Ocean Village does a good line in wooden sculptures, wicker baskets and small furniture manageable even on a plane. There's also a gorgeous **art gallery** and shop at Harmony Hall, ten minutes' drive out of Ochi on the way to Tower Isle. Set in a beautifully restored great house, the gallery features small but comprehensive and ever-changing collections of work by renowned contemporary Jamaican artists, and a variety of crafts, Caribbean books, aromatherapy oils and women's clothing. The site hosts excellent occasional art and craft fairs.

For **books**, try Everybody's Bookshop in Ocean Village Plaza which carries a good selection of titles, some published only in Jamaica, plus magazines and foreign newspapers. Frontline Books in Island Plaza have a good selection of titles of Rasta, black history and reggae. For **music**, Disc and Dat in Island Plaza stocks the latest dancehall, reggae, R&B and hip hop, as do Vibes Music Shack in Ocean Village Plaza.

Listings

Airlines Air Jamaica has a local office (☎974 2566) for flight confirmations and information; for other airlines see Montego Bay listings, p.271. Air Jamaica Express (☎975 3254 or 922 4661) runs internal flights to and from Boscobel Aerodrome.

American Express Grace Kennedy Travel, shop 11b, Taj Mahal Shopping Centre, Main St; ☎974 5482.

Banks and money Most of the banks are on Main St opposite Ocean Village Plaza, though Citizens Bank is on Newlin St. For currency exchange at better rates, try Cambio King at 12 Ocean Village Plaza (Mon–Sat 9am–5pm), or Cambioman at 19 Main St (same hours). On the east side of town, Jamswi car sales at 135 Main St have a licensed cambio (Mon–Sat 9am–5pm), as do Meldam Real Estate at Coconut Grove shopping centre (Mon–Fri 9am–4pm). Wire transfers are available through the Western Union outlet at *Pier View* hotel; for other local outlets call toll-free on ☎1-888-991 2056.

Car and bike rental Many of the internationals have in-hotel branches in Ochi, or there's Bargain, Pineapple Place Shopping Centre (☎974 5298) and Hertz, Shop 5, Coconut Grove Shopping Centre (☎974 2017). You'll often get a better deal from local companies such as Caribbean Cars at 1 Evelyn St (☎974 2123 or 2513); Island at 4 Carib Arcade, Main St (☎974 2666 or 2334); Don's at *Shaw Park* hotel (☎974 7726) and Sunshine at 154 Main St (☎974 2980). For cycles and motorbikes, reliable companies include Abe in Ocho Rios Mall, 73 Main St (☎974 7787 or 1008), and G&B at 6 James Ave (☎974 8247 or 9832).

Doctors Most hotels have a resident doctor or nurse. Otherwise, try Dr Michael James at 11 Carib Arcade (☎974 5413), for a paediatrician call Dr Horace Betton at 14 Carib Arcade on Main St (☎974 2005 or 5413). The Holistic Medical Centre at 40 Ocean Village Plaza (☎974 6403–4) offers homeopathic and chiropractic therapy alongside regular medical care, and also have a link to an air ambulance (☎974 6404; 24hrs).

Hospitals The nearest is at St Ann's Bay (☎972 0150 or 2272), a fifteen-minute drive from Ocho Rios. In an emergency call ☎119, or ☎974 6403–4 for a private ambulance.

Internet The cheapest (but somewhat unreliable) option is Global Communications on James Ave, which offers Internet access for J$180 per hour (Mon–Sat 8am–11pm, Sun 8am–6pm). Higher prices but more comfortable surroundings are on offer from the computer shop at 3 Island Plaza (Mon–Fri 9.30am–5pm; US$6 for half an hour, US$10 per hour).

Laundry Carib Launderette, 6 Carib Plaza (Mon–Sat 10am–7pm), offers self-service wash and dry for J$200; add JS$50 for a service wash. A little further east and slightly cheaper, Pauline's, on Main St opposite the *Jamaica Inn* hotel offers self-service wash and dry for J$80, and a service wash and dry for J$150.

Pharmacies Ochi pharmacies are plentiful, well-equipped and often open late; best are The Great House Pharmacy on Main St next to the *Little Pub* (Mon–Thurs 9am–7.30pm, Fri–Sat 9am–9pm), or Ocho Rios Pharmacy in Ocean Village Plaza (daily 8.30am–8pm).

Photography Frank Bailey Studio at 2 Rennie Rd and Pugh's Photo Lab in the Mutual Security Building, 70 Main St, both offer Kodak film, photographic supplies and 1hr developing.

Police The police station (☎974 2533 or 4588) is on Evelyn St behind the Texaco garage that faces the clocktower; in emergencies call ☎119.

Post office The permanently busy post office is on Main St opposite the main craft market (Mon–Fri 8am–5pm, Sat 8am–noon).

Supermarkets General Foods in Ocean Village Plaza is Ochi's largest and carries a wide range of imported food alongside Jamaican staples. Fruit and vegetables are cheaper and better at the market, which is located off the bypass and adjacent to Evelyn St.

Taxis Reliable operators include Al's Taxi Service, also reasonable for day charters (☎933 7978 or 1997 7573); Maxi Taxi (☎974 2971); Rising Bird (☎974 7339 or 5929), and United (☎974 4755).

Telephones Pay phones are dotted around town; expect long queues. Local phonecards are available from *Mother's* on Main St, the post office and pharmacies. Worldtalk cards are available from most gift shops. Inexpensive overseas calls can be made at Global Communications on James Ave (Mon–Sat 8am–11pm, Sun 8am–6pm). You can send faxes from the Xerox Centre in Ocean Village Plaza.

East of Ocho Rios

As the clamour of Ocho Rios recedes, the A3 coast road narrows as if to make way for some of the most beautiful scenery on the north coast. Lushly vegetated cliffsides almost overwhelm the tarmac, and the region's languid allure is markedly different to the in-your-face glitz of Ochi. The main settlements, **Oracabessa** and **Port Maria**, are slow, close-knit communities where tourism is only just starting to take hold, and the small guesthouses and excellent little restaurants that pepper the roadsides are generally overlooked by those who prefer sports bars and jet skis to peace and quiet exclusivity. Low-key glamour has a lengthy history here, however: though ostensibly quiet, the area has long been a favourite haunt of the rich and famous – Noel Coward and James Bond creator Ian Fleming both lived here in the 1950s and 60s, and their old homes, **Firefly** and **Goldeneye**, are still standing, with Firefly transformed into a prime tourist site and Goldeneye the centrepiece of a luxury villa complex. Surface tranquillity masks a steady hum of industry here, mostly the work of

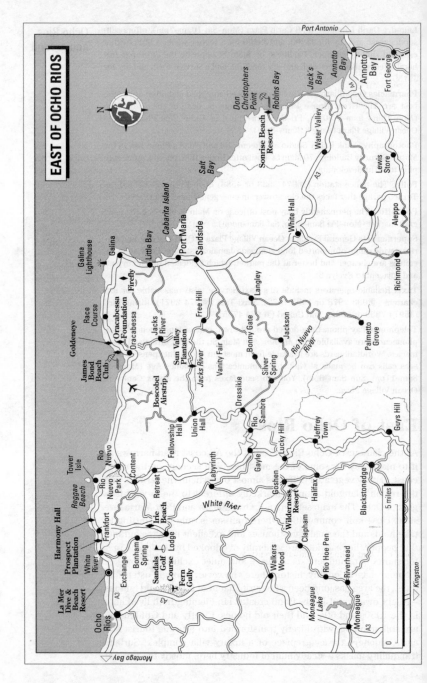

EAST OF OCHO RIOS

music impresario Chris Blackwell's **Island Outpost** company, which has concentrated a sizeable part of its operations in Oracabessa and has fully exploited the 007 connection at the stylishly designed **James Bond Beach** complex, the first phase of a tourist development plan that looks set to put the region firmly on the tourist map.

The Island influence and the physical presence of tourism infrastructure extends about as far as pretty Port Maria; beyond the town, the road swings inland and the coastline extends in an unbroken series of forested outcrops interspersed by deserted, volcanic-sand miniature beaches reachable only by foot or boat. Hikes or drives around here uncover breathtaking vistas as the peaks of the Blue Mountains (see p.126) shimmer into view.

Accommodation

In addition to two large **all-inclusives**, there are some really lovely small-scale **guesthouses** around Oracabessa and Port Maria, which range in price and facilities from the very cheap to the extremely plush.

Belretiro Inn, PO Box 151, Port Maria; ☎994 0035. Lovely, breezy location on the cliffside in Galina with various standards of clean, basic rooms with private bathrooms; some have a TV or a verandah and all can use the kitchen. There's a salt-water pool, good snorkelling and sea swimming, and the best rates in the area. ①–②.

Blue Harbour, PO Box 770, Questa, New Mexico USA; ☎994 2262, fax (in US) 505 586 1087, *www.villasetal.com/blueharbour*. Built in the 1950s by Noel Coward, and pretty much as he left them, these three seaside villas overlooking Port Maria bay offer the best views in the area. There's a saltwater pool, a small beach and plenty of seclusion; meals (and meal plans) are available. ④.

Bolt House, Galina; (☎ 994 0303, fax 975 3620, *www.islandoutpost.com*). Built by Blanche Blackwell (mother of Island impresario Chris), this gorgeous villa on a bluff below Firefly affords the same stunning views of Port Maria bay. Still much as Mrs Blackwell left it, with her shell collection on the mantelpiece and china in the cabinets, this is the epitome of tasteful, secluded luxury, with two bedrooms, dining and living rooms and a lovely pool, all set in landscaped gardens. ⑧.

Boscobel Beach Hotel, PO Box 63, Boscobel; ☎975 7331 or 7336, fax 975 7370; *www.superclubs.com*. Sprawling family-oriented all-inclusive on the outskirts of Oracabessa. Nice rooms, a large white-sand beach, petting zoo, playground, pools, tennis courts, watersports, gym, disco and numerous bars, plus constant childcare and an exhaustive kids' activity schedule. One child under 14 per adult stays free. Three night minimum stay. ⑧.

Caribbean Pearl, PO Box 127, Port Maria; ☎994 2672, fax 994 2043, *caribbeanpearl@cwjamaica.com*. German-oriented and spotlessly clean guesthouse on a hillside just west of town. The spacious rooms have rattan four-poster beds, and there's a lovely pool and bar with views of the bay. ⑤ Breakfast is included in the rates.

Casa Maria Hotel, PO Box 10, Port Maria; ☎994 0006, fax 994 0005, *nwas@owt.com*. Plenty of very faded grandeur but popular with Jamaicans who get a far more appropriate rate than tourists for the basic rooms. There's a pool, bar and restaurant on site. ③.

Goldeneye, ☎975 3354, fax 975 3620, *www.islandlife.com*. Understated class at what must be Jamaica's most exclusive hotel, a regular haunt of the rich and famous. Centred on Ian Fleming's beautifully restored Jamaican home, the one- to three-bedroom villas are secluded and indescribably inviting, with outdoor showers and all the delightful extras you'd expect. Each has access to the private beach where Fleming cooled his toes, and rates include all meals, drinks and watersports. ⑧.

*Golden Seas
hotel (see
opposite) run
a regular shut-
tle service to
Ocho Rios
(US$8 one
way) and
Dunn's River
(US$10 one
way), a conve-
nient and
inexpensive
way of getting
into town.*

Golden Seas, PO Box 1, Oracabessa PO; ☎975 3540–41 or 975 3094, fax 975 3243, *julane@infochan.com*. Relaxed, Jamaican-owned resort hidden behind trees next to the roundabout, with 1970s-style decor, a medium-sized yellow-sand beach with rather murky water, watersports, fitness centre, a pool with swim-up bar and a tennis court. Rooms have a/c, satellite TV, phone and a balcony overlooking the river or ocean. ⑥.

Lovely Spot Villas, Race Course, Oracabessa PO; ☎975 3322 (in US ☎617/361-4416). Signposted off the A3 just before *Goldeneye*, a small, friendly if a bit chaotic family-run resort of self-contained villas at the sea's edge, with access to wonderful swimming and snorkelling. Discounts for stays of a week or longer. There's a small bar area and meals are available, though there are cooking facilities. ③.

Nix-Nax Rainbow Isle of Light, off Main St, Oracabessa PO; ☎975 3364. Small American/Jamaican-run guesthouse with an unashamedly collective ambience – walls are adorned with consciousness-raising adages and alternative medical treatments are available. The eclectic collection of rooms are basic but nice and clean with shared or private bathroom and a communal kitchen. ①–②.

Reef Point, Port Maria; ☎994 0817. Newish collection of gorgeous wooden cabins built into the cliffside, with a/c, cable TV, fridges and balconies overlooking Port Maria bay and Cabarita Island. Peacocks wander through the pretty grounds, hopefully avoiding the sea-facing pool and bar/restaurant. Extremely friendly and accommodating – the best in its price range. ⑥ Breakfast is included in the rates.

Tamarind Great House, Crescent Estate, Oracabessa PO; ☎ & fax 995 3252, *www.cariboutpost.com/tamarind*. Palatial, newly-built home of an English expat family with ten spacious guest rooms, all luxuriously decorated with four-poster beds, TVs and lovely views of the valley below. Fruited gardens and a pool surround the house, and sailing and snorkelling trips aboard the family yacht are available, as are meals; a bus ride to the beach is included in the very reasonable rates. ④.

Trade Winds, Galina; ☎994 0420–2, fax 994 0423. Fairly new resort sprawling down the cliffs on the outskirts of Port Maria. Cool and clean if uninspiring, rooms have a/c, phone, radio and views of the crashing sea below. There's a pool, restaurant and bar on site. ④.

Oracabessa

Lit in the afternoons by an apricot light that must have prompted its Spanish name *Orocabeza*, or "Golden Head", **ORACABESSA**, some sixteen miles east of Ocho Rios, is a leisurely, friendly little one-street town centred around a covered fruit and vegetable market (main days Thursday and Friday), a police station and a few shops and bars. A centre for the export of **bananas** until the early 1900s, the wharves around the small natural harbour closed in 1969, taking with them the rum bars, gambling houses and most of the workers. Oracabessa became something of a ghost town, snoozing quietly until the mid-1990s when the **Island Outpost** corporation cemented owner Chris Blackwell's family connections with Oracabessa, buying up seventy acres of prime land from Jack's River to the west of town to the Goldeneye estate at the eastern outskirts with a mission to develop it into a rather exclusive community resort with a policy of promoting "seamless tourism", a sharp contrast to the usual fenced-off enclosures in which regular Jamaicans figure only in a servile role. To kickstart the project, the **Oracabessa Foundation** has been established to foster the sense of leadership, independence and community responsibility which will be vital to the success of the project. From their office on the second floor of a concrete shopping plaza on Main Street (☎ 975 3393; Mon–Sat 9am–5pm), the Foundation organize various community activities, as well as acting as an unofficial **tourist information centre**.

Unless you stay at *Goldeneye* or stop off at the Foundation office (and a quick visit is essential if you're spending any length of time here), Outpost's efforts are, for the moment, visible only at the **James Bond Beach Club** (Tues–Sun 9am–6pm; US$5), just off Main Street along Old Wharf Road. Already Jamaica's most stylish strip of sand, the beach is a sprawling collection of distinctively styled, brightly painted changing rooms, watersports centre, bar and restaurant grouped around a slim but pretty white-sand beach lapped by translucent waters. The expansive lawns are often used to stage large-scale concerts such as the Air Jamaica Jazz and Blues Festival in November (see p.43).

If you prefer to stay away from the glitterati, the small adjacent **fisherman's beach** is an equally appealing place to swim (though the showers and changing rooms are rather less so), and the Rasta carvers who've built a shack on the sand sell seafood meals and drinks as well as putting on the odd sound-system dance.

East of the turnoff for James Bond beach and the town's petrol station, Oracabessa merges into the residential community of **Race Course**. Here, gates, walls and trees mask **Goldeneye** (see also p.205), the unassuming white-walled bungalow designed and purpose-built by Ian Fleming, sometime military man and creator of James Bond, who wrote almost all of the James Bond novels within its walls.

Right on the other side of town and before the market, a roundabout crowded with fruit vendors (and serving as an unofficial **taxi rank**) forms the junction of the coast road and the B13 inland road. The latter wreathes through attractive residential communities towards the well-signposted **Sun Valley** (daily, 1hr 30min tours at

East of
Ocho Rios

For more on 007's connection to Oracabessa, see the box on p.210.

Island Outpost also operate The Caves, Jake's *and* Strawberry Hill *in Jamaica (see pp.309, 345 & 133).*

From James Bond beach, guided jet-ski safaris along the coast cost US$50 for half an hour.

East of Ocho Rios

007's Jamaica

From Errol Flynn to Ralph Lauren, Jamaica has always attracted the rich and famous, but the island has also served as inspiration for the ultimate (albeit fictional) symbol of glamour – **James Bond**. As a commander in the Naval Intelligence Division of the British army, Bond's creator Ian Fleming first visited Jamaica in 1943 on military business. Staying in the Blue Mountains, he was immediately taken with the island's sensual pleasures, and declared that he'd be back to put down permanent roots as soon as the war ended. By 1947, he'd paid £2000 for a plot of land on Jamaica's north coast that had once served as Oracabessa's race course, and engaged local workers to build the simple, elegant beach house that he'd designed himself. Naming it after a bungled NID anti-German operation that he'd been involved in, **Goldeneye** became his winter retreat and a source of competition with neighbour **Noel Coward**, who insisted that his Blue Harbour (see p.207) was far superior to Fleming's spartan bachelor pad. A series of magazine articles penned by Fleming on the joys of his island paradise soon began to encourage a glamorous, fashionable set to Jamaica, and Goldeneye played host to such luminaries as Sir Anthony and Lady Eden to Truman Capote, Lucian Freud, Graham Green, Eveyln Waugh and Cecil Beaton. However, cocktails by the pool and snorkelling expeditions with his "Jamaican wife" Blanche Blackwell (mother of Island Records' Chris Blackwell) took up most of his time, and it wasn't until his other long-term lover, and soon-to-be wife, Lady Anne Rothermere (ex-wife of the British newspaper baron) became pregnant in 1952 that he got down to any serious writing, cracking out *Casino Royale* on a rickety old Remington typewriter with the jalousies shut to block out the distracting sea view.

Fleming took his hero's name from the author of the classic book *Birds of the West Indies* and many of his characters from various Jamaican friends; Pussy Galore, in the *Goldfinger* novel, was said to be a tongue in cheek representation of Blanche Blackwell. Clearly besotted with the island, Fleming exploited the Jamaica connection in his writing wherever possible: two novels, *Doctor No* and *The Man with the Golden Gun* were set here (scenes were filmed in Kingston and Westmoreland respectively), and the island served as the fictional San Monique in *Live and Let Die*, while 007 wouldn't have dreamed of drinking any other coffee than his favourite Blue Mountain brew. Fleming later wrote "Would these books have been born if I had not been living in the gorgeous vacuum of a Jamaican holiday? I doubt it."

A regular routine developed, with Fleming returning to Goldeneye each January, spending a couple of months writing, and returning to England in March. However, the years of hard drinking and partying were beginning to take their toll, and by the late 1950s, his health had deteriorated. Fleming survived long enough to supervise Cubby Broccoli's movie of *Dr No*, filmed in Jamaica with Chris Blackwell as location manager. In the first few months of 1964, Fleming returned to Goldeneye where he wrote his last 007 novel, *The Man with the Golden Gun*, infusing the pages with a strong sense of nostalgia for Jamaica. His strength was waning, however. Though his Bond novels had by then sold some 40 million copies, Ian Fleming died on August 12, 1964 without ever really knowing what a sensation he had created; four months after his death, the release of the movie version of *Goldfinger* signified the beginning of a worldwide Bond mania that continues to this day.

9am, 1pm & 2pm; US$12), one of the north coast's most attractive plantations, though one of its smallest. This working family-owned estate concentrates on bananas and coconuts, and the tour explains their growth processes, takes in some interesting trees, flowers and bushes, and includes drinks, a light meal and some fruit-tasting.

Eating, drinking and entertainment

For a splurge, the *Sea Palm* restaurant at *Golden Seas* hotel serves huge portions of well-executed Jamaican dishes as well as pasta, kebabs and imaginatively prepared seafood; it's also a good option for breakfast in comfortable surroundings. Directly opposite, *Big Mamma's Jerk Centre* offers good, cheap jerk chicken or pork and Jamaican staples. From her tiny *Total Delight* restaurant in the market, Miss P bakes the fare for miles around, including sesame-seed topped ackee, callaloo and cheese patties, cakes and pastries as well as delicious shrimps in curry, pineapple or orange sauce, and baked, fried or brown stew chicken and fish. Perched atop a cliff on the other side of town and by far the best option in the area, jovial and friendly *Dor's Sea Cliff Fish Pot* in Race Course has juicy fresh fish or lobster dinners, superlative conch and fish soups and a nice circular bar for lounging and chatting (daily; 24hr) – the brilliant wall murals of 1970s style north coast scenes are also pretty good.

Unless you visit a hotel or head into Ochi, your **drinking** choices are limited to hole-in-the-wall rumshops such as *Cheers Bar* in Oracabessa town or the *Country Jug* between Race Course and Galina – a circular outdoor bar that serves basic Jamaican food to soak up the white rum. James Bond Beach is good for a drink on Friday evenings, when the more well-heeled local people descend for a few after-work Red Stripes, while the regular Latin Nights here are well worth checking out, taking place roughly once a month. *Nix Nax*, a large concrete building in Oracabessa (opposite the hotel of the same name), is a roomy indoor bar run by a friendly couple, but probably the liveliest place, and the only chance to **dance**, is *Tropical Hut*, a fairy-light-strewn bar set back from the road in Race Course – the "lawn" is often fenced-off to provide a venue for brilliant oldies parties (the venerated Merritone sound are regulars) and more raw dances with the likes of Stone Love.

Port Maria

The diminutive capital of St Mary, **PORT MARIA** is one of Jamaica's most picturesque towns, nestled around a crescent bay with lots of cut stone and faded gingerbread fretwork alluding to more auspicious times, and far more in the way of shops and offices than Oracabessa. However, once you've taken in the bay view and strolled the few shopping streets, there's little to keep you here.

The town's main attractions are all on its outskirts. As you round the twisting outcrops that protect the natural harbour, a stunning

For guided hikes in St Mary contact Sonrise Beach Retreat in Robins Bay (☎ & fax 1-999 7169, sonrise @in-site.com).

East of
Ocho Rios

The Tacky Rebellion

In the late eighteenth century, Port Maria saw one of Jamaica's bloodiest rebellions against slavery, an uprising that sowed the seeds for emancipation eighty years later. Led by a runaway slave known as **Tacky** (a European spelling of the Ghanaian name Tekyi or "the great") who was said to have been a chief of Coromantee descent, the rebellion sparked violent protests throughout the island and aimed at a complete cull of whites and the creation of an all-black colony. The revolt began on Easter Sunday 1760, when Tacky and a small group of slaves from local estates murdered their overseers and marched to Port Maria, killing the storekeeper at Fort Haldane and seizing arms and ammunition. Five months of fighting ensued, with £100,000 worth of damage done to nearby plantations. However, the thousand-strong slave army could not compete with the military force of the British, who utilized loyal slaves and Maroons (in accordance with the 1739 treaty) in the guerrilla warfare. The rebellion was savagely quashed and severe punishments meted out to the freedom fighters; Tacky was captured by Maroon marksmen and killed, his head cut off and displayed on a pole in Spanish Town. Others were chained to stakes and burned alive, gibbeted or hung by irons and left to die as an example to others contemplating sedition; however, it's said in one last gesture of defiance, Tacky's sympathizers removed his body under cover of night and gave their leader a proper burial. After Tacky's death, many of his followers committed suicide rather than live enslaved. In all, 300 Africans died fighting, 50 were captured and executed and 300 transported abroad, but only 60 whites lost their lives.

view of tiny and forested **Cabarita Island** is revealed right in the middle of the bay. You can arrange a combined fishing trip and island visit with one of the fishermen who moor their boats on the rather grubby grey-sanded central fishing beach. Around the next outcrop and marked by two sizeable Royal palms at its gates is the beautiful cut-stone **St Mary Parish Church**, dating back to 1861. The cemetery extends down to the sea, and its weathered gravestones stand testament to the abrasive properties of salty air. To the right of the church is a playing field which fronts the parish library; in the middle of the grass is a monument to black freedom fighter **Tacky** (see box); opposite is the old police station, gutted by fire in 1988 and currently being refurbished. Just beyond, the attractive clapboard building housing the Office of Health Department faces the covered fruit and veg **market** (main day Friday), a maze of dingy paths wreathing through the piles of yams, bananas and assorted local produce. A bridge crossing the murky Ochom River brings you into the town centre, where the streets of yellow stone or clapboard buildings are laid out in a rough grid formation.

Port Maria's church and old police station are immortalized in scenes in the classic Jamaican movie Countryman.

Firefly

Perched on a hilltop about two miles west of town, Port Maria's only organized attraction is **Firefly** (daily 8.30am–5.30pm;

US$10), the Jamaican home of Noel Coward and partner Graham Payn from its construction in 1956 to Coward's death in 1973. The house was built on what had once been the site of a Taino settlement (many artefacts have been found here), and later the stamping ground of pirate extraordinaire Sir Henry Morgan (see p.110), who used the spot as a vantage point during his reign as governor three hundred years ago; gun slits in what is now the on-site bar recall the buccaneer days. Coward stumbled upon the site during Jamaican holidays, when he stayed at his **Blue Harbour** beachhouse on the coast below, and bought it from local politician Roy Lindo for £150.

Acquired by Island Outpost in 1992, the house remains much as Coward left it, his studio set up with a painting on the easel, the drawing room – where illustrious guests from Sophia Loren to Audrey Hepburn and Joan Sutherland were entertained – complete with two polished pianos, kitchen cupboards full of yellowing bottles and packets, and the table freshly laid as it was on the day the Queen Mother came to lunch in 1965. Coward died here in his bedroom and is buried on the property, and a statue of him by UK-based artist Angella Connor still overlooks his favourite view.

Island are currently developing the site to give more focus to its Taino and pirate history, and the organized tours of the house, which include excerpts from a BBC TV documentary on his life – may be discontinued. Even if you're not a Coward fan, it's worth coming up to Firefly for the view alone. One of the best on the island, the panorama takes in Port Maria bay and Cabarita Island to the east, with the peaks of the Blue Mountains poking through the clouds, while to the west lies **Galina Point** and **lighthouse**, the most northerly tip of Jamaica – you can even see Cuba on a clear day.

Practicalities

Port Maria has plenty of small **restaurants** for simple, cheap Jamaican fare; among the more reliable are the unceremonious *Almond Tree* at 56 Warner St, and *Essie's Faith*, in the town square next to Courts furniture store. For more upmarket dining, the *Santa Maria* restaurant at the *Casa Maria* hotel offers continental, American and Jamaican breakfasts, and a nice selection for lunch and dinner including sandwiches, salads, seafood fritters, burgers, steak, pork chops, spaghetti and meatballs, which make a change from the roster of Jamaican staples. Another worthy but quiet hotel option is *Trade Winds* in Galina: the breezy terrace is nice for a drink or cocktail, and the restaurant serves cook-to-order Jamaican food. Port Maria has **rum bars** aplenty; a few play rocksteady into the night on Saturdays and Sundays, and the weekend "ben-dung" (literally, "bend down", with items spread out on the ground) market adds a bit of bustle.

East of Ocho Rios

Most full moons see fabulous "Moonlik" parties on the Firefly lawns – bring a blanket and watch it rise to the strains of venerable Jamaican artistes such as Della Manley and Ernie Smith. Entrance is J$500; call ☎ 994 0920 for details.

There are buses to Port Maria from Ocho Rios, Montego Bay, Kingston and Port Antonio.

East of Ocho Rios

There are various hole-in-the-wall shops and rum bars on the road between Port Maria and Annotto Bay, but you might want to stop off at the Puss-a-Foot Rest, Bar and Jerk Stop *in Albany for the name alone.*

Day passes to the Sonrise *property cost US$6, which covers use of the showers and changing rooms, as well as volleyball, tennis and a bounce on the trampoline.*

Robins Bay and around

Past the strip of bars and restaurants on the eastern outskirts of Port Maria, the potholed A3 swings away from the coast, over a series of clattering Bailey bridges and through tiny settlements where kids play at the edge of the ever-frayed tarmac and chickens pick through the dust. Keep an eye out for the roadside stall bedecked in all shapes and sizes of aluminium saucepans, including the ubiquitous Jamaican favourite, the squat "Dutch pot", used for cooking on open fires. About four miles from Port Maria, a large sign for *Sonrise Beach Retreat* marks a newly re-covered road towards the sea at **ROBINS BAY**. The coastline here is fabulous, with cattle pastures on one side of the road and a series of deserted **white-sand coves** on the other; further east, development tails off completely, and there are scores of gorgeous, little-visited black-sand beaches and **waterfalls** to explore. The area's idyllic aspect was first exploited in the 1970s, when the free-love shenanigans of American hippies at the long-gone *Strawberry Fields* campsite drew sighs of consternation from local people.

These days, the campsite has been re-opened as *Sonrise Beach Retreat* (☎ & fax 1-999 7169, *sonrise@in-site.com*; ④–⑥), a Christian-oriented hotel centered around the pretty white-sand cove from which Spanish governor Don Christobel Arnaldo de Yssasi fled the island in 1660. Cabins are scattered throughout the extensive grounds (some have shared bathroom, others a kitchenette) and there's a gazebo on the cliffs for chilling out or watching the sun come up. *Sonrise* is popular amongst local church groups, many of which attend the weekend Family Fun Days, and owner Bro' Bob conducts various eco-oriented **tours** of nearby beaches and waterfalls, costing US$50–70 and including lunch.

Past *Sonrise*, the tarmac gives way to dirt and stones and the atmosphere lightens as you pass through a friendly Rasta-oriented community, signified by the *Natural Vibes* bar, a cool and breezy hangout on the cliffs which rents out snorkelling gear (US$5 per half day) and conducts boat trips to nearby deserted black-sand bays (US$10 per person). Night-time bonfires and Rasta drumming sessions provide evening entertainment, but it's great for a drink at any time: natural juices are particularly good, as are the seafood and Ital stew meals. A few minutes' walk further west along the road takes you to *River Lodge* (☎ & fax 1-995 3003; ①), the most alluring place to stay for miles. Owned and run by German expat Brigitta Fuchslocher, this restful complex on the inland side of the road is built around the restored ruins of a seventeenth-century Spanish fort. Rooms make full use of the stone walls, with attractively minimal decor and shared or private bathrooms. A river running through the grounds has swimming possibilities during the wet season, and the beach is steps away. Cooking mostly vegetarian food and set under an open-sided, thatched-roof gazebo, the restaurant and bar are delightful, particularly after a day spent walking along the coast.

East of Ocho Rios

The coastline east of Robin's Bay is covered in Chapter Two; see pp.179–182.

Rio Sambre and inland St Mary

Firmly off the tourist track, the gorgeous scenery of the St **Mary interior** is well worth exploring if you have a car or can hire a driver for the day, and there are several opportunities for a fresh-water swim if the going gets too hot. A mile or so east of Port Maria, turn inland at the tiny community of **SANDSIDE**, and right again at a sign for the *Rio Sambre* resort. The road clambers up a steep hill which provides eyecatching views of the rolling St Mary countryside and the Port Maria coastline below, and passes a waterfall at Preston Land and orange groves at New Road. You'll hardly notice the hamlets of Langley, Bonny Gate and Silver Spring, but at the slightly more substantial **DRESSIKIE**, you can **swim** at the deep turquoise Zennor Hole, at the roadside opposite the *D&B Groove Scene Pub*. From here, continue towards Gayle and follow the signs for a couple of miles to *Rio Sambre* (☎975 8146, fax 975 8967; entry US$10, camping US$30; ②). A campsite-cum-lido centred around the clean, fast-flowing river from which it takes its name, *Rio Sambre* is popular with Jamaicans who come to swim in the wide, deep **river pool**, play cricket and volleyball or to go-kart, usually followed by drinking and dominoes or a meal at the restaurant. If you want to **stay**, there's one hexagonal cabin to rent, with kitchen, hot water, fans, satellite TV, VCR and a balcony overlooking the property, and you can also hire a good quality tent which sleeps three to twelve people and comes equipped with air beds (tent and beds are included in the rates). Guided **hikes** of the surrounding area are included in the entry fee (which also covers use of the changing rooms and showers), and you can also explore on **horseback** (US$10 for half an hour or so).

From Rio Sambre, it's a short drive through Gayle, Lucky Hill and Goshen to Wilderness Resort (see p.198).

West of Ocho Rios

Though the coast between the top resort towns sees plenty of tourist traffic, the craft stalls, "Welcome to Jamaica" billboards and fruit vendors are generally restricted to the coast, and even in the swiftly developing resort neighbours of **Runaway Bay** and **Discovery Bay**, tourism is pretty low-key. With its thriving market and Georgian architecture interspersed with gently weather-beaten clapboard houses, St **Ann's Bay**, just west of Ochi, is the small, unpretentious capital of St Ann, with ruined Spanish capital **Sevilla Nueva** a few minutes' walk away. Working west along the coast, historic but unkempt **Rio Bueno** marks the boundary of St Ann and Trelawny parishes and a distinct change in the landscape, from languid hills to rugged hillocks. Unexpectedly energetic interior villages, such as **Brown's Town**, perch on the fringes of Cockpit

Midway between Ochi and St Ann's Bay, behind the Roaring River generating station, is the now-private beach where Ursula Andress emerged from the sea as Honey Ryder in the 007 movie Dr No.

Country (see Chapter Four) and the panoramic views over deep valleys are constantly spectacular. The interior remains largely undeveloped save for the **Bob Marley Mausoleum** in central St Ann and some excellent tourist-oriented rum factories and river-rafting operations around **Falmouth**, capital of Trelawny and an architectural goldmine.

Just east of St Ann's Bay, Drax Hall is the annual venue for the huge Easter Monday kite festival, which attracts amateur and professional kite flyers from all over the world and draws thousands of spectators; for more information call ☎ 972 9607.

St Ann's Bay and around

Eight miles west of Ocho Rios and stretching up the hillside from the coast, **ST ANN'S BAY** is characterized by its porticoed shopfronts, sloping streets and old-fashioned atmosphere. Small enough to cover on foot in an hour, it consists of two central thoroughfares, Bravo and Main streets, which meet in a crossroads. Main Street hogs all the action, lined with shops and a **market** which spills out onto the street on Fridays and Saturdays, selling everything from reggae tapes to string vests.

Marcus Garvey

Born at 32 Market Street in St Ann's Bay on August 17, 1887, the **Right Excellent Marcus Mosiah Garvey** was one of the most powerful black rights activists of the twentieth century. His outspoken denunciations of colonialism and racism and his concrete efforts to unite and empower the African diaspora influenced politicians, musicians and academics alike. His legacy remains one of the most significant in Jamaican history – Rastafarians call him a **black prophet** and his philosophies form the basis of their faith (see "Religion" in Contexts, p.394).

Reputedly of Maroon descent, Garvey's early years were dominated by the uncompromising attitude of his father, a master stonemason who earned enough to pursue multiple law-suits against those he felt had slighted him on racial grounds. Though lack of funds ended the young Garvey's formal education at fourteen, he continued to be tutored privately and spent long hours in his father's extensive library. Prodigious from an early age, Garvey was made foreman of his uncle's Eclypse Printery at eighteen, but small-town living offered scant opportunities, and in 1906 he moved to Kingston and found work as a printery foreman – a significant coup at a time when supervisors were usually white – and became an activist in the fledgling trade union movement. Disturbed at the institutionalized injustice meted out to black workers, Garvey left Jamaica in 1910 to search for better prospects in Costa Rica, where he worked as a time-keeper on a banana plantation and set up two workers' newspapers to highlight the deplorable conditions for West Indian migrants. During a stint in England in 1912, he took classes at Birkbeck College and read up on other black nationalists such as Booker T. Washington, whose seminal text *Up From Slavery* was highly influential in fostering Garvey's ever-increasing militancy. In 1914, he returned to Jamaica and formed the **Universal Negro Improvement Association** (UNIA) "to champion Negro nationhood by redemption of Africa; to make the Negro race conscious, to advocate self determination, to inspire and instil racial love and self respect", but

The town's distinctive 1860 **courthouse** dominates from its perch at the top of Main Street – you can enter as an observer during trials, though the bureaucratic rigmarole of the Jamaican court system is often more arresting than the cases themselves. Continuing down Main Street, and in the middle of a roundabout, sits an ornate monument to Christopher Columbus by Spanish artist Michele Geurisi – the adventurer strikes a noble pose above his sunken ships. Just before the road forks, the church of **Our Lady of Perpetual Help** is one of the few remaining Catholic houses of worship in Jamaica; the stone it's made of was resurrected from the original structure – Peter Martyr Church, the first stone church in Jamaica, built in 1524 by the Spanish as a part of Sevilla Nueva.

The quieter left fork of Main Street holds the **library** (Mon–Sat 9.30am–6pm), with its **Marcus Garvey memorial statue** on the front lawn. The outsize bronze stands before the words "We Declare to the World – Africa Must Be Free". Other than a parade in the town centre every August 17, the statue is the only distinctive evidence of

West of Ocho Rios

Snorkelling and diving are excellent around St Ann's Bay – Seascape Dive Resort (☎972 2573), just outside town, will rent equipment and offer guided trips.

Jamaica's middle classes weren't ready to embrace such a radical and he emigrated to the USA in 1916 to seek a more sympathetic audience. Black Americans identified so strongly that by 1920, the UNIA had become the largest black pressure group ever to exist in the US, with a membership estimated from two to six million. Despite being outlawed in most of the colonies, his self-published *Negro World* newspaper achieved the largest circulation of any black paper in the world, and with the financial backing of thousands who bought shares, Garvey formed the Black Star Line Shipping Company to foster trade links between black nations and enable repatriation to the African homeland.

Though known principally as a "Back-To-Africa" advocate, Garvey was equally concerned with improving the cultural and economic situation of blacks wherever they found themselves. His assault on post-colonial nihilism was his greatest achievement; eschewing the sense of inferiority and powerlessness fostered during enslavement, he advocated black pride and self-determination, using the historical achievements of Africans to animate blacks: "Up you mighty race, you can accomplish what you will."

Marcus Garvey was regarded a subversive in the US by white America and his supporters saw his 1922 imprisonment on a trumped-up mail fraud charge as an attempt to muzzle the message. After two years in Atlanta Federal Prison, pressure from UNIA members secured his release, and in 1927 he was deported back to Jamaica on a wave of publicity. However, his imprisonment had caused a loss of campaign momentum; the Black Star Line had foundered, and Garvey never recaptured his early success. Tiring of constant battles with authority, he moved the struggle to the UK, where he died in obscurity in 1940. His importance was only recognized posthumously – in 1964 his remains were returned to Jamaica by the state and interred in Kingston's National Heroes Park. In the 1970s, music inspired a resurgence of Garveyism in Jamaica, with Rastafarian musicians like Burning Spear immortalizing his life and work in song, and today his ideas remain central to the Jamaican national consciousness.

Garvey's local connection (the house where he was born – 32 Market St – is a private residence), although the library itself is a good source of information on his life and work.

Seville

St Ann's Bay is bordered to the west by the old Spanish village of **SEVILLE**, Jamaica's first Spanish settlement (see box), but now an overgrown wasteland dotted with the crumbling remains of once-impressive buildings. On the other side of the road to the site of old Seville village is **Seville Great House and Heritage Park** (Tues–Sat 9am–5pm, 45min tours; J$150). Managed by the Jamaica National Heritage Trust, this is one of the few true heritage sites on the island, focusing on the lives, customs and culture of Tainos and Africans rather than celebrating plantation owners or "discoverers". A video presentation gives a detailed overview of Seville's history, and the

---

Christopher Columbus and the Tainos at Seville

The north coast is often referred to as "**Columbus Country**" – and though a little jaded the title is certainly apt, as the conquistador got his first sight of Jamaica at St Ann's Bay. Sailing into the bay during his second voyage in 1494 to claim new territories on behalf of King Ferdinand and Queen Isabella of Spain, Christopher Columbus was so impressed by its beauty that he named it **Santa Gloria**. He was rather less enamoured during his fourth and final voyage in 1503, when the unseaworthy state of his worm-eaten, weather-beaten caravels forced him and his crew to spend an unhappy year marooned here in makeshift shacks, awaiting rescue from Spanish compatriots in Hispaniola. Plagued by illness and worried by the partial mutiny of his men, Columbus used a mixture of bribery and super-stition (his prediction of a solar eclipse led them to believe he was a god), to coerce Taino Indians into providing food until their eventual rescue in 1504, after a year and a day on the beach.

Columbus died in Spain in 1506 but his son **Diego** was appointed Governor of the Indies and directed **Juan de Esquivel** to establish the first Spanish colony on the island – **Sevilla Nueva** – at what is today called Seville, in 1510. Situated on the site of the Taino (or Arawak) village **Maima**, the development of Sevilla Nueva eradicated Jamaica's Indian population in fifty years. The *encomienda* system of serf labour – the antithesis of the previously unfettered Taino lifestyle – was introduced and brutally enforced, and Caciques (Taino chiefs) selectively murdered; with their society in tatters and their forms of authority destroyed, the confused Indians were easily branded and enslaved, and along with Africans trans-ported to the island by the Spanish, were conscripted to build the new city. Less robust than the Africans, the Amerindians were unable to bear a life of slavery; ill-treatment and European diseases soon eradicated those who didn't commit suicide, but while the Tainos expired, New Seville rapidly developed into a sizeable town, with churches, castles, irrigation and drainage sites and a wharf. However, its occupation lasted only until 1534, when the marshy, disease-inducing environment was abandoned in favour of Villa de la Vega or Spanish Town (p.115).

---

museum displays intricately crafted Taino *zemis* (talismans used to ward off evil spirits) and other artefacts. Hidden in cattle pastures and woods, the ruins of Seville itself are not visible from the main road, but staff at the great house may be persuaded to accompany you on a walking tour of what remains – a water wheel, parts of the Spanish Catholic church (the first on the island), sugar mill and the governor's castle, as well as the sites of Taino villages and slave settlements. A better way to see the site is on a **horseback trail ride** courtesy of Hooves (☎972 0905; 2hr 30min Beach Ride; US$60), which meanders through the bush from the great house to Seville, winding past what's left of the buildings and finishing up riding your mount in the sea.

Around St Ann's Bay: Priory to Chukka Cove

The short coastal stretch west of St Ann's Bay is dotted with minor roadside communities. A mile and a half along is tiny **PRIORY**, little more than a roadside strip but a favoured selling spot of jerk vendors, who set up reams of smoking oil-drum barbecues each evening. Running parallel to the main strip are the appealingly deserted, clear waters of **Alterry beach**, a favoured local swimming spot and occasional venue for sound-system dances; the circular bar is also a nice place for a drink.

Half a mile or so west of Priory, the mountains recede back from the coast and the road cuts through the cattle pastures and sugarcane flats of **Llandovery**, once home to a huge sugar plantation, the Llandovery-Richmond estate, established in 1674 by the English – you can just make out the factory chimneys from the road. Just west is **Chukka Cove**, the most prestigious equestrian facility and polo ground in Jamaica – matches are open to observers most weekends; call for schedules (☎972 2506). The immaculate stables also offer a fabulous three-hour beach ride (daily 9am & 2pm; US$55); after a gentle hack through cattle pastures, you swim your snorting mount in the sea. They also run a four hour mountain bike tour (daily 9am & 2pm; US$50); you're bused up into the hills, then glide down to the sea for swimming and snorkelling. Costs for both trips cover return transportation and drinks. Chukka also serves as the main north coast venue for Carnival celebrations each April – for more details, contact the JTB in Ocho Rios (see p.189).

A mile or so past Chukka Cove, a tiny paved road cuts inland toward the signposted **Cranbrook Flower Forest** (☎770 8071; daily 7.30am–4.30pm; US$10), an exquisitely landscaped, 130-acre nature park with several grassy lawns, a fishing pond, a family of resident peacocks and a swift-running river with plenty of marvellous swimming spots. Run by a friendly Jamaican family who wanted to create a space where visitors and local people could retreat from urban clamour, Cranbrook is an overwhelmingly peaceful spot. No ghetto blasters or vendors are allowed, and it's the perfect place for

West of Ocho Rios

Hooves also offer the Bush Doctor Mountain Trail (2hr; US$50) into the hills toward Higgin Town.

Inland of Priory, Circle B Farm (☎913 4511; daily 10am–5pm; US$12) offers interesting, low-key walking tours of a working plantation.

Lillyfield Great House, set in the hills behind St Ann's Bay, offers guided tours and lunch (☎972 6045).

Chukka Cove's barren volcanic cliffs were used as a backdrop for scenes from the screen epic Papillon.

a quiet picnic and river swim: you can bring your own food and drink, or buy it from the tuck shop, housed in a pretty cut-stone building that was originally an outbuilding of the sugar estate which flourished here. To the right of the tuck shop is the **fishing pond**, a flower-wreathed man-made pool that's well stocked with tilapia. Caught with the aid of a customized bamboo pole, it costs US$5 to have your fish scaled, seasoned, roasted and served with roast yam or rice and peas etc (order before 10am). The stretch of river next to the pond has several shallow pools ideal for splashing children. Beyond the pond is the largest of the lawns, and, to the left, a series of mesh-covered walkways sheltering a staggering variety of **orchids** and **anthuriums**. Past here, pathways overhung with enormous tropical flowers, tree ferns, philodendrons and sheaves of giant bamboo parallel the riverbank. Strategically-placed steps lead down to the deeper pools, but for Cranbrook's best swimming, you'll need to walk half a mile to the **riverhead**, a gorgeous 20ft-wide pool where the river gushes up from the rocks. Overhung with lush greenery, the deep turquoise water is cool, refreshing and absolutely clean, having been freshly filtered through the limestone.

Accommodation

Though **accommodation** choices are few around St Ann's Bay, you escape the dust and bustle of Ochi while staying close enough to enjoy its good points, and can relax in less restricted surroundings. If you really want to rough it, *Starfish Beach Camping* (no phone; US$5 per tent), at the end of the road beyond *Seascape Dive Resort*, offers **camping** in an unfenced field by the sea.

Chukka Cove Villas, PO Box 160, Ocho Rios; ☎913 4851. Luxury two-bedroom villas with a/c, full kitchen, living room and large verandahs – each comes with a cook and maid. All are dotted around lush gardens with fruit trees and a mineral pool, and have access to deep-sea swimming and excellent snorkelling – paradise if you can afford it. ⑧.

High Hope Estate, PO Box 11, St Ann's Bay; ☎972 2277, fax 972 1607. A ten-minute drive inland from Priory, just west of town, an eclectically furnished seven-room hotel that's both intimate and luxurious, with fantastic views, a pool, extensive gardens, excellent food and free access to a private beach club. ⑦.

Seascape Dive Resort, Priory; ☎ & fax 972 2753, *seascapedivers @cwjamaica.com*. Supremely friendly, Jamaican-run scuba divers' paradise set in lush, expansive gardens at the seas' edge, with spacious, air-conditioned rooms, comfortable villas and camping. Meals and watersports are available, and there's a pool on site. To get there, go down the slip road for *Jamel Jamaica* hotel and look for the sign. ④.

Eating and entertainment

Patty shops and small **restaurants** line Main Street in St Ann's Bay; *Square One* on Bravo Street is especially good for cheap Jamaican meals or snacks – chicken, patties, callaloo loaf and pastries. Fabulous sit-down meals are served at *The Mug* (☎972 1018), on the coast road opposite the turnoff to St Ann's bay, one of the north coast's best seafood restaurants; Jamaicans come from miles around for the excellent conch, fish, lobster and shrimp, served with sublime bammy, rice or chips. Wednesday is "Mug Night", when barbecued fish and chicken are added to the menu and opening hours are extended until 1am. Elsewhere, check out the *Seafood Specialist*, a breezy, enduringly popular eatery just off the road between St Ann's Bay and Priory – it specializes, unsurprisingly – in some of the best seafood around, from sublime conch soup and fish tea to brown stew or fried fish and chicken, fish and chips or "crack conch": marinated, deep-fried pieces of tender meat so-called because like the drug, you'll keep going back for more. *Jus' Cheers* jerk centre, on the coast road just west of St Ann's Bay, is a popular jerk joint and a nice place for a drink – they often set up a sound system at weekends, too. For **entertainment**, sound-system dances and stageshows are regularly held at the open-air *Windsor Lawn* in St Ann's Bay (☎972 2940), and occasionally at Alterry beach – look out for promotional posters at the roadside or listen out on Irie FM.

Runaway Bay and Discovery Bay

Sitting halfway between Ocho Rios and Falmouth, two mini-resorts bask in isolated indolence, bayside oases where the "Jamaica no problem" maxim seems to ring true. Dominated by lavish all-inclusives, **Runaway Bay** is the more developed of the two, though beyond the razor-wired fences and Italianate marble lobbies, life jogs along at a slow lick, with few organized attractions to draw in the crowds. Even more pacific than its neighbour, the crescent harbour of **Discovery Bay** is dominated by the red-stained sphere of the Kaiser Bauxite plant, with fewer hotels but a fantastic public beach. However, the recent opening of the ultra-racy *Hedonism III* all-inclusive (sister resort of the legendary Negril original) in Runaway Bay may soon speed up the pace hereabouts, and with another huge resort in the making at Pear Tree River, on the outskirts of Runaway, the future of the bays looks set to change.

Theories abound as to the **naming** of the twin bays; while it's usually assumed that the "runaways" were Spanish troops fleeing the strong arm of the British in the late seventeenth century, it's more likely that the name refers to Africans who made the risky ninety-mile canoe trip to Cuba and freedom from slavery. Survivors were baptized into Catholicism, and calls for their return were denied on the grounds that Catholics couldn't be expected to live among sectarians.

Arrival and getting around

As both communities spread out from the coast road, getting lost is practically impossible, though the barely paved tracks of the Cardiff Hall satellite community can seem a bit maze-like. Most things you'll want to do are within walking distance, but you may find it easier to

Contrary to popular belief, Discovery Bay does not hold the dubious honour of being the place where Columbus first stepped onto Jamaican shores; that accolade goes to Rio Bueno a few miles down the road.

*Petrol stations
are located on
the main A1
road, opposite
Cardiff Hall
beach in
Runaway Bay
and Puerto
Seco Beach in
Discovery Bay.*

*The area's
cheapest inter-
national phone
calls, fax ser-
vice and
Internet access
(J$180 per
hour) are
offered by
Global
Communi-
cations (daily
8am–10pm) at
the Northern
Shopping
Complex in
Runaway Bay.*

jump in a shared taxi for the ride to Puerto Seco; these run constantly along the coast road. **Buses** from Montego Bay and Ocho Rios arrive and depart from the small square outside the post office and *Patty Place* snack bar in Runaway Bay, and from the A1/ B3 intersection in Discovery Bay. Regular **taxis** are available from any of the larger hotels, while shared taxis shuttle constantly between Discovery Bay, Runaway Bay and Ochi. **Car rental** is available from Caribbean Car Rentals in Runaway Bay (☎973 3539) or from Salem, in, of course, Salem (☎973 2564), while Jake's (☎973 4403), also in Runaway Bay, rents motorbikes and the odd bicycle – ideal for hopping between the bays.

Accommodation

All-inclusives dominate the bays, but there are still some lovely small **hotels** and **guesthouses** towards Discovery Bay and around Hampton Road in Runaway Bay. There are also lots of luxury **villas** in the area, which can be cost-effective for large groups – a four-bedroom place rents from around US$2000 per week. For further information, contact JAVA (☎974 2763 or 2508). *Sunflower Resort* (see p.224) has some reasonably priced villas in the hills above Runaway Bay, while the three- and four-bedroom villas operated by *Portside Villas* (see opposite) are a little more luxurious with pools, all mod cons and fabulous views of Discovery Bay from their hilltop perches.

Caribbean Village, Salem, Runaway Bay; ☎973 3453 or 5070. Functional, good-value three-bedroom apartments in the *Sunflower* complex with a/c and full kitchen. The gorgeous private beach is steps away, and there's a pool on site. ⑤.

Cliff's Apartments, PO Box 33, Runaway Bay; ☎973 2061. Popular with Jamaicans and budget-conscious Europeans, this collection of apartments and rooms on Hampton Road enjoys the ambience of a Jamaican home – kids running around and lots of hanging out. ②.

Hampton View, Runaway Bay PO; ☎973 4337. Self-catering apartments in a characteristic Jamaican abode on Hampton Road – not flash but comfortable and homely, with kitchen and shared verandah. ②.

The Pantharosa, 100yd down the A3 Brown's Town road; ☎973 5553. These thoroughly Jamaican self-contained, spacious and spotless rooms and apartments with cable TV and VCR are one of the best deals in the area. There's a lively bar in the backyard and home-cooked meals are available. ② Breakfast is included in the rates.

Pastel Villa, Salem, Runaway Bay; ☎973 5070. Spacious five-bedroom apartment above a family home; rooms can be rented singly or with the kitchen. Each has a/c and cable TV, and there's a plunge pool on the verandah. ③–④.

Piper's Cove, Runaway Bay PO; ☎973 7156, fax 973 7714. Newly built complex of one-bedroom apartments in a prettily landscaped garden next to *Hedonism III*. Each unit is attractively decorated with rattan fittings, fully equipped kitchen, living room, a/c, fans, cable TV and balcony. Meals are available, there's a pool on site and access to the sea (but no beach). ⑤.

Portside Villas and Apartments, PO Box 42, Discovery Bay; ☎973 2007 or 3135, fax 973 2720. Characterful, popular complex of rooms, studios and one- to three-bedroom apartments overlooking the sea; all have kitchenette, a/c and satellite TV, and there's a pool, jacuzzi, tennis court, a bar and restaurant and a small beach with watersports equipment. Evening entertainment ranges from beachside fish-fries to limbo shows and karaoke. ④–⑤.

Runaway HEART Country Club, PO Box 98, Runaway Bay; ☎973 2671–4, fax 973 2693, *runaway.heart@cwjamaica.com*. Outstanding service at reasonable rates in a government-sponsored hotel training school. Immaculate gardens overlooking the golf course, great patio restaurant, pool, daily beach shuttle and good rooms with balcony, a/c, cable TV and phone; children under 12 stay free. ⑤.

Tamarind Tree, PO Box 235, Runaway Bay; ☎973 4819 or 4106–7, fax 973 5013. One of the few remaining "old school" hotels and struggling to keep up with the all-inclusives, this has a quiet, friendly atmosphere, restaurant, large pool, disco, and a choice between rooms and three-bed cottages. Not far from some public beaches. ④–⑦.

Village of Portside, PO Box 42, Discovery Bay; ☎973 2572, fax 973 3543. Sprawled over the hillside on the opposite side of the A3 to *Portside Villas*, these spacious rooms, studios and one-bedroom apartments have great views of the bay, a/c and satellite TV; some have full kitchens. There's a pool and jacuzzi on site, and the catchment clientele are "singles who want to meet other singles." ③–④.

Villa Rose, Runaway Bay PO; ☎973 3216. Basic, clean rooms in a block behind the owner's bar on the west side of town. Each has a large bathroom, ceiling fan, fridge and TV (you pay $5 extra for a set hooked up to cable), and rooms overlook a small slip of beach. ②.

Whilby Resort Cottages; PO Box 111, Runaway Bay; ☎973 6308. Easy-going home-from-home right at the end of Hampton Road. Sweeping lawns, a garden full of herbs and flowers, camping, laundry facilities, bicycles to borrow and a good spread of rooms and self-contained apartments. ②–③.

All-inclusives

Breezes, PO Box 58, Runaway Bay; ☎973 2436, fax 973 2352. The largest all-inclusive in the area, with a huge range of activities – gym, all watersports, scuba, pools, tennis courts, 18-hole golf course across the road, nightclub, a super-perfect beach (with a clothing optional area) and an emphasis on fun for over-16s. ⑧.

Club Caribbean, PO Box 65, Salem, Runaway Bay; ☎973 3507–8 or 4702, fax 973 4703, *clubcar@cwjamaica.com*. Appealing, unpretentious all-inclusive with a 1000ft beach, pool, tennis courts, gym, watersports, English-style pub, disco, supervised children's activities and pleasant rooms with all the usual facilities – garden cottages are the most basic option. Children under 12 stay free. ⑤.

Franklyn D. Resort, PO Box 201, Runaway Bay; ☎973 4591–8, fax 973 3071. Well-run family resort with cheerful atmosphere, attractive suites with terraces, numerous children's activities, small beach, all watersports, a pool, gym and disco, and loads of capable nannies. Excellent meals and a designated children's restaurant. Children under 16 stay free. ⑧.

Northern Laundromat at Northern Plaza, Salem (☎973 7365; daily 7am–11pm) have self-service machines and a pick-up and delivery service.

The superb Superclubs golf course opposite Breezes hotel is open to non-guests; there's also a restaurant, bar and clubhouse on site (☎973 2436).

Hedonism III, ☎973 4100, fax 973 5402, *www.superclubs.com*. Ultra-luxurious "adult" resort that tries hard to cultivate a risqué feel – and succeeds. Two beaches ("nude" and "prude"), three pools (one with a three-storey water slide that cuts through the disco before reaching the water), four restaurants, five bars, four jacuzzis, a beachside trapeze and trampoline and all the sports facilities you could wish for. The swim-up rooms (a first in Jamaica) feature marble bathrooms with jacuzzi, while the evening entertainment pushes libidos to new heights. ⑧.

Sunflower, PO Box 150, Runaway Bay; ☎973 4809–10, fax 973 4650, *sunflower.r@cwjamaica.com*. Inexpensive, friendly and popular with Europeans, the one- to- three-bedroom apartments on this sprawling complex have kitchenettes, fan and balcony; a/c is on request. There's a pool, a shuttle to the beach and low-key evening entertainment. Non all-inclusive plans are available. ④–⑥.

Runaway Bay

Little more than a roadside strip, **RUNAWAY BAY** stretches lazily along the coast for three miles or so, a sun-bleached and lackadaisical melee of bars and hotels running to the satellite community of **SALEM** to the east, where you'll find the majority of shops and restaurants. The **all-inclusives** are clumped together in a single block in front of the best beaches (and the neatest strip of highway). Runaway Bay is not a resort on the scale of Ocho Rios or Montego Bay, and as most holiday business takes place inside the all-inclusives, the place appears pretty somnolent and easy-going. However, as the new kid on the block of north-coast tourism and with several large hotels in the making, what little indigenous character there is may soon be eradicated.

Other than the flurry of activity as buses come to a honking halt and vendors hawk their piles of cane and fruit around the open space in front of the post office, there is little obvious activity in town, though there's plenty just up the B3 at **Dover Raceway** (☎975 2127), a motor-racing track with regular advertised meets. For swimming, sugary-sanded **Cardiff Hall public beach**, opposite the Texaco petrol station, is popular with locals who congregate under the tree for dominoes and a beer. **Salem Paradise Beach**, at the Salem end of town, is not the promised elysium field – sound-system dances are occasionally held here and nobody clears up the debris.

Midway between the two bays are the **Green Grotto and Runaway Caves** (daily 9am–5pm; US$3.50), the area's sole managed attraction. Thought to have been used as a hideout by fleeing Spanish troops and possibly as a Taino place of worship, the limestone caves are expansive and well lit with a crystal-clear underwater lake 120 feet below sea level. The guides who take you through are particularly good, injecting plenty of humour into their tours and pointing out bats and vaguely discernible animal shapes in the rock formations as they relate a little of the cavern's history. The tour ends with a rum punch or fruit juice taken in an area of the cave that was once

---

Plantation culture and the story of sugar

When the British took control of Jamaica in 1655, they found three ram-shackle **sugarcane plantations** recently deserted by the Spaniards, who had brought the plant to the island from southeast Asia but failed to develop it; a hundred years later, there were well over four hundred plantations on the island. Having already established successful plantations in Barbados, the British were eager to transform Jamaica into a giant sugar-producing factory, offering thirty acres of land to any Englishman settling on the island. Hundreds took up the offer and the commercial cultivation of sugarcane began in earnest. Small concerns were quickly bought out and by the early eighteenth century, huge plantations covered practically all of Jamaica's most fertile land, with African slaves shipped in to do the dirty work and absentee owners reaping tremendous profits.

By the mid-eighteenth century, tax and trade incentives made Jamaica the largest sugar producer in the world and the richest of England's colonies. The planters celebrated their wealth by building the lavish **great houses** that still overlook cane flats from breezy hilltop perches. However, the abolition of the slave trade in 1834 and full emancipation in 1838 left a labour gap and marked the decline of the sugar trade. The Sugar Equalization Act of 1846 ended preferential treatment for sugar produced in the colonies and despite the influx of indentured workers from Africa, India and Europe (who were paid wages for the first time), the industry could no longer compete with cheaper sugar produced in Cuba and Brazil. In the twentieth century, the sugar industry is still Jamaica's single largest employer and accounts for nearly twelve percent of its overall exports, but poor rates of pay make industrial action a regular occurrence and inadequate technological advancement has seen a slide in productivity.

---

used as a nightclub – the stage still stands, and there are plans to reinstate a disco here. For the moment, though, the only music is provided by a fatigued-looking Rasta guitarist who strums Bob Marley tunes as you drink your juice.

Discovery Bay

DISCOVERY BAY is more a coastal clutch of shops, snack bars and houses than a town. The **bauxite industry** is very visible here – the orange-stained wharf and dome-shaped storage chamber are even attractive in their immense ugliness. Jamaica exports over two million tons of "red gold" to US refineries annually, much of it from the plant at Discovery Bay; local big cheese Kaiser Bauxite pays its dues by financing all sorts of community projects, even sponsoring the push-cart derby held every August on the cricket pitch behind the plant (a good laugh if you're around).

A rangy shopping complex is the main focus of Discovery Bay; bang opposite, **Puerto Seco beach** (daily 8am–5pm; J$100) is the best swimming spot in the bays that's not attached to a hotel; the name is derived from the old Spanish title meaning "dry harbour" in reference to Columbus's reluctance to land in a bay with no fresh

Kaiser Bauxite's Discovery Bay loading plant became Crab Cay, the fictional base of Dr Julius No, in the first of the James Bond movies.

See p.358 for more on bauxite.

Watersports in Discovery and Runaway bays

There are over twenty luxuriantly lively dive sites in the area, including sunken ganja planes and a Mercedes car. All are visited by the Jamaqua dive shop at *Club Caribbean* (☎973 4845, *jamaqua@infochan.com*), which rents equipment and offers taster dives, PADI certification courses and guided night and day dives. They also operate glass bottom boat rides (20min; US$11.50) and a "reef adventure" snorkelling tour (1hr 30min; US$17.50). The other reliable scuba operator in the area is Resort Divers based at the *FDR* hotel (☎973 2830 or 5750, *www.resortdiver.com*). Also from *Club Caribbean*, Broadreach Cruises offer catamaran trips along the coast to Dunn's River Falls – call for prices and availability (☎973 5155 – ask for Cottage 4). Kayak rental (US$10 per hour); banana boat rides (US$10 per ride); sailing trips (US$20 per hour), and deep sea fishing (4hr; US$250) are offered by Reef Divers at *Sunflower* resort (☎973 4400).

water (see p.252). Despite gleaming sand and crystal-clear water, it's relatively deserted on weekdays, and the gently shelving shoreline is good for families. There are full facilities and a good snack bar. The adjacent **Discovery Bay beach**, east down a rutted dirt track and separated from Puerto Seco by a fence, is free but has no facilities and is in need of a bit of a clean up. Past here, the eastern curve of Discovery Bay's horseshoe is dominated by luxurious villas owned by the likes of Jamaican entrepreneur Gordon "Butch" Stewart, owner of Air Jamaica and the *Sandals* resort chain, while on the opposite outcrop, the University of the West Indies Marine Research Laboratory (☎973 2241) houses the island's only **decompression chamber**.

Much of the go-karting footage in the movie Cool Runnings *was shot in Discovery Bay.*

The broken-down structure as you round the bay is **Quadrant Wharf**, built in 1777 by British fearful of possible French attack; its cannons have long disappeared, and only the basic stone structure and some rusting ironware remain. **Columbus Park** (daily 9am–5pm; free), on the western curve of the bay, is a slick, well-signposted yet rather dull open-air museum exploiting the local Columbus link. The colonial-era artefacts include a water wheel and cannon, and there's an expensive craft market on site. The needle-straight stretch of road beyond Columbus Park was used as an **illegal airstrip** by ganja exporters in the 1970s – in the still of the night, they'd set up impromptu roadblocks, land their small planes and load bales of ganja aboard with the motor still running. The government finally wised up and installed concrete bollards at the roadside, smashing the planes' wings and putting a halt to proceedings on this part of the road at least.

Eating

The bays' fancy **restaurants** are predominantly within hotels, and as most are all-inclusive you have to buy an expensive day or evening pass to eat there. However, there are several Jamaican eateries serving hearty fare at attractive prices, and you can buy cheap and delicious soup, jerk, fried fish and bammy or chicken and rice at any of the roadside stalls which set up along the main road in Runaway Bay. Patties and callaloo loaves are available from the *Patty Place* in Runaway Bay, and from the small bakery at Columbus Plaza, behind the shopping complex in Discovery Bay; here, there's also a reliable, inexpensive Chinese takeaway.

Supermarkets are located in the plazas that line the main road in Runaway Bay – A & B Value Mart is the largest and cheapest and has a pharmacy (Mon–Sat 9am–8pm, Sun 9am–3pm). The shopping complex by the petrol station in Discovery Bay has another that's open daily from 7am to 11pm.

Afiya, Cardiff Hall Boulevard, Runaway Bay. Set back from the main road, this well-signposted vegetarian restaurant and health food store cooks up succulent and imaginative wholefood fare, from cornmeal porridge to soups and vegetable stews served with brown rice and peas, as well as great soya, vegetable and corn patties and delicious cakes. Closed Sunday.

Auntie May's Bluebird, Runaway Bay. Good old-fashioned Jamaican restaurant with some tables overlooking the sea. Huge breakfasts, sublime conch, beef, or mannish water soups, a few Chinese dishes and all the local staples, from oxtail to lobster in curry butter. Takeaway is available, and there's a full bar.

Cardiff Hall Restaurant, *Runaway HEART* hotel. Reliable Jamaican and international cuisine and wonderful service at the formal in-house restaurant of this hotel training school.

Charlante, Salem. Small indoor eatery serving good Jamaican breakfasts of ackee and saltfish and mackerel run-down, and pizza, chicken or fish for lunch and dinner.

Mackie's Bar and Jerk Centre, off the A1 between the bays. Open-air circular bar and restaurant serving good, cheap jerk chicken and pork.

Northern Jerk and Steak Pit, Northern Plaza, Salem. Super-efficient shiny-countered indoor jerk house, with a selection of soups and a confectionery counter for late-night munchies. Open daily till midnight.

The Rising Sun, Runaway Bay; ☎973 2907. Reliable Swiss-run bistro opposite Cardiff Hall beach, serving salads, sandwiches, burgers, pizza, seafood, chicken, steaks and Swiss specialities. Deliveries available.

Seafood Giant, Runaway Bay. Breezy dining area under an open-sided thatch roof, with a couple of rope swings for kids to play on. From stuffed baked crab backs to shrimp, fish, lobster and conch cooked in every imaginable style, the seafood here can be a little greasy, but it's mostly passable and the conch or fish soup is the highlight.

In restaurant listings, we have given a phone number only for those places where you might need to reserve a table.

Sea Shanty, *Portside Villas*, Discovery Bay. Attractive, semi-open-air setting on the waterfront, and imaginative, varied meals from solid local and "international" breakfasts to lunchtime salads, burgers, sandwiches and a great fish chowder. Dinners include fettucine Alfredo, steamed fish and okra and Jamaican staples.

Tek it Eazy, Runaway Bay. Unassuming rooftop restaurant and bar serving inexpensive Jamaican food alongside the rum and beer.

Ultimate Jerk Centre, on the A1 opposite Green Grotto cave. Lively and popular, this roadside jerk centre serves up spicy and delicious helpings of pork, chicken and sausage. Tables are dotted in the grounds, and it's usually open until at least 1am.

Drinking and entertainment

There are several **bars** at the Salem end of Runaway Bay, many of which serve as go-go clubs these days – plenty of rude, semi-naked gyrating and not for the faint-hearted. Of these, the *19th Hole Club* is popular, and also has a pool table; *Classique Nite Spot* in Discovery Bay is equally well-patronized. *Dougie's One Stop Rest* in Salem is a nice, local-style bar, while just down the road at Runaway Bay, the suitably-named rooftop bar *Tek it Eazy* has piped music most nights, and occasional live music – including a one-man country and western band – at the weekends. Don't bother with the seafood at *Seafood Giant* at the far western end of Runaway Bay – it's far better for a leisurely drink under the huge circular thatched roof, and there's a happy hour between 5 and 6pm each Saturday. The seafront setting of the *Sea Shanty* bar at *Portside Villas* in Discovery Bay is also an appealing place for a few drinks, while midway between the bays and opposite the Green Grotto cave, the *Ultimate Jerk Centre* is good for a purely Jamaican lime, with plenty of white rum drinking and oldies on the stereo.

As most people head into Ocho Rios for their nightlife, the twin bays are not exactly jumping at night, though occasional live shows and sound-system dances are advertised on roadside billboards. Most of the **entertainment** is centred on the all-inclusives. Non-guests can buy an evening pass (US$35–60), which covers dinner, drinks, some kind of floorshow and access to the disco – *Breezes* and *Club Caribbean* are particularly lively. Alternatively, the *Tamarind Tree Hotel* disco is intermittently open to the public at weekends, though it's usually very quiet (cover around US$5). Finally, if you're around in August, look out for posters advertising Kaiser Bauxite's **Family Fun Days**, an uproarious blend of children's activities, push-cart racing, live music, sound systems and amateur comedy/cabaret.

Brown's Town

High in the hills above the twin bays, bustling **BROWN'S TOWN** hums with the dynamism and industry absent along the coast below. Reached on the B3 from Runaway Bay, Brown's Town is a sizeable inland community with fantastic views and a booming central **market** (main days are Wednesday, Friday and Saturday): the stalls that line the main road overflow with fresh produce – six-foot pillars of sugarcane, yams and dasheens caked in red alluvial earth, and oranges tied into strings of ten – ferried in by small-scale farmers and sold by formidable-looking female higglers. Food is much better bought here than on the coast – quality improves once you near the source and people are too busy to bother about ripping you off. Bootleg name-brand clothing and tawdry knick-knacks also sell by the bucketload – this is the place for china figurines and fake flower displays. Even the proper shops are worthy of a root – Charley & Son on Main Street is a treasure-trove of ancient books with yellowing covers, tacky postcards and intriguing miscellany.

The **restaurants** and **bars** along Main Street are good for plates of steaming Jamaican food or a few white rums, and if you want to **stay** and soak up the atmosphere, try the basic but comfortable rooms at *Meditation Heights*, just past the Esso petrol station on Huntley Avenue (☎975 2588; ②). Buses from Runaway Bay arrive two or three times a day; taxis are much more convenient.

Marley's mausoleum and the St Ann interior

Both the B3 from Runaway Bay and the inland road from Discovery Bay lead toward **ALEXANDRIA**, a tiny hamlet where you turn left for the only tourist attraction in the St Ann interior, Bob Marley's Mausoleum, at his former home of **NINE MILE**. Though the scenery here is stunning – the red-earthed pastures, distant Cockpits and sweeping hills and gullies of the Dry Harbour mountains are a photographer's dream – there are few specific points of interest, and the viciously potholed road will demand most of your attention. You'll need to have your own transport or charter a taxi to get here; a round trip in a taxi from Runaway or Discovery bays should cost around US$80–90 and from Ochi US$90–100, but bargain as you may be able to haggle down the rate. Small communities such as **CLARKS TOWN** bear the names of European estate keepers and missionaries, and history is everywhere in a landscape strewn with the crumbling chimneys of unidentifiable sugar factories and stone churches built by Baptist missionaries.

From Alexandria, the narrow road off the B3 to the **Bob Marley Centre and Mausoleum** (☎999 7003; daily 8am–8pm; US$12) winds through the hills past **Alva** and **Ballintoy** – you know you're in Nine Mile when you see the red-gold-and-green flags flying high above a fenced-off compound stretching up a hillock to the side of the main road. If you're driving, you'll be directed into the compound car park, from where you proceed directly to the ticket office where all visitors must sign in. There's also a vegetarian restaurant here, as well as a small gift shop selling tapes and Marley memorabilia. Once you've paid your fee, you're assigned to one of the throng of Rasta guides and are taken up the hill and into the centre proper. There's a prayer space to the left at the first plateau, sometimes occupied by orthodox Rastafarians who come to worship and hold "reasoning" sessions. To the right is the wooden shack that Marley lived in between the ages of six and thirteen, complete with the "original" single bed he sang of in *Is This Love*. Opposite is an outdoor barbecue where Marley cooked up Ital feasts during rural retreats at the height of his career, and the Rasta-coloured "meditation stone" where he rested his head for contemplation with a marvellous view, immortalized in the song *Talkin' Blues*. You leave cameras and shoes outside before entering the **mausoleum** above, a concrete building painted with Rasta colours and depictions of Black angels that encases the marble slab which holds

Bob Marley – King of Reggae

The legacy of the original ambassador of reggae is impossible to overemphasize; Jamaicans tend to regard their most famous compatriot with an emotional and religious reverence and his lyrics continue to strike a chord across every social strata. Born February 6, 1945, **Robert Nesta Marley** was the progeny of an affair between 17-year-old Cedella Malcolm and 51-year-old Anglo-Jamaican soldier Captain Norval Marley, stationed in the Dry Harbour mountains as overseer of crown lands. Marley's early years in the country surrounded by a doting extended family (particularly his grandfather and formidable "myalman" Omeriah Malcolm) and by the rituals and traditions of rural life had a profound effect on his development. Unlike most Jamaicans of mixed parentage, Marley clung to the African side of his heritage and revelled in the solidarity, freedom and rich cultural life of downtown Kingston, where he spent most of his later life. Marley was known as an intensely spiritual individual, emanating an almost-tangible energy and charisma. He was also a lover as well as a thinker: his 1970s membership of the influential Twelve Tribes Of Israel – a Rastafarian sect that divides members by birth month into "houses" with a name and a colour – gave him the title of Joseph, "a fruitful bough" according to the Bible, and though his 1966 marriage to **Rita Anderson** lasted until he died, his appetite for women was great and he fathered eleven children by various women.

Fusing African drumming traditions with Jamaican rhythms and American rock guitar, Marley's music became a symbol of unity and social change worldwide. Between 1961 and 1981, his output was prolific. Following their first recording *Judge Not* on Leslie Kong's Beverley's label, his band, The Wailers (Marley, Bunny Livingstone and Peter Tosh), went on to record for some of the best producers in the business – Joe Higgs, Clement "Coxsone" Dodd, Clancey Eccles and Bunny Lee – though most agree that the finest material was recorded in collaboration with innovative and volatile musical genius Lee "Scratch" Perry. In 1963, the huge hit *Simmer Down* (a warning to Kingstonians to cool down the increasing tension) meshed perfectly with the post-independence frustration felt by young Jamaicans, and the momentum of success began in earnest, the Wailers' lyrics providing a script for the island's development from rude boy to Rasta (see "Music" in Contexts, p.398). International recognition came when the Wailers signed to the Island label – owned by Anglo-Jamaican entrepreneur Chris Blackwell, who Marley saw as his "interpreter" rather than his producer. The first Island release was *Catch a Fire* in early 1973, and the eleven albums that followed all became instant classics. With the help of Blackwell's marketing skills, reggae

Marley's remains. A stained-glass window filters red, gold and green sunlight over the stone, while candles, incense, fresh flowers and scribbled tributes make the mausoleum one of the more uplifting aspects of a place that in celebrating Marley's death seems only to succeed in highlighting the yawning gap left by his passing. Many Rastafarians – who eschew the concept of physical death – argue that Nine Mile is not his final resting place and that, like Haile Selassie, Bob Marley's bones will never be found.

became an international genre. Differences with Blackwell – particularly over his obvious concentration on Marley – led to the departure of Peter and Bunny in 1974, but the group continued to tour the world with new musicians and a new name – Bob Marley and the Wailers.

Inevitably, the socially aware Marley became embroiled in the factionalized and violent confusion of Jamaican politics, and in the run-up to a headline performance at the 1976 Smile Jamaica concert, staged by the government to quell rising tensions in an election campaign so dogged by violence that Prime Minister Michael Manley declared a state of emergency, gunmen burst into Marley's Kingston home and tried to **assassinate** him. The attempt was bungled, and most of the shots hit manager Don Taylor (who made a full recovery), though Bob and Rita incurred minor injuries. Undeterred, a bandaged Marley went on stage under heavy security. After the concert, Marley left Jamaica to recover and record in Britain and the States, but as his international reputation grew, so did his popularity at home, and Jamaicans began to embrace fully their homegrown megastar. Two years later, he returned to the island for the first time since the shooting. Met by two thousand fans on the runway, Marley was back to perform for his people at the historic **One Love Peace Concert**, the result of an unprecedented – and short-lived – truce between the political garrisons of the PNP and JLP. The headline act of a line-up that also included Peter Tosh singing solo and spitting vitriol at the politicians, Marley ended his performance by enticing arch-enemies Michael Manley and Edward Seaga on stage to join hands in a show of unity – a huge coup. But Marley's call for unity and freedom was not restricted to Jamaica; one of his greatest triumphs was performing the protest anthem *Zimbabwe* at the independence celebrations of the former Rhodesia, the last African country to free itself from colonial rule.

See p.331 for the Peter Tosh story.

In the midst of a rigorous 1980 tour, Marley was diagnosed as suffering from cancer, and despite treatments at an alternative clinic in Austria, he died a year later in Miami, honoured by his country with the Order of Merit. The Honourable Robert Nesta Marley OM died without making a will, and years of costly legal wrangles over his US$46 million estate ensued, with his widow eventually granted the lion's share. Rita Marley's Bob Marley Foundation continues to sponsor the development of new Jamaican artists, and many of the Marley children have forged their own musical careers – Ziggy, Cedella and Sharon have found success abroad as the Melody Makers, Junior Gong, his son by 1976 Miss World Cindy Breakespeare, is a respected DJ, and another son, the US-based Kymani, is fast becoming a national heart-throb – but in the hearts of Jamaicans, the master's voice can never be equalled.

Marley fans may also be interested by the Bob Marley Museum in Kingston; former home and a monument to Jamaica's greatest musical legend (see p.90).

In some ways, the centre is a bit of a disappointment, particularly if you're expecting some kind of theme-park ambience; there's also an undercurrent of hustle to the whole thing (you'll doubtless be offered overpriced ganja). Nothing can detract from the beauty of the locale though; the home of the original "Natural Mystic".

If you want to linger in Nine Mile, you can stay in the relatively basic **hotel** opposite the complex, run by extended members of the Marley family; rooms cost around US$35 and you can have meals

cooked for you or use the kitchen yourself. Campers with their own
tents can pitch them for free in the complex. Otherwise, the place
comes alive every **February 6**, when Marley's birthday is celebrated
with a jump-up and sometimes a live show featuring the Melody
Makers. For details contact the Bob Marley Foundation in Kingston
(☎978 2991) or simply turn up on the day (see also Basics, p.41).

Rio Bueno to Duncans

A Spanish-built stone bridge marks the St Ann–Trelawny border and
the entrance to **RIO BUENO**, a destitute-looking village of crumbling
eighteenth-century buildings, too many skinny dogs and a peeling
police station, all cowering in the shadow of a towering silver animal-
feed factory – fortuitously absent when the town was used as a set for
A High Wind in Jamaica. Yet despite its unprepossessing appearance, the town has a place in the history books. Having spent a night
anchored off St Ann's Bay during his so-called discovery of the island
in 1494, **Christopher Columbus** sailed west along the coast seeking
a bay to land and find fresh water; with its rapidly running river and
horseshoe dimensions, Rio Bueno is popularly agreed to be the
"crescent harbour" he decided upon and recorded in his diary
account. Columbus made a fortuitous choice – despite its diminutive
size, the bay is one of Jamaica's deepest harbours.

The town today is nothing to write home about, though the British
presence is evident in a ruined **fort**, named after Henry Dundas,
British Secretary of War, and dating back to 1778, and the neat,
blue- and white-painted **St Mark's Anglican Church**, built at the
sea's edge by the British in 1833. The original **Baptist church** was
burnt to the ground in that same year by hostile Anglicans – the present incarnation on the hill above town was erected in 1901.

The town fell into decline following the abolition of slavery,
though there are proposals for its development as a heritage site;
until this comes to fruition, the only reason to linger is to peruse the
collection at Gallery Joe James, an **art gallery** set in a seventeenth-
century warehouse on the western fringes of town that also serves as
a hotel, restaurant (see opposite) and the studio of James himself, a
well-known Jamaican artist who has lived in Rio Bueno for some
years. Pieces on display – by both James and other local luminaries
– range from paintings to Africanesque masks and a stunning cedar
Medusa with flowing locks of men and snakes. The knowledgeable
Mr James is usually on hand to talk you through the work, most of
which is for sale.

If you're after more pastoral delights, head for a swim in the rapidly running **Rio Bueno River** – the best spot for a dip is at the
Dornoch Riverhead pool, a deep, cliff-edged swimming hole surrounded by silk cotton trees and throngs of mosquitoes. It's reached
on the B10 from Discovery Bay through Queenhythe and Rising Sun,
but it's hidden from the road and you'll probably need local help to

pinpoint it. Baptist missionary and anti-slavery activist William Knibb used to baptize converts here, and a spiritual, slightly spooky ambience lingers.

Practicalities

Although there is no earthly reason to stay in Rio Bueno, a vast all-inclusive has seen fit to open two miles down the road. *Grand Lido Braco*, Rio Bueno PO, Trelawny (☎954 0000, fax 954 0020; ⑨) is a sprawling complex that strives to recreate a "real" Jamaican town – it even has its own town square (though obviously minus the traffic, goats and dirt). It's a mishmash of architectural conceits, and it's fabulous; rooms are spanking new, the grounds are beautifully landscaped and amenities – gyms, pools, private 9-hole golf course, watersports, bars – are exhaustive. There's also an "au naturel" section in which guests spend every waking hour in the nude. In Rio Bueno proper, *Gallery Joe James* (☎954 0046, fax 954 0049; ⑤–⑦) offers an eclectic selection of atmospheric but overpriced rooms and suites overlooking the sea. Guests and non-guests alike can eat at the hotel restaurant, *The Lobster Pot*, where seafood lunches and dinners and solid Sunday brunches (US$10) are served in an open-air dining room right on the water. The breezy indoor bar is also an inviting place to sink a few Red Stripes. Just out of town, *Richie Rich's Yow Jerk Centre* sells great jerk, fish, chicken, fish tea, conch soup and very popular breakfasts, while in between Braco and Duncans, the *Plane Stop* (so-named for the carcass of a crashed ganja-smuggling plane that stands outside) is an open-air jerk centre which does tasty chicken and pork or roast yam and saltfish at the weekends, and refreshing juices – June plum, beetroot, soursop and roots tonics – throughout the week.

Just west of town, the Rio Bueno Travel Halt *(daily 8.30am–5.30pm) has a restaurant, gift shop and spotless bathrooms.*

Signposted Arawak Sunset Bar, *on the main road west of Rio Bueno, is opposite a small undeveloped cave; the owner acts as unofficial guardian and guide (for a small fee of course).*

Duncans and the beaches

A peaceful village huddled under the hills of Cockpit Country, **DUNCANS** consists of little more than a supermarket, a few small-scale restaurants and bars, a pharmacy and a clocktower with a timepiece that hasn't worked for fifteen years. There's a huge villa complex set back from the coast road just east of town, *Silver Sands*, PO Box 1, Duncans (☎954 2001, fax 954 2630; ②–⑦), where the mostly privately-owned holiday homes are decorated in varying styles and degrees of luxury, and the sense of seclusion makes for some fantastic beach life away from the resorts. Directly opposite, the *Sober Robin* (☎ & fax 954 2202; ②–③) has an eclectic selection of rooms with various combinations of fan, a/c, TV and fridge; a pool and restaurant are on site, as well as an ageing jukebox and numerous written reminders that the great Harry Belafonte once lived here – allegedly. Just east out of town and suffering from its isolation, the dirt-cheap, dependable and friendly *Montgomery's Holiday House*, PO Box 36, Duncans PO, Trelawny (☎954 0263; ①) stands alone in

West of
Ocho Rios

*The B10 road
that runs
straight from
the clocktower
in Duncans is
the easiest
route into
Cockpit
Country from
the north
coast.*

a sparsely-developed pasture set back from the main road. The comfortable if spartan rooms are fantastic value, with tiled floors, ceiling fan and hot and cold water. The owners also run the *Café Braco*, a rest-stop-cum-jerk-pit which also occasionally moonlights as a disco.

The **coastline** parallel to Duncans is sublime – powdery white sand and big waves, though as the area is quite sparsely populated, you'll need a car to see the best of it – most buses will flash by full. The best beach is attached to the *Silver Sands* resort, though non-guests can normally use it for a fee; enquire at reception. Wide and windswept, the sand is famously white and the swimming superlative. Alternatively, there's Duncans **public beach**, basically a facility-free fisherman's beach that's so rocky it's hard to imagine how the boats ever manage to leave the shore. The turn-off for *Montgomery's Holiday House* marks a series of completely deserted bays – the water is quite shallow with some sea grass, but they're ideal spots for a secluded day by the sea. When you get **hungry**, try the *Prestige Fish Pot* at the roadside in Duncans town; for **drinks** head to the *Rainbow Tavern* next door.

Falmouth

Trelawny's capital reflects the history of the parish; at the height of the plantocracy there were 88 **sugar estates** in the region worked by thousands of slaves, and **FALMOUTH** – named for the English birthplace of parish Governor Sir William Trelawny – became the main port of call for sugar ships. Slaves were traded on the wharves and goods for the plantations unloaded while planters snapped up land and built elegant townhouses in Georgian style. In the late eighteenth century, Falmouth boasted more than 150 houses and a cage where the market now stands (akin to the one still standing in Montego Bay's Sam Sharpe Square – see p.260), used for locking up drunken sailors found on the streets later than the 6pm curfew. Though slavery was almost at an end when the town was dedicated as parish capital in 1790, Falmouth's central location and natural harbour ensured Trelawny's prosperity, and the town thrived where others declined, even after emancipation in 1838. However, the advent of the steamship – the first docked at Jamaican shores in 1837 – spelled the first step in the town's declivity. The harbour wasn't deep enough to accommodate these larger vessels, trade was diverted to bigger harbours, and by the 1890s Falmouth became something of a ghost town – the planters and traders had left for Montego Bay or Kingston, and their houses began to rot slowly in the sun and salty air. In 1896, the Albert George Market was built at the edge of the square, and Falmouth instead became Trelawny's main **market town**, a status it still enjoys. Each Wednesday, a bustling "bend down" market spills out on to the streets – traders set out fruit and veg, bootleg clothing and garish arrays of brightly-coloured plastic fripperies along the pavements, and customers pour in from miles around, causing a day-long traffic jam and a flurry of complaints from those who see the market as a safety hazard.

Falmouth is a somewhat forgotten but nonetheless compelling place these days, entirely unaffected by tourism and rich with architectural interest. The town boasts the highest concentration of **Georgian architecture** in Jamaica – possibly in the whole of the Caribbean – but many buildings are in a terrible state of disrepair: two-hundred-year-old timbers crumble onto the tarmac, and once majestic buildings serve as dilapidated shelters for chickens and stray dogs – a visible symbol of the decline of the sugar industry and the failure to develop new business. Despite periodic calls for Falmouth to be granted some kind of official protection as a "heritage town", there's been no noticeable effort to capitalize on its historic status so far, and as there are no easy-access managed "attractions", most visitors pass through without a second glance. However, a wander through the streets provides an unadorned – and sometimes chilling – glimpse into Jamaica's past, and the lack of touristic glitz just adds to Falmouth's easy-going charm.

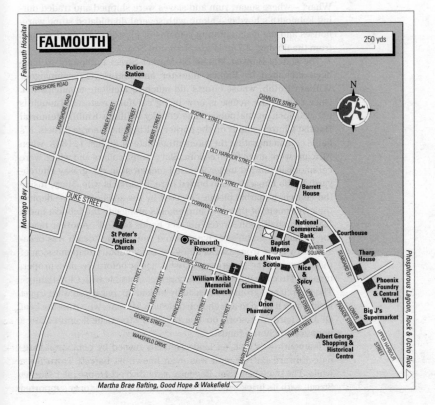

*Buses to
Montego Bay
and Ocho Rios
arrive and
depart outside
Courts in
Water Square.*

The Town

The town centre retains its original grid formation, neatly bisected by the busy A1, the western continuation of the A3. Most of the activity is centred on **Water Square**, named in allusion to Falmouth's status as the first Jamaican town with access to piped water. The non-functioning central fountain marks the spot of a stone reservoir which once held fresh water pumped by water wheel from the Martha Brae river, and though marred by the lurid facade of a furniture chain, the antiquated aspect of the wooden shopfronts that remain, combined with cane and coconut vendors and crowds of shoppers and people waiting for buses, lends the square plenty of character.

Some of Falmouth's most impressive constructions – the sagging **Tharp House**, with a huge termite nest on the roof, the porticoed **post office** in the middle of Market Street, and the old **courthouse**, built overlooking the sea in 1895 – are still in commercial or municipal use, though badly in need of structural attention. Immediately striking as you enter or leave town to the east is the conical roof of the 1810 **Phoenix Foundry**. It's behind the locked gates of **Central Wharf** – where sugar, rum and slaves were shipped and traded during Falmouth's heyday – along with several dilapidated stone warehouses and the disintegrating remains of plasterboard set dressings from the filming of *The Wide Sargasso Sea*.

The stately **Baptist Manse** on Market Street is thought to have been inhabited by Baptist minister and anti-slavery campaigner **William Knibb**, whose efforts did much to facilitate emancipation. Once ruined, the manse is now being carefully restored, though is not yet open to the public. The chunky **William Knibb Memorial Baptist Church** stands on the corner of King and George Streets, it's name commemorating the momentous date of August 1, 1838, when Africans were given full freedom. Slave irons, collars and whips were ceremonially buried under a raised memorial in the grassy churchyard; Knibb himself is also buried here, beside his wife, Mary. Inside the church, a marble plaque "erected by the sons of Africa" depicts their interment of the slave implements alongside the biblical quote "Ethiopia shall soon stretch out her hands to God". Another marks the demise of Knibb's twelve-year-old son, whose "death was occasioned by fever from excess of joy" at the voluntary manumission of their slaves by the congregation, who, a year before freedom proper, managed to conclude that "slavery is incompatible with Christianity". The church and grounds are usually locked up, but if you want to get inside, you'll need to ask church treasurer Mr Mac, who runs the Leaf Of Life hardware store on nearby King Street; he'll appreciate a donation to church funds.

Falmouth was built on land originally owned by plantation magnate Edward Barrett, and was even known as Barrett Town for a while. The once-beautiful, Regency-style **Barrett House**, at 1 Market Street, with its brick base and weather-board upper storey supported by wooden columns, was built in 1799 as the family's appropriately fine domicile. It's now in a state of near-collapse, though, seemingly liable to cascade into the street below at any minute; current owners the Methodist Mission have embarked on repairs, but for now you can't go inside. The house also has a tenuous literary connection; having survived his three sons, Edward Barrett left his Jamaican estates to his daughter on the condition that the man she married took the Barrett name – the house was built by her husband, Charles Moulton Barrett. The family moved to England and had two sons, one of whom fathered the poet **Elizabeth Barrett Browning**. Finally, the 1791 **St Peter's Anglican Church** on Duke Street is a sepulchral structure, perfumed by wax polish and surrounded by a sun-bleached cemetery, brimming with faded gravestones and generously sprinkled with the droppings of a resident herd of goats.

Out of town

Several more attractions lie immediately outside Falmouth. The most visible is **Jamaica Safari Village** (☎954 3065; daily 9am–5pm; US$10), a somewhat haphazard menagerie on the A3 five minutes' drive west of Falmouth that has recently been overtaken and refurbished by the owners of the Black River safari tours (see p.341). Like many small zoos, it's a bit depressing, but it's the only place on the north coast where you can see Jamaican **crocodiles**. Ranging from tiny babies to alarming twelve-footers, the crocodiles look fairly content, and there are various other indigenous animals on display. Incidentally, this is the place where James Bond used crocodile heads as stepping stones in *Live and Let Die*.

Half a mile east of Falmouth at **Rock**, **Oyster Bay phosphorous lagoon** owes its name to the incandescent illuminations of microorganisms. After dark, the water shines bright green when agitated and you can see the trails of fish darting about. *Fisherman's Inn*, a restaurant and hotel right on the lagoon (☎954 3427; see p.239) offers night-time boat trips costing US$10 for a twenty-minute jaunt (US$5 if you eat at the restaurant); bring your swimsuit and plunge into the eerie depths. Wide and wild **Burwood public beach** is 200 yards east down the road from *Time'n'Place* (see p.239) – there are no facilities but it's clean, with good swimming and snorkelling, and usually completely deserted.

Heading inland from Falmouth, a lone road threads from Water Square toward the **Martha Brae River**, Trelawny's longest waterway, notable cheifly because of the popular **raft trips** that glide through its waters. If you want to have a go, follow the battered signs from Water Square for about three miles to the put-in point at Rafter's Village (☎952 0889; daily 9am–4pm; 1hr 15min; US$36 per two-person raft). The leisurely trip takes you past banks overhung with silk cotton and mango trees and under towering banyans festooned with vines. There are a few craft stalls on

Set along a two-mile stretch of mostly undeveloped white-sand beach just east of the phosphorous lagoon, the well-signposted Time'n'Place is the best place in the area for a drink or meal with an ocean swim.

the riverbank, floating bars and a constant mosquito offensive – bring repellent.

The Martha Brae road is also the route to **Good Hope Great House**, a Georgian dream home overlooking its 2000-acre working plantation – follow the signed turn-off along a muddy and rutted road. Built in creamy English stone and set in gardens full of flowers and hummingbirds, this beautifully furnished Tharp family home is a serene nod to colonial excess; though, as the house itself is rented as an exclusive villa, it's only accessible to those who rent it out. However, you can explore the grounds on **horseback**, and the estate offers some of the best riding around (as well as some very well-kept mounts); you go at your own pace, and it's a very different kettle of fish to the staid trail rides of the resorts – if you're lucky, it'll be just you and your guide alone. A hack (call ☎1-610 5798 to book; 1hr 30min; US$30) takes you past original cut-stone estate buildings such as the aqueduct and water wheel – the old sugar processing room is now used for the packing of Good Hope oranges, ugli fruit and papaya – and then on through citrus and coconut plantations, with a stop at a small waterfall on the Martha Brae where you can take a dip.

Still inland and west of Good Hope **Hampden Estate** (☎954 6394 or 6395; Mon–Fri 9am–3pm; US$12) – a smoke-belching rum distillery surrounded by vast sugarcane flats and a road littered with fallen cane from the trucks that shuttle between field and factory in the summer cutting season. The estate's great house is closed to the public, but in any case, Hampden's main draw is its distinctly no-frills **sugar factory tour** (by appointment only), where the hot, dirty process of extracting sugar and rum from raw cane unfolds. The walkways are narrow and some steps a bit wobbly, so children under 10 are not allowed. The cobweb-festooned distillery is thick with the sickly-sweet smell of fermenting cane, and you get to sample the abrasive "jancro batty" overproof white rum – at about 170 percent proof, the innocuous-looking liquid could strip paint. To get to Hampden (referred to by most local people as "Amblin"), turn inland at Falmouth following the signs for Martha Brae rafting, and turn right at Wakefield.

Accommodation

With Montego Bay so near, few people choose to **stay** in and around Falmouth. However, there's a fair spread of accommodation, and the area is certainly a more relaxing place to rest your weary head for a night or two while exploring the town and surrounding attractions.

Bodmint Resort, Rock; ☎954 3551. A range of rooms and villas set in pretty gardens next to the phosphorescent lagoon. Rooms are clean with fan or a/c, and the villas with fully equipped kitchens and screened porches. Tasty Jamaican food, baby-sitting and various water-based trips are available. ③/⑤.

Falmouth Resort, Duke St; ☎954 3391. Managed by English returning residents, this quiet place is the only option in the centre of Falmouth. The small, basic rooms have a/c and TV, and there's a bar and restaurant on site. ③.

FDR Pebbles, Rock; ☎973 7651, fax 973 4600, *www.fdrholidays.com*. Brand new family-oriented all-inclusive slung along 600ft of lovely white-sand beach, with heaps of activities for all ages of children from toddlers to teens. The one-bedroom suites are spacious and appealing, and meals are good. Children under 16 stay free. ⑨.

Fisherman's Inn, Rock; ☎954 3427, fax 954 3078. Right on the phosphorous lagoon, these comfortable, sparklingly clean rooms have a/c, satellite TV and balconies overlooking the lagoonside pool. Rates include continental breakfast, and there's a restaurant on site. ④.

Good Hope, PO Box 50, Falmouth; ☎610 5798, fax 979 8095. Tastefully restored and utterly classy great house rented as a private villa with space to sleep seventeen. The furnishings are mostly antique, and there's an unmitigated feel of grandeur about the place, overlooking the stunning estate below, itself ringed by the conical hillocks of Cockpit Country and best seen when the mists roll away at dawn. ⑧.

Time'n'Place, PO Box 93, Falmouth; ☎ & fax 954 4371; *timenplace @cwjamaica.com*. Easily the most inviting choice in the area, just off the main road five minutes' drive east of Falmouth, these Thai-style stilted wooden cabins right on a beautiful white-sand beach have porches, a/c, satellite TV; those with pull-out futons are good for families. The bar and restaurant are steps away and the atmosphere is extremely friendly. ④.

Trelawny Beach, PO Box 54, Falmouth; ☎954 2450–8, fax 954 9923, *trelawnybeach@cwjamaica.com*. Budget-conscious, cheerful all-inclusive east of Falmouth. With tiled floors, breezy balconies, a/c, satellite TV and sea or mountain view, rooms in the main high-rise block are far more appealing than the dark and stuffy two-bedroom apartments close to the splendid white-sand beach, where watersports and scuba are available. There's a pool, kids' playground, tennis courts, supervised children's club, nightly entertainment and a disco. ⑤.

Eating

For **snacks**, *Nice and Spicy* on Water Square sells pastries and patties, and there are loads of **restaurants** around town – many, like the *Ackee Tree* at Salt Marsh, are your basic jerk stop or curry goat and oxtail shack. *Glistening Waters* at the Rock marina does a good line in seafood served up right next to the water – but bring repellent as mosquitoes are rampant. Just down the road from Rock and a little more upmarket, *Fisherman's Inn* offers tasty fish, shrimp, lobster, jerk chicken and curry goat in a cool, indoor dining room. Also east of Falmouth, the fabulous beachside café/bar *Time'n'Place* is the perfect place to hang out, despite the resort that's sprung up on the doorstep. The food ranges from tasty burgers and fries to jerk chicken, steak, fish, key lime pie and fruit smoothies laced with rum – there's also hammocks, a white-sand beach, great swimming and snorkelling, boat trips on the phosphorous lagoon, domino tournaments and occasional parties. A little further east, the presence of the sprawling *Trelawny Beach* all-inclusive has spawned a couple of eateries; directly opposite, *All Nations* offers inexpensive Jamaican lunches and dinners of stew pork, oxtail, curry chicken and good conch soup or fish tea, eaten amid some nicely kitsch wall murals, while the nearby *Ponderosa* has passable Chinese food. Busy *Down South* west of Falmouth, cooks fish any way you like it and makes a mean carrot juice.

Travel details

Other than the Air Jamaica Express (☎923 6664) internal flights to Boscobel airstrip near Ocho Rios, the only public transport along the coast is the haphazard bus system. Coasters, minibuses and the occasional old-style country bus ply the road between around 6am and 7pm, with a reduced service on Sundays, and little or nothing after 5pm. There are so many buses shooting along this stretch of the coast that we haven't put frequencies below – but you shouldn't have to wait any longer than thirty minutes for a bus; for pick-up points see relevant areas. The interior is a different matter entirely; areas that are covered have only one daily service, usually departing at the crack of dawn and returning to base in the early evening.

Buses

Falmouth to: Duncans (20min); Montego Bay (30min); Ocho Rios (1hr 15min); Runaway Bay/Discovery Bay (40min); St Ann's Bay (55min).

Ocho Rios to: Duncans (55min); Falmouth (1hr 15min); Kingston (2hr); Montego Bay (1hr 45min); Oracabessa (30min); Port Maria (45min); Runaway Bay/Discovery Bay (30min); St Ann's Bay (20min).

Runaway Bay/Discovery Bay to: Brown's Town (30min); Duncans (20min); Montego Bay (1hr 15min); St Ann's Bay (20min).

Flights

Ocho Rios (Boscobel) to: Kingston (3 daily; 15min); Montego Bay (3 daily; 25min); Negril (2 daily; 35min); Port Antonio (3 daily; 15min).

Chapter 4

Montego Bay and Cockpit Country

Montego Bay was once unashamedly Jamaica's tourist capital. Hundreds of foreigners flooded in every day, seduced by a heavily marketed Caribbean dream of swaying palm trees, lilting reggae and cocktails at sunset. In recent years the steady flow of tourists has slowed down or moved on to the more expansive charms of Negril or laid-back Treasure Beach. In many ways though, Montego Bay still delivers; sitting pretty in a sweeping natural harbour, hemmed in by a dazzling labyrinth of protected offshore reefs, and cradled by a majestic arc of hills, making it furnished with enough natural attributes to fill any brochure. The town itself, though marred by uninspired architecture, over-development and beaches which charge, remains the reigning old madam of Jamaican resorts; gossipy, belligerent and overdressed but also absorbing, spirited and lively, particularly during its world-renowned summer reggae festival.

Concentration upon the traditional pleasures of the Caribbean fantasy has left the surrounding countryside largely undeveloped, save for the public plantations and converted great houses on the fringes

---

Accommodation price codes

All the hotels detailed in this guide have been graded according to the following price categories. Note that the prices have been calculated as those for the cheapest **double** or **twin room** during low season, normally mid-April to mid-December. During high season, rates are liable to rise by up to 25 percent (though this is rare at the cheap hotels), and proprietors may be less amenable to bargaining. Although the law requires prices to be quoted in Jamaican dollars, most hotels give rates in US dollars; payment can be made in either currency. For more details see p.27.

① under US$20	④ US$51–70	⑦ US$151–200
② US$21–35	⑤ US$71–100	⑧ US$200 and above
③ US$36–50	⑥ US$101–150	

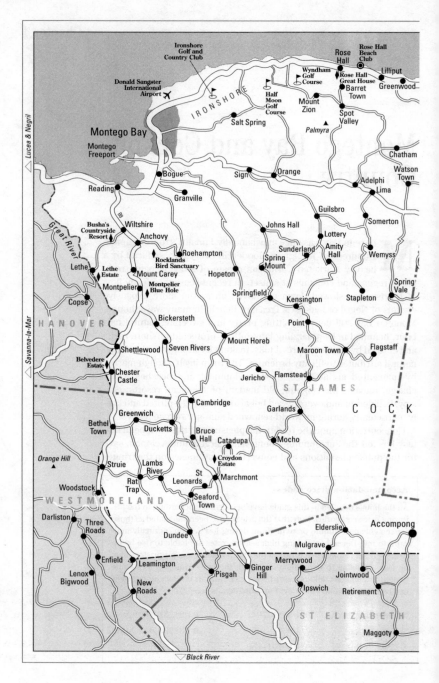

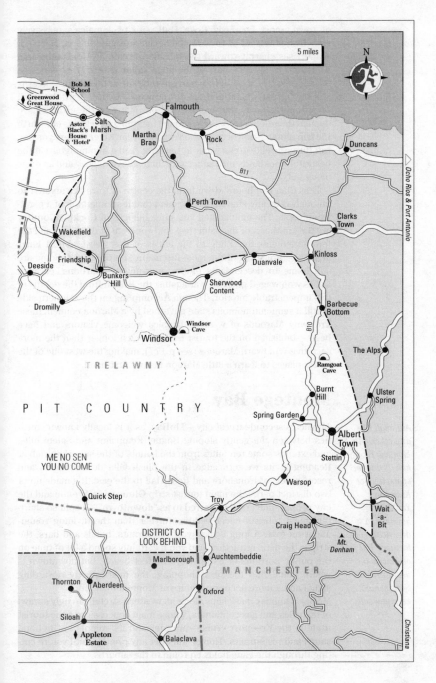

of town, most famously **Rose Hall**, site of Jamaica's massively embellished legend of voodoo and sexual intrigue. Inland, the landscape rises sharply toward the hillside retreats of **Montpelier** and **Kensington**, all once part of the huge **sugar estates** that were the backbone of the area before tourism took off in the 1920s. Sugar is still big business here, and the downtown air is thick with the smell of burning cane during harvest season. Many of the estates have opened their doors to visitors, and the magnificent settings are worth the trip alone. Elsewhere, in the verdant **Great River valley**, you can raft through silky green water at **Lethe** or feed a hummingbird at the beautiful **Rocklands bird sanctuary**, high above the bay and an oasis of serenity.

Less than two hours' drive from the centre of town lies an area so untouched by any kind of development that it's something of a parallel universe. The uninhabited limestone hillocks of **Cockpit Country** are the antithesis of the palm trees and concrete of the coast, and the few settlements that cling to the edges of this weird, almost lunar landscape are some of the most fascinating on the island. Some are still home to descendants of the once-mighty **Maroons**, escaped slaves who waged guerrilla war against the British from the depths of this impenetrable interior. Though **Accompong** on the southern side is still a semi-autonomous state governed by a Maroon council, these Trelawny Maroons of western Jamaica welcome visitors and have been established on the tourist trail for much longer than the more secretive Windward Maroons (see p.177), making the west one of the better places to learn a little Maroon history first-hand.

Montego Bay

Although like any other city, Montego Bay has its danger spots, it's not Kingston. You'll be hounded to distraction by hustlers, but otherwise the usual precautions should keep you safe.

Jamaica's second-largest city – **MoBay**, as it is locally known – nestles between the gently sloping Bogue, Kempshot and Salem hills, and extends some ten miles from the haunts of the suburban rich at Reading at its western edge to the plush villa developments and resort hotels of Ironshore and Rose Hall to the east. It's made up of two distinct parts: the main tourist strip **Gloucester Avenue** and the city proper, universally referred to as "**downtown**" – a split so sharp that most tourists never venture further than the dividing roundabout on foot. A long walkway of restaurants, hotels and bars, the strip is the main attraction, and you'll certainly spend a lot of time on the public portions of its postcard-perfect beach, but downtown is where you'll find the best shopping, the most quietly rewarding sights and a more accurate picture of Montegonian life.

MoBay's holiday mask slips along its **western** stretch, an ugly sprawl of factories and gas containers, whose main concession to the tourist trade is the **Freeport cruise-ship pier** and its complex of in-bond shops and restaurants. Things don't get any prettier until you're cutting through the cane fields en route to the suburbs.

Some history

When Columbus anchored briefly in Montego Bay harbour during his 1494 voyage to the island, he was charmed enough to name it *El Golfo de Buen Tempo* (The Bay of Good Weather). The Spanish were less romantic, dubbing it *Manterias*, a derivation of *manteca* or pig fat, after the lard they produced and shipped from here in large quantities. Eventually, the English corruption, "Montego", stuck.

Spanish occupation was short-lived and half-hearted; by the time the Spaniards hastily fled the island in 1655, Montego Bay was little more than a village – a few haphazard buildings around a harbour. Its subsequent development was heavily influenced by two factors. The first was the presence in neighbouring Cockpit Country of **Maroons**, an African-Jamaican band of militarily skilled rebel slaves whose frequent attacks on British settlements cowed the government and kept the town from prospering until a peace treaty was signed in 1739. By this time, **sugar production** was booming throughout Jamaica and the turnover of the area's many plantations saw the harbour thronging with ships, and lavish cut-stone town houses and travellers' inns spreading back from the waterfront. Plantation culture built Montego Bay and nearly destroyed it; the 1831 **Christmas Rebellion** (see p.260), the first and most important of the violent slave revolts that prefaced emancipation, began in the foothills behind the town and burned almost all the estates to the ground.

See p.370 for more on the Maroons.

After the collapse of the sugar trade, the city spent a hundred-odd years in limbo; many of the grander buildings were destroyed by fire or hurricanes and it was not until the early twentieth century that Montego Bay entered another period of growth, beginning when Sir Herbert Baker advocated the redemptive powers of the Doctor's Cave waters (see p.257) in the 1920s. Since then, Montego Bay has thrown full weight into its metamorphosis as the ultimate **tourist town**. Initially the trade was restricted to rich North Americans and Europeans who built holiday homes around Doctor's Cave or arrived on a banana boat to stay in the town's first hotel, the *Casa Blanca*. Sangster International Airport grew from the original single airstrip built in the late 1940s, and the town was poised for development as a major resort. Its population increased four-fold between 1940 and 1970, with Jamaicans from all over the island moving in to work at the hotels that sprang up alongside the best of the beaches. In the 1960s, the Freeport peninsula was manually constructed on land reclaimed from the sea, and Montego Bay's position as a premier port of call on any Caribbean cruise was assured.

More recently, Montego Bay achieved fame as the base for Jamaica's **reggae festivals** – the first ever Reggae Sunsplash took place here in 1978 and newcomer Sumfest is resident today – but over-development and a reputation for aggressive hustlers led to a decrease in tourist arrivals in the late 1980s and early 1990s.

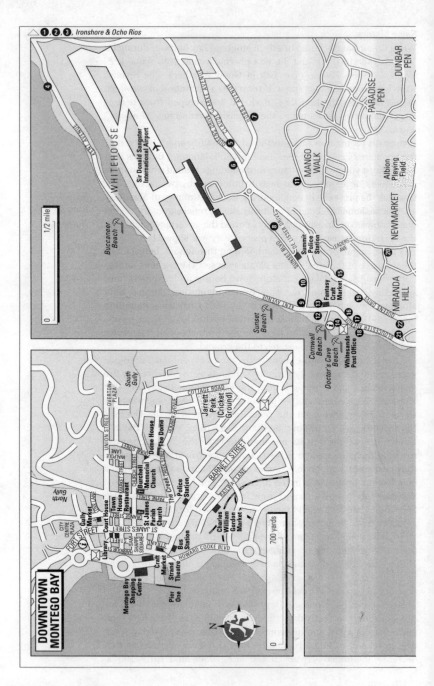

DOWNTOWN MONTEGO BAY

WHITEHOUSE

Sir Donald Sangster International Airport

Buccaneer Beach

DUNBAR PEN

PARADISE PEN

MANGO WALK

Albion Playing Field

NEWMARKET

MIRANDA HILL

Summit Police Station

Fantasy Craft Market

Sunset Beach

Cornwall Beach

Doctor's Cave Beach

Whitesands Post Office

0   1/2 mile

City Centre Plaza

Overton Plaza

South Gully

North Gully

Cottage Road

Jarrett Park (Cricket Ground)

Montego Bay Shopping Centre

Library

Craft Market

Strand Theatre

Pier One

Court House

Town House Restaurant

Burchell Memorial Church

The Dome

Dome House

St James Parish Church

Police Station

Charles William Gordon Market

Bus Station

Barnett Street

Howard Cooke Blvd

N

0   700 yards

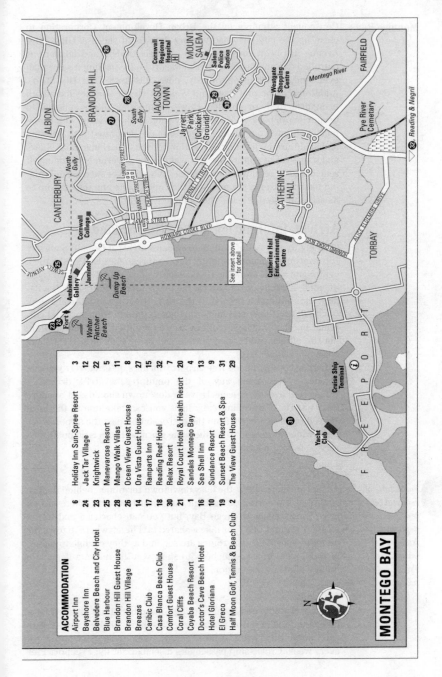

ACCOMMODATION

Airport Inn	6
Bayshore Inn	24
Belvedere Beach and City Hotel	23
Blue Harbour	25
Brandon Hill Guest House	28
Brandon Hill Village	26
Breezes	14
Caribic Club	17
Casa Blanca Beach Club	18
Comfort Guest House	30
Coral Cliffs	21
Coyaba Beach Resort	1
Doctor's Cave Beach Hotel	16
Hotel Gloriana	10
El Greco	19
Half Moon Golf, Tennis & Beach Club	2

Holiday Inn Sun-Spree Resort	3
Jack Tar Village	12
Knightwick	22
Manevarose Resort	5
Mango Walk Villas	11
Ocean View Guest House	8
Ora Vista Guest House	27
Ramparts Inn	15
Reading Reef Hotel	32
Relax Resort	7
Royal Court Hotel & Health Resort	20
Sandals Montego Bay	4
Sea Shell Inn	13
Sundance Resort	9
Sunset Beach Resort & Spa	31
The View Guest House	29

MONTEGO BAY

Consequent attempts by the Urban Development Corporation to clean up the city have had varying degrees of success. Gloucester Avenue has been largely cleared of street traders and hustlers, is patrolled day and night by special Resort Police making it safer than ever, and, rather incongruously, now calls itself "The Hip Strip". Additionally Doctor's Cave and Walter Fletcher beaches have both been attractively overhauled. However, more ambitious schemes to bring visitors back to Montego Bay such as the creation of a three-mile seafront promenade, Reggae Avenue, decorated with painting and sculpture by local artists, and proposed aquariums, boat shows and a festival of culture are still waiting for government funding. It remains to be seen whether Montego Bay will ever succeed in bringing back tourists in the numbers they once came and thus live up to its self-appointed title of "The Complete Resort".

Arrival, information and getting around

Over eighty percent of visitors to Jamaica arrive at **Donald Sangster International Airport**, right by the sea three miles east of the town centre and a mile from the Gloucester Avenue tourist strip. As you'd imagine, it's fully geared up for the newly arrived tourist, with a 24-hour **cambio** and a branch of the NCB bank, a tourist-board desk (daily, 9am–10pm) and numerous hotel, ground transport and car-rental booths. **Luggage trolleys** aren't permitted past immigration, but the official red-capped porters will carry your bags for a small charge (J$20 per bag).

Larger hotels provide free airport transfers; alternatively you can charter a **taxi** from any of the omnipresent JUTA drivers – Gloucester Avenue, Queens Drive or downtown should cost no more than US$10. If travelling *very* light you can take one of the local **shared taxis** that leave from the petrol station past the airport's car park, which charge J$30 for the same journey. There is no public bus service from the airport.

By road

For details of regional bus services departing from the terminus, see Travel Details, p.288.

All **bus** journeys end at the busy downtown **terminus**, behind the fire station at the corner of Harbour and Barnett streets. There are no city buses serving Montego Bay, but you can charter a taxi to the strip for around US$7, or take a shared taxi to anywhere in town for no more than J$20. The routes are set, and as they change frequently you'll need to ask somebody to show you the relevant departure point within the bus station.

By boat

Though visitor harassment and high disembarkation charges have taken their toll in recent years, some 250 ships still drop anchor here each season, carrying approximately 4000 passengers into town every week. Cruise-ship passengers disembark at the **Freeport Pier** (*www.cruisemontegobay.com*) centred in its own complex of shops and restaurants. Reps board the boats offering bus transport to designated in-bond shops and attractions, or you can negotiate a price with one of the many taxis that await ship arrivals. If travelling on a private craft, full marina facilities are available at the nearby Montego Bay Yacht Club (☎979 8650).

Information

The main **Jamaica Tourist Board** office (☎952 4425; Mon–Fri 8.30am–4pm, Sat 9am–1pm) is just to the left of the turnstile entrance to Cornwall Beach, with a nearby information kiosk on Gloucester Avenue and others at Harbour Street Craft Market and the cruise-ship pier. All carry maps and informative freesheets and can advise on hotels, restaurants and attractions. **The Cage** in Sam Sharpe Square (see p.260) is an excellent informal information centre. The twice weekly *Western Mirror* and weekly *North Coast Times* both advertise local events. As in all other parts of Jamaica, musical events – concerts and special club nights – are usually announced by lurid fluorescent banners tied to trees and lamp-posts. For comprehensive information on Montego Bay check out *www .montego-bay-jamaica.com*.

Local radio station HOT 102 has good coverage of MoBay events.

Getting around

Unfortunately there is no public transport serving downtown Montego Bay or the strip. The shortlived Soon Come Shuttle which carried visitors down to the Montego Bay Mall, along Gloucester Avenue and out as far as Rose Hall for a set fare no longer exists due to predictable opposition from local taxi drivers. Consequently any tourist walking the streets will be assailed with offers by passing taxis. Be prepared to haggle and always settle the price before you get in; from Gloucester Avenue to the Fort Street craft market should cost around US$6. The cheapest place to pick up a **private taxi** is the downtown taxi park at the intersection of Market and Strand streets, but there are also stands opposite Doctor's Cave and Cornwall beaches. For trips further afield, don't be afraid to follow the local example and cram into a **shared taxi** which charge a flat rate of J$20 per person for anywhere in the city, and J$30–50 for trips out of town; most leave from the bus station or Gully Market (see p.259), but there are unofficial pick-up/drop-off points along the strip outside Walter Fletcher and Cornwall beaches. Alternatively **walking** is your most convenient option. You shouldn't experience any problems along the strip even at night, but in the middle of town it's better to walk in company until you get your bearings.

See p.273 for a list of reliable taxi firms.

Constant tailbacks during the daily rush hours (8–10am and 4.30–6.30pm) make **driving** a frustrating experience in town, although you might want a car for independent sightseeing elsewhere. International **car rental** companies have booths at the

Montego Bay

One breathtaking way to see Montego Bay and Cockpit Country is on a helicopter ride from Helitours (☎974 1108, fax 974 0306). Tours start at US$65 per person.

Hundreds of **tour companies** operate out of Montego Bay; most have booths at the airport and offices along Gloucester Avenue and offer similarly priced trips to independent plantations and great houses. The **best operators** are slightly more adventurous: Barrett Adventures, Rose Hall (☎995 2796, fax 979 8845, *advent@n5.com.jm*) puts together customized packages to off-the-beaten-track waterfalls, farms and beaches from US$100 per person per day; Glamour Tours, LOJ Shopping Mall (☎979 8207) organizes bob cart races, treasure hunts and trips to a Jamaican farm fair from US$40 per person; Tourwise, 10 Queen's Drive (☎952 4943) has horse riding and mountain bike excursions through picturesque villages and farmland, and Caribic Vacations, 69 Gloucester Ave (☎979 3421), offers island-wide specialist and reggae tours and trips to Cuba. Alternatively, hire a **local driver** and do some independent sightseeing; both Kenneth Watson (☎952 2723) and Percell Pusey (☎079 0377 or 770 1268) are recommended.

Listed below are the best tour sites and most popular organized excursions. All can be seen independently as well as on a package.

Appleton Estate, Siloah, St Elizabeth (☎963 9215, *www.appletonrum.com*; Mon–Sat; US$12). This classic half-day tour crosses the edge of Cockpit Country into St Elizabeth to the orderly Appleton rum distillery in Siloah. You see the progression of cane to molasses and finally rum, view the ageing stills, taste various varieties and come away with your own miniature bottle.

Croydon in the Mountains, Catadupa, St James (☎979 8267, *thenry@infochan.com*; Tues, Wed & Fri; US$45). Half-day tour to Croydon Estate, a 132-acre working coffee and pineapple plantation in the foothills of the Catadupa mountains in the St James interior. Barbecue lunch and fruit tasting included in the price.

Hilton High Day Tour, St Leonards, St James (☎952 3343, *www.montego-bay-jamaica.com/hilton*; Tues, Wed, Fri & Sun; US$55). So-called because it once included a balloon ride – now a little short on thrills but still enjoyable. Visitors are bused up Long Hill through Montpelier and Cambridge to the diminutive Hilton plantation house, whose small grounds contain a piggery and stables. Breakfast and lunch are included, as are a stroll around the village and local school, a bus ride to the German settlement of Seaford Town and its museum, and a drive back through the western outskirts of Cockpit Country.

Maroon Attraction Tours, 32 Church St (☎979 0308; Tues, Thurs & Sat; US$50). The only tour company granted permission by Maroon officials to carry visitors to Accompong (see p.286). Includes a stop at Kensington to view the Sam Sharpe monument, tours of Accompong and Maroon Town, with introductions to "authentic" Maroons. Breakfast, lunch and live Maroon/mento band included. The views and countryside passed are spectacular and it's a hassle-free path to Accompong.

airport, while most local operators are located along the lower section of Queen's Drive/Sunset Boulevard (listed on p.271). Rates are high, but most operators offer reductions for weekly rentals; expect to pay around US$50–70 per day. Motorbikes (from US$35 per day), scooters (from US$25 per day) and bicycles (from US$10 per day) are also available from most of the local companies.

Accommodation

As you would expect, the range of **accommodation** in one of Jamaica's top tourist cities is staggering. This is prime **all-inclusive** territory, with the swankiest enclaves out at suburban Ironshore just east of town. Most people, however, stay along the Gloucester Avenue **strip** – busy, buzzing and swarming with hustlers. Opting for a hotel on **Queen's Drive**, the road just above the strip, reduces the likelihood of being accosted as soon as you step outside. Hotels **downtown** are considerably cheaper though you'll probably make up the difference getting taxis to and from Gloucester Avenue's nightlife. Many hotels include free airport transfers in their rates, and more distant properties throw in a free beach shuttle. As this is tourist territory, places are up to international standards and, unless otherwise stated, rooms come with air conditioning, TV and phone.

Montego Bay's wealthiest visitors head for Round Hill *resort, eight miles out of Montego Bay near Hopewell (see Chapter Five, p.292). It's the island's classiest hotel and literally swarming with the rich and famous.*

Most **budget** options are downtown, with a few more opposite the airport, but in such a tourist-oriented town, even the cheapest rates are pretty high. With so much to choose from, it's rarely difficult to find a vacancy, unless you hit town during Sumfest season – mid-July to mid-August – when it's practically impossible to find accommodation if you don't have a reservation.

Gloucester Avenue and the beaches

Bayshore Inn, 27 Gloucester Ave; ☎952 1046. Cheerful gingham rooms above a great jerk restaurant at the less frantic end of the strip. Reduced-rate weekly rentals available. ③.

Belvedere Beach and City Hotel, 33 Gloucester Ave; ☎952 0593, fax 979 0498. Friendly small hotel with a restaurant, bar and pool opposite Walter Fletcher beach. Rooms are slightly shabby. Live jazz once a month. ③–⑤.

Blue Harbour, Sewell Ave; ☎952 5445, fax 952 8930, *www. fly.to/jamaica .com*. Quirkily decorated small hotel perched above the strip with good views, a nice pool and a restaurant serving breakfast and lunch. A range of rooms, all scrupulously clean; the cheapest are a bit gloomy. ③.

Caribic House, 69 Gloucester Ave; ☎979 6073, fax 979 3521, *caribichse@hotmail.com*. Small hotel popular with European backpackers. Clean rooms, some with ocean views. ③.

Coral Cliffs, 165 Gloucester Ave; ☎952 4130, fax 952 6532, *www.montego-bay-jamaica.com/coralcliff*. Colonial-style hotel with comfortable rooms, restaurant and pool fronted by very popular gaming lounge. ⑤.

Doctor's Cave Beach Hotel, Gloucester Ave; ☎952 4355 or 4359, fax 952 5204, *info@doctorscave.com*. One of the better strip hotels, with bright

Montego Bay

interiors and gorgeous tropical garden, pool, Jacuzzi, restaurant, bar and small gym, across from Doctor's Cave Beach. Rooms are pretty uniform, but the friendly atmosphere wins lots of points. ⑥.

Hotel Gloriana, 1–2 Sunset Blvd just off Gloucester Ave; ☎979 0669–71, fax 979-0698. Cheap and cheerful hotel which is popular with backpackers. Rooms are basic but nice pool and poolside bar, with state of the art hot tub. ③–④.

Knightwick, Corniche Rd; ☎952 2988, fax 971 1921. Several large comfortable rooms in the elegant hacienda-style building which houses the restaurant *Tapas*; conveniently situated above the Coral Cliff. Run by friendly live-in couple with breakfast on the verandah included. ③.

Manevarose Resort, 17 Claude Clarke Ave, Whitesands PO; ☎952 1842, fax 940 3881. Small property overlooking the airport, so a bit loud. Airy rooms, a large pool, rooftop bar and restaurant and a canary cage out back. ②.

Ocean View Guest House, 26 Sunset Blvd; ☎952 2662. Modest guesthouse situated between the strip and the airport with basic rooms but convivial atmosphere. ②.

Reading Reef Hotel, PO Box 225, Reading; ☎952 5909, fax 952 7217, *www.montego-bay-jamaica.com/jhta/reefclub*. Superbly appointed hotel, right by Bogue Lagoon. Large private beach, bright rooms, restaurant, bar, beauty salon and pool. ⑤.

Relax Resort, 26 Hobbs Ave; ☎952 6944, fax 952 7218, *www.fantasyisle .com/relax.htm*. Tranquil place on a side road above Sunset Boulevard with pretty landscaping, spanking new rooms and apartments, a pool, shop, restaurant and bar. ⑤–⑥.

Royal Court Hotel and Health Resort, 13 Sewell Ave; ☎952 4531, fax 952 4532. Big on natural healing and weight loss, this resort with adjoining alternative health clinic has fancy rooms, some with kitchenette, juice bar, pool, hot tub, steam room, gym and restaurant. "Healthy holiday" packages available. ④.

Sea Shell Inn, Mabel Ewen Drive, Whitesands PO; ☎979 2984, fax 979 9836, *d.chin@cwjamaica.com*. Excellent location, back from the road opposite Cornwall Beach. Restaurant, bar and pool in pleasant tropical gardens. Rooms are clean, functional and popular with Europeans on a budget. ④.

Sundance Resort, 1 Kent Ave; ☎952 4370, fax 952 6591, *sundance@ cwjamaica.com*. Cheerful hotel with friendly staff and pretty grounds centred around a 200-year-old breadfruit tree. Rooms are attractive, with wooden furniture and balconies, and there's a pool, several restaurants and sports bar on site. ④.

Queen's Drive and downtown

Airport Inn, Queen's Drive; ☎952 0260, fax 929 5391. Two minutes from the airport, and clean and reliable. All rooms have kitchen facilities, and there is a pool and bar/restaurant. ③.

Brandon Hill Guest House, 28 Peter Pan Ave, Brandon Hill; ☎952 7054, fax 940 5609. Rooms are airy and neat with ceiling fan. There's a bar, pool and large lounge adorned with Jamaican art. ③.

Brandon Hill Village, 11 Coke Ave, Brandon Hill; ☎952 2563, fax 971 7832. Funkily designed rooms and self-contained apartments; good value for those on a budget. All units have fans; apartments have TV. Bar and cheap cook-to-order restaurant. Most guests are Jamaican, and the atmosphere is friendly and quiet. ③.

Comfort Guest House, 55 Jarrett Terrace, Barnett View Gardens; ☎952 1238. Family-run place with a Christian slant – ideal for those seeking a reserved but friendly atmosphere. Comfortable rooms, TV lounge, sun deck and home-cooked meals. ③.

El Greco, Queen's Drive; ☎940 6116, fax 940 6115, *www.montego-bay-jamaica.com/jhta/elgreco*. New resort with self-catering apartments perched high above the strip, conveniently located by lift via the *Montego Bay Club Resort*. Tennis courts, pool and laundry service. Bright modern rooms with optional in-suite cooking and baby-sitting services. Lacking in atmosphere but good value. ③.

Mango Walk Villas, Mango Walk; ☎952 1472 or 1473, fax 979 3093, *www.mangowalkresort.com*. Spacious, inviting villa complex in the hills above Queen's Drive, with big, bright studios and apartments, a pool, restaurant and small shop. ③.

Ora Vista Guest House, PO Box 351, Richmond Hill, Union St; ☎952 2576. A superb, friendly guesthouse with unrivalled atmosphere and great views. Rooms are simple, with no a/c, but clean and homely, and there's a pool, bar, kitchen, sun deck and communal lounge. Excellent Jamaican food available. ②.

Ramparts Inn, 5 Ramparts Close; ☎979 5258. A quiet, friendly small hotel just off Queen's Drive, with elegant rooms, a pool, bar and restaurant. ③.

The View Guest House, Jarrett Terrace, Barnett View Gardens; ☎952 3175. Commendable guesthouse with a real Jamaican flavour; good food, fair-sized pool, nice views and big function lounge. Rooms are comfortable and basic; a US$5 supplement gets you a/c. ②.

All-inclusives

Breezes, Gloucester Ave; ☎940 1150–7, fax 940 1160, *www.superclubs.com*. Fancy-looking resort with turrets and walkways which towers over Doctor's Cave Beach. Amenities are comprehensive – pool, Jacuzzi, gym, watersports, tennis courts, games room, restaurants, bars, poolside grill and nightly entertainment – but the rooms are poky and the resort characterless, though the shrieks of happy holidaymakers can be heard on the adjoining beaches. Very popular disco. Minimum stay two nights. ⑧.

Casa Blanca Beach Club, Gloucester Ave; ☎952 0720, fax 952 1424, *www.montego-bay-jamaica.com/casablanca*. This unobtrusive resort was the first hotel in MoBay, and although slightly shabby now it has two pools, a wonderful tiled foyer, vast beds and rooms right on the water. Recommended if you're looking for character rather than immaculate plumbing. ⑦.

Coyaba Beach Resort, Little River PO, Ironshore; ☎953 9150–3, fax 953 2244, *www.coyabajamaica.com*. Classy resort with elegant rooms and a tranquil atmosphere. Pool, all watersports, restaurant and bar, tennis courts and free tennis lessons, particularly beautiful beach and good offshore reef. ⑦.

Half Moon Golf, Tennis and Beach Club, Ironshore; ☎953 2211, fax 953 2731, *www.halfmoon.com.jm* (in US ☎1-800/237-3237; in UK ☎020 7730 7144, fax 020 7938 4793). Lauded as the most luxurious property on the island, short on atmosphere but with brilliant amenities: a shopping village, equestrian centre, 18-hole golf course, lovely half-mile beach, all watersports, three public and 49 private pools, tennis courts, croquet lawns, spa, sauna and Jacuzzi, disco, six restaurants and various bars. Guests can stay in one of 220 rooms or a villa which comes equipped with antique furniture, cook, gardener and private pool. ⑨.

Holiday Inn Sun-Spree Resort, Ironshore; ☎953 2485, fax 953 9480. MoBay's only family-oriented resort, with childcare facilities and daily activities. Recently refurbished but still disfigured by ugly room blocks. Facilities include restaurants, bars, disco, beach, watersports, pool, tennis and basketball courts, gym, slot machines and games. Children under 12 stay free; 13–19s pay US$50 per night. ⑨.

Jack Tar Village, 2 Gloucester Ave; ☎952 4340, fax 952 6633. Friendly and comfortable, with oceanfront rooms and a lovely private beach with "clothing optional" section, watersports, pool, gym, sauna, Jacuzzi, tennis courts, restaurant, beach grill and bars. Loud and lively entertainment and piped music all day long. Newly renovated. ⑥.

Sandals Montego Bay, Whitehouse; ☎952 5510, fax 952 0816, *www.sandals.com*. MoBay's largest Sandals property, with the emphasis on fun and frolics for a young and racy clientele. Tucked behind the airport in Whitehouse, it's all here for the taking: a huge private white-sand beach with watersports, tennis courts, gym, disco, lavish nightly entertainment, four restaurants and four bars that keep most guests permanently on the property. Two night minimum stay. ⑨.

Sunset Beach Resort and Spa, Montego Freeport; ☎979 8800, fax 979 8039, *www.sunsetbeachresortspa.com*. Located just outside Montego Bay on the Freeport Peninsula this popular, and friendly, resort caters for singles, couples and families. Comprehensive facilities include tennis, pool, watersports, spa and three sheltered beaches, one nude. ⑨.

The strip: Gloucester Avenue and the beaches

Though it stretches for less than two miles, Montego Bay's glittering oceanfront tourist strip is the focal – sometimes only – point of many a Jamaican vacation. Occupying the whole of **Gloucester Avenue** and stretching north into **Kent Avenue**, this holiday highway builds to a bottleneck around Doctor's Cave Beach during the daytime with hair braiders, taxi drivers and hustlers shadowing your every move and identikit gift shops competing for business; as night falls the action switches to MoBay's most happening joint, *Margueritaville*, and street vendors stake out jerk chicken stands and pushcarts selling sweets and snacks. Gloucester Avenue is where you'll find the majority of MoBay's tourist hotels and restaurants as well as the best beaches, bars and clubs, so even if you don't check into a strip hotel, you'll find that you spend a lot of time here.

The best of the strip's countless bars and restaurants are reviewed on p.266 and p.268.

Starting at the roundabout that filters Howard Cooke Boulevard, Queens Drive and Fort Street traffic, the first stretch of Gloucester Avenue is a kind of no-man's land split in two by an elevated section of a one-way traffic system and bordered by the only sizeable undeveloped beach in town (see p.259). Easily missed on the upper section of Fort Street and overtaken by the adjacent craft market, **Fort Montego** is an uninspiring hulk of stone with an even less impressive past. Dating back to the eighteenth century, the fort was built by the British to guard against foreign attack, but its cannons were fired only twice, both times with disastrous results; in a salute to celebrate the capture of Havana in 1760, one of the corroded guns misfired and killed its operator, later in 1795 – in the fort's only recorded attempt at a defensive attack – it mistakenly opened fire on one of its own vessels, the schooner *Mercury* carrying a cargo of dogs imported to hunt down Maroons. Inevitably the shots missed. Infinitely more absorbing, **Fort Street Craft Market** is a favourite haunt of persistent hair braiders but a relatively relaxed spot for a bit of bartering. Loosely arranged around steep steps that make a useful short cut to Sewell Avenue and Queen's Drive, stalls sell the usual array of carvings and T-shirts.

Though Gloucester Avenue runs parallel to the sea, the water is mainly obscured by the hotels and bars that carve the beach into private sections. The only place to fully appreciate the sweep of the bay is from the strip's only **green space**, more of a thoroughfare than a public park, in the old hospital grounds opposite the restaurants and bars at Miranda Ridge, just above the strip. The bucolic illusion is rudely shattered just past the park at **Margueritaville** (*www. margueritaville.com*; daily 10am–3am), a mini-lido-cum-restaurant-cum-bar that proudly displays the tackiest facade along the strip, a mock-stone clad, neon-flashing shrine to the worst in US kitsch and glitz. The bar and outdoor eating deck are built right over the sea; below there's a watersports area with boat berths and

The MoBay hustle

The constant tourist presence in Montego Bay has spawned a multitude of young hustlers trying to earn a living selling crafts, ganja, hair braiding or their services as a guide (or gigolo – see p.301). However with the introduction in 1996 of a special tourist police force, the Resort Patrol, who pace the strip day and night, much of the heat has gone out of the hustle. Still unless you're encased in an all-inclusive, you will at some point be accosted by someone trying to sell you something. It's tiring, it's irritating, and it's easy for visitors to lose perspective, bristling with tension and regarding every encounter as adversorial. You can't really blame the hustlers for trying, though, and whether or not the harassment becomes a problem depends largely upon your attitude. Resign yourself to being frequently approached, and learn how to deal with it. Hustlers play on guilt and use psychological trickery. Lines like "Don't you remember me from the hotel/car rental shop/airport/beach?" are designed to suck you into dialogue – of course you've never met them, but once you've stopped, the sales pitch begins. If you ignore the outstretched hand or catcall the response is often "Wh'appen, you too good to talk to a black man?". If you're white, don't fall into the liberal trap of buying things you don't want just to avoid looking racist. Don't try to avoid the issue by giggling or hinting that you may be interested another time; if you mean no, say no, in a friendly but straightforward manner. Keep your sense of humour and treat street sellers as people, and you'll minimize potential problems and maybe even make some friends.

swimming platforms, while on the roof there's a Jacuzzi, sun deck, and – best of all – a 110ft water slide (US$5 or free to spending customers) which sluices down into the sea and draws tourists and locals alike in their hordes.

The strip builds in intensity as it approaches the magnificent Doctor's Cave Beach, becoming a seamless parade of bars, cafés and identical in-bond shops that doesn't slacken up until past Cornwall Beach. Behind the last few stores here is diminutive **Fantasy Craft Market**, massively oversold by its vendors who spend more time outside trying to induce you in than tending their stalls. The hotels peter out as Gloucester becomes **Kent Avenue** at the junction with Sunset Boulevard and continues to hug the coast. Locally known as Dead End Road, Kent Avenue passes tiny Buccaneer Beach (also known as Dead End Beach) (see p.259) before ending abruptly at the wall marking the distant section of the airport runway. The last of the strip proper, **Sunset Boulevard** is home to a small complex of forlorn shops and bars, countless car rental outlets and the rather grand **Summit Police Station**, the only one in Jamaica with its own pool. At the airport roundabout, the boulevard becomes part of **Queen's Drive**, an inland road that runs parallels to Gloucester Avenue – essentially a fast traffic route straight through MoBay (and popularly known simply as the top road, Gloucester Avenue being the bottom), pavements are sporadic and walking can be risky, though the views over the bay are fantastic. After a mile or so, the road forks left to the small fishing community of **WHITEHOUSE**, a quiet residential zone – bar the noise from the airport – seldom visited by tourists and refreshingly hassle-free. Roadside vendors sell excellent fried fish and festival, and the sand at **Tropical Beach** (see p.259) is as fine as you'll find anywhere.

The beaches

Cornwall (J$80 entrance charge), Doctor's Cave and Walter Fletcher beaches (J$100) are open daily between 9am and 5pm.

The strip, of course, wouldn't exist were it not for Montego Bay's prize asset: a dazzling bay with miles of protected coral reef (see box opposite) and some beautiful beaches. Much of the coastline has been snapped up by the hotels and carved into private chunks, but there are three main managed **public beaches**, all with showers, changing rooms, snack outlets and watersports concessions and a minimal entrance fee.

Opposite Fort Street Craft Market, **Walter Fletcher Beach** is closest to downtown and, following its extensive 1999 re-invention as the Aquasol Theme Park, has the most comprehensive sports facilities of the three – all watersports (rates for half an hour: jetski US$40; glass bottom boat rides US$8; snorkelling US$8), tennis and basketball courts and a go-kart track (J$150 per ride). An attractive decked bar (which stays open until late every night), decent seafood restaurant and the wide expanse of gently curving sand have made the beach popular with young tourists and the attendant hangers-on as well as

Montego Bay Marine Park

Though offshore MoBay became officially protected in 1974, regulations were seldom enforced, and the reefs remained open to attack from plunderers, spear fishers, snorkellers, divers, boat anchors and industrial pollution. In an attempt to stem the destruction, **Montego Bay Marine Park** was created in 1991 – Jamaica's first national park, with environmental regulations strictly enforced within its boundaries. Running west from Sangster Airport to Great River, just past Reading, the park comprises over nine square miles of coral reef, sea grass beds and mangroves, zoned into watersports, fishing and fish nursery areas and patrolled by four rangers. Within the park it is illegal to mine sand, damage or move coral, shells and seaweed, fish without a permit or drop litter. Mooring buoys have been introduced along the major reefs, spear fishing has been banned, and a larger mesh is being used in wire traps. With two days' notice, rangers lead educational diving and snorkelling expeditions; there's no charge but donations in cash or kind (particularly depth gauges) are gratefully accepted. Unfortunately the Marine Park organization is desperately underfunded and in urgent need of financial support; if you're interested in helping out details are available from the Resource Centre at Pier One (☎971 8082, *www.montego-bay-jamaica.com /mbmp*). For more on the conservation movement in Jamaica, see p.390 of Contexts.

Jamaican families. An all-inclusive beach picnic (US$60) takes place every Tuesday and Friday.

Half a mile further north lies the famous **Doctor's Cave Beach**, Montego Bay's premium portion of gleaming white sand and see-through water. The beach was put on the map in the late nineteenth century when local doctor and sea-bathing advocate Alexander McCatty founded the *Sanatorium Caribbee*, an exclusive private bathing club that's still in existence today (though a lot less choosy); in the 1920s visiting English chiropractor Sir Herbert Baker was so impressed by the curative potential of the waters that he published an article in the English press extolling their efficacy. The beau monde flocked and MoBay's tourist industry was born. The rapidly deepening waters really are the best in town and facilities are excellent, though there is little shade and it gets very crowded at the weekend.

Separated from Doctor's Cave by unattractive breeze-block walls, **Cornwall Beach** is the most intimate and laid-back of MoBay's public beaches. It's a young person's beach, with music pumped out from giant speakers and topless bathing common (though theoretically prohibited); inevitably, it's popular with Jamaican gigolos, and female visitors should expect constant, usually good-natured approaches. There's a lively bar, built around a giant almond tree, favoured by local professionals and off-duty policemen who stop by to drink, play dominoes and catch the sunset.

If the big three are too crowded for your tastes, head past the strip to Whitehouse (see p.256) and **Tropical Beach** (daily

Montego Bay

Thrill-seekers can parasail from Margueritaville *(☎952 4285) and Cornwall Beach (☎957 1234) at a rate of US$45 for 15 minutes, while jet skis are available all over the place for US$40 for half an hour.*

WATERSPORTS

Montego Bay is justifiably famed for its deep turquoise waters and abundant reef systems, some close enough to swim to from the main beaches. Discarded rum bottles and tyres can be disconcerting, but the deeper reefs are alive with fish, rays, urchins and the occasional turtle and nurse shark. There are hosts of similarly priced **watersports operators** on each beach and within the larger hotels; naturally, we list the most reputable below. Pamphlets and information are always available from the Montego Bay Marine Park office (see box p.257).

DIVING AND SNORKELLING

The following offer guided dives (around US$40), certification courses (from US$350) and equipment rental (from US$15). Like every other watersports operator in Montego Bay, they also rent **snorkel gear** for around US$10 a day – most also offer guided snorkelling tours of the best reefs.

Captain's Watersports and Dive Centre, *Round Hill Hotel*, Hopewell (☎956 7050, ext 378).

Fun Divers, Wyndham, Rose Hall (☎953 3268).

Jamaica Scuba Divers, *Half Moon Hotel*, Ironshore (☎953 9266).

Resort Divers, *Jack Tar Village* and *Holiday Inn* (☎940 1183 or 953 9699).

BOAT TRIPS

Boat trips, with an open bar and sometimes lunch, are always popular and usually fun, if bawdy on-deck humour is your bag. Most depart from the Pier One complex downtown and sail around the bay to the airport reefs with a stop for snorkelling. Pick of the bunch are those run by the excellent Captain's Watersports, Calico Cruises, the only wooden sailing ships in town (☎952 5860; 3hr daytime cruise; US$35; 2hr evening cruise; US$25) and *Sun Cat* (☎952 5860; 3hr cruises; US$40) a 52ft catamaran whch includes a stop at *Margueritaville* (see p.268) to ride the water slide. *Sandals Montego Bay* operate a similar wet 'n' wild cruise party on their catamaran *Tropical Dreamer* (☎979 0102; 3hr cruises; US$40).

Glass-bottom boats operate from all the main beaches and sail out to the airport reefs for around US$10 for half an hour; particularly recommended is *Birthday*. MoBay Undersea Tours, adjacent to *Margueritaville* (☎940 4465; 2hr; US$30) has several semi-submersible vessels which take you ten feet underwater. Go in the morning for the best light or try a night tour to catch the nocturnal marine life. If you'd rather go it alone, you can rent out a semi-sub, *Sharky*, for US$150 per day with a maximum of fourteen passengers. Alternatively a fully equipped **sport fishing boat** costs around US$700 per day; try the *Irie Lady* (☎953 3268), *No Problem* (☎936 6702; *dptaylor@n5.com.jm*) or Captain's Watersports which has several boats and also rents out *Stoshus*, a 36ft yacht (see *www.montego-bay-jamaica.com/stoshus/index.html*, for details of special trips; US$120 per hour or US$600 per day).

Fort Charles' cannons, Port Royal

Different draughts

Cliff jumping, Negril

Royal Palm Reserve, Negril

West End waters, Negril

Cornwall Beach, Montego Bay

Beach at Alligator Pond

Fruit seller, Mandeville

Sound system session

YS Falls, St Elizabeth

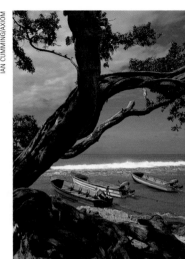

Treasure Beach, St Elizabeth

Bamboo Avenue, St Elizabeth

9am–5pm; US$1), a much quieter private white-sand stretch that nonetheless offers windsurfing and jet skis, and has a nice shady area with seating and occasional stageshows. Alternatively, right by the airport, and consequently dogged by the racket of landings and take-offs, **Buccaneer Beach** (or Dead End Beach) is a thin but attractive strip of public sand popular with Jamaicans. The water is shallow and there are no facilities, but snorkelling is good and the view over the bay is fabulous, providing the best free sunset seat in town.

Downtown

After the flamboyance of the strip, **downtown** announces itself with its very own stretch of undeveloped shoreline right opposite the dividing roundabout. **Dump-Up Beach** looks pretty enough, particularly from a distance, with a gentle curve of white sand, but this is one of the dirtiest parts of the bay; overflow from the Catherine Hall sewage plant, alongside untreated human waste and garbage from downtown squatter settlements, drain directly into the sea via the many rainwater gullies. It's not a place to swim or spend much time, although it's the popular venue of local soccer matches and packed gospel meetings with Jamaicans in their Sunday finery overflowing the marquees erected for such occasions.

This is a prime area for pickpockets – don't take out wads of cash when paying for small items, use ATM machines in daylight, and keep cameras in a closed bag.

Shooting off from the roundabout, the main route into the centre of town is **Fort Street**, a clamorous thoroughfare with dancehall flooding out from storefronts and all manner of pushcarts and vehicles jostling for space with the thick human traffic. A short way along, there's a little garden area housing the useful **parish library** (☎952 4185, Mon–Fri 9.30am–5.30pm, Sat 9am–4pm), which carries a fair stock of Caribbean books; it would be a tranquil spot were it not for the cigarette, newspaper and Rizla vendors who noisily tout their wares from the garden wall. Past here, over the bridge across North Gully, you enter town proper. The covered market to the left is popularly known as **The Gully** (the correct name, William Street Market, is seldom used), a lively fruit and vegetable market where hardough bread and callaloo are sold out of supermarket trolleys and bartering is common at the stalls; a Jamaican companion will ensure reasonable prices.

Star Wholesale in The Gully give big reductions on bulk buys of three or more of the same item – it sells everything from cigarettes to saltfish.

Running parallel to Fort Street, **Orange Street** is lined by shabby shops and dingy bars that back onto the Canterbury squatters' community. The zinc-roofed clapboard dwellings cover the entire valley behind Orange Street, petering out at the red-earthed playing fields of MoBay's main high school, Cornwall College.

Sam Sharpe Square and the craft market

St James Street comes to an abrupt end at **Sam Sharpe Square**, the heart of downtown. Characterized by its central fountain and seemingly permanent stream of screaming traffic, this cobbled pavement

Sam Sharpe and the Christmas Rebellion

During the course of just over a week, slavery in Jamaica received the blow that would kill it forever. The **Christmas** or **Baptist Rebellion** began on December 27, 1831; by its end on January 5, 1832, twenty thousand slaves had razed nearly 160 sugar estates, causing damage to the value of £1 million – a massive drain on the British exchequer. It was the largest slave uprising in Jamaican history, and set in motion the process that led to the abolition of the slave trade in 1834 and full emancipation in 1838.

The rebellion was led by **Sam Sharpe**, a house slave working for a MoBay solicitor. Though this nascent martyr took on the surname of his master in accordance with tradition, his sideline as deacon of the town's Burchell Baptist Church made him anything but servile – at the time, the Baptists were Jamaica's most radical and outspoken critics of slavery and were rightly seen as a threat by the British establishment, particularly as religious congregations were the only gatherings legally allowed to slaves. The church taught Sharpe to read, and through international newspapers he learned of English anti-slavery sentiments and became convinced that emancipation in Jamaica was imminent, a reality that planters were trying to suppress. A powerful orator, Sharpe formed a secret society dedicated to banishing slavery, and planned a non-violent withdrawal of labour over the Christmas period. Talk of the insurrection spread fast through St James estates and even the planters became uneasy as December 1831 drew to a close. By the night of the 27th, passions were running high. The peaceful protest soon degenerated into anarchy; tipped off by the estate owners, the militia were out in force, and the more miltant slaves responded by lighting bonfires at the highest point of the Kensington estate to signify the start of a full-scale rebellion. Others followed suit and within days western Jamaica was burning as the cane fields and great houses were destroyed one by one. The response of the British militia was brutal. Though damage was predominantly restricted to property and only fourteen whites died, soldiers gunned down one thousand slaves and Montego Bay magistrates handed down a further three hundred execution orders during the emotionally charged six-week trial that ensued. Sharpe himself was hanged in the MoBay square that today bears his name and buried in the harbour sand, though his remains were later exhumed and interred in the vault of Burchell Memorial Church.

area was until recently dominated by illegal vending rackets, every pavement obscured with displays of leather sandals, cheap watches, toys and bootleg designer imports presided over by knife-wielding Kingstonian immigrants. Vociferous local complaint has succeeded in moving most of the vendors on, but it's still a good idea to watch where you tread.

The square is bordered by a jumble of old and new architecture, including **The Cage**, built in 1806 as a lock-up for disorderly seamen and runaway slaves whose custodial shenanigans so damaged the original wooden walls that they were replaced with the red-brick and stone that stands today. In 1811, the rooftop belfry was installed, used to ring out a 2pm curfew warning; after the second ring at 3pm, any slaves still on the streets were locked up. The building is now a telephone and fax centre (Mon–Sat 9am–6pm), run by Irish exile Michael Maher, and a good place to stop for directions and local information. Just outside, National Hero Sam Sharpe (see opposite) is commemorated in a **bronze statue** by Jamaican sculptor Kay Sullivan, which depicts him in full evangelical flow before a crowd of converts.

Just off the square beyond the junction with Market Street the site which once held the old courthouse, long since destroyed by fire, is being redeveloped into a Town Hall, complete with theatre and museum. Market Street itself is unremarkable; even the **Burchell Memorial Church**, where Sam Sharpe lies buried, is hulking, unattractive and uninteresting. Market Street ends at the junction with Harbour Street where you'll find the town's main **craft market**, a surprisingly hassle-free place to shop if you don't treat the inventive sales pitches as bamboozling. The 200-odd stalls sell every type of Jamaican craft (see p.270), and there are a couple of good, cheap restaurants patronized mostly by the vendors.

Church Street

The four streets that feed off Sam Sharpe Square are MoBay's busiest, packed with stores and offices. Of these, **Church Street**, branching off from the square's southern corner, is the most architecturally interesting. Dominating the street is **St James Parish Church** (if locked, ask at the office opposite or call ☎952 2775), built from creamy cut stone in the shape of a cross – it was considered the showpiece of the parish when the original structure was completed in 1782. In 1957, an earthquake destroyed the foundations and the building underwent major repairs. Inside the church, the virtues of Rosa, first wife of John Palmer of Rose Hall (see p.274), are commemorated in a John Bacon verse and sculpture, set to the left of the altar. Outside, the well-maintained graveyard contains the ornate but weathered graves of deceased planters, many standing at erratic angles since the earthquake.

Facing the church is the elegant facade of the **Town House**, its weathered stone walls and stately grace rendering the surrounding concrete even more ill-favoured. Constructed in 1765 by local merchant David Morgan, the building has served as a private home, church manse, Masonic lodge, warehouse, synagogue and hotel – Queen Victoria spent the night – before becoming the smart restaurant, favoured by lunching ladies and visiting dignitaries, it is today (see "Eating", p.266).

Dome Street and Jarrett Park

At its very top Church Street becomes **Dome Street**, which loops down to Water Lane, Creek Street and the South Montego Gully. The principal feature of an otherwise quiet street is **Dome House**, built as a wealthy planter's residence in the late eighteenth century and now restored to its former glory after a long period of disuse. It's still a princely building, with the classic proportions of plantation architecture; large sash windows, cool cut stone and an interior rich with original mahogany floors and fittings – it's currently a rehearsal and performance space for dance and theatre groups. Aqueous street names hint at the centrality of water to the history of this part of town; the now disused well in front of Dome House was originally linked to the **Dome** on Creek Street below – a solid stone circle topped with a peeling wooden roof that looks rather incongruous these days in the midst of what has long been the building site for a new drainage system and racing traffic. Originally built over the stream that provided Creek Street with a name (it's still flowing along concreted banks), the Dome's thick walls mask two floors; the upper portion was originally occupied by the "Keeper of the Creek", who supervised collection from what was Montego Bay's main and only source of fresh water until a piped supply was made available in 1894.

For details of forthcoming events at Dome House, call ☎952 2571 or 1134.

Moving west from the Dome along Creek Street, you reach the junction with the second half of **St James Street**, downtown's liveliest shopping strip. Tatty hole-in-the-wall emporia vie for space with neon storefronts and sidewalk vendors, all fighting to be noticed against a background symphony of non-stop reggae and shouts of "sky juice" and "peanuts and Wrigley's". East of here, Creek Street rises sharply uphill, changing names and eventually reaching **Jarrett Park**, MoBay's premier cricket ground and the original site of Reggae Sunsplash (Bob Marley and the Wailers made their only festival appearance here in 1979). Even if you're not a cricket fan, attending a match is highly entertaining, as much for the crowd-pleasing dancehall that booms out during every break in play as for the aficionados' impassioned running commentaries. Tickets (US$4–8) are sold at the gate, but you should get to the larger games early to ensure a seat; alternatively, you could follow the local example and catch the match for free from one of the surrounding hills.

Cricket matches are well advertised in local papers and on MoBay's HOT 102 radio station.

Barnett Street and Charles William Gordon Market

The least tourist-friendly part of downtown, **Barnett Street** – reached by following St James Street south from Sam Sharpe Square – is a raucous belt of supermarkets and mini-malls choking in a constant fug of traffic fumes. After St James Street, this is where you'll find the best shopping in town, though not of the duty-free T-shirt and packaged rum variety. Look out for the artistic storefront of Lyle's Intensified Inn, featuring caricatured policemen and Rastas and a strongly worded admonition to any prostitutes or pimps foolish enough to linger outside. Barnett Street is also the site of the town's notorious main **police station** and lock-up, so run-down that the inmates sleep ten to a cell on concrete floors and the officers make regular appeals for donations. Turn down Railway Lane for the main fruit and vegetable outlet, **Charles William Gordon Market** (also known as Fustic Market). Straddling the disused railway tracks and the impoverished houses that make up MoBay's most notorious "ghetto" (though it's luxury by Kingston standards), the market is a visceral whirl of tarpaulin-covered stalls selling enormous mounds of earth-covered yams, sweet potatoes and cassava alongside deep-orange pumpkins, bunches of scallion and thyme, fat fingers of green bananas or plantain and a kaleidoscope of fruits. Goat belly and cheap chicken back are bartered in the pungent indoor meat section, where higglers make up temporary beds beside their pitches at the end of a day's trade. Main days are Wednesday and Saturday, but goods are always on sale and you get better deals here than at Gully Market. You can refresh yourself with a jelly coconut or Day-Glo sky juice from one of the ever-present vendors – look for the lone guy selling fresh cane juice, a far more refreshing choice.

At the end of Barnett Street, the traffic opens up and passes over Montego River. Here, the roadside takes on an incongruously lush aspect; giant bulrushes and emerald reeds flourish in the greyish semi-sewage and egrets roost in the few remaining poinciana and palm. Beyond the river is Westgate shopping centre, where a fairly good road branches off towards Adelphi and ultimately Cockpit Country.

West of town

Barnett Street shoots off from the dividing roundabout to become the A1, and takes you through MoBay at its least inspiring, a grim industrial estate perfumed by the slaughterhouse. The flotsam-filled yards and warehouses don't let up until well past the painted zinc fence circumventing **Catherine Hall Entertainment Centre**, stageshow venue and home of Reggae Sumfest (see p.44). The road ends at a fork, the right prong leading to **Freeport Peninsula**, a depressingly empty thoroughfare suspended in a limbo of factory fronts and abandoned marshland backing onto the Bogue Lagoon. The shipping wharves seem to sum up the desolation; fuel silos block out the view of the bay and hundreds of cars sit marooned until their owners can afford to get them through customs. The sole sign of life is at the **cruise-ship piers**, an incongruously flashy mass of expensive shops and restaurants that springs into action on docking days. Otherwise, you might wander up here for an early evening drink on the roof of the *Houseboat* restaurant which overlooks Bogue Lagoon or a game of pool and a tasty lunch at the posh **Yacht Club**, ostensibly for members only but covertly accessible to tourists; if so, shared taxis ply the route.

The left fork takes you past the rambling wilderness of Pye River Cemetery, from which a turn left and another right leads through mile upon mile of undulating cane to **Barnett Estate**, a 3000-acre plantation occupying most of the MoBay basin and still owned and

Across the
courtyard
from Belfield
Great House is
the sumptuous
restaurant
Belfield 1794
(see opposite).

run by the Kerr-Jarrett family. The estate no longer runs its jitney tour but it is still possible to be shown round **Belfield Great House** (daily 10am–5pm, tours last 45min; US$10 free if dining in the restaurant). Less stately than Rose Hall or Greenwood great houses (see pp.274 and 276), Belfield's sweeping verandah and gleaming cream paintwork make it look contemporary, though it dates from 1735. Inside, the refurbishment is slick, with fittings brought in from all over the island: "pineapple" beds laid with best linen, Dresden china in showcases, eighteenth-century kitchen implements and a spectacularly bad life-size model of former owner David Kerr, all crimson cheeks and outraged expression.

Right of Pye River, the A1 takes you out of town through more cane fields, skirting the coast at Bogue and the lavish villas of the well-to-do at **READING**. More of an extended residential zone with a petrol station than a town, Reading is notable mostly as site of the **Desnoes and Geddes factory**, producer of national brew Red Stripe. The private life of founder Paul Geddes came under the public microscope in 1995 when his estranged common-law wife won a J$6m palimony lawsuit in recognition of the 32 years she had spent supporting him while he built up his empire – which would have been a significant victory for women had she not lost the lot on appeal. A few hundred yards further on, clipped bougainvillea hedges and a milestone ("Montego Bay 5") on the shoreline are the only markers for a roadside **mineral spring**, maintained by a talkative Rasta, who has built his home adjacent to the brackish pool and will perform his small repertoire of dives if you ask nicely (and give a contribution towards the spring's upkeep). The cool, clear, pitch-black depths are slightly unnerving to enter but wonderfully refreshing once you're in, and the Montegonians who visit this low-profile little spot swear by its rejuvenative powers.

A mile or so further down the coast road is **Budhai's Gallery** (daily 9am–5pm; free), owned and run by Cuban-born artist Neville Budhai, charismatic leading light of the local arts scene and recipient of the prestigious Institute of Jamaica Centenary Award. His distinctive line-drawings, watercolours and lithographs are on sale, but the man alone makes the gallery a worthwhile stop.

Eating

Montego Bay's resort status ensures a fair share of swanky **restaurants** alongside the more usual Jamaican eateries, though many offer bland "international" fare or watered-down Jamaican dishes at inflated prices. Pricier tourist restaurants almost always offer free pick-ups; look out for flyers around town with various seasonal deals and special offers. Aside from notable exceptions such as *The Native*, Jamaican food is at its best from small-scale cookshops and restaurants; for **fish**, head for Whitehouse. There are plenty of US-style **fast-food** outlets around town, including the

Snacks

Patties, callaloo loaf, coco bread and pastries are generally found only at downtown pastry shops, though vendors wheel pushcarts of them into the strip's craft markets. The best **bakeries** are *Butterflake Pastry* on Harbour St, *Viennese Pastry* on the corner of St James and Union streets, *Chin's* on Market St and *Juci Beef* on St James St. The **Montego Bay (LOJ) shopping centre** on Howard Cooke Boulevard has an excellent **food court** with a great view over the bay: decent purveyors include*Chicken Internationa Café*, *Jamanda's* and *Pizza Delite*. Vegetarians should head for the *Adwa* juice bar in the City Centre Mall which serves delicious fruit/vegetable juices and smoothies, and Ital style vegetable stews at lunchtime. Elsewhere, cheap and tasty jerk is sold at the *Pork Pit* on Gloucester Ave, delicious box lunches (meat with rice and peas) come from *Wayne's* cookshop in the Fantasy Craft Market opposite Cornwall Beach and the counter at the front of the *Sunset Deli* on Gloucester Ave. Also on the strip *Tony's Pizza* (☎952 6365) has graduated from a permanently parked red-and-white van opposite Cornwall Beach to a small shop in the same location, very popular with the locals, which sells pizza and sub sandwiches until 2am. *Tony's* also delivers locally free of charge. Downtown *24-7* on the corner of St. James St and the Gully Market serves **all-night** macaroni cheese or callaloo and saltfish with dumplings, but be prepared to jostle with crowds of hungry Jamaicans fresh from the clubs. Sweet teeth can be satisfied at the **frozen yoghurt** outlet underneath the *Pork Pit* while *24-7* is the best **ice cream** outlet downtown. Tourists desperate for a decent cup of coffee should try *The Coffee Mill of Jamaica* on Gloucester Ave for very good cappuccino, caffe mocha etc; the café is not cheap but it's a perfectly located spot on the strip for watching the MoBay hustle pass by.

Caribbean's largest *KFC* and an adjacent *Pizza Hut* opposite downtown Dump-Up beach, *McDonald's* at the Baywest Shopping Centre on Harbour Strreet and the Blue Diamond mall in Ironshore and a *Burger King* on Gloucester Avenue. The concrete balustrades of Buccaneer Beach are a popular spot for takeaway consumption.

Queen's Drive and downtown

Belfield 1794, Barnett Estate, Fairfield; ☎952 2382. Renovated sugar mill provides a grand and romantic setting for a restaurant serving good nouvelle Jamaican cuisine. A special occasion place.

Canton Express, Union St. Basic but tasty Chinese food to eat in or take out Portions are large and very cheap; local workers queue down the street at lunchtime. Sweet and sour fish particularly recommended.

Crafts Cafeteria, Harbour St Crafts Market. Excellent open-air bar and restaurnat serving very reasonably priced Jamaican food, cooked to order. Popular with both stall-holders and tourists; the atmosphere is friendly and surprisingly hassle-free.

Georgian House, corner of Orange and Union streets. Attractive eighteenth-century building with a garden, serving well-made, inexpensive Jamaican food.

In restaurant listings, we have given a phone number only for those places where you might need to reserve a table or you'd like to take advantage of a free pick-up.

Montego Bay

The Houseboat, Freeport Rd; ☎979 8845. Lovely old boat moored in Bogue Lagoon with a wooden-panelled restaurant aboard, specialising in fondue, and a highly entertaining host, wartime pilot Timothy Moxon. The rooftop bar is the breeziest spot in Montego Bay, worth visiting in the summer to escape humid nights. Evenings only.

I'N'I Paradise, Queen's Drive. Rastafarian vegetarian restaurant just beyond the airport serving authentic Ital food in attractive red-gold-and-green bamboo shacks. Excellent natural juices including roots wine and cane juice.

Rite Stuff, Westgate Plaza. Bustling breakfast and lunch café popular with office workers. Soup and cheesecake are the highlights, but there are lots of salads and very good vegetarian options too.

Smokey Joe's, 19 St James St. Cheap and tasty local, serving no-nonsense Jamaican lunches and dinners in a comfortable atmosphere.

Sunset Gardens Restaurant, Queen's Drive. Home-cooked Jamaican food at very reasonable prices in a peaceful and pleasant garden setting complete with tiled swimming pool.

Tigers, 23 St James St. Buffet-style Jamaican café frequented almost exclusively by locals. All the usual dishes with some vegetarian food available. Enormous Jamaican breakfast served from 7am.

The Town House, 16 Church St; ☎952 2660. Fashionable basement restaurant in a beautiful eighteenth-century building (see p.261), reeking of old-world gentility. The dinner menu (New York steak, red snapper papillot, shrimp and lobster creole) is expensive, but the daily lunch special, taken at one of the pews in the lounge area, is great value.

Gloucester Avenue and the beaches

The Brewery, Miranda Ridge, Gloucester Ave. Late-opening spot above the strip. Extremely varied menu with daily specials (like oysters in lemon butter), a big burger selection, lots of salads and some Mexican. Good value and pretty views.

Dragon Lounge, Kent Ave, Whitehouse. Laid-back terrace under almond trees with its proximity to the airport making it perfect for plane-spotting albeit somewhat noisy. Specialises in seafood with some Chinese dishes. Good mix of local old boys playing dominoes and tourists wanting very freshly-caught fish.

Evelyn's, Kent Ave, Whitehouse; ☎952 3280. Famous for its unusual way of preparing roti, usually a spicy split-pea pancake but reinvented as a flat fried dumpling to back up fried fish or curry chicken. Call ahead for the conventional version served with dahl. Other dishes span the Jamaican spectrum, with lots of seafood.

Guangzhou, Miranda Ridge, Gloucester Ave. The only Chinese restaurant on the strip, and very good it is too. The indoor dining room is a bit gloomy in the daytime, but a 15 percent weekday lunch discount pulls in the punters.

Jen's Coffee Place, 166 Gloucester Ave. Friendly breakfast café and ice-cream parlour with reasonably priced pancakes, eggs and bacon and club sandwiches.

Margueritaville, Gloucester Ave. The loudest place on the strip. International menu with a Mexican flavour, and American-style service with the emphasis on fun. Hidden behind an aquatic wall mural, *Marguerites* (☎952 4777) next door has elegant decor, upscale atmosphere and a continental menu specialising in seafood; there's a flambé grill for table-side cooking as well. Outdoor terrace dining over the bay makes it very popular with honeymoon couples.

The Native, 29 Gloucester Ave; ☎979 2769. The best place on the strip for a sit-down Jamaican meal – not cheap so take advantage of reduced-rate buffets and lunch specials. Try the "Boonoonoo's Platter" of ackee, curry goat, jerk chicken and escovitched fish, rice and peas and plantain.

The Pelican, Gloucester Ave; ☎952 3171. Long-established restaurant popular with locals and tourists. Highlights include cornmeal porridge or American/Jamaican breakfast, the daily lunch specials (fricassee chicken to cow foot) and desserts – rum pudding and coconut or banana cream pie.

PJ's, 17 Kent Ave. Excellent open-air jerk centre, serving platters of curried lobster, steamed fish and vegetables as well as jerk meats and all the trimmings.

Raine's, St James Place, Gloucester Ave; popular kiosk café situated between Doctor's Cave and Cornwall beaches with all day breakfasts, burgers, and home-made cakes.

Spaghetti Factory, Gloucester Ave. Upstairs restaurant painted in lurid shades of red and green, with tiny balcony opposite Doctor's Cave Beach. Large and tasty pasta dishes range from basic tomato sauce to fancy cream and lobster combos. Loud Italian ice-cream music completes a pleasingly eccentric atmosphere.

Sunset Restaurant and Bar, Gloucester Ave. Tiny, easily missed place that's the only really authentic Jamaican bar and restaurant along the strip, as suggested by the clientele – taxi drivers and Jamaican couples. Recommended, especially the home-made ginger beer.

Tapas, Corniche Rd; ☎952 2988. Innovative and delicious Mediterranean food in a place that's upscale but affordable, and blessedly detached from the strip; take the small road to the left of *Coral Cliff* hotel.

Drinking, nightlife and entertainment

Surprisingly, Montego Bay is not particularly lively at **night**; the strip takes on a ghostly hush as the cruise ships glide out of the harbour and visitors hole up in their all-inclusives. Official attempts to get tourists out after dark with a Monday night mini-carnival along the strip have faltered and what Monday night action there is has moved to beach parties at Cornwall and Walter Fletcher beaches. Elsewhere along the strip the straggle of bars is home to a desultory collection of gigolos hunting for fresh meat, North Americans and business-suited Jamaicans glued to big-screen NFL action and the unwary pickling themselves in rum punch. For the most part though, MoBay's nightlife is conveniently situated at the ubiquitous *Margueritaville* on Gloucester Avenue, the only place in the city full every night of the week. *The Brewery, Hurricanes Disco* at *Breezes* and *Pier One* are popular enough at weekends and downtown certain enjoyably seedy joints attract a crowd of die-hards most nights; all get going by 11pm and keep the pace until the small hours. Cover charges vary, but you're unlikely to pay more than US10. The weekend is ritually celebrated throughout downtown, with small-time **sound systems** setting up on street corners and the rum flowing free; these are local parties, not the preserve of tourists, but you

Exercise some caution if you venture away from the strip at night – take a taxi and leave your valuables at the hotel.

should be fine with a Jamaican escort – recommended for all downtown bars and clubs.

Bars

The Brewery, Miranda Ridge, Gloucester Ave. Friendly preppie style bar, permanently packed at the weekends with young Jamaicans and large parties of American tourists, who spill out onto the attractive decked bar. Tuesday and Friday are karaoke nights, popular with both game locals and partying tourists. Highly entertaining.

Dead End Bar, Kent Ave. Open 24hr, a laid-back spot perfect for sunset- and plane-watching. Thursday night is given over to a beach party, with a comprehensive mix of reggae, soca and hip-hop. Sunday is oldies night with classic reggae and rocksteady churned out until the last punter leaves.

Hi-Lites Café, 19 Queen's Drive. Very sleepy bar, but a great escape from the strip and worth visiting for the wonderful view across the bay.

Margueritaville, Gloucester Ave. Hugely popular bar, club and restaurant Aquatic activity takes a backseat to American sports (admission charge for big games). Lively theme nights, special offers, drinks promotions and fabulous bay views but an irritating token payment system for drinks. 52 different flavours of marguerita and 32 ounce 'bongs of beer' help keep the atmosphere buzzing.

Paradise Pool Bar, Gloucester Ave. Late night pool bar frequented by local (harmless) hoodlums. Good place for a cheap 2am beer and you'll be largely ignored – playing the game is what counts here.

PJ's, 17 Kent Ave. Outdoor bar with roller-blading rink, attractively set under towering bamboo and silk cotton trees. There's nightly live reggae, happy hour and Monday night carnival with craft stalls. Persistent rent-a-dreads and ganja hustlers are the only drawback to an otherwise entertaining scene.

Richmond Hill Inn, Union St; ☎952 3859. The overpriced 'international' cuisine at this rather gloomy hotel isn't that exciting, but do go for a sunset drink. The setting – on its very own hill at the top of Union St – is spectacular and intensely romantic; the view covers the whole bay.

Clubs

Bottle Inn, 11 Union St (nightly). Late-opening club with ultra-violet light and a certain louche charm. Wednesday is dancehall night, Thursday is old hits. Recommended for a taste of real Jamaican clubbing.

Diamonds Nite Club, Blue Diamond Shopping Centre, Ironshore (nightly). Popular with a ritzy Jamaican crowd who follow the strict dress code, and improved by a breezy outdoor area. Various theme nights, with a usual cover of US$5 for men, free for ladies.

Flamingo, Sugarmill Rd, Ironshore (nightly). The usual X-rated go-go dancing and all-round lasciviousness occasionally make way for phenomenally popular jams by the best of the Kingston-based sound systems. Cover US$5.

Goldfingers, Market St (nightly). Dingy dancehall club downtown favoured by kissing couples and expert Jamaican dancers – make sure you know your butterfly from your body-basics.

Hurricanes Disco, *Breezes*, Gloucester Ave (nightly). Brand new, state-of-the-art hotel club, with dancehall, Euro-techno and R&B until dawn. Heaving on

Saturday, with the gigolos out in full force. Cover US$12, including all drinks and the first one hundred women get in for free.

The Keg, 2 Barnett St (nightly). Friendly local hangout on the corner of Harbour St with a popular oldies session every Wednesday. Cover US$3.

Lollypop on the Beach, Sandy Bay; ☎953 5314 (weekends only). Though it's ten miles out of town, many Montegonians trek west to this seaside venue for the occasional stageshow, while tourists are bused in for live reggae shows on Friday, Saturday and Sunday nights (cover US$15–20). Basic accommodation exists on site should you wish to stay over (②).

Margueritaville, Gloucester Ave (nightly). Incredibly popular venue with themed nights (Wednesday is pyjama parties, US$15 all-inclusive and half-price if you come suitably attired, Thursday is Latin), two for one drink promotions, live music on the roof and a permanently packed holiday-hits style disco. If you're looking for guaranteed action this is the place and if you don't mind gigolos galore and sunburnt tourists it's great fun. Dance floor opens at 10pm and there's a weekend cover of US$7.

Pier 1, Howard Cook Blvd (nightly). Oldies on the boardwalk during the week (free) and a pumping club at the weekends; Friday is busiest, with upfront dancehall and R&B until dawn. The club's a bit rough round the edges but entertaining nevertheless. On Thursday and Sunday *Sharky's* party boat goes out to sea (9pm–midnight) for an all-inclusive cover of US$7.

Randles, Hart St. Brilliant oldies club (ska, R&B, soul) in a large open-air building downtown (Thurs & Sun only). Popular with a eclectic mix of Jamaicans, and though you won't feel unwelcome this is strictly non-tourist territory so go with a local. Cover US$4.

Entertainment

Unless you're content with a diet of tired in-hotel floor shows, you'll often be climbing the walls for live entertainment in MoBay. Music is the town's strongest suit, with regular live reggae at various strip venues and at the beaches, where you'll occasionally find stageshows and open-air sound-system nights, generally more pleasant than the hot and smoky indoor venues. **Walter Fletcher Beach** is a popular venue for sporadic visits from Jamaica's top DJs, as is **Pier One**. Usually ad-hoc affairs at Tropical Beach or *Club Inferno* in Rose Hall, the major events (including Reggae Sumfest; see p.44) are held at the **Catherine Hall Entertainment Centre** on Howard Cooke Boulevard. August and the whole winter tourist season are the best time to catch the larger **annual shows** such as Sumfest, Sting and Reggae Kwanzaa, which move from venue to venue across the island. Traditionally the suicide season for those in the tourism business, rainy October sees the **All That Heritage and Jazz** festivities, a week-long series of concerts on the strip with world music and jazz alongside the reggae. If you're feeling lucky, the **Coral Cliff Gaming Lounge** has over a hundred slot machines, free drinks for punters and a US$50,000 jackpot. The *Coral Cliffs* hotel also hosts an annual dominoes competition at the end of January, which is wildly popular with the local aficionados. For a more sedate evening, the hotel hosts live jazz every Sunday, as does

For more details on MoBay's annual events see p.41.

the *Coyaba* in Ironshore on Fridays, as an accompaniment to its half-price cocktail hour.

There are two **cinemas** in town: the characterful, rather shabby Strand Theatre downtown at 8 Strand St (☎952 5391) and the smarter Diamond Cinema at the Blue Diamond Shopping Centre in Ironshore (☎953 9540). **Roots plays** are staged at the Strand and occasionally at the Chatwick Gardens Centre, 10 Queen's Drive (☎952 2147). For serious theatre catch one of the excellent Montego Bay Little Theatre Movement productions at Fairfield Theatre (☎952 0182).

Shopping

As a major cruise-ship port, much of MoBay's consumer activity centres around **in-bond shopping**, with countless flashy malls given over to identical jewellery, perfume and leather goods outlets. They're all much of a muchness, but City Centre Mall on Fort Street is the least ostentatious. The Montego Bay Shopping Centre – usually referred to as the LOJ (Life of Jamaica) Mall – on Howard Cooke Boulevard, is better for general purchases and has a couple of decent clothes shops, as well as a branch of the excellent Fontana Pharmacy, which is great for gimmicky souvenir mugs, pens, stationery and knick-knacks. The Baywest Mall on Harbour Street, is also recommended for clothes; particularly good here is Sahara for linen shirts and shorts.

You can't move for **crafts** in MoBay. The best market is the huge Harbour Street complex (daily 7am–7pm; see p.261) packed with straw and wicker work, belts, clothes, jewellery, T-shirts and woodcarvings; more unusual woodcarving can be found at unit 4 while Betty at unit 81 will sew the design of your choice onto a range of baskets. The Fort and Fantasy craft markets along the strip (daily 8am–7pm) are worth a look but tend to be a little more expensive with less variety. Elsewhere, check out Things Jamaican at 44 Fort St or Irie Creations upstairs in the City Centre Mall. The **Bob Marley Experience** at Half Moon Shopping Village has the largest collection of Bob Marley T-shirts in the world, as well as all kinds of other Marley memorabilia.

Head downtown for the best **art** shopping – the Gallery of West Indian Art, 11 Fairfield Road, Catherine Hall (*www.galleryof westindianart.com*) has a huge range of works and is renowned for its hand-carved and painted wooden animals. The tiny Heaven's Art Gallery, 1 Church Lane, houses, among the tombstones (carved and engraved here), the wonderful paintings of the late Hector Heavens, Montego Bay's most talented naive artist. For Jamaican and Cuban prints and originals, at upscale prices, try also Budhai's in Reading (see p.264) and Ambiente Gallery at 10 Fort St. On the strip, below the Cultural Arts Centre at 31 Gloucester Ave, Elgo's exhibits and sells the Cubist paintings of the eponymous artist, and Jenny's

Boutique, 60 Gloucester Ave, sells attractive handpainted clothes, cards and paintings of local scenes.

Downtown **record stores** offer the Jamaican speciality of custom-made reggae tapes (around US$3) as well as CDs and vinyl. Worth a visit, for the enthusiasm of owner Ainsworth Palmer coupled with his large collection of classic sounds, is Federal Records, 14 Strand St. Other shops include El Paso at 3 South Lane overlooking Sam Sharpe Square and Top Rank in Westgate Plaza. For sound-system session tapes and bootleg recordings of recent stageshows (US$5) check Clapper's Mobile Music Box in the Church Lane car park; the quality is surprisingly good, but ask for a test play before you buy.

For miscellaneous odds and ends, browse around the untouristy stores downtown. St James Street holds a branch of the dependable Sangster's **book** chain and Dominion Stationery, with an excellent selection of 1970s postcards and a small but quality selection of yellowing books, while Barnett Street is best for useless souvenirs. If you want to take home some **rum**, the cheapest option is to club together and buy it wholesale from C&J Liquors on Harbour Street, though the Jamaica Farewell pre-packed boxes from in-bond shops are easier to carry and only a little more expensive.

Listings

Airlines Air Jamaica (☎952 4300); American Airlines (☎952 5959); British Airways (☎952 3771) and Continental (☎952 4460) are all based at Sangster International Airport.

Airport enquiries Sangster International Airport's ticket, flight and baggage information line is ☎952 3124.

American Express Grace Kennedy Travel Ltd, 2 Market St (☎979 5912).

Banks and money Several banks congregate around Sam Sharpe Square; most efficient are Bank of Nova Scotia (also at Westgate Shopping Centre) and NCB (with other branches on Gloucester Ave opposite Cornwall Beach and at the airport); all have ATMs. Citizens Bank is at Montego Bay (LOJ) Shopping Centre, also with an ATM. Cambios are at Chin's Pastry, 10 Church St, King Midas, 37 Gloucester Ave, and Alvin Wallace, Unit 144, Harbour St Craft Market. Alternatively most of the in-bond shops on Gloucester Ave operate unofficial cambios. Wire transfers can be collected from Western Union above Hometown Supermarket on Church St, or at The Pelican on Gloucester Ave, though Moneygram is a little cheaper – pick-up points are the Lotto Shop, 6 Market St or downtown branches of NCB.

Car and bike rental All the major car rental companies have offices at the airport or on Queens Drive/Sunset Boulevard: Avis (☎952 5195); Budget (☎952 3838); Hertz (☎979 0438) and Thrifty (☎952 5825). Local operators are usually cheaper, most reliable for regular cars are: Alex's, 1 Claude Clarke Ave (☎952 3242); Beaumont's, 32 Queen's Drive (☎940 1494); Horizon, 2 Sunset Boulevard (☎952 0185, *delkerlew@cwjamaica.com*); Prospective, 28 Union St (☎952 3524, *prospective@cwjamaica.com*); Sunshine, 1 Queens Drive (☎974 2359, *selective@cwjamaica.com*); United (also rents out jeeps), 49 Gloucester Ave (☎952 3077, *unicars@n5.com.jm*). For motorbike rental try Kryss (☎940 0476) or Sun Cruise (☎979 0614) both of which are at Miranda Ridge, or Montego Bikes, 21 Gloucester Ave (☎952 4984).

Consulates Only the Canadian Consulate (☎952 6198) and US Consulate (☎952 0160) have offices in Montego Bay, and both are on Gloucester Ave. Embassies and other consulates are all based in Kingston (see p.7).

Dentists Dr Marlene Foote, 14c Market St (☎952 3016), or Dr Vernon Gardiner, 90 Barnett St (☎952 5742).

Doctors Most hotels have a doctor or nurse on duty or on call. Recommended practitioners are Dr Anthony Vendryes, whose surgery is at the *Royal Court* hotel on Sewell Ave (☎979 3333), or Dr Shirley Campbell at 15 Union St (☎952 0305).

Hospitals Cornwall Regional Hospital, Mount Salem (☎952 5100 or 6683) is the best public hospital outside Kingston. The best private institution is Doctor's Hospital in Fairfield (☎952 1616) or the Mobay Hope Medical Clinic at Half Moon Shopping Village, Rose Hall (☎953 3649 or 9310). In an emergency dial ☎119 for an ambulance.

Immigration Immigration Office, Floor 3, Overton Plaza, Union St (☎952 5381; Mon–Thurs 8.30am–4pm, Fri 8.30am–4pm). Visa extensions, lost passports – go early to avoid the queues.

Internet Places from which to collect and send email, at a rate of US$3–5 per half hour, include: Cigar King opposite the *Casa Blanca* hotel on Gloucester Ave (☎953 4318, *cigarkingjamaica@hotmail.com*); Teleworld Services on Miranda Ridge (☎940 7415, *teleworld@cwjamaica.com*) and Internet West, 17 Harbour St (☎971 6057, *iwesti@hotmail.com)*. The St James Parish Library has a small computer lab which allows half an hour of free Internet access.

Laundry Most hotels have a laundry service but there are some fairly good laundries. Bay Fabricare Centre at 4 Corner Lane (☎952 6987) is chaotic but central, and its one-hour dry cleaning service is convenient. Superwash below Upper Deck Condos on Sewell Ave (☎940 5501) is friendly, with a good pick-up and drop-off service. Wonder Wash in Westgate Plaza (☎940 1143) and underneath Baywest Mall on Harbour St has MoBay's only coin-operated machines.

Pharmacies There are plenty of pharmacies downtown. Best equipped are Clinicare on Sam Sharpe Square (Mon–Sat 9am–8pm, Sun 10am–6pm), Fontana, Montego Bay (LOJ) Shopping Centre (Mon–Sat 8am–7pm), and Hilton's Pharmacy, 27 St James St (Mon–Sat 9am–8pm). There are no pharmacies on the strip; the Sunset Supermarket sells basic toiletries.

Photography You can buy or develop film at Photo Express, Fort St (☎952 3120), at Salmon's, 32 St James St (☎952 4527), and at Ventura at 22 Market St (☎952 2937).

Police Montego Bay has four police stations. The largest and newest is inconveniently located in Catherine Hall (☎952 4997) and the nearest downtown station is at 14 Barnett St (☎952 1557). If your car is impounded, you should go to the station at 27 Church St (☎952 5310); visitors are usually told to take complaints or crime reports directly to the Tourism Liaison Unit at Summit station on Sunset Boulevard (☎952 1540). In an emergency, dial ☎119; the Woman Inc rape crisis line is (☎952 9533).

Post offices The two main post offices are named Number 1, on the corner of Fort St opposite the library, and Number 2, at 120 Barnett St. There is a postal agency (Whitesands PO) on Gloucester Ave next to Doctor's Cave Beach; you can pick up post-restante mail at all three, but Whitesands is the least frenetic.

Supermarkets There are large supermarkets in Westgate Plaza on Barnett St, Overton Plaza on Union St and Blue Diamond Shopping Centre in Ironshore. Hometown at 19 Church St is the best of the downtown bunch. Mini-marts on Gloucester Ave are pricey but convenient; try Sunset Supermarket and Deli opposite *Casa Blanca* hotel or New Eagle Supermarket in the *MoBay Club* building, which opens until 10pm daily.

Taxis Reliable taxi ranks on the strip are operated from both *The Quality Inn* and the *Coral Cliffs*; best of the lot, though, is the Doctor's Cave Stand (☎952 0521) opposite the *Doctor's Cave Beach Hotel*. Downtown locals take taxis from the Market St Stand. Recommended drivers for longer distances and custom-made tours are Keith Tomlinson (☎971 5420 or 990 5637) or Danny Paterson (ask for him on the strip).

Telephones The strip is fairly well served by public phones and there's a large bank of them opposite the Cable and Wireless building on Church St. Overseas calls are cheapest from the call centre in the City Centre Building, though you can also call home from The Cage in Sam Sharpe Square.

Travel agents Friendly Travel Service, 18 Strand St (☎979 5797); International Travel Service, 14b Market St (☎952 2485); Vaughans, 3 Corner Lane (☎952 5140).

Around Montego Bay

Away from the shops and the beaches, there's plenty to see around Montego Bay, and though many of the attractions – like **Rose Hall**, with its ghoulish reputation and theme-park ambience – are so hyped-up that you couldn't miss them if you tried, others, such as the **Rocklands bird sanctuary** or the **Belvedere Estate**, have a quiet charm and natural beauty that are effortlessly seductive.

Other than **rafting** down the Great River from Lethe, few people head into the **St James interior**, which is a shame because the rolling hinterland pastures are spectacular in places. St James was prime plantation territory under the British and a few of the old estates have kept their land and opened it up to the public. Polished boiling pots and repointed stone mills illustrate the mechanics of the sugar industry, and lavishly restored great house interiors froth over the planters' lifestyles, but there's little to commemorate one of the most significant phases in Jamaican history: the **Christmas Rebellion** of 1831 that began in St James and set the wheels in motion for the abolition of slavery (see p.260).

East along the coast

With its endless reefs and postcard beaches, the eastern stretch of coast beyond Montego Bay has long been the preserve of the more expensive all-inclusive hotels. As a consequence, the A1 coast road is a pleasure to drive; straight and smooth, it zips through the plush

Around Montego Bay

Ironshore's all-inclusives are covered along with Montego Bay accommodation on p.253.

residential belt of **IRONSHORE**, home to two of the island's best **golf courses**, the independent Ironshore Golf and Country Club (☎953 2800) and the Half Moon Golf Club (☎953 2211), host of the Red Stripe Pro-Am tournament (July/August). The area was once part of a vast sugar plantation; from Sugarmill Road you can see the remains of crumbling chimneys and an aqueduct.

Some of the island's best **horse-riding** is found at the Rocky Point Stables at the Half Moon complex (☎953 2286; daily 9am–5pm). Beginners are welcome on the Jungle Jaunt, a forty-five-minute trek that starts with a short lesson (US$50); more experienced riders can take the Tryall Trail, a longer ride along bridle paths into the Jamaican countryside (1hr 45min; US$60). Dressage, showjumping and polo lessons are also on offer.

Rose Hall

Meals on Wheels, a roadside café in an old van between the Half Moon Hotel and Rose Hall, is a favourite haunt of local workers and taxi drivers who stop for a cheap box meal and a game of dominoes under the trees.

Romanticized plantation history comes into its own at **ROSE HALL**, six miles east from MoBay and site of the infamous **Rose Hall Great House** (daily 9am–6pm; US$15), inspiration for Jamaica's best-loved piece of folklore, the tale of a voodoo practitioner who ruthlessly disposed of her husbands and is still said to haunt the corridors. Built between 1770 and 1780 by its first owner, planter and parish custos (the old English term for a mayor) John Palmer, the dazzling white stone structure, set back from the A1 and surrounded by gardens, woods and a swan-filled pond, is difficult to miss. Rose Hall makes much of the vastly embellished legend of Annie Palmer, the "White Witch of Rose Hall", and the rather mechanical guided tours that run every fifteen minutes milk it shamelessly. You gasp at blurred photos that supposedly show the face of an unknown woman in the mirror, and gawp at Annie's bedroom, symbolically redecorated in shades of red, and the terrace from which she allegedly pushed a maid to her death. As the house was unoccupied and widely looted during the nineteenth century, almost all of its current contents have been transported from other great houses or from overseas. The silk wallpaper, magnificent mahogany staircase and furnishings are attractive (if not from the right period), but the fake food and on-site Olde English pub – legacies of a gaudy refurbishment in the mid-1960s – rather spoil the romance.

For more on Rastafari, see p.391 of Contexts.

Nevertheless, the grounds are lovely, although these too have a violent past, this one authentic. In 1963 the district was the site of the "**Coral Gardens Massacre**", a bloody altercation between police and Rastafarians – then commonly viewed as vicious, anti-white, drug-crazed maniacs – whose right of way through the Rose Hall grounds to their vegetable plots was being threatened by property speculators developing the house into the tourist attraction it is today. After months of contention, a policeman sent to arrest the dissidents was attacked with a spear and a petrol station was set on fire. The army was called in, and during the ensuing bloodbath eight

Rastas died and others throughout the island were thrown into jail. Obviously, nothing marks the spot, and it's ironic that Rose Hall glorifies a violent fairy story while ignoring the blood spilt to make it so glamorous.

The Rose Hall empire extends a few miles east along the coast to the nondescript roadside community of **LILLIPUT**. Just past the signs for the Jamaican Bush Doctor and Palm Reader, where roots wine and bush medicine are dispensed alongside negligible clairvoyant advice, lies **Rose Hall Beach Club** (daily 9am–6pm; US$8); a recently landscaped beach with full tourist amenities that's advertised as the safest in Montego Bay – presumably because the locals can't afford to swim there any more. Every Thursday, the beach hosts the Miskito Cove Beach Picnic (☎817 5439; US$60) an all-

---

The White Witch of Rose Hall

Jamaica's most famous horror story centres on **Annie Palmer**, the "White Witch of Rose Hall". A beautiful young woman of Anglo-Irish descent, Annie Mary Patterson's early years are cloaked in mystery. Born in either England or Ireland, she was the only child of small-time property owners John and Juliana Patterson, who brought her to live in Haiti as a little girl, where she learned the voodoo art. The date of her arrival in Jamaica is unknown, but it's said that she came to Kingston as a fresh-faced seventeen-year-old in search of a husband. Being young and white, she was granted access to high society functions and her brooding good looks soon captured the attention of John Palmer, incumbent of Rose Hall and grandnephew of its architect, John Palmer. They married in March 1820, but the union was not a happy one; seven years on and bored with her insipid husband, Annie took a young slave lover. Palmer found out and whipped her severely; Annie took her revenge by placing poison in his wine, smothering the dying man with a pillow. She went on to stab and strangle two more husbands, and seduce and murder a succession of white book-keepers and black slaves. Even to those slaves she wasn't sleeping with, she was a cruel and sadistic mistress, meting out excessive punishments for minor misdemeanours.

However, Annie's cruelty proved to be her undoing, and she was murdered in her bed in 1831. No-one knows for sure whose hands encircled her neck, but some accounts point to an old and powerful balmist whose pretty granddaughter had been in competition with Annie for the attentions of a young English book-keeper, until the older woman set an "ol' hige" vampire upon her rival, killing her within a week.

Gripping as it is, there's barely a shred of truth in the story. Annie Palmer did exist (she's buried in a concrete grave to the left of the house), but by all accounts she was a peaceful woman with no discernible tendencies to sadism or lechery. She may have become confused over the years with Rosa Palmer, the original mistress of Rose Hall who did have four husbands, but she was said to be unwaveringly virtuous. Nonetheless, most Jamaicans choose to believe in something more sinister, and visiting mediums swear to strange visions and the discovery of buried effigies in the grounds.

Herbert DeLisser's bodice-ripping The White Witch *of Rose Hall is a thrilling narrative version of the story; see "Contexts", p.421.*

---

inclusive fun day comprising an open bar, lunch, watersports and a cruise.

The towering *Wyndham Rose Hall* resort (see below) dominates the rest of the Rose Hall district. Its expansive (and expensive) **golf course** contains a beautiful waterfall seen in the Jamaican James Bond classic *Live and Let Die*, and is an excellent spot for a walk even if you don't play golf – though you should check at the hotel before entering. The hotel is also home to the **Sugar Mills Falls**, a water complex billed as the Caribbean's most spectacular with cascading waterfalls, a 280ft thrill slide, three terraced pools and bridges from which to watch all the fun. Unfortunately, the falls are only open to guests at *Wyndhams* though the friendly management may make an exception for visitors keen to test the waters.

Practicalities

The *Wyndham Rose Hall* **hotel** (☎953 2560, fax 953 2617, *www.wyndham.com*; ⑦) is an ugly high-rise with an incongruously plush lobby, a pristine private beach, five bars and restaurants. A simpler place to stay is *Dunns Villa* two miles inland, Little River PO (☎997 5077; ③), a small family-run resort with a pool, Jacuzzi, restaurant and mountain bikes for rent. Rooms are pleasantly decorated but overpriced so haggle.

The best place to **eat** in the area is the *Ambrosia Restaurant* at *Wyndham Rose Hall* (☎953 2560 ext 459), serving top-notch, topwhack Mediterranean dishes with an accent on seafood.

Greenwood

Five miles east from Rose Hall, the A1 passes through scrubby mangrove swamps and opens up with a magnificent sea view at diminutive **GREENWOOD**. Perched on a hill overlooking the sea, the dull grey stone of **Greenwood Great House** (daily 9am–6pm; US$12) dominates the few houses and bars below. Surrounded by luscious flowering gardens, the house itself has none of the flashy allure of Rose Hall, and has managed to retain most of its original contents as well as a listless eighteenth-century ambience. Built in 1790 by relatives of the Barrett family of Wimpole Street fame (see p.237), the house was used primarily for recreation and entertaining and contains their original library and a wonderfully eclectic collection of objects including ancient musical instruments, a court jester's chair and custom-made Wedgwood china. The Barretts clearly had an eye for scenery as the forty-foot verandah commands a panoramic view of the sea unbroken by land, and, doubtful as it may seem, you really can see the curvature of the earth. The tour, which ends in the bar set up in the original kitchen area, is much more enjoyable than the breakneck run round Rose Hall, but is soured by a rather cavalier attitude to the property's slave history; there's just a cursory reference to a man trap used to catch runaways and a leg iron displayed on the wall like an ornament, while, with an apparent lack of irony, the young female guides are dolled up as eighteenth-century servants.

Nearby, **Cinnamon Hill Great House** was also built by the Barretts, but is now the private home of country and western star Johnny Cash, a local hero both as a singer (country music is incredibly popular in Jamaica) and for his regular contributions to children's charities and schools. Just outside Greenwood, fluttering flags and red, gold and green huts mark the first buildings of the **Bob Marley School for the Arts**, an ambitious project which is currently being built in two hundred acres of land. The school, which aims to be the island's premier musical training centre, is the brainchild of reggae expert Astor Black; check out his website for further details (*www.bobartsinstitute.edu*).

Practicalities
You can stay at the headquarters of the Bob Marley School for the Arts at nearby Scarlett Hall, two miles east of the school and based at Flamingo Beach (☎954 5252; ③). The hall offers spacious roots-style rooms with beautiful wicker furnishings, clover-shaped skylights, fans, patio doors and a fantastic view of the coastline; the housekeeper will cook-to-order for guests. Otherwise, there are all-inclusive, self-contained apartments at *Sea Castles* (☎953 3250, fax 974 3062, *www.comfortresorts.com*; ⑥) in a huge property right on the coast between the *Wyndham* hotel and Greenwood, with a pool, private beach, watersports and two restaurants. On the same stretch of road is the *All Seasons Resort* (☎953 1448, fax 953 1449, *allseasons68@hotmail.com*; ⑤), an intimate grouping of white apartments around a driftwood decorated bar.

For **eating and drinking**, the *Far Out Fish Hut*, eastwards along the A1 just half a mile beyond Greenwood, has good fish and bammy. More Jamaican food is available at *Turtles Inn*, half a mile further down the road and worth a visit for the home-made conch soup alone. Best of all the roadside joints and a mile past Lilliput is *Last Chance*, a laid-back spot overlooking the sea with delicious fish and friendly staff.

The St James interior

Shooting off from Reading on Montego Bay's western flank, the well signposted B8 inland road plunges straight into tropical St James. The initial steep incline, known as Long Hill, that parallels the Great River valley affords occasional glimpses of the lush palms and ferns of the chasm below. Most visitors venture here to raft the river and hike at **Lethe**, although there are more worthy attractions further on, including the superlative **Rocklands Bird Sanctuary**, the interesting **Belvedere Estate** plantation and the unique German settlement of **Seaford Town**. The B8 is the quickest route to Savanna-la-Mar and the south coast, so traffic is pretty heavy. Striking west out of downtown Montego Bay, Fairfield Road takes you into a strikingly beautiful landscape. Country roads overhung with dripping foliage pass over swift streams and hug the edges of the Cockpit foothills, and the tarmac barely grips the edges of steep valleys lined by tiny hamlets such as **Kensington**, the key flashpoint of the Christmas Rebellion.

If you don't have a car, you'll often find **transport** a problem in the interior. Buses are practically non-existent towards Kensington, so your best bet, if you're heading somewhere fairly near the B8, is to hop on a Savanna-la-Mar bus, get off as near as possible and complete the journey on foot. It's usually much easier to join an organized tour or hire a private driver (see p.201).

Lethe and around

Less than ten miles south from MoBay and well signposted from the B8, **LETHE** is a pretty village set amid cool and vividly green hills, with a graceful stone bridge, built by slaves in 1820, straddling the gushing Great River. The rafting and plantation tour that it is locally famous for encourages plenty of tourists and a money-grabbing streak in some of its locals, though it's otherwise a very friendly community.

The village's focal point, on your left as you enter, is **Lethe Estate** (☎956 4920, *lethe@cwjamaica.com*; daily 9am–4pm; ⑥) a banana plantation chock-full of touristic opportunities. Most visitors opt for a jitney tour of the grounds (from US$12), with further options of lunch, fruits, liqueur-tasting and a stop-off at **Rheas World**, a rather contrived set-up of labelled flowers, morose-looking caged coneys and squawking geese. There are plenty of combinations available, but it's all a bit over-packaged, and your best option by far is to ignore the jitneys and naff "village tours" and opt instead for a tailormade-**hike** (you decide on the distance) from Lethe into the surrounding hills and it's a better way to get a flavour of the countryside (guides from the estate set their own prices, but expect to pay US$10; ask for Johnny). **Rafting** is another huge pleasure – the 45-minute trip (US$30 for two people) takes you past banks dripping with vines and overhung by trees. It rains a lot up here so the usually clear water often takes on a muddy aspect, but it's still safe for swimming. There are a few rather turbulent spots where the shallows tumble and bubble over rocks; the bamboo rafts scrape the bottom a little, but the punt-handlers are far too experienced to sink. You can **stay** on the property in lovely but expensive rooms with balconies overlooking the river, a breezy verandah restaurant, bar, TV lounge and a huge pool.

On the road up to Lethe you'll notice the signs for **Busha's Country Resort Hotel** (☎952 0712; ③), three hundred acres of usually deserted private land that contain the remains of an old slave village. The Jamaica National Heritage Trust has removed most of the artefacts but a few scant vestiges remain – rusting sugar kettles lie half covered by earth and weather-beaten gravestones struggle to stay upright. The hotel barely functions these days though it's worth calling in if there's a group of you in search of peace and quiet. Close to *Busha's*, and again on the way to Lethe, several miles along an appallingly potholed track is **Nature Village Farm** (daily 10am–7pm). Principally the venue for local football matches and known as Wembley, the site is a very scenic spot on the Great River with manicured lawns, bamboo groves and an open-air restaurant overlooking the water.

Just two miles beyond Lethe at Copse, a right-hand fork takes you down to **Animal Farm** (☎815 4104, *www.homestead.com /animalfarm*; Mon–Fri tours by arrangement, Sat & Sun 10am–5pm; US$5), a well-tended smallholding run on solar energy with exotic birds, herb garden and petting zoo which is worth a visit especially if you're travelling with small children.

Rocklands Bird Sanctuary and Feeding Station
Reached along a terrible road off the B8 just before the right turn for Anchovy, **Rocklands Bird Sanctuary and Feeding Station** (☎952 2009; daily 2–5pm; US$7) is unique in Jamaica. The flow-ered home and gardens of celebrated ornithologist Lisa Salmon, it's the only place on the island where hummingbirds are confident enough to drink sugar water while perched on your outstretched fin-ger. Feeding peaks at around 4.30pm when the air thrums with tiny wings; over a hundred varieties of bird have been known to visit, including orange quits, vervain and national bird the streamer-tailed doctor. Ill health and age mean that Ms Salmon is seldom seen, but her assistant Fritz is extremely knowledgeable and can take you on bird-watching trails through the property and beyond (US$10) – a nature walk through the gardens is included in the entry fee; serious ornithologists should call ahead to arrange more specific bird-watching hikes.

Montpelier and Belvedere Estate
About three miles further along the B8 from Anchovy is **MONTPE-LIER**, 2000ft above sea level and surrounded by citrus groves, arable land and cattle and ganja fields. The crumbling stone buildings in front of the hilltop Anglican church – declared a National Monument in 1999 – reached along a muddy track off the main road, are all that's left of one of the largest sugar estates in western Jamaica, burned to the ground during the Christmas Rebellion (see box, p.260). A rusting plaque marks the spot of the ensuing skirmish between British forces and the "black regiment". If you're in Montpelier visiting the church it's worth knocking on the door of the adjacent rectory; the Rev Antony Otty is a highly entertaining

Although Anchovy itself consists of little other than a school, post office and a couple of snack bars, it is the location for one of the most popular dance-halls in the area, Bojangles; party goers travel from miles around to see some of Jamaica's top DJs perform here.

character and welcomes visitors. Pat, his wife, is an authority on the history of the village and its environs.

A further fifteen minutes' drive along the track, the eight-hundred-acre **Montpelier Blue Hole Nature Park** (☎0909 9002; daily 9am–4pm; US$4) claims to be a botanical garden but is more like a pastoral retreat. The views across the hills are awesome, and there is a huge swimming pool, an aqueduct dating back to 1747 and a series of breathtaking swimmable and climbable waterfalls along the Blue Hole River, a tributary of the Great River. You can **camp** in the park for US$6 per person; simple **food** is available from the thatched bar if you call ahead, or you can bring your own picnic.

Just beyond Montpelier, the B8 forks; right takes you over the interior mountains to Shettlewood and on to Savanna-la-Mar in Jamaica's far west. It's an incredibly pretty route with, in season, the accompanying smell of orange blossom from the surrounding citrus plantations. The communities along the road are diminutive; only **Ramble** boasts a petrol station and a police station. The left fork takes you to the most attractive open plantation in the area, **Belvedere Estate** (☎952 6001 or 957 4170; daily 9am–4pm; US$10), a well-organized fruit and cattle farm that does good business with tour operators. The standard tour round the estate is unusually imaginative with a traditional mento band and samplings of jerk pork and sugar cane juice. Also enjoyably explored independently, the coconut, citrus and banana fields are impressive, and the waterfall and pool (managed by a three-hundred-year-old dam) provide excellent swimming.

*Christmas
Rebellion
leader Sam
Sharpe was
once a slave at
Belvedere (see
also p.260).*

Seaford Town

From Belvedere it's an hour's drive along an inconsistently tarmacked road to **SEAFORD TOWN**. At first glance, this is just another rural community, but you'll soon notice that a lot of the older residents are white. In 1834, the British administration, fearing that forthcoming emancipation would result in widespread chaos and a mass exodus from the sugar plantations, began a pre-emptive programme of European settlement throughout the island's interior. To establish a "civilizing" white presence throughout Jamaica, and, more importantly, snap up the best land and labour before the slaves could, it drafted in over a thousand Germans over the next two years, promising them land and prosperity after a set period of indentured toil. Between 1834 and 1836, 251 Germans settled in Seaford Town, a five-hundred-acre plot of land donated by Lord Seaford of nearby Montpelier. The rest of the immigrants scattered throughout Jamaica's interior and blended into existing communities; Seaford Town remains the only Jamaican town to be deliberately established by the government.

*For an easier
route to
Seaford Town,
turn left at the
Montpelier
fork of the B8,
then head
right at
Marchmont.*

The new arrivals, many unused to farm labour, found life in rural Jamaica difficult, and when the rations they'd been allocated for the first year ran out, became as impoverished as their black neighbours. Intense hardship and tropical diseases depleted their numbers, and within just a couple of years many of the survivors emigrated to the US. Enough remained, however, for their legacy to be obvious today. Despite some racial intermixing over the years, a tradition of inbreeding has ensured that quite a few of the town's residents still have blonde hair, blue eyes and (almost) white skin.

The diminutive **Seaford Town Historical Museum** (daily 9am–5pm; US$2), on a grassy knoll below the Catholic Church of the Sacred Heart, tells the story of Seaford's German heritage, with photographs of the original settlers and a plaque listing their names and occupations (one man was a comedian). As the museum is usually locked you'll need to ask at the church to enter. However, beyond the proudly displayed artefacts in the museum, little German culture has been retained around town. Traces are seen in the pointy roofs and gingerbread fretwork of some of the older houses, but German speakers are restricted to the very old, and people are more likely to have rice and peas than sauerkraut for their dinner.

The Cockpit fringes and Kensington

From Seaford Town, you can drive east through the pretty hilltop village of **ST LEONARDS**, site of the Hilton High tour (see p.250). Just north of here, the ragged road takes you through tiny **MARCHMONT** – look out for the red-gold-and-green-painted board home of the local bush doctor just off the road. Just a short way beyond Marchmont, you pass signs for **Croydon Estate**, 132 acres of pineapple plantation occupying the last stretches of accessible land before the Cockpit hillocks make large-scale farming a commercial impossibility. A mile north down the same road is **CATADUPA**, once the main tourist stop of the now-derelict train line that ran from Montego Bay to Kingston. Today, cows and goats pick at the grassed-over sleepers, though the gingerbread-style station house, with its peeling paint and panelled walls, exudes a faded romance.

From Catadupa, the road lurches crazily along the western fringes of Cockpit Country, passing lazy-looking communities like **MOCHO** where untethered goats stare wild-eyed at the sun and housewives hang their washing out to dry on hedges. City folk disparage the residents of this backwoods village as unsophisticated country bumpkins. There are several villages called Mocho in Jamaica, all located in remote rural areas. A common colloquial insult is to tell someone they're from "up a Mocho sides", and the *Dictionary of Jamaican English* interprets the name as "a place of symbolic remoteness – a rough, uncivilized place".

Three miles on at diminutive **FLAMSTEAD**, the road splits; right heads for **MAROON TOWN**, which despite its name has no contemporary Maroon connections, while left takes you the four miles north to **KENSINGTON**. Despite huge historical significance as the place where the first fires of the Christmas Rebellion were lit (see p.260), the only hint of the past is a roadside plaque. Past Kensington, the views over gaping valleys are marvellous; John Crow vultures whirl high on the thermals and you get the occasional glimpse of the sea behind the trees. You're only thirteen-odd miles from Montego Bay, but the contrast couldn't be more striking. If you want to **stay**, head for *Orange River Ranch* (☎979 6523; ④), set in 1000 acres of land complete with a swimmable river, a 110-year-old great house and countless groves of raggedy banana trees. Rooms are simple and functional with a balcony, and there's a restaurant, bar and pool as well as some of the nicest hotel staff you'll encounter. Horse riding (1hr; US$25 per person) and hiking are both available from the hotel.

Cockpit Country

The Cockpits are believed to be the stamping ground for all manner of spirits and duppies and are avoided by more superstitious Jamaicans.

The most bizarre landscape in Jamaica, **COCKPIT COUNTRY** is an uncanny series of improbable lumps and bumps covering roughly five hundred square miles of Trelawny Parish, just south of Montego Bay. Thousands of years' worth of rain and river water flowing over the porous limestone surface has created a rugged karst topography of impenetrable conical hillocks dissolved on each side by a drainage system of sinkholes and caves. The region is one of the most intriguing parts of the island, not least because of the place names peppered throughout it: Me No Sen You No Come, Wait-a-Bit, Quick Step and Rest and Be Thankful District, though the last appears on aged maps only. Cockpit Country is also known as The District of Look Behind in reference to the justifiable paranoia of English soldiers who made hot, comfortless and usually ill-fated missions through the area tracking Maroons, whose superior local knowledge and guerrilla strategies brought most of the sorties to a bloody end.

Save for a few pockets on the outskirts and along the central ten-mile trail from Windsor to Troy, Cockpit Country is uninhabited. Hunters make regular forays into the interior in search of feral pigs, but otherwise the few locals congregate at **Windsor**, **Albert Town** and **Accompong**, their economy based on small-scale farming, coffee-production and – cloaked by the region's thick foliage – ganja-growing.

Only a fraction of this land is accessible, and you can't get far independently, so what follows is not a geographical tour but a few of the highlights. Wherever you go, the scarcity of tourists and the lack of environmental damage make Cockpit Country unmissable: a sanctuary of incredible untouched beauty, particularly in the early mornings when low-lying mists and a silence broken only by bird calls give it an almost primeval feel. Plans to turn the whole of this region into a National Park funded in part by the World Bank will ensure, with careful management, that the area remains protected and unique.

Hiking and caving in the Cockpits

Despite popular disbelief, **hiking trails** do exist in Cockpit Country, usually maintained by local residents, though the further you get into the interior the rougher they become. Windsor and Albert Town are the most accessible starting points for hiking, where you should pick up a local guide, essential not only to stop you getting lost but in case of any accident – if you fall down a hole here, there will be nobody around to get you out. The main ten-mile trail through Cockpit Country starts at Windsor and runs straight through the middle to Troy on the southern outskirts, though it gets very overgrown towards the middle. The first few miles are relatively easy and foliage-free, but in the heat of the day it's an arduous eight-to-ten hour trek that few would want to undertake; you're in the midst of foliage most of the time so there are few open vistas and little to interest you after the first couple of hours, but you'll certainly feel a sense of achievement if you complete it. Of course, you don't have to go the whole way; the first couple of hours from Windsor give you a pretty good idea of what's to come. If you set out from Troy, the trail is mostly downhill and a lot easier-going – the best plan is to base yourself at Windsor, hire a guide there and drive to Troy early enough to make the hike back to Windsor before nightfall.

Informed and well-organized **guided tours** pointing out rare plants and birds seen along the pig-hunting trails that network the Cockpit interior are available from Sun Venture in Kingston (☎960 6685, *www.sunventuretours.com*). For basic hikes around the more open land near Albert Town, try local community group Cockpit Country Adventure Tours (☎610 0818, *stea@cwjamaica.com*) who also organize nature walks, trips to caves and campfire picnics in the bush. As the going is rugged you'll need a stout pair of shoes or boots with good grip, something waterproof, something warm (winter evenings are pretty cold), a torch, water bottle, and heavy-duty mosquito repellent to deter the mosquitoes: Cockpit Country's limestone pools are an ideal breeding ground. Allow double your usual walking time, as an ostensibly simple trek can take hours longer if you have to chop at foliage to clear your path.

Cavers would find Cockpit Country irresistible were it not for the lack of infrastructure. Though 250-odd caves network the area, only Windsor is easily accessible; the rest are little explored and there is no specialized group to guide you. However, both Sun Venture and Cockpit Country Adventure Tours run trips into local caves; recommended is the cathedral-sized **Quashie River Sink Cave** though it's a tough scramble down steep slopes to reach it and is not for the unfit or fainthearted. Alan Fincham's essential *Jamaica Underground* lists and measures all the island's caves, but is difficult to get hold of – try the excellent Caving in Jamaica website, *www.villa-jamaica.com/links* for information and related topics.

Getting there and around

If you're **driving** in from Montego Bay, you can take either of the roads that lead off the A1 near Westgate Plaza, though as these are narrow, potholed country lanes, a quicker route is to drive along the coast to Falmouth (see p.234) and head inland at Rock along the B11. As with most of the Jamaican interior, Cockpit Country is

Never hike alone or unguided in Cockpit Country; maps are useless, sinkholes extremely dangerous and there's no one to help if you run into problems.

Cockpit Country

Non-ornitholo-gists can join the Cockpit field trips made by the Gosse Bird Club, Kingston (☎ 927 8444, mclevy@cwja-maica-com).

Flora and fauna

Though soil forms only a thin cover over the Cockpit limestone, under-ground rivers ensure enough irrigation for flourishing **plant life**, in some cases so thick that a chainsaw would be more appropriate for chopping your way through than the conventional machete. Close inspection of tree trunks often reveals miniature orchids, and giant bromeliads hang from the boughs overhead. The Cockpits are also great for **ornithologists**; this is one of the few places where you'll see – and hear – profusions of shriek-ing green parakeets. The rare Jamaican blackbird is also seen here – and the forests support all 27 endemic Jamaican species of bird. The feral **pigs** that root through the undergrowth are descended from those reared by the Maroons, and with hundreds of caves, **bats** are common – all 22 Jamaican varieties are found in the region. The limestone also provides a perfect cover for the **Jamaican boa** or **yellow snake** as well as the **black racer**, a venomous variety that was thought extinct until pig hunters began to report bites on their hunting dogs.

poorly served by **buses**. For Windsor, a limited daily service runs from Falmouth to Clarks Town and Sherwood Content, the best places from which to catch a lift to Windsor itself; buses for Albert Town also depart from Falmouth. If all that sounds like hassle, you might want to consider joining an **organized tour** from MoBay (see p.250); Maroon Attraction Tours (☎952 8753; from US$50 pp) are the only carriers authorized to visit Accompong, but big companies like Caribic offer trips to Windsor on demand.

Once you're there, by far the best mode of transport is a **car**. Most makes of regular car will suffice, but a four-wheel-drive is preferable. Otherwise local people are extremely amenable with **lifts**, usually for free but sometimes for a small charge; just flag down anything that passes.

Windsor

Smack in the middle of Cockpit Country's accessible northern edge and reached via a dirt track from the tiny village of Sherwood Content, **WINDSOR** is the most heavily visited settlement in the region, as tour buses pull in to its star attraction, **Windsor Cave**. Documented to stretch as far as three miles underground, the cave itself is an eerie maze of dripping water and huge twisting columns of fused stalagmites and stalactites. Its innocuously small mouth exhales a constant, clammy wind, except at dusk, when hundreds of bats – the cave is home to seven species – sweep majestically out on feeding forays. Experienced cavers or the foolhardy can follow the slippery path for about two and a half hours, emerging deep into the mountains and walking back to Windsor overground. As it's com-pletely undeveloped and pitch black inside, the best way to see it is with a guide. Franklyn Taylor, owner of the village's convivial red-gold-and-green painted bar, and his brother lead tours for US$10–20 dependent upon group size; the duration of the tour depends on the requirements of the group but averages at around ninety minutes.

Franklyn's also your man for **hiking**, a big activity here as Windsor is the starting point for the only trail that crosses Cockpit Country. There's not much else to Windsor save for a couple of nice swimming spots along the Martha Brae River which rises by the cave, a few fields of coffee and the stately **Windsor Great House** (☎997 3832, *windsor@cwjamaica.com*; ②), recently renovated and privately owned, with a huge open verandah and a couple of facility-free **rooms** for budget travellers – though only those with a committed interest in Cockpit Country are really welcome. Every Wednesday the house's owner, Mike Schwartz, hosts a "meet the biologists" meal (four courses with wine, US$25 per head), part of an ongoing project to develop Windsor into a research station for scientists and other related parties.

Albert Town

The best way to see the southern Cockpits is from **ALBERT TOWN**, an isolated but friendly hillside community at the southeastern edge of the area. It's fairly small, with thirty-odd buildings dotted around a central square and residential areas extending down into the valley below. It's also the best starting point for any trips, hiking or other-wise, into the area; the excellent **South Trelawny Environmental Agency** or S.T.E.A. and their tour company Cockpit Country Adventure Tours (☎610 0818, *stea@cwjamaica.com*) are based here and offer a wealth of advice, useful information and official guides.

Albert Town is also the location for the annual **Trelawny Yam Festival**, a hugely popular celebration of the area's most typical food, held in the week before Easter. Tens of thousands of people, locals and tourists, jam the streets to witness culinary displays, best dressed goat and donkey competions, yam head balancing races and ultimately the crowning of the Yam King and Queen.

Practicalities

The easiest route into Albert Town is via the B11 from the north coast at Rock. At Clarks Town, you join the B10, a poor excuse for a road that offers fantastic views and some of the best white-knuckle driving in Jamaica. The road takes you past the **Barbecue Bottom** district, notable for the scarily steep cliffs that sheer off from the roadside and provide superlative views of the Cockpits and cane fields below. Off the road just south of Barbecue Bottom is **Ramgoat Cave**, another pitch-black abyss that you'll need a knowledgeable guide to find, let alone enter.

There's no formal **accommodation** in Albert Town, but a number of local families offer bed-and-breakfast, most with private bath-rooms and meals at extra cost (contact S.T.E.A. for reservations;

②–③). Basic but tasty Jamaican **food** is available from the three-storey *Ataurus Restaurant and Bar*, the best place in town to sink a few beers and admire the stunning views from the back verandah, and *Alice's Restaurant*, at nearby Dutch Hill, serves delicious lunches in a friendly local café. A fried chicken vendor, small mini-mart and a petrol station are all found in the town square. Weekend **jams** take place at the *Upstairs Club* in the centre of town.

Accompong

Herbal medi-cine is still the tonic of choice in Accompong; a booklet, Welcome to the World of Maroon Traditional Medicine *is locally avail-able (US$3). Ask to see Carlton Smith if you want a consultation.*

Sitting on one of the precipitous hillocks that make up outer Cockpit Country, **ACCOMPONG** boasts breathtaking views and is the last remaining Maroon settlement in western Jamaica. Named after the brother of Maroon hero Cudjoe, Accompong came into being in 1739, when, as part of the peace treaty that ended the first Maroon War, the British granted the Maroon people 15,000 acres of land (see p.370) upon which to create a semi-sovereign community (however a missing zero meant that only 1500 acres were made available, a matter of continuing contention). Several such communities, including Trelawny Town in St James, were also given land and the Maroons set about a peaceful life in the hills, raising animals and farming. In 1795, however, a Trelawny Town Maroon caught stealing a pig in downtown Montego Bay was publicly flogged, ironically by one of the runaway slaves the Maroons had captured and returned to the plantations in accordance with the peace treaty. His kinsmen rebelled once again and the second Maroon War flared up. Though the Trelawny Town Maroons could muster only 300 fighters, the British took no risks and sent in 1500 soldiers and hunting dogs to track them down and wreck their villages. Accompong, the only Maroon village in western Jamaica that chose to remain neutral, was allowed to stand.

Still ruled by a Colonel, the citizens of Accompong are beginning to doubt the benefits of their semi-autonomous status; though the Colonel still makes judgements and the residents pay no taxes or rates, this independence has meant years of state neglect; roads are fixed only when the Maroons can raise the money and the whole town is served by one public phone box. Modern Accompong clings to its heritage, but it's fighting a losing battle. A one-street village with a church, school and a bar, only the palm-thatched roof and woven bamboo walls of the local community centre belie an alternative history. Though older residents claim direct descendancy from fearsome Maroon leaders Nanny and Cudjoe, there are relatively few "real" Maroons left in the town and during the last thirty years over two thirds of the population have left to pursue jobs in urban areas or abroad. The secret "Coromantee" language has vanished from daily use, resurfacing only in traditional songs and ceremonies and the survival of Maroon culture has become less important to a younger generation more interested in dancehall than Goombay drums or Akan chants.

Accompong Maroon Festival

Every January 6, Accompong Maroons from all over the island come
home to celebrate the most important day in their calendar – the anniversary of the 1739 peace treaty. Like everything else in Jamaica, the
Accompong festivities start late. Under a towering mango tree on the outskirts of the town, a suckling pig (always male according to Maroon tradition) is roasted on a spit and eaten communally just before the real highlight of the day, when Maroon leaders, adorned by the vines used as cam-
ouflage by their ancestors, make their way up from the Peace Cave where
they have drummed, danced and chanted since dawn. Goombay drums
beat complicated rhythms in anticipation and the town's aged hornblower
sends the haunting tones of an abeng horn (a cow horn once used as a
musical instrument and means of communication) echoing across the
hills, signalling the approach of the elders. The drumming reaches a climax as the parade arrives and the assembled mass joins in with call-and-
response Akan war songs. The procession moves through the village, paying respects at the homes of former Colonels and those too old to participate, finishing at the town square for speeches and performances from traditional Maroon dance groups who whirl around and are sprinkled with a
traditional dash of white rum. Eventually, the drums make way for towers
of speaker boxes, and the party continues in an all-night sound-system
jam.

Today, Accompong feels more or less like any other rural
Jamaican village, though a rush of would-be guides craftily try to
impose an entrance fee (there isn't one, though a donation to the
school is always appreciated). Its sights consist of a musty **church** on
a hillock overlooking the main town, a **memorial to Cudjoe**, co-sig-
natory of the 1739 treaty, set on a small concreted podium that
serves as the town square, and a tiny **craft centre** opposite that's
usually locked – vendors will open it up and show you the goods but
other than the odd goatskin drum they differ little from what's on
offer in resort markets. In a valley below the town is the **Peace Cave**
where the treaty was signed. You should be able to arrange for somebody local to take you there, but it's so small and insignificant-look-
ing that it's hard to imagine that history was made here; it's a couple
of miles' walk through pretty, undulating hinterland that's more of an
attraction than the destination. The best and most interesting time to
visit is for the annual **Accompong Maroon Festival**, held on January
6 to celebrate the signing of the peace treaty (see box). Additionally,
the S.T.E.A. (see p.285) organize a monthly event, with transport
provided, known as Maroon Members In The Moonlight, which
showcases Maroon culture with drumming, dancing and the opportunity to taste local dishes.

Practicalities

There are several ways to get to Accompong, the easiest by heading
north from Maggoty in St Elizabeth (see p.351) to Vauxhall, and

asking from there. You can also drive up from Albert Town, skirting the southern edge of Cockpit Country along the B10/B6, or travel via Elderslie and Jointwood. Other than arranging to **stay** in a private home (ask around when you get there), you can rent one of the three basic rooms at *Peyton Place Pub* (①) just up from the town square; it also serves **food**.

Travel details

Buses

Buses from the main bus station in Montego Bay can take you throughout the island, but you'll have to change midway for longer journeys. The terminal is pretty well organized by Jamaican standards and even has signs directing you to each route, but as there are no timetables your best bet is to turn up the day before and ask, particularly if your destination is off the beaten track. Below are the main routes covering places listed in this chapter. Services run from around 6am until 6pm. There is a reduced service on Sundays, with little or nothing after 5pm.

Montego Bay to: Anchovy (10 daily; 40min); Catadupa (4 daily; 1hr 30min); Falmouth (every 20min; 30min); Reading (every 30min; 10min); Rose Hall (every 30min; 15min); Savanna-la-Mar (every 40min; 40min).

Flights

Montego Bay to: Tinson Pen, Kingston (Mon–Fri 8 daily, Sat–Sun 5 daily; 35 min); Negril (3 daily; 20min); Port Antonio (Mon & Thurs–Sun 3 daily, Tues & Wed 2 daily; 45 min).

Chapter 5

Negril and the west

T hough Jamaica's **western tip** is often associated only with the seven miles of sand at **Negril**, there's a lot more than beach life to the parishes of Hanover and Westmoreland. At only 174 square miles, **Hanover** is the island's smallest parish, and despite the deceptively steep-looking coastal rise to the 1789ft peak of the central Dolphin Head range, it's also the flattest, ensuring the **lowest rainfall** in Jamaica and invariably sultry weather in the extreme west. Sleepy capital **Lucea**, with its Georgian buildings and decaying grandeur, is slated for heritage development, but for now remains a languid and charming shrine to the past. Other than the ever-hopeful roadside refreshment stops and craft shacks, there's little tourism development along its stretch of coast. The smooth cattle pastures and deserted white-sand coves beg for exploration, while the odd abandoned windmill and crumbling walls of long-deserted estates remain untouched.

Split in two by Hanover and Westmoreland, sybaritic **Negril** has a front-row sunset seat, the longest continuous stretch of white sand in Jamaica and a geographical remoteness that provides this ultimate chill-out town with a uniquely insouciant ambience. "Discovered" by

---

Accommodation price codes

All the hotels detailed in this guide have been graded according to the following price categories. Note that the prices have been calculated as those for the cheapest **double** or **twin room** during low season, normally mid-April to mid-December. During high season, rates are liable to rise by up to 25 percent (though this is rare at the cheap hotels), and proprietors may be less amenable to bargaining. Although the law requires prices to be quoted in Jamaican dollars, most hotels give rates in US dollars; payment can be made in either currency. For more details see p.27.

① under US$20	④ US$51–70	⑦ US$151–200
② US$21–35	⑤ US$71–100	⑧ US$200 and above
③ US$36–50	⑥ US$101–150	

Montego Bay

Round Hill Bluff

Bull Bay Beach

North West or Pedro Point

Lucea Harbour

Mosquito Cove

Sandy Bay

A1 Hopewell

Reading

Fort Charlotte

Lance's Cove

Davis Cove

Negro Bay

Green Island Harbour

Orange Bay

Green Island

Lucea

B9

Cousins Cove

Blenheim

Prospect

Santoy

Westfield

Logwood

The Great Morass

Cave Valley

Springfield

Negril

Sheffield

Mount Airy

Revival

Orange Hill

Little Bay

Homers Cove

Little Bay

South West Point

South West Point

Broughton

Cabarita Point

Savanna-La-Mar Fort

Peter Tosh Mausoleum

Dias

Askenish

Dolphin Head

Mayfield Falls

Kendal

Grange Hill

Frome

Little London

Savanna-la-Mar

Wakefield

Paradise Park

Bluefields Bay

Belmont

Mount Edgecumbe

Auchindown

Culloden

Whitehouse

Scott's Cove

Fustic Grove

Mosquito Cove

Cold Spring

Cascade

Pondside

Birchs Hill

Alexandria

HANOVER

Cacoon Castle

Great River

Tryall

Ramble

Fort William

Haddo

Roaring River

Petersfield

Whithorn

Orange Hill

WESTMORELAND

Amity Cross

Ferris Cross

Darliston

Seaford Town

Three Roads

Enfield

Cave

Bognie Content

Lenox Bigwoods

New Roads

Blackwood Hill

Pondicherry

Lenox

Beeston Spring

Hopeton

Orange Grove

Kilmarnoch

Bluefields

Bluff Point

SURINAM QUARTERS

CARIBBEAN SEA

0   6 miles

wealthy hippies in the 1970s, Negril is still immensely popular with those who favour fast living and corporeal indulgence, and is easily the best place outside Kingston for **live reggae** and **nightclubs**, though its reputation as "sin city" means an over-quota of ganja and cocaine hustlers and an inevitable edginess. However, even though the main menu is sun, sea, smoke and sex, there are plenty of natural attractions around Negril, including the **Great Morass**, the **Royal Palm Reserve** and some marvellous **reefs**. Beyond Negril, the landscape stretches out into the flat south-coast plains and tourism gives way to agriculture. Irrigated by the meandering Cabarita River, **Westmoreland** was once Jamaica's foremost **sugar-growing** parish and though rice is now an equally popular crop, cane plantations still surround the main commercial town and parish capital **Savanna-la-Mar**. Exports have significantly declined in recent years, leaving districts without tourism receipts struggling to find new industries and lending an air of pastoral neglect to the quiescent coastal villages.

Until long-standing plans for a huge all-inclusive near Whitehouse are realized, the **southwesterly point** remains deliciously quiet, with beaches dedicated to fishing rather than aloe massages and sun loungers. **Bluefields** and neighbouring **Belmont**, birthplace of the late **Peter Tosh**, are small but lively once you scratch beneath the surface, and have the best undeveloped beaches in Westmoreland. Fishing also dominates **Whitehouse**, a main port of call for north-coast hotel food buyers; both towns are ideal if you want peace, quiet and few other foreign faces.

West towards Negril

The west tip begins where Montego Bay ends. Past the bridge over the mouth of Great River, the A1 coast road twists and turns past **Hopewell**, home of one of the finest hotels on the island, and villages that decrease in prosperity the further they are from the tourist towns. Though the haunting coastal scenery is a constant enticement into the interior, there's little to occupy you other than the swimming at **Mayfield Falls** or the mini-museum at Alexander Bustamante's **Blenheim** birthplace, and as most people choose to remain within sight of the Caribbean Sea much of the land remains uncompromisingly indifferent to tourism; even the many hiking possibilities of the central **Dolphin Head** range are unexploited. Market town **Lucea** breathes a little life into the area, and further west the build-up to Negril begins, with a closer concentration of roadside bars and rest-stops around **Green Island** and **Orange Bay**. Riding and diving at bounteously situated **Rhodes Hall Plantation** and swimming at the marvellously secluded **Half Moon Bay** beach are the last vestiges of calm before the onslaught of Negril.

Hopewell

The first sizeable town west of Montego Bay, dormitory town **HOPEWELL** is quite content to let MoBay deal with the tourists, to the extent that some residents positively seem to resent a foreign face. Other than browsing through the general stores that surround the bedraggled and unjustifiably pricey **vegetable market** (main day Saturday), there's little in this one-street town to keep you busy. The hills around are scattered with multiple zinc and plaster fundamentalist **churches** – *The Watchtower* is the unofficial village newspaper – and an evangelical mood dominates, broken only on Friday evenings, when a local sound system strings up on the main road and blocks traffic way into the night. The **coastline** around town is not ideal for swimming, but there are occasional sandy spots; most popular is **Steamer Beach** just past the murky fishermen's beach, marked by the rusting iron shell of a wrecked boat. The slim white stretch gets packed in the early evening and on weekends when kids

*Shared taxis
run between
Hopewell and
MoBay; fares
are around
J$40, cars
leave every
10min from
the main street
and terminate
in St James
Street.*

descend for an after-school bathe and dominoes slap down on the verandah tables of the *Old Steamer Tavern*. Before moving on from Hopewell take time to visit the small **gallery** of local potter Sylvester Stephens – it's just past the Shell petrol station on your left as you drive west – his garden, in front of the gallery, is a bizarre collection of giant pots and clay figures nailed to wooden posts.

There is just one **hotel** in Hopewell – *Round Hill*, PO Box 64 (☎956 7050, fax 956 7505, *www.roundhilljamaica.com*; ⑧) draped across an entire hillside just east of town – but it is one of the classiest in Jamaica. Designed in part by Ralph Lauren, with an elegant 36-room hotel and 29 eclectically furnished villas, the 98-acre property exudes taste and opulence. JFK and Jackie O, Audrey Hepburn, Clark Gable and Queen Elizabeth II gave the hotel a reputation for glamour which today attracts an autograph book of famous names. Ordinary Joes may use its facilities – the main pool, tennis courts, gym, art gallery, restaurant and all watersports – for a US$50 daily fee. On Mondays, *Round Hill* hosts a wonderful candlelit beach party with tables and chairs shifted onto the sand, barbecued food and live music (US$55 per head). Otherwise in Hopewell, there are plenty of possibilities for **private rentals** if you ask around, and as the town is nicely detached from MoBay but close enough to to enjoy its benefits, it's worth having a go.

You won't go hungry in Hopewell. There's an excellent bakery renowned for its hardough bread, and a couple of very good **restaurants**, *Love Bird* on Bamboo Hill, which churns out ackee and saltfish, chicken and curry goat to its local regulars and further up the hill, *The Real Kitchin*, with a slightly grander menu. Just west of town, seafood dominates at three restaurants directly in front of the fishing beach, all serving comforting conch and fish soup as well as steamed or fried fish: *Shoreline* is the most upmarket.

Tryall and Mayfield Falls

Three miles west of Hopewell, a towering **water wheel** at the roadside marks the old **Tryall Estate**, a once huge sugar plantation detroyed in the Christmas Rebellion (see p.260) that's now Jamaica's most prestigious **golfing hotel**. Until 1996, *The Tryall Club*, PO Box 1206, Montego Bay (☎956 5660, fax 956 5658, *www.tryallclub.com*; ⑧) hosted the annual Johnny Walker World Championship tournament. The smoothly undulating eighteen-hole course is the best-kept, and reputedly most challenging, on the island, though you'll need deep pockets to examine it; non-*Tryall Club* guests pay US$150 per round plus mandatory caddie service. The hotel, in the plantation's refurbished great house, is unstintingly luxurious; rooms come with every conceivable trapping and most of the self-contained villas have private pools. The 800yd beach is fully equipped for watersports and there are tennis courts and a waterfall pool on site.

The road that turns inland here overlooks the foothills of the Dolphin Head Mountains, a languid series of low-lying hills said to resemble a dolphin (though no-one seems to know *where* you get this perspective). Most of the hillocks are partially cultivated by small-scale farmers, and there's none of the cool air or remoteness of full-scale ranges like the Blue Mountains (see Chapter Two). A right fork at Cold Spring leads to the appealing surrounds of Pondside and Cascade, where there are plenty of undeveloped waterfalls – you'll need local help to find them, and to do any walking in the area, as this is prime ganja-growing territory. However, the best way to get a flavour of the Dolphin Head surrounds is to visit the 22 mini-cascades and numerous swimming spots at Mayfield Falls (daily 9am–5pm; US$10). Two private tour operators, Original Mayfield Falls (☎957 4729) and Riverwalk at Mayfield Falls (☎974 8000) have sites a hundred yards apart on the same stretch of river, which offer the identical experience of a tranquil walk through bamboo-shaded cool water with swimming holes every twenty yards – a fabulous, sensuous treat compared to the contrivances of the more famous Dunn's River Falls (see p.194). Mayfields Falls is not though, the easiest of places to find: signs dot the route from Tryall via Pondside, but you'll probably have to ask about a dozen times. To avoid getting lost, go with a local or join a tour offered by Riverwalk at Mayfield Falls with transport from Montego Bay or Negril and lunch included (US$65 per person). The procedure for starting your tour is similar with both operators: upon arrival you'll be allocated a guide (leave a tip) who helps to carry belongings, points out the easiest route and the best naturally formed swimming pools, and will tell you the local names of the trees, flowers and vines along the banks. Wear a swimming costume and bring flip-flops as the stones are tough on bare, wet feet – mosquitoes can also be a problem. Once at the end, you walk back through richly fruited, hilly pastures dotted with yam banks and fluffy clusters of bamboo. Hiking guides are available for walks in the surrounding mountains, and additionally on Tuesdays and Fridays, the Original Mayfield Falls puts on a show of African song and dance (1–3pm; no extra charge) in front of the bar.

West towards Negril

From Cascade you can drive south straight to Savanna-la-Mar (see p.328), though the road is abominable in places.

Divine Tours Limited (☎957 9777) offers full-day tours to Mayfield Falls from Negril, including a brief stopover at Lucea market; US$54 covers transport, snacks, lunch and entrance fee.

Sandy Bay and Mosquito Cove

Three miles west of Tryall, sleepy, suburban SANDY BAY was founded by Baptist missionaries as a free village for newly liberated slaves. Today it's just a strip of shops, cafés, bakeries and bars, with great views back along the coast to distant Montego Bay, and the incongruous *Lollypop on the Beach* (☎956 2788), a seaside entertainment venue packed to the rafters on weekend nights for its cheesy tourist-oriented reggae shows with a cover charge of US$15–20; it also hosts occasional sound-system nights and stageshows.

Just west of town, pretty MOSQUITO COVE is named for the perfect breeding ground of the Maggoty River shallows; several

See p.376 of Contexts for more on the free villages.

tributaries meet here, spanned by a tiny stone bridge. The pesky mites didn't deter the Amerinidians – remains of **Taino settlements** have been found around here, though there's not a hint of them today. Instead there's a small **beach** of pebble-strewn yellow sand lined by wind-bent palms – assorted flotsam and jetsam hint at the strong undertow that makes swimming risky, so stick to paddling. There are a couple of bar-cum-jerk spots and craft stalls at the edges of the bay.

Inland of Mosquito Cove, horses graze in clipped pastures dotted with the odd run-down windmill, relics of the plantation days when the land was part of the Kenilworth estate. A superb example of old industrial architecture, Kenilworth's **great house** now serves as the HEART Academy (Human Employment and Resource Training), a further education college, signposted off an inland track just past the cove (daily 9am–5pm; free). There are no guided tours, but you can go in and have a look around the surrounding mills, boiling houses and distillery, all now listed buildings under the protection of the Jamaica National Heritage Trust.

Lucea

Built around a crescent-shaped natural harbour, where Henry Morgan (see p.110) moored ships during his respectable period as lieutenant-governor of Jamaica, **LUCEA** (pronounced Lucy) was a flourishing port town during the plantation era, its wharves thronged with ships exporting locally produced sugar. These days, only the occasional shipment of molasses leaves the docks, but the town has another card up its sleeve: the exceptionally tasty **Lucea yam**. A floury-textured tuber with excellent storing properties, it was exported in vast quantities to the thousands of Jamaicans who migrated in the late-nineteenth century to work on sugar plantations or as labourers on the Panama canal, and is still crucial to Lucea's economy.

Despite being the capital of Hanover, Lucea is no showpiece; peeling paint pervades, and even the best buildings display the odd broken window or sagging wall. The faded allure of the Georgian town hall and gingerbread fretwork of the older houses have long prompted calls for Lucea's development as a heritage resort, though in true "soon come" style, nothing much has yet happened, although the town hall is under renovation, and Lucea remains a sleepy sort of place. It's a beguiling town, a perversely aesthetic jumble of austere stone architecture and salt-and-sun-bleached clapboard houses, gaudy storefronts, and snack and rum bars, all clustered around a seething central bus park that hums with the raucous shouts of minibus touts and peanut vendors and the tinny strains of reggae tape stalls. The A1 twists straight through the centre of Lucea, past the bus park and the covered entrance of **Cleveland Stanhope Market**, which spills out onto the streets on Saturdays and draws villagers from miles around.

Just beyond the bus park is the imposing exterior of the once-majestic **town hall** and old **courthouse**, recently restored after years of neglect to its original Georgian grandeur. The roof of the courthouse is topped by an incongruously large **clocktower**. Still keeping perfect time after 170 years, the size of the clock betrays its misplacement – it was originally destined for St Lucia (Lucea's Spanish name was Santa Lucea) but was mistakenly sent to Lucea. Locals became so attached to it that they refused to exchange it for the more modest timepiece originally ordered, raising the difference through public collections. The tower was built with funds donated by a local planter of German origin on the condition that he had a hand in its design, hence the distinctive nippled dome of a German army helmet that forms its roof. The town hall overlooks the official town square, which serves as a traffic roundabout. Formally dedicated as **Alexander Bustamante Square** by England's Queen Elizabeth in 1966, the square was used as a period set for parts of the movie *Cool Runnings*.

Lucea's western portion contains most of the older buildings; particularly noticeable from the road is the towering cut-stone steeple of **Hanover Parish Church**, which dates back to 1725. The church boasts some fine monuments, one by the British sculptor John Flaxman. The cemetery's walled area is a **Jewish burial ground**, presented in 1833 to the large Jewish community who settled here during Lucea's commercial heyday. Toward the sea behind the church, **Rusea's School** (Mon–Sat 8am–4pm; free) was established in 1777 by a benefaction from French religious refugee Martin Rusea, who was so grateful for the help he received when washed ashore at Lucea that he bequeathed his accumulated estates to the parish upon his death in 1764; his disgruntled relatives were not quite so benevolent and contested the will for ten years without success. Originally located at the current Wesleyan mission house, the school was moved to the present site, an old army barracks, in 1900. Just past the school, through a small truck repair yard, is near-derelict **Fort Charlotte**, restored in 1761, though no one is sure when the foundations were first laid. Three of the original cannons remain, and the fort gives a fabulous sweeping view across the harbour.

The Lucea **Infirmary** is adjacent to the museum, just off the main road leading to Negril and adjoining Watson Taylor Park (☎956 2911). The infirmary was the inspiration for the setting up of JAFI (Jamaican and American Friends of the Infirmary), an American charity founded following a trip to Jamaica by gerontologist Paul Scott Rhodes. The charity brings practical aid, such as wheelchairs, sheets and toiletries, to these cash starved homes for the elderly and also encourages visits to the residents who welcome company. If you wish to help or take part in JAFI's annual working vacations, contact JAFI in the USA (☎310 249 7112, *gikirk@aol.com*) or ring the infirmary directly.

West
towards
Negril

See p.391 of Contexts for more on Jews in Jamaica.

As you leave town towards Negril, scrubby playing fields mark the way to Lucea's main bathing spot, windblown **Watson Taylor public beach**. This is not one of Jamaica's best and it's generally the preserve of locals who pick up the rubbish and maintain the rudimentary facilities. The miniature cove is sheltered by rocks, and there's a little sea grass, but the swimming is good and the water clean. Overlooking the beach is the excellent **Hanover Museum** (Mon–Sat 10.30am–4.30pm; J$100). A former British barracks, the red-brick building has also seen service as a prison, police station and firing range – you can see the original stocks and lock-up rooms complete with newly concreted stone "beds". Blackened timbers purport to the fire that almost destroyed the structure in 1985; it suffered a further battering from Hurricane Gilbert in 1988, the year it was awarded the prestigious Heritage Architecture Award. In honour of the settlements discovered at nearby Mosquito Cove (see p.293), recreations of Taino dwellings and canoes stand in the backyard, flanked by a traditional canoe hollowed from a silk cotton tree. Other artefacts have been made by present day Amerindians living in South America and the Caribbean. The main museum offers a surprisingly comprehensive glimpse into local history, with several aerial photos of Hanover, old English weights and measures displayed alongside records of the west African ancestors of various Lucea citizens, maps, "jackass rope tobacco" (a long coil of dried tobacco leaves, resembling the rope used to tether a donkey and smoked by poor Jamaicans in the nineteenth century), a chunk of Lucea yam, and a copy of a harbour map hand-drawn by Captain Bligh who lived in Lucea for four years. The Ian Robinson research centre upstairs has a small collection of West Indian history books and there's a good gift shop selling locally made crafts.

Lucea-based Hanover Historical Society (☎956 2584, www.jamaica history.com) is the best source of in-depth local information.

Around Lucea

From the town centre, a twenty-minute drive inland along the B9 will take you to **BLENHEIM**, birthplace of National Hero Alexander Bustamante. The shack in which Jamaica's first prime minister grew up has been converted into a small but interesting museum (daily 9am–5pm; J$130) celebrating Bustamante's life and achievements. The grounds surrounding the museum make a great picnic spot with a large mango tree for shade and staggering views over the hills.

The other inland road parallels the Lucea East River and circumvents the Dolphin Head Mountains, an undeveloped wilderness area known for its abundant bird life and 23 endemic plants including species of orchid and bromeliad. At present there are no **organized tours** into the area; you may be able to arrange an ad hoc guide at the tiny village of **Askenish**, the nearest settlement to the highest peak, or at Mayfield Falls (see p.293).

West of Lucea, the coastal scenery is immensely attractive; foliage drips down over the road from the inland side and deserted coves

Chief Busta

Wild-haired and brutishly handsome, Sir William Alexander Bustamante's physical stature, charismatic appeal and legendary appetite for women earned him a fond notoriety in the ribald world of Jamaican politics. Born Alexander Clarke on February 24, 1884 into an impoverished family working on the Blenheim estate, Bustamante was architect of his own destiny, rising to political prominence through a mixture of insight, cunning and cynical manipulation of the illiterate populace who came to worship him as "Busta" or simply "Chief".

He left Jamaica at nineteen in search of better prospects, and his years away are veiled in mystery. Though he's said to have begun cutting cane and labouring alongside other migrants, he returned nearly thirty years later with an assumed surname and enough wealth to become a small-time money lender, a shrewd move that gave him clandestine influence before he entered the political arena.

Settling in Kingston, the Jamaica he returned to was still firmly under Britain's imperial grip and languishing with it; pay and working conditions for those lucky enough to have a job were abysmal, and the polarities between the ruling brown-and-whites and the black majority were as sharp as ever. Bustamante allied himself with the workers and became their unofficial spokesman; his outspoken condemnation of these inequalities began to win support. By 1938 his "fire and brimstone" warnings of racial violence and black revolution (designed to scare the colonial authorities into action) were almost realized; fanned by Bustamante's inflammatory rhetoric, a violent confrontation between police and workers broke out at the West Indies Sugar Company in Frome, Westmoreland, sparking a wave of rebellions and strikes that brought the whole island to a near-standstill for months. Eclipsing the tentative support for black nationalist labour leader William Grant, Bustamante formed the **Bustamante Industrial Trade Union** – still the island's main union – and became the leader of the labour movement among the rank and file.

*See p.327 for
more on
Frome.*

In 1940, distressed at the volatility of his speeches, the government seized on Bustamante's union involvement and imprisoned him as the ringleader of the 1938 unrest – he spent seventeen months in jail plotting his future. On his release in 1942 he formed the **Jamaica Labour Party** and swept to victory at the island's first election in 1944, trouncing his first cousin Norman Manley's People's National Party so decisively that Manley lost even in his own constituency. Though the PNP enjoyed a few years of power between 1955 and 1961, it was the JLP who ruled when Jamaica was granted independence in 1962, and Sir Bustamante – he was knighted by Queen Elizabeth II in 1954 – who danced with Princess Margaret during the ensuing celebrations. He remained active in politics until 1967 and died a National Hero on August 6, 1977, aged 93.

swing temptingly into sight around each precarious corner. **Bull Bay Beach**, five minutes west of Lucea, is a nice spot for a swim; the two pristine white-sand coves are usually deserted and *Sally Faithful's* across the road provides refreshments. At **Lance's Bay**, three miles west of Lucea, **Ron's Arawak Cave** (daily 9am–5pm; 2hr tour; US$10) is signposted from the road. The impressive cave is a mile long with plenty of intricate stalactite and stalagmite formations, a mineral pool and faint markings on the wall made by bat guano miners, long since gone, to help them navigate the various chambers and tunnels. Ron himself is an engaging tour guide, pointing out anthropomorphic shapes in the cave walls and playing the stalagmites like a musical instrument. There are possibilities to rent a room in a private house on the pretty beach at Lance's Bay; just ask around.

Practicalities

You can see Lucea's sights on foot in a day, but it's an engaging kind of place and if you do choose to **stay**, better options than the overpriced, anonymous *West Palm Hotel* (☎956 2321; ②) are *Global Villa* (☎956 2916, in the UK ☎0121 554 1410; ②) a small clean guesthouse situated slightly west of town at Esher, or Mrs Cousin's homely rooms at *Leila Cousins*, Malcolm Heights, PO Box 4742 Lucea (contact Marguerite Curtin at the Hanover Museum, ☎956 2584; ③ with breakfast included). For **eating**, there's the Rasta-striped shack *Vital Ital*, on your right as you enter Lucea from Montego Bay, serving delicious bowls of soup and vegetable stew; for spaghetti and burgers try the *D&S Restaurant and Grill* in town and if it's Jamaican food you're after any number of cookshops in the large market do delicious box lunches of chicken, rice and peas. Taking an ironic slant on the well-known chain of the same name, the *Hard Rock Café* by the town hall is another worthy Jamaican eatery.

Practically all of the **buses** and **minibuses** that connect MoBay and Negril terminate at Lucea's central bus park; you simply change services to complete the journey. To avoid long waits, ignore the touts and choose a bus that's almost full. The fare from Lucea to Negril is around J$60.

Green Island, Orange Bay and Rhodes Hall

Several miles out of Lances Bay, **COUSINS COVE**, a small roadside community with a welcoming cafe, *Joe's*, was widely but controversially acknowledged to be the inspiration behind *One People*, Guy Kennaway's hilarious novel about Jamaican village life (see p.422). There are very few good reasons to stop in **GREEN ISLAND**, a scruffy harbour town six miles west of Lucea, which is also home to the only secondary school for miles around – consequently most of Negril's burgeoning youth population commutes to it daily. However, well worth a visit is the yard of Abdel Mason, master woodcarver whose bold sculptures (particularly of women) have won high acclaim; his place is adjacent to the post office. Just out of town, the *Crystal Bar* is a spanking new rest-stop facility for drinks or basic Jamaican meals, and small, clean, fan-cooled **rooms** are available at *JJ's Guesthouse* (☎956 9159; ②), on a breezy hill off the main road.

Three or four miles down the coast, **ORANGE BAY** boasts the unspoilt **Half Moon Bay Beach** (☎957 6467; daily 8am till late;

J$80 entrance, redeemable at the bar), full of the paradisical charm that originally brought tourists to Negril. The wide curve of white sand has no braiding booths, jet skis or hassle, just a little sea grass and some small islets; nude bathing is perfectly acceptable and snorkel equipment cheap, and the **restaurant** (daily 8am–10pm) serves excellent chicken, fish and sandwiches. The overgrown flat track behind the restaurant was once an illegal airstrip used for ganja smuggling; today it hosts occasional dirt-bike races. Set back from the sand, there are two wooden cabins (②) for overnight stays; **camping** is also possible (US$5, US$10 if you rent a tent) and security provided. The *Hurricane Bar*, in the small strip of bars past the beach, is the perfect place for a seafront beer.

Just past Orange Bay, **Rhodes Hall Plantation** (☎957 6333; *www.fantasyisle.com*) is a 550-acre coconut, banana, plantain, pear and coconut farm with two private **beaches** – one a shallow sea-grassy reef beach with a freshwater mineral spring bubbling under the brine, the other a more conventional sugar-sanded curve. Volleyball and football pitches and a restaurant/bar back onto the beaches, as do two luxurious two-bedroom **cottages** (⑨). **Horse-riding** is also an option; the well-kept mounts trot into the hills and along the beach (US$30-50, depending on length of ride). The property also covers an area of pristine **mangrove swamp**, home to a few wild Jamaican **crocodiles** – if you can't see any in the open section, you'll usually find some sunning themselves in a fenced-off enclosure.

Negril

Jamaica's shrine to permissive indulgence, **NEGRIL** has metamorphosed from deserted fishing beach to full-blown resort town in little over two decades. Though it's hard to imagine once you've seen today's overdeveloped strip, in the late 1960s the population was well under a hundred and the only visitors were day-tripping Jamaicans. By the 1970s, hippies had discovered a virgin paradise of palms and pristine sand, and the picture of beach camping, ganja smoking and chemically enhanced sunsets set the tone for today's free-spirited attitude. Thanks to deliberately risqué resorts like the infamous **Hedonism II**, Negril is widely perceived as a place where inhibitions are lost and pleasures of the flesh rule. The traditional menu of ganja and reggae – Negril has a deserved reputation for its **live music** – draws a young crowd, but the north-coast resort ethic has muscled in too – all-inclusives pepper the coast and are encroaching on the only remaining undeveloped section of Negril's seven miles of beach, Bloody Bay, while hustling has increased to an irritating degree.

Nonetheless, Negril shrugs off its minor irritations and remains supremely chilled-out – every conversation starts and ends with

For a humorous and entertaining introduction to Negril, read resident and hotelier Mark Conklin's novel, Banana Shout, *based on the outlandish real-life events that shaped the beginnings of Negril as a tourist resort.*

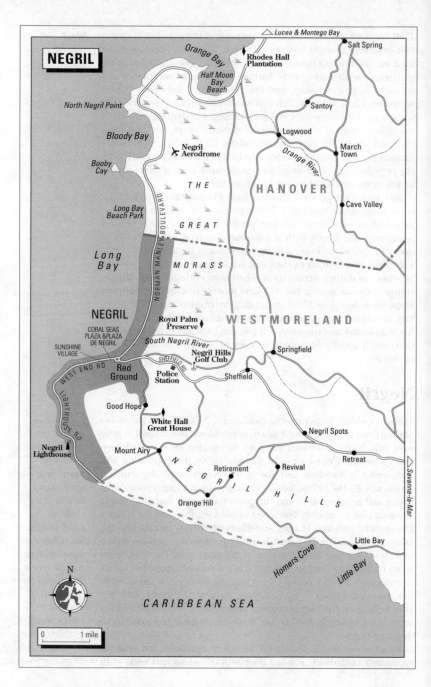

"Rent-a-dread"

Jamaica is a carnal kind of country, and while there's no sex tourism industry as such, monetary-based holiday liaisons are a well-established convention. Fuelled by tropical abandon and the island's pervasive sexuality,
the lure of the "big bamboo" prompts some unusual partnerships. Middle-
aged women strolling hand in hand with handsome young studs has
become such a normality that pejorative epithets – "**Rent-a-dread**" or
"**Rastitute**" – for the young men who make a career out of these cynical
liaisons have entered the lexicon.

The butt of many jokes, conventional specimens are muscle-bound
models of the latest mini-trunks and expensive sneakers topped off with
dreadlocks – or hair extensions if they can't manage the real thing.
However, not all gigolos come in the same package; a "Rastitute" is equally likely to appear in the form of an Ital-style Rasta who woos with talk of
natural living and postulates sex with white tourists as an expression of
racial unity.

In a country of scant possibilities and high unemployment, becoming a
gigolo is a practical career move for many young Jamaicans. Negril is a
centre for this kind of trade-off, and many women regularly return specifically to partake of an injection of "Jamaican steel", some forming relationships that span several years of holiday time. This makes life rather difficult if sex is not a part of your holiday vision as single women are almost
unanimously assumed to be out for one thing only – prepare yourself for a
barrage of propositions.

Male tourists are less involved in the holiday romance scenario, but
female prostitutes are common and men should expect to be frequently
propositioned; in Negril the prostitution scene is firmly ingrained. If you
do choose to indulge, make sure that you practise safe sex; one in five
prostitutes are HIV-positive and STDs – including syphilis – are rife (see
Basics, p.31).

"Irie" or "no problem" – and addicts come back year after year for the
best sunsets in Jamaica and a resort that offers pretty much everything anyone could ask for on holiday. Pristine miles of sand with
comprehensive watersports facilities, open-air dancing to rated
Jamaican musicians, a wide range of eating and drinking joints and
gregarious company are all on offer here. Many visitors have stayed
on permanently and the consequent blurring of the distinctions
between tourists and locals make for a relaxed, natural interaction
that's a refreshing change from other resorts.

Some history

Negril's isolation – until very recently completely cut off from the
mainland by the Great Morass, Long Bay and the smaller Bloody Bay
– has been central to its history; even its Spanish name *Punto de
Negrilla* or "dark point" referred to the west tip's remoteness as
much as to the black eels that once thrived in its rivers. During
British rule, Negril's seclusion was used both to protect British ships
sailing home under the cover of armed men-of-war and to attack

Spanish vessels straying off course to Cuba. It also provided an ideal hideout for **pirates** in the eighteenth century (see box below), and for the export of **ganja** in more recent years. In 1996, over-zealous coast guards opened fire on a seaplane owned by Island Outpost boss Chris Blackwell, assuming that the cargo was drugs rather than, as was the case, various members of the band U2 and country and western singer Jimmy Buffet; fortuitously the volleys missed and pop fans were spared a tragedy, though the shame-faced coast guards were cornered into a public apology. The town has also played a part in war: in 1814, fifty English warships and some 6000 men, including 1000 Jamaicans from the West Indian Regiment, sailed from Negril to Louisiana to fight the Battle of New Orleans.

In 1959, a coast road was laid from Green Island, and Negril was for the first time connected to the rest of Jamaica. Its beauty was soon discovered by foreign hippy travellers, who brought Negril's charms to wider attention and spawned a **tourist industry**. Developers were quick to step in, and by the early 1980s the once-empty curve of beach was smothered with all the trappings of a full-blown resort. International attention was captured by tales of debauchery at the notorious *Hedonism II* resort, and Negril's reputation as Jamaica's devil-may-care holiday hotspot was assured.

In recent years the town has worked hard to solve its infrastructural problems: Negril now has an efficent central sewage system, a new mains supply of water, and is also on its way to being linked to

---

Negril's women pirates

One of Negril's proudest moments came when the reign of **Calico Jack Rackham**, the most famous and notorious buccaneer to terrorize Jamaican waters, was brought to an end here in November 1720. Rackham – called "Calico" in reference to his preferred underwear – and his crew had moored their captured sloop in Bloody Bay to celebrate recent plunders along the north coast, unaware that their every move was bring shadowed by one Captain Barnet of the British navy. Made inattentive by rum punch, the pirates were quickly overwhelmed. Some surrendered instantly, but two, in particular, put up a mighty struggle – even turning their weapons on their more malleable crew members. Eventually, these last two were subdued – at which point naval officers were atonished to find that they were **women** in disguise. Famously ruthless and bloodthirsty in battle, **Anne Bonney**, Rackham's former mistress, and **Mary Read** formed a courageous double act and were instrumental in earning Rackham his infamy as a freebooter. At their trial, victim Dorothy Thomas noted that "they wore men's jackets and long trousers... each of them had a machete and a pistol in their hands, and cursed and swore".

Rackham was executed, his body displayed in an iron frame at the Kingston cay that now bears his name. Bonney and Read were also sentenced to death, but were spared when they declared themselves pregnant and eventually reprieved. Anne Bonney disappeared from recorded history, while Mary Read died of yellow fever and is buried in St Catherine.

Montego Bay (and the airport) by a brand new coast road. The flip-side of all these improvements is that the resort continues to grow and the whole of Bloody Bay, the last piece of virgin beach remaining in Negril, is now staked for hotel development. Nevertheless it is still possible to find the laid-back charm and gorgeous scenery that first brought tourists to Negril.

Arrival and information

Arriving in Negril is straightforward; **buses** from Lucea drop off on the A1 just before the central roundabout – if you're staying on Norman Manley Boulevard, bus drivers will drop you off outside your hotel. Buses from Savanna-la-Mar terminate at the top end of Sheffield Road, from where you can charter a taxi to the West End or beach (see below) for about US$5. Domestic **flights** land at Negril Aerodrome at Bloody Bay; taxis are waiting but fares can be ridiculous – a reasonable price is between US$7 and US$10.

Buses to Savanna-la-Mar and Lucea depart every half-hour; the fare is J$50–60.

The **Jamaica Tourist Board office** is on the first floor of Coral Seas Plaza opposite the roundabout (☎957 4597; Mon–Fri 9am–5pm, Sat 9am–1pm), it stocks various local freesheets, all of which carry local maps, listings and news. Pretty-pink JTB **information booths** are located at the main craft market by the roundabout and on West End Road opposite *Tensing Pen* hotel.

Alternatively the Yacht Club (☎957 9224, *www.yachtclub.com*) on West End Road has set itself up as a one-stop shop, offering not only accommodation, watersports, bike rental and taxi services but also informal advice; the staff are friendly and trustworthy.

For bike and car rental outlets and taxis on the phone see pp.325 and 326.

Orientation and getting around

Negril doesn't really have a "town centre", just a roundabout right on the coast that feeds its three streets: **Norman Manley Boulevard**, which runs parallel to the Long Bay and Bloody Bay beaches and the Great Morass wetlands; the quieter **West End/Lighthouse Road** which winds along the cliffs to Jamaica's west tip; and **Sheffield Road**, the route to Savanna-la-Mar.

You don't need a **car** if you're going to stay in town. **Shared taxis** run the length of the beach and West End Road all day every day, and charge between J$20 and J$50 from the roundabout to the lighthouse or Bloody Bay – you can flag them down anywhere en route. **Chartering a taxi** can be expensive, particularly at the far reaches of the cliffs, but competition is high, so you should be able to haggle – US$5 from the roundabout to Bloody Bay is reasonable. There is no local bus service to the roundabout from the beach or cliffs. Other than **walking**, by far the most popular way of getting around is moped, motorbike or bicycle. **Dirt bikes** rent for around US$40 per day, mopeds from US$30 and bicycles from US$10. Alternatively you could take a **water taxi** from the Yacht Club on the West End to

Private taxis charge around US$70 for the MoBay to Negril ride; alternatively try hitching a lift with a hotel transfer bus for approx US$20 per person each way.

the beach (US$5 each way) or, if you're staying on the cliffs try flagging down a glass-bottomed boat on its way to the beach – *Famous Vincent Elvira* is a good choice.

Organized tours

As Negril tends to attract those who want to stay put and relax, the roster of available tours in Negril is pretty paltry in comparison to Ocho Rios or Montego Bay. Most tour operators offer the same roster listed in the Montego Bay chapter (p.250) and a few options in southern Jamaica. Standard trips include a Black River safari (approx US$60 per person) with a visit to the YS Falls, a typical Jamaican lunch and finishing with a crocodile search along the Black River, a nature tour to Mayfield Falls (US$55 per person), and a beach party (US$35 per person) with folklore show, creole picnic and rum punch on the beach. Try local operators Divine Tours Limited (☎957 9777, *www.divine.tours@cwjamaica.com*) and Jameka Tours (☎957 0129, *www.jahhiya.com*) who offer all of the above tours and are amenable to bargaining.

Bicycle tours are an excellent way to explore the countryside; Rusty's X-cellent Adventures, situated past the lighthouse on West End Road (☎957 0155, *www.webstudios/rusty.com*), has a series of trails through the ganja landing strips and deserted beaches of greater Negril; the top-of-the-range mountain bikes and the pace demand good riding ability. Rusty's is also the headquarters of the Jamaica Mountain Bike Association which organizes an annual Fat Tyre Festival in Negril (during the second week in February) with championship mountain bike races and bicycle bashments. Or you

---

Spring Break

Every year, between the end of February and the Easter weekend, upwards of twenty thousand American college students arrive in Jamaica for **Spring Break** – a non-stop carnival of fun if you're nineteen, and a rude shattering of the (relative) peace if you're not – and well over half go straight to Negril. Heavily promoted by the Jamaican Tourist Board in their widening quest for niche markets, Spring Break in Jamaica is the one time of the year when hotels can still guarantee one-hundred-percent occupancy with many given over entirely to Spring Breakers. If wet T-shirt competitions, drinking challenges and dancing in pina-colada flavoured foam are your thing, then this is the time to head for Negril – otherwise be warned. *Margueritaville* is the self-appointed headquarters for Spring Break, in both MoBay (also popular with Spring Breakers) and Negril; *Legends*, *Risky Business* and the *Yacht Club* all put on special events, and the season is sponsored by both Red Stripe beer and Appleton's Rum. This is also a good time to see **live music** with some of Jamaica's best DJs and bands making the most of a large, enthusiastic audience.

Travel agents that specialize in Spring Break packages include *Apple Vacations* (in US ☎1-800 727 3400), *Student Travel Services* (in US ☎1-800 648 4849) or *Sunsplash Tours* (in US ☎1-800 426 7710).

---

could try Superherb, a genial local (☎773 3335 mobile) who knows every inch of the area and sometimes takes groups out on bikes.

Alternatively, hire a **local driver** and set off on your own; Tony Vassell at Tykes Bikes (☎957 0388) opposite *Tensing Pen* hotel, and Kenny Tours taxis which operate from *Rockhouse* are both recommended. Otherwise call the Negril branch of JUTA (☎957 4620, 9699 or 9197).

Accommodation

Negril has over two thousand **beds**, split between the cliffs and beach. Easily the more popular location, the **beach** reeks of commercial vitality. Most hotels have commandeered semi-private areas of beach with sun loungers and security guards, while smaller hotels and those on the inland side of the road simply use whatever piece of sand is closest. Inland properties are often cheaper, but as they back straight onto the Great Morass, bugs can be a problem. The all-inclusives congregate towards **Bloody Bay**, well away from the polluted South Negril River. The quieter **West End** has a degree of privacy lacking at the beach, though steep open-access cliffs make it a bad choice if travelling with children. There are more budget options here and rates are often open to negotiation, especially if you're planning a long stay; *Dreamscape Villas* (☎957 4495) has serviceable, well-equipped "efficiency apartments" on the cliffs for extended rental. Try also *Divor Realty* on West End Road (☎957 4346, fax 957 0251, *divorrealty@cwjamaica.com*), which has a couple of two- and one-bedroom cottages for rent, all with kitchen facilities and fan, and rates from US$385–900 per week with a group rate for renting all these units together at US$3000 per week for up to twelve people max. *Freedom Villa*, opposite the beach on Norman Manley Boulevard (☎957 3181, fax 957 3181, *www.jamaica-villa.com*) is a rather fine five-bedroom colonial-style mansion which can accommodate up to twelve adults and costs US$2178 for the whole villa per week, or US$449 per room per week.

As Negril's planning regulations prevent building anything higher than a palm tree, a lot of accommodation is in traditional circular palm-thatched **cottages**. Though much cooler than concrete, many of these are ludicrously easy to break into. Also popular in Negril is the **pillar cabin**, a round cottage set on top of a stone column, with a shower below and the advantage of catching the best breezes. Locals cite the lonely reaches of West End Road as problematic in terms of **security**; wherever you stay, always make sure that doors and windows are secure and check ID before you let anyone in. Twenty-four-hour security is sensible if you plan to **camp**, though if you're willing to rough it and risk it, there are plenty of cabins and campsites with few facilities and negligible security on the morass side of Norman Manley Boulevard.

The beach

Beachcomber Club, PO Box 98, Norman Manley Blvd; ☎957 4170, fax 957 4097. Sparsely planted gardens with garishly painted accommodation blocks. Spacious rooms with four-poster beds, plus pool, games room and popular Italian restaurant. Under 12s stay free and baby-sitting is available. ⑤.

See p.312 for the map of Negril – Long Bay

Charela Inn, PO Box 33, Norman Manley Blvd; ☎957 4277, fax 957 4414, *www.charela.com*. French–Jamaican-owned place with gardens, pool, carpeted rooms with four-poster beds, and an air of cultured elegance. Rates include a cruise, watersports and folklore shows. Three night minimum stay. ⑥.

Chippewa Village Hotel, Norman Manley Blvd; ☎ & fax 957 4676, *www.chippewavillage.com*. Friendly and laid-back resort with attractive self-contained apartments and wooden cabins. Overlooks the Great Morass and Negril hills. Swimming pool, sun deck and communal dining area. ④.

Country Country, Negril P.O, Norman Manley Blvd; ☎957 4273, fax 957 4342, *www.countrynegril.com*. Brightly-painted cottages set in a garden on particularly lovely stretch of beach. The rooms are spacious and have a fridge, a/c and ceiling fans. There are two good restaurants, one of which is the only Chinese restaurant in Negril. ⑥.

Firefly, PO Box 54, Norman Manley Blvd; ☎957 4358, fax 957 3447, *firefly @jamaicalink.com*. Rooms, studios and cottages, with an outdoor whirlpool, beach bar and free access to the *Swept Away* hotel's sports facilities. ⑤.

Golden Sunset, PO Box 21, Norman Manley Blvd; ☎957 4241, fax 957 4761, *www.thegoldensunset.com*. Long-established and reliable, though across the road from the beach. Clean rooms or cabins with fan, kitchenette and private or shared bath. ④.

Negril Cabins, PO Box 118, Norman Manley Blvd; ☎957 5350, fax 957 5381, *www.negril-cabins.com*. Well-equipped cabins in a garden backing onto the Great Morass. Excellent food and a full range of facilities, including a "private" section of Bloody Bay. Good for kids; under-12s stay free and there's a playground on the beach. ⑤.

Negril Tree House, PO Box 29, Norman Manley Blvd; ☎957 4287, fax 957 4368, *jackson@cwjamaica.com*. A clean, comfortable and appealing complex of rooms and villas. Two bars, one built round a tree and restaurant, pool and watersports. ⑤.

Negril Yoga Centre, PO Box 48, Norman Manley Blvd; ☎957 4397, *www .negrilyoga.com*. Yoga centre and guesthouse overlooking the Great Morass. Attractive cottages of varying degrees of comfort surrounded by heaps of greenery. Wholefood cooking and yoga classes available. ②.

Nirvana on the Beach, Negril PO, Norman Manley Blvd; ☎957 4314, fax 957 9196, *www.nirvananegril.com*. Semi-luxurious wooden cottages in an unusually beautiful sand garden shaded by tall trees and dotted with sculptures and hammocks. Friendly atmosphere, kooky decorative touches and free pass to *Swept Away*'s sports facilities nearby. ⑥.

Perseverance, PO Box 17, Norman Manley Blvd; ☎957 4333. Budget accommodation across the road from the beach; clean and comfortable with fan and shared or private bath. ②.

Rondel Village, PO Box 96, Norman Manley Blvd; ☎957 4413, fax 957 4915, *www.negril.com/rondmain.htm*. Lots of greenery surrounding the fully equipped villas and comfortable rooms with tiny TV and occasional kitchenette. Pool, jacuzzi, restaurant and beach bars. ⑤.

Roots Bamboo, Norman Manley Blvd; ☎957 4479, fax 957 9191, *rootsbamboo@toj.com*. Friendly, efficient place that's one of Negril's most popular budget options and live music venue. Cottages are small but cosy; some have private showers or there's a communal row. Cheap Jamaican restaurant and a campsite with 24-hr security and showers. Often noisy due to thrice-weekly gigs. ②.

Sea Gem, Norman Manley Blvd; ☎ & fax 957 4318, *www.negril.com*. One of the beach's classiest hotels with imaginative and stylish Mexican tiling, calico fabrics and large bathrooms. Good restaurant on site. ⑤.

Sea Splash, PO Box 3123, Norman Manley Blvd; ☎957 4041, fax 957 4049, *www.seasplash.com*. Spacious, clean, upscale one-bed units with screens, lounge and kitchenette. Attractive gardens with a pool, Jacuzzi, mini-gym, beach bar and gourmet restaurant; meal plans available. ⑤.

Sunny Cottages, Norman Manley Blvd; ☎957 4741. Friendly guesthouse on the beach. Basic rooms, with hot water and fans. Breakfast café and shop on site. ②.

Westport Cottages, PO Box 2626; ☎957 4736. Budget travellers' haven at the roundabout end of the beach. The basic cabins are starkly furnished but comfortable, with fan, mosquito nets, outdoor bathroom and communal cooking area. ①.

Whistling Bird, Norman Manley Blvd; ☎957 4403, fax 957 3252, *www.negril.com*. Beach cottages set in a lovely garden with cook-to-order restaurant. Very private. ⑤.

West End

Addis Kokeb, PO Box 78, Summerset Rd; ☎818 7331. Communal living in the main building or handsome hardwood cabins in fruited and flowered gardens. Cooking facilities are shared, and you can use the pool at *Summerset Village* next door. ②-③.

See p.316 for the map of Negril – West End.

Banana Shout, PO Box 4, Lighthouse Rd; ☎ & fax 957 0384, *www.negril.com/bananashout*. Simple but attractive cottages in lily-ponded gardens or right on the cliffs. Kitchenette, ceiling fan, hammocks on the verandah and Haitian art. The cliff portion has a diving platform, sun deck, its own cave and exceptional sunset views. ③.

Blue Cave Castle, PO Box 66, West End Rd; ☎957 4845, *www.negril.com/bluecavecastle*. Pastel-painted castle on the rocks, a curious mix of high kitsch and careful luxury. Individually decorated rooms built over a cave that extends underneath the road (excellent swimming). ③.

Catcha Falling Star, PO Box 22, Lighthouse Rd; ☎957 0390, fax 957 0629. Attractive gardens crisscrossed by pathways, lots of grassy sunbathing spots and excellent sea access. Most of the split-level cottages have verandahs with hammocks, a few have waterbeds, and all have fridge and access to the communal kitchen. Rates include full breakfast. ⑤.

Drumville Cove, PO Box 72, West End Rd; ☎957 4369, fax 957 9198, *wadrommond@colif.com*. Imaginative cliffside setting with a quiet serenity and eclectic accommodations. There's a bar, swimming pool, diving platforms, sun deck, table tennis and restaurant. ④.

Heart Beat, PO Box 95, West End Rd; ☎957 4329, fax 957 0069. Family-run collection of cabins, cottages and rooms, all featuring lots of wood and Balinese fabrics. Two swimming/sunbathing decks and a cliffside gazebo. ③.

Negril

Home Sweet Home, PO Box 2, West End Rd; ☎957 4478, *www .homesweethomeresort.net*. Small cheerful resort popular with young Americans. All rooms have ocean view. Swimming pool, Jacuzzi, restaurant, cliffside sun deck. ⑤.

Jackie's on the Reef, Negril PO, Lighthouse Rd; ☎957 4997. Breezy alternative-style place with all sorts of holistic therapies on offer – massage, yoga, t'ai chi, you name it. Private cottages or expansive units in the main house, all simply but carefully decorated – there's a saltwater pool if the sea gets too rough. Four night minimum stay. ⑥.

Lighthouse Park, PO Box 3, Lighthouse Rd; ☎957 4490. Sprawling, densely vegetated section of clifftop with basic but serviceable A-frame cabanas, villas and camping. There's a communal kitchen and a gazebo with hammocks. Gay friendly. ①—③.

LTU Villas, PO Box 2875, West End Rd; ☎957 0382, *www.negril.com /ltuvillas*. Spacious rooms in quiet gardens opposite one of Negril's best bars the *LTU Pub*. A great-value option offering rooms with lounge, fridge and balcony. ③.

Mariners Inn, PO Box 16, West End Rd; ☎957 4474, fax 957 0391, *www .negril.com/marinersinn*. Medium-sized retreat with attractive wood-panelled rooms and facilities including a dive centre, swimming pool and games room patronized by local pool wizards. Great sea swimming and a boat-shaped bar. ③.

Mirage, PO Box 33, West End Rd; ☎957 0386, fax 957 4414. The round cottages (often privately rented), or tile-floored oceanfront rooms are much nicer than the hotel rooms, but all enjoy a large gazebo, sun deck, and cliff access with diving board. ④.

Moonlight Villa, West End Rd; ☎957 4838, *moonlightvilla@excite.com*. Spacious rooms in attractive oceanfront villa, all with large beds and fridge. Private sun deck and outside grill for barbecues. ③.

Native Shelter, Negril PO, West End Rd; ☎957 0159. Self-contained apartments above and around a private home, with good security and a tranquil family atmosphere. ③.

New Moon Cottage, West End Rd; ☎957 4305. Clean and quiet rooms in a Jamaican family home with cooking facilities. Camping available. ②

Ocean Edge, PO Box 71, West End Rd; ☎957 4362, fax 957 4849. Atmospheric, budget-friendly property straddling the road. Accommodation is split between rooms, some with kitchenette, and two private cottages, and there's a cliff diving board, pool, Jacuzzi, restaurant and bar. ③—④.

Primrose Inn, c/o Gus Hylton, Negril PO; ☎957 4399. Basic "home from home" set back from the road in a yard dominated by a large ackee tree. Rooms are off an open corridor laced with hammocks; all have fan and double bed and most have a cold-water bathroom. Bad dogs take care of security. ①.

Rockhouse, PO Box 3024, West End Rd; ☎957 4373, fax 957 0557, *www .rockhousehotel.com*. Enviable location, Mediterranean styling, magnificent thatched bar/restaurant and saltwater pool on a rock peninsula ensure unique and stylish comfort. Thatched studios or villas with glass-doored patio overlooking the ocean, outdoor shower, fan and bamboo four-poster beds draped with muslin nets. Innovative and deservedly expensive restaurant. ⑤.

Secret Paradise, PO Box 56, Lighthouse Rd; ☎ & fax 957 4882. Rambling resort that's quiet to the point of inertia but attractive and very private. Large clover-shaped pool, landscaped cove with nude bathing area, restaurant and bar. Rooms are pretty basic but very clean with fan; some have kitchen. The five-bed units are good value at US$45 per person per night. ③–④.

Summerset Village, PO Box 80, Summerset Rd; ☎957 4409, fax 957 4078. Set in seven fruited acres with a large pool, restaurant, bar and games room, the eclectic accommodation ranges from regular room blocks to a five-bed wood-panelled thatch house at US$45 per person per night. ③–④.

Tensing Pen, PO Box 13, Lighthouse Rd; ☎957 0387, fax 957 0161, *www .tensingpen.com*. Stylish and exclusive retreat in pretty clifftop gardens with imaginatively decorated bamboo and wood cottages graced with individual touches, and a well-equipped communal kitchen/lounge. Some of the cliffs are linked by a tiny suspension bridge. ⑤.

Villas Sur Mer, Negril PO, Lighthouse Rd; ☎957 0377, fax 957 0177. Thoughtfully designed and decorated luxury villas right on the cliffs, with marble bathrooms, breezy living rooms, full staff and a wooden boardwalk complete with pool and Jacuzzi. ⑤.

Xtabi, PO Box 19, West End Rd; ☎957 4336, fax 957 0827, *www .xtabi-negril.com*. Well-organized West End veteran with flowering gardens and a network of caves. Oceanside rooms are wooden cabins with private sun deck and sea access or two-storey concrete cottages with kitchen. Pool, open-air restaurant and bar and countless swimming platforms. ④.

All-inclusives

Beaches Negril, Negril PO, Norman Manley Blvd; ☎957 9270, fax 957 9269, *www.beaches.com* (in US ☎305/284-1300, fax 667-8996; in UK ☎020 7581 9895, fax 823 8758). One of two *Sandals* family-oriented resorts in Negril (the other being neighbouring *Beaches Inn*), but as children over two years old can only stay in one of the more luxurious rooms (there are nine categories) and singles pay a US$110 surcharge, the excellent facilities don't come cheap. Three restaurants, pasta bar, beach grill, five bars, two pools, all watersports, tennis courts, a fitness centre, disco, nightly entertainment and supervised children's activities. Babies under two stay free, children up to 16 pay US$70 per night. Three night minimum stay. ⑧.

The Caves, PO Box 3113, Lighthouse Rd; ☎957 0270, fax 957 4939, *www .islandoutpost.com*. Gorgeous small hotel set behind Fort Knox gates and patronized by celebrities who are helicoptered in. Cottage-style rooms are funkily designed and include batik bathrobes and CD players. On-site facilities include a spa, Jacuzzi and sauna. ⑧.

Grand Lido, PO Box 88, Norman Manley Blvd; ☎957 5010, fax 957 5138, *www.superclubs.com*. One of the island's swankiest all-inclusives in a dream location on Bloody Bay, and altogether mellower than its nearby cousin *Hedonism II*. All watersports are included, as is a nightly cruise on the luxury *M/Y Zein*, former yacht of Aristotle Onassis, and there are four top-quality places to eat – book early for the fantastic *Piacere* restaurant. ⑧.

Hedonism II, PO Box 25, Norman Manley Blvd; ☎957 5200, fax 957 5214, *www.superclubs.com* (in US ☎954 925 0925, in UK ☎01749 677200). Anything goes at *Hedonism II*, a fast-paced, singles-bar-on-sea, complete with nudist beach and popular late-night Jacuzzis. Though there are plenty of couples, the raunchy reputation attracts far more men (mostly North Americans) than women, and it can feel like one long stag night, but it's great fun if you're in the mood. ⑦–⑧.

Point Village, PO Box 105, Norman Manley Blvd: ☎957 5170, fax 957 5351, *www.pointvillage.com*. Great location opposite Booby Cay Island with several beaches, one nude, and excellent dive and watersports centre. Tranquil and unpretentious atmosphere, which is particularly popular with German families. Rather dated accommodation blocks and some apartments are time-share. ⑦.

Swept Away, PO Box 77, Norman Manley Blvd; ☎957 4061, fax 957 4060, *www.sweptaway.com* (in US ☎1-800/545-7937 or 305/668-0008, fax 668-0111). Extensive landscaped gardens and copious sports facilities make this one of Negril's finest; there's tennis, squash, basketball and racquetball courts, gym, regular and Olympic-sized pool with lap lanes, Jacuzzis, saunas, steam rooms, aerobics room, fitness circuit, spa facilities and watersports. Rooms are elegantly furnished, the beach grill and veggie bar serve up healthy snacks, and the main restaurant is award-winning. Three night minimum stay. ⑧.

The Town

Negril doesn't really have a centre – just a roundabout feeding its three main roads – and most people leave the beach or cliffs only to change money, buy petrol or find a ride out of the area. However, **Sheffield Road** is the least tourist-oriented part of town and the closest approximation of a real heart. The police station, market stalls, petrol station, restaurants and constant crowds dodging beeping mopeds create an animation that's absent in the boulevard's beach-life or the West End's studied tranquillity. To the right of the roundabout are two **shopping plazas** – Coral Seas Plaza and Plaza de Negril; the car park in front is known as **Negril Square**, a base for

---

Negril's drug culture

As any aficionado can tell you, Jamaica's best **ganja** (marijuana) grows in the fertile Westmoreland earth – well-flavoured and incredibly potent – and the trade to eager tourists plays a significant if covert part in the local economy. Many devotees make annual pilgrimages to find a place to chill out and partake of the local weed. Herb is a part of daily life in Negril, so don't be surprised if your first potential supplier is your hotel porter and you lose count of the men who hiss "sensi" as you pass them in the street. Don't feel that you can light up wherever you choose, though – marijuana is as illegal here as it is anywhere else on the island, and there are plenty of undercover police around town who can and do arrest tourists and locals alike for possession.

Though Negril has been an unofficial ganja centre since its hippy heyday, there's also a great deal of **cocaine** and **crack** use around town. It's not especially noticeable and crack-heads won't accost you on the street, but a certain furtiveness around the late-night beach bars lets you know that it's there for the taking. Negril is also one of the few places on the island where you're likely to be offered locally abundant **magic mushrooms**, considerably larger and stronger than those in cooler countries. Some restaurants include them in cakes, omelettes or pizzas, and *Miss Browns* on Sheffield Road is the traditional spot for foul-tasting mushroom tea while next door *Tedds* mixes up mushroom-flavoured daiquiris.

---

taxi drivers, black-market currency touts and would-be guides. Nestled behind is **Red Ground**, a seldom-visited residential area that houses most of Negril's permanent population.

The beach

Negril beach is a near-perfect Caribbean seashore. The whiter-than-white sand is lined by palms and sea-grapes, the water is translucent and still, and the busy reefs ornately encrusted. It's also packed with tourists, locals and holidaying Kingstonians, and while it's great for lively socializing – the banter runs as freely as the rum cocktails, and everyone and everything is on show – the high concentration of human traffic inevitably draws a hard core of vendors and hustlers. The hassle is constant and high-octane, and as well as the usual crafts, hair braiding and aloe massage – the last must have been invented in Negril – you'll be offered sex and drugs with alarming frequency.

Though hotels guard "their" portion of beach with security men and strings of floating buoys, the law keeps beaches public up to the shoreline and you can walk the entire seven miles in an hour or so, though it's a hot and thirsty business in the sun. The beach is roughly divided by the bank of all-inclusives at the outcrop splitting Long Bay and Bloody Bay. Beginning at the roundabout, **Long Bay** is the most heavily developed, by day a rash of bronzing bodies and flashing jet skis; by night a chain of disco-bars dedicated to reggae, rum punch and skinny dipping. At the far end, the hotels give way to the grassy stretch of **Long Bay Beach Park**, with picnic tables, changing rooms, a snack bar and considerably fewer people. Towards the northern end of Long Bay on the Morass side of the boulevard is **Anancy Fun Park** (daily 11am–7pm; free), a themed entertainment centre with miniature golf, a small museum with rather humdrum exhibits on Jamaican life, a mini-steam train ride (US$1.50) and boating and fishing out into the Great Morass aboard paddle boats (1hr; US$6). The tilapia and perch that inhabit the dark and peaty waters cost US$1 per pound caught. Tackle is supplied, you pay US$1 to fish and can have your catch cooked on the spot.

If you prefer a quieter strip of sand, head for crescent-shaped **Bloody Bay** beyond Long Bay Beach Park. Named for the crimson innards of whales once butchered on the beach, this is the "private" domain of the luxury all-inclusives and has sadly been earmarked as the location of three new hotels. Still, for the moment it remains the least-developed stretch of beach in Negril, much favoured for nude bathing and deserted enough to merit keeping a beady eye on your belongings – the sand backs straight onto scrawny bush, and robberies are not unknown. Stick close to the open-air barbecue towards the centre of the beach and you're sure to be looked after. The small forested islet in the centre of Bloody Bay, **Booby Cay**, appears in Jules Verne's epic movie *20,000 Leagues Under the Sea*. It's named

Cosmo's, towards Bloody Bay, is one of the best places to hang out if you're not staying at a beach hotel, with a pretty stretch of sand strung with hammocks (J$40 entrance).

The island's largest wetland, also called the Great Morass, is covered on p.313.

after the **booby bird** or sooty tern, an ocean dweller that takes a brief respite to lay eggs on offshore cays, though centuries of egg collection and hunting mean you're unlikely to clap eyes on one these days. The all-inclusives hold barbecues here, though you can usually get a local fisherman to transport you for around US$12 – ask at the fishermen's beach behind the main craft market. On Bloody Bay's northern side is an attractive rocky inlet with rope swings slung over the trees and an excess of sea grass that negates swimming.

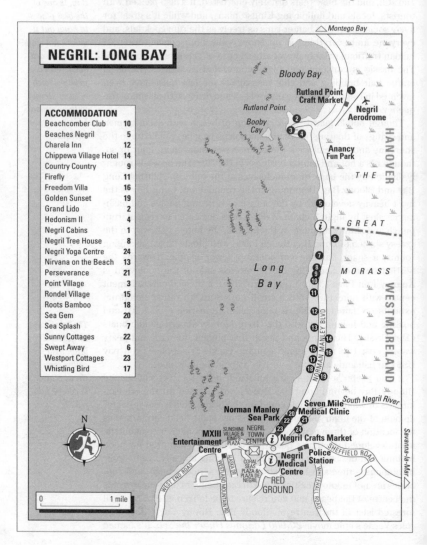

NEGRIL: LONG BAY

ACCOMMODATION

Beachcomber Club	10
Beaches Negril	5
Charela Inn	12
Chippewa Village Hotel	14
Country Country	9
Firefly	11
Freedom Villa	16
Golden Sunset	19
Grand Lido	2
Hedonism II	4
Negril Cabins	1
Negril Tree House	8
Negril Yoga Centre	24
Nirvana on the Beach	13
Perseverance	21
Point Village	3
Rondel Village	15
Roots Bamboo	18
Sea Gem	20
Sea Splash	7
Sunny Cottages	22
Swept Away	6
Westport Cottages	23
Whistling Bird	17

Watersports

Two large reefs running parallel to the West End cliffs and four along the beach make **snorkelling** and **scuba** major Negril highlights. Reefs are sumptuous despite environmental damage, crowded with soft and hard coral, brilliantly coloured sponges and fish, octopuses, starfish and even the odd turtle or nurse shark. There are several **sunken wrecks** that have become artificial reefs, including a ganja smuggling plane that misjudged its landing at Negril airstrip and one that was sunk deliberately. Snorkel equipment is available at most hotels and from all watersports operators at around US$5 per day. For snorkels, scuba gear, guided dives and certification courses try Dolphin Divers (☎957 4944), Marine Life Divers (☎957 4369, *www.negril.com/marinelife*), Mariners Dive Centre (☎957 0392, *www.negril.com/mimain.htm*), Negril Scuba Centre (☎957 4425, *neg.scuba.centre@cwjamaica.com*), and, West Point Water Sports (☎957 5521). Both **water-skiing** (US$25 per lesson) and **jet ski** hire (US$40 per hr) are available on the beach; **parasailing** is also possible (try Aqua Nova Sports at *Mariner's Beach Club*, ☎957 4420, US$30 for 20mins).

Glass-bottom boats are well represented along the beach and cost roughly US$15 for a 90 min trip; touts also sail along the cliffs, as do **canoe owners**, offering impromptu pleasure or fishing trips. Rates vary greatly depending upon the mood of the owner but average at about US$40 per half day; you can also ask at the fishermen's beach behind the craft market. If you're really serious you can hire a **sport fishing boat** from most of the cruise operators listed below – try also The Spread Eagle Fishing Co (☎957 5170) or Stanley's (☎957 0667) – and go after deep-water blue marlin, sailfish, wahoo and tuna. Bait, tackle, ice and beverages are usually included in half-day rates of around US$400. **Cruises** are an excellent way to see the local coastline, particularly at sunset (US$30 per person), although daytime cruises include Rhodes Hall Plantation or Half Moon Beach (US$50–55); most operators throw in snorkelling and snacks and all have an open bar. Try Cool Runnings (☎957 4323, *gaynair@ cwjamaica.com*), Indigo Cat (☎957 0382), Wild Thing (☎957 5392) or Willowdean (☎957 9224).

Tiny Mary Gate of Heaven Catholic Church opposite the Beachcomber Club is worth a visit if only to see the jalousied windows and brightly painted heart-shaped fretwork.

Beyond Bloody Bay, past the Orange River bridge, there are several deserted white-sand coves fringed by mangroves, creepers and trailing vines, favoured by Jamaicans for weekend beach parties. To get to them, take any of the dirt tracks that lead into the trees. Past reports of robberies and assaults make going in a group sensible.

The Great Morass and Royal Palm Reserve

Jamaica's second largest **wetland**, the **Great Morass** comprises 6000 acres of rivers, peat bogs and grasses running directly parallel to the beach. Fed by rivers flowing down from the Orange and Fish River hills, the morass lies at the bottom of Negril's watershed recharge area and is crucial to the area's supply of fresh water. Acting as a giant natural filter, the wetlands also protect the reefs from being smothered by silt and earth run-offs and are a sanctuary for insects, shrimp, rare plants and birds – commonly seen species include Jamaican euphonias, parakeets and woodpeckers. Land crabs enjoy one of the few remaining perfect habitats in Jamaica, and are a common sight during the summer breeding months – often, unfortunately, squashed at the roadside.

This rare habitat has long been threatened by pesticide and sewage pollution and proposals to remove peat fuel, but public outrage at the obvious destruction put a stop to the cut-and-drain activities of the government-owned Petroleum Company of Jamaica, and the 200-acre **Royal Palm Reserve** was created in the 1980s towards the south side of the morass as a means of protecting this crucial wetland and the plants and animals within. Tall and graceful but devoid of coconuts, the royal palm cluster is one of the largest single collections in the world, and it's magnificent; wreathed in creepers and vines springing up from the nutrient-rich bog below, in places the palms are thick enough to block out the hills behind and their stately presence lends a patently tropical air. Peat channels are now fishponds, there's a rickety bird-watching tower and a system of boardwalks which allows you to go deep into the morass without getting wet.

The land is still owned by the PCJ, but apart from limited maintenance, little has been done to encourage or facilitate visitors, and despite being one of the most attractive sites in the Negril surrounds,

---

Environment matters

Rapid growth and unplanned development have had a devastating effect upon Negril's delicately balanced eco-systems. Norman Manley Boulevard cuts straight through what was originally swamp land while jet skis and anchors have played havoc with the reefs and mangrove-felling has allowed the sea to slim down the precious beach and smother portions of reef with earth and sand that the trees once filtered. The population explosion has meant that until recently houses built on captured land lacked water supplies, garbage removal services and sanitation facilities. However, the long-term picture is far from hopeless: Negril now has a US$15 million water treatment plant and reservoir at nearby Logwood, which ought to minimise the amount of untreated sewage flowing into the sea, although link-up is proving beyond some peoples' means. With healthy support from Negril citizens, the **Negril Coral Reef Preservation Society** (NCRPS) has placed 45 mooring buoys at key points on the reefs and successfully lobbied for marine park status, granted in March 1998, like that afforded the Montego Bay waters (see p.257). The **Negril Environmental Protection Trust** (NEPT) has a wider brief, declaring 80 square miles from Green Island to Salmon Point as the **Negril Watershed Environmental Protection Area**. To find out more about both groups, or to become a member of NCRPS (and receive the excellent monthly publication *Reef Rap*), visit their offices above the community centre in the main craft market (PO Box 27, Negril; ☎957 3735, fax 957 4473, *www.fantasyisle.com*).

---

the area remains difficult to get to. In 1996, local environmental groups put in a bid for the lease, documenting plans to create a wildlife centre and nature tourism destination, which was not taken up. Following an eighteen-month interlude when the park was run unsuccessfully by Kingston businessmen, the reserve remains ostensibly private and closed to visitors. However, it's usually possible to go in and have a walk by paying a small fee to the caretakers who inhabit the block of decaying rooms at the gates. Finding it can be tricky, but most locals know the way from the Negril Hills golf club. At present, other than the paddle boats at Anancy Fun Park, there are no organized boat trips into the morass, but you may be able to hire one of the fishing boats moored at the mouth of the South Negril River for a glimpse of its perimeter.

The West End

Beyond the overpriced cocktails and hallucinogenic sunset-watching at the infamous *Rick's Café*, the West End cliffs are the last vestige of truly laid-back Negril. Traffic is infrequent, as hairpin bends and potholed tarmac are traumatic enough for pedestrians, but the ostensible serenity masks the depression of an extended period of decline. Disruptive sewage works between 1995 and 1997, combined with the more obvious appeal of the beach, have almost eclipsed the West End's formerly massive popularity, though the remoteness, immaculate reefs and the thrill of diving from a cliff straight into fifteen feet of the crystal-clear Caribbean remain unbeatable, and the quietude often means that you've got some of the best places entirely to yourself.

The West End begins at the roundabout in the centre of town and meanders along the cliffs for some three miles, becoming Lighthouse Road at Negril lighthouse and winding inland to Orange Hill and ultimately Sheffield Road. The first stretch is the liveliest, with jerk shacks, bars, juice stalls and craft shops – including the official A Fi Wi Plaza **craft market** – lining the inland side and restaurants hanging over the sea's edge; there are a couple of ramshackle **beaches** where fishermen moor their canoes but the murky water makes swimming inadvisable. The road opens up a little once you get to the fancy Kings Plaza and Sunshine Village shopping malls, but the true West End begins over the next blind bend; the road narrows, the water clears and the hotels that carve up the rest of the cliffs begin in earnest.

As this is Jamaica's extreme westerly point, the **sunset view** from the West End is the best you'll see; most evenings the sky blazes with absurdly rich oranges, pinks and blues that intensify as the sun dips behind the horizon, eventually merging into the deepest of blues with a moon reflected way out to sea. Sunset-watching is an institution; most bars and restaurants offer sunset happy hours (see p.322) and the half-hour or so before dusk is the closest the West End gets to

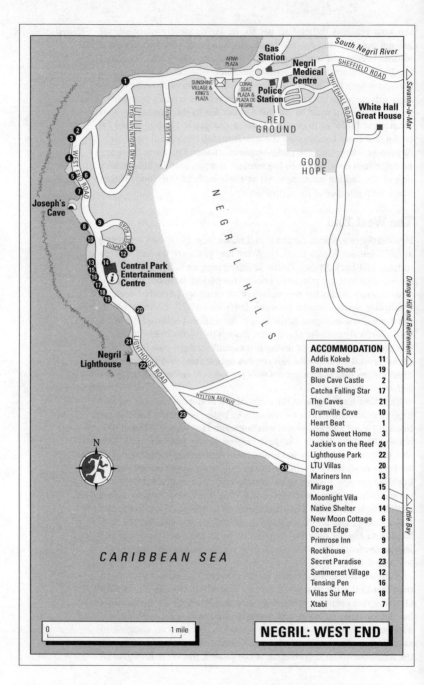

ACCOMMODATION

Addis Kokeb	11
Banana Shout	19
Blue Cave Castle	2
Catcha Falling Star	17
The Caves	21
Drumville Cove	10
Heart Beat	1
Home Sweet Home	3
Jackie's on the Reef	24
Lighthouse Park	22
LTU Villas	20
Mariners Inn	13
Mirage	15
Moonlight Villa	4
Native Shelter	14
New Moon Cottage	6
Ocean Edge	5
Primrose Inn	9
Rockhouse	8
Secret Paradise	23
Summerset Village	12
Tensing Pen	16
Villas Sur Mer	18
Xtabi	7

NEGRIL: WEST END

The West End's top spots

Many hotels will let you swim from their piece of cliff for the price of a drink, and though they all look pretty similar, some stand out. *Drumville Cove* has a friendly attitude towards non-guests and a spectacular portion of cliff, while *Rockhouse* boasts a stylishly surreal saltwater swimming pool, a bar, excellent sea access and complete seclusion. The limestone cliffs are riddled with **caverns**, with a popular network below *Xtabi* hotel, though the ever-popular *Pickled Parrot* watering hole is in prime position for the exploration of **Joseph's Cave**, one of the largest along the West End, made famous in the movies *Dr No*, *Papillon* and *20,000 Leagues Under the Sea*; the daredevil swings and waterslide above help to draw in the crowds as well. The cliffs are at their highest around *Rick's Café*, the venue of daily **cliff-diving** demonstrations; a less prominent place to have a go yourself is the *LTU Pub* next door. Below the lighthouse is a beautiful **cove** unconnected to any hotel, reached via a precarious wooden ladder, with rocks smooth enough to lie on and a small cave. Past the lighthouse, the cliffs peter out, coastal winds whip the sea into a frenzy and swimming becomes a little risky, but there is a sheltered spot just past the point where Lighthouse Road turns inland – turn straight onto the piece of undeveloped land and climb down the rocks.

hectic. Coach parties descend in droves upon Negril's biggest tired cliché: undeservedly popular **Rick's Café** has the trade sewn up – you pay for your drinks with plastic tokens, cameras click and local lads play the jester by diving off the cliffs for dollars.

Rick's marks the last of the major development; from here on the road becomes a country lane and the hotels are interspersed with near-wild coastline. A main point of interest is **Negril Point Lighthouse**, standing 100 feet above sea level at Jamaica's westernmost tip. Built in 1894, the 66-foot tower flashes a solar-powered beam ten miles out to sea and still contains the carefully preserved acetylene gas canisters that first provided the power, the original hand-wound pendulum that once regulated the beam and plenty of brass fittings. Port authority workers who live on site are usually willing to take you up all 103 leg-quivering steps to the top. Look out for the quaint crumbling outhouses preserved as listed buildings and the far-reaching roots of a huge silk cotton tree.

Negril Hills

Beyond the lighthouse the coast swings out of sight, but there's plenty of undeveloped land perfect for exploration by **bicycle** (see p.304 for outlets and cycling guides). As the cliffs and calm water diminish into a windblown ruggedness, there are fewer people, practically no hassle and a markedly rural atmosphere. Inland, the terrain rises into the dry limestone peaks of the **NEGRIL HILLS**, habitat of the non-venomous **yellow boa snakes** occasionally seen slithering across the road. The coast road becomes a dirt track here, and the tarmac swings into the interior through quiet **ORANGE HILL**, with flowered duck ponds on its outskirts and a host of quietly convivial **bars** along its single street. Orange Hill merges into residential **RETIREMENT**, home to the innocuous **Jurassic Park Restaurant and Lounge**. Marked by giant cast-iron painted flamingos at the gates, this is the creative outlet of a local ironworker, whose enormous metal pterodactyls, hibiscus flowers and a five-foot-long centipede overlook the basketball court, bar, restaurant and a shady gazebo set up for domino tournaments.

Past Retirement the route either continues to weave round to Little Bay (see below) or loops back to Sheffield Road, giving wonderful views of the cane fields in the basin below and passing **Whitehall Great House**, a crumbling piece of colonial architecture that enjoyed a brief stint as a disco in the early 1980s, but has lain uninhabited since being gutted by fire in 1985. Only the stone shell and black-and-white floor tiles remain, but you can climb the foundations for a magnificent sweep over West End, the beach and the Great Morass. A peaceful spot for **horse rides**, the 187 acres of grounds contain an enormous silk cotton tree with grotesquely twisting limbs and quite possibly the widest girth of any on the island. The estate is also home to the grave of Robert Parkinson, a plantation owner, who had the dubious honour of giving his name to Parkinson's disease. There's a **bar** adjacent to the house staffed by men who will offer to guide you round the house and grounds for a small tip.

Homer's Cove and Little Bay

If you're heading for the coast immediately east of Negril you can either continue on from Retirement or go directly from Negril along the shore (although you won't be able to drive all the way; a bicycle is a much better bet for traversing the dirt track) until you arrive at the pleasant but rather dishevelled inlet of **HOMER'S COVE** (also known as **Brighton Beach** to locals). The once-pristine beach has been mostly eroded by sand-mining, but it's still a nice place for a swim and there are a few vendors selling drinks and snacks.

Past Homer's Cove lies **LITTLE BAY**, the last piece of unspoilt coastline in the Negril hinterland and for now an extremely attractive, tranquil place; it may not remain so for much longer. Increasingly escapees from the noise and mania of Negril are choosing to visit, and even stay in, Little Bay. **Accommodation** options include **Bob Marley's Place**, an attractive wooden house built by Bob Marley in 1972, which was lived in by him and then girlfriend Ester Anderson for several years and was also the setting for Marley's *Talking Blues*. The house is now owned by an American couple who rent out rooms by prior reservation (in US ☎608 244 8886; ②) and has a small mineral spring which is just about swimmable. Further along the bay, *Romie's Bar* has several simple cabins (☎770 3840; ②) as well as bikes for hire. The *Humble Boy Club* is the closest Little Bay gets to a hotel with restaurant, bar and rooms (☎700 0198; ②) set on the loveliest stretch of the beach. **For eating** *Uncle Sam's* has delicious conch soup and fresh fish served in the grooviest bar around; follow the signposted right fork just before *Bob Marley's Place*. *Uncle Sam's* is also the venue for one-off sound-system dances and an annual unmissable **Donkey Derby** (held on the first Sunday in February). You can also camp here at US$10 per pitch.

Eating

Negril caters to a cosmopolitan crowd and the classiest, albeit somewhat pricey, dining is likely to be found in hotel restaurants; the best of these are included in the listings below. Negril's hippy associations are manifest in the high proportion of **vegetarian** options alongside the usual chicken and fish, and you'll also find a lot of **pasta**, as many restaurants attempt to cater for the huge number of young Italians who visit en masse in the early summer. Vendors based at the first stretch of West End Road sell roast or fried fish, jerk chicken and soup; as many of these are no more than a shack, names come and go and phones are infrequent, but generally the less flashy the place, the cheaper the product. Particularly recommended for jerk chicken is *Roy's Spice and Spice* stand opposite *Sips and Bites* on the West End Road. Many of the smarter restaurants offer free pick-up; call in advance. Ganja (aka special) cakes turn up on menus occasionally, particularly along West End Road. Thankfully the fast-food giants haven't yet reached Negril though there is a hot dog stand on the beach, *Hot Diggety Dog* and the beach bars catering to American students, *Risky Business*, *Legends* and *Margueritaville* all serve various forms of hamburger and chips.

Sheffield Road

Sweet Spice, Sheffield Rd. The best place on Sheffield Rd for cheap, delicious Jamaican food to take away or eat in.

In restaurant listings, we have given a phone number only for those places where you might need to reserve a table or take advantage of a free pick-up.

Snacks

For snacks and patties, try *Tan-Tan* at the back of the Plaza de Negril – its callaloo and cheese loaf, vegetable and beef patties are by far the best and cheapest in town. *3C's Pastry* at the start of the West End Rd is open 24hr for chicken, fish and curry goat alongside the pastries. *Mr Slice's Pizza* (☎957 3520) opposite the Yacht Club on the West End and at the beach sells real thin-crust pizza, the best for miles and will deliver. Ice cream and fruit vendors make regular rounds of the beach if you can't be bothered to move, otherwise, the *Yogurt Hut* at the *Bar-B-Barn* hotel sells frozen yoghurt flavoured with tropical fruits, and Devon House "I-Scream" is available at *Cecile's Café* on Norman Manley Boulevard.

Three Sisters Restaurant, Sheffield Rd. Quite a way up, but worth the trip for Jamaican cooking in a friendly atmosphere. Peanut soup, pepper steak and oxtail curry goat as well as the usual chicken and rice. Carrot and beet or okra juice too.

The beach

Alfred's Ocean Palace, Norman Manley Blvd; ☎957 4735. Hearty American-style breakfasts accompanied by an early-morning pianist. Crepes and sandwiches at lunch and seafood, blackened chicken and pasta in the evenings.

Beach Beans, *Mariner's Beach Club* hotel, Norman Manley Blvd; ☎957 4220. Pizzeria and ice cream parlour on the beach with really good coffee, milkshakes, sundaes and home-made cakes.

Blue Mountain Coffee Shop, Norman Manley Blvd; deservedly popular breakfast-joint run by friendly couple. Excellent coffee, banana pancakes, callaloo omelettes.

Cosmo's, Norman Manley Blvd; ☎957 4330. One of the best, busiest spots on the beach, equally popular with Jamaicans and tourists. Excellent seafood – conch soup is a speciality – and the usual selection of chicken variations.

Gambino's Italian Restaurant, *Beachcomber Club*, Norman Manley Blvd; ☎957 4170. Celebrated Italian eatery; dishes include fettucine with lobster, grilled fish, lasagne, carbonara and so on. Usually pretty busy.

Ristorante da Gino, *Mariposa* resort, Norman Manley Blvd; ☎957 4918. Excellent Italian restaurant set on pretty outdoor terrace. The usual range of pasta and seafood dishes; scallopine al burro (scallops in butter) is particularly good, as is lobster linguine.

Hunan Garden, *Country Country* hotel, Norman Manley Blvd; ☎957 4359. Excellent Chinese restaurant in attractive dining room with vast menu. Eat in or take out.

Kuyaba, *Sea Gem* hotel; ☎957 4318. Thatch-roofed, open-sided restaurant with innovative decor, consistently good food and regular crowds. The frequently changed blackboard menu includes lobster in white wine and garlic, imported Italian pasta, steaks, snapper stuffed with crab in an orange sauce and vegetarian dishes.

Office of Nature, Bloody Bay. Funky barbecue joint under canvas on the beach. Lobster, fish and chicken cooked to order.

Sonya's, *Freedom Villa* hotel, Norman Manley Blvd. Delicious Jamaican food cooked over a wood fire at the entrance to the hotel and the classiest patties in Negril,; try the Italian with tomato and mozzarella.

Tanya's, *Sea Splash* hotel; ☎957 4041. Gourmet poolside restaurant, with seafood specialities, chicken crepes and beef tenderloin.

La Vendome, *Charela Inn*; ☎957 4648. Celebrated, sophisticated French/Jamaican cuisine – duck à l'orange, veal with velouteé sauce, snapper in coconut, home-made ice cream and excellent bread – and a good wine list. Some vegetarian dishes.

West End

The Carrot, West End Rd. Natural juice bar and vegetarian café with on-site herbal consultant. Seafood dishes include excellent conch soup.

Chicken Lavish, West End Rd; ☎957 4410. Choice spot for domino players, serving chicken and fish, Jamaican and Chinese style, steaks and pork chops.

Choices, West End Rd. Brightly painted outdoor café with all the Jamaican staples. Popular with both locals and tourists, particularly at breakfast.

Culture Yard, Lighthouse Rd. The menu is a bit limited – the main dish is hemp burger (soy burger with nuts and *real* ganja seeds), but they're delicious, high in fibre and quite unable to inebriate.

Ericas, Small shack opposite the *Rockcliff Hotel*, West End Rd. Home cooking by Erica herself; seafood is a speciality with excellent, and reasonably priced, lobster.

Happy Bananas 11, West End Rd; ☎957 0871. Relaxed pub atmosphere with hospitable English proprietors, an attractive cliffside setting and for the adventurous a trapeze swing over the bar. Mixed menu with seafood including curried lobster, Tex-Mex and excellent pasta.

Hungry Lion, West End Rd; ☎957 4486. The best vegetarian food in town, with seafood as well. A walled courtyard affords privacy, and the food – meatless shepherd's pie with green lentils, lobster in lemon butter, black bean chilli, pasta primavera – is always good. The coconut cream pie is unmissable.

Jackies on the Reef, Lighthouse Rd; ☎957 4997. Meals have to be ordered in advance but the menu is innovative and health-food oriented and the setting romantic and unusual. Dishes include grilled tuna with sesame noodles, sun-dried tomato pasta and chicken marinated in rosemary.

Just Natural, West End Rd. Inexpensive, fresh Jamaican food, callaloo omelettes, pasta, burritos and vegetarian options, in a beautiful shady garden.

Lighthouse Inn, Lighthouse Rd; ☎957 4052. Classy German/Jamaican run restaurant way out by the lighthouse with grilled kingfish, conch steak and good salads. The lobster lasagne is very popular. Good wine list.

LTU Pub, West End Rd; ☎957 0382. Laid-back venue with cliffside dining, relaxed atmosphere and a mixed menu; seafood, stuffed jalapeno chillis and chicken filled with callaloo and cheese. Some German dishes.

Marios, West End Rd. No-frills seafood restaurant right at the beginning of the West End, with charming and friendly service. The roof has great views over the ocean.

Pickled Parrot, West End Rd; ☎957 4864. Popular and efficient American-style bar and grill. The extravagant clifftop original serves large portions of tacos, fajitas and burritos alongside jerk chicken, seafood, formidable burgers and pizza.

Rockhouse, West End Rd; ☎957 4373. Romantically set on a boardwalk right over the sea, with excellent service and a menu that includes vegetable tempura, seafood linguine with garlic and conch fritters.

Roy and Felix Serious Chicken, West End Rd. The fowl-heavy decor competes for your attention with wonderful chicken, fish and vegetarian options. Unintrusive musical accompaniment from a huge CD selection.

Shorty's, West End Rd. Cut-above-the-rest jerk chicken joint, probably the best in Negril; served with rice, peas and salad. Funky and very friendly.

Silver Star Café, West End Rd. Long-established café with excellent hippy breakfasts – yoghurt, muesli, banana pancakes – some vegan meals and peaceful veranda set back from the road.

Sips and Bites, West End Rd. Laid-back shack serving unadulterated Jamaican cuisine at very reasonable prices.

Drinking and entertainment

Most **bars** want you to spend the **sunset** with them and provide drinks promotions or happy hours as an incentive. As the cliffs give the best view, bars along the West End tend to be livelier at dusk, with the action moving to the beach after dark. The larger places are distinctly tourist-oriented, with neon, imported drinks, satellite TV and an air of enforced indulgence. If you want some local flavour try the darkened interiors of the **rum bars** and **beer shacks** along Sheffield Road or West End Road near the roundabout.

As there are only two proper **clubs** in town, most of the week-night dancing is offered by **beach bars** using their portion of sand as a dancefloor. These have agreed a nightly rotation system to share the business around a little; DJs play dancehall or Euro-disco and the **live music** usually consists of a no-name reggae band singing Bob Marley covers. Ask around to see which is on each night – Tuesdays, Fridays and Sundays at *Alfred's* and Saturdays at *De Buss* are particularly lively. Nights vary and new venues pop up with alarming regularity, but most locals keep abreast of the current hot spots, and as the beach venues are free you can walk from one to another in any case.

Large **stageshows** featuring well-known reggae artists are advertised on roadside billboards and through a car-with-megaphone system, and are supposed to start at 9.30pm and finish at 1.30am, but rarely begin before 11pm and often go on until 3 or 4am. Well-known artists and DJs perform regularly during the winter season; if a major artist is scheduled to play, it's always worth checking that they are actually there before you pay your money, as some have a reputation for unreliability. Main **venues** for large shows are *Roots Bamboo* on the beach which hosts big name bands several times a week and less regularly *MXIII* in the West End; cover charge is usually in the region of US$7. *The Samsara Hotel* and *Central Park* (both places are on the West End Road) have occasional live events and open up properly during the Spring Break period in March; the *Bella Donna* restaurant on Summerset Road has live music on Wednesdays and sporadic big name gigs. The *Lighthouse Inn* plays host to the wonderful Count Lebbie mento band every Saturday night for an all-inclusive buffet (US$30 per person). Other all-inclusive buffets include a particularly popular *Icebreaker* evening at *Mariners Inn* every Tuesday with limbo-dancing, fire-eating and deafening karaoke.

Sound-system jams take place every weekend in Red Ground, Orange Hill and the surrounding communities. There's often a jam at the large lawn in front of the *One Love Rastawant*, off West End Road behind Coral Seas Plaza. Though the Negril Reggae Festival is a thing of the past, there's usually a huge **reggae extravaganza** around Spring Break. Two set fixtures in the local calendar are **Negril Carnival**, held annually in late April with costume parades and all-night dancing in the streets – contact the JTB for further information. The other main event is the annual **Bob Marley Birthday Bash** at *MXIII* each February 6, which usually attracts top reggae performers. See p.41 for details of both.

Bars

Alfred's Ocean Palace, Norman Manley Blvd. Busiest bar on the beach with thrice-weekly live reggae and crowds of happy holidaymakers dancing on the sand. This is where all the action is and it's great fun but watch out for the hustlers, particularly on gig nights.

De Buss, Norman Manley Blvd. The trademark London bus used in *Live and Let Die* stands outside; inside there's piped or live music every night in a covered area and section of the beach. The jerk chicken is famously good.

Errol's, Norman Manley Blvd. Small 24hr beach bar with reggae videos, an overdose of fairy lights and hard-core drinking by guests who rent basic but adequate rooms in the yard behind the bar. Freshly squeezed orange juice during the day.

Jahmerican, West End Rd. Breezy upstairs spot for drinking and dominoes.

LTU Pub, West End Rd. Very cool bar, and vastly superior to next-door *Rick's*; cliffside drinking, diving, snorkelling and food to boot. Ask the barman to make you a Bob Marley – and then try and drink it.

Margueritaville, Norman Manley Blvd. Large beach bar with nightly bonfire, beach volleyball, two-for-one drink offers and big TV screens for sports fans. Karaoke on Sundays and Mondays and an all-inclusive party on Friday evenings (US$34 per person). Hugely popular with American students.

Mi Yard, West End Rd. High-rise bar that's tourist-friendly but positively Jamaican. Open 24hr for music, dominoes, drinking and jerk; always packed once the beach bars slow down after 2am.

Natural I, Lighthouse Rd. Groovy 24hr bar run and frequented by Rastas. It's a long way from downtown Negril which makes it chilled out and quietly sociable.

Peachy's, West End Rd. Dark but atmospheric 24hr bar and restaurant popular with hotel workers.

Pickled Parrot, West End Rd. The cliffside venue with water slide and swing gets very busy during the daily happy hour (3–5pm) and is an essential stop-off for sunset cruisers. If nude Hedonists and swingers seriously misbehaving (don't ask) are not your chosen drinking companions then this isn't the place for you.

Rick's Café, West End Rd. Overpriced tourist trap with an appallingly tuneless band playing reggae cover versions alongside the traditional spectacle of local boys diving from the high cliffs. The West End's main sunset event.

Risky Business, Norman Manley Blvd. Popular American-style beach bar complete with big-screen sports via satellite, Thursday two-for-one drinks offers, and Appleton Ladies' Nights on Mondays and Saturdays when women drink for free.

Three Dives, West End Rd. Mellow drinking spot with nightly bonfire in cliffside garden and good food.

Yacht Club, West End Rd. Large thatched bar, with a long and colourful history, overlooking the sea. Cheap Red Stripe all day until 7pm, live music at weekends and wonderfully shady clientele. Come for a heavy drinking session with the hippies who "discovered" Negril and other local characters; the staff are helpful and friendly, it's surprisingly safe and often great fun.

Clubs

Close Encounters, Kings Plaza, West End Rd (nightly). Every town has one, and this is Negril's go-go club, where scantily clad women gyrate for the drinkers. Cover US$4.

Compulseion, Plaza de Negril (nightly). Negril's largest indoor disco and pick-up joint, at its most entertaining and sweaty each Wednesday and Saturday. An experience not to be missed for the dodgy chat-up lines alone. Occasional visits from top dancehall DJs. Cover US$5, including a drink.

Shopping

Crafts are available practically everywhere you go in Negril. Dedicated craft shops pepper the West End and though the resort police and Chamber of Commerce have cracked down on mobile vendors by building dedicated plazas and patrolling the streets, plenty still roam the beach. The best place to buy is the main craft market at the roundabout end of Norman Manley Boulevard, with around a hundred stalls and a full spread of merchandise. Also good is A Fi Wi Plaza on West End Road between the roundabout and Sunshine Village. The Rutland Point market opposite Bloody Bay deals mostly with guests of the all-inclusives, so it can be more expensive but it's often quiet enough to make bartering worth the vendors' while as is the ramshackle collection of huts opposite the *Rockhouse Hotel*.

For unusual items try the shop at *Kuyaba* restaurant on the beach, which prides itself on stock that you can't find anywhere else in town, like painted tin "country buses" and primary-coloured enamelled tropical fish. Well-known Negril-based artist Geraldine Robins sells excellent batik and hand-painted T-shirts and fabrics from her shop at *Margueritaville*, and Gallery Hoffstead in A Fi Wi Plaza has prints, originals and sculpture by owner Lloyd Hoffstead. Sarongs to Go on the West End Road has the best and cheapest selection of beach wraps while the adjacent stall Think Positive sells an intriguing mix of cute wooden animals, old records and natural insect repellent; its chatty Rastafarian owner is a self-appointed philosopher and is more than happy to give free advice about Negril. Roots Man Corner on the main Negril roundabout is the place to get natural remedies as well as knitted shoes and leather sandals. Ja-Ja Originals sells elegant gold and silver jewellery and will create custom-made items; you'll find their workshop just beyond the aptly-named Time Square mall on Norman Manley Boulevard which specializes in thousand-dollar watches. Other in-bond shops are situated in hotels or Sunshine Village which is also the best choice for kitsch holiday souvenirs and swimwear.

Basic **food** needs are met by the well-stocked Hi-Lo in Sunshine Village, or the smaller Valuemaster in Plaza de Negril. The stalls at the top end of Sheffield Road have cheaper and fresher fruit and vegetables. If you don't want to stray too far from your hotel, *Café Taino* on Norman Manley Boulevard has a small selection of deli items and wine; *Twin Stars*, near *Rick's Café*, is a comprehensive grocery store and incredibly convenient if you're loathe to leave the West End. Daley's liquor store near the post office on West End Road offers discounts on bulk buys of **beer** or **spirits**; a good idea if you have a fridge in your room. Don't be surprised by Negril's high **prices**; the isolation means that all fresh food has to be transported in and you'll often be forced to pay over the odds for simple items.

Listings

Airlines Air Jamaica (☎952 4300 or 4100); Air Jamaica Express (☎957 5251); American Airlines (☎952 5950); British Airways (☎952 3771); Continental (☎952 4495, or in US ☎1-800/230-0856); Timair (☎957 5374); only Air Jamaica Express and Timnair have offices in Negril.

Airport The information line for Negril aerodrome is ☎957 3016.

American Express Bank of Novia Scotia, Plaza de Negril (Mon–Thurs 9am–2pm, Fri 9am–4pm).

Banks and money The Bank of Nova Scotia, Plaza de Negril, has a 24hr ATM machine as does the National Commercial Bank in Sunshine Village (☎957 4117; Mon–Thurs 9am–2pm, Friday 9am–4pm); there's also an ATM at the Petcom petrol station by the Negril Aerodrome. Both banks offer currency exchange and cash advances on credit cards; rates are substantially better than in hotels but around the same as the town's best official cambio, Gold Nugget on Norman Manley Blvd (Mon–Sat 9am–5pm). Black market touts hang around Negril Square; if you choose to risk using them, try and get a Jamaican to accompany you. Moneygram wire transfers can be collected at the National Commercial Bank and the cambio at the Time Trend Financial Co on Norman Manley Blvd (Mon–Fri 9am–5pm, Sat 9.30am–4pm; ☎957 3242); Western Union (Mon–Thurs 9am–5.30pm, Fri & Sat 9am–6pm) has an outlet at Hi-Lo supermarket in Sunshine Village.

Car and bike rental Action Car Rental (☎957 3259); Jus Jeep, West End Rd (☎957 0094 or 0095); Vernon's, Plaza de Negril and Norman Manley Blvd (☎957 4522 or 4354). Bikes can be rented from Dependable (☎957 4764), Elvis (☎957 4732) and Jah B's (☎957 4235), all on Norman Manley Blvd; Banmark (☎957 0197), Kool Bike Rental, (☎957 9224) and Tykes Bikes (☎957 0388) on West End Rd.

Doctors and clinics There are plenty of doctors and private clinics; try Negril Minor Emergency Clinic on Norman Manley Blvd (☎957 4888; open 24hrs), Negril Medical Centre on Sheffield Rd (☎957 4926) or Dr Dale Foster (☎957 9307). There is an optician in Kings Plaza, West End Rd.

Golf Negril Hills Golf Club (☎957 4638), an extremely hilly and attractive 18-hole, 6,600 yard, par 72 course in the hills above town. The topography makes for a challenging game and there's a clubhouse and restaurant on site.

Hospitals The nearest hospitals are at Savanna-la-Mar (☎955 2533 or 2133) and Lucea (☎956 2233). In an emergency dial ☎119 for an ambulance.

Internet You can pick up and send emails (from US$3 per hr) from *Negril Cyber Café* (☎957 9659); Cigar King, Time Square Mall (☎957 3315, *cigarkingjamaica@hotmail.com*); Caribbean World Network (☎957 4759, *www.negrilbiz.com*), or *Café Taino*, all on Norman Manley Blvd. On the West End, try the *Yacht Club* (*www.yachtclub.com*).

Laundry Most hotels will wash clothes but it's cheaper to hire a local lady; ask around – a load should cost US$5–7. West End Cleaners (☎957 0160) is rather inaccessible off Hylton Ave at the top of Lighthouse Rd but will pick up and deliver between 8am and 10pm daily. Washing costs J$30 per pound including soap. The Village Laundry (☎957 0165) on the back road behind Coral Seas Plaza is more expensive but convenient.

Massage Massage is a Negril institution; try Nadine Loeb at *Catcha Falling Star* hotel (☎957 0390); *Jackie's on the Reef* (☎957 4997); Catherine McLean (c/o *Tensing Pen*, ☎957 0387); or Beverly Haslam at the *House of Dread* bar on West End Rd (☎957 4833). Peggy Daugherty (☎818 0682) is a naturopathic doctor specializing in deep tissue and cranio-sacral massage.

Petrol Negril has two petrol stations: on Sheffield Rd at the junction of the right fork to Whitehall and Retirement (daily 6.30am–11pm) and Petcom by Negril aerodrome (6.30am–11pm).

Pharmacies Key West Pharmacy is at 11 Sunshine Village (Mon–Sat 9.30am–8pm, Sun 10am–6pm); Negril Pharmacy is at 14 Coral Seas Plaza (Mon–Sat 9am–7pm, Sun 10am–2pm).

Photography Colour Negril, Plaza de Negril, and Photo Prints, West End Rd; both offer free pick-up and delivery and one-hour processing.

Post office Negril post office is on West End Rd next to A Fi Wi Plaza; open Monday to Friday 9am to 5pm.

Taxis Candycabs (☎957 9224, or 972 0190, *www.candycabs.com*).

Telephones and communications There is a bank of phone boxes opposite the main craft market and another in Plaza de Negril; phone cards are available from pharmacies or the post office. Other than Sunshine Village, the West End is poorly served; there are two booths at the Twin Stars grocery stores and one by the *House of Dread* bar. Office Solutions, Bouganvillea Complex, West End (daily 8am–11pm) offers relatively cheap local and overseas calls and a fax service, as does the Negril Calling Centre (9am–11pm), Plaza de Negril; you can also send faxes from the Negril Chamber of Commerce office at A Fi Wi Plaza (Mon–Fri 9am–5pm).

East of Negril

After Negril's glittering hedonism, the rest of the southwest can come as quite a surprise. Restaurants remain wholeheartedly Jamaican with mannish water and eye-rollingly insouciant service replacing waffles and exhortations to "have a nice day". Locals tend to be more genuinely friendly, if a little surprised that you've torn yourself away from a resort, and unfettered by high-rises and serviceable roads, the countryside is magnificent. Westmoreland's longest river, the multi-tributaried **Cabarita**, meanders down central hills through the vast cane fields around **Frome Sugar Factory** and the alluvial plains surrounding the concrete capital of

Savanna-la-Mar, where brisk trade and honking horns fight against the soupy humidity. A few miles to the east, **Roaring River** marks its entrance above ground with a spectacular blue swimming hole, having carved out an inky cave on its way. Water is central to Westmoreland: irrigating the sugarcane and reducing turf to swamps or noticeable by its absence as you near the parched fields and dry riverbeds towards St Elizabeth. Since Indian workers first entered the scene in the mid-nineteenth century, the region's extensive wetlands have been mostly employed for the cultivation of rice. The potential for bird-watching and boat safaris has not been capitalized as it has further down the south coast, nor have the miles of beach at **Bluefields** or the unhurried charm of fishing villages **Belmont** and **Whitehouse**.

Little London and Frome

Once out of Negril proper, Sheffield Road opens up into the pock-marked, fast-moving and truck-dominated route to Savanna-la-Mar, sweeping past cane fields neatly bordered by the stunning Fish River hills. After about nine miles, a cluster of buildings around a gas station signifies the start of **LITTLE LONDON**. Though the years have blurred racial origins, the local population was at one time dominated by Indians who came to Jamaica in the nineteenth century as indentured workers to labour in the cane fields and sugar factories. Most people pass through Little London with hardly a sideways glance, as there's little of obvious interest. However, it's a world away from the commerciality of Negril, and boasts some excellent places to **eat** and **drink**; try the gaily painted *Malcolm X Bar*, *First Choice* or *HQ Jerk Chicken*. Best of the lot is the *Kingfish Kitchen* for traditional Jamaican cooking; the large lawn out back serves as an occasional venue for sound-system dances and the proprietors and regulars usually have a small party on a Sunday. There's no **accommodation** in Little London proper but turning right at the central crossroads in town will take you down a tortuous road to **BROUGHTON**, and the *Lost Beach Resort* (US ☎800 626 5678, outside US 1 734 761 7444, fax in US 734 663 7477, *www .lostbeach.com*; ③) which has spacious rooms on Hope Wharf fishing beach, swimming pool, restaurant and bar. Horse-riding and watersports are also available and the place itself is an idyllic getaway spot.

*See p.123 for
more on the
Indian
immigration.*

Flat savannah lands ideal for the cultivation of cane have long meant strong local ties to the **sugar industry**. The largest cane-processing factory in the area is **FROME**, about five miles northeast of Little London, which handles most of the cane from neighbouring plantations (see box on p.328). Though the factory is not officially open to the public, you should be able to arrange a tour by calling ahead (☎955 6080).

Sugar wars

The centre of some of Jamaica's most violent labour disputes, **Frome
sugar factory**, was built in 1938 by British company Tate and Lyle's sub-
sidiary West Indies Sugar Company as the most modern facility in the West
Indies, and is now government-run under the Sugar Company of Jamaica.

The factory has long been beset by industrial disputes; constructed during a period of high unemployment, the promise of work drew job-seekers
in their thousands, most were unlucky, and even those who were given
jobs received a pittance far lower than the salary they'd been promised.
Under the fiery leadership of Alexander Bustamante, the workers banded
together in protest and the dispute swiftly turned ugly; cane fields were set
on fire and a full-scale riot broke out on May 3, 1938, which left four dead
from police bullets and one hundred demonstrators, including
Bustamante, in jail.

Frome's volatile reputation endures and it has been the centre of more
recent difficulties, triggered by the decline of the Jamaican sugar industry.
Machinery has never been updated, leaving the factory unable to compete
with more efficient producers and operating at a loss and re-mechaniza-
tion is mooted as the only solution. However, the inevitable loss of hundreds of manual jobs has understandably generated animosity – Frome
remains the largest single employer in Westmoreland and its success is
crucial to the overall prosperity of the area.

Savanna-la-Mar

Capital of Westmoreland it may be, but there's little to keep you in
the rather soulless confines of commercial **SAVANNA-LA-MAR**. It's
the area's main shopping centre, but as the profusion of low-lying
concrete keeps the air still and makes it a hot and uncomfortable
place to wander about, most people depart as quickly as possible and
there are no developed tourist attractions. The elements have given
the town a battering – successive hurricanes flattened it in 1748,
1780, 1912, 1948 and 1988; in 1748 the wind drove the sea far
enough up central Great George Street that boats were left dry-
docked in the middle of the road.

Other than a couple of attractive gingerbread dwellings on the
outskirts, you're stuck with the negligible appeal of **Great George
Street**, the needle-straight main thoroughfare. The **courthouse**
and parish administrative offices stand next to a cast-iron **fountain** with the warning "Keep the pavements dry" inexplicably
inscribed on each side. The rest of the street is taken up with pharmacies and general stores, most selling the usual assortment of
imported designer bootlegs, though if you want some true yard-
style ragga string vests, Jamaican flag bandannas or barely-there
dancehall attire, this is the place to go. Great George Street ends
abruptly at the seashore; here you'll find the main fruit and vegetable **market** (main day Saturday), and the ruins of **Savanna-la-
Mar Fort**, declared the worst fort in Jamaica by a visiting admiral

in 1755, who discovered that though vast sums had been devoted to defending the town, the fort was unfinished and one third of what there was had collapsed into the sea. Opposite is the West Indies Sugar Factory **pier**, from which sugar from the Frome factory is loaded for export. There's little to see other than crumbling walls and moored fishing boats.

Practicalities

Savanna-la-Mar is a main junction of the Montego Bay/Negril route; all **buses** stop at the main bus station at the top of Great George Street and you can connect with services to the south coast and beyond. With so many pleasant options nearby, few choose to **stay** in Savanna-la-Mar, but you could join Jamaican regulars and rent a basic but air-conditioned room at *Orchard Great House* (☎955 2737; ②); there's a restaurant, bar and a pool on site. Simpler but much more attractive is the *Lochiel Guest House* east of town on Sheffield Road (☎955 9344; ①), an atmospheric old house in lovely grounds. For **food**, try the *Chicken Place Restaurant and Bar* on Rodney Street.

If driving to Montego Bay, take the A2 east to Ferris Cross and keep straight on at the petrol station – the signposts are very confusing.

Around town: Roaring River Park

An easy escape about five miles north of Savanna-la-Mar is gorgeous **ROARING RIVER PARK** (daily 9am–5pm; US$10) near the small community of **Petersfield**, approached on a rutted road that you'll probably need directions to find, though there are plenty of signposts from town. Set in a former plantation and still surrounded by cane fields, a dazzling blue **mineral pool** and extensive **caves** have been developed with tourists in mind, though not on the scale of Dunn's River (see p.194). The site's reputation for unpleasant hassling has largely been dealt with by its current managers, the TPDCO (Tourist Product Development Company): a guide meets you as you arrive, leads you helpfully to the ticket office and then takes you on a trip round the caves and surrounding gardens. It's all very pretty – watercress grows wild along banks planted with palms and crotons and the forested hillside rises up unbroken. Steps up to the mouth, concrete walkways and lighting let you appreciate the full magnitude of the caverns, which range from broom cupboard to auditorium in size. Bats flit about, and there are two mineral pools for a disquieting swim in pitch-blackness – the water is said to rejuvenate. The caves are marred only by graffiti carved into the rock and jagged edges where the quartz has been levered off and sold.

The village is located further on past the main swimming spot at **Blue Hole Garden** (daily 8am–6pm; US$5). Overhung with trees and flowers, this thirty-foot-wide natural spring of refreshing chilly azure water is said to be bottomless – the true depth has never been charted. The surrounding gardens are well kept but not over-landscaped, packed with unusual trees, anthuriums, narcotic white trumpet flowers, every variety of heliconia and several spots to immerse yourself amid gushing mini-waterfalls.

If you want to **stay** in Roaring River, there are two cool thatched cabins (②) in the Blue Hole Garden. Facilities (outdoor shower, mosquito screen and pit toilet) are simple but the setting is incredible. You can also **camp** at perfectly appointed tent sites for US$10. **Food** and **drink** are available from the *Lover's Café* in Blue Hole Garden; for a relatively remote spot, the menu is excellent and includes vegetable patties, garlic bread, spicy dumplings and fish.

Bluefields and Belmont

East of Savanna-la-Mar, the coast road becomes the A2 and after the crossroads at Ferris Cross sticks close to the sea on its way to Bluefields and Whitehouse. Just before Ferris Cross, **Paradise Park** (daily 9am–6pm; US$5) marked by a drive of royal palms, is an extensive cane plantation offering swimming in the Sweet River, hiking in beautifully varied terrain (guides are available), and two-hour horse rides (between 9am and 3pm; US$20) – a worthwhile diversion before you reach **Bluefields** and **Belmont**, contiguous, laid-back communities of picturesque fishing beaches and reef-fringed shallows.

Henry Morgan (see p.110) sailed from **BLUEFIELDS** in 1670 to attack Panama, and the calm seas and sheltered bay have attracted every generation of Jamaican settlers; it was one of the first Spanish settlements, and the dynamic local community association (see below), is attempting to reopen the old Spanish road to Martha Brae in Trelawny as a hiking route – though the distance and thick plant cover make this a rather distant possibility. The most interesting building in modern Bluefield is privately owned **Bluefields House** next to the police station, once a temporary home to "father of Jamaican ornithology" and inventor of the modern aquarium Philip Gosse, who researched *Illustrations of the Birds of Jamaica* and *A Naturalist's Sojourn in Jamaica* during an eighteen-month residence in 1844–45. In the gardens stand a **breadfruit tree** said to be the first in Jamaica, planted by Captain Bligh when he brought seedlings from Tahiti. The house is virtually derelict now but it is possible to stay, in very basic but wonderfully atmospheric accommodation (②).

*See p.161 for
more on
Captain Bligh
and the bread-
fruit.*

Bluefields merges imperceptibly into **BELMONT**, birthplace of the late **Peter Tosh** (see box opposite). His body lies in a small red-gold-and-green **mausoleum** (daily 9am–5pm; donation) just off the road, decorated with cobwebs, stained glass and press cuttings. It's much less of an affair than the Marley mausoleum in St Ann (see p.229) and usually deserted.

Peter Tosh

Consciously controversial, **Peter Tosh** (born McIntosh) was Jamaica's best-known lyrical agitator. Born an only child in Belmont on October 19, 1944, he was raised by an aunt in the West Kingston tenement yards dominated, at the time, by the explosion of hopeful harmony groups that transformed post-independence Kingston into a hotbed of aspirations. Every newly arrived country "bhuttu" (or bumpkin) wanted to be a singer and Tosh followed suit, embarking on a mission to reveal home truths from a ghetto perspective. He saved to buy his first guitar and in 1964 formed vocal trio The Wailers with teenage allies Bunny Livingstone and Bob Marley. In 1972 the Wailers signed to Chris Blackwell's Island label, and recorded *Catch a Fire* and *Burnin'* together while Tosh put out tracks on his own Intel Diplo HIM label (Intelligent Diplomat for His Imperial Majesty), all the time becoming increasingly bitter over pay and personal disputes with the man he referred to as "Whiteworst". By 1974, he and Bunny Livingstone had gone their separate ways.

Having already earned a reputation as the Wailers' social conscience and an uncompromising egotist, Tosh took on the mantle of chief critic of what he called Jamaica's "Babylon shitstem", publicly berating politicians for double standards and hypocrisy and lighting spliffs on stage with a cool disregard for the law. His bellicose militancy did him no favours with the island's police; in 1975 he was busted on a trumped-up ganja charge and beaten to within an inch of his life. As soon as his wounds had healed, he answered back with *Whatcha Gonna Do*, a cocky release chiding the futility of police brutality, smokers' anthem *Legalize It*, and the defensive *Can't Blame the Youth* – inevitable airplay bans ensured record sales and Tosh cemented his position as the roots reggae revolutionary.

Tosh stayed in Jamaica, but his ever-increasing status and fortune – collaboration with the Rolling Stones in 1978 and a deal with EMI attracted global recognition – drew awkward parallels with the sufferers' lot he expostulated. In a country where money and fame draw a barrage of demands from old friends, needy causes and shady characters, the intensely spiritual and suspicious Tosh began to display signs of paranoia, believing himself both a victim of an establishment assassination conspiracy and haunted by duppies. His prophecies of destruction were fulfilled on September 11, 1987, when gunmen opened fire in Tosh's living room, killing him and two friends, and wounding five others. Rumours of the motive spread swiftly, some arguing that head assassin and renowned "bad man" Dennis "Leppo" Lubban was demanding financial retribution for a recent prison stint he saw as Tosh's rap, others muttering of a government-backed gagging.

Remembered by Jamaicans as a formidable ladies' man with a razor-sharp wit, Tosh himself provided his best biography; the "Red X" tapes shot on scratchy film in a darkened room show him philosophizing on his personal mantra, reggae and Rastafari and form part of the essential Tosh documentary *Stepping Razor Red X*.

Practicalities

The two villages are served by hourly **buses** from Savanna-la-Mar. If you want to **stay** in **Bluefields**, try *Casa Mariner*, Cave PO (☎995 9897; ②) to the west of town, which has nine budget rooms with fan and air conditioning, a restaurant, popular bar, pool tables and slot machines, and an upstairs "conference room" that serves as a weekend disco. Another inexpensive and unusual option, *Shaftson Great House*, c/o Frank Lohmann, Bluefields PO (☎0997 5076, *www .shaftson.com*; ①–③) sits above the bay (call ahead for free pick-up) with fabulous views, and offers large attractive rooms with en-suite or shared bathroom. There's a pool, bar and cheap restaurant, pool table, lots of hammocks and extensive grounds; camping costs US$10. Frank is a useful source of local knowledge and often takes guests out sightseeing. Just past the police station in Bluefields is *Cool Runnings* (①), with simple rooms, self-catering facilities and private beach. If you're looking for a luxurious option, scattered through the bay are five beautifully designed and furnished villas which comprise the casually elegant *Bluefields Villas* complex (in US ☎202 232 4010, fax 703 549 6516, *www.bluefieldsvillas.com*; ⑧).

In **Belmont**, both *Sunset Cottage* and the *Belmont Cabins* offer basic but clean accommodation at low prices (②). By far the most exciting place to stay in the area, though, is the fabulous *Moun Tambrin Retreat* (☎918 4486, fax 918 4487, *www .jamaicaescapes.com*; ⑧) at **Darliston** in the hills above the bay; it's the private work in progress of American artist Russ Gruhlke, with one of the loveliest gardens in Jamaica, a stupendous view and an on-site collection of bizarre but beautiful follies, sculptures and woodcarvings. All meals are included in the rates and there's a three-night minimum stay.

A few **bars** and **restaurants** group around the police station and post office in the "centre" of Bluefields. *KD's Keg Lawn and Restaurant* (aka *Sands* to the locals) and the cavernous *Ocean Edge Pub and Restaurant* are both fine, but for really good local food cooked al fresco try *Roberts* at the far end of Belmont. Also good is the *Fresh Touch* fish restaurant in the Bluefields Beach Park; the park is a rather characterless collection of landscaped units selling snacks and drinks and is part of a new highway project which now bypasses the beach. In Belmont, *Sands* hosts a very popular disco on Sunday evenings and is the usual venue for the annual **Peter Tosh birthday celebration** in mid-October, a live concert featuring "roots and culture" performers.

For all local **information**, contact the excellent Bluefields People's Community Association (☎955 8792, fax 955 8791; Mon–Thurs 9am–5pm, Fri 9am–1pm), whose ongoing programme of community tourism, including the running of a local radio station, *Radio Bluefields*, operates from headquarters next door to the *Ocean Edge Pub*.

Whitehouse and Scott's Cove

As you continue along the A2 – through land known as **Surinam Quarters** in honour of the English who resettled here when the

British colony was captured by the Dutch in 1667 – the scenery becomes drier but more agricultural, with swathes of pasture and plenty of cattle and goats. The road swings away from the coast but there are still some nice places to swim; ask locals to direct you to the best spots.

One of the main fishing ports on the south coast, **WHITEHOUSE**, five miles down the road, offers little beach life but plenty of commercial bustle. Turn off the main strip of shops at the fruit and vegetable **market** (Wednesday & Saturday); passing some dusty cows and resigned-looking higglers, the track deposits you in the midst of the clapboard shacks and run-down bars at the **fishing beach**. If you get there early enough, you can watch the chicken wire traps being baited up with cow skin, balanced on canoes and sailed out to the shallows where the meat attracts lobster and fish. Huge hessian bags of flapping specimens are weighed and bartered over, while women scale furiously and cats prowl for scraps. Fish caught at Whitehouse is transported island-wide, and this tiny place hums with action (and odour) as the boats return from trips that can last as long as a week. A new octagonal-shaped fish market is the work of the project for development of small-scale fisheries in Jamaica and was completed in 1999 with a grant from the government of Japan as a token of friendship and co-operation between the two countries. An attempt to shift the market to the new yard has so far failed miserably; it's used occasionally for dancehall events and fish is sold as it was before.

Past Whitehouse, the coast road marks the Westmoreland/St Elizabeth border with a cache of purpose-built fish and bammy stalls at **SCOTT'S COVE**, manned by a friendly team of vendors who crowd around anything that stops. The fish is usually excellent, but ensure that your bammy has been soaked and fried – it's become commonplace to offer tourists the uncooked supermarket version.

Practicalities

There are quite a few places to **stay** in Whitehouse, most of them – like the large, airy *South Sea View Guesthouse* (☎963 5172, fax 963 5763; ③) – deserted. A better option, and never empty, is *Natania's* (☎ & fax 963 5342; ⑤) in Culloden around two miles west of town. Rooms are beautifully simple with fan only – request an ocean-facing unit. There's a deck overlooking the sea, a pool, bar and a small beach, and its **restaurant** is very good. Best bet of all for both accommodation and food, however, is the neighbouring *Culloden Café* (☎963 5344, *www.cullodencafe.com*; ④ including breakfast) where you can stay in one of several bohemian cottages in the grounds and facilities include a small beach and waterfront bar. A superb restaurant serves modern Jamaican cuisine at ridiculously reasonable prices and the café hosts a popular karaoke night on Sunday evenings, and live music every Friday.

Travel details

Buses

Tour company buses make daily runs from Sangster airport in Montego Bay to Negril (US$30), but public buses are as haphazard as everywhere else in Jamaica.

Lucea to: Montego Bay (16 daily; 1hr); Negril (20 daily; 40min).

Negril to: Lucea (20 daily; 40min); Savanna-la-Mar (20 daily; 40min).

Savanna-la-Mar to: Bluefields (9 daily; 40min); Montego Bay (20 daily; 1hr); Negril (20 daily; 40min); Whitehouse (16 daily; 50min).

Flights

Negril to: Kingston (2 daily; 1hr 15min); Montego Bay (3 daily; 20 min); Port Antonio (1 daily; 1hr 15min).

Chapter 6

The south

M ass tourism has yet to reach Jamaica's southern parishes. None of the all-conquering all-inclusives have opened here yet and the beaches aren't packed with sun-ripened bodies, but there are some fantastic places to stay and great off-the-beaten-track places to visit. It takes a bit of extra effort to get here – and you'll need a car or a tour to see one or two of the "hidden" highlights – but it's definitely worth it. If you're after watersports and heavy-duty nightlife, stick to the coastal resorts, but if you want to catch a glimpse of Jamaica as it was before the boom, head south.

The parishes that make up south-central Jamaica are immensely varied, with the landscape ranging from mountain to scrubby cactus-strewn desert, and from typically lush vegetation to rolling fields more redolent of the English countryside. To the west, in the beautiful parish of St Elizabeth, **Black River** is the main town – an important nineteenth-century port that today offers popular **river safaris** and a handful of attractive colonial-era buildings. If you're after somewhere to stay and swim, **Treasure Beach** is a better target – an extremely laid-back place with decent beaches and some lovely accommodation options – and if you want to tour around you can

---

Accommodation price codes

All the hotels detailed in this guide have been graded according to the following price categories. Note that the prices have been calculated as those for the cheapest **double** or **twin room** during low season, normally mid-April to mid-December. During high season, rates are liable to rise by up to 25 percent (though this is rare at the cheap hotels), and proprietors may be less amenable to bargaining. Although the law requires prices to be quoted in Jamaican dollars, most hotels give rates in US dollars; payment can be made in either currency. For more details see p.27.

① under US$20	④ US$51–70	⑦ US$151–200
② US$21–35	⑤ US$71–100	⑧ US$200 and above
③ US$36–50	⑥ US$101–150	

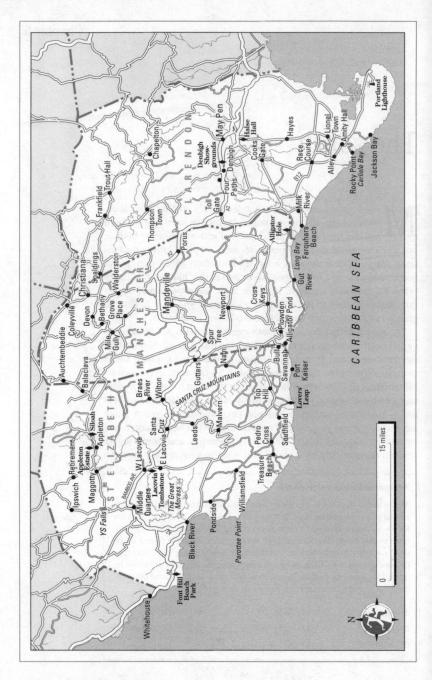

make for the **rum factory** at Appleton, the fabulous **YS waterfalls**, or drive around the tiny villages of the attractive and untouristed **Santa Cruz Mountains**.

Further east, the parishes of Manchester and Clarendon are less diverse and a little less appealing. Manchester has the major town of **Mandeville** – a possible inland touring base that makes a pleasant if unspectacular change from the coast – and the much smaller market town of **Christiana**, an unspoilt retreat with a single, delightful old hotel. The coast is less accessible, although a new road through the wild scenery between Alligator Pond and Milk River has opened up **Gut River**, one of the most picturesque spots on the entire island. The parish of Clarendon is total farming country, with large citrus groves in the north and sugarcane fields everywhere else, and offers a handful of unusual places to visit, from the mineral spa at **Milk River** to the seventeenth-century **Halse Hall**, just south of the market town of **May Pen**.

Bauxite is the crucial economic commodity in the area, mined at seams in the central highlands (particularly around Mandeville) and processed at refineries scattered over the parishes. **Agriculture** is also key: despite the dry climate (particularly west of the Santa Cruz Mountains), St Elizabeth produces much of the country's agricultural surplus and is known as Jamaica's breadbasket. Recently, **tourism** has begun to make a limited impact, though it is unlikely ever to approach north-coast levels – the emphasis is on small-scale "community tourism", avoiding the disruption to traditional lifestyles that the industry has caused elsewhere on the island.

Getting around

Regular **buses** and **minibuses** ply the main routes between Kingston and Negril, giving easy access to the main towns of May Pen, Mandeville, Santa Cruz and Black River. From these centres, a network of buses fans out to smaller towns like Christiana, Treasure Beach and Malvern, though these services are much less frequent. Be warned, also, that many of the main attractions in the interior, like the YS Falls, Apple Valley and Appleton, are somewhat off the beaten track and can be hard to reach by public transport. **Driving** is the best way to see the hidden parts of the south; the roads are mostly good, but watch out for gullies on the smaller, coastal roads – they'll take the bottom out of your car if you hit them too fast.

The south coast

New roads have opened up large parts of Jamaica's **south coast** in the last few years and it's now possible to drive along large stretches of it, particularly between Black River and Milk River, without losing sight of the sea. The scenery is often wild and unspoilt down here, though you'll need a car to see most of it as buses and minibuses tend to stick to the main, inland roads, making side-trips down to coastal villages as required.

Just east of Whitehouse (covered in Chapter Five), **Font Hill Beach Park** has a particularly lovely stretch of pristine sand to relax on before starting your south-coast tour. Beyond Font Hill, **Black River** merits a visit for its crumbling architectural gems and **river safari** into the Great Morass, and, further round the coast, laid-back **Treasure Beach** is probably the best place on the island to just stop, chill out and de-stress for a couple of days. Further east still, there's a great coastal drive from Alligator Pond to the tiny nature reserve at **Alligator Hole**, and you can stop off for a splash in the vividly blue **Gut River**. Finally, and usually the quietest place of all, the mineral spa at dry and dusty **Milk River Bath** is the perfect place to soothe away any aches and pains.

If you spend any time in this part of Jamaica, you'll appreciate the importance of the local **fishing industry**. Tiny fishing villages are scattered along the coast with boats pulled up on stretches of the beach; even in tourist areas like Treasure Beach, fishing remains vital to the local economy. Many of the fishermen head for the **Pedro Banks**, about eighty miles south, for the best possibilities, with several thousand of them living on small islands there – known as the Pedro Cays – at any one time. If you're interested in going out on a fishing boat, ask around at any of the fishing villages; many fishermen will be grateful for the extra cash, but make sure you clarify whether you'll be expected to help out with the work.

Font Hill Beach Park

Still little known by tourists, the **FONT HILL BEACH PARK**, which runs alongside the main road three miles east of Whitehouse, is all that's currently open to the general public of the **Font Hill Wildlife Sanctuary**. It's a lovely stretch of clean, white sand with good snorkeling at several off-shore reefs and restaurant and bar on site (Tues–Sun 9am–5pm; J$100).

The sanctuary, a three-thousand-acre reserve originally established to provide some unspoiled land for swimming and nature walks, continues to serve as a refuge for the endangered **American crocodile**. About two hundred of the crocodiles live in the swamps at the eastern edge and many bird species – doves, pelicans, egrets and herons – also inhabit the sanctuary. The Petroleum Corporation of Jamaica, who own the land, apparently have plans to re-open the place and if you have a special interest in wildlife or ecology you may well be able to enter the park anyway (phone in advance, ☎929 5380, or consult *www.pcj.com*). **Buses** regularly pass the entrance on the main road and will drop you off outside if you ask.

Black River

Although it's St Elizabeth's largest town, **BLACK RIVER** is a quiet spot, and most travellers only nip in briefly to take a boat trip on the river. It wasn't always this way: in the mid-nineteenth century the town derived substantial wealth from the trade in **logwood**, used to produce black and dark-blue dyes for the textiles industry and exported in great quantities from Black River's port. For a brief period the trade helped to make the town one of the most influential in Jamaica, with electricity, the telephone and the car all first introduced to the island here, and a big racecourse west of town. However, with the introduction of synthetic dyes, the trade in logwood began to dry up and, today, the only signs of those illustrious days are some wonderful but decrepit old gingerbread houses. If you have time to spare, Black River's somnolent charms are worth a couple of days gentle exploration.

For details of the Black River boat safari, see p.340.

Buses and **minibuses** stop behind the market, just off the High Street. Five minutes' walk away, the **Jamaica Tourist Board** (☎965 2074; Mon–Fri 9.30am–4.30pm) has a small office on the upper floor of the Hendrick's building, 2 High St, but don't expect much in the way of useful information.

Accommodation

Given that few tourists stop over in Black River, there's a surprisingly good selection of **places to stay**. Most of the cheaper options are just east of town on Crane Road, across the iron bridge, but there are several good choices in the town centre.

Bridge House Inn, 14 Crane Rd; ☎965 2361, fax 965 2081. The rooms are nothing special but this is a friendly place and pretty good value on the east side of town. ②.

Invercauld Hotel, High St; ☎965 2750, fax 965 2751. Attractive restored house on the seafront and a comfortable option close to the centre of town. ④.

Irie Sands, 67 Crane Rd; ☎965 2756, fax 966 4844. Small guesthouse and restaurant run by friendly proprietor. Clean and comfortable rooms overlooking the sea. ③.

South Shore Guesthouse, 33 Crane Rd; ☎965 2172. Small, tidy guesthouse, with very well-stocked bar, on the beach east of town. ②.

Sunset Beach Club, 29 Crane Rd: ☎965 2462. Quite possibly the most eccentric hotel in Jamaica: three buses converted into very basic rooms, set on a pretty stretch of beach adjoining a friendly local bar. Owner Cliff Senior is highly entertaining. Not for the faint-hearted. ①.

Waterloo Guesthouse, 44 High St; ☎965 2278. The first hotel in Black River, central with good restaurant, pool and lots of character. ①.

The Town

The nicest thing to do in Black River itself is to take a stroll along the **waterfront**, particularly attractive towards sunset, and check out the old wooden buildings, many with gorgeous colonnaded verandahs and gingerbread trim and most in a perilous state of collapse. The **Waterloo Guesthouse**, built in 1819, is reputed to have been the first place in Jamaica to get electricity – installed to provide air conditioning for racehorses kept in the old stables – and to have boasted the island's first telephone. Nearby, the gleaming white **Invercauld Hotel**, built in 1889, reflects the confidence of the town during its heyday. Heading back towards the town centre, goats roam in the grounds of **St John's**, the tidy parish church which dates from 1837 and has marble monuments to Robert Munro and Caleb Dickenson, benefactors of two of the schools at nearby Malvern.

There are a couple more attractive old buildings in the town centre, particularly the brightly coloured **Hendrick's building** beside the bridge, built in 1813 and now housing the Jamaican Tourist Board. From here you can wander down to the shore where you'll see men and boys fishing and maybe the odd crocodile feeding or hanging out by the ocean. Scant traces of the once fashionable town can be found a couple of miles west of here along the main road: **Abundant Spring** is an old spa, once attracting people from all around the area with its restorative waters but now a run-down and forlorn spot by the sea, while nothing at all remains of the nineteenth-century **racetrack** that stood across the road.

The Great Morass and the Black River safari

The main reason most people come to the town is for a **boat safari** on the **Black River** which, at 44 miles, is Jamaica's longest. The river – so named because of the peat moss lining the river bottom that makes the crystal-clear water appear an inky black – is fed by various tributaries as it makes its way down from Balaclava, on the Manchester/St Elizabeth border, and is the main source for the **GREAT MORASS** – a 125-square-mile area of wetland that spreads north and west of Black River and provides a swampy home for most of Jamaica's surviving crocodiles as well as some diverse and spectacular bird life. It's the best place to spot the crocodiles, a rapidly dwindling bunch, now protected by law, who once lived in great numbers around the coast of Jamaica until hunting and the deterioration of the swamplands began to take their toll.

The boat tour is a very pretty trip into the Great Morass, although the term "safari" promises rather more excitement than it delivers. You do have a virtually guaranteed sighting of crocodiles (albeit fairly tame ones), and there are some marvellous **mangrove swamps** where you can normally spot flocks of roosting egrets as well as whistling ducks, herons and jacanas, and you may run into the occasional shrimp- or crab-fisherman in his dug-out canoe. The boats run about eight miles upriver to Salt Spring Bridge, where you can get some refreshment and take a swim – most people decline the opportunity, though crocodiles are rarely spotted this far north – before heading back down. To go on the ninety-minute tour, (5 daily; US$15 per person), turn up at the dock or contact St Elizabeth River Safari (☎965 2229) or Black River Safari Boat Tours (☎965 2513). Otherwise try the fisherman's bar, *Boney's*, at the back of the marketplace and ask for Teddy; he advertises a mini-cruise which goes beyond the bridge and up to Cheese Rock. If you're interested in further exploration of the river, Jacana Aqua Tours (☎965 2211) is run by wetland ecologist Lloyd Linton who not only puts a more scientific spin on the standard safari tour but also runs **specialized ecology trips** (by prior arrangement only; rates negotiable) with birdwatching experts, fishing trips and occasional forays into virgin stretches of the morass.

Eating and nightlife

Black River is a quiet town and, though there are a couple of good **places to eat**, the evening **entertainment** options are strictly limited. If you're **snacking** during the day, there are a couple of good bakeries on the High Street and you'll find the odd jerk chicken vendor plying his trade nearby.

Abundant Spring, west of town. Open-air and inexpensive restaurant alongside the old mineral spa serving roast fish and Jamaican staples. Only open sporadically for lunch but worth checking out; the food is home-cooked and really delicious.

Bayside, 17 High St. Reasonable café serving the usual chicken and fish dishes and a good selection of cakes and ice cream.

Bridge House Inn, 14 Crane Rd. Often rather low on atmosphere, and an official lunch venue for coach tours doing the safari but the Jamaican food is consistently good and moderately priced.

Jacinta's, Brigade St. Small classy restaurant on the edge of the market with excellent Italian and Chinese food.

King Lion Reggae Centre, Black River bus park. Tasty Ital food in Rasta decorated hut – with fierce biblical quotations on the walls – which doubles up as a record shop. Nineteen different natural juices.

Turns, High St. Popular ice cream parlour also serving snacks and standard Jamaican fare. Its central locality and large windows makes this a good spot for watching the town go about its business.

Drinking and entertainment

Most of your drinking and entertainment will be done at the places listed above. For an early evening drink, the bar of the *Waterloo Guesthouse* is often the busiest spot in town, popular with Black River's professionals. On Fridays the *Riverside* bar by the St Elizabeth River Safari offices has an after-work jam and is an easygoing place for a waterfront drink on other nights. East of town along Crane Road, the *Sunset Beach Club* has a similarly earthy feel, with locals playing dice and drinking rum while nearby *Cloggys on the Beach* hosts regular dancehall and live music events (US$7 cover).

Treasure Beach and around

From Black River, a minor road cuts south to the coast beyond
Parottee Point, passing some bizarre ironshore rock formations and
a string of deserted bays en route to snoozy **TREASURE BEACH**.
Though it's a tiny spot, with no watersports or nightlife worth mentioning, this easy-going community attracts those who simply want
to unwind, and has become the main tourist centre on the south
coast, particularly popular with a hip bohemian crowd. There is a
good range of **accommodation** options, including a delightfully
eclectic collection of villas and beach cottages to rent, some great
places to **eat** and a couple of diverting attractions, while the bays
that make up the area boast some pretty **beaches**.

The **Santa Cruz Mountains** (see p.354) rise up from the sea just
east of Treasure Beach and run northwest, providing a scenic backdrop for the village and protecting the area from rainclouds coming
from the north. As a result, Treasure Beach has one of the **driest** climates in the country, and the scrubby desert-like landscape – strewn
with cactuses and acacia trees – often looks like the setting for a
western. Despite the dry weather, though, this is very much farming

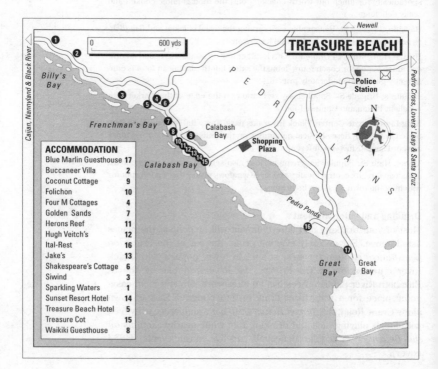

TREASURE BEACH

0   600 yds

Billy's Bay

Frenchman's Bay

Calabash Bay

Calabash Bay

Shopping Plaza

Police Station

Newell

Pedro Cross, Lovers' Leap & Santa Cruz

Cajian, Nannyland & Black River

PEDRO PLAINS

Pedro Ponds

Great Bay

Great Bay

ACCOMMODATION

Blue Marlin Guesthouse	17
Buccaneer Villa	2
Coconut Cottage	9
Folichon	10
Four M Cottages	4
Golden Sands	7
Herons Reef	11
Hugh Veitch's	12
Ital-Rest	16
Jake's	13
Shakespeare's Cottage	6
Siwind	3
Sparkling Waters	1
Sunset Resort Hotel	14
Treasure Beach Hotel	5
Treasure Cot	15
Waikiki Guesthouse	8

country, and you'll see plantations of carrots, scallions, thyme, onions and watermelons scattered around the area.

Treasure Beach itself is made up of a string of loosely connected fishing settlements. The chances are that you'll stay on the long sandy sweep of **Frenchman's Bay** where tourism has displaced fishing as the main industry or smaller **Calabash Bay**, where you can still see brightly coloured fishing boats pulled up on the beach below the newly constructed hotels and guesthouses. To the east, **Great Bay** remains a basic fishing village with just a couple of guesthouses and some lovely beaches, while west of Frenchman's Bay the road runs out of town past **Billy's Bay**, home to several of the classiest villas in Treasure Beach, a series of shacks and a lot of goats.

Nannyland, Caijan and Lovers' Leap

Right beside the road five miles west of Treasure Beach, **Nannyland** (daylight hours; J$100 entrance to the museum) is a sprawling seaside site dedicated to black heroes – particularly the Maroon leader, Nanny – with statues of and monuments to Martin Luther King, Paul Bogle and Sam Sharpe scattered around the grounds. A bizarre collection of strident homages to black culture and unrelated bits of junk constitute a small-scale museum. It's usually deserted, with a bleak and slightly eerie feel, but the location, just above the ocean, is superb. A little further west, and less easy to reach, **Caijan** is a mountain retreat where Rastaman Brother John Deer has built an extraordinary house into the mountainside, using the rocky outcrops as floor, ceiling or wall as required. The house is full of artefacts that John has collected on his world travels, including paintings, musical instruments, bits of pottery and other paraphernalia. Entrance is up a steep hill (you'll need a four-wheel-drive or the legs of a mountain goat), marked by an ancient pink Ford Prefect; you're better off getting John to come and pick you up (☎990 6441). He makes an interesting and knowledgeable guide; his collection is free to visit though donations are welcome.

On the other side of Treasure Beach, the Santa Cruz Mountains drop nearly two thousand feet to the sea at the sheer cliffs of **LOVERS' LEAP**, signposted off the main road at Southfield seven miles east (☎965 6634; Mon–Thurs 9am–6pm, Fri–Sun 9am–7pm; J$100 entrance fee). According to legend, two young lovers – slaves at a nearby plantation – came here while running away from their owners. They were followed to the edge of the cliffs and, preferring to die rather than be separated again, threw themselves into the sea. The views over the cliffs and out to sea are pretty spectacular, and if you're feeling reckless you can scramble part of the way down for an even better look at the drop. There's a new **café** and **viewing platform** on the site, too, though it rather spoils the feeling of isolation.

Arrival, information and getting around

Public transport links with Treasure Beach are not great, although
several minibuses and shared taxis run daily from Black River; a
regular taxi costs around US$25 each way. If you're driving, there
are two approaches to the village. Most traffic arrives via the road
from Pedro Cross, passing the police station and post office north of
the village. A turn-off to the left leads to Great Bay while the main
road continues towards Calabash Bay, where most of the recent
tourist development has taken place. The newer, coastal road from
Black River runs into the village from the west past a string of small
bays and intermittent guesthouses.

Treasure Beach has a comprehensive **Web site**, *www
.treasurebeach.net* which lists accommodation and local sites of
interest. There's an **internet centre** (☎965 3067, *borris
@jamaicans.com;* daily 9am–1pm & 4–9pm; except Thurs) next to
South Jammin which also serves as an information and call centre;
additionally Jason Henzell at *Jake's* is incredibly helpful even if
you're not a guest.

*For informa-
tion on off-
shore trips, see
p.346*

If you're interested in seeing the YS Falls, Gut River or other parts
of the south from a base here, Treasure Tours (☎965 0126) runs a
good and reasonably priced **tour service** (from US$35 per person);
otherwise independent tour guide Paul Henningham (☎965 3048),
born and bred in Treasure Beach, knows every inch of the area and
will customize trips to suit your will (by prior arrangement only;
rates negotiable). If you're more adventurous Red's Treasure Beach
Tours takes cycling trips on off-road tracks in the area (☎965 3101;
US$30 per person with snorkelling included) while both *Golden
Sands* (☎965 0167) and the *Waikiki Guesthouse* (☎965 0448)
rent **bicycles** for around US$10 per day.

Accommodation

There is a wide variety of **accommodation** in Treasure Beach, and
more guesthouses are springing up all the time. Seemingly every
other house is a rentable **villa**; these vary from simple beach cottages
to luxurious and elegant homes with all mod-cons. Otherwise **camping** – available at *Caijan*, *Nannyland* (see opposite) and *Four M
Cottages* for around US$10 per tent – is more feasible than in most
parts of Jamaica.

Hotels and guesthouses

Caijan, west of Billy's Bay; ☎990 6441 or c/o *Jake's*. Fabulous mountainside
setting with camping sites and a couple of cottages about seven miles west of
town on the coastal road to Black River, the entrance marked by an old Ford
Prefect. No electricity, but great views and atmosphere. You'll need a sturdy
four-wheel-drive to get up there or ask to be collected. ②.

Four M Cottages, Frenchman's Bay; ☎965 0131. Six small, simply furnished
rooms in a friendly house opposite the *Treasure Beach Hotel*. ②.

Golden Sands, Frenchman's Bay; ☎965 0167. Long-standing and deservedly popular budget option on the beach, with basic rooms and self-catering facilities. ②.

Ital-Rest, Great Bay; ☎965 3231. Two cottages only at this gentle and beautifully landscaped place near the beach, each with separate rooms upstairs and down (ask for upstairs for the views and the breeze). Small bar with ping-pong table, restaurant and herbal steam room on site (US$50 for a steam and massage). Turn right just before the *Seacrab* restaurant and then take the first right. ③.

Jake's, Calabash Bay; ☎965 0635, fax 965 0552, *www.islandlife.com*. Casual but delightful venue on its own tiny beach, with six brightly coloured cottages and an easy-going but cultured atmosphere. If you're not after luxury, this is one of the most charming options in Jamaica. ⑤.

Lovers' Leap Guest House, Lovers' Leap; ☎965 6004. Friendly place with fairly spartan rooms, and snacks and drinks at the bar downstairs. ①.

Nannyland; ☎962 0522. A couple of tatty cabins and camping space by the sea, in this sprawling shrine to Jamaica's black heroes. ②.

Shakespeare's Cottage, Frenchman's Bay; ☎965 0120. Cheapest place in town, with four basic but clean rooms and a self-catering option. ①.

Siwind, Billy's Bay; ☎965 0582. Small tranquil hotel with amazing views and steps down to a private beach. Rooms are classily simple and clean. ④.

Sunset Resort Hotel, Calabash Bay; ☎965 0143, fax 965 0555, *www .sunsetresort.com*. Incongruously and fabulously kitsch resort in a lovely seaside setting. Huge comfortable rooms with all mod cons. ⑤.

Treasure Beach Hotel, Frenchman's Bay; ☎965 0110, fax 965 2544, *www.treasurebeachjamaica.com*. Big, attractive resort with two pools and suites with oceanfront views on one of the best stretches of beach. ⑤.

Waikiki Guesthouse, Calabash Bay; ☎965 0448. Budget option with basic wooden cabins on large lawned garden opposite *Tiffany's* restaurant. ①.

Villas and cottages

The villas and cottages listed below are a recommended selection of dozens available in Treasure Beach – it's worth bearing in mind that while some of these options are simply much cheaper and more private than a hotel, several of the more expensive villas are very beautiful indeed with spectacular oceanfront settings. Prices quoted are for the whole property.

Blue Marlin Guesthouse, Great Bay; ☎965 0459. Located on the site of a Taino (Arawak) settlement; the house is strewn with Taino artefacts, as well as colonial-era heirlooms collected by the owner. The guesthouse – rented by the week only – costs US$1000 for up to four people.

Buccaneer Villa, Billy's Bay; bookable through *Jake's* on ☎965 0635. The most spectacular villa of the lot, designed in funky Santa Fe style by Sally Henzell who created *Jake's*, though it's not cheap at US$500 per night or US$3000 per week. Facilities include Jacuzzi, satellite TV, cook (though all food and drink is extra) and four bedrooms.

Coconut Cottage, Frenchman's Bay; ☎473 7595. Sweet cottage with two en-suite bedrooms, garden and roof terrace opposite the beach in downtown Treasure Beach, which rents for US$45 per night.

Folichon, Frenchman's Bay; ☎904 5454. Close to *Jake's*, this place has four rooms (though only one double bed) and costs US$120 per day.

Herons Reef, Frenchman's Bay; ☎904 5454. Adjacent to *Folichon*, and with the same owners, there are two rooms, sleeping four, costing US$60 per day.

Hugh Veitch's, Frenchman's Bay next to *Jake's* (ask for Gita Hill at the small house in front of Hugh's). Classily simple three-bedroomed beach house with roof terrace and seafront patio at a rate of US$50 per night.

Sparkling Waters, Billy's Bay; ☎965 0486, or ask for Arnie at the *Trans-love Café*. Two small bedrooms and a fabulous verandah right over the water are on offer here; US$1100 per week for two guests with extra guests a further US$250 each.

Treasure Cot, Calabash Bay; ☎965 0635. Just east of *Jake's* is this atmospheric two-bedroom guesthouse on the beach that rents for US$100 per day.

The beach

If you're in the mood for sightseeing, there are a couple of places worth checking out just outside Treasure Beach (see below). Otherwise, it's just you and the **beach**. The swimming is good, though you'll need to watch the undertow, which can get strong at times – ask at your hotel about present conditions. Although rocky headlands create occasional obstacles, you can stroll for miles on certain parts of the beach, particularly west of the *Treasure Beach Hotel*, and the bluff which protects the shore at Great Bay is a lovely place to walk and look out for the local seabirds.

Fishing trips with the local fishermen can normally be arranged without difficulty for around US$25 per person for a half day – ask the people at your hotel to put the word out that you're interested. **Boat trips** along the coast to Black River and out to Sunny Island, a tiny spit of land with safe off-shore snorkelling cost around US$30 per person; ask at *Jake's*. That's pretty much your limit when it comes to watersports in Treasure Beach – there's no scuba diving or jet skis here – and the community is keen to keep it that way.

Eating and nightlife

Evenings are pretty low-key in Treasure Beach but there are a few good options for **food** and a couple of **bars** which keep late hours and get very full at the weekends. The roads aren't lit at night though, so you'll be wandering between places in the moonlight.

Blossom's Pizza and Jerk Centre, Calabash Bay adjacent to Kingfisher Plaza. Takeaway joint with excellent pizza.

Fishermen's Bar, Frenchman's Bay. Thatched bar up the lane beside *Tiffany's*, with a small disco and pool table out back. Easy-going local hangout that's open after everywhere else has closed. Very popular at the weekends with both locals and tourists, particularly Sunday nights.

Jake's, Calabash Bay; ☎965 0365. Good option for dinner and usually one of the busiest places in town, with a blackboard menu that changes daily but normally includes fish and lobster.

Little Treasure Café, Calabash Bay. Tasty Jamaican food with seafood a speciality and great breakfasts; right on the sand.

Natural Vibes, Frenchman's Bay. Basic and tasty home-cooking with some tables out on the main street. Open late.

Seacrab, Great Bay. Friendly local restaurant, near *Ital-Rest*, with good and inexpensive Jamaican staples like escovitched fish and curry goat.

South Jammin, Frenchman's Bay. Unpretentious and popular bar with a comprehensive mix of burgers, pizza and seafood. Pool table and cute pocket-sized garden.

Tiffany's, Frenchman's Bay; ☎965 0300. Attractive restaurant serving excellent lobster, octopus and fish dishes from around J$200.

Trans-Love Cafe, Frenchman's Bay. Laid-back thatched patio and the essential stop for breakfast or brunch, with fresh bread, cakes and fruit salads, as well as regulars like ackee and saltfish and good jerk chicken.

Yabba, *Treasure Beach Hotel*; ☎965 0110. Good hotel food and enthusiastic service, though it's often quiet and consequently low on atmosphere.

Alligator Pond to Alligator Hole

At first glance, the ramshackle fishing village of **ALLIGATOR POND** – ten miles east of Treasure Beach – is not one of the most attractive spots on the south coast. But if you're passing, it's worth stopping to get the feel of a part of Jamaica completely unsullied by tourism, and to eat some superb **seafood**. A number of small shacks sell lobster and fish fresh from the boats; the most popular is *Little Ochi*, right on the beach just to the west of the town square, which fills up at weekends and holidays with hungry folk from Mandeville or even Kingston. There's little reason to **stay** but, should you need to, the uninspiring *Sea-Riv Hotel* (☎962 7265; ②) – west of town en route to the Port Kaiser bauxite-loading pier – is right on the beach, while

---

Manatees

The **manatee** – an aquatic mammal that looks rather like a large, fat seal – is found in the warm waters of the Atlantic Ocean and in the Caribbean Sea. Also known as the sea cow, it's a very secretive creature; little is known about its reproductive habits, for example, and studies have found it tricky to monitor numbers. The nature park at Alligator Hole is the only place in Jamaica, and one of few places in the world, where you can see them in the wild.

Fully grown, manatees can reach up to fourteen feet in length, although the great size is no cause for concern as they are strictly vegetarian – eating as much as four hundred kilos of sea grass per day – and known for doting on each other and their young. Columbus probably spotted them when he first came to Jamaica in 1494 (although he claimed that he had seen mermaids), and there were certainly plenty around. Sadly, their slow and gentle lifestyle meant that they were (and are) easy prey for fishermen; accordingly, even though they are now protected, fewer than 3000 are believed to survive in the Caribbean and only 100 in Jamaica.

---

just one mile to the east at Wards Bay, *The Venue Sunset Lounge*
(☎965 4508; ①) is a small, friendly guesthouse with a bar and
seafood joint.

From the square in Alligator Pond, a road leads east for eighteen
miles to Alligator Hole and Milk River. Recently laid, this gives a pretty drive through an isolated area known as **Canoe Valley** or the Long
Bay Morass, much of it along the coast, with goats and seabirds usually your only company. The area is barely touched by development
and remains a naturalist's paradise, with the dry, cactus-strewn
slopes in the west giving way to mangrove swamps as you head further east – brilliant for bird-watching. Halfway along the road you'll
cross **Gut River**, one of the most picturesque places on the south
coast. The river runs under the road towards the sea, emerging in a
clear blue stream edged by coconut palms, where you can swim,
snorkel and jump off the rocks. Frigate birds and egrets flap lazily
around, and even the best efforts of local developers, who have put
up a **café** and **bar** with very basic **accommodation** (①) or camping,
can't spoil the beauty.

Continuing east towards Milk River, you'll pass the tiny nature
park of **Alligator Hole** (daily 9am–4pm; free), the part-time home of
a small number of **manatees**. It's a peaceful place to stop, with a
rather shabby visitor centre. If you're lucky, you'll see the gentle
creatures come in for their daily feed, usually in the late afternoon,
supplied by the caretaker-managers who hang out by the park, drinking, playing dominoes and selling cold beer and soft drinks. A boat
trip downriver to look for the manatees is highly recommended
(J$200 per person); ask to go all the way to the end where the river
flows into the sea and there's a tiny deserted beach. It's a truly para-
disiacal spot. **Crocodiles** (known locally as alligators) also inhabit
the area, although they are seen less often.

Milk River Spa

*Infrequent
buses run to
Milk River
from May Pen
(see p.365).*

The **hot mineral springs** near **MILK RIVER**, only a couple of miles
inland from Alligator Hole, were first discovered in the early eighteenth century. Mineral spas were subsequently built in the area –
first opened to the public in 1794 – and are today housed in the basement of the *Milk River Hotel* (☎902 4657, fax 902 4974; ②). The
hotel is a lovely old wooden building, with comfortable rooms and
inexpensive meals on offer, and, though there's nothing spectacular
about the area, the dry climate and the laid-back atmosphere make it
a very pleasant place to spend a night.

Many of the guests at the hotel and spa are return visitors who
swear by the curative powers of the water for a range of ailments
from rheumatism to gout, nerve diseases and sciatica. Other visitors find their curiosity tinged with concern about the high radioactivity levels of the baths – more than fifty times that of the waters
at Vichy in France – although the staff will assure you that this is

quite harmless. The nine sunken tiled baths are big enough to have a good splash around in during the recommended fifteen minutes, although you'll probably just want to lie there and soak up the steam. You get free use of the spas if you're staying at the hotel; if you're visiting, they cost J$80 per time.

Other than the spa, there's little to the village of Milk River other than the usual crowd of schoolchildren and smattering of churches, although there are rumoured plans to build a large all-inclusive hotel close to the spa. The river itself is named for its colour in the early morning, when it is shrouded in mist, but given that it is the home of a number of local crocodiles, swimming is not a great idea. You could try the **Milk River Mineral Pool** – an open-air swimming pool 150 yards from the hotel – though it's only filled these days on special occasions. Two miles beyond the spa, past rows of giant cactuses, is the tiny fishing village of **FARQUHARS** which has, at its western end, a passable black-sand beach where you can swim in the ocean.

East of Milk River

From Milk River, you can either head north to the main road for Mandeville and May Pen or continue east towards Lionel Town. After six miles, the latter B12 road passes through the quiet village of **ALLEY**, where **St Peter's Church** is one of the oldest and most attractive churches on the island. Founded in 1671 the present building mostly dates from the early eighteenth century. Inside the church, check out the tablets on the upper west wall, engraved with the Lord's Prayer and the Ten Commandments, and the 1847 organ. Outside there are a mass of crumbling tombs, many of the inscriptions ravaged by time. If the church is locked try asking for the key at Amity Hall library (see below).

Beyond Alley you'll pass a unique octagonal building at tiny **AMITY HALL**. Originally a sugar mill, probably built around 1800, the building now houses the **parish library** (Mon–Fri 11am–5pm), with the rooms above occupied by a local family (though you can ask to look around). Constructed from imported brick, rather than Jamaican limestone, this was an unusual building even in its own time. Ruins of the old sugar works, which closed in 1926, are dotted around nearby and there is a present-day refinery at **Monymusk**, a mile away. Unlikely as it now seems, Amity Hall was the site of an important battle during the French invasion of 1694. The French landed at Yallahs in the east of Jamaica (see p.145) and crossed the island, destroying sugar estates as they went. At Amity Hall, though, they lost over a hundred men in one short engagement with the British (probably on the site of the sugar mill) and fled, never to return, burning the coastal village of **Carlisle Bay** in spite as they left.

East of Amity Hall, the B12 road turns north for the bustling market town of **LIONEL TOWN**, crowded with traders, fruit and vegetable stalls and schoolchildren, or you can continue past the turnoff and head south for some of the most isolated places in Jamaica. JACKSON BAY, roughly five miles from Lionel Town, is a scruffy fishing village with a not particularly attractive beach. A much better option for a swim is the gorgeous strip of sand 500 yards to the west; take the right-fork on your way down to Jackson Bay. Very few tourists ever come to this part of the island, and your presence will awaken considerable local interest. If you have a four-wheel-drive vehicle, you can head east before you reach the bay and a rough track carries you out along the deserted and scrubby **Portland Ridge** past mangrove swamps and muddy plains dotted with stunted acacia trees. Inhabited only by a few fishermen and the occasional abandoned car the peninsula is an eerily atmospheric place. The track continues on through the private grounds of the PWD Hunting and Sporting Club, which are closed to the public, and comes to a halt at Portland Lighthouse. For the adventurous, a canoe ride through the mangrove swamps and inland swamp-lakes may be arranged with some of the local fishermen at Portland Cottage, starting at the Beach, or, in local parlance at "Bar Mout".

Inland to Mandeville

The A2 highway speeds inland from Black River, passing through some attractive countryside before making the long climb up Spur Tree Hill to **Mandeville**. The main road passes through **Bamboo Avenue**, with its walls of tall bamboo, and there are several interesting detours worth taking, particularly in the interior of St Elizabeth. There are gorgeous **waterfalls** at YS, **hiking** possibilities in the **Black River Gorge**, and the quiet and completely untouristed villages of the **Santa Cruz mountains**. You can also visit a **rum factory**, beautifully placed among fields of sugarcane at Appleton, on the southern edge of Cockpit Country (see Chapter Four).

Accommodation options in the area are limited, though there are a couple of decent places at Santa Cruz and Maggotty, and you may want to consider visiting on day-trips from a base on the south coast or in Mandeville. **Getting around** is a breeze if you've got a car; public transport links into the interior are not brilliant though buses do run to most parts – for a couple of places, including YS, you'll need to take a taxi for a short part of the trip.

Middle Quarters and YS Falls

As you drive northeast from Black River, you'll reach an intersection directing you north for Montego Bay or east towards Santa Cruz and Mandeville. Head east and you'll soon pass **Middle Quarters**, a small crossroads where groups of women sell spicy, salty **shrimp** from the Black River. Feel free to sample from the proffered bags before you

buy; reckon on around J$100 for a small bag. The shrimp taste okay
on their own, though better with hardough bread which the vendors
occasionally have. Buy some to add to your picnic if you're heading
to the YS waterfalls or take a few minutes out to crunch them on the
roadside and have a chat with the women. Incidentally, don't be
intimidated by the fiercely competitive approach of the sellers – they
are often all members of the same family and if one is lagging in sales
for the day, she will usually be thrust forward to clinch the deal.

Shortly after Middle Quarters, a left turn takes you two and a half
miles north to **YS**, an area dominated by the **YS farm**, home of the
magnificent YS Falls. The name is thought to derive from the farm's
original owners in 1684, John Yates and Richard Scott, whose initials
were stamped on their cattle and the hogsheads of sugar that they
exported. Today the farm covers around 2500 acres and raises pedigree **red poll cattle** – a Jamaican breed that you'll see all over the
country – and grows papaya for export.

*For more on
the medicinal
uses of
Jamaican
plants see p.32.*

The **YS Falls** a series of ten greater and lesser waterfalls, are great
fun (daily 9.50am–3.30pm; April–Dec closed Mon; US$10). A jitney
pulls you through the farm's land and alongside the YS river to a
grassy area at the base of the falls. You can climb up the lower falls
or take the wooden stairway which leads to a platform beside the
uppermost and most spectacular waterfall. There are lianas and
ropes for aspiring Tarzans, pools for gentle bathing at the foot of
each fall, and you can swim under the main falls and climb up into a
cave behind them. Early morning is a good time to go, before the
tour buses arrive; take a picnic and a book and you can comfortably
spend a few hours loafing around on the grass and in the water. Cold
beers and soft drinks are always available nearby.

A **car** is extremely handy if you're heading for the falls, as they're
a little off the beaten track, but if you're relying on public transport,
buses run along the main A2 highway south of YS between Black
River and Santa Cruz. Ask the driver to drop you at the junction, and
you can usually find taxis waiting to run passengers up to the YS farm
– make sure you negotiate a price before you get in (around J$150 is
standard). There's nowhere to **stay** at YS – the nearest options are
Maggotty (see below) or Black River (see p.341).

Maggotty

East of YS and seven miles from the main A2 highway, **MAGGOTTY**
resembles a small Wild West frontier town. It's a dry, dusty place,
most of whose inhabitants work at the **Appleton rum estate** nearby
(see 352), and, though there's little to see in town, there is some
beautiful scenery nearby – including the YS Falls – and a couple of
good accommodation options.

Just south of town, the red-roofed *Apple Valley Guesthouse*
(☎963 9508; ③) is a colonial-era great house with five comfortable
rooms. It's also a handy base for some good walking, and the owners

can provide guides. The best **hike** is across the local farmland and down into the **Black River Gorge**, a deep and attractive ravine carved by the island's principal river. Around twenty minutes' walk from the guesthouse you reach the first of a series of 28 **waterfalls** and you can either wallow around there or trek for an hour or so down to the bottom. It's a straightforward walk to get down into the gorge although the climb back up can be a bit strenuous.

The guesthouse's industrious owners also run the **Apple Valley Park** opposite, a small nature park with ducks and geese, paddleboats for kids, explanations of the medicinal value of Jamaica's herbs and a little farm. Unfortunately a decline in custom means that the park is only open by appointment these days; you might be lucky and arrive at the same time as a school group (J$250 if you're not booked with a party). The park has a couple of very basic cabins (①), but the simple, clean rooms at *Poinciana Guesthouse* (①), up a slight hill opposite the police station, are more comfortable. Each of the guesthouses will provide **meals** as required, or you can get typical Jamaican food in town at the *Valley* restaurant or *The Sweet Bakery and Restaurant*, just up the road from the *Apple Valley Guesthouse* and run by the owners, which does vegetarian and Chinese meals as well.

Infrequent **minibuses** run to Maggotty from Black River and Santa Cruz. If you're **driving**, the road north from the A2 highway is in far better condition than the road running east/west between Maggotty and YS.

The Appleton rum estate

Three miles east of Maggotty, the **Wray and Nephew rum estate** at **APPLETON** (☎963 9215, *www.appletonrum.com*; Mon–Sat 9am–3.30pm; US$12) has a great setting in the Black River valley among thousands of acres of sugarcane fields. At 250 years old, this is the oldest rum producer in the English-speaking Caribbean and the best known of Jamaica's several brands. All of the rum produced here is sent for barrelling in Kingston (though some barrels are sent back here to age) and blending and bottling are also carried out in the capital.

You'll need a car to get here, or you can take a taxi from Maggotty. Though you're free to drop in, it's a good idea to call ahead to arrange a guided visit, if only to avoid your visit coinciding with a big tour party. The thirty-minute **tour** starts with a complimentary drink and video session, followed by a whirlwind tour through the factory and warehouses and then outside to an old press, where donkeys used to walk in circles to turn a grinder that crushed juice out of the sugarcane. Today it's all mechanized, though a donkey has been put back into service to demonstrate old techniques. All sorts of pots, boilers and barrels used for the production process are placed artistically around the site. The tour

Rum and raison d'être

Rum – once known as rumbullion or kill-devil – is the island's national drink, and you couldn't choose a better place to acquire a taste for the stuff. Jamaica was the first country to make rum commercially and it still produces some of the world's finest. **Overproof** is the drink of choice for the less well-off – it's cheap, lethally strong (64 percent alcohol) and, supposedly, cures all ills. If you can't handle the overproof, the standard **white rums** are the basis for most cocktails, while more refined palates go for the **darker rums**. During the ageing process these rums acquire colour from the oak barrels in which they are stored and, as they get older, you'll find they slip down increasingly smoothly with no need for a mixer.

Distilling of sugarcane juice started in Jamaica during the years of Spanish occupation, stepping up a few gears when the British took over in 1655, and rum became famous as the drink of the island's semi-legitimate **pirates** and **buccaneers**. The production process hasn't changed much over the centuries, although it has become fully mechanized, putting a number of donkeys out of work in the process. The sugarcane is squeezed to extract every drop of its juice, which is then boiled and put through a centrifuge, producing molasses. In turn, the molasses are diluted with water and yeast is added to get the stuff fermenting away. After fermentation, the liquid "dead wash" is sent to the distillery, where it is heated, and the evaporating alcohol caught in tanks. It sounds simple enough and it is, but when you discover that it takes ten to twelve tonnes of sugarcane to produce half a bottle of alcohol, which is then blended with water and a mixture of secret ingredients – molasses is almost certainly among them – to make the finished product, you begin to appreciate all those fields of swaying cane a little more.

concludes in a "saloon", where you get to sample all sixteen kinds of rum and various rum-based liquors.

Bamboo Avenue and Lacovia

Back on the main A2 highway, **Bamboo Avenue**, halfway between Middle Quarters and Lacovia, enlivens the drive to Mandeville. For several miles *bambusa vulgaris*, Jamaica's largest species of bamboo, has grown up on either side to create a pretty arch over the road. The place was once almost completely shaded by the bamboo but the sun now streams in through gaps created by Hurricane Gilbert and, some say, by official neglect.

Just east of Bamboo Avenue, the village of **LACOVIA**, one-time capital of St Elizabeth, was once an important inland port for shipping sugar and logwood down to Black River for export. Today it is most notable for its **twin tombs**, just outside the Texaco petrol station, believed to contain the bodies of two young men killed in a local duel in 1723. One of the deceased is named as Thomas Jordan Spencer and the coat of arms on his tombstone suggests a connection with the family of Winston Churchill and Diana Spencer. Lacovia is also home to the **Cashoo Ostrich Park** (☎771 6000; Sat & Sun

10am–5.30pm; US$10); take a right turn over the old Lacovia bridge and follow the signs towards Slipe. The park, named after its former crop of cashew nuts, is a family-orientated place which offers a petting zoo and play area as well as the ostriches themselves. Jamaicans haven't yet warmed to the appeal of eating ostrich and they're being bred here for export. A guided tour of the grounds concentrates on ostrich facts but also takes in the park's comprehensive and rather pretty herb garden. Pond fishing (J$100 per pound caught) and pony rides for children (J$100 for 20 mins) are available and the park hosts seasonal special events – an Easter egg hunt and an annual shrimp festival held over the third weekend of November.

Santa Cruz, Malvern and Spur Tree Hill

If you're in this part of the country, sooner or later you're likely to pass through **SANTA CRUZ**, the main settlement along the A2 and reckoned to be the hottest place in Jamaica. This rapidly expanding market town, once famous as a livestock trading centre, is noisy and frenetic at the best of times and there's no particular reason to stop off here, although you can fill up on fresh patties and delicious juices at *Paradise Patties* on Main Street. If you need to spend a night, the friendly *Danbar Guest House* (☎966 9382; ①), at Trevmar Park just south of the main road towards the west side of town, has seven very cheap rooms and the owners will cook to order. Fans of dancehall might want to stay for **Club Classique**, run by Irie FM disk jockey G.T. Taylor and often featuring the best of Jamaica's dancehall DJs; check out Wednesday nights in particular (Wed–Sun; J$150–300 cover dependent on the popularity of the DJ or act).

The road south from Santa Cruz to Treasure Beach and the coast (see p.342) is a beautiful (if slow) drive over the Santa Cruz Mountains. The drive takes you through a series of tiny villages and the quiet town of **MALVERN**. Like Christiana further north (see p.363), this is one of Jamaica's **coolest** towns, at around two and a half thousand feet above sea level, and, earlier this century, was an important summer retreat for foreigners and wealthy Jamaicans, though it's now almost bereft of tourists. Today, apart from a handful of top-notch schools and colleges established here in the 1850s, there's not much to the town, although the presence of returning residents who've made their money abroad is injecting an air of affluence – with grand houses springing up on the hilltops – and it's a pretty place to cruise around for a little while. There's nowhere to stay, although the nearby *Chariots Hotel* (☎966 3860; ②) in **LEEDS**, midway between Santa Cruz and Malvern, has a small pool and decent rooms. *Dolly's* restaurant and ice cream parlour, next to the petrol station in Malvern, has standard Jamaican food if you're after some lunch.

Heading east from Santa Cruz, the A2 continues to **Gutters**, on the Manchester/St Elizabeth border, where it begins the long and rather tortuous climb up **Spur Tree Hill** to Mandeville. Once known as "man bump", the switchbacking hill provides dramatic views over the southern plains, the Santa Cruz Mountains, and down to the sea, and there are a couple of good **bars** and **restaurants** to stop off at and enjoy the view: *All Seasons* has a variety of local dishes and a verandah while, 400 yards further up, a handful of small bars specialize in curry goat and mannish water – *Alex's Curry Goat Spot* is known island-wide.

Mandeville and around

You can almost feel the wealth in **MANDEVILLE**, Jamaica's fifth largest town. Big money started to arrive here in the 1950s as a result of the very visible **bauxite industry** that grew up around the town. More recently, returning expatriate Jamaicans, attracted by the cooler climate and the relatively low crime rate, have begun to invest their accumulated savings in large homes and small businesses around town. Tourism has been rather an unimportant sector in recent years, although from the early days of the *Mandeville Hotel* in the 1890s, the town was popular with British soldiers who came to escape the heat of the coastal areas and to recuperate from their fevers and diseases.

*For more on
Jamaica's
bauxite indus-
try, see p.358.*

Nowadays, Mandeville is still a quiet town and by no means an essential stop on your tour of the island. However, it is a pleasant place to get away from the hustle and bustle of Jamaica's more touristed areas – you'll probably notice the lack of hassle – and makes a reasonable base for exploring the south and centre of the island. If you're here for any time, check out the old great house at

---

Community tourism

The creation of big tourist "ghettos" on the north coast has completely disrupted traditional lifestyles there and means that, often, the only contact overseas visitors have with Jamaicans is when they are serving drinks or driving tour buses. In the face of its own gradually developing tourist scene, Jamaica's south coast, where the absence of large-scale beach resorts offers visitors more of a feel of the "real" Jamaica, is keen to escape such insensitive development. Planners and hoteliers are showing increasing interest in the concept of **"community tourism"**, which aims to contain and control tourism by fostering closer connections between the tourist and the community – through visits to schools, farms and craft centres – and persuading developers not to despoil the area. It's a positive, optimistic approach, but it remains to be seen whether the organizers' noble intentions will rein in some of the short-termist developers, beginning to sniff big possibilities on the south coast. For more information on the scheme, contact the Sustainable Communities Foundation at Mandeville's *Astra Country Inn* (☎962 3725, fax 962 1461, *scf9@hotmail.com*), where you'll also find the community tourism operator Countrystyle Ltd.

*See p.26 of
Basics for more
on community
tourism in
Jamaica.*

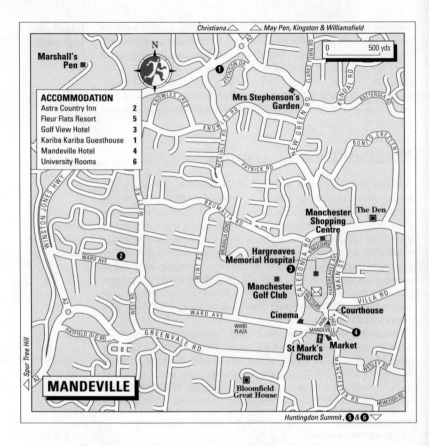

N

0   500 yds

Marshall's
Pen ■

ACCOMMODATION

Astra Country Inn	2
Fleur Flats Resort	5
Golf View Hotel	3
Kariba Kariba Guesthouse	1
Mandeville Hotel	4
University Rooms	6

Mrs Stephenson's
Garden

Manchester
Shopping
Centre   The Den

Hargreaves
Memorial Hospital ❸

Manchester
Golf Club

Cinema   Courthouse

WARD AVE
WARD
PLAZA

St Mark's
Church   Market

MANDEVILLE

Bloomfield
Great House

Marshall's Pen and the more contemporary mansion at **Huntingdon Summit,** or while away an hour with a visit to a local **factory.**

Arrival, information and getting around

Buses into Mandeville arrive at the south end of Mandeville Square, a small village green in the town centre surrounded by banks, supermarkets and, usually, a crowd of people. Buses and minibuses for Kingston and Christiana (less often for the west and north coasts) leave from the same place at regular intervals, and the town's main **taxi rank** is alongside. If you're **driving** there are three separate entrances to town signposted from the highway – it's simplest to take the middle one, at the major roundabout, and follow New Green Road all the way into town. For sightseeing, a car is definitely a major asset; although you can see everything in the town centre on foot, getting out to Marshall's Pen or Huntingdon Summit will require wheels.

There is no longer a **tourist board office** in Mandeville, so you'll have to rely on your hotel staff and the usual flyers around town for news of what's going on. Diana McIntyre-Pike at the *Astra Country Inn* is especially helpful and a great source of information on the local area. The *Astra Country Inn* and the *Mandeville Hotel* both organize tours of the local sights, as does the *Kariba Kariba* guesthouse whose genial owner, Derrick O'Connor has a lovely retreat, **Little Rippon Farm** in Mile Gully, to which he takes guided visits through the fruit orchards, carefully planted flowering shrubs and woodland trails.

Accommodation

Mandeville's **hotels** largely cater for business travellers as tourists are relatively few here, although there are a couple of decent budget places. Countrystyle Tourism (c/o the *Astra Country Inn*, see below) can organize bed and breakfast accommodation in some of Mandeville's loveliest homes.

Astra Country Inn, 62 Ward Ave; ☎962 3725, fax 962 1461, *www.access-ja.com/countrystyle*. A little out of the town centre, and a bit short on character; the place used to be a nursing home and still feels a little sterile though major renovations are underway. There's a small pool, the food is good and the hotel is the base for the area's community tourism scheme (see box p.355). ④.

Fleur Flats Resorts, 10 Coke Drive; ☎962 5109. Tidy self-catering apartments in a small hotel complex a five-minute drive from town – follow the Manchester Road south from the central square, keeping right at the petrol station, and take the first left. ③.

Golf View Hotel, 51/2 B Caledonia Rd; ☎962 4471, fax 962 5640. Modern, well-equipped hotel designed around a central courtyard that holds a small pool. ④.

Kariba Kariba Guesthouse, Winston Jones Highway (A2), New Green Road roundabout; ☎962 8006, fax 962 5002. Friendly little guesthouse on the edge of Mandeville whose rates include breakfast. ③.

Mandeville Hotel, 4 Hotel St; ☎962 2460, fax 962 0700, *manhot @cwjamaica.com*. One of the oldest hotels in Jamaica and, though almost totally reconstructed and refurbished, still a pleasant and easy-going place to stay right in the heart of town. Facilities include a large pool. ④.

University Rooms, Northern Caribbean University, Manchester Road; ☎625 2296, fax 962 0075, *taicentre@wicollege.edu*. Clean, spacious and comfortable rooms catering for visitors to the university, though tourists may be welcome if the rooms are not booked. Rates include breakfast. ④.

The Town and around

Mandeville was founded in 1814 and still retains something of its early colonial air – most noticeably at the very English **Manchester Golf Club**, just west of the town centre. The first buildings were set out around **Mandeville Square**, a rather unkempt grassy space now also known as Cecil Charlton Park after a former mayor (see p.359), and this is the best starting point for a brief walking tour of the centre.

Built in 1819, **St Mark's Church** is on the south side of the park, behind the massed ranks of taxis, buses and vendors. The interior is pretty ordinary but, as usual, there are plenty of goats nosing around in the churchyard, and you could happily spend a few minutes wandering among them and checking out the nineteenth-century tombstones. On the other side of the park, the limestone **courthouse** is one of Mandeville's original buildings, completed in 1820 and still normally crowded, while the **rectory** (now a private home) alongside the courthouse dates from the same year. The nearby **police station** – once the town jail and workhouse – is the last of Mandeville's original structures.

North of here, at 25 New Green Rd, there is a **private garden** that will be of interest if you've a passion for anthuriums. Carmen Stephenson has the most impressive collections of plants in town, and she is a regular winner at the Mandeville Flower Show every May. Visitors are free to drop in for a tour of the garden (daily during daylight hours; US$2) with its well-ordered collection, which includes the rare white anthurium, orchids and **ortaniques** – a cross

---

Jamaica's bauxite

Bauxite, the raw material from which aluminium is produced, is present in abundance in Jamaica's earth. Large-scale extraction began here during the 1950s, when three North American companies started local operations, and the mining and processing operations remain very visible as you travel around the country's interior. Much of the mining is open-cast, resulting in gruesome-looking red mud lakes like the one just outside Mandeville, while the ugly refineries spoil the landscape at various places around the country.

It may not be pretty, but the "red gold" is vital to Jamaica's economy. After tourism, it's the second most important contributor, employing around five thousand people and, more importantly, contributing about a quarter of the government's income and a half of the nation's export earnings. A third of the raw bauxite is shipped abroad for processing; the rest is processed at the island's four alumina refineries, and the resulting alumina is then sent abroad for conversion to aluminium. This last stage – the most profitable part of the process – cannot economically be carried out in Jamaica because of the lack of a cheap energy source.

The industry took a big hit during the 1970s, when Michael Manley's PNP administration imposed higher taxes on the multinational companies involved in extraction. The bauxite companies scaled down their operations dramatically and, in the face of increasing world competition and a declining price, it was a decade before the local industry recovered to a perceptible degree. Today, the industry remains under pressure, with world prices relatively low and new production centres in Australia and South America challenging Jamaica's market position. With little else to fall back on, the island has to hope that the industry it has relied on so heavily for nearly five decades can survive its modern challenges.

between the orange and the tangerine and Mandeville's contribution to the world of fruit.

Marshall's Pen and Huntingdon Summit

Mandeville's more interesting sights are both a bit of a drive out of town. **Marshall's Pen** (tours daily by appointment, ☎904 5454; US$10) is a lovely old great house, built around 1795 and originally used in the preparation of coffee beans for export. The driveway you enter through was the "barbecue", where the beans were laid out to dry in the sun, and the ground floor of the house, with its massive cedar floorboards, was where they were polished prior to their shipment to the US and UK for roasting and grinding. Nowadays this area has been converted to living quarters and also serves, together with a couple of rooms upstairs, as an interesting **museum**. The Suttons, owners of the house, have collected relentlessly over the generations; there are fabulous collections of shells and stamps, both from Jamaica and abroad, Japanese and Chinese artefacts, and a tiny array of Taino relics.

The grounds are great for **bird-watching** and serious ornithologists can arrange to stay at the house for around US$30 per person per night. Even if you are just passing through you are likely to see a doctor bird or two flitting around the gardens. Robert Sutton has co-written a leading book on Jamaica's birds; he and his wife Ann are loaded with information on the country's natural history and occasionally lead natural history tours of the south coast and Cockpit Country. If you have a particular interest, ask.

A more modern mansion is **Huntingdon Summit** (daily by appointment ☎962 2274; free), a Jamaican version of Elvis Presley's Graceland that's the home of the town's former mayor and self-made millionaire Cecil Charlton – you'll see his **off-course betting shops**, from which he made his fortune, all over town. The octagonal extravagance features a giant living room replete with antique furniture, seven bedrooms colour coded by their carpets and often esoteric furnishings, and a library stuffed with trophies and photographs of the great man meeting Jamaican and foreign dignitaries. The extensive grounds of the house have their own bamboo avenue and swimming pool with swim-up bar that you enter via a tunnel inside the house, as well as great views over the neighbouring countryside. The whole place is gloriously kitsch and offers an interesting perspective on Jamaica's nouveaux riches. If Mr Charlton is at home try and persuade him to show you round – he's predictably a larger-than-life character.

To get there, follow the Manchester Road south out of Mandeville, keeping right at the Texaco station. At the T-junction where the road ends, turn right onto Newport Road, then first left onto May Day Road for just under a mile, turning left down George's Valley Road until you reach the big green gates on your left.

Coffee, chocolate and Pickapeppa sauce

If you have some time to kill while you're in Mandeville you can visit a nearby factory. The **coffee factory** of Jamaican Standard Products (☎963 4211; Mon–Fri by appointment; free) is a couple of miles north of the town centre in Williamsfield. JSP makes a number of different foodstuffs – including tea, sauces and spices – but coffee, which they've been producing since the 1950s, is their mainstay; the factory roasts, grinds and packages beans for the superior Blue Mountain coffee as well as JSP's own "High Mountain" brand. Since seventy percent of coffee drunk in Jamaica is instant most of the coffee packaged here is exported – largely to Japan. The tour of the coffee plant is brief but informative and the place smells wonderful; afterwards you have a chance to buy the products at pretty good prices.

On the same street, the **chocolate factory** of the Pioneer Chocolate Company (☎963 4216; Mon–Fri by appointment; free) is a small family-run business that has been producing chocolate products since the 1920s. The cocoa beans are roasted here to give a chocolate flavour and the crushed beans are then put into a melter and separated into cocoa butter and cocoa powder. Much of the cocoa butter is exported for use in pharmaceuticals, like tanning lotion, while the powder is used for popular items like drinking chocolate. Pioneer also produces excellent chocolate bars, though it has only a tiny share of the domestic market. The owners have recently started to discourage visitors, mainly because of the risk of accidents, but if you have a keen interest it's worth calling to try to arrange a tour.

The Magic Toy factory, in nearby Walderston, is a good place for souvenirs – see p.363.

Finally, there's the **Pickapeppa factory** (☎962 2928; Mon–Fri by appointment; free), just beyond Williamsfield at the bottom of Shooter's Hill. In operation since 1921, the factory is active for nine months of the year (normally March–Nov) producing its unusual spicy sauce, made from home-grown tomatoes, onions, mangoes, spices and hot peppers. Though you'll see the distinctive bottles at restaurants across the island, 98 percent of the factory's production is for the export market.

Eating, drinking and nightlife

In restaurant listings, we have given a phone number only for those places where you might need to reserve a table.

As you'd expect from such a peaceful town the **nightlife** is pretty tame, but there are plenty of good **restaurants** and a lot of fast-food options and snack outlets at the ubiquitous malls (particularly at the Manchester Shopping Centre). The central bus park at twilight is your best bet for jerk chicken and delicious roasted yam. You'll also find a handful of decent **bars** and **nightclubs**.

Restaurants and snack bars

Astra Inn, 62 Ward Ave; ☎962 3725. Good and moderately priced hotel restaurant, though not worth the trip out if you're staying in town.

Bamboo Village, Ward Plaza, 35 Ward Ave; ☎962 4515. Pretty good Chinese restaurant, halfway between the town's main square and the *Astra Inn*.

Bloomfield Great House, Bloomfield; ☎962 3116, Wonderfully restored great house with a beautiful verandah offering one of the best views over Mandeville and an imaginative exhibition space on the restaurant walls. The food is top-notch, a mix of international cuisine and nouvelle Jamaican with home-made pasta, fresh lobster and spicy chicken dishes. Puddings include cheesecake and tiramisu. If you're not eating come anyway for an early evening drink.

Bluebells, Midway Mall, Caledonia Rd. Reasonable spot for a cheap Jamaican breakfast or lunch, serving the usual staples.

Centenary Rastarant, marketplace. Tiny café with superb freshly squeezed orange juice and home-cooked Jamaican food. A great spot for watching the hustle and bustle of the market.

Central Restaurant and Bar, Caledonia Rd; ☎962 1546. Just across from the more popular *Den* and serving similar meals, *Central* is less refined but the food is still good.

The Den, 35 Caledonia Rd; ☎962 3603. One of Mandeville's busier restaurants, with curry chicken and other typical Jamaican dishes served indoors or out. The Friday night jam here plays host to live music in the garden, often jazz.

Gee's Café, Manchester Shopping Centre. Best of a number of good eateries, juice bars and pastry shops at the back of this shopping plaza, with excellent Jamaican breakfasts and good cheap food throughout the day.

International Chinese Restaurant, 117 Manchester Rd; ☎962 1252. Chinese food from an extensive menu, a short drive from town.

Mandeville Hotel, 4 Hotel St; ☎962 2460. Consistently good central hotel restaurant, though often low on atmosphere, with a varied menu of steaks, fish and curry goat. Excellent breakfasts are served on a poolside terrace.

Steo's Grill and Bar, Caledonia Rd. Friendly jerk meat joint in yard close to the *Golf View Hotel* (see p.357).

Bars and clubs

Manchester Arms, at the *Mandeville Hotel*. Pleasant quiet bar, fashioned after an English pub.

Manchester Club, corner of Caledonia Rd and Ward Ave. Definitely a colonial feel at this golf club, but a decent place for an early evening drink if you're cruising around.

Medina Sport's Bar & Grill, 8B Caledonia Rd. Popular basement bar with slot machines and outside yard. Hosts occasional visits by top Jamaican bands and DJs.

Merv's Cocktail Bar, Caledonia Plaza, 11 Caledonia Ave. Simple, easy-going bar – good if you're looking for a bit of local colour.

N'Somnia, 33 Ward Ave, next to the Ward Plaza (open Wed–Sun). Small dark venue that gets seriously crowded at weekends belting out dancehall music. The best place for a dance in the town itself.

Ward 21, Manchester Shopping Centre (open Wed–Sun). Local disco which gets busy at weekends, playing a mix of dancehall, reggae and soca.

Shopping

Shopping malls are everywhere in Mandeville. Probably the most extensive is the Manchester Shopping Centre, opposite the junction of Caledonia Road and New Green Road, where you'll find banks, an excellent Hi-Lo supermarket, craft stores, and a number of fast-food restaurants. Bookland at the shopping centre has **books** on Jamaica and recent UK and US **newspapers** and **magazines**. There are two more **supermarkets** – Moo-Penns and Super Plus – beside Mandeville Square on East Park Crescent, and a good **record shop** at Leroys, Leaders Plaza, 41 Main St. The vibrant and colourful local **market** is at the southeast corner of Mandeville Square and a great place to shop for fruit and vegetables.

If you're nearby, drop in at the SWA Craft Centre, 7 North Racecourse behind the Manchester Shopping Centre, which evolved as a way of dealing with the problem of youth unemployment for girls. They are trained in various craft skills, such as embroidery, dress-making and cooking, and many of the products are sold in the centre. If you're not interested in the crafts there's normally some cooking going on and patties or plantain tarts worth trying.

Listings

Banks Numerous banks around town include NCB at the Mandeville Centre (☎962 2161) which is situated at the top end of Manchester Rd just off the main square, and Bank of Nova Scotia at Caledonia Rd (☎962 2842) and also the Manchester Shopping Centre (☎962 3139). If you're changing money, there are cambios at the Moo-Penns and Super Plus supermarkets on East Park Crescent.

Car rental Candi, Caledonia Rd, opposite Manchester Shopping Centre (☎962 3153); Hemisphere, 51 Manchester Rd (☎962 1921); Maxdan, 183 Ward Ave (☎962 5341). From US$60 a day.

Dentist Manchester Dental Associates, 11 Manchester Rd (☎962 1560).

Golf The nine-hole Manchester Golf Club (☎962 2403), at the corner of Caledonia Rd and Ward Ave, is the oldest club in the Caribbean and costs around US$20 for a round and a caddy.

Hospitals The public Mandeville Hospital is at 32 Hargreaves Ave (☎962 2067); the private Hargreaves Memorial Hospital shares the same address (☎962 2040). In an emergency call ☎119 for an ambulance.

Internet Email can be collected and sent from Internet Solution, Brumalia Mall, 2 Perth Rd (☎625 2023, *gwhits@cwjamaica.com*; US$3 per hr).

Library The Manchester Parish Library (Mon–Fri 9.30am–5.30pm, Sat 9am–1pm) is on Hargreaves Ave, just above the hospital.

Pharmacies Haughtons, 18 West Park Crescent (Mon–Sat 8am–10pm, Sun 9am–9pm); Fontana, Manchester Shopping Centre (Mon–Sat 8am–7pm).

Police The main station is on the north side of Mandeville Square (☎962 2250). In an emergency call ☎119.

Post office is on South Racecourse (Mon–Fri 8.30am–4pm).

Taxis The main rank is on the south side of Mandeville Square, near the parish church, or call Garth Taxi Service (☎625 5681).

Travel agents Praise Travel Ltd, Midway Mall, Caledonia Rd (☎625 4514).

Christiana and May Pen

The south's two other main towns sit in splendid isolation, with the emptiness of the interior between them. North of Mandeville, the hills around the small market town of **Christiana** offer a view of a very different, more rural, Jamaica, while unattractive **May Pen**, to the east, is only worth a visit for its annual agricultural show, or for the impressive great house at nearby **Halse Hall**.

Christiana and around

The steep Shooter's Hill heads north from Mandeville, climbing up above the ugly Alcan bauxite plant, with its lake of red mud. Just over halfway up the hill you'll come to **WALDERSTON**, a small village at the crossroads; turn left and left again up a dreadful track for the sweet little **Magic Toy factory** (☎603 1495; daily 9am–5pm). The small workshop makes the very colourful wooden fish, jigsaws and similar playthings that you'll see in hotel gift shops all over Jamaica – you can buy them here at a considerable discount – and is housed in a lovely old house with attractive gardens and fabulous views over the surrounding area.

Continue ten miles north for **CHRISTIANA**, a small market town for the surrounding agricultural community, where potatoes, yams, ginger, coffee and cocoa are grown. Lofty and cool, three thousand feet up in the hills, the town was a popular resort for "old-style" tourism in the 1940s and 1950s when beaches and tanning were less fashionable than they are today. It's a simple one-street town with just a single hotel and not a huge amount to see – though you can organize a hike or two and a spot of caving – but if you're looking for a peaceful escape from the heat of the coast, it's an excellent choice. If you have a car, Christiana also makes a decent base for visiting Appleton and Maggotty to the west (see p.351) or Bob Marley's mausoleum to the northeast in Alexandria (see p.229).

A hike to the lush gorge at **Christiana Bottom** is the big thing to do here. Take a right turn by the post office in town and then follow the left fork at the crossroads to a standpipe where you can park if you're driving, though it's perfectly walkable from the centre of Christiana. Continue down an often muddy track – it's not easy to find the way so if you get lost ask for the "blue hole" – through prolific ferns and bamboo to a **waterfall** and a cold but refreshing **pool**. North of town, beyond the village of Coleyville, the **Gourie State Park** (daily during daylight hours; free) has a number of hiking trails through its pine woods; the nearby **Gourie Caves** and **Oxford Caves**

Christiana and May Pen

offer some challenging caving, and tours can be arranged through the *Hotel Villa Bella*. With a good flashlight you can explore on your own, though the underground routes are tricky and a guide is strongly recommended.

If you have a car, it's also worth taking a brief trip west of Christiana to **BETHANY**. Head back downhill towards Walderston, take a right turn beside the petrol station and bear left down a winding road that leads through the cute village of **Devon** and some very English scenery. Nineteenth-century Moravian missionaries – the first Christian missionaries to come to Jamaica – built a number of **churches** in the local area, and Bethany's, modelled on one in Hernhut, Germany, and perched on the mountainside, is the most impressive. The large, red-roofed church was founded in 1835 and the views over the Dom Figuereroa Mountains and up to Cockpit Country are staggering. There isn't much to the church interior but, if it's locked, you can get a key at the adjacent rectory, prettily gabled with gingerbread trim. The countryside around here is green, rolling and quite un-Jamaican with its hedgerows and dry-stone walls, but don't come out this way if you're short of time – it's easy to get lost driving around as there are no roadsigns and minor roads spin off all over the place.

Practicalities

Hotel Villa Bella (☎964 2243, fax 964 2765, *www.go-jamaica .com/inns*; ④), three miles from the town centre (see below) and the only **hotel** in Christiana, is one of the most delightful small hotels in Jamaica. There's no pool or unnecessary fripperies, but the place retains a colonial-era feel and is dotted with interesting curiosities – plenty of art deco furniture, nineteenth-century china, old prints and the hotel's original guest book from 1941. The *Villa Bella* also organizes a variety of **tours** of the local area, including mountain-biking, caving and hiking, for between US$10 and US$35 per person. If *Villa Bella* is full or you prefer an even quieter location, *Glencoe Bed and Breakfast* (☎964 2286; ②) in **Spaldings** – a tiny agricultural centre three miles east of Walderston – is a lovely old farmhouse dating from 1891, with spacious, well-kept rooms.

Villa Bella is the best place around for **food**, many of the ingredients originating from its own garden, with delicious, experimental Jamaican dishes from around US$10 for lunch or dinner. Options in town include *Christiana*, a cheap restaurant serving local meals, which is opposite the Syldian Court shopping centre, and *KenSheilas Fry Chicken* just beyond the Shell petrol station. Otherwise the main road has a smattering of inexpensive snack bars and patty shops. **Nightlife** is quiet, but the *Lamplight Club* in town is open late every night and has occasional live music or dancers.

Regular **minibuses** run up Shooters Hill from Mandeville and head straight into town – ask them to drop you off if you're heading for

Hotel Villa Bella. If you're driving, the hotel is signposted on your right just before you enter town; bear left and keep straight on for the town itself.

May Pen and around

Heading east from Mandeville, the A2 road runs out of the parish of Manchester through **Porus** – a lengthy village easily identified by its displays of citrus fruit strung up by the roadside (though the planned Kingston–Montego Bay highway bypasses this colourful place) and into **Clarendon**, one of Jamaica's least enthralling parishes. A right turn at Toll Gate takes you down to Milk River Bath on the south coast (see p.348), while continuing straight ahead brings you to the capital of **MAY PEN**, a light industrial centre and an important market town with a population of over forty thousand. The highway actually bypasses the town, which is handy as there is no reason at all to stop there unless your bus is breaking its journey. However, if you're here during the **Denbigh Agricultural Show**, a three-day fair held in the Denbigh showgrounds just west of town – normally over the last weekend in July or the first weekend in August – then it's certainly worth stopping off. The event features displays of each of the country's parishes' agricultural produce, exhibits of prize livestock and a showjumping event. There's also plenty of live entertainment including singers, dancers and reggae bands and the usual array of food vendors and craft stalls. If you're planning to stay over, try to arrange a room well in advance.

See p.43 of Basics for more on the show.

The best place to **stay** in town is the *Hotel Versalles*, just off the highway at 42 Longbridge Ave (☎986 6384, fax 986 2709, *www .hotelversallesjamaica.com*; ④). If you're driving, take the right-hand exit towards May Pen at the main roundabout and there's a small signpost for the hotel about 400 yards down on your left.

Otherwise try *King Led's Palace*, five minutes from the centre of town on Anderson Drive (☎986 4527; ②). Bed and breakfast accommodation in May Pen can be arranged through Countrystyle in Mandeville (see p.357).

The **restaurant** at *Versalles* serves reasonable food, but there's an excellent café and ice cream parlour, *La Maria*, in the Crown Eagle Centre on Brooks Avenue. The café is also the centre for the Clarendon Countrystyle Tourism Association and offers all kind of local information. You'll find a number of **patty shops** around the clocktower in the market square (where most of the buses originate and terminate).

The Versalles *hotel has its own private yacht,* The Versalles Queen, *moored at nearby Salt River, which is bookable for special events and chartered excursions (☎986 2102).*

Halse Hall

The great house at **Halse Hall**, due south of May Pen, is certainly worth a visit. However, the house is no longer officially open to the public, and tours have to be arranged through its present owners, bauxite company Jamalco (☎986 2561). The basic structure was

Christiana and May Pen

built in the late seventeenth century by Thomas Halse, an English soldier who was active in the war against the Spanish, although the present building mostly dates from the 1740s. The wealth of the erstwhile owners is evident from the interior design; the sturdy mahogany doors and window frames in the airy living room are particularly impressive. The front of the house (you drive up at the back) has commanding views over miles of plantations and, to the south, over the less attractive alumina works of Jamalco. Don't miss the tiny **cemetery** behind the house, which holds the tombs of Halse and some of his descendants.

Halse Hall is just off the A2 highway from May Pen. Take the exit south from the main roundabout towards the Jamalco alumina plant and the house is one mile down on your right. Several **buses** a day run past the house en route from May Pen to Lionel Town (see p.349).

Travel details

Buses and minibuses

It is impossible to predict accurately the frequency of buses and minibuses running the following routes – services are often chaotic and delays and cancellations frequent – so the figures given below are only rough estimates. However, on the most popular routes you should be able to count on getting a ride within an hour if you travel in the morning; things normally quieten down later in the day. On less popular routes, you're best off asking for probable departure times the day before you travel.

Black River to: Kingston (3 daily; 5hr); Mandeville (5 daily; 2hr 15min); May Pen (3 daily; 3hr 30min); Montego Bay (4 daily; 2hr 15min); Negril (2 daily; 2hr 20min); Santa Cruz (8 daily; 1hr); Treasure Beach (3 daily; 1 hr 15min).

Christiana to: Kingston (3 daily; 3hr); Mandeville (8 daily; 30min).

Mandeville to: Christiana (8 daily; 30min); Kingston (6 daily; 2hr 45min); May Pen (6 daily; 1 hr 15min).

May Pen to: Kingston (6 daily; 1hr 30min); Milk River (3 daily; 1hr); Spanish Town (8 daily; 1hr).

Part 3

Contexts

The historical framework

The first human inhabitants of Jamaica were the Tainos, an Amerindian people speaking the Arawak language, who arrived in Jamaica around 900 AD. The Tainos originated from present-day Venezuela and Guyana in South America, making their way between the Caribbean islands by way of dug-out canoe. They were a peaceful people with a primitive stone age culture – fishing and foraging for subsistence – and they lived in scattered settlements all over the island, settling around sites with a good water source. Estimates of Taino numbers at the time of Columbus's arrival in Jamaica are hugely varied, but it is possible that there were as many as a million. Although Tainos living in the small islands of the eastern Caribbean were under attack by the more war-like Caribs by the fifteenth century, there is no evidence of any Carib attacks on Jamaica.

The arrival of the Spanish

Christopher Columbus made his first expedition from Spain in search of a western sea-route to Asia in 1492. During his second "voyage of discovery", he landed at Rio Bueno on Jamaica's north coast, on May 6, 1494. The Tainos had learned of the violence of Columbus's men from their neighbours in Hispaniola (today's Haiti and Dominican Republic) and there was a brief skirmish, easily won by the Spanish with their armour, dogs and superior weaponry. Columbus had little interest in the island (which he named Santiago) but claimed it for Spain and moved on in search of China. During his fourth and last voyage in 1503, Columbus made an unfortunate return to Jamaica, his ships running aground on the coral reefs at St Ann's Bay. The explorers were marooned on the island for a year before a rescue ship could be summoned from Hispaniola, carrying them back to Spain where Columbus died two years later.

Spanish settlement of Jamaica began in 1510, when a group of settlers from Hispaniola, headed by Governor Juan de Esquivel, set up a base at Sevilla Nueva on the north coast. The initial plan was to look for gold but, other than the few trinkets the Tainos had collected in trade with other islands, there was none to be found. Nor was Sevilla Nueva a good site; surrounded by swampy land, the tiny Spanish population soon found its numbers threatened by fever. In 1534, King Charles I permitted a transfer of the capital, and the Spanish decamped to a better location near the south coast; Villa de la Vega, known today as **Spanish Town**, was to remain the island's capital until 1874.

Despite the successful settlement of Spanish Town, and the agricultural bounty that the country offered, Jamaica remained a backward colony until well into the seventeenth century. Early colonists established farms across the country – introducing cattle, horses and various food crops such as bananas and sugarcane – but mostly the island served as a stopping-off point between the mother country and the richer colonies of the Spanish Main. Ships stopped for cleaning and repairs and supplies of maize, cassava, pork and beef were taken on. Despite the low level of activity on the island, though, the Spanish soon managed to obliterate any traces of the native population. The Tainos fell victim to European diseases in their thousands, suffering severely, too, from the legendary cruelty of the Spanish, and by the time of the British conquest of Jamaica in 1655, not a single Taino remained alive.

Because of the inability of the Tainos to provide the Spanish with the labour force they required, the importing of **slaves** from Africa began within a decade of the Spanish settlement of Jamaica. This was not a novel practice – slavery from Africa had been going on for centuries – but the new gold and silver mines of South America required a mass labour force, and the trickle of slaves slowly became a flood. Again, most of the traffic bypassed Jamaica but there was a steady growth, and there is evidence of the first runaway slaves, who gradually developed settlements of their own and were to prove a constant thorn in the side of the British after 1655 (see box below).

The British conquest

Spanish Jamaica was not a well-protected colony. In 1596, Sir Anthony Shirley, an English adventurer, landed with five hundred men at Passage Fort near present-day Kingston and

completely **sacked** Spanish Town. In 1643, the same thing was done by a small force led by a Captain William Jackson. Spain provided little or no assistance in defending the place, and gave scant impression of caring for its colonists.

In 1654, Britain's "Lord Protector" Oliver Cromwell, distrustful of sections of his armed forces whom he suspected of plotting the restoration of the monarchy, decided to send them against Spain's American possessions, far away from home. The British were well aware of the immense Spanish wealth in the area and, for over a century, British pirates and buccaneers like Francis Drake had been making a good living from looting their ships and cities. Cromwell sent fifteen ships under the command of General Robert **Venables** and Admiral William **Penn**, the father of the founder of Pennsylvania. The ships were fitted out in British Barbados before launching an assault on the city of Santo Domingo, capital of Hispaniola.

The Maroons

The Spanish armed and freed most of their slaves when they finally quit the island in 1660; these Africans joined comrades who had escaped from Spanish owners previously, and formed a band known as the *cimarrones*, a Spanish word meaning "wild" or "untamed" that the British corrupted to **Maroons**. These Maroons lived in small communities in inaccessible parts of Jamaica's mountains and forests – particularly in the Blue Mountains in the east and Cockpit Country in the west – and, after the British arrival, found their numbers gradually swollen by new runaway slaves, particularly after slave rebellions such as the Clarendon revolt of 1690.

Most of the original Maroons were of **Coromantee** descent, from the region of modern-day Ghana, and, despite the upheaval of slavery, their shared language and traditions helped them to organize strong communities in their new environment. As their numbers grew, they periodically plundered British settlements for arms, animals and supplies, and they proved an effective deterrent to colonists who were considering settling in inhospitable areas like Portland.

Although British soldiers made regular forays against them, by the 1720s the Maroons had

become such a serious threat that it was decided to take conclusive action against them once and for all. Forts and barracks were built at the edges of their territory and the British military might was turned towards wiping out this troublesome fifth column. Special troops were brought in, including a large party of Mosquito Indian trackers from Nicaragua, but, in extremely difficult and confusing terrain, they were often outmanoeuvred by the skilled **guerrilla tactics** of the Maroons. In places that now carry evocative names like "The District of Look Behind", whole parties of British soldiers were slaughtered, though one was normally left alive to carry the message of comprehensive defeat back to the authorities.

By 1739, though, the superior firepower of the British had gained the upper hand, although it was apparent to them that winning a war against this "invisible enemy" would be costly and drawn-out. Accordingly, the First Maroon War was ended by a **peace treaty**, signed in the Maroon stronghold of Trelawny Town by British commanding officer Colonel Guthrie and old **Cudjoe**, the Maroon chief. The terms were that the Trelawny Maroons should stop attacking British settlements, return all future

The assault on Hispaniola was a catastrophe for Penn and Venables. The Spanish resistance was well thought-out and the British troops were incompetently managed, retreating to their ships having lost around a thousand men yet without having properly engaged the enemy. There was little will for fighting on, but the leaders knew that to return to Britain without anything to show for their trip would be fatal. Jamaica was known to be a modestly prosperous and poorly defended place, so they set sail for the island, landing at **Passage Fort** in May 1655.

After the previous sackings, there were few Spanish left to fight for Jamaica: Spanish Town was quickly overrun, but the Spanish settlers were able to withdraw to the north coast, where they held the British at bay for another five years. The Spanish king hadn't given up entirely: in 1657, an invasion force from nearby Cuba engaged the British, but were defeated at the battle of Los Chorreros, present-day Ocho Rios. In

1660, British governor Edward D'Oyley led a force that defeated the Spanish at the battle of **Rio Nuevo**, near Ocho Rios, and the last of the Spanish finally left for Cuba. In the process of leaving, the Spaniards freed and armed their slaves to continue the fight; these freed slaves proved an important boost for the growing band of Maroons.

Having anticipated further incursions, the Spanish had removed their valuable goods to the mountains before 1655, so there was little booty to show for the capture of the island. Penn and Venables returned to Britain and, despite the conquest, were promptly imprisoned in the Tower of London. Nevertheless, despite his disappointment over Santo Domingo, Cromwell soon came to appreciate the strategic importance of Jamaica and issued a proclamation encouraging emigrants, from Britain and from other colonies like Nevis, and offering land to settlers.

runaway slaves and provide assistance in the event of internal rebellion or foreign invasion. In return, they were granted freedom, fifteen hundred acres of land around Cockpit Country, and a remarkable degree of autonomy, including the administration of justice in all cases except for those involving the death penalty. One year later, the Windward Maroons – those encamped in the Blue Mountains – signed a similar deal with the British.

For two generations the peace held, and Maroons lived as a semi-sovereign state within Jamaica. Both sides kept to the agreement, most notably in 1760 when a major **slave rebellion** broke out in St Mary, led by a runaway slave named **Tacky** (see p.212). Tacky and his followers took to the mountains, anticipating support from the Maroons, only to find that the poacher had turned gamekeeper, helping the British to suppress the uprising. However, in 1795, the public flogging of two Maroons in Montego Bay outraged the Maroon community in Trelawny and, with temperatures raised and neither side prepared to compromise, hostilities quickly flared again. Plantations were burned and planters killed, and the British army rushed to quell this internal conflict. For a while, the **Second Maroon War** followed the path of the First, with soldiers ambushed as they ventured

into unfamiliar territory, and the Maroons inflicting heavy losses.

However, the British were better organized this time and had at their disposal both enormous hunting dogs – imported from Cuba and quite terrifying to the Maroons – and warriors and trackers from Jamaica's other Maroon settlements. A generous peace offer was made by British General Walpole and the Maroons surrendered their arms, although not until several days after the terms of the peace offer had lapsed. Using this pretext, the British revoked the promise that the Maroons should be allowed to stay on their land, and five hundred of the Trelawny Maroons were **deported** to the freezing cold of Nova Scotia, although not before General Walpole had resigned in disgust at the authorities' duplicity. The deported Maroons stayed in Nova Scotia for just a year, setting sail for Sierra Leone from where, generations earlier, many of their ancestors had been brought to Jamaica as slaves.

Most of the Maroon communities in Portland and at Accompong in Cockpit Country remained relatively undisturbed by the ructions of the Second Maroon War and, protected by the 1739 peace treaty, continued to maintain a semi-independent status within the island.

Port Royal and the buccaneers

Immediately after the British conquest, large tracts of Jamaica were divided up between the officers who had served with Penn and Venables, their legacy still very apparent today. Officer Thomas **Hope** was given a huge estate near present-day Kingston, while Thomas **Halse** and John **Colbeck** established properties at or near modern-day Halse Hall and Colbeck Castle. The first priority of these new British settlers, though, was defence, to ensure that they could keep their newly won colony. Recognizing the strategic position of what is now Kingston harbour, they began immediately to build **fortifications** on either side of it, particularly on **Port Royal**. Five separate forts were built on the uninhabited island including the still-standing Fort Cromwell, renamed Fort Charles in 1660 when King Charles II was restored to the British throne.

In 1661, Edward D'Oyley became Jamaica's first non-military governor and, in 1664, the first **local assembly** was summoned. Sir Thomas Modyford became governor and encouraged local **"buccaneers"** to make Port Royal their base for attacks on Spanish dominions. These buccaneers had started out as a ragged collection of outlaws from their European homes, living on the island of Tortuga near present-day Haiti. By the mid-seventeenth century, they had evolved into a disparate but skilled collection of pirates, attacking ships around the region. The British saw a way of using these buccaneers to their advantage. By giving them official sanction as "privateers" and letting them use Port Royal as a base, they would provide some defence for the young colony; equally important, they would harass the Spanish enemy, attacking their treasure ships, and would be obliged to deliver ten percent of their haul to the British authorities in Jamaica.

Port Royal became a boom town. The security provided by the forts and the wealth provided by the privateers encouraged traders to set up, exporting sugar and spices and importing slaves and supplies for the growing population. Although Spanish Town remained the capital city, government figures set up home on the island alongside the merchants, and Port Royal became one of the wealthiest places in the world, with rents rivalling London's classiest districts. However, its ascendancy was to be short-lived; a devastating **earthquake** in 1692 plunged most of Port Royal into the sea, and sent its residents fleeing for a new home across the harbour in modern-day Kingston.

By the 1670 **Treaty of Madrid**, the Spanish recognized British rule in Jamaica, and the brief era of the privateers was over, though there was to be one last fling. Henry Morgan, most famous of the privateers, launched an attack on the Spanish colony of Panama, sailing from Bluefields Bay on Jamaica's southwest coast. Though he claimed that he was unaware of the peace treaty, Morgan and Governor Modyford were recalled to Britain. Modyford was sacked to appease the Spanish, while Morgan, having insinuated his way into royal favour, was made lieutenant-governor in his stead, returning to Jamaica with a new brief – to stamp out piracy by persuading his former colleagues to turn to a life of peace.

Naturally enough, many of the buccaneers, now officially termed **"pirates"** to mark their loss of favour, refused to give up their thrilling and financially rewarding lifestyles and continued to torment shipping throughout the Caribbean throughout the eighteenth century. But their heyday was past, and a succession of high-profile successes by the authorities – particularly the capture in 1720 of Calico Jack Rackham, with his female aides Anne Bonney and Mary Read – inexorably turned the screw on the remaining bandits.

Sugar and development of the Jamaican economy

After the British had taken possession of Jamaica, and particularly after peace was made with the Spanish in 1670, settlers were encouraged to come out from the mother country with the offer of land grants and other financial incentives. Slowly, the island began to embark on the massive transformation from tiny colony towards its present shape, and the key factor in that change was **sugar**. Though first imported and grown by the Spanish, cultivation of sugarcane was to become a major phenomenon only under British rule, turning its West Indian colonies into much-prized possessions.

At first, there was little enthusiasm for sugar. **Tobacco** was the crop of choice, but the Jamaican harvest was unable to compete with the produce of Virginia. However, the settlers quickly realized the potential of sugar, which flourished in Jamaica's tropical conditions, and as the taste for the stuff boomed in Europe, the cultivation of sugarcane grew in leaps and bounds. The number of sugar estates in Jamaica expanded eight-fold between 1673 and 1740 and, during the course of the eighteenth century, the island became the **biggest producer** of sugar in the world.

As Jamaica developed, more and more settlers were tempted out from the mother country, although most of the estate-owners, known as **"planters"**, were absentee landowners, who spent most of their time in Britain and delegated control of their estates to overseers. The planters amassed extraordinary fortunes from their Jamaican possessions and, as their wealth increased, it brought with it significant political power and influence in London. In turn, this new-found influence was used to nourish and protect the sugar trade, with huge duties levied on sugar imported from elsewhere and the price of Jamaican sugar kept artificially high. Given the lavish lifestyle led by the planters in Britain, practically none of the profits of sugar were ploughed back into the colony, although every plantation had its "great house" – the elegant mansions that often survive today (despite the fact that they were normally the first target during any slave revolt).

Slavery

The success of the sugar industry, and the wealth of the planters, was, of course, predicated upon the appalling inhumanity of **slavery**. Like sugar, slaves had been in Jamaica during the Spanish rule, but on a tiny scale. Under the British, the development of the sugar estates called for a mammoth workforce and, with no indigenous labour available, the planters embarked upon the importation of slaves from Africa, a business which had already been in existence for many years, providing labour throughout the Americas.

The **slave trade** was dominated by British merchants. Their ships sailed first to the west coast of Africa – from where most of the slaves were taken – carrying trinkets and other goods to barter for the human cargo. From Africa, the ships were loaded with slaves, and sailed direct to Kingston, the most important transshipment point in the region, where the "chattel" (slaves were not considered worth referring to as human beings) strong enough to have survived the **"Middle Passage"** were unloaded into warehouses and sold at auction. From there, the ships

would return to Britain, now laden with the Jamaican products of sugar, rum and spices. It's estimated that between twelve and fifteen million people were transported from Africa as slaves, and this triangular traffic brought great wealth to the traders, reflected among other things in the development of the major port cities of Bristol and Liverpool. Little attention was paid, though, to the plight of the west Africans, drawn principally from the tribes of the Coromantee, the Fula, the Ibo and the Mandingo. In the early days of slavery, many of these Africans were already prisoners before they were shipped, bought from local **chieftains** who had captured them in war.

As the needs of the colonies expanded, **raiding parties** were sent into the African interior to hunt for more victims, who were then marched across the continent to stockades on the coast. From there, the journey to Jamaica could take between six and twelve weeks, with the slaves kept in chains in the hold of the ship, packed into galleries one above the other, and jammed into spaces so small that they couldn't stand or lie at full length. With no sanitation facilities and barely any food, huge numbers died of disease or malnutrition; many others committed suicide if the chance arose, sometimes leaping from the ship rather than continue in captivity.

Despite the high rate of loss, it continued to be profitable for the slavers to ply their trade and, every year, several thousand slaves survived to become labourers on the estates or, on a smaller scale, domestic workers in the home. Unsurprisingly, many of the transported slaves – uprooted from home and family and prohibited from using their own language – found the prospect of life on the plantations impossible, and there was continual **conflict** between slaves and slave-owners. Discipline, accordingly, was fierce, with severe punishment for any wrongdoer and torture followed by a slow, painful death commonly imposed as a deterrent to others.

Though the **living conditions** of the slaves varied a little from estate to estate, it's clear that they were all utterly squalid, with little living space or privacy. Slaves were at the whim of cruel overseers, few of whom would ever be taken to task, however badly they treated those in their charge. As time went by, however, conditions improved slowly, albeit very marginally. Religious conversion played a part in this – once converted, slaves were usually given Sundays off to attend church – and encouraged slave-owners to treat slaves as human beings for the first time. When food supplies to the island were disrupted, for example in the 1770s during the American War of Independence, slaves suffered badly; as a result, they were often given the opportunity to cultivate and market their own foodstuffs.

Yet this was hardly an altruistic gesture – malnourished slaves did less work, so it was in every planters interest to keep his lifeblood alive at the least possible cost to himself. For every slave-owner who made some effort to ensure the physical well-being of his slaves, there were ten more who cared little or nothing for their wellbeing – if a few slaves died, it was easier and cheaper to simply buy some more. Hence life on the plantations remained unimaginably horrible for all but the slave-owner.

Rebellion

Given the harsh living conditions, it's hardly surprising that **slave revolts** were a feature of Jamaican life from the time of the British conquest right up until emancipation in 1838, always dreaded by the authorities and invariably crushed with appalling brutality. Insurrection was commonly punished by the insurrectionist being slung up from the waist in the sun for four days, before being taken down to have the soles of the feet and the armpits seared, the heart and entrails removed and burned in front of the still-living victim, and then to be quartered, with the body parts displayed as a warning to others considering rebellion. Despite such grisly punishments, slave rebellions in Jamaica – occurring, on average, every five years during the eighteenth century – were both more numerous and on a larger scale than in the United States or elsewhere in the British West Indies.

There were a number of reasons for this. First, there was an unusually **high ratio of slaves to whites** and, particularly during the seventeenth and eighteenth centuries, a relatively high ratio of African slaves to creole slaves (those born on the island and generally considered less rebellious). The island's mountainous geography encouraged rebels, by providing places to which they could escape and hide, and the high level of absentee slave-owners probably also encouraged revolts either through the cruelty of those left in charge or, conversely, because of a lack of attention to the risks of rebellion. In addition, though not exclusive to Jamaica, **social and religious ideas**

fomented disorder, particularly at the turn of the nineteenth century, as abolitionists argued the case against slavery and missionaries challenged the religious orthodoxy about keeping black people in their "place". Finally, Toussaint L'Ouverture's revolution in **Haiti** in 1799, which threw out the French colonialists and created the first independent black republic in the world, provided slaves with a concrete example of a successful revolt.

The first major slave rebellion faced by the British came in 1673, when around three hundred Coromantee slaves from present-day Ghana, working at a large plantation in St Ann, murdered their owner and fled inland, massively swelling the ranks of the Maroons. Their success encouraged further revolts and, in 1690, five hundred slaves from the same part of Africa instigated a rebellion in Clarendon, though most were either killed or captured.

Tacky's rebellion in 1760 (see p.212), again with Coromantee slaves at its heart, was the major slave revolt of the eighteenth century, occurring during Britain's Seven Year War against France and Spain and lasting for five months. For the first time, a rebellion spread island-wide; sixty whites were killed, more than a thousand slaves were either killed or transported from the island, and there was colossal damage to property across Jamaica. After the rebellion, the British authorities continued to fortify the island, bolstering the armed forces and encouraging firmer dealings with the slaves.

For a while, the level of revolts died down but, in 1831, the **Christmas rebellion** was to prove the most serious slave uprising in the island's history. Though it lasted for just ten days, as many as 20,000 slaves were involved. By now, Jamaica's slaves were aware of moves towards abolition in Britain, and of the fierce hostility to such a move felt by the island's planters. There were strong rumours that slavery had actually been abolished, and that no one in Jamaica was going to tell the slaves.

Sam Sharpe, the rebel leader, was a slave in Montego Bay, reasonably educated and a leader in the Native Baptist church. Through the church, he organized a campaign of passive resistance, designed to coerce the slave-owners into declaring the end of slavery, but this had little chance of success and quickly erupted into a full-blown revolt throughout the island's western parishes. Though Sharpe and another five hundred slaves were either killed or executed, the seriousness of the rebellion and the brutality with which it was crushed intensified the abolition debate, both in Jamaica and in Britain, and accelerated the emancipation that Sharpe had been seeking.

Foreign affairs 1670–1800

The threat of slave rebellions, and the two wars with the Maroons, were not the only problems faced by the Jamaican authorities during the eighteenth century. Although Spain had recognized British control of the island in 1670, the risk of **foreign invasion** was far from removed. In 1694, Ducasse, the French Governor of nearby San Domingo (present-day Haiti), launched an invasion of Jamaica; troops landed in St Thomas in the southeast and did tremendous damage to sugar estates across the country before they were repulsed at the battle of Amity Hall. Regular skirmishes with the French followed, with British Admiral Benbow killed during another defeat of Ducasse in 1702.

The frenzy of **fort-building** with which the British began their occupation of Jamaica was continued, with military establishments being put up around the coast, as well as in parts of the interior where regiments were being maintained to contain the threat of the Maroons. All of Britain's great naval commanders served time on the island, normally based at Port Royal, and the presence of such force undoubtedly contributed to the fact that there was not to be another foreign invasion.

In 1775, the **American War of Independence** had a profound effect on Jamaica. The Jamaican assembly sympathized with the thirteen colonies when they made their declaration of independence, but the British refused to concede and blockaded the eastern coast of North America, depriving the island of its ability to trade with the Americans. The resulting food shortage was dramatic – around fifteen thousand slaves are believed to have died of starvation – and prompted significant change on the island. Estate owners began to encourage slaves to grow food on small allotments, while the introduction of the **breadfruit** from Tahiti in 1793 helped the island take a big step towards self-sufficiency in food.

The French were not slow to take advantage of Britain's war with its former colony in North America, and a series of invasions of her West Indian possessions left Britain holding just Jamaica, Barbados and Antigua. In Jamaica itself, invasion seemed inevitable, but a crucial sea battle off the Windward Islands in 1782 – the Battle of **Les Saintes** – saw the destruction of the French navy by British forces under Admiral Rodney, and removed the threat of attack from the island for several generations.

Jamaican politics 1700–1834

From the early days of British occupation of Jamaica, the chief authority on the island was the governor, appointed from Britain. An assembly of estate-owners was convened in 1661 to advise the governor on local matters, but control of key issues was kept in the hands of the British Crown. However, it wasn't long before conflicts arose between the interests of the early settlers and of the mother country, coming to a head towards the end of the century in discussions over the abolition of slavery. As creole society developed, and a new generation grew up who had actually been born in Jamaica, there were increasing demands for political power to be kept entirely on the island. Accordingly, in 1729 the British Crown recognized the local assembly as the source of all legislation on Jamaican matters.

Throughout the eighteenth century, power remained in the hands of the white planter class, with the right to vote given only to property owners. Gradually, given the sexual proclivity of the planters, a "mulatto" or **mixed race class** emerged who looked to their white fathers for an education and opportunities that were denied to people of pure African origin. Although this mulatto class were not officially granted equal rights until 1832, many of its members exercised considerable political influence, and were to prove far more sympathetic to the black cause that anyone from the planter class had previously been.

By the end of the eighteenth century, the present-day **racial composition** of Jamaica was already pretty much in place, with the black population outnumbering the whites by over ten to one. Though political power rested with the whites, forces inside and outside Jamaica were soon to bring about a sea-change in the fortunes of the different racial groups.

The abolition of slavery

In 1807 the British parliament prohibited its colonies from trading in slaves, but the **abolition of slavery** itself – heavily opposed by the West

Indian lobby, who feared the collapse of the local economy – was not finally passed until 1834. Despite the island-wide jubilation, though, the slaves were not yet given unconditional freedom; they were expected to continue working for their former masters, unpaid, for a six-year "apprenticeship". In 1838 the apprenticeship system was abandoned and the former slaves were, at last, free to demand wages or work elsewhere.

Many former slaves left the hated estates at the first opportunity, renting or squatting on a little landholding and establishing small farms. Across the country, missionaries set up "free villages", buying land, subdividing it and either selling or donating it to former slaves, who would also normally help with building the local church and school that the villages were based around.

The drain of workers from the estates, and the reluctance of many estate-owners to pay proper wages, forced them to turn to alternative sources of cheap labour. Already, during the 1830s, 1,200 Germans had been brought to Jamaica, with the promise of land grants once they had worked on the estates for five years. Other workers were brought from China, the Middle East and other parts of Europe, but it was India that was to provide the great majority of the new **indentured labour**.

Under a scheme approved by the Jamaican assembly in 1845, 35,000 Indians were brought to the island before the Indian government banned further traffic in 1917. The estate-owners promised that, once the workers had paid off the cost of their passage from India, they would be able to earn decent money to send home, before returning themselves at the end of their contracts. In practice, the Indians became the new slaves – working for scant pay under appalling conditions – and the majority never had the chance to return home.

Jamaica's sugar industry took another major blow in 1846, when a **free-trade** minded British government passed the Sugar Duties Act, forcing Jamaica's producers to compete on equal terms with sugar producers worldwide. At the same time, the development of **beet-sugar** in Europe also hurt the industry, contributing to the drop in the price of sugar and reducing demand for the West Indian product.

Although the sugar industry was far from dead, this series of setbacks forced the island to diversify out of its reliance on a single crop. A Royal Commission report recommended the

encouragement of peasant proprietors and the substitution of other tropical products – such as coffee, coconuts and citrus fruits – for sugarcane. **Banana** cultivation was introduced in the 1860s and, for a while, became the boom crop as demand for the new fruit soared in Europe and America. By the end of the nineteenth century the older economic pattern of the Jamaican community had faded completely and a new organization was emerging. Only the scattered ruins of the plantation great houses and sugar mills – still found in even the remotest districts – now speak of the once great days of sugar.

Post-emancipation problems

Jamaica's estate-owners were given a total of **£20 million compensation** for the loss of their slaves (most of which went to repay debts owed to merchants in Britain). There was no such compensation for the newly freed slaves. Life for them was far from easy and, in the mid-nineteenth century, there were two issues which caused black Jamaicans particular concern.

The first problem was **land**. Unless they could get somewhere to farm, black Jamaicans had little choice but to return to the plantations and work as poorly paid wage labourers; getting their own plot of land guaranteed a degree of independence and gave them a bargaining tool for higher wages. Unfortunately for black Jamaicans, the planters were equally aware of this issue, and made it as hard as possible for the ex-slaves to get land, imposing high rents and taking action against squatters who tried to take possession of unused land. The second, related, issue was the one-sided **administration of justice**; the landowners generally dominated the magistrates' courts, and imposed heavy-handed penalties for squatting and other minor wrongs.

The downturn in the country's economy that followed the abolition of slavery and the introduction of free trade in sugar also took its toll on the freed slaves. Wages were kept pitifully low, taxes were imposed and unemployment rose as plantations were downsized or abandoned altogether. There were numerous **riots** and conspiracies, particularly in the early years of emancipation as rumours of re-enslavement were given strong currency, and there was even talk – fuelled by dissatisfied planters – of the island being annexed to the United States as a slave state. The last straw came during the American

Civil War of 1861–65, when naval blockades cut off crucial supplies to Jamaica, causing food shortages and intensifying the economic problems of the poor.

The grievances of Jamaica's black population came to a head in 1865, when a major **rebellion** broke out in **Morant Bay** in St Thomas. Problems here were particularly acute, and compounded by the authorities, who removed a magistrate seen as too impartial and also removed from the parish council **George William Gordon**, a mixed-race businessman openly sympathetic to the cause of the poor black Jamaicans. On October 11, a band of rebels marched on the town, looting weapons from the police station, releasing prisoners from jail and attacking the courthouse, killing eighteen soldiers and council members.

The attack on the courthouse was swiftly followed up by minor rebellions on outlying plantations in the area, and fearing that the rebellion would spread throughout the island, Governor Eyre ordered a show of strength from the armed forces. Little mercy was shown as 437 people were killed and executed, including the rebellion leader, **Paul Bogle**. The government also took advantage of the situation to execute leading political dissidents such as Gordon. Thousands more people were flogged and terrorized, and the brutal suppression caused horror throughout Jamaica and Britain. For more on Paul Bogle and the rebellion, see p.148.

After Morant Bay

Although the Morant Bay rebellion did not spread outside St Thomas, and there was no evidence of an island-wide conspiracy, it provoked considerable change in the colony. After the rebellion, Governor Eyre was ordered back to Britain and dismissed for his part in the atrocities. His assembly abolished itself, and in 1866, Jamaica became a **Crown Colony**, with direct rule from Britain. This meant that, rather than having elected representatives, the governor appointed members of a legislative council who were responsible for policy on the island. Although this set back the cause of responsible government on the island for almost a century, it enabled certain reforms to be passed that would never have got past the planters and their representatives in the assembly.

Governor Grant, who replaced Eyre, brought in important measures that helped to give Jamaican society a more modern shape. New courts were established, a new police force created and the Church of England was disestablished on the island. Roads and irrigation systems were improved, more money was spent on education and, in 1872, the capital city was transferred from Spanish Town to **Kingston**. This move was long overdue – most of Jamaica's trade – from slaves to rum – had been processed through Kingston's harbour for two centuries, bringing colossal wealth in its wake, and by any criteria the city was the right place for the seat of government.

There were downsides to the changes, of course. Taxes were raised to finance the reforms, and the unrepresentative political system frustrated the island's fledgling democratic movement for nearly eighty years. There was scathing criticism of the government by landowners for financial extravagance and inefficiency, while black leaders bemoaned the lack of any radical change and the continuities with the old system of government. On the whole, though, the new system kept the peace while preserving the status quo; the whites retained all political and social authority, while the blacks were sufficiently mollified that there was little threat of upheaval for the rest of the century.

Away from politics, meanwhile, innovation in Britain's prized colony continued as the mother country continued to reap the rewards of its industrial revolution. In 1845 Spanish Town and Kingston had been joined by **railway** – the first outside Europe and North America – while, in 1891, the **Jamaica Exhibition** was held in Kingston and Spanish Town and drew a crowd of around 300,000 people. Also during the 1890s, early **tourists** were brought to Jamaica, many sailing from North America on the banana boats that plied between the US east coast and Port Antonio in Portland. Trends were being started that would prove of crucial significance in the coming century.

Jamaica in the twentieth century

The early twentieth century saw considerable **economic prosperity** in Jamaica, with particular booms in the banana and tourism industries. And the new wealth was no longer confined to the whites – **George Stiebel**, Jamaica's first black millionaire – had used his fortune to design some fine buildings, particularly Devon House in Kingston, and his example proved an inspiration to others. Inevitably, though, most of the new wealth bypassed the black masses, and serious **poverty** remained throughout the island. People were increasingly drawn to the new capital city to look for work, but many were left stranded in slums on the city's western edge with little prospect of income or employment. **Natural disasters** also took their toll. In 1907, Kingston was partially flattened by a devastating earthquake, and there were major hurricanes throughout the 1910s.

By the 1930s, as the **Great Depression** took hold worldwide, the positive effects of the economic boom had pretty much evaporated. The banana crop had been decimated by disease, never to regain the exporting heights of the early century, while sugar exports fell precipitately as overseas demand dried up. In the face of the depression, US immigration laws tightened up, and the blocking of this perennial pressure valve resulted in further problems, sending unemployment figures spiralling. Riots in Kingston and around the island were commonplace, and **strikes** erupted too, with a major clash in 1938 between police and workers at the West Indies Sugar Company factory in Frome leaving several people dead. Protests and looting followed island-wide.

1938, in fact, was to prove a key year in the development of modern Jamaica. Partly as a result of the battle in Frome, strike-leader **Alexander Bustamante** founded the first **trade union** in the Caribbean – the Bustamante Industrial Trade Union (BITU). An associated **political party** was born too, with the foundation of the People's National Party (PNP) by the lawyer **Norman Manley**. Both events gave a boost to Jamaican nationalism, already stirred by the campaigning of black consciousness leader **Marcus Garvey** during the 1920s and early 1930s, and increased the pressure for political reform and improvement in the condition of the workers.

World War II and after

As it did worldwide, **World War II** fuelled the pressure for change in Jamaica, dramatically weakening European countries and loosening their grip on their colonies. It was also a major catalyst for development in economic terms – Jamaica was an important Allied base during the war and Britain was obliged to increase financial aid to the island. Jamaica was also called on to provide increased supplies of food to the mother country and, as sugar and other food industries expanded again, the disruption of shipping supplies led to the creation of local servicing industries and small manufacturing businesses. This all continued after the war and was boosted by major tourism and bauxite, whose commercial export began in 1952.

On the political front, a **new constitution** in 1944 introduced universal adult suffrage and the same year saw the first elections for a government to work in conjunction with the British-appointed governor. In 1943, Bustamante had split from Manley's PNP to form the Jamaica Labour Party (JLP) and it was the JLP that won the elections, succeeding on a populist appeal for "Bread and Butter", rather than the PNP's more intellectual call for independence. The two parties gradually drifted in different ideological directions, with the JLP adopting a basic liberal capitalist philosophy, and Manley's PNP leaning towards democratic socialism. The JLP won again in 1949, not ceding power to the PNP until the election of 1955.

Taking office in 1955, one of Norman Manley's first priorities was the issue of independence. Both he and the British government considered that it was impractical for the Caribbean islands to "go it alone", and the idea of a West Indian federation was floated. However, right from the start such a federation faced awesome challenges. First, **economic development** in Jamaica and in Trinidad and Tobago during the 1950s – fuelled by the exploitation of bauxite and oil respectively – convinced many in both countries that they were strong enough economically to stand on their own feet. Second, **public opinion** in the large islands was largely anti-federation, with traditional rivalries between islands coming to the fore and many Jamaicans suspicious that they would have to subsidise the others. Third, the progress of self-rule, albeit somewhat limited, in Jamaica, created a class of local **politicians** who felt they could manage the island's affairs themselves, and were reluctant to share power with others in the Caribbean.

Accordingly, though the **West Indies Federation** was launched in January 1958, with its capital in Port of Spain, Trinidad, it never really stood a chance. Jamaica refused to accept the principle of federalism, arguing that it must be allowed to protect its own economic interests, even where these clashed with the other islands.

Following the threat of sanctions from the federal government, Bustamante declared his opposition to the union in 1960 and, in a **referendum** called by Manley in September 1961, the Jamaicans voted categorically to leave, prompting the rapid disintegration of the federation. Disheartened though they were, the British had little choice but to accept the decision of the electorate. Within a year they had granted Jamaica its **independence**.

Independence

On August 6, 1962, Jamaica became an independent state within the British Commonwealth, with Bustamante as its first prime minister. The early years of independence were marked by rising prosperity, as foreign investment increased, particularly in the bauxite industry. **Hugh Shearer** succeeded Bustamante after his retirement in 1967 and the JLP continued in power until the key elections of 1972. By then, the difference between the two main parties had become marked, with the JLP espousing a US-friendly liberal economic programme and the PNP – now led by Norman Manley's charismatic son **Michael** – an avowedly democratic socialist party.

Michael Manley's victory in 1972 led to eight years of PNP rule, a period regarded by almost all Jamaicans as instrumental in fashioning the country of the late twentieth century. Until 1972, economic and political power had rested predominantly with the whites and the mixed race Jamaicans. Manley's slogans, such as "Power for the people", set out his desire to improve the conditions of the black majority and, to accomplish this, he would have to challenge the status quo.

The major reforms introduced by the PNP included a minimum wage, a literacy campaign, the distribution of land to small farmers, more public housing, and an improvement in funding for the island's education and health-care sectors. To finance these "**people's projects**", Manley turned to businesses which had been largely protected from taxation, in particular the internationally owned bauxite industry. Increased levies on the industry proved counterproductive, though, as bauxite companies promptly scaled down their Jamaican operations, reducing the country's foreign exchange earnings. This blow was quickly followed by the effects of the 1973–74 oil crisis, which led to a tripling in the cost of the island's imported oil and further increased pressure on government spending. In the light of this, Manley sought to promote a greater degree of **self-sufficiency**, encouraging the use of Jamaican, rather than imported products.

In **foreign affairs**, too, Manley followed a different line to his predecessors. Rejecting close ties with the United States, the prime minister turned to the non-aligned movement, calling for increased aid and better terms of trade for third world countries, and forged particularly close ties with Fidel Castro's Cuba. Needless to say, the American reaction was furious; economic sanctions were applied and it became increasingly difficult for the island to attract foreign investment. Manley's problems were compounded by the **exodus** of wealthy white Jamaicans, withdrawing their capital and skills from the island at the time that they were most needed. Most left through fear of higher taxation and even the introduction of communism, but the rhetoric of Manley and his supporters didn't help as they gave broad hints to anyone dissatisfied with his regime that there were plenty of flights leaving the island every day, and if they didn't like it, they should get on one.

During the Manley years, politics in Jamaica became as polarized as they had been since self-rule was reintroduced in 1944. The opposition JLP, led now by **Edward Seaga**, launched blistering attacks on the "communist" administration, and the 1976 election – won by the PNP again – saw a disturbing increase in **political violence**. This was particularly true in the ghetto constituencies of Kingston which the political parties had turned into "garrisons" – distributing guns to their supporters and encouraging them to recruit voters and drive opponents away through intimidation. Despite criticism from human rights groups, Manley's response to the violence was to impose a **state of emergency**. The government established a non-jury "Gun Court" and passed severe anti-crime legislation providing, for example, a life sentence for anyone convicted of unlawful possession of a firearm.

During the PNP's **second term**, the lack of capital to finance his projects sounded the death knell for Manley's brand of democratic socialism. Foreign investment had fallen precipitately, local capital had been withdrawn from the island and, despite the empty shelves in the supermarkets, the cost of imports continued to outstrip exports.

The government was forced to turn to the International Monetary Fund for assistance, and the resulting curtailment of public spending and the drastic cuts in social programmes alienated many erstwhile supporters. Violence flared again during the 1980 election campaign, with hundreds of people killed in shoot-outs and open gang warfare and, amid the carnage, the Jamaican people turned to the JLP for a new vision for their country.

The JLP in power

Immediately after Ronald Reagan won the 1980 US presidential election, Jamaica's new prime minister Edward Seaga was the first foreign leader to visit him in Washington, and the **re-alignment** of the two neighbouring countries was perhaps the most important change in policy that Seaga brought about. The US took steps to open its markets to foreign imports and to encourage outward investment, most notably with the enactment of the Caribbean Basin Initiative (economic aid in return for free elections and co-operative governments), and foreign capital began to find its way back to Jamaica. However, Seaga was obliged to continue the cutback of government services, begun under the PNP, and his honeymoon with the Jamaican people proved short-lived.

In 1983 Jamaican troops assisted the US **invasion of Grenada**, launched to depose the Marxist leaders who had overthrown and executed prime minister Maurice Bishop. Taking advantage of a brief surge in popularity (and the absence of opponent Manley from the island), the JLP called a snap election. In protest at government tactics, the PNP boycotted the election, leaving the JLP in sole control of Jamaica's parliament, and re-elected prime minister Seaga gave himself various portfolios in the resulting government, including minister for finance, defence and culture. However, although his skills as minister of finance were widely praised, Seaga was unable to give the island's economy the boost it required and, in the face of rising poverty and unemployment, his lack of charisma and the concentration of power in his hands led to a fall in support. In 1989, Michael Manley and the PNP were returned to office.

Despite widespread fears of a return to the politics of the 1970s, the new-look Manley administration proved very different. The emphasis now was on continuity of policy and, although foreign relations with Cuba were restored, there was no more of the anti-American and anti-white rhetoric.

The demands of the World Bank and the IMF continued to be met and a generally liberal economic policy followed. In 1992 Manley resigned the premiership on the grounds of ill-health, leaving his successor, **P.J. Patterson**, to continue the policy of continuity. In 1993 Patterson – the first black man to become Jamaica's prime minister – defeated Seaga and the JLP in the general election, and since then Seaga hasn't been able to recover his previous levels of support.

Jamaica today

The backbone of the modern Jamaican economy is provided by tourism, bauxite and agriculture. A colossal amount of money is spent on encouraging **tourism** and counteracting the negative images of the island that have been seen abroad in recent years, although arrival figures have been pretty stable for several years at a little over a million people a year. **Bauxite** production has recovered from the blow the industry took in the 1970s although falls in prices worldwide have meant overall lower earnings.

Agriculture – particularly sugar and bananas – accounts for around twenty percent of export earnings. The potential of the sector remains vast, with great products and superb farming conditions, but the imagination required to expand and diversify output has been sorely lacking. A daunting problem that Jamaica faces alongside West Indian islands is the recent removal by the WTO of their privileged access to European markets, leaving small-scale and often inefficient Jamaican farms unable to compete with the giant US-owned and funded plantations in Latin America. Also on the agricultural side, **ganja** farming and export – illegal but very widespread –makes a major, if unofficial, contribution to the island's economy, despite the efforts of the US' "War on Drugs".

Unfortunately, Jamaica's export earnings from these industries are quite unable to keep pace with the nation's spending habits. Jamaica carries a substantial burden of **debt** to foreign banks, and much of the foreign currency earned is required to repay interest and capital on that debt. As a result there is little money available for urgently needed domestic programmes, such as education, roads or public transport. Retrenchment, built on interest rates of nearly 50 percent, has hit hard – officially, unemployment stands at around seventeen percent (though the real figure is probably significantly higher), and the glamour of the tourist resorts belies a lot of poverty in Kingston and rural areas.

The imbalance between earnings and spending has been compounded in the last decade by a staggering increase in foreign **imports**. The streets and shopping malls of the cities and towns are chock-full with flash cars and other foreign accessories, though there is no sign of any corresponding increase in export production to pay for it all. **Remittances** from Jamaicans working overseas help to reduce the earnings gap but even this is creating problems – it is widely felt that "easy money" from relatives abroad is creating a class of idle youngsters, who refuse to countenance the prospect of hard work.

On the **political** scene, major ideological differences remain a thing of the past. In 1995, JLP veteran Bruce Golding left the party to set up a third political force, the **National Democratic Movement**. There is little to indicate that the party has any new ideas on dealing with the country's problems at the start of the twenty-first century, and the political scene continues to limp along, with P.J. Patterson cutting a rather insipid figure with little popular support, despite his second victory in the 1997 election. Many of the important political issues today are familiar ones throughout the Caribbean, although given the size of the island, relative to its smaller neighbours, they are often felt more extremely in Jamaica than elsewhere.

Crime is the key topic for most people. The "garrison communities", first established by politicians in Kingston and Spanish Town, have become safe havens for gangsters and drug barons these days, no longer in need of political support. Convicted Jamaican criminals have been deported to their home country from North America and Britain but, as they have committed no local crime, they are free as soon as they arrive home. With their overseas contacts, these deportees (numbering around 1500 a year) have reinforced the gangs and turned the drug business into a billion dollar industry. Gang warfare is a serious problem in the city ghettos, occasionally spilling out into "uptown" areas and thereby provoking more calls for action.

Political corruption is another much-lamented problem, with the party in power seen to dispense favours to its supporters and believed to use every available ploy to get itself re-elected. In the face of this cynicism, and a general feeling that successive governments have done little to alleviate poor economic conditions, disillusionment with politics is growing and a selfish materialism and a dangerous fatalism have both taken over large sectors of society.

Despite these problems, there remains much to be positive about in Jamaica. Democracy is still firmly rooted and there is a vigorous **culture of debate**, most noticeable in the numerous talkshows that compete with reggae for radio airtime. There is growing enthusiasm for another attempt at serious regional co-operation, one example of which is the prime minister's support for a Caribbean Court of Appeal, to replace the British Privy Council as Jamaica's highest appellate court. Leading entrepreneurs – most notably **Chris Blackwell**, former head of Island Records, and **Butch Stewart**, owner of Sandals – have elected to stay in Jamaica and invest their considerable fortunes in the island's development; Stewart's purchase and overhaul of the once-decrepit Air Jamaica has been particularly inspiring.

Nonetheless, those not in a position to enjoy the prosperity enjoyed in some sectors of the tourism industry continue to find life in Jamaica extremely hard, and small-scale street protests are a regular feature of island life. In early 1999, reacting to an unprecedented (and later retracted) forty percent hike in gasoline tax, the masses took to the streets, demonstrating over three days in Ocho Rios and Montego Bay as well as uptown and downtown Kingston. Nine people were left dead, and the damage was said to run to millions of dollars. Though no tourists were harmed (most were blissfully unaware of any trouble), the industry was hit hard, with cruise ships striking Jamaica from their itineraries and tour operators pulling out of the island; slowly, though, the big guns are drifting back, no doubt reassured by the strenuous governmental efforts to assert that Jamaica is a safe place for visitors, and a world away from the volatile war-zone it's often made out to be.

Away from politics, Jamaican culture remains vibrant and the island continues to produce leading figures in **music** and **sport**, from Ziggy Marley and Buju Banton to the Reggae Boyz and Courtney Walsh, who became the leading wicket-taker in the world in early 2000. Whatever the challenges, it is hard to quench the island's spirit as Jamaica heads into the twenty-first century, and while many islanders predict that "things will get worse before they get better", Jamaica's future, on balance, seems bright.

The environment

Jamaica's four thousand-plus square miles make it the third largest island in the Caribbean archipelago after Cuba and Hispaniola. Unlike many of its neighbours, however, more than half of it stands over 1500ft above sea level, providing mist-shrouded peaks as well as brilliant white-sand beaches.

Jamaica's landscape and topography vary immensely – from parched savannah plains and dry limestone forest to low-lying rainforest and wetland swamps, with richly vegetated undulating hills and lush pastures in between. Other than the metamorphic, sedimentary and igneous volcanic rocks of the Blue Mountains – Jamaica's oldest geological feature – most of the island's surface area is covered with soft, sedimentary limestone, at its thickest in central and western areas such as Cockpit Country (see p.282), where rivers have carved out a labyrinthine network of conical hillocks surrounded by deep sinkholes and caves. Also abundantly present in Jamaica's earth is bauxite (see p.358), though the island's largest export mineral comes at a price – the caustic red mud deposits, still inadequately disposed of in unlined pits which seep into the watersheds and poison rivers and lakes.

There are about 120 **rivers** in Jamaica, the longest being the 44-mile Black River in St Elizabeth. **Mineral springs** bubble up from the earth throughout the island, many within caves and a few hot, such as at Bath in St Thomas (see p.152).

Over half of the land area is given over to **agriculture**, with vast plantations cultivating coconuts, bananas, sugarcane, cocoa, coffee, citrus, rice and tobacco. However, farming has had a negative effect upon the island's environment; unstable mountain slopes are cleared for cultivation, resulting in landslides and soil erosion, while use – and misuse – of pesticides and fertilizers has led to loss of productivity. Slash-and-burn farming methods destroy acres of forest and animal habitats annually. The Jamaican gardener's adage "whatever you throw, it grow" is borne out in the island's abundance of trees and plants; of the **3003** varieties of flowering plant, some 28 percent are endemic, and many have been introduced by successive colonists. Jamaica has always been an island, so all of its fauna and flora have evolved from ancestors that crossed a marine barrier. There may be relatively few indigenous species, but as Jamaica boasts many

Natural disasters

Jamaica's geographical location and geological origins make the island highly susceptible to the elements, particularly during the rainy seasons, which run roughly from May to June and September to mid-October, when pre-hurricane tropical storms can cause flooding, landslides and road closures island-wide. After a few days of relentless sun and calm seas, these intense tropical storms can be exciting, but it's wise to avoid swimming or golfing during a violent electric storm.

Though the Caribbean is ranked third in the worldwide scale of annual **hurricane** occurrence, full-scale tempests are relatively rare in Jamaica. Twenty hurricanes hit between 1886 and 1991, the worst being Allen in 1980 and Gilbert in 1988 (see p.151), with the season

running from June through to November. News bulletins carry regular updates on the position and force of storms in the region, the Office of Disaster Preparedness, 12 Camp Rd, Kingston 5 (☎972 9941 or 4101) issues guidelines for coping with a strike, and most hotels are well prepared during the season.

Jamaica is also prone to **earthquakes**; the most violent occurred in 1692, destroying Port Royal (see p.105), and in 1907, when much of Kingston was levelled. Most of the major faults are found in the east of the island – there have been over twenty earthquakes per century in Kingston and St Andrew, but only five in the western region. The last earthquake occurred in Kingston on January 13, 1993, a scale two quake that caused extensive damage.

variations found only on the island, it's an important centre of **endemism**.

Aside from its creepy crawlies and bats, Jamaica's animal life is pretty poor in comparison to its flora, and there are few large mammals. **Camels** made a brief and embarrassing appearance in the eighteenth century, transported by planters to carry sugar and rum on the estates, but their preference for smooth ground and sand dunes made them unsuited to Jamaica's uneven and precipitous terrain. They spooked other livestock and had more or less died out by the late nineteenth century when historian Edward Long described them as "the most useless animals on the island".

Trees and shrubs

Though only five percent of Jamaica's natural woodlands remain, the island's tropical fertility ensures a richly variegated landscape. Trees are often planted for their shade-giving properties; the **guango**, with its symmetrical spreading branches, is popular, but the most arresting and majestic is the towering **silk cotton**, which often reaches more than 130ft in height, its buttressed roots spreading elegantly to meet the ground. Regarded as sacred in Ashante folklore, the silk cotton is surrounded by superstition; the silver roots are said to hide duppies, and the trees are associated with Myalist ceremonies. Naturally buoyant and easily carved, silk cotton trees were hollowed out into dug-out canoes by Tainos, and the fruits contain the cotton-like kapok. **Logwood** is extremely common, and was once grown commercially for the dark-blue dye extracted from the trunk and roots – and in 1893 surpassed cane and coffee as the island's main export – until synthetic alternatives ended the trade. Bees flock to the perfumed yellow blossoms, and logwood honey is said to be the best available. The **annotto** was also exploited for the intense orange-red dye extracted from seed pods growing in clusters around its attractive pink flowers – Tainos used it as their principal body paint and it was a prime commodity during Spanish occupation – though it's extremely rare today.

You'll encounter the marbled blue-tinted wood of national tree the **mahoe** in countless craft items. Fast-growing and indigenous, the mahoe has a short straight trunk that grows up to 65ft, broad leaves and distinctive hibiscus-like flowers that change from yellow to orange and deep crimson as they mature. The rich red wood of Jamaican **mahogany** is regarded as the best in the world and has been so heavily exported that few trees are left – the custom of stripping the bark from young trees to extract a dye also helped to decimate populations. Those remaining grow in remote areas such as Cockpit Country and the Blue and John Crow mountains, and can attain a height of 130ft. Another prized tropical hardwood, true **ebony** is found only in Jamaica and Cuba, though trees called "ebony" grow in other places. Now rare in primary forest, the orange and crimson flowers make it a popular garden shrub if trained.

Characteristically Caribbean, there are several varieties of ornamental **palm** in Jamaica. Often used to mark out driveways, the graceful **royal**, at around 100ft, is shaped like the perfect postcard palm, while close relative the **cabbage palm** manages a whopping 130ft, and has thicker, messier-looking fronds. There are several pseudo-palms in Jamaica – the unusual **screw pine** is easily distinguishable by its yucca-like leaves and spidery "silt-roots" that branch off from the bottom of the central trunk. Commonly planted in hotel gardens, the most attractive pretender is the magnificent **travellers' palm**, a member of the banana family – the name refers to mini-ponds at the base of the leaves that provide a convenient water source. Fronds fan out from the base in an enormous peacock's tail shape that can measure 30ft.

Flowering trees and shrubs

If you fly over Jamaica's interior or look closely at any rural panorama, the greenery will doubtless be broken by occasional patches of deep red, courtesy of the **African tulip** or "flame of the forest". Flowering sporadically throughout the year, the clusters of blooms often cover entire outer branches; each bud contains a pouch of water which children squirt out to make a natural water pistol. Commonly planted in towns and hotel gardens for its distinctive and gorgeous crown of deep-scarlet blossoms, the **poinciana** or "flamboyant tree" produces long brown seed pods, often polished and used as shaker instruments. Equally popular and familiar as a Christmas pot plant, the **poinsettia** displays a huge spread of bright green leaves that turn deep red in the cooler winter months; however the leaves are highly poisonous if imbibed. Twenty-nine varieties of **cassia** are found in Jamaica; most common are the pink and yellow flowering types, widely planted in urban parks. The showy blossoms cascade downward in tight clusters and develop into brown seed pods up to 2ft long. The smaller shrub *Cassia occidentalis* is equally pretty but known as "piss-a-bed" and "stinking weed" due to its nauseating odour.

The tree of life, **Lignum vitae** – so called because of its many medicinal uses – blooms with Jamaica's **national flower**, a subtle light blue shower that covers branch tips and makes a splendid show from afar. Trees are fairly small with twisting branches, heart-shaped fruits and a dense cover of dark and waxy leaves. Highly resinous, the wood is heavy enough to sink in water, and was extensively used in shipbuilding and as a suitably painful material for truncheons. The gum has long been used as a purgative and a treatment for syphilis and gout, while the detergent action of the leaves still usurps soap powder in remote areas. An urban staple known as "poor man's orchid", the **bauhinia** is a prolific purple-flowered shrub also known as bull hoof in reference to the cloven-shaped leaves.

Fruit trees

Bearing Jamaica's national fruit, the 30ft **ackee** tree is one of the most common in Jamaica, with glossy ovoid leaves and crimson seed pods, the latter bursting open when ripe to reveal the yellow arils (see p.34 for more). Almost as prevalent are the spreading branches of the **breadfruit**, decorated by serrated, hand-like leaves and pockmarked, matt-green fruits; less widespread is its cousin the **breadnut** tree, similar in appearance but producing a two-inch edible nut.

Cashew trees are common and produce both fruits and nuts. Similar in appearance to red ackee pods, cashew apples produce the cashew nut but can also be cooked and eaten. The oily liquid in the shell is poisonous, while the sap produces an indelible ink. The **calabash** is a 30ft spreading tree bearing large globular fruits which are hollowed and dried for use as dishes and containers, or filled with pebbles to make musical instruments like the "shakka" or maraca. It's an odd-looking tree with leaves clustered in condensed spirals along long, thin branches. **Cocoa** trees are easily identifiable, with shiny dark-green or red leaves and ten-inch oval pods that grow

in clusters from branches or sometimes the trunk, turning from light-green to brown when ripe; the sweet pulp around the beans inside can be eaten when raw.

Versatile **coconut palms** are everywhere, with every part of their fruit used – be it for food or floor mats. The Jamaica Tall coconut palm has been largely eradicated by lethal yellowing disease and is widely replaced by the hardier hybrid **mayapan**, a squat ten-footer with straggly yellowed leaves and orange-tinted nuts. Diminutive **guava** trees grow wild throughout the island and are also cultivated commercially for their green-skinned, pink-fleshed fruits. Fairly common in the interior, **jackfruit** trees grow up to 65ft and produce a globular, strong-smelling sweet fruit with pronounced pimples that can weigh as much as 40lb. With a satisfyingly rounded crown of leathery leaves over a short trunk, **mangoes** are one of the most beautiful trees in Jamaica, also boasting admirable shade cover and delectable fruits. Stumpy and rather nondescript, **naseberry** trees grow to around 50ft, with hairy brown fruits better known as sapodillas. Suited to wet areas, **nutmegs** attain a height of 60ft with plain but oily dark-green leaves and inconspicuous flowers which spawn a creamy yellow fruit that contains the nutmeg kernel. When ripe, the fruit splits to reveal the red aril (mace) and the nutmeg, soft enough to be chewed at this stage.

Coastal trees

Mangrove swamps grow along the Jamaican coast and are central to the health of coastal ecosystems, affording protection from hurricane surges, filtering earth sediments and nutrients and providing a protected nursery for fish and crustaceans. Yet they often fall victim to short-sighted development, bulldozed to make way for housing and to facilitate sand-mining or used as fuel for charcoal kilns. Though not naturally a coast-dweller, the **Indian almond** can withstand drought and flourishes along the length of Jamaica's shores. Branches grow symmetrically, and though they don't taste much like conventional almonds, the nuts can be eaten once the outer pods turn brown. A staple of all Jamaican beaches, the **sea grape** varies considerably in shape according to its environment; on exposed shores it lies low and twisted, but with less buffeting can attain a height of 50ft. The flat, round leaves are distinctively veined and turn a deep red as they mature. Once they've turned purple, the grapes are edible if a little sour. Fortunately very rare and definitely one to avoid is the **manchineel**, which grows to about 40ft with a wide-spreading canopy dotted with indistinct green fruits and flowers, all of which are extremely poisonous – even standing below a manchineel during rain incurs blistering. Luckily, you're only likely to chance upon a manchineel in the most remote areas, and cases of run-ins are unheard of.

Plants

Borders and fences island-wide are enlivened by the multicoloured **croton** shrub; the yellow, red, orange and green leaves are extremely hardy and are also used in bush medicine. More than 550 species of **fern** thrive in Jamaica's hot, moist climate; silver and gold ferns are common, coated with a waxy substance on the underside which makes a natural tattoo. **Cactuses** are best suited to the dry scrub of the Hellshire Hills and south coast plains, where some, such as the two **dildo** varieties, grow as tall as 20ft stretching skywards between clumps of visciously-thorned **makko** bushes. The inner stems of **torchwood** cactuses are dried and lit as homemade torches in rural areas and bear a yellow fruit, while the **dildo pear** (*Stenocereus hystrix*) has a red fruit; both are edible. **Prickly pear** and the "smooth

pear" or **cochineal cactus** are also common, the latter known as "roast pork" for its taste when cooked. Of climbing cactuses, most spectacular is the **queen of the night**, which boasts a huge and powerfully scented flower that only blooms at night. The endemic **god okra**, with edible stems and crimson fruits, is often vested with supernatural powers as its aerial roots spread so far over rocks and trees from their triangular main stem that they appear to have no earth to support them. The epiphytic **spaghetti cactus** has 6ft skinny green stems that hang down from dead or living trees and bears miniature white flowers and berries. The flat-lobed prickly **tuna** cactus is widely used in bush medicine, said to cure dandruff, reduce swelling and relieve chronic pain.

Of Jamaica's **vines**, the rampant forest **cacoon** has a huge circular bean pod the colour of a burnished conker, while the rare, triffid-type **duppy fly trap** bears the largest flower in Jamaica – an eight-inch purple heart-shaped centre from which 23-inch fly-catching spurs extend. A rotting-meat odour attracts flies to the inside of the flowers, where they are covered in pollen and released to pollinate other plants – contrary to popular belief, the insects are not consumed. Strings of shiny red and black seeds from the **John Crow bead vine** turns up on craft stalls island-wide; dangerously so, as this is one of Jamaica's most toxic plants. Growing prolifically throughout the island, the mimosa family's

---

Ganja cultivation

Though there are two annual growing seasons, Jamaica's most infamous crop is mainly reaped between August and October, when the buds have received the full benefit of the summer sun. Plantations – usually small, very remote and planted amongst other tall crops – of 7ft bushes are harvested, the outer leaves discarded and the potent buds hung up and cured. Marijuana, or **ganja**, is not particularly easy to raise – many cultivators liken the task to bringing up a sickly child. Seeds must first be carefully germinated, then planted in open ground and stringently guarded against pests and birds. As buds attain maturity, the farmer must spend increasing amounts of time at the plot, feeding, watering and tending his crop as well as defending the valuable stems against thieves. Many farmers use pesticides and

expensive conventional fertilizers, though this is frowned upon and seen to produce a tainted version of the real thing; organic fertilizers such as bat guano are preferred to ensure top potency. Growers also face losing it all to the hands of the Jamaica Defence Force, who conduct regular eradication programmes as the fields reach maturity. Helicopters scour the hills for likely plantations while a ground crew sweeps through the countryside burning or spraying the plants with powerful insecticide. Unscrupulous soldiers are frequently known to accept a bribe in return for burning only a portion of the fields or not arresting the farmer, though as many policemen sell or smoke cannabis themselves, undocumented and highly profitable confiscations are reputedly common.

---

fascinating **shame'o'lady**, resembling a miniature bracken, closes its leaves to expose thorns on its stem at the slightest touch as protection against foraging animals. Equally intriguing is the epiphytic **wild pine bromeliad**, its 3ft pineapple-like leaves flourishing wherever there's a tree to host it. The rainwater collected between the leaves supports a variety of insects and even frogs, and the most protected specimens boast a pale crimson flower.

Flowers

Jamaica's perennial summer keeps flowers constantly in bloom, and the rich soil supports a huge variety of **flowers**, from the lavish exotics of the lowlands, exported worldwide, to the delicate iris, begonia and azaleas of cool mountain climates. One of the most familiar sights is the brush-like deep pink **red gingers**. The bracts hide the small white true flower that grows from each tip once fully open, and the shiny, banana-like leaves are teamed with the blooms as a staple of flower arrangements. A close relative is the **torch ginger** which boasts one of the showiest heads in the world, a deep-crimson cluster of thick waxy petals nestled among leaf blades that grow to 15ft. Also ubiquitous are the forty vividly coloured varieties of the **heliconia** genus. Most popular are the various red shades of aptly named **lobster claw** and the red, gold and green cascade of the **hanging** heliconia, which looks like a series of fish hanging from a rod. Equally prevalent is the artificial-looking **anthurium**, a heart-shaped and shiny red, pink or white bract with a long penile stem protruding from the centre, and the spectacular **bird of paradise**, a mauve, bent stem which resembles a bird's head graced by a deep orange crest.

Jamaica boasts 237 species of **orchid**, approximately 25 percent of which are endemic. Most are epiphytic and grow on living or dead plant or tree matter, and many are so small that you'll need a magnifying glass to appreciate them. There are far too many varieties to mention, but some of the most notable are pea-sized miniature orchids like **Lady Nugent's purse**, commonly seen in the pristine Blue Mountain and Cockpit Country forests.

Hedges and fences are beautified by several varieties of **flowering shrub**; the ubiquitous **bougainvillea** ranges from red to deep magenta, white, orange and pink, the colour provided not by the comparatively insignificant flowers but by the surrounding papery bracts. **Hibiscus** take on an abundance of hues and shapes but are distinguishable through the generic pollen-tipped stamen that grows from the centre. The lacy **coral hibiscus** has a cluster of tiny curling red petals and an unusually long stamen topped by another red frill, and there are hundreds of hybrid varieties. **Mexican creeper** is a clambering shower of delicate pink or white flowers used to beautify fences and walls. The unusual **angel's trumpet** boasts large white horn-shaped flowers that are mildly hallucinogenic, so don't get too close when inhaling the musky scent. **Bladderwort** is a carnivorous plant found mostly in the Black River morass, bearing trailing yellow flowers that float on water and feeding on insects lured by sweet nectar.

Fauna

Jamaica's geological isolation precludes a rich variety of animals, and human habitation has decimated indigenous mammal species, with an estimated 37 species becoming extinct since the first settlements. Much damage was done by the introduction of the **mongoose** in 1872, which wiped out the Jamaican cane and rice rat population in little more than three years. Together with rats and mice first introduced via the galleys of Spanish ships, burgeoning populations of mongoose pose a significant threat to other Jamaican creatures, including traditional victim the Jamaican hutia or **coney**, a nocturnal rabbit-sized rodent that lives in hollowed trees or rock crevices. Other than **feral pigs** first introduced by the Spanish and still living wild in the interior 200 years later, Jamaica has no large land mammals, although semi-feral cats, dogs and, particularly, goats roam every corner of the island, especially prevalent in urban areas. The only other indigenous mammal is the **bat**, of which there are 21 varieties, referred to along with the country's huge moths as "rat-bats". Some are solitary tree-dwellers, but huge colonies inhabit Jamaica's caves, from which their droppings or guano have been harvested as a fertilizer, particularly prized for its effect on ganja plants.

Birds

Approximately 250 species of bird frequent Jamaica's skies, though many are migratory or come to the island only to breed. There are 25 indigenous species and 21 varieties found nowhere else in the world, which represents a greater level of endemism than in any other Caribbean island. Quick-moving, brightly coloured **hummingbirds** epitomize Jamaican bird life at its most spectacular; the red- or black-billed streamertail or **doctor bird** is the national bird, though only males have the characteristic trailing double tail feathers (reminiscent of an old-fashioned doctors' coat) and iridescent green breast. At under two inches, the **vervain** or bee hummingbird is the second smallest bird in the world. Its darting aerial techniques, surprisingly loud squeaky call and bee-like buzzing are far more notable then its grey-brown plumage. The endemic two-tone black and purple **mango hummingbird** is seldom seen in the urban flower gardens frequented by its braver cousins, preferring peace and quiet and defending its rural nesting sites with dive-bombing assaults and a sharp curved beak. Another nectar addict, the black and yellow **banana quit** punctures flowers with its curved bill and often hangs upside down from a twig to ensure a favourable feeding position. Equally eye-catching is the bright green back and red crest of the Jamaican **tody**, which digs a nest two feet underground during its breeding season. Squawking green **parakeets** and rare red- and black-billed parrots are found in quiet forested areas, like Cockpit Country. Glossy black, sharp-beaked **greater Antillean grackles** are to Jamaica what pigeons are to England. Their staring yellow eyes have resulted in the common name "shine eye" though they are also known as "cling clings" or "tinglings". Noisy and social, they live in groups and their harsh clacking call broken by a gentler whistle forms a constant background music wherever there are food scraps to be found. Commonly seen around cattle, the **white egret** often roosts on a ruminating rump in a mutually rewarding relationship that provides the egret with a constant supply of insects and the cow some relief from bloodsuckers.

Few sights are more evocatively Jamaican than the sight of a distant **John Crow vulture** swooping high over the hills. Though ugly and awkward on the ground, this scavenging carrion bird comes into its own in the air as it scans the land for the scent or sight of dead meat. Typically scrawny, its messy black plumage and bald red neck and head make it a convenient euphemism for people considered dirty, lazy or ugly. Easily recognizable by its harsh rasping cry is the 2ft

red-tailed chicken hawk, dark-brown and black with a white breast and russet tail feathers, which feeds on rats, mice and occasionally chickens. Jamaica has two types of night-hunting **owls**, both surrounded by superstition. The unworldly call of the **"screech owl"** or white owl is said to bring bad luck, despite its useful function as a vermin exterminator. Owls are generically referred to as **patoos** (their Ghanaian name), and the **Jamaican brown owl** is rarely known as anything else. Seldom seen away from country areas, the patoo feeds on moths and lizards and has a deep, hoarse cry that's said to be a harbinger of death and destruction – it's certainly disquieting on a dark night. The charismatic sea-dwelling **brown pelican** or "old Joe" frequents fishing harbours feeding on discarded scraps, though out at sea they dive for fish. Despite their dull brown coat, old Joes are facially expressive; the squat body, thin neck and long hooked bill with a food pouch on the underside give a faintly ridiculous aspect.

Reptiles and amphibians

There are 24 species of **lizard** in Jamaica including the **iguana**; the Jamaican version *Cyclura collei*, native of the Hellshire Hills near Kingston, is found nowhere else in the world. A dinosaur-like beast, it attains a body length of 5ft. However, most of the lizards you'll see are one of the seven varieties of *Anolis* lizard – all are despised by many Jamaicans who refuse to enter the same room as a lizard and squash them like vermin. *Anolis lineatopus* has a mixed pattern of brown markings, while *Anolis grahami* and *garmani* are bright green and can darken their body skin if threatened. A variety of gecko, **croaking lizards** provide a throaty night-time call and are extremely common. The 2ft-long, dark-brown **galliwasp** has a particularly unfortunate reputation that has led to a massive decline in numbers; African superstition falsely argues that the bite is fatal and that if bitten, you must run to the nearest water source – if you get there before the galliwasp, you'll live. Though decimated by the mongoose, there are still six varieties of **snake**. Only the **black racer**, thought extinct but recently rumoured to have been spotted in Cockpit Country, is poisonous. Most snakes inhabit remote forests but are found in small numbers throughout the island. The largest is the Jamaican **yellow boa** or nanka, which grows to around 7ft and is bright yellow/orange when young, maturing into a beautiful yellow and black, though during the day it rests in trees and sinkholes and is rarely seen. Popularly called the trophy dophy, the 0.5m **thundersnake**, cream-coloured with rows of brown squares along a russet stripe, is said to be able to soothe sprains; chunks of its body are marinated in white rum which is rubbed into the skin – its willingness to be handled makes it easy to catch. Jamaica's two species of **grass snake** (*Arrhyton funereum* and *dromicus*) are also known as black snakes, both attaining a size of 0.5m and uniformly brown with a white underside, found under logs or leaf litter. The **two-headed snake** or worm snake is so named because of its tiny head and larger tail, which comes equipped with a small "thorn" used to burrow into the earth. Fairly common throughout Cockpit Country, you'll usually find one through lifting stones or digging.

South-coast swamp inhabitant the American **crocodile** has been so extensively hunted that it is now classed as endangered and has been protected by law since 1971. The Black River Morass is one of the last places it lives wild, growing up to 12ft, though smaller specimens are more common. Generally non aggressive unless threatened, Jamaican crocodiles live mostly on small fish. The only native amphibians, there are 22 varieties of **frog** in Jamaica. Since their introduction in 1890 by the then-governor's wife Lady Blake, who apparently found their sound soothing, whistling frogs provide a regular night-time chorus throughout the island. There is one variety of **toad**, commonly called "bull frog", introduced from Barbados in 1844 as an insect killer, but most often seen squashed flat on country roads.

Insects

By far the most noticeable Jamaican insects are the 120 varieties of **butterfly** and moth ("rat bats" to Jamaicans), which appear in all shapes, sizes and colours. Most striking but extremely rare is the six-inch **giant swallowtail** butterfly, seen only in the lower slopes of the eastern John Crow Mountains, matched in size by the multiple species of giant moths. One variety of solitary **wasp** (*Auplopus bellus*) prefers meat to pollen and stores its food in a self-built larder of loosely connected mud cells, incarcerating spiders by chewing their legs off, while cave-dwelling flies capture prey with silken home-spun fishing lines dangled from the ceiling. **Spider** species are comparatively

few, and though there are none of the huge and hairy tarantula types, there are some pretty big ones; the orange, red and black **silk spider** measures around six inches. Its many-layered webs are an arachnaphobe's nightmare, at 3ft wide with attachment lines extending as far 6ft, they have been known to trap small birds. Encountered only by the foolishly inquisitive, **brown** and **black widows** live under rocks and leaves, and though dangerous do not carry a fatal bite. Heavily armoured, dull brown and apparently without a sense of direction, **news bugs** are easily recognizable by their habit of bumping into walls and people; if one lands on you, it's said that important news is to come. Diamond-shaped, lime-green and with an equally poor sense of direction, "stinkie bugs" are named after their offensive smell. Often referred to as white ants, Jamaica's seventeen species of **termites** construct huge nests along tree trunks and wooden buildings.

Marine life

Much diverse marine life is found around Jamaica's reefs. The sixty or so coral varieties include rotund **brain** coral, patterned with furrowed trenches, branching umber **elkhorn** and **staghorn**, stalagmite-like **pillar** coral and coolgreen **star** coral. Extremely striking are the **gorgonian** group of intricate soft coral **sea plumes**, **sea whips** and purple **sea fans**. Around the reefs, brilliant yellow **anemones** and red, brown, purple and green **sponges** provide a splash of colour, some growing up to three feet in diameter. **Crabs**, **Caribbean spiny lobsters** and spotted **moray eels** inhabit the crevices between corals. Harmless unless provoked, when they can inflict serious bites, morays open and close their mouths in a constant snarl as they draw oxygenated water over the gills. The patches of sandy seabed and sea grass fields between reefs provide a habitat for many animals; spiny black sea **urchins** are an obvious hazard – their needle-sharp barbed and venomous spines splinter off into the skin if stepped on (see Basics, p.31). Often picked up for a closer inspection by scuba guides, the spines of round white urchins are too short to puncture skin. **Sea cucumbers** are long, thin and off-white, sifting through the sea floor to feed on deposited nutrients, while five-armed orange and green **starfish** and queen **conch snails** move slowly along encircling grass blades with their stomachs to ingest encrusted organisms. One of the most stunning inhabitants of the sea floor is the flat manta or **stingray**, often partially buried in sand. Though non-aggressive, the serrated tail spine is venomous but can only be used if the ray is partially immobilized by a bite or a badly placed foot. The camouflaged **scorpion fish** rests motionless on coral or sand looking exactly like a barnacle-encrusted rock – the spines of its dorsal fin carry a virulent poison.

Despite the effects of over-fishing (see "Threats to the environment", below), there are still over seven hundred varieties of **fish** in Jamaican waters. The commonest include multicoloured **parrot** fish, electric-blue creole **wrass**, red and yellow **snappers**, ornate **damselfish**, striped **grunts**, glassy sweepers, spiny puffers and rarer **tarpon** and **trigger fish**. The slender yellow and blue **trumpetfish** suspends itself vertically in the water awaiting smaller victims to drift by and into its mouth. Larger fish include **groupers**, **jackfish**, **dolphin**, **kingfish**, **tuna**, **marlin**, **bonita** and **wahoo**. The scourge of spear fishermen, silvery-sleek predatory **barracudas** impart a nasty bite if provoked, though the common **nurse shark** is benign unless attacked or cornered. In deeper water, **dolphins** are a common companion to boats, and pleasure cruisers often carry a conch shell to blow in answer to their squeaks.

Though increasingly rare, hawksbill and logger-head **turtles** still lay their eggs on Jamaican shores, despite the continuing threat of capture. Though it is illegal to kill, capture or posses any part of a turtle living or dead, the trade in their meat and shells is lucrative. The Caribbean **monk seals** that once inhabited offshore cays are now believed to be extinct, and Jamaica's most engaging sea mammal, the **manatee** or sea cow, is extremely endangered; there are only about a hundred left in Jamaican waters, mostly along the less developed inlets of the south coast.

Threats to the environment

As a developing country, the Jamaican environment has long suffered the effects of unplanned development and a lack of environmental awareness. While many of its **reefs** are still the beautiful underwater gardens of hotel brochures, they are under serious threat; a recent study reported that the island has damaged 95 percent of its reefs in the last fifteen years as a result of over-fishing (and destructive fishing practice), sand-mining, coral collection, industrial pollution and mass tourism. Dynamiting and chemical bleaching, which stun fish up to the surface for an easy catch have had disastrous effects upon reefs, which depend upon clean, clear water for their survival. A symptom of unusually high sea temperatures throughout 1995, coral bleaching was reported on eighty percent of reefs around Jamaica's shores – killing the algae within the polyps and leaving the still-living coral to starve.

On land, **deforestation** and its associated problems are a major concern. Stripped slopes are overly susceptible to soil erosion and landslides, threatening hundreds of already rare animal and insect species and wreaking havoc with the island's ecosystems. Deforestation has been particularly severe in the Blue Mountains, which represent the watershed for the entirety of eastern Jamaica, causing annual droughts, and water restrictions in the corporate area and an increasingly shallow Mona Dam. For an island with such a high rainfall, Jamaica is in the perverse situation of facing a permanent drought entirely of human making. In the Yallahs Valley, a century of misuse – slopes cleared for coffee cultivation or slash-and-burn farming techniques – has left the area vulnerable to the torrential rainy season deluges, which have flooded the valley and dumped huge amounts of earth onto former farmlands, leaving the slopes above bald and impossible to cultivate. The situation became so desperate that the government intervened as early as 1961, creating the Yallahs Valley Land Authority to rehabilitate the area through planting Caribbean pine, mahoe and eucalyptus to restabilize the slopes, although a lack of funding has resulted in poor maintenance.

Elsewhere, though eighty percent of household waste is collected by the government, the remaining twenty percent is simply dumped in open areas and gullies, resulting in poor hygiene, increasing levels of vermin and polluted water.

However, all is not lost. Thanks to the efforts of non-governmental conservation organizations there has been a marked increase in public awareness over the last few years. Jamaica has established three **national parks** (Montego Bay Marine Park and the Blue and John Crow Mountains National Park) as the first phase of the 1995 Protected Areas Resource Conservation (PARC) Project, and the area offshore of Negril has also been designated a marine park. A further six sites are proposed for protected status, including Cockpit Country, Black River, the Hellshire Hills and the coastline around Port Antonio.

Environmental and conservation associations

Environmental matters in Jamaica are the responsibility of the **Natural Resources Conservation Authority**, 53 1/3 Molynes Rd, Kingston 10 (☎923 5155, fax 923 5070), which devises and enforces environmental legislation – you can report environmental outrages via the NRCA's toll-free hotline ☎0888 991 5005. More directly active are the voluntary conservation agencies, also useful for obtaining information on specific environmental concerns. The **National Environment Societies Trust**, 46 Duke St, Kingston 8 (☎922 0667, fax 922 0665) and the **Jamaica Conservation and Development Trust**, 95 Dumbarton Ave, Kingston 10 (☎960 2848, fax 960 2850) act as umbrella organizations for those listed below.

Bluefields People's Community Association, Bluefields PO, Westmoreland (☎955 8792, fax 955 8791).

Friends of the Sea, 6 James Ave, Ocho Rios (☎974 9832, fax 974 6494).

Gosse Bird Club ☎927 1864.

Jamaica Environment Trust, 58 Half Way Tree Rd, Kingston 10 (☎960 3693, fax 929 1074).

Negril Coral Reef Protection Society and **Negril Environment Protection Trust**, PO Box 27, Negril (☎957 3735, fax 957 4473).

Portland Environmental Protection Association, 6 Allen St, Port Antonio (☎993 9632, fax 993 3407).

South Coast Conservation Foundation, 91a Old Hope Rd, Kingston 6 (☎978 4050, fax 927 3754).

Southern Trelawny Environmental Agency, Albert Town PO, Trelawny (☎610 0818, fax 610 0819, *stea@cwjamaica.com*).

St Ann Environmental Protection Agency, PO Box 21, Runaway Bay (☎ & fax 973 4305).

St Elizabeth Environment Association, 2 High St, Black River (☎965 2074, fax 965 2076).

Trelawny Environment Protection Agency, c/o Trelawny Chamber of Commerce, Shop 6, Albert George Shopping Centre, Falmouth (☎ & fax 954 4087).

Wildlife and Environment Conservation Action Now, Hope Zoo, Royal Botanical Gardens, Kingston 7 (☎927 1085).

Religion

With over 250 denominations and the highest number of churches per capita in the world, religion is a Jamaican vocation. Most Jamaicans are devoutly religious, and in this fundamentally non-secular society, faith features in every aspect of daily life. Over eighty percent of the population describe themselves as Christian, but there are also Jews, Quakers, Moslems and Hindus practising on the island alongside the American-influenced fundamentalist Church of God, Pentecostal, Seventh Day Adventist and Jehovah's Witness faiths. Popular ideology is governed by Biblical dogma, and most Jamaicans have an astonishing ability (and propensity) for quoting lengthy passages of scripture. Sunday piousness is fervently observed, reggae stars read from the Bible on stage and devote entire performances to unadorned preaching, graffiti artists decorate Kingston walls with apocalyptic Biblical verse rather than obscenities and the most popular newspaper agony columnist is addressed "Dear Pastor". Churches are at the heart of all Jamaican communities, providing subsidized housing, education, healthcare and a strong social focus – and this centrality is fundamental to Jamaican religion, in all its myriad forms.

The development of Jamaican religion

The antecedent of most contemporary Jamaican cults and Christian sects is a wider **African** religious tradition that arrived with the first wave of slaves. Considered as living machines with no Christian or human rights, slaves were denied formal religious instruction until the late eighteenth century. This privation, together with the constant influx of new slaves, allowed for a continuing reinforcement of African tradition – although the planters attempted to quash it by banning drumming and persistently breaking up ceremonies.

Missionaries began arriving on the island in the late eighteenth century. Fighting against the indifference of the planters, they slowly began proselytizing increasing numbers of slaves, while also pressuring the planters that slavery in itself was inherently un-Christian. Owners were faced with a choice between having their slaves attend church on a Sunday or flaunt their heathen proclivities on a daily basis; they grudgingly bowed to the former, and a mass church culture was born.

Sunday mass became the only sanctioned gathering for slaves, and, ironically, contributed to emancipation, as firebrand black-activist preachers used their sermons to whip congregations into political action.

After emancipation, the British took a belated interest in the spiritual lives of black Jamaicans, and tried to "civilize" them into orthodox Christianity, but decades of religious neglect had permitted African belief systems to survive and flourish, and former slaves preferred to openly practise aspects of their folk culture or combine their traditions with western Christianity. The time was ripe for a uniquely African-Jamaican phenomenon.

Some twenty years after the abolition of slavery, a new religious fervour swept Jamaica, initially carried along by the momentum of the newly popular Native Baptists and other Christian denominations but essentially resting upon the Revival, Pukkumina, Zion and Myal Afro-Jamaican cults that have remained active in Jamaica ever since. The **Great Revival** of 1860–61 was one of several religious revivals (also in 1831, 1840, 1865 and 1883) that signified a resurgence both of religious practices banned under slavery and a desire among blacks to rediscover and celebrate their African origins. It marked the beginning of a Jamaican religious tradition that threatened carefully constructed colonial hierarchies, and white Jamaicans were horrified at this "grossly perverted religious fervour" and "scenes of debauchery and hideous caterwauling".

By the end of the nineteenth century, the Jamaican elite was panic-stricken by the phenomenal popularity of the church led by self-declared messiah (and eventual lunatic) **Alexander Bedward**. His August Town branch of the Native Baptist Church adapted conventional theology, proffering a combination of black power and faith healing – he blessed the waters of Hope River and thousands flocked to Kingston for baptism or a miracle cure. He also prophesied

Jamaican Jews

Though numbers have never risen much higher than 1000, **Judaism** has been practised in Jamaica since the sixteenth century, when small numbers of Sephardic Jews fled to Jamaica from Spain and Portugal during the Spanish Inquisition. Though they still had to worship in secret in a Spanish colony, the "Portugals" or "Marranos" could at least live without the threat of being tortured to death. Eager to avoid continued persecution, Jamaican Jews assisted the English in their capture of Jamaica by piloting ships and acting as negotiators in the Spanish surrender. Under English rule, Jews were not only able to worship openly, but were granted both English citizenship and the right to vote, going on to play a prominent role in contemporary civic and commercial life despite making up less than one percent of the population. Numbers were only minutely increased by the **"Syrian"** Jews that emigrated to Jamaica from the Middle East in the late nineteenth century. Though Jamaican Jews have only one recognized synagogue – the United Congregation of Israelites in Kingston, where the majority of believers are based – their commercial success has attracted anti-Semitic sniping, though the community's prime economic position in Jamaican society means that Jews suffer little direct persecution.

that he would sprout wings and fly to Zion on December 31, 1921, and Bedwardites from all over Jamaica and the Caribbean descended upon Kingston to witness his departure; Bedward stayed put, but used the mass gathering as an opportunity to spread the message. Inevitably, Bedward's black nationalist tendencies led to several clashes with the state; in 1895 he was tried for sedition but acquitted on the grounds of insanity, and eventually he was arrested as a vagrant and committed to Kingston's Bellevue asylum, where he died in 1930.

Christianity

Christianity arrived in Jamaica with the Spanish, who built the island's first **Roman Catholic** church at Sevilla Nueva in St Ann (see p.218) in 1524. The British promptly outlawed Catholicism in 1655, and it was not freely practised until 1792; only between five and eight percent of Jamaicans are Catholic today.

The British replaced Catholicism with the Church of England, and divided the island into the ecclesiastical **parishes**, each of which had a church as its spiritual centre. The Church later became known as the **Anglican Church of Jamaica** and is far and away the island's dominant faith, though the Moravian, Baptist and Methodist missionaries who arrived on the island from 1754 established denominations that still thrive in force today.

The second-largest Christian denomination is **Baptism**, first brought to Jamaica by African-American ex-slaves **George Lyle** and **Moses Baker** in 1783. The Native Baptist movement, as it was then known, incorporated numerous African rituals into more orthodox forms of worship and was widely supported at its peak, with impressively large and still-functioning churches springing up all over the Jamaican interior throughout the nineteenth century. Following emancipation the Baptists were the first to set up **free villages** for liberated slaves, and became a main instigator and provider of free education for black Jamaicans.

Approximately ten percent of Jamaicans are **Methodists**, a faith strongly influenced by the African religious tradition and often connected to Revivalism (see below). Many black Jamaicans were converted to Methodism by missionaries from the Wesleyan Missionary Society who arrived in Jamaica in 1789 to set

up the Coke Church in Kingston, assuring potential converts that their own religious traditions would survive within the blanket of the Methodist Church.

In recent years, the fundamentalist tenets of US Bible Belt churches have started proving immensely popular, with many Jamaicans becoming Seventh Day Adventists and Jehovah's Witnesses, while Pentecostals and the Church of God also have significant followings.

Revivalism and Kumina

Essentially spiritualistic, the **Revival** movement, which came into being during the Great Revival, combines African and European religious traditions into a uniquely Jamaican form. It centres on the African acceptance of a synthesis between the spiritual and temporal worlds; an "animist" philosophy of a supernatural power that organizes and animates the material universe. Spirits are seen to have a distinct influence upon the living and, accordingly, must be respected, pacified, praised and worshipped through ritual dances, offerings and prayer. There are two branches within Revivalism; **Zionism** and **Pukkumina**. More overtly Christian, Zionism deals only with the heavenly spirits and angels of the Bible, while the more African Pukkumina worships earth-bound "ground spirits" such as deceased ancestors. Known as **bands** (the collective plural is always used), Revivalist congregations have a female (**mother**) or male (**shepherd** or **captain**) leader who acts as general advisor and governs meetings. Ceremonies are held in consecrated **mission/seal grounds** or **poco yards** which are specifically designated by spirits and marked by a tall central pole flying coloured flags to attract passing spirits and identify the site. The **tabernacle** is either in the open air, in a temporary bamboo structure or, increasingly, in a concrete building, decorated with symbolic candles, fruits, herbs, flowers and holy pictures, and containing an earthenware jug of water used in the rituals. Liturgies include the singing of "Sankeys" (hymns penned by the American evangelist Ira David Sankey), dancing, drumming, clapping and multiple-spirit possession (sometimes called **trumping**) induced by the hypnotic rhythms, controlled circular wheeling and dancing movements and the technique of **overbreathing**, a self-induced hyperventilation

African death rituals

A prime time for the release of wicked duppies, **death** is still surrounded by rituals designed to smooth the passage from one world to another, though these days many are remembered only by the elderly and restricted to rural areas. Within hours of expiration, the body is washed by two family members who begin at the head and feet and meet in the middle; the water is saved and poured into the grave. Mirrors are turned against walls to prevent reflections that may portend further deaths, and the house is ritually swept out with new palm brooms. If death occurred in bed, the body is placed so that the head rests at the foot of the bed to confuse any lurking duppies, and the mattress may be turned over. Once the corpse leaves for the funeral home, the bed is left outdoors for three days to air out any negative spiritual residue. **Nine Night**, or "death watch" ceremonies traditionally take place over the nine days and nights following a death, with friends and relatives "setting up" to remember and celebrate the deceased and ensure that their duppy doesn't return to haunt the living; food is cooked and consumed, stories told, rum imbibed and traditional dances performed. Today observance is usually restricted to the ninth night only, and sound-system speakers often take the place of drums and anecdotes.

which results in a trance-like state of possession. Once inside a physical host, the spirit becomes an advisor to the whole flock and is controlled by the shepherd who interprets messages received in "tongues" or through the movements of the possessed. The drumming, chanting and dances are all of African origin, as are the traditional goatskin burru or kette drums (see "Music", p.398). Revivalism is concentrated in the eastern end of the island, and flocks are typically comprised of the working-class, with a higher proportion of women than men. Followers wear flowing white or coloured robes and cover their heads in a turban-style wrap.

Usually described as the most African of Jamaican cults, **Kumina** (also concentrated in the east) is less formally organized than Revival, and though still centred on connections between spiritual and temporal worlds and the evocation and worship of dead ancestors, **music** plays a far greater role. Indeed, Kumina is regarded as an art as much as a religion; the intricate and precise patterns of its **drumming** have had far-reaching influence upon latter-day forms such as reggae, and Jamaica's national dance company NDTC incorporates numerous Kumina **movements** into performances. Call-and-response chants backed by complicated drumming rhythms provide the music for the worshippers, who dance around the players in a ring; women often take an aggressive, sometimes sexual stance, dancing their male partners into the ground in a proud show of female power.

Obeah

Obeah (from the Ashante term *obayi*, meaning a malicious spirit) is the belief in a form of spiritual power or witchcraft that can influence events – from curing disease to providing good fortune or wreaking revenge – and that also manifests itself in individual ghosts or **duppies** (see box on p.394). Though dismissed by some as primitive nonsense – and theoretically outlawed, though prosecutions are rare – obeah, or "duppy business", is taken seriously, and it's not uncommon to call upon the services of an obeah practitioner in special circumstances. **Obeah-men** are paid to invoke or dispel a curse and usually dole out brown bags of special powders – the "powder of compliance", for instance, is comprised of roots and herbs, ashes, earth, blood, feathers – to sprinkle on the subject and bring on the desired effect – reversible only by a more powerful obeah-man. "Good" obeah-men are sometimes called **myalmen**; they use specific ceremonies to counteract evil or mischievous obeah and rid those possessed by duppies in a "shadow catching" ceremony, commonly held around the roots of a silk cotton tree where duppies are said to hide. Myalmen are usually respected members of rural communities who prescribe herbal medicines for physical and spiritual complaints (see Basics, p.32) and minister at ceremonies to mark births, illness, and death – dangerous times when spirits are particularly active.

Duppies

The Jamaican name for ghosts, **duppies** can be good but are almost always seen as malevolent. The idea of the duppy originates from the African belief that each person has two souls; after death, one goes up to heaven while the other may linger in the temporal world and can be easily persuaded by an obeah-man to do good or evil to the living. Believers consult obeah-men if they feel they've been "fixed" or cursed, and there are countless rituals, charms and substances used to ward off or invoke the spirits. A traditional superstition warns that when walking on lonely roads at night, you should carry handfuls of stones or matches and drop them as you go to ensnare any inquisitive ghoul – unable to count beyond three, the duppy is forced to remain on the spot in a perpetual inventory.

Alongside the ghosts of regular people, there are also specific fiends that haunt children's bedtime stories and have become intermeshed with Jamaica's folklore and culture. The **Ol' Hige** is a bloodsucking hag who leaves her skin at night to seek out succulent babies and feast on their blood. A crossed knife and fork and Bible are kept near a child's crib to ward off her attentions, but she can only be stopped by finding her skin and dousing it with salt and pepper. The **Rolling Calf** is a staple night phantom that appears as an enormous red-eyed bull draped with clanking chains and walking with a sickly rolling gait; to see it is dangerous, and to be attacked means certain death. Missing a foreleg, the **Three-Foot Horse** is sometimes ridden by the **Whistling Cowboy** and its breath is said to be deadly. The only duppy to appear during the day, the **River Mumma** combines the African belief in a river spirit with the Western mermaid legend. Appearing as a ravishing young woman, she sits near deep pools on river banks and exposed rocks, bewitching passing males with her beauty; once beguiled, the love-struck victims are pulled down to the river bed and drowned. The River Mumma is also one of the most commonly invoked spirits in Revivalism, particularly when ceremonies are held near running water.

Rastafari

From the reds, golds and greens that colour everything from shop hoardings to belts and buses, and the beaming dreads that adorn commercials and tourist brochures, the outer trappings of Jamaica's newest and most visible religious movement are inescapable. **Rastafari** has influenced all aspects of society from art and craft to politics, academia, language and particularly music (see p.401), but the movement was not always looked upon so favourably. The last thirty years have seen a complete societal volte-face from widespread revulsion and persecution (a favourite police pastime in the 1960s was to arrest Rastas on ganja charges and shear off their locks; as sacrilegious as the cutting of hair is to Sikhs) to the tentative acceptance of today. Nevertheless older Jamaicans still retain a deepseated prejudice against the "Blackheart Man", and despite a few notable exceptions, dreadlock-wearing Rastafarians are poorly represented within the professions. Their more prestigious supporters prefer to defend the faith without displaying the frowned-upon outer trappings – wearing locks is not deemed essential to "knowing" Rastafari as followers assert that they do not merely "believe" in Rastafari, but know and feel their faith.

The development of the faith

Kick-started in 1930s Kingston by Marcus Garvey, the **Rastafarian** movement centred on the capital and quickly attracted some vociferous advocates, and provoked widespread antagonism in the broader society. One of the most provocative early sympathizers was **Claudius Henry**, head of the self-made Kingston-based African Reform Church, and something of a charlatan. Aligning himself with Rastas through public speeches on white corruption and the necessity of repatriation, in 1959 he enraged the poorest sections of Jamaican society through the sale of thousands of cards purporting to be tickets back to Africa. Hundreds of eager exiles sold all their furniture and descended upon Kingston on October 5, only to be disappointed as Henry reneged on his promises. The movement was further maligned when Henry's church was raided and a quantity

Women in Rastafari

Inherently patriarchal, the traditional Rastafarian attitude towards **women** takes direction from Biblical concepts of an evil, impure and a potentially corrupting influence upon man. Initially, women ("daughters" or "sistren") could only be recognized within the movement and be shown their own innate sin through the guidance of a "king-man", the physical and spiritual ruler of the Rasta queen who takes responsibility for balancing her thoughts and for her spiritual development – without a man, women cannot know the faith. Women are expected to be receptive to spiritual instruction at all times, and – unlike males – they are required to cover their hair when praying. They must never be seen in public without a hat or headscarf, and must dress modestly,

avoiding revealing clothes (particularly trousers) and make-up. They are considered unclean during menstruation, when they are not permitted to prepare food for others or attend communal prayer sessions, and in camps are often completely isolated and excused from chores. Traditionally, women are also greatly excluded from worship, prohibited from leading rituals and sharing the chalice and sometimes excluded from the most significant nyabinghis. However, since the 1970s, and the rise of the more egalitarian Twelve Tribes group, women have begun to assert themselves within the movement, often with the active support of progressive, usually young, male Rastas, taking respected positions in the hierarchy and participating in all celebrations.

of detonators, guns, swords and conch shells packed with ganja were seized. Henry was imprisoned, but reports that his son was training a crack team of armed Rastas in preparation for an overthrow of the government led to a national manhunt and an island-wide state of emergency; a public relations disaster for a movement that prides itself on pacifism and tolerance.

Among early Rasta elders of a more sincere nature, **Leonard Howell** stands out as one of the most influential father figures. He established a Rasta commune at **Pinnacle**, an abandoned great house near Sligoville in St Catherine, where converts lived a self-sufficient lifestyle praising Jah, growing food crops and cultivating ganja. Despite countless police raids, the community flourished for over thirteen years until Howell's 1953 arrest and permanent committal to the Bellevue asylum. Those Pinnacle members who were not incarcerated drifted back to the slums of West Kingston, establishing the Back'o'Wall and the Dungle strongholds described in Orlando Patterson's seminal novel *The Children of Sisyphus* (see "Books", p.422) and setting up Jamaica's oldest Rastafarian camp at Bull Bay, east of Kingston. By the late 1950s, Rastafari was a serious faction in the volatile sphere of Jamaican religion, with at least fifteen different sects practising in Kingston alone. Yet the wider view, fuelled by hysterical press reports, was of a drug-crazed, violent underclass plotting the mass murder of white Jamaicans. Police harassment

ensued throughout the 1960s, with Rastafarian communities bulldozed without notice and countless followers beaten and thrown into jail.

However, by the 1970s, things began to look more favourable. Poor Jamaicans in their thousands began to identify with the movement's militant analysis of a wicked state and its apparent disdain for the lot of the black sufferer. The socialist Michael Manley was the first politician to use the Rasta faith to his advantage. During a visit to Ethiopia in 1970, Manley was presented with an ornamental staff by Haile Selassie; a sacred relic that he dubbed the "**Rod of Correction**" and transported to every election meeting in every small village during the 1972 election campaign. Always up for a little showmanship, Jamaicans greeted the appearance of the sacred rod with evangelical fervour, and Manley reinvented himself as the Rastas' ally, employing their lexicon in speeches and calling himself the "people's Joshua", able to lead Jamaicans into deliverance. He swept to victory on election day with the tacit support of the Rastafarian community and its many sympathizers. Governmental recognition of Rastafari was lent untold weight by the worldwide influence of **Bob Marley and the Wailers**, who brought international attention to Jamaica and forced an acknowledgement of the movement's legitimacy at home, and suddenly – almost overnight – the tide of public antipathy turned. Dreadlocks became chic and reggae Jamaica's number-one

Rastafari Web sites

members.aol.com/rasjoshi/rastafariring.htm
The Rastafari Ring has links to the best Rasta-oriented pages on the net; an essential first stop.

members.xoom.com/MindfulJDK/
Nice, basic overview of the faith.

web.syr.edu/~affellem/raslinx.html
Slow to load, but thoughtful and with some good links.

www.rastafari.org
Good-looking site with a chat room, music-based features and links.

www.webcom.com/nattyreb/rastafari
/everlasting.html
Collection of biblical scripture relating to Rastafari

export, but these halcyon days were short-lived. With popularity came a certain commercialization of the faith, with many Rastas turning to the financial gains of the international ganja trade rather than to Jah. Conspiracy theories about infiltration by the CIA were supported to a degree even by Manley, who believed that his programme of "economic socialism" was deliberately destabilized by the US government. Twinned with the death of chief ambassador Marley in 1981, this general degeneration meant a loss of international prominence and local momentum, but Rastafari continues to develop its political and ideological strategies on home ground, remaining one of the most unique, challenging and fascinating of twentieth-century religions.

Though true figures are probably far greater, it is estimated that there are around 100,000 Rastafarians in modern Jamaica, many now describing themselves as "twenty-first century Rastas"; they allow women a more prominent and egalitarian role (see box on p.395) and even question the divinity of Selassie and criticize his questionable human rights record. It's worth bearing in mind though, that not all contemporary Rastafarians are orthodox followers. Many embrace the faith superficially, wearing locks as a hairstyle rather than an expression of faith, becoming "Rent-a-dreads" (see p.301), smoking the sacred herb and pontificating about Jah, Ethiopia and their personal friendship with brother Bob but lacing their ganja with cocaine and washing down their jerk pork with a white rum.

Beliefs and rituals

The Rastafari faith has its roots in the teachings of black activist and National Hero **Marcus**

Garvey (see p.216). He advocated an anti-imperialistic, pro-black philosophy and prophetically urged Jamaican followers to "Look to Africa, where a Black King shall be crowned". When **Ras Tafari Makonnen** was crowned Negus of Ethiopia in 1930, taking the title Emperor Haile Selassie, King of Kings, Lord of Lords, Conquering Lion of the Tribe of Judah, Jamaicans looked to their Bibles and interpreted his title as proof of divinity; Garvey was christened the **Black Moses** and Selassie became a messiah sent to redeem black people from their suffering at the hands of white oppressors.

Rastafari places Africans as the direct descendants of the original Hebrew Israelites and Africa as the promised land, offering a restructuring of black identity and an emphasis on black culture lost and maligned by centuries of "slave mentality". As a colonized country, Jamaica is part of the white, Western system of corruption and "downpression" – **Babylon** – which will ultimately destroy itself through its own innate wickedness in an appropriately apocalyptic manner.

The first tenet of Rastafari is the acceptance of Haile Selassie as the second coming of God or **Jah**. *Kebre Negast*, the Ethiopian version of the Christian bible, places him in a legendary line of Ethiopian kings stretching directly back to King Solomon and Queen Sheba; it states that the Ark of the Covenant (and therefore the God of Israel) rests in Ethiopia rather than Jerusalem, and that Selassie is the 225th incarnation of the divinity – a latter-day Christ. Though the Rastafarian elders granted a private audience with Selassie during his 1966 visit to Jamaica report him saying "Holy priests, warriors and traitors, be still and know that I am He", Selassie never publicly acknowledged himself as a god and was said to be frightened rather than gratified by the adulation he received. Selassie died in 1975, but to Rastafarians, he became even more powerful – it is believed that only the evil truly die, and as the Rastaman lives his life in the appropriate spiritual manner, his soul is immortal.

A second central doctrine is African **repatriation**, which became a real possibility through Haile Selassie's gift of land at Shashamene in Ethiopia for black people to return "home" to. Though the few who made the journey found life equally as harsh as in Jamaica, the belief in Africa – particularly Ethiopia or **Zion** – as a spiritual home persists amongst older Rastas. Younger followers, though, point to 1966, when Selassie publicly advised Rastafarians that they should "liberate themselves in Jamaica" before removing to Africa. The new cry of "liberation before repatriation" emerged, alongside a new politicization – traditionally, Rastas do not vote and refuse to enter the corrupt world of "politricks" – but following Selassie's words, the movement became intensely political, with popular adherents such as Peter Tosh publicly decrying the manifestations of the bloodsucking Babylon "shitstem".

Most Rastafarians abide by basic principles taken from the Bible. Proverb 15:17 "Better is a dinner of herbs where love is, than a stalled ox and hatred therewith" directs the strict **Ital** (natural and unprocessed) **diet**: no salt in cooking, no meat (pork, lobster and shellfish are particularly avoided, though many eat small fish – anything larger than 12in is probably predatory and representative of cannibalistic Babylon), and few dairy products. Some even abstain from rice and bread, eating only home-grown vegetables and pulses. Animal by-products such as lard are also prohibited, as are alcohol, cigarettes and chemical stimulants. **Ganja**, however – or "herb", as Rastas prefer to call it – is seen as a religious sacrament, as referred to in Psalm 104:14 "He causeth the grass to grow for the cattle, and the herb for the service of man". Though many followers smoke pretty much continually to aid their meditations or "reasonings", ganja is primarily used at prayer meetings when the communal pipe (chalice, cutchie or chillum) is stoked with the finest herb available, blessed with a prayer and passed round the group to the left. Alleged to have first grown around King Solomon's grave, the "holy herb" is said to enable deep penetration of thought as well as permitting a higher level of spirituality that transcends the petty distractions of the Babylonian world. **Reasoning** is central to the Rastafari faith, designed to reveal truth and elucidate the wickedness of the world and the Rasta position within it. Alongside these ad hoc sessions, Rastafarians hold more organized gatherings, usually outdoors, known as **grounations** or **nyabinghis**, which go on for as long as three days.

Dreadlocks are also a biblical directive; Leviticus 21:5 commands that "They shall not make baldness upon their head, neither shall they shave off the corner of their beard, nor make cuttings in the flesh". Orthodox Rastafarians cover their hair in a wrap or a knitted hat called a **tam**, believing it indiscreet and immodest to show it off. The reference to cutting the flesh informs Rasta opposition to surgery; most prefer to trust in herbal **bush medicine** and supplement their diet with a variety of stamina-building fruit drinks and herbal tonics such as the "roots wine" concoction consumed by Rastas and non-believers island-wide.

Finally, the Rastafarian **colours** of red, black, gold and green have a deep significance. Red symbolizes the blood spilled in Jamaican history, black is the African skin of 97 percent of the population, gold is the hope for the victory over oppression and green represents the fertile land of Jamaica – and Ethiopia.

Sects

Though there have been many attempts to co-ordinate the Rastafarian movement, there are hundreds of divergent belief strands, sects and methods of worship. The **Rastafarian Centralization Organization** represents the newest attempt to unify the disparate chapters of Rastafari, holding yearly conferences and speaking for the wider movement on common issues. In recent years, the development of new sects with differing interpretations of the faith have caused some level of internal division. Some (including several of the Marley family) have moved towards the more Christian-oriented **Ethiopian Orthodox Church**, while others (like Marley himself) have opted to join the **Twelve Tribes of Israel** sect. Well-organized and well-connected, Twelve Tribes is now one of the more prosperous branches of Rastafari, with chapters in the UK and America, as well as one of the more progressive, with women taking a far more equal role. Members must read a chapter of the

Houses and colours of the Twelve Tribes of Israel

The houses and colours of the Twelve Tribes of Israel begin in April according to the ancient Egyptian calendar used by the Hebrews or "Children of Israel". They are: April: Reuben, silver; May: Simeon, gold; June: Levi, purple;

July: Judah, brown; August: Issachar, yellow; September: Zebulun, pink; October: Dan, blue; November: Gad, red; December: Asher, grey; January: Naphtali, green; February: Joseph, white; March: Benjamin, black.

Bible every day, and are assigned a name and a colour based on twelve "houses" related to birth months (see box), and music plays a strong part in ceremony. Controversially, Twelve Tribes believe that redemption will be limited to only their 144,000 chosen few, and use the names Haile Selassie and Jesus Christ interchangeably when referring to God. At the other end of the spectrum, members of the reclusive and strictly orthodox **Bobo Shanti** sect are the high priests of

Rasta, following the teaching of the late Prince Emmanuel Charles Edwards in choosing to reject wider society and live self-sufficiently in semi-rural communes called **camps**, wearing their locks wrapped tightly in a cloth turban rather than the conventional knitted tam. Prayer meetings are continuous, and members leave only to sell the palm brooms and leather sandals made on site or to purchase foodstuffs that the commune is unable to produce.

Music

Close your eyes practically anywhere in Jamaica and you'll hear music. Radios blare on the street, buses pump out non-stop dancehall and every Saturday night the vibrations of a thousand sound systems waft through the evening air. Music is a serious business here, generating an average of a hundred record releases per week and influencing every aspect of Jamaican culture from dress to speech to attitude. Reggae, and specifically DJ-based

dancehall, dominates, but Jamaicans are catholic in their musical tastes: soul, hip-hop, jazz, rock-n-roll, gospel and the ubiquitous country and western are popular.

The evolution of Jamaican music

Jamaica has long been a musical island. The simple rhythms of the Amerindian Tainos were adopted by the Maroons; the drumming, Coromantee chants and songs of their **Myal** religious ceremonies and related **Kumina** dance movements (see "Religion", p.392) became the island's first established musical form. Principal instruments included the bamboo and Coromantee nose flutes, abengs (cow horns), conch shells and strum-strums – home-made banjos fashioned from a hollowed calabash strung with horsehair. These provided the melody, but by far the most important instruments were the gumbe and ebo **drums**, supplemented by **percussion** from shakers, scrapers and graters. But while the Maroons were sounding their drums and abeng horns through the hills, plantation slaves were expressing

Traditional Jamaican dance forms

The syncretism of African and European culture in the plantations and beyond is particularly visible in traditional **dance**. Much of it emanates from the moves performed at Myal or Revival religious ceremonies, and most dances are purely African, often revolving around "dip and kotch" up-and-down movements or shuffling, hip-swinging styles that parallel the counter-clockwise movements of ritual dance. One of the most interesting dances is **etu**, danced at Nine Night Festivities (see "Religion", p.393), but otherwise performed only in Hanover by descendants of the original community of Nigerian slaves. It revolves around a process called "shawling", where the Revival Queen throws a scarf around the neck of a fellow dancer who is ceremoniously dipped back, giving each individual a chance to demonstrate some solo footwork from the standard pose of a slight but flat-footed bent-kneed crouch. Still actively practised in Portland, **brukin' party** is danced to celebrate the emancipation of Africans from slavery; groups of red and blue sets perform in a mock contest before the king and queen of each colour.

Many of Jamaica's most well-known dance forms are incorporated into performances by the island's professional dance companies, and you can see practically every style ever danced at the annual Heritage Festival held each October all around the island (see Basics, p.43).

themselves in a considerably more restricted environment. Recognizing the drum as a principal instrument of African warfare, the British tried to smother the provocative music of their minions, going so far as to prohibit "the beating of drums, barrels, gourds, boards or other such-like instruments of noise".

Yet African musical traditions survived on the plantations, most notably in the annual **Jonkonnu** masquerade parade, contemptuously dubbed "Pickaninny Christmas" by the whites. Jonkonnu was originally a religious ceremony using music and dance to evoke spirits – and named for its principal rhythmic component, the jawbone of a cow or horse played by scraping a stick across the teeth – and appropriated on the plantations to become a secular travelling pantomime. It incorporated British fife and drum marching rhythms and featured the fixed characters of a cow- or horse-headed leader followed by a king, queen and policeman, with companies of **Set Girls**, grouped by coloured sashes and skin tone. Jonkonnu is resurrected today as a tourist attraction. Other celebrations, such as those marking the end of the plantation year, were more European in flavour, with English maypole and morris dancing, and French quadrilles.

Another significant development was the rise of the **folk song**, created by workers in the cane and banana fields as a way to alleviate the arduous hard labour – an oral tradition that survives today. In the enormous canon of Jamaican folk music, there are traces of African, British, Irish and Spanish musical and vocal traditions, and heavy doses of Nonconformist hymns, arrangements and singing styles. Each of these influences is blended with characteristic Jamaican wit, irreverence and creativity. There are songs for courting, marrying, digging, drinking, playing ring games, burying – and just for singing, too. One of the all-time classics is "Hill and Gully Rider", a timeless ode to transport on an island strong on hills and weak on roads.

The roots of reggae: burru to mento

After emancipation, the influx of free African workers rekindled support for the less European aspects of Jamaican music and society. The Great Revival of 1860–61 (see p.392) saw a massive resurrection of support for Myal, Kumina and Afro-Pentecostal Revival religious forms within which drumming, chanting and singing form an integral part of worship. The new prominence of the master **burru** drummer and his topical, wickedly humorous social commentary signified the return of the **drum** to the heart of Jamaican music. A version of the African griot (a travelling one-man information agency who brought gossip and news to rural communities), the burru man originally accompanied fertility rites and played in plantation cane fields to keep machetes swinging to a steady pace, but later became a sort of smutty strolling minstrel. Burru songs were commonly associated with sinful and indecent practices, and dealt with situations seen as taboo in everyday speech. Musically influenced by Pukkumina and Revivalist drumming, the burru man would accompany himself on a three-part set of drums known today as **akete**, with complicated rhythms that would eventually work their way into Rastafarian music and develop into ska, rocksteady and finally reggae.

Over time, the burru man added a booming rhumba box (a wooden box with a hole on one side covered by metal strips which are plucked for an elementary bass sound) and home-made bamboo fifes, piccolos and fiddles to his repertoire. By the turn of the twentieth century, groups of burru men were banding together to perform at jump-ups and parties, singing souped-up and sophisticated versions of traditional folk songs – burru had become **mento** and Jamaican popular music was born. With a syncopated rhythm that got hips gyrating and bodies dipping forward or back in Kumina-esque abandon (a style of movement revived in the "bogle" dance of the early 1990s), pelvis-centred mento was closely related to calypso – the music of nearby Trinidad and Tobago – both through a predilection for rhythmic and lyrical sexual bawdiness and its humorous social commentary, and it dominated the Jamaican music scene for the first decades of this century. You'll still see mento trios–often referred to as calypso bands – performing welcome songs at north-coast hotels or forming the "authentic Jamaican culture" portion of an all-inclusive floor show.

Big bands to ballads

By the early 1940s, mento was waning in popularity as thousands left the island to fight for Britain in World War II or find work in Cuba, Latin American and the US. They returned with a taste for new rhythms and musical styles – rhumba, salsa and merengue – as well as new musical technology; phonograph records and cheap radio sets, widely available and affordable for the first time. Taking their influence from Count Basie and Duke Ellington, **big bands**, such as the Eric Deans Orchestra, found moderate success playing international standards and cleaned-up versions of mento hits at hotel floor shows. The best of these were put on vinyl by West Indies Recording Limited (WIRL), a record label owned by then-entrepreneur and later prime minister Edward Seaga. However, despite the quality of these tightly orchestrated performances, the big bands were bypassed by the majority of Jamaicans in favour of the radio stations beaming black American R&B from transmitters in Florida.

By the early 1950s, Jamaica's music scene was concentrated largely in a few pockets of southwest Kingston that were later to spawn the island's best-known musical luminaries. The desperately poor communities of Trench Town, Jones Town, Denham Town and Greenwich Farm offered plenty of dancehalls and street corners where quick-thinking impresarios like **Duke Reid**, **Prince Buster** and **Clement "Coxsone" Dodd** played for the people on huge mobile disco sets, taking the latest R&B or blues to areas where few could afford to see a big band play live. Reid and Dodd were the first to exploit the full commercial potential of the **sound system** (see box on p.403), vying with each other to see who could spin the best selection, often acquired on record-buying sorties to the US, and employing the braggadocio that characterizes today's dancehall posturing. An ex-policeman who always carried a firearm, Reid was prone to arrive at a dance dressed to the nines in sequins and leather, his guns cocked and ready to discipline any contenders to his throne.

By the mid-1950s, R&B's star had faded and the fickle Jamaican consumer was tiring of American imports. Quick to catch on to a new opportunity, men like Reid, Dodd and Leslie Kong began recording music themselves – primarily soft and soulful ballads – using established vocalists and players who had cut their teeth on the big band circuit. The Gaylads, Jackie Edwards, Owen Grey, Jackie Opal, Laurel Aitken and Bunny and Skully were backed by some of the best session musicians Jamaica has ever produced – Roland Alphonso, Tommy McCook and "Deadly" Headley Bennett on saxophone, Don Drummond and Rico Rodriguez on trombone, Jerome "Jah Jerry" Haines and Ernest Ranglin on guitar, Lester Sterling on trumpet and keyboard virtuoso Jackie Mittoo. Initially, the producers used the WIRL (now Dynamic) and Federal (now Tuff Gong) studios to record, but as soon as finances allowed, Reid and Dodd (among others) built their own rudimentary studios, giving them the names of their most popular labels, **Treasure Isle** and **Studio One** respectively. Around this time as well, in 1959, Chris Blackwell founded Island Records, which would go on to become arguably the most famous label in Jamaican music. It was a halcyon age for Jamaican music, a time of co-operation and innovation described by Ken Boothe, who began his career with Coxsone in the late 1950s: "Music was nice in them times; you could just go and sing on a corner, go look for some other singers and everybody used to talk and smoke and sing together."

Ska licks

By the late 1950s, musicians and singers began flirting with the philosophies of **Rastafari**. Some went down to the Dungle in Kingston or Adastra Road in the Rasta-dominated Wareika foothills and jammed with master drummers like **Count Ossie** (Oswald Williams) and his **Mystic Revelation of Rastafari** band, collaborations that produced the first ever recording for the Jamaica Broadcasting Corporation (JBC). Reworked in 1993 to massive commercial success by Jamaican DJ Shaggy, their *Oh Carolina* was one of the most influential tracks recorded, a perfect example of the fusion of Kumina drumming, harmonic singing and unique rhythm that was later to develop in to ska, rocksteady and finally reggae. The Rasta drummers became well known on the Kingston entertainment scene via the popular Vere Johns Opportunity Knocks variety show (held every week at the Ambassador Theatre in Jones Town) when star Marguerita Mahfood refused to appear unless she was backed by Ossie and Mystic Revelation. Unwillingly, Johns complied; to his surprise the drummers were a huge hit and went on to perform regularly at Kingston venues.

For Jamaican musicians, the late 1950s and early 1960s were a time of intense creativity, a period of exploring new rhythms and pushing the boundaries of jazz, R&B and Rasta drumming – an explosive combination that sometimes saw drummers and instrumentalists pitched against sound-system wattage. Meanwhile, session musicians were conducting their own experiments using the exaggerated shuffle rhythm of R&B and syncopated mento sounds, until somewhere along the way, the staccato, guitar-and-trumpet-led sound of **ska** emerged and captured the Jamaican musical imagination with effortless ease.

Following independence from British colonial rule in 1962, the future seemed full of possibilities. You can hear the euphoria in the music – joyous, up-tempo ska tunes that seem now not to express a care in the world – and it was the small independent record labels in West Kingston who were at the cutting edge. Ska lyrics provided a window into the evolution of Jamaica and its music, and with its home-grown roots and dancefloor beat, ska expressed the mood of the ghetto dweller. Tommy McCook grouped together the cream of the session musicians to form the now-legendary **Skatalites**, who released a host of massively popular instrumental tracks, like *Guns of Navarone*, and backed most of the era's popular singers – including Millie Small, who shot to international fame with *My Boy Lollipop*, produced by Chris Blackwell for Fontana. Other prominent ska tracks included Justin Hinds and the Dominoes' *Carry Go Bring Come*, the Ethiopians' *Train to Skaville* and a host of others on Beverley's, Federal, Treasure Isle and Coxsone's Studio One and Coxsone labels.

Rude boys to rocksteady

As the post-independence glow began to fade, the ghetto youth became increasingly dissatisfied with their meagre slice of the pie and the **rude boy** era of violence, police brutality and ghetto dissent began, cinematically celebrated by Jimmy Cliff's portrayal of urban rebel Ivan in *The Harder They Come*, and musically documented in early Wailers cuts like *Rule Them Rudie* and *Let Him Go (Rudie Get Bail)*, a fractious stance that had generated 1964's *Simmer Down*, an appeal for calm among the youth.

While the musical critique of free Jamaica continued in releases like the Skatalites' 1966 *Independent Anniversary Ska*, subtle changes occurred in the music itself as Jamaicans began to demand something more leisurely. Producers accorded and began to slow down the tempo, guiding their artists toward a more benign lyrical output. Though the rude boy lament continued in cuts like *007 (Shanty Town)* from Desmond Dekker and the Aces, by 1966 Hopeton Lewis had produced *Take It Easy*, Stranger and Patsy were singing emollient **rocksteady** tracks about love and relationships in *When I Call Your Name*, while *Happy Go Lucky Girl* and *Only A Smile* by John Holt and the Paragons, *Queen Majesty* and *You Don't Care* by the Techniques with Slim Smith and Pat Kelly and *You Don't Need Me* and *I Caught You* by Brent Dowe's Melodians did something to temper the pressure in West

The art of the rhythm track

Through what's known in Jamaica as the **rhythm track**, the basslines and chord sequences laid down during the rocksteady and reggae eras have become the foundation for practically all Jamaican music recorded thereafter. Realizing that there are only so many chords to play or pressed for time when studios charge by the hour, musicians and producers like Bunny Lee (one of the first to release multiple versions of the same rhythm) have capitalized on the best chord and bassline combinations, manipulating and reinterpreting them so often that most of the classic rhythm tracks have established names, usually gleaned from the song title with which they first appeared. Working as full-time studio session musicians throughout the rocksteady and early reggae eras, the likes of singer, bassist

and arranger **Leroy Sibbles** created many of the rhythms that backed hundreds of 1970s' reggae cuts and are still reworked into today's dancehall; hence the famous bassline which underpinned Eric Donaldson's *Cherry Oh Baby* was reworked by UB40 in the 1980s with their cover version and by Tony Rebel in the 1990s with *Sweet Jamaica*. Many of the older rhythm tracks (and some new ones) have been digitally reworked to become hugely popular backing tracks, and surface on as many as six hundred versions. The upshot is that listening to Jamaican music can feel like an exercise in déjà vu; you may or may not have heard a particular song before, but once you've listened to a fair portion of rocksteady and early reggae, you'll certainly be familiar with most of the classic rhythm tracks.

Kingston. Characterized by the addition of the "one drop" drumming style and a more melodic tone, rocksteady carried the swing and swiftly eclipsed the ska sound. The king of the era was Alton Ellis, who put a name to the movement with his *Get Ready Rock Steady* track. It was a prolific time for Jamaican music, with labels like Studio One and, primarily, Treasure Isle literally pumping out the tunes, many set to rhythm tracks which still continue to be heard to this day (see box, above). However, rocksteady was a short-lived movement, and by 1968 it had been superseded by the tighter guitars, heavier bass and sinuous rhythm of reggae.

Reggae to roots rock

So many artists contributed to the development of **reggae** that it's impossible to say who originated the genre – it's most likely that this ubiquitous Jamaican sound developed organically as a natural progression from rocksteady, but Toots and The Maytals' 1968 single *Do The Reggay* (sic) certainly cemented a name that Rastafarians will tell you derives from *rex*, meaning king. Hence reggae is the "king's music" – an apt allegory, as the appearance of reggae coincided with an explosion in the popularity of the Rastafarian movement.

From 1970 onwards, Jamaican music took an increasingly religious stance, with its main

lyrical themes drawing reference from the tenets of Rastafari; repatriation, black history, black pride and self-determination. "**Roots and culture**" were the lick and reggae became a fully fledged protest music – anathema to the establishment, who saw a menacing, subversive message from a dirty and violent source, and banned it wherever possible; though the rum bar jukeboxes played whatever the radio stations wouldn't. Not until the international acclaim that greeted Bob Marley and the Wailers after they signed to Island Records in 1972 (see p.230), was reggae given islandwide approval for the first time.

A time of intense musical productivity, the 1970s stands out as the classic period of Jamaica's best roots reggae. But while **Burning Spear** was singing *Marcus Garvey* and *Slavery Days* and Joseph Hill's **Culture** provided apocalyptic warnings of the time when *Two Sevens Clash*, the era also offered a sweeter side; the angelic crooning of more mainstream artists like **Dennis Brown** or **Gregory Isaccs** found an eager audience, their style becoming known as **lovers' rock**. Though lyrics rested mostly on love and affection, lovers' artists also had some bite; tracks like Junior Byles' *Curly Locks* (a song about the controversial move of falling in love with a Rastaman) highlight the uneasy relationship that Rasta and reggae still had with wider Jamaican society.

Dub to DJ business

As the 1970s wore on, studio technology became increasingly sophisticated and producers began manipulating their equipment, using reverb or echo machines, over-dubbing techniques and snatches of dog barks or gun shots to produce some of the most arresting and penetrating music ever to emerge from Jamaica – **dub**. Using a remarkable level of inventiveness with often limited means, Jamaican engineers such as dub pioneers **King Tubby**, **Prince Jammy** and **Scientist** pre-dated the advent of the digital sampler by ten years and brought reggae back to basics, stripping down songs so that only bass, drums and inflections of tone remained. Snippets of the original vocals were then mixed in alongside sound effects and two-line DJ sound-bites. Like ska, dub remained a primarily instrumental music for a short time; before long, scores of DJs clamoured to produce a dub voice-over, and producers plundered their archives and released dub versions of old cuts, while DJs provided the voice-over and even vocal tracks had a dub flipside.

The cult of the DJ had begun in the sound systems, with resident DJs improvising a couple of lines of introductory patter at the beginning of a record. The ecstatic crowd responses encouraged them to spin it out, and soon they were delivering full-length monologues over the music,

The cult of the sound system

Since the mid 1950s when Duke Reid and Coxsone Dodd discharged the first shots in a battle of heavy wattage, mobile discos known as **sound systems** have been intrinsic to the Jamaican music scene. Laying the foundations of each stage in reggae's development, sound systems provide an opportunity to test crowd response to new lyrics or rhythms, and inspire Jamaicans to follow their sound of choice with vehement loyalty. A simple arrangement of high-powered amplifiers and momentous columns of speakers customized to give a heavy, belly-rolling bass, the sound system began (and remains) as a way of bringing the music to those who can't afford nightclub or stage show cover charges, and is now the major form of entertainment for young Jamaicans. Some come to hear their favourite **selector**, the man who employs an almost clairvoyant intuition to play just what the crowd wants, while others come for the prospect of hearing DJs chatting live lyrics over a rhythm track – a tradition that began with a couple of introductory one-liners as the music played and expanded to full-blown commentaries. Overall though it's the unique "dancehall vibe" that most people come to savour. Whether it's a country dance or a high-fashion session in downtown Kingston, the panorama is the same: packed with sweaty patrons bubbling alone or intertwining loins in a sensuous exchange of body heat as rum and ganja fumes mingle with the steam and smoke from pots of mannish water soup or jerk barbecues, and the shouts of "Wheel and come again!" ("play that one again") as the music reaches its peak.

Since the early days when Dodd could set up on an opposite Kingston corner to Reid and try to poach his crowd with a mightier bass and a craftier playlist, **rivalry** has been central to sound-system culture, with the battle to be known as the best fought out at "clashes", where two sounds play on one night, and crowd appreciation is the mark of the winner. Buying a larger amp or a new set of speakers is one way of achieving dominance, but the most popular method is still to spin an exclusive record, a one-off "dub-plate" acetate voiced over by the latest DJ or singer.

At the start of the new millennium, the main players in the Jamaican sound-system scene are Stone Love, whose raw reputation and killer selectors Rory, Billy Slaughter and Wee Pow prompt followers to travel for miles to hear them play. Other sets to watch out for are the Twelve Tribes sound, Jah Love, as well as Adonai, Skyy Disco, Travellers and Renaissance, the latter popular amongst more well-heeled Jamaicans. Even with this glory, though, the position of the sound system in its land of origin is increasingly fragile. Following noise pollution legislation and the closure of Kingston clubs such as *House of Leo* and *Skateland* in the late 1990s, the days when a sound system could simply set up in the street and play until the early hours are drawing to a close.

The Producers

From the late 1950s to the late 1960s, Duke Reid and Coxsone Dodd dominated Jamaica's music scene, commanding heavyweight respect among the music fraternity and churning out the majority of the island's hits. This pair of musical titans are widely credited with controlling Jamaican recording as the industry shifted focus from ska to rocksteady. Their "big fish in a small pond" infamy has shaped the way that the industry works at a basic level. A producer raises enough funds to buy a studio, he then hires a team of musicians or a master keyboard programmer to lay down the rhythm tracks and scouts for a talented arranger to look after the daily running of recording sessions and auditions of hopeful vocalists. The producer then selects the right combination from his pool of vocalists, songs and rhythm tracks, puts it all together, presses vinyl copies and releases it, sometimes taking no chances on it's success by handing out favours to ensure the tunes are played on the radio and at dances.

Though the reign of Dodd and Reid remained watertight until the late 1960s, the prevailing mood had changed by the early 1970s. Artists got sick of being paid a single fee while the producers reaped the royalties, and in-house arrangers balked at doing all the work while the producers sat back and enjoyed the rewards. As starting a label was merely a matter of raising the funds for studio time and record pressing, a new breed of **independent producer** emerged. Many lasted no longer than a couple of releases, but the likes of Jack Ruby, Harry "J" Johnson, Bunny "Striker" Lee, Henry "Junjo" Lawes,

Sonia Pottinger and Clancy Eccles were more longstanding, and produced some of the finest reggae of the era. The most infamous and instrumental independent producer, though, was the eminent "Upsetter", **Lee "Scratch" Perry**, who started out as a bouncer for Prince Buster and graduated to running Coxsone's Studio One, where he worked with Marley and the Wailers on the definitive singles (*Small Axe*, *Sun Is Shining*, *Duppy Conqueror*, *Satisfy My Soul*) that were later reworked on albums for Island Records. In the late 1960s, Perry built his **Black Ark** studio and established the famous Upsetter label, releasing classic tracks such as Junior Murvin's *Police and Thieves*, Max Romeo's *Sipple Out Deh* (*War Inna Babylon*) and the definitive roots reggae LP *Heart of the Congos*. Perry remained at reggae's cutting edge until the late 1970s, becoming one of the chief innovators of dub (see p.403) as a patron of the late King Tubby, before his legendary – and often consciously cultivated – mental instability (planting records in his garden, and burning down his studio in a fit of pique) and refusal to compromise to his increasingly eccentric musical vision led to a decline in sales.

In the digital age (see p.406), dominated by electronically-generated dancehall rhythm tracks, producers were able to release material with even fewer resources behind them. Producers such as Prince Jammy have taken centre stage alongside fellow luminaries King Tubby, Bobby Digital, Gussie Clarke, Mikey Bennett, Donovan Germaine, Dave Kelly, Philip "Fatis" Burell and Steely and Cleevie.

discussing topical events as well as the state of play on the dance floor. The craft was mastered by **U-Roy** – inspired by the earlier efforts of Count Machouki and Sir Lord Comic – who released talk-based singles to great success throughout the 1970s with roots sound systems like the venerable King Tubby's Hi-Fi, Tippertone, Sir George and Killermanjaro providing the backing for their live appearances. Meanwhile, the DJs' trade was expanded when Big Youth started talking over records in his cultural style, followed by the likes of King Stitt, Dennis Alcapone, I-Roy, Jah Stitch, Tappa Zukie, Prince Jazzbo and Dillinger, whose

Cocaine Running Around My Brain scored a hit in the UK. As the violent elections of 1976 and 1980 saw the pressure in Kingston building up, the sound systems multiplied and the DJs "chatted" on the mike about the times, analyzing the position of the ghetto youth in Jamaica from a dread perspective, and offered cultural distractions by setting the Psalms to song. Newcomers U-Brown, Ranking Joe, Josey Wales, Charlie Chaplin and Trinity continued in the same vein, touring Jamaica and the Caribbean with sound systems, and paving the way for the dancehall explosion of the 1980s.

In 1981, the Jamaican reggae industry was left in shock as Bob Marley succumbed to cancer and the music fraternity realized the enormity of their loss. Jamaica came to a standstill for two days as mourners viewed his coffin and lined the roads to watch the entourage on the final procession to Nine Miles. Though not the greatest singer to emerge from Jamaica, Marley's influence and songwriting talent were immeasurable, and following his demise, reggae struggled to regain its direction and purpose. Groups like **Black Uhuru** recorded a succession of roots albums for Island, but the musical tide had already turned towards the DJ and Marley's legacy of cultural consciousness began to seem less appropriate to the world of cocaine-running and political warfare in the ghettos. The scene also took a blow in 1999 with the death of the "Crown Prince of Reggae", Dennis Brown, one of Jamaica's most prolific – and sweetest – singers.

Slackness in the dancehall

These days, you're far more likely to be assailed by a clamorous barrage of raw drum and bass and shouted patois lyrics than hear Bob Marley or Burning Spear booming out from Jamaican speaker boxes. The two-chord sound that earned DJ Shabba Ranks two Grammy awards in the early 1990s is the most popular musical form in contemporary Jamaica, named **ragga** (from "ragamuffin", meaning a rough-and-ready ghetto-dweller) or **dancehall** because that's where it originated and where it is best enjoyed. The genre first surfaced in around 1979, and was cemented in 1981 when a flamboyant albino DJ named **Yellowman** exploded on to the scene with his massive hits *Married in the Morning, Mr Chin* and *Nobody Move*. Yellowman's lyrical bawdiness and huge popularity signified the departure from roots reggae and cultural toasting to the sexually explicit and often violent DJ-ism that took hold in the 1980s. Though none were rawer than Yellow, who added energetic stage performances and self-deprecating humour to the expletives, other DJs – fuelled by a positive response from their Jamaican audience – emulated his lewd approach, and sexually explicit lyrics – or **"slackness"** – began to proliferate.

In 1985, Wayne Smith's hit *Under Me Sleng Teng* – voiced for King Jammy-created rhythm of the same name – heralded the start of the computer age in the dancehall. Studios switched from analogue to digital recording formats and

---

Dancehall queens

Weekends in Jamaica mean sound-system dances islandwide, and fashion goes hand-in-hand with the music. In a society where women are often the sole breadwinner of a single-parent family, parties are a time to let loose and forget the domestic drudgery in favour of some of the rudest dancing and most glittery glamour on the planet – as demonstrated in the 1998 Jamaican movie *Dancehall Queen* (see p.420). Whether it's a latticework leatherette g-string and bra ensemble or a concoction of carefully arranged silver plastic straps, topped-off with a neon wig, thigh boots or killer heels, dancehall wear is loud, proud and deliberately ostentatious. The costumes are for one purpose: the sheer hype and self-promotion of "modelling" for the crowds who'll step aside to watch the wearers "skin out" and "shock out" performing the suggestive gymnastics of the latest dances (see below) to the most overtly sexual tracks. Dancehall queens, as the wearers are called, are the icons of sound-system culture, a league of ghetto princesses ruled by a light-skinned uptown Kingstonian named Carlene, whose killer dress sense, athletic dancing style and pneumatic body have earned her the local status of a Hollywood film star. Other luminaries include Eva, whose steamy performances at stageshows have earned her a legendary reputation.

Each new rhythm that appears on the dancehall scene spawns not only a hundred DJ or singer versions but – if it becomes really popular – a **dance** of its own, usually based around sensual, gyrating of the hips and lower body, and always best displayed by dancehall queens. The "winding", "skanking" or "water pumping" of the early 1980s were a fairly innocuous way of slow-dancing, but in recent years, some of the dances have become ever more explicit. Some of the best to look out for – or have a Jamaican companion demonstrate, are the classic bogle and butterfly or the more current Jerry Springer or Angel.

Reggae Web sites

Below are some of the best reggae-related Web sites. As new pages pop up with increasing frequency (and we've only the space to list a few), it's well worth conducting your own search too.

www.afflictedyard.com/menu.htm
The "Noise in the yard" section of this excellent site has downloads of the best and most current sound clashes and stageshows.

www.bobmarley.com
Official Bob page, with essays on the man and his life, music clips, and information on the continuing activities of the Marley clan.

www.dancehallminded.com
One of the best dancehall sites, with reviews, pictures, features, music downloads and links to the cream of like-minded sites.

www.niceup.com
Essential all-round site better known as the Jammin Reggae Archives, with excellent background material and up-to-date information on every aspect of reggae and dancehall, plus hordes of links.

www.reggaeambassadors.org
Culture oriented, with heaps of links, music downloads, features, but rather unappetizing to look at.

www.reggaejams.com
Pretty site with sound clips, artist profiles, lyrics, pictures, charts and good links.

www.reggaesource.com
News, reviews, charts, features, interviews and links, all nicely-presented.

www.reggaetrain.com
Reviews, charts – and the weather in Kingston.

www.reggaeweb.com
US-based site, with a good selection of features, interviews, reviews and a few music clips from sound-system dances.

www.thereggaeboyz.com/rootz/
Despite the name, this is a cultural, Rasta-oriented reggae (not dancehall) site, with interviews, links, reviews and thoughtful editorial comment.

www.yardie.com/reggae.htm
Yardie.com's exhaustive list of reggae-related links.

producers seized upon computerized rhythms as a quicker and cheaper way of putting out a record. The mixing board had become an instrument unto itself, with a new breed of producers like Bobby Digital, Donovan Germaine, Mikey Bennett, Dave Kelly and Patrick Roberts becoming the Reids and Dodds of the 1990s and DJs becoming the island's biggest stars. Vocalists also clamoured to ride the digital rhythms – singers like Frankie Paul, Michael Palmer, Little John, Beres Hammond, Barrington Levy, Pinchers, Wayne Wonder and Sanchez got the sweetness out of the rhythms and continue to record today.

Dancehall is massive in contemporary Jamaica, though it's not to everyone's liking. Many charge the genre with wider moral decline as the DJs become the gangsta rappers of reggae with gold chains, flash cars, and in some cases, a seemingly limitless enthusiasm for automatic firearms and violent sex. However, though some songs do seem intent on a glorification of violence, most simply reflect the lives of a thousand ghetto dwellers for whom violence and guns are a daily reality. Essentially, dancehall is a raw, rude, hardcore music designed to titillate and tease its Jamaican audience on home ground and beyond. Whether you like the lyrics or hate them, it's unlikely that you'll be able to resist dancehall's compelling rhythm and infectious hype, and while you're in Jamaica, it's futile to try.

Reggae in the twenty-first century

Undoubtedly, dancehall dominates contemporary Jamaican music. Yet those worried about moral depravity can take heart: dancehall culture is going through another transitional phase, as the battle between cultural and slackness artists intensifies. In 1993, the conscious lyrics and staunch Rastafarian stance of singer **Garnet Silk** managed to conquer the dancehalls at the time

For the definitive history of Jamaican music, consult Steve Barrow and Peter Dalton's *Rough Guide to Reggae*, and for a musical trip through the years, try Island's unbeatable *Tougher Than Tough* four-CD collection.

when "gun bizness" and sexual slackness were the sole signifiers, and his immense popularity started the momentum for today's resurgence of cultural reggae. In 1994, Silk was killed in an explosion, but the likes of the massively popular Morgan Heritage (*www.morganheritagefamily .com*) and Luciano have carried on where he left off, using musicians rather than keyboards and writing their own material. It seems that the righteous are triumphing over the slack. In the late 1990s, even the original "gold teeth, gold chain don gorgon" **Ninjaman**, a long-term crack addict and firearms advocate, resurrected himself as Brother Desmond, a gospel singing born-again Christian, while megastar **Buju Banton** – who famously encouraged the murder of homosexuals, to mercifully widespread condemnation – has renounced his early lyrical vitriol, converted to Rastafari and now sings of Jah to the sufferers (though he also continues to record rather lascivious material). Meanwhile, "veteran" artists John Holt, Leroy Sibbles, Ken Boothe and the Mighty Diamonds do the stageshow rounds to satisfy the current demand for **"oldies"** hits. Sizzla,

Anthony B and Capleton (who made a conscious decision to sing positive lyrics after his conversion to Rastafari) keep up the cultural pressure in the dancehall and singers Sanchez, Singing Melody, Beres Hammond and Richie Stevens provide sweet love songs for the romantically inclined. Reggae has even made moves into the pop arena: Grammy award winner Shaggy scored worldwide hits in the late 1990s with *Boombastic* and the *Train Is Coming*; Chaka Demus and Pliers' *Murder She Wrote* and *Tease Me* provided the now-staid Island Jamaica label with the biggest crossover hit in years, and reggae's current leading light, Beenie Man, has scored a UK chart hit in 1998 with *Who Am I?*

The on-going DJ feud between **Beenie Man's** Shocking Vibes stable (*www.shockingvibes.com*) and Bounty Killer's Scare Dem crew continues to rumble on – Sumfest 1999 offered two dancehall nights only because Bounty and Beenie refused to perform on the same bill. Meanwhile, other luminaries such as Mr Vegas, Zebra and Spragga Benz, many working out of label-based crews such as Main Street or Scare Dem, continue to keep the dancehall scene alive.

You'd be hard-pressed to find anywhere with a music scene as influential, vibrant and liberated as Jamaica's, and with thousands of young Jamaicans dreaming of being the next Marley, Tanya Stephens, Merciless or Lady Saw, it looks as though reggae's future prosperity is secure.

DISCOGRAPHY

COMPILATIONS

Various, *Tougher than Tough: the Story of Jamaican Music* (Island, UK; 4-CD set). This is quite an investment but it would be hard to imagine a better compilation of Jamaican music. The discs cover just about every phase of the Jamaican musical story, from 1958 to 1993, beginning with a superb selection of pre-ska R&B, then moving through the ska and rocksteady hits of the 1950s and 60s to

an overview of reggae's manifold styles and sub-genres. The songs are gathered from a wide variety of labels – not just from the Island catalogue – and there are superb, virtually book-sized sleeve notes from Steve Barrow.

Various, *This is Reggae Music Volumes 1–5* (Mango, UK). More crucial anthologies, if you prefer to pick your reggae years.

ROOTS AND MENTO

Count Ossie and his Mystic Revealers of Rastafari, *Grounation* (various labels). Traditional Rasta drumming accompanied by bebop and cool jazz horn lines, apocalyptic poems, and much chanting.

The Jolly Boys, *Pop'n'Mento* (Cooking Vinyl, UK/First Warning, US) and *Sunshine'n'Water* (Rykodisc, US). Sunny and lewd, this is classic good-time mento from a band who have been playing it for decades. Strongly recommended.

Continued...

Luciano, *Where There Is Life* (Island Jamaica, UK). An exceptionally well-crafted set that's a landmark in modern roots music.

Various, *Drums of Defiance* (Smithsonian Folkways, US) and *The Roots of Reggae* (Lyrichord, US). Two excellent, well-annotated anthologies of the deepest roots music of Jamaica from the Maroon communities.

Various, *From Kongo to Zion and Churchical Chants of the Nyabinghi* (Heartbeat, US).

Traditional Rasta music from nyabinghi ceremonies.

Various, *Jamaican Roots: Bongo, Baccra and Coolie, Volumes 1 & 2* (Folkways, US). The first volume includes more or less the only Kumina music on record, plus Indian Hindu (baccra) music; the second has Revival Zion plus carnival music.

SKA AND ROCKSTEADY

Alton Ellis, *Cry Tough* (Heartbeat, US). Alton invented the sound of rocksteady, and the name – with his song *"Get Ready to Rock Steady"*.

Ethiopians, *The World Goes Ska* (Jetstar, UK). Classic 1960s ska, with songs full of ghetto life in Kingston.

Skatalites, *Music is my Occupation* (Trojan, UK) and *Hog in a Cocoa* (Esoldun, France). Led by trombonist Don Drummond, the Skatalites had an all-star musical cast, and produced simply the greatest ska sounds. The first

disc here is a showcase for Drummond, Tommy McCook and Baba Brooks; the second has them backing the best singers of the 1960s at Duke Reid's studio.

The Techniques, *Run Come Celebrate* (Heartbeat, US). Classic rocksteady from one of the great vocal trios.

Various, *Duke Reid's Treasure Chest* (Heartbeat, US). Rocksteady gems from the producer who ruled the sound.

REGGAE

Abyssinians, *Satta Massagana* (Heartbeat, US). A legendary dread album.

Big Youth, *Hit the Road Jack* (Trojan, UK). This was one of the great toaster records of the 1970s.

Dennis Brown, *The Dennis Brown Collection* (Jetstar, UK). A fine, wide-ranging hits compilation from 1993.

Burning Spear, *Marcus Garvey* and *Garvey's Ghost* (Mango, UK). Spear's 1976 Marcus Garvey tribute was full of exquisite vocals and horns, and given a sublime dub treatment on *Garvey's Ghost*, packaged with it on this bumper CD. Spear's 1990 album, *Mek We Dweet* (Mango, UK), marked a return to form, updating his sound with heavy guitar hooks.

Jimmy Cliff, *The Harder they Come* (Mango, UK). No reggae collection is complete without this 1972 movie soundtrack, combining early reggae standards with Cliff songs like the title track and *"Many Rivers to Cross"*.

Culture, *Two Sevens Clash* (Blue Moon, UK/Shanachie, US). The band never equalled this debut with its gorgeous vocals.

Eek-a-Mouse, *Wa Do Dem* (Greensleeves, UK/Shanachie, US). One of the wittiest, most imitated 1980s toasting discs.

Marcia Griffiths, *Naturally* (Sky Note, Jamaica). Greatest hits compilation from Jamaica's top woman singer, and former leader of the I-Threes, Bob Marley's backing trio.

Ijahman, *Haile I Hymn* (Mango, UK). Ijahman Levi's unique, soulful, meditative brand of reggae at its (1978) best.

Gregory Isaacs, *Night Nurse* (Mango, UK). Isaacs has been releasing Jamaica's best love songs for the past thirty years. This set, from 1983, is the finest of the lot to date.

King Tubby and Yabby You, *Time to Remember* (Yabby You, Jamaica). Ethereal and heavy dub – just as it should be.

Bob Marley and the Wailers highlights include: *Songs of Freedom: the Complete Bob Marley Collection* (Tuff Gong/Island, UK). The definitive Bob anthology: four CDs and 78 songs, dating from 1962 to his death in 1980, including virtually all the classics, plus lots of rare treasures.

Legend (Island, UK). If you want just a single disc, this is a near-faultless "best of" selection.

Burnin' (Island, UK). The sound of the original Wailers in 1973 with Marley and Tosh at their songwriting best on *"Get Up, Stand Up"* and *"I Shot the Sheriff"*.

The Lee Perry Sessions (Charly, UK). Many consider these the greatest of all Bob's recordings: songs include *"Lively up Yourself"*, *"Sun is Shining"* and *"Kaya"*.

Mighty Diamonds, *Mighty Diamonds* (Mango, UK). Fine selection from one of reggae's best vocal harmony groups.

Morgan Heritage, *Don't Haffi Dread* (VP, US). The best release yet for this family-based band, featuring the smash hit title track as well as the uplifting *Reggae Bring Back Love* and *Send Us Your Love*.

Junior Murvin, *Police and Thieves* (Mango, UK). The title song, inspired by election violence in Jamaica, was a massive hit on the island and in Britain in 1977. Lee Perry produced and shared writing credits.

Augustus Pablo, *King Tubby Meets Rockers Uptown* (Jetstar, UK). Pablo and producer King Tubby (the Upsetters' keyboard player, Glen Adams) invented dub in the early 1970s and perfected things on this wonderful and innovative album.

Frankie Paul, *20 Massive Hits* (Sonic Sounds, UK). One of the best – of innumerable – Frankie Paul compilations.

Lee "Scratch" Perry and the Upsetters, *Reggae Greats* (Mango, UK). Jamaica's greatest and craziest arranger is responsible for too many classic reggae albums to mention. This compilation has generous doses of his 1970s *"Super Ape"* outings, with wild dub. For true devotees, Greensleeves have released three triple-CD sets which pull in most of Perry's greatest moments, with the Upsetters and as arranger. These are titled: *The Upsetter Compact Set*, *Open the Gate*, and *Build the Ark*.

Sly and Robbie, *Reggae Greats* (Mango, UK). This drums and bass duo are even more prodigious producers than Lee Perry. This is

their own stuff – dub at its most sophisticated.

Mikey Smith, *Mi C-yaan Believe It* (Island, UK). An album of powerful dub poetry from a radical exponent, Mikey Smith, murdered by JLP gunmen shortly after its release.

Third World, *Reggae Greats* (Island, UK). Third World were often too slick for their own good, but their late 1970s songs like *"96 Degrees in the Shade"* and *"Now That We Found Love"* are pop reggae at its sweetest.

Toots and the Maytals, *Reggae Got Soul* (Mango, UK). The title says it all – Toots Hibbert is the man who put soul together with reggae.

Twinkle Brothers, *Twinkle Inna Poland Style* (Twinkle, UK). And if Toots put soul into reggae, the Twinkles' Norman Grant was the man who put Polish folk into the genre, on this, the latest of a series of recordings with the Trebunia family. Strangely enough, it works brilliantly.

Peter Tosh, *Legalise It* and *Equal Rights* (Virgin Frontline, UK). These two records were recorded after Tosh split from the Wailers, with most of the band along. They're militant songs with razor-sharp backing.

Yellowman, *Reggae on the Move* (Ras, US). Yellowman was the biggest toaster of the 1980s, and his slack lyrics, full of crudity and anti-feminist and anti-gay raps, were a precursor of the more offensive contemporary ragga habits. This is one of his better outings.

Various, *Chatty Chatty Mouth Versions* (Greensleeves, UK). Twelve cuts of this hugely popular rhythm.

Various, *If deejay was your trade: the Dreads at King Tubby's 1974–77* (Blood & Fire, UK). Sixteen dynamite tracks from Kingston's premier DJs of the 1970s – U Roy, Dr Alimantado, Dillinger, Tapper Zukie and others – produced by Bunny Lee.

Various, *Solid Gold, Coxsone Style* (Heartbeat, US). The likes of John Holt, the Abyssinians and Dennis Brown singing their hearts out for Studio One.

Continued...

DANCEHALL AND RAGGA

Buju Banton, *Voice of Jamaica* (Polygram, UK), *'Til Shiloh* (Loose Cannon, UK), *Inna Heights* (VP, US). The first album has bad-boy Buju at his baddest, the second sees him in more reflective cultural mood, and the third builds on the Rasta theme, though with the odd lascivious track.

Beenie Man, *Many Moods of Moses* (VP, US), *The Doctor* (VP, US). Two seminal albums from Jamaica's hottest and most versatile DJ, including the hits over the last few years.

Bounty Killer, *My Xperience* (VP, US). Double album by this hardcore ragga DJ, with a generous portion of major reggae hits alongside some scintillating fresh material.

Capleton, *One Mission* (J&D, US), *Prophecy* (DefJam, US). Two shots of Capleton's own brand of feiry cultural ragga, complete with nyabinghi drumming to boot.

Cocoa Tea, *Kingston Hot* (Ras, US). A silky-smooth dancehall voice, produced by Henry "Junjo" Lawes.

Chaka Demus and Pliers, *Tease Me* (Mango, UK). Mid-1990s ragga, mixing in Curtis Mayfield soul and hip-hop rhythms, and produced by the ever-inventive Sly and Robbie.

Lovindeer, *One Day Christian* (TSOJ, UK). Dancehall, poco-style, from its finest exponent.

Sugar Minott, *Slice of the Cake* (Heartbeat, US). Sweet sounds from "Sugar Sugar", including the great "No Vacancy".

Shabba Ranks, *As Raw as Ever* (CBS, US). Hip-hop meets reggae in this pioneering ragga album from 1991.

Garnett Silk, *It's Growing* (Vine Yard, UK; VP, US). The album that established the late Garnett Silk as one of the prime vocalists of the 1990s – a celebration of physical and spiritual love.

Sizzla, *Praise Ye Jah* (Xterminator/Jet Star, UK), *Black Woman and Child* (Greensleeves, UK). The deeply serious bobo-dread Sizzla chatting over the pick of the rhythms from Philip "Fattis" Burrell and Bobby Digital.

Mr Vegas, *Heads High* (Greensleeves, UK). Mr Vegas' best-recieved album, including the smash title track.

Various, *Reggae Hits – Volumes 1–25* (Jetstar, UK). Essential dancehall and lovers' rock compilations from 1984 on.

Jamaican art

Though the island has a centuries-old artistic tradition, interesting Jamaican art is very much a modern phenomenon. Before the 1920s, Jamaicans were, on the whole, simply too busy making ends meet to turn to art. Today, however, the island is considered one of the artistic centres of the Caribbean.

The earliest Jamaican art was the work of the Amerindian Tainos, who lived on the island prior to the arrival of Columbus in 1494. A few relics of their art remain – **cave paintings**, for example, at Mountain River Cave, near Spanish Town – and suggest that they were rather primitive woodcarvers and painters. The Spanish, who controlled

the island from 1513 to 1655, imported artisans from Spain to produce **limestone carvings**, notably for the now-destroyed governor's castle at Sevilla Nueva on the north coast, and these carvings incorporated Jamaican subject matter such as the figures of Taino women. In contrast, the dominant features of art in Jamaica during the period of British rule were **commemorative sculpture** – produced in Britain by British sculptors – and **portrait and landscape paintings** by British artists who paid occasional visits to the island.

Some of Britain's finest sculptors had their work commissioned for the Jamaican market. **John**

Bacon (1740–99) produced the Spanish Town memorial to Admiral Rodney and the smaller but more impressive monument to John Wolmer in the Kingston Parish Church. **John Flaxman** (1755–82), probably the finest English sculptor before Henry Moore, carved the monument to planter Simon Clarke that sits in the church at Lucea. More interesting is the "documentation" of eighteenth- and nineteenth-century Jamaica in the landscape paintings of **George Robertson** and **Joseph Bartholomew Kidd**, who paid visits to Jamaica during the 1770s and the 1830s respectively, and the nineteenth-century photographic records of **Adolphe Duperly** and **V.P. Parkhurst**. A more voluminous artistic legacy of the period is a series of portraits of governors and wealthy planters and their families painted, again, by itinerant British artists like **Philip Wickstead** who was in Jamaica in the 1770s.

A new art movement

Even after the abolition of slavery, it inevitably took three or four generations before a true Jamaican art began to flourish. Ironically, the prime mover in the new phase was an English sculptor – **Edna Manley** (1900–87) – who had married prime minister-to-be Norman Manley and moved to Jamaica in 1921. Several of her sculptures may be seen as turning points in Jamaican art. *Beadseller*, from 1922, is the small wood figure of a Jamaican street vendor, carved in a way that echoes European cubist and art deco movements of the period; her 1935 *Negro Aroused* – a black body uncoiling out of bondage – depicts early enthusiasm for national independence in art form.

In 1939, around forty artists in Manley's circle stormed into the annual meeting the island's main (and rather sedate) art museum, the Institute of Jamaica. They demanded an end to the domination of Anglophile attitudes to art and the replacement of the colonial portraits that hung in the art galleries with works by local artists. The event was more symbolic than revolutionary, marking a new departure point for Jamaican painters and sculptors; classes began at the Institute in 1940, organized initially by Manley, and helped to give direction to a new wave of Jamaican artists.

For several decades the primary aim of these pioneers of the island's new art movement – painters like **Albert Huie** (born 1920), **Carl Abrahams** (born 1913) and **Gloria Escoffery** (born 1923) – was to represent Jamaican people and their surroundings. Whereas earlier painters had focused on the simple beauty of nature, ignoring local people, artists now showed the landscape as a place where Jamaicans lived and worked. Paintings like *Crop Time* by Albert Huie, for example, showed the sugar plantations in action, with workers cutting, bundling and loading the cane, while in *Constant Spring Road*, his citizens go about their daily business on the streets of Kingston – chatting, selling and reading newspapers.

There were two distinct artistic styles in the work of this new wave of painters and sculptors. The predominant style was **European-influenced**, following twentieth-century trends in European art. Plenty of Jamaicans studied in Britain on British Council scholarships during the 1940s and 1950s, and an exposure to foreign art trends is reflected in much of their work. Most followed a classical approach, with artists like Huie and **Barrington Watson** (born 1931) using natural forms and landscapes as reference points, though Watson's later paintings, like *The Banana Loaders*, show the influence of post-impressionism. Of the early European-influenced painters, Escoffery shows the greatest interest in abstract art, stretching her figures along wide, panoramic canvases which depict a range of subjects from quiet pastoral scenes to the traditional Saturday market.

More distinctive, the **Afro-Caribbean approach** was characterized by the paintings of the self-taught, known as "intuitive", artists. One of the first, and most unusual, of these intuitives was the prodigious **John Dunkley** (1891–1947). Dunkley was a barber in Kingston, famous for covering every square inch of his shop with pictures of trees, vines and flowers; his later paintings continued his obsession with dark, brooding scenes from nature. Though scorned by the critics during his lifetime, Dunkley's work has become far more appreciated and sought after in recent years, and is excellently represented at the National Gallery in Kingston.

As you would expect in an island where religion plays such a large role, many of the island's other successful intuitive artists have focused their art around **religious imagery**. **Mallica Reynolds** (1911–89) – the shepherd (head) of a Revivalist group in Kingston, better known as **Kapo** – is the best known of these artists. During the 1950s he became the first self-taught Jamaican painter to be fully accepted by local and foreign viewers, and is still seen as the island's foremost intuitive sculptor and painter. Other intuitives such as **Albert Artwell** (born 1942) and **Everald Brown** (born 1917) – a priest in the Ethiopian Coptic Church – concentrate on Rasta beliefs, their paintings rich in religious symbolism and Rasta colours, showing kings and queens living an idyllic existence in heaven (Zion).

Jamaican artists grew in confidence during the 1960s and 1970s, many of them spurred by the promises and hopes of nationalism and independence. **Black iconography** was prominent in the work of artists like **Osmund Watson** (born 1934), who painted miniature portraits of a black Christ and black madonnas, as well as large, spiritual African archetypes. At the same time Jamaican art became more experimental, most noticeably in a specifically Jamaican surrealism, represented by the work of **David Boxer** (born 1946) and Australian-born **Colin Garland** (born 1935). Garland's paintings, inspired by the works of Haitian intuitives, seem to tell a story but instead dissolve into bizarre fantasy – his triptych,

In the Beautiful Caribbean, for example, appears to be a familiar summary of the island with its jumble of birds, fish and religious figures, until you spot the incongruous parachutist and the soldier with a seashell on his head.

Today, Jamaica's art scene continues its diversity. At the bottom end, it is dominated by the huge carving and painting industry which has grown up around mass tourism and, although much of it is relentlessly mediocre, there is some reasonable quality art at the craft markets in Kingston and across the north coast. At the higher end of the market, the tourist industry helps to expose artists to an audience they would otherwise struggle to reach, and some hotels – like *Mockingbird Hill* in Port Antonio, co-owned by local artist Barbara Walker – have set up exhibition areas for top-quality work. More importantly, the establishment of the National Gallery in Kingston in 1974 has given the island's art an important institutional infrastructure, and its regular exhibitions of the best of Jamaican art continue to encourage the development of young painters and sculptors, as witnessed by the proliferation of studios and galleries island-wide.

Language

Jamaicans enjoy nothing better than a good debate – you can join in at any rum shop or simply switch on the radio. They take great delight in outwitting each other in verbal

battles that Anancy the sharp-brained spider who's a favourite Jamaican folk hero (see box opposite) would be proud of. Although Jamaica's official language is English, patois is the working mode of expression for most Jamaicans. Its validity as a legitimate language or corrupted slang continues to provoke much debate on the island.

Jamaican patois is an incredibly creative and constantly evolving idiom; new words are coined almost daily to suit every development and fall into common use with astonishing speed while older phrases – yesterday's "buzzwords" – disappear without trace. Sex and related topics are generously covered in the patois lexicon; there are no less than four names for the penis in its various stages from boyhood ("pem pem") to teenage years ("tutu"), and countless names for the female genitalia. Patois also forms the basis for Jamaica's

Rasta linguistics

The Rasta challenge to all things Babylonian includes an assault upon all that "downpresses" the black man in the English language. As a means of resistance, Rastas have embarked on a new classification of words that attempt to correct what is seen as bias against their experiences, perceptions, personal choices and world view as black people. While this may sometimes seem pedantic (greeting a Rasta with "hello" might illicit the cool response "We're not in hell and I'm not low"), language does have a strong effect upon the formation of hierarchies and prejudices, and Rasta linguistics is one of the most creative elements of Jamaican patois. Rastas generally counteract negatives with positives and vice versa, breaking down each word and analysing its syllabic connotations, often reading significance into every nuance; hence understand becomes **overstand** (because if you comprehend something,

you're above it rather than beneath it), oppress (up-press) becomes **downpress**, and Selassie I is interpreted as proof of the deity's omnipresence; **Sela**see eye. It isn't difficult to see why there are so many cryptic messages embedded in 1970s roots reggae lyrics. The most recognizable aspect of Rasta linguistics is the use of "I" to emphasize unity (Inity) and positivity as well as to protest against the coercive control of language. Hence create becomes **I-rate**, continually becomes **I-tinually**, creation is **I-ration**. Rasta linguistics are not restricted to the Rastafarian community; the Rasta greetings "hail", "yes Rasta" or the acknowledgement of understanding in "seen Iyah" have become normal phrases for Jamaican (particularly male) youth. Rasta words that have slipped into daily usage are listed below. For a full description of the Rasta lexicon read Velma Pollard's *Dread Talk*.

myriad **proverbs**, spouted by grannies and rudeboys alike, such as "what sweet nanny goat ago run him belly" ("what you like may not necessarily be good for you"); "every hoe have him stick a bush" ("there's an ideal partner for everyone") or "tree nah grow in yuh face" ("you're not ugly").

An explanation of some of the more obvious idiosyncrasies will go some way to unravelling the labyrinth of patois. If you want to delve deeper, consult the books listed on p.425, and keep your ears wide open.

• Women are commonly referred to as "him": "Wha! Shelley pregnant! Him never tell me!"

• "H" is often not voiced, but makes up for the discrepancy by adding itself to plenty of other words. Hence "So yu is 'Enry from Hin-glan, don't?" ("don't" is used to mean "aren't you", or "isn't it?").

• There are plenty more inexplicable additions and absences: "shrimp" is often "swimp", "spliff" is "scliff", "vex" is "bex", "little" is "likkle", "ask" is "aks".

• Plurals are either ignored or conveyed by adding "dem"; hence "two feet" becomes "two foot", and "the girls are cooking for me" is "de gyal dem a cook fe de I".

• If somebody calls you "fatty", "whitey" or "big batty gyal", they are simply being direct rather

than attempting to insult. Follow Jamaicans in their directness and convey your meaning as simply as possible. Don't waste time with endless unnecessary pleasantries – please and thank you will suffice.

Anancy

The Twi word for spider, **Anancy** is a Jamaican hero and the principal character of most of the island's traditional folk stories; even tales without him are often referred to as "Nansi stories". Living by intellect rather than substance, the half-man, half-spider Brer Anancy always outwits his adversaries in a triumph of cunning over force – an allegory of the historical and contemporary struggles of black Jamaicans.

Anancy's Machiavellian use of deception and cunning in his triumphs mean each story has to end with the words "Jack Mandora, me no choose none" – Mandora is the keeper of heaven's gates, and the narrator has to disassociate him or herself from Anancy's wicked ways. Anancy stories are best told in Louise Bennett's *Anancy and Miss Lou* (see "Books", p.421).

Patois glossary

The common words and phrases below have been written semi-phonetically, a sometimes clumsy medium but the only way in which to convey their sound in the available space.

Ago Verb meaning will or going to do something: "Me ago check yuh tomorrow".

Agony Rough sex (or just sex).

Almshouse Militant or negative behaviour, a favourite attitude during sound-system clashes.

Babylon Government or the established and oppressive social system; also an insulting title for police.

Baby mother/father A person with children.

Baggy Female underwear.

Bakra White man, traditionally a slave-owner, probably derived from the Ibo "mbaraka".

Baldhead Non-Rasta, or person of unsound views.

Bandulu Trickery or a swindle.

Bangarang Noise or disruptive commotion, often caused by rival sound systems: "Pack up yu old time bangarang" ("Pack away your pathetic array of tinny equipment").

Bare Only; as in "she ave bare plantain fi sell".

Bashment A huge party or dance, or anything or anybody current, appealing and worth making a fuss over; also shortened as in "me ave one **bashy** dress fe wear to de dance".

Battery dolly A woman who makes a habit of having sex with more than one man simultaneously.

Batty Backside/bottom.

Battyman/boy Homosexual male.

Batty riders Tight lycra hot-pants worn by dancehall queens for maximum buttock exposure.

Bawl Cry out or call, particularly to register anguish: "Him a bawl out over the taxi fare".

Beenie Small or diminutive: "Me buy a likkle beenie amplifier".

Bhuttu Unsophisticated, simple country-bumpkin; used as an insult.

Big Up Boost yourself up (verb): "Big up yu chest" or "Big up yu status/yuself".

Bimma BMW: "Who got the keys to my bimma?".

Blood Principally a swear word used with claat and hole. Can also be used as a respectful greeting signifying unity; as in "Wh'appen, blood?".

Blouse and skirt An exclamation of surprise.

Bly An opportunity, chance or escape from an unwanted chore: "De rain gimme a bly – me nah haffe go a wuk".

Bombo Offensive expletive meaning backside, usually used in conjunction with claat or hole: "Move yu bombo-claat face from me".

Boops Rather 1980s term for a man who financially supports his (usually much younger) girlfriend.

Bow Verb meaning to indulge in oral sex; "**bow cat**" is a participant.

Breddah Friend, usually male: "Yes mi breddah!". **Bredren** is the plural form, used both as a noun and as an adjective.

Browning Light-skinned woman.

Buck To meet somebody: "Me will buck up wid yu later".

Buddy Penis.

Buff Bay Relating to the vagina; if a woman is said to come from Buff Bay, she has large and appealing vaginal lips.

Bumper Backside/bottom.

Bun or **burn** To smoke, usually ganja.

Cat Vagina.

Chalice Pipe for smoking ganja, usually communally.

Charged Intoxicated, stoned: "Me get charge las' night".

Check Pay a visit: "Me ago check yu tomorrow". Also a term of platonic or sexual appreciation, as in "Me check fe di man's argument" and as a term for sexual advances: "De young bway try an' check big woman".

Chronic Ganja, borrowed from US hip-hop lingo.

Claat/clot Literally, cloth, used with ras, pussy, bumba as an expletive: "Tek yuh blood-claat hands off me!"

Clean de rifle Perform fellatio.

Cook an' curry Everything's been taken care of, as in "Me clean de whole house; everything cook an' curry now".

Copasetic Cool, good: "Everyting copasetic".

Cork Full, as in "the dance cork tonight".

Cotch Rest up, chill out: "Sit dung and cotch with me". Also a verb to mean where a person sleeps: "Me a cotch by Evelyn's". Also used to denote bracing something: "Cotch de wheel wid' a rock".

Continued...

Craven Greedy, desperate.

Criss Attractive, beautiful: "Maxine a criss, criss gyal".

Criss-biscuit Anything of excellence but seldom used these days.

Crub Dance with a partner slowly and suggestively.

Cuss-cuss Argument.

Dads Don, a well-respected man: "Zekes a de dads fe Matthews Lane" ("Zekes runs Matthews Lane").

Dally To go: "Me mus dally now".

Dawta Young woman, interchangeable with **sistah**.

Dead-stock Quiet, a non-event: "Dem promote pure dead-stock dance".

Deh-deh Be somewhere: "Me deh-deh" ("I am here").

Deportee Humorous term used for the huge number of Japanese estate cars imported in recent years, so-called because like wayward Jamaicans deported from "foreign", the unwanted cars have been sent here because no-one else wants them.

Dis Disrespect: "Him a dis de programme" ("He's rudely disrupting our plans").

Don Respected male: "Him a de don". Also used in conjunction with gorgon or dada to mean the best or the toughest: "Me a di don gorgon/don dada" ("I'm the man!")

Draw card To trick or deceive; pull something sneaky.

Dread A person with locks (not necessarily of Rastafarian faith), or an adjective used to describe a bad situation: "De times dread".

Duns/Dunsa Money.

Dutch pot Heavy cooking pot.

Eat under a table A man performing oral sex on a woman.

Facety Impertinent, rude: "De touris' facety to rass".

Fassy Nasty, dirty, foolish, as in: "Yow, fassy-hole, who you talk to so?" Also sores on the body.

Feel no way Don't worry about it.

Fire Often used as a respectful greeting; originally popularized through songs such as Anthony B's hit *Fire Pon Rome*, and since a Rasta condemnation: "fire pon P.J. fe de gas hike!"

Fish Homosexual man.

Flex A person's way of behaving: "Ah so me flex my yout" ("That's how I operate, young man").

Flop Losing face, usually in public and often associated with the performance of an artist or sound system.

Fowl pill Poultry steroid taken by women to increase the size of their breasts and backsides.

Friend Apart from the usual meaning, can be used (rather confusingly) to refer to one's sexual partner.

Fuckery Irritating, bothersome, out of order: "dis man is pure fuckery" ("this man is badly behaved").

Ganja Marijuana.

Ganzey String vest or light-knit T-shirt.

Ginnal Con man or trickster.

Glamity Female genitals.

Gravalicious Greedy or avaricious.

Grind To have sex.

Grindsman is a particularly skilled man between the sheets.

Guidance An inspirational goodbye meaning "Let God be with you".

Gwan Go on or carry on (verb). Also used to mean "go away" or "going to".

Gweh Go away. Can also be used as an affectionate retort to foolish actions or speech.

Gyal Girl or woman.

Heartical Conscious esteemed person: "He's my heartical bredren".

Herb Ganja, herbal marijuana.

Higgler Female market trader, or a woman who brings goods to Jamaica from abroad to sell, often also called an **ICI** (Informal Commercial Importer).

Hol' it down Be cool and restrained, to be on a low profile or stay quiet.

Hood Penis, also called a **wood**.

Hottie-hottie An attractive female: "She one hottie-hottie gyal".

I an' I Me, I, we, mine, myself. **I-man** equally applies.

Idren Used by Rastas to mean friends or bredren.

Irie Adjective meaning fine or good: "You lookin' Irie tonight". Also used as a greeting.

Iron bird/fish Airplane or boat; used mostly by Rastas.

Ishence Ganja.

Continued...

Ital Anything natural (an Ital car wash is a river) or pure (a spliff without tobacco). Also describes Rastafarian meatless food cooked without salt.

Iyah Greeting to a friend: "What a gwan Iyah".

Jagabat Nasty, unclean, sluttish woman.

Jamdown Jamaica. JA is also frequently used.

Joe White man.

Joe Grind Term for a man sleeping with someone else's partner.

Jook Stab or pierce: "De rass fish hook jook me". Also a common term for the act of penetrative sex.

Juggling Sound-system tactic of playing several tracks on the same rhythm, mixing them smoothly via two decks. Also just playing records in a dance.

Kiki man Ganja dealer.

Kiss me neck! An expression of surprise: "Kiss me neck! Price of cornmeal gone down!".

Labrish Gossip, small talk.

Let off Give something; "She nah let off she tings" ("She won't have sex with me").

Lick To strike a blow: "(H)im a lick down the pear tree". Also to smoke: "Me a lick de chalice Iyah". Also an adjective meaning hot: "Beenie Man a de lick!" ("Beenie Man is the best").

Lick shot Literally or figuratively firing a gun to demonstrate appreciation in the dancehall.

Likkle more See you later.

Live blanket Human body, as in "Darlin', you need a live blanket?" ("Would you like to have sex with me?")

Lock off Cease, desist; also hold a low profile.

Maaga Thin, scrawny: "You sorry fe a maaga dog, maaga dog turn an bite you".

Maama man Effeminate, probably gay man.

Mampy Fat woman, not necessarily derogatory.

Massive Crowd of friends or people: "Strictly for de dancehall massive".

Matey Girlfriend, often used to denote one of an attached man's multiple sexual partners.

Men Used in the plural form to denote a homosexual male.

Merino Mens' tank top or string vest.

Modeller Fashionable, attractive woman, not necessarily a model.

More time Another way of saying "See you soon".

Mule Woman without children, usually incapable of conceiving. Also a person that smuggles cocaine internally.

Natty Used as an adjective or adverb to describe dreadlocks, also a greeting to a Rasta: "Wh'appen, Natty?".

Navel string Placenta; it's traditional for a new baby's naval string to be planted under a young tree.

Nuff Abundant or copious: "Me have nuff gyal". Often twinned with respect as a courteous greeting: "Nuff respect me breddah".

Nyam To eat, from the Hausa word "nyamnyam".

Obeah Jamaican witchcraft.

One love Greeting or farewell salutation. "Love" is used in the same way: "Love Iyah".

Ongle Only.

Oonu You, them: "Oonu wan' eat tonight?" ("Do you want any dinner?")

Pappy show Something utterly ridiculous and foolish.

Phat Adjective applies to a fit, attractive woman, so-called because she has all the right things in all the right places "Pussy, Hips, Ass and Tits".

Piece A gun, a girl, or sex: "Me get a nice piece las' night" ("I had sex with an attractive woman last night").

Pikney Child.

Pirogue Fishing canoe.

Pon On or upon.

Prentice Apprentice or protégé, usually young man; also prenta.

Profile Status; someone who's intent on showing off their designer clothes is profiling.

Pum pum Vagina.

Punaani Vagina – again.

Pussy or punny printers Shorts even tighter than the batty rider.

Queen Respectful title for a woman, usually a Rastaman's partner.

Raggamuffin Respected and wily ghetto sufferah, often used in a musical context. Also used to refer to "street" style.

Rahtid Mild expletive or an expression of surprise.

Ramp Usually used as "Ramp wid", meaning to interfere with or irritate.

Rass An expletive when used with claat or hole: "Wha de rass claat man a deal wid?" ("That man is one nasty rasshole"). Can also express surprise or emphasize a point.

Rastitute See "Rent-a-Dread", below. Not to be confused with Ras, the abbreviation for Rasta.

Rat-bat Large moth – or regular bat.

Reason Discuss and debate a subject: "Me a reason wid mi bredren".

Red Used to refer to a lightskinned person "See de red man deh". Red also describes someone who has been smoking ganja.

Red-eye Greedy, envious.

Renk Extreme insolence or rudeness: "De man talk to me so renk it is a shame". Also foul-smelling, nasty.

"Rent-a-Dread" A man with locks who makes a living out of sexual relationships with tourists.

Respect Perhaps the most commonly used greeting or farewell in Jamaica.

Risto From "aristocrat"; someone from (or who thinks they're from) high society.

Roughneck Ragamuffin rascal.

Rude bway Bad boy.

Runnings Happenings, things that are going on: "Bway, runnings hard dis year" ("Things are tough this year").

Rush Assail: "Watch dem rush de gates" ("Look at them forcing their way in").

Schoolers Schoolchildren.

Science Obeah.

Screw Be annoyed, and look like you are. A **"screw face"** is a miserable character.

Seen Understand or comprehend what someone is saying. Usually used as a reply to a statement, as in "Uh-huh".

Sensimillia High-grade herbs; also shortened to sensi.

Shock-out Looking good: "Me ago shock-out tonight ina mi criss new Versace".

Shotta Rude boy, with all the appropriate notoriety that such status demands.

Sipple Slippery, precarious, as used in Max Romeo's hit song *Sipple Out Deh*.

Skank Rip off, con: "Me get skank at the mechanic today". Also an old-time dance.

Sketel Promiscuous, provocatively dressed woman.

Skin-out Abandoned dancing or enjoyment, usually with sexual connotations.

Slackness Improper, lowdown, dirty behaviour; also used to describe rude dancehall lyrics.

Slam The sexual act.

Spar Friend.

Spliff Marijuana joint.

Star Used as a salutation or qualifier in greetings: "Wh'appen, star".

Stoosh Snooty, condescending from a position of assumed superiority.

Structure The body: "Min' you structure" ("Get out of the way").

Sufferah Poor but righteous ghetto-dweller.

Sweetboy Man who is financially supported by his lover.

Talawah Small but strong, applied to Jamaica itself in the motto: "She little but she talawah".

Talking to can also be used to mean sleeping with someone, as in "she been talkin' to de man for de longest time".

Tan Stay or stand: "Tan so back" ("Hold back").

Ting Object or woman; "A my ting dat" ("That's my girlfriend"). "Tings" can be male and female genitalia. Also the Jamaican pronunciation of things: "Tings a gwan rough sah".

Trace To curse somebody.

Version A cut of a popular rhythm track.

Vex(ed) Irritated or annoyed.

What a gwan "What's going on?"

Wind/Wine Dance closely and suggestively.

Wuk Regular work or sex.

Wutless Combination of worthless and witless: "Pure wutless bway me meet at the show" ("I met some awful men at the show").

X-amount Huge, incalculable amount: "Me have x-amount of loving".

Yahso Here: "Park yuh car yahso".

Yard Home, also used as an alternative name for Jamaica: "No where no better dan Yard".

Yush A greeting.

A short history of Jamaican film-making

How does an island with a relatively small population and a lack of technical infrastructure compete in the global market place against multinational media empires? Independence in 1962 gave Jamaicans the right to political self-determination, but it didn't provide an opportunity to see themselves or their cultural traditions represented in film. In the same year Jamaica became the primary location for *Dr No*, the first in the series of James Bond films. *Dr No* set the pattern for the first type of "Jamaican" film making: the island is exploited as a tropical back-drop against which tales of international adventure and romance, aimed at the North American and European market places, are set. Films like *Club Paradise* and *The Mighty Quinn* continue the tradition of Hollywood's many re-mixes of the "Jamaican experience" on celluloid, but the competing, alternative strand of Jamaican film making, which came into being with *The Harder They Come* in 1972, continues to gain ground and respect both at home and abroad.

The Harder They Come

In 1972, for the first time in the nation's history, a film set out to document island life and placed its distinct regional history and culture at the centre of its narrative. **The Harder They Come**, directed by Perry Henzell, is both the story of Ivan, played by Jimmy Cliff, as he comes to try to make a better life for himself in the city, and an indictment of Jamaican society that implicates the church, music industry and police in Ivan's eventual estrangement from authority, new career as a criminal, and violent death. The film has become the standard by which authentically Jamaican films are judged. Its radical synthesis of social realism, political consciousness and popular culture introduced a new regional voice to world cinema that built on the artistic traditions established within the Caribbean through carnival celebration and religious worship. The film sets out to document contemporary social injustice but places these elements of realism in a critical flux with imported conventions from American crime and spaghetti western genres. In the same way that ska and reggae throughout the 1950s and 1960s transformed imported American rhythm and blues songs to generate a totally Jamaican style of popular song, *The Harder They Come* appropriated an eclectic range of influences, drawn from America and Europe, to produce a unique cinematic vernacular that spoke directly to the majority of Jamaican citizens.

Finance for *The Harder They Come* was raised from a small network of Jamaican investors, and the film took three years to make, with two long breaks in the shooting schedule. During these interludes Perry Henzell, the film's producer, co-writer and director edited material and hunted down more funds to complete the project. At home the film was a success, winning the first of many box office clashes between indigenous and imported titles, while abroad the film gained almost universal critical acclaim but suffered from limited distribution.

Directed by Jamaican playwright, and co-writer of *The Harder They Come*, Trevor Rhone, the hilarious **Smile Orange** (1974) features Ringo, a head waiter in a resort hotel, played by Carl Bradshaw, who uses all his guile and wit on tourists to overcome the harsh economic realities of contemporary

Jamaica. "If you're a black man and you can't play a part, you'll starve to death", he advises a novice waiter under his training. The film's drama tests Ringo's ability to manage other people's perceptions of him, as he alternately seduces and cheats American tourists out of their dollars, while avoiding being caught in the act by his wife and the hotel manager. Finally, his acting skills pay off when the hotel manager mistakenly believes that Ringo made a concerted effort to save a guest who drowned in the hotel pool and rewards him financially. Like Henzell's earlier film, *Smile Orange* also deals with the economic dominance of America and the class and race divisions within Jamaica. Unlike Ivan, Ringo chooses to make a truce with the repressive forces of the wider society if only the better to fool them into granting him a chance for a more profitable survival. Social injustice and discrimination are an occasion for farce and satirical commentary in this film rather than anger, violence and revolt.

The 1980 film **Children of Babylon**, written, directed, edited and produced by Lennie Little-White, focuses on Jamaican society through a set of character archetypes: a beautiful Marxist graduate student, a bourgeois painter, a Rastafarian farmer, a white plantation owner and a mute servant girl. The story follows these characters through a series of romantic affairs set on a plantation that reveals the class and ethnic divisions in Jamaican society. The film featured the seminal reggae songwriter Bob Andy, as Luke the Rastafarian farmer. Bob Andy had given up on music at that time in favour of acting with the theatrical workshop at the University of the West Indies. The film's cinematographer, Franklyn St Juste, maintained that the film's poor critical reception in America was due to the fact that it confounded long-held expectations about the low-budget visual style of third-world cinema.

"Dread at the Control"

The continuing worldwide popularity of **Jamaican music** has set the commercial pattern for most Jamaican film production. **Rockers** (1978) by Greek film-maker Theodoros Balfaloukos featured a cast of contemporary Jamaican musicians playing both themselves and fictional roles. Balfaloukos lived in Jamaica for two years before shooting the film, making personal contact with the musicians who came to feature in it. The story is a modern-day fable in which the Rastafarian

musician, played by Leroy "Horsemouth" Wallace as himself, takes revenge on the Trench Town gangsters that have stolen his bike. The film points to many of the cultural tensions within Jamaican society. Such tensions are exemplified in scenes like Leroy and Dirty Harry's hijacking of the turntables at a disco to play reggae to the well-off Jamaicans who patronize the club. "Dread at the control!" shouts Leroy as he replaces the imported sounds from America with Rastafarian rhythms. Throughout the 1970s and early 1980s it was the music of Jacob Miller, Gregory Isaacs, Burning Spear, Robbie Shakespeare, Big Youth, Dillinger and Theophilos Beckford, all cast members in *Rockers*, and the counter culture of Rastafari that came to be Jamaica's best-known cultural export and therefore a vital component of an emerging film industry.

Chris Blackwell has long been able to see the potential export value of Jamaican music and has devoted himself to establishing profitable links with Europe and North America. After acting as location scout on *Dr No* in 1962, Blackwell came to London and as co-founder of Island records promoted and recorded Jamaican music in Britain, eventually releasing the classic film soundtrack album from *The Harder They Come* on his Island label. In the early 1980s, following the enormous international success of Bob Marley, Blackwell sought to extend Island Record's portfolio into film production. He envisaged that advances in technology, especially the advent of home video recorders, would eventually circumvent the traditional chain of cinema distribution, and he established Island Pictures in 1982 with the production of **Countryman**, directed by Dickie Jobson. The film exchanges the urban realism of *The Harder They Come* or *Rockers* for a bucolic mysticism inspired by its eponymous hero's deep faith in Rastafarian theology. The plot revolves around a scheme operated by corrupt governmental officials to discredit the political opposition through the framing of two innocent Americans as CIA gunrunners to the island during a forthcoming election. Through Countryman's religious beliefs, kung-fu fighting skills and certain supernatural helpers the young Americans are rescued from the corrupt politicians and allowed home. The film's endorsement of the Rastafarian rejection of the modern world and its materialism contrasts strongly with Ivan's quest in *The Harder They Come* to better his conditions of living by all means at his disposal. *Countryman* was made during a time of almost open civil war between Jamaica's two main parties, the JLP and PNP, but whereas *The Harder They Come* had attempted to expose the economic motivations behind this new breed of political gangsters, *Countryman* wanted to avoid the political implications of its own timely plot in favour of a more supernatural contest between a rural spiritual faith and the urban forces of corrupted and westernized "progress".

During the 1980s Blackwell concentrated on the non-Jamaican side of his film company, achieving international success with productions such as *Kiss of the Spider Woman* and *She's Got To Have It.* Eventually he sold his film and record companies, while continuing to manage them, to European entertainment giant Polydor. For small independent producers based in Jamaica at this time the costs involved in feature production seemed prohibitive. In Britain, television in the form of Channel 4 acted as a crucial catalyst for feature film production, but in Jamaica film and video producers were forced to actually buy air time on JBC themselves before broadcast was possible.

In 1991 Blackwell returned to Jamaican subject matter with the **Lunatic**, directed by American songwriter and music video director Lol Creme. Like *Smile Orange*, the film makes broad comedy out of the Jamaican tourist industry and featured Aloysius, played by Paul Cambell, who has an affair with Inga, played by British actress Julie T. Wallace. The pair become embroiled in a plot to rob the local white landowner which has hilarious consequences. Adapted by Jamaican author Anthony Winkler from his own novel the film is an engaging, achingly funny mixture of burlesque humour, folklore and satirical comment on the sexual tourism prevalent in Jamaica.

Digital Futures

In the 1990s the cost of feature film productions were greatly reduced by the arrival of new digital video technology. Chris Blackwell's hope at the start of the 1980s that technological progress would eventually lead to greater opportunities for smaller producers operating outside Hollywood now seemed much closer to reality. Blackwell eventually left Polydor and went on to form Palm Pictures. Both **Dancehall Queen** (1997) and **Third World Cop** (1999) were financed by Blackwell

and made on a limited budget using small digital cameras for release onto the video market; although they were eventually given a theatrical release by the transference of the digital format to film. *Dancehall Queen*, directed by British music-video veteran Don Letts and Rick Elgood, adapts elements of the musical and crime genres to a Jamaican context. The film follows the fortunes of its heroine, Marcia, played by Audrey Reid, as she struggles to break free from her existence as a street vendor and to distance her daughter from the sexual advances of "Uncle" Larry. Her escape route is to become queen of the dancehall and receive the cash prize that goes with it. The film generated controversy in Jamaica upon its release, as it was seen to raise difficult questions over the representation and exploitation of women within society, and in the island's cinemas its popularity ensured it competed successfully with *Men in Black. Third World Cop*, directed by Christopher Brown, continues the ongoing creolization of American cinema conventions by Jamaican producers. It takes the stock characters, action sequences and narrative cliché associated with the modern Hollywood action thriller and fleshes them out with distinctively Jamaican motivations and language.

Almost thirty years after the release of *The Harder They Come*, there are still only limited film production opportunities on the island and producers are often forced to seek an audience outside Jamaica to gather a return on their investment. American studios, on the other hand, continue to take advantage of local tax concessions and dollar exchange rates. Don Letts, director of *Dancehall Queen*, warns that digital technology can only bring down the cost of what takes place behind the camera, not in front of it. For the time being at least, it seems those wishing to make films about the reality of Jamaican society will continue to occupy a disadvantaged place within the world's media, while the processes of globalization continue to support the dominance of European and North American culture. Although the number of authentic Jamaican films produced over the years has been small, within this handful of films is the beginning of a cinematic tradition: one that turns its own economic disadvantages into positive aesthetic values and absorbs foreign cultural influence to transform it into the unique historical synthesis that is Jamaican cinema.

John Fortnum

Books

The following books should be readily available in the US, UK and/or Jamaica. We have given the publishers for all of the in-print titles: the US publisher first, separated where applicable from the UK, and then from the Jamaican. Where a book is only published in one country, we have specified which. Most of the titles listed as being out of print (o/p) should be easy enough to find in secondhand bookstores, or online via sites such as www.amazon.com – also a good general source for all the titles listed here.

Travel and diaries

Patrick Leigh Fermor, *The Traveller's Tree* (o/p). The classic Caribbean travelogue describing Leigh Fermor's visit in the late 1940s, before tourism had really started in the region, though only the last chapter covers his time in Jamaica, with specific reference to the developing Rastafari movement in West Kingston.

Margaret Hodges (ed), *Blue Mountain Guide* (JA Pear Tree Press). Useful pocket guide to the peak trail, with a sketch map of the stages up and accounts of the surrounding environment, geology, fauna and flora, and human impact.

Matthew Lewis, *Journal of a West Indian Planter* (o/p). Fascinating diaries of Lewis, an early nineteenth-century English novelist, describing his brief visits to his Jamaican estates and cataloguing the lifestyle and living conditions of the island's slaves.

Margaret Morris, *Tour Jamaica* (JA & UK Gleaner). A Jamaican's view of Jamaica, recommending seventeen different driving tours around the island. Lots of history and folklore titbits, and plenty of detail, but short on practicalities.

Lady Maria Nugent, *Journal of Residence in Jamaica 1801–5* (JA Institute of Jamaica). Lady Nugent was the wife of one of Jamaica's governors, and her diary, though often naive and patronizing, paints an interesting picture of how the "ruling class" lived.

Anthony Winkler, *Going Home to Teach* (US & UK LMH Publishing). Engaging story of novelist Winkler's own experience, as a white Jamaican, returning to live on his native island during the "anti-white" climate of the late 1970s. Very good on the politics and atmosphere of the period.

Paul Zach (ed), *Jamaica: Insight Guides* (US Houghton Mifflin/UK APA). Glossy guide, short on practical information but long on colour photographs, and a decent souvenir book.

Fiction

Louise Bennett, *Anancy and Miss Lou* (JA Sangster's). Jamaica's oral tradition of storytelling may be fading, but these are the classic folk-tales – from the greatest of modern Jamaican storytellers – told in patois and including the story of the crafty spider Anancy.

Colin Channer, *Waiting In Vain* (US & UK Ballantine). This tale of modern-day romance between a Jamaican man and an American woman perfectly evokes the Jamaican communities of England, New York and Jamaica itself.

Mark Conklin, *Banana Shout* (US Fusion Press). Engaging and occasionally hilarious account of an American draft dodger's adventures as he sets up home in Negril during the 1970s, and an essential oral history of the development of the resort. The easiest way to get hold of a copy is via the Web site www.authorlink.com.

Herbert de Lisser, *The White Witch of Rose Hall* (UK Macmillan). A blend of Gothic horror and purple prose, this richly embellished account of the island's best-known ghost story tells the tale of Annie Palmer, mistress of Rose Hall Great House, whose three husbands all died in suspicious circumstances.

Lorna Goodison, *Baby Mother and the King of Swords* (US & UK Longman). Rather dark collection of contemporary short stories set in Jamaica.

Victor Headley, *Yardie* (UK Pan/JA X Press). Easy-reading, thought-provoking (if not that well-written) tale of a drug-running "mule" who rises to the top of a UK-based drugs racket, shedding light on the whole sordid business along the way.

Perry Henzell, *Power Game* (US Hastings House/JA Ventana). Long, entertaining story of power-seekers at different levels in Jamaican society – politics, the army, the banks, the drug traders. Henzell catches local language and atmosphere with the same skill he used in his movie *The Harder They Come*.

Evan Jones, *Stone Haven* (US/UK Heinemann). Long-winded but readable historical novel that picks its way through modern issues, from 1920s attitudes to colour to the problems of post-independence.

Guy Kennaway, *One People* (US Canongate/UK Payback Press). Entertaining and humorous take on life in a tiny coastal town in Westmoreland that perfectly evokes rural life; an essential read.

Roger Mais, *The Hills Were Joyful Together*, *Brother Man* and *Black Lightning* (US/UK Heinemann). *Hills* is a bleak, compelling picture of life in a Kingston ghetto in the 1950s, with a harsh look at law and order Jamaica-style, by one of the country's earliest novelists. *Brother Man* details the emergence of Rastafari in Kingston via the gentle "Brother Man" himself, while *Black Lightning* is an intense and atmospheric account of the life of a brooding sculptor living in the Jamaican bush.

Terry McMillan, *How Stella Got Her Groove Back* (US Mass Market/UK Penguin). In Macmillan's lightweight but enjoyable tone, this semi-autobiographical tale tells the story of a holiday romance that turns serious, written as a result of the author's experiences during Jamaican holidays.

Colin Moone, *Obeah* (US/UK X Press). Fascinating and sinister fictional introduction to the world of Jamaican witchcraft.

Orlando Patterson, *The Children of Sisyphus* (US/UK Longman). Famous, uncompromising picture of the poorest of Kingston's poor, fighting for survival on the margins of society, and of Dinah, a prostitute who tries to leave them behind and move up in the world. One of the first novels to try to present a fair picture of the Rasta community.

V.S. Reid, *The Jamaicans* (JA Institute of Jamaica). Juan de Bolas was a slave liberated by the Spanish when the English captured the island in 1655; Reid's fictionalized account tells of his life in hiding and struggle against the English.

Jean Rhys, *Wide Sargasso Sea* (US W.W. Norton/UK Penguin). A view of post-emancipation Jamaica, with Antoinette, a young creole girl, and Rochester, her English boyfriend, trapped by declining financial circumstances and his inability to understand the realities of local life. Written as a "predecessor" to Bronte's *Jane Eyre*.

Kim Robinson and Leeta Hearn (ed), *Twenty-two Jamaican Short Stories* (US/UK LMH Publishers/JA Kingston Publishers). Excellent short story book that covers some of the more chilling psychological aspects of Jamaican life. Venerable authors include Olive Senior, Dennis Scott, Hazel Campbell and Trevor Fearon.

Tony Sewell, *Jamaica Inc* (US/UK X Press). Gripping and intelligent fictional history of a strangely familiar political family dynasty.

Vanessa Spence, *The Roads Are Down* (US/UK Heinemann). Excellent and amusing first novel of a cross-cultural love affair, set in modern-day Kingston and the Blue Mountains.

Michael Thewell, *The Harder They Come* (US Grove Press/UK X Press). Novel inspired by Perry Henzell's brilliant movie, telling the story of Rhygin – country boy turned rude boy – who comes to Kingston and gets caught up in gangs and ganja.

Anthony Winkler, *The Great Yacht Race*, *The Painted Canoe* and *The Lunatic* (UK LMH Publishers/JA Kingston Publishers). Set just before independence, *The Great Yacht Race* is a hilarious look at the lifestyle of Montego Bay's erstwhile "ruling class" as the lawyers, journalists and hotel-owners go through scandal after scandal in preparation for their annual boat race. *The Painted Canoe* is a powerful, evocative tale of a Jamaican fisherman and his relationship with the sea, while *The Lunatic* is a poignant but amusing tale of a Jamaican madman, who wanders the island talking with the trees and bushes, and his encounter with Inge, a sexually voracious German tourist (see also p.420).

History and politics

Warren Alleyne, *Caribbean Pirates* (US Media Publishing/UK Caribbean Publishing). Alleyne debunks the myths about the region's leading pirates – from Blackbeard to Henry Morgan – in a series of brief portraits.

Clinton Black, *Port Royal* and *Tales of Old Jamaica* (UK Longman). *Port Royal* is a solid history of the city once known as the "wickedest place on earth"; *Tales* has brief accounts of some of the key events in the island's past, recalling the capture of Jamaica by the British, the story of "Three Fingered" Jack Mansong, and the women pirates, Anne Bonney and Mary Read.

Mavis Campbell, *The Maroons of Jamaica 1655–1796* (US Bergin & Garvey/UK Africa World Press). Scholarly work that traces the origins of the Maroons during the English invasion of Jamaica in 1655 and follows their development as a community up to the Trelawny war of the late eighteenth century.

James Ferguson, *A Traveller's History of the Caribbean* (UK Windrush Press). This concise and well-written overview provides a good introduction to the region's history.

John Gilmore, *Faces of the Caribbean* (UK Latin American Bureau). Excellent and essential sociohistory of the Caribbean, covering everything from slavery to reggae, cricket and the environment.

Gad Heuman, *The Killing Time: The Morant Bay Rebellion* (US University of Tenessee Press/UK Macmillan Heinemann). Detailed and articulate study of the 1865 rebellion, its causes and the aftermath, and a review of the tradition of protest in Jamaica.

Rupert Lewis & Patrick Bryan (ed), *Garvey: His Work and Impact* (US/UK Africa World Press). Twenty-one articles on the historical background to Garveyism, his influence on Jamaica and his worldwide legacy.

Darrell E. Levy, *Michael Manley: The Making of a Leader* (US University of Georgia Press). Detailed biography of the controversial leader, though it never really captures Manley's sparkle, and Levy lets him off rather lightly on some of his acknowledged errors.

Michael Manley, *The Politics of Change – A Jamaican Testament* (US Howard University Press/UK Andre Deutsch). Interesting overview of the proposed transformation of the island under Manley's PNP government, written as it got underway in the early 1970s.

J. P. Parry, Philip Sherlock & Anthony Maingot, *A Short History of the West Indies* (UK Macmillan Heinemann). The best concise history of the region, taking the story up to the mid-1980s, and good on general issues such as regional co-operation and debt crisis.

Carey Robinson, *The Fighting Maroons of Jamaica* (JA Sangster's). Accessible, general history of the Maroons up to 1800, fairly easy to get in Jamaican bookshops.

Olive Senior, *The A-Z of Jamaican Heritage* (JA Heinemann). Concise but useful dictionary, with brief entries on everything from Garvey to Manley, Rastas to Pocomania.

Tony Sewell, *Garvey's Children: The Legacy of Marcus Garvey* (US Africa World/UK Macmillan). Readable account of Garvey's black power movement and the inspiration it has provided for black nationalists in Jamaica and abroad.

Verene Shepherd, *The Experience of Indians in Jamaica, 1845–1950* (JA Peepal Tree). Short, scholarly look at Indian indentured labour and its social and economic consequences.

John Stewart (ed), *In Old St James* (JA Sangster's). Small collection of stories of the early English settlers, focusing particularly on the ancestors of Elizabeth Barrett Browning.

Religion, culture and society

Mervyn Alleyne, *Roots of Jamaican Culture* (US Frontline). Academic but fascinating exploration of African-Jamaican culture and society covering history, language, music and religion.

Leonard Barrett, *The Rastafarians* (US/UK Beacon Press) and *The Sun and the Drum* (UK Heinemann/JA Sangster's). The former is one of the most comprehensive accounts of the movement, explaining its origins and politics, and looking at related religious movements like the Twelve Tribes of Israel sect. The latter is an in-depth look at the influence of African traditions in Jamaican culture, including language, witchcraft and folk medicine.

Marcel Bayer, *In Focus Jamaica: A Guide to the People, Politics and Culture* (UK Latin America Bureau). Excellent little handbook, with lucid and relevant sections on history, politics, the economy, society and culture.

Derek Bishton, *Black Heart Man – A Journey into Rasta* (o/p but usually available online via www.amazon.com). Succinct, well-researched foray into the origins and development of the Rastafarian movement in Jamaica, with discussion of Garvey and a host of less well-known black theorists.

Adrian Boot and Michael Thomas, *Babylon on a Thin Wire* (UK Thames and Hudson). Evocative photographic portraits of 1970s Kingston, backed up by cynical and informed text.

Edward Kamau Braithwaite, *Folk Culture of the Slaves in Jamaica* (JA New Beacon). Fact-packed mini-book with an excellent introduction to black culture under slavery as seen through the eyes of a contemporary black Jamaican university professor. Detailed descriptions of the customs among slave societies, including death rituals, religion, music and dance, dress, entertainment tastes, language and even household decor.

Horace Campbell, *Rasta and Resistance from Marcus Garvey to Walter Rodney* (US Africa World/UK Hansib). Academic but militant discussion of the development and influence of the Rasta religion and philosophy.

Laurie Gunst, *Born Fe Dead* (US Henry Holt/UK Payback Press). Gripping account of the dark side of political and drug-related violence in Jamaica. Ably researched with the help of Jamaicans in Kingston and New York, this traces the development of Jamaican posses from political lackeys to drug-trafficking gangsters.

Polly Pattullo, *Last Resorts – The Cost of Tourism in the Caribbean* (US Monthly Review Press/UK Continuum). Important, well-researched critique of the tourist industry and its impact on the islands.

Edward Seaga, *Revival Cults in Jamaica* (JA Jamaica Journal Publications). Anthropological descriptions of the beliefs, rituals and practices within Pocomania, Kumina and Zion religions by former prime minister Seaga.

M.G. Smith, Roy Augier and Rex Nettleford, *Report on the Rastafari Movement* (JA UWI Press). Published in 1960, the first academic study of Rastafari. Dated but accurate description of the contemporary make-up, history, beliefs and rituals of Rasta.

Andrea Taylor, *Baby Mother* (UK X Press) One mother's journey through single parenthood – Jamaican style. Also published by X Press, Patrick Augustus's *Baby Father* and *Baby Father 2* (UK X Press) provide the male point of view.

Anita Waters, *Race, Class and Political Symbols – Rastafari and Reggae in Jamaican Politics* (US/UK Transatlantic Publications). Academic but thought-provoking study of the manipulation of Rasta and reggae by Jamaican politicians, with a thorough discussion of shenanigans around the volatile 1976 and 1980 elections.

Music, art and sport

Petrine Archer Straw & Kim Robinson, *Jamaican Art* (UK/JA Kingston Publishers Limited). Comprehensive account of the development of modern Jamaican art, well-illustrated with examples of all of the major painters and sculptors, from Edna Marley to Kapo.

Steve Barrow and Peter Dalton, *The Rough Guide to Reggae* (US/UK Rough Guides). Comprehensive, definitive handbook on reggae music, with sections on the UK, US and African scenes as well as a comprehensive rudown on things in Jamaica.

Cedella Booker, *Bob Marley* (UK Penguin). Very personal account of Marley's life and death written by his mother, light on the music but heavy on family anecdotes, plus the occasional (and most entertaining) catty swipe.

Stephen Davis, *Bob Marley – Conquering Lion of Reggae* (US Schenkman/UK Plexus). Businesslike and exhaustive examination of Marley's life and work, with lots of gossip thrown in.

Claire Forrester, *Merlene Ottey – Unyielding spirit* (JA West Indies Publishing). Enthusiastic biography of Jamaica's revered sporting hero, written before Ottey's career was shattered by a wrongful positive drugs test.

Dermott Hussey & Malika Lee Whitney, *Bob Marley* (US/UK Pomegranate Art Books). Coffee-table heavyweight, with lavish illustrations, interviews with all the principal characters and text by Jamaicans who were part of the unfolding scene.

Brian Jahn and Tom Weber, *Reggae Island* (US/UK Da Capo Press). The story of reggae told mainly through interviews with key players, from the young Garnet Silk to Buju Banton, Bunny Wailer, Ken Booth and Mykal Rose, but somewhat lacking in contemporary insight.

Michael Manley, *A History of West Indies Cricket* (UK Andre Deutsch). The late prime minister's superb history of the Caribbean contribution to the world's greatest game.

Anton Marks, *Dancehall* (US/UK X Press). A slippery slide into the steamy world of the dancehall, bringing the familiar players to life and providing an informed slant on ghetto politics.

Don Taylor, *Marley and Me* (US Barricade Books/UK Kingston Publishers). Taylor was Bob Marley's one-time manager, and his chatty if rather badly-written account – focusing on girlfriends, politics and controversy – is more sensationalist than White's (below).

Timothy White, *Catch a Fire* (US Owl/UK Omnibus). Exhaustive and loving biography of Bob Marley (including a detailed discography), with an in-depth look at the early Jamaican music scene and plenty of obeah and superstition.

Language and humour

L. Emile Adams, *Understanding Jamaican Patois* (US/UK LMH Publishers). User-friendly and intelligent description of patois grammar and language use, with a small dictionary.

S. Knight and T. Lowrie, *Hustling Jamaican Style* (JA Jamrite Publications). Light-hearted and sarcastically incisive trip through the familiar tourist town hustlers.

Kim Robinson, Harclyde Walcott & Trevor Fearon, *The How To Be Jamaican Handbook* (JA Jamrite Publications). Humorous lessons on appropriate behaviour in the resorts and beyond, with painfully accurate tourist caricatures.

Flora and fauna

C. Dennis Adams, *Flowering Plants of Jamaica* (JA UWI). Useful introductory guide to Jamaican flora.

James Bond, *Field Guide to Birds of the West Indies* (US/UK Houghton Mifflin). The classic bird book, from which Ian Fleming took the name of his fictional hero, though generally considered to have been supplanted by the Downer/Sutton book.

Audrey Downer & Robert Sutton, *Birds of Jamaica: A Photographic Field Guide* (UK Cambridge University Press). The definitive field guide on the island's birds, with handy sections on the island's principal habitats and birding "hot spots".

Eugene Kaplan, *A Field Guide to the Coral Reefs of the Caribbean and Florida* (US/UK Houghton Mifflin). Attractive guide to the region's reefs.

G.W. Lennox & S.A. Seddon, *Flowers of the Caribbean; Trees of the Caribbean; Fruits and Vegetables of the Caribbean* (US/UK Macmillan). Handy pocket-sized books, with glossy, sharp, coloured pictures, and a good general introduction to the region's flora.

Diane Robertson, *Jamaican Herbs* (JA De Sola Press). Thorough description of the medicinal properties of commonly used herbs, roots, fruits and vegetables, with advice on preparation.

Food and drink

Norma Benghiat, *Traditional Jamaican Cookery* (UK Penguin). Handy and engagingly written guide to the island's traditional dishes, from ackee and saltfish to curry goat and rice and peas, with all of the classic recipes and a lot more. Also by Norma Benghiat and John Demers, *The Food of Jamaica* (US Periplus/UK Tuttle) is another reliable option.

Mike Henry, *Caribbean Cocktails and Mixed Drinks* (US Mass Market/UK Kingston Publishers). All of the classic recipes based mostly around rums and fresh juices.

Laura Osbourne, *The Rasta Cookbook* (US Africa World Press). The low-down on classic Ital cooking with main courses, puddings and (of course) blended health drinks.

Caroline Sullivan, *Classic Jamaican Cooking* (US Interlink Publishing/UK Serif). The Jamaican version of Mrs Beeton, little changed since its first publication in 1896. Excellent recipes, anecdotes and the essential "Herbal Remedies and Household Hints".

Helen Willinsky, *Jerk – Barbecue from Jamaica* (US/UK Crossing Press). DIY jerk manual.

Index

K

Stay in touch with us!

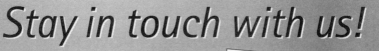

ROUGH*NEWS* **is Rough Guides' free newsletter.
In four issues a year we give you news, travel
issues, music reviews, readers' letters and the
latest dispatches from authors on the road.**

I would like to receive ROUGH*NEWS*: please put me on your free mailing list.

NAME . . . .

ADDRESS . . . .

Please clip or photocopy and send to: Rough Guides, 62–70 Shorts Gardens, London WC2H 9AH,
England or Rough Guides, 375 Hudson Street, New York, NY 10014, USA.

ROUGH GUIDES: Travel

Alaska
Amsterdam
Andalucia
Argentina
Australia
Austria

Bali & Lombok
Barcelona
Belgium &
  Luxembourg
Belize
Berlin
Brazil
Britain
Brittany &
  Normandy
Bulgaria
California
Canada
Central America
Chile
China
Corsica
Costa Rica
Crete
Croatia
Cuba
Cyprus
Czech & Slovak
  Republics

Dodecanese &
  the East Aegean
Devon &
  Cornwall
Dominican
  Republic
Dordogne & the
  Lot
Ecuador
Egypt
England
Europe
Florida
France
French Hotels &
  Restaurants
  1999
Germany
Goa
Greece
Greek Islands
Guatemala
Hawaii
Holland
Hong Kong &
  Macau
Hungary

Iceland
India
Indonesia
Ionian Islands
Ireland

Israel & the
  Palestinian
  Territories
Italy
Jamaica
Japan
Jordan
Kenya
Lake District
Languedoc &
  Roussillon
Laos
London
Los Angeles
Malaysia,
  Singapore &
  Brunei
Mallorca &
  Menorca
Maya World
Mexico
Morocco
Moscow
Nepal
New England
New York
New Zealand
Norway
Pacific
  Northwest
Paris
Peru
Poland
Portugal
Prague
Provence & the
  Côte d'Azur
The Pyrenees
Romania
St Petersburg
San Francisco

Sardinia
Scandinavia
Scotland
Scottish
  highlands and
  Islands
Sicily
Singapore
South Africa
South India
Southeast Asia
Southwest USA
Spain
Sweden
Switzerland
Syria

Thailand
Trinidad &
  Tobago
Tunisia
Turkey
Tuscany &
  Umbria
USA
Venice
Vienna
Vietnam
Wales
Washington DC
West Africa
Zimbabwe &
  Botswana

AVAILABLE AT ALL GOOD BOOKSHOPS

ROUGH GUIDES: Mini Guides, Travel Specials and Phrasebooks

MINI GUIDES

Antigua
Bangkok
Barbados
Beijing
Big Island of Hawaii
Boston
Brussels
Budapest
Cape Town
Copenhagen
Dublin
Edinburgh

Florence
Honolulu
Ibiza & Formentera
Jerusalem
Las Vegas
Lisbon
London Restaurants
Madeira
Madrid
Malta & Gozo
Maui
Melbourne
Menorca

Montreal
New Orleans

Paris
Rome
Seattle
St Lucia
Sydney
Tenerife
Tokyo
Toronto
Vancouver

TRAVEL SPECIALS

First-Time Asia
First-Time Europe
Women Travel

PHRASEBOOKS

Czech
Dutch
Egyptian Arabic
European
French
German
Greek

Hindi & Urdu
Hungarian
Indonesian
Italian
Japanese
Mandarin
  Chinese
Mexican
  Spanish
Polish
Portuguese
Russian
Spanish
Swahili
Thai
Turkish
Vietnamese

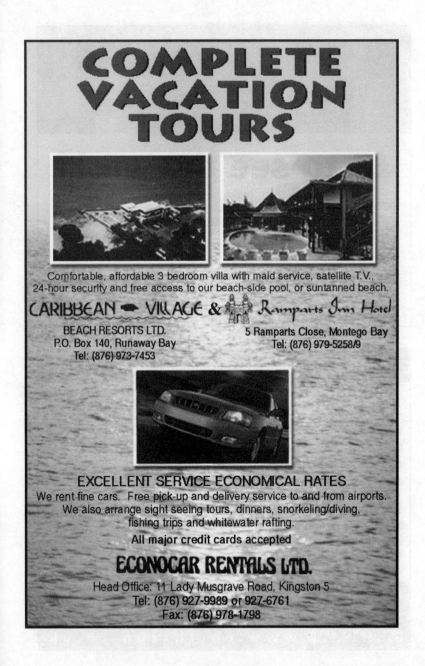

#1 In Jamaica.

- Largest Rent-a-Car Fleet in Jamaica
- Efficient Personalised Service
- Reliable
- In Terminal Airport location
- Wide Selection of Cars, Jeeps & Buses
- Best Rates
- Unlimited Mileage
- 24 Hour-Emergency RoadSide Assistance
- Chauffeur Service
- Private Transfers
- Excursions & Day Tours

HEAD OFFICE: 17 Antigua Avenue,
Kingston 10, Jamaica
KINGSTON: International Airport Terminal
MONTEGO BAY: International Airport Terminal
OCHO RIOS: Main Street

Island car rentals, ltd

RESERVATIONS
(876) 926-8861/8012 Fax: (876) 929-6987
1-800-892-4581 (USA/CAN)